CRIMINOLOGY

Sixth Edition

John E. Conklin

Tufts University

Allyn and Bacon

Boston   London   Toronto   Sydney   Tokyo   Singapore

Editor-in-Chief, Social Sciences: Karen Hanson
Editorial Assistant: Elissa Schaen
Marketing Manager: Karon Bowers
Editorial-Production Service: DMC & Company
Text Designer: Donna Merrell Chernin
Photo Researcher: Martha Shethar

Editorial Production Administrator: Susan Brown
Cover Administrator: Linda Knowles
Cover Designer: Susan Paradise
Prepress and Composition Buyer: Linda Cox
Manufacturing Buyer: Suzanne Lareau

Copyright © 1998 Allyn & Bacon. Previous edition copyright © 1995 by Allyn and Bacon. Previous editions copyright © 1992, 1989, 1986, and 1981 by John E. Conklin.
A Viacom Company
160 Gould Street
Needham Heights, MA 02194
www.abacon.com

All rights reserved. No part of the material protected by this copyright notice may be reproduced or utilized in any form or by any means, electronic or mechanical, including photocopying, recording, or by any information storage and retrieval system, without the written permission of the copyright owner.

Photo Credits

Chapter 1: p. 3: Michael Newman/Photo Edit. p. 10: Billy E. Barnes/Stock Boston. p. 6: Daytona Beach News Journal/Sygma. p. 23: Corbis-Bettmann. **Chapter 2:** p. 39: Sandra Baker/Liaison International. p. 43: Corbis-Bettman. p 45: Peter Menzel/Stock Boston. p. 52: Jeff Greenberg/Photo Edit. **Chapter 3:** p. 70: Christopher Brown/Stock Boston. p. 94: B. Nation/Sygma. p. 101: John Maher/The Picture Cube. **Chapter 4:** p. 105: Michael Weisbrot/Stock Boston. p. 128: Les Stone/Sygma. p. 135: Reuters/Corbis-Bettmann. **Chapter 5:** p. 145: Reuters/Corbis-Bettmann. p. 149: Photofest. p.167: Barbara Alper/Stock Boston. p. 171: UPI/Corbis-Bettmann. p. 179: UPI/Corbis-Bettmann. **Chapter 6:** p. 184: Mike Greco/Stock Boston. p. 188: R. Maiman/ Sygma. p. 199: Haruyoshi Yamaguchi/Sygma. p. 208: Lester Bob Larve/Sygma. p. 222: Gary Wagner/Stock Boston. **Chapter 7:** p. 232: Don West/The Picture Cube. p. 248: Rafael Macia/Photo Researchers, Inc. p. 262: B. Bachmann/The Image Works. p. 266: Myrleen Ferguson/Photo Edit. **Chapter 8:** p. 274: James Carroll/Stock Boston. p. 280: Photofest. p. 298: James Shaffer/Photo Edit. p. 312: Tannenbaum/Sygma. **Chapter 9:** p. 318: Michael Newman/Photo Edit. p. 320: David M. Grossman/Photo Researchers, Inc. p. 327: Wiley ©1996 Washington Post Writer's Group, reprinted with permission. p. 336: John Coletti/The Picture Cube. **Chapter 10:** p. 345: The Bettmann Archive. p. 349: Reuters/ Bettmann. p. 364: UPI/Bettmann. p. 369: Gary Wagner/Stock Boston. **Chapter 11:** p. 372: A. Ramey/Woodfin Camp & Associates. p. 389: Sygma. p. 397: Reuters/Bettmann. **Chapter 12:** p. 403: Dede Hatch/The Picture Cube. p. 405: Alex Farnsworth/The Image Works. p. 420: UPI/Bettmann. p. 429: Day Williams/Photo Researchers, Inc. **Chapter 13:** p. 433: James Shaffer/Photo Edit. p. 445: Reuters/ Corbis-Bettmann. p. 452: Billy E. Barnes/Stock Boston. p. 462: Elin Schoen/Sygma. **Chapter 14:** p. 474: The Bettmann Archive. p. 488: Michael Newman/Photo Edit. p. 489: John Eastcott/Yva Momatiuk/ Photo Researchers, Inc. p. 515: Bob Daemmrich/The Image Works. **Chapter 15:** p. 527: Halstead/Gamma Liaison. p. 540: Michael Siluk/The Image Works. p. 544: Michael Newman/Photo Edit. p. 551: Tony Freeman/Photo Edit.

Conklin, John E.
      Criminology / John E. Conklin. — 6th ed.
            p. cm.
      Includes bibliographical references and index.
      ISBN 0-205-26478-6
      1. Criminology   I. Title.
      HV6025.C59   1997
      364—dc21   97–1116
                                                              CIP

Printed in the United States of America
10 9 8 7 6 5 4 3 2 1   00 99 98 97

CONTENTS

PART II   THE EXTENT AND NATURE OF CRIME   37

PART III   THE CAUSES OF CRIMINAL BEHAVIOR   143

PART IV REACTIONS TO CRIME   401

CHAPTER 12 Community Reactions to Crime   403

CHAPTER 13 The Criminal Justice System   433

BOXES

Crime and the Media

Crime on Campus

Cross-Cultural Perspectives

Using Criminology

*New to this edition

PREFACE

This book remains organized around a conceptual scheme, unlike the core of most textbooks, which use a "crime-of-the-week club" approach (for example, a chapter on violent crime, a chapter on organized crime, a chapter on white-collar crime, and so on). This book contains as much material on those crimes as other books, but the material appears in chapters that treat conceptual issues, such as the social and economic sources of crime or the organization of criminal behavior. In revising this book, I have, as usual, paid close attention to professional journals and books in criminology and sociology. This literature develops and tests hypotheses and theories; it is conceptual in nature, rather than focused on telling the reader everything he or she might like to know about a particular type of crime. I believe that such a conceptual approach is the best way to understand crime and the most useful way to introduce students to the tools and ideas with which to analyze criminal behavior.

New to this edition of Criminology are eight boxes on the theme of crime and the media. A complete list of these boxes, which deal with the way crime is reported as well as the impact of the media on behavior, appears after the Table of Contents. Also new is a section of Chapter 6 that deals with gender and feminist criminology; gender structure, ways of enacting masculine scripts, and power-control theory are all covered. A new section of the first chapter looks at the ways that crime is socially constructed as an issue, focusing on the cases of rape, child abduction, and serial murder.

Another change is that the three chapters in the fifth edition on deterrence and incapacitation, retribution, and rehabilitation have been condensed and combined into a single chapter in this edition. I have edited those three chapters to retain the important material that appeared in earlier editions, while reducing the proportion of the book devoted to those topics. This book remains the only criminology textbook to treat retribution in any detail and cover deterrence research in depth.

This edition benefits from graphics that are greatly improved over previous editions. Many more pie charts, bar graphs, and diagrams appear throughout the book to illustrate points made in the text.

Review Questions appear at the end of each chapter. These questions are useful to readers in reviewing the material and to instructors in developing essay questions for examinations. Important terms are highlighted in the text, listed at the end of each chapter, and defined in the Glossary at the end of the book. Each chapter has a detailed but concise Summary. References in the text are to an end-of-text Bibliography, which is followed by a Name Index and a Subject Index.

I would like to thank the following people for their comments and suggestions for this sixth edition: Randy Blazak, Portland State University; Leonard Dobrin, Old Dominion University; and Kathleen Casey Jordan, Western Connecticut State University.

I would also like to thank Karen Hanson, Editor-in-Chief, Social Sciences, at Allyn and Bacon, for her very useful suggestions for improving this book. Thanks are also due to Donna Chernin for her professional production work, to Martha Shethar for her photographic research, and to Cecilia Thurlow for copyediting the manuscript.

I am indebted to my daughter, Anne Adamsky, for spending hours designing the pie charts and bar graphs that appear throughout the book. I also appreciate the time that Kathleen Szostek and Frances Fu-Chung devoted to scanning the fifth edition of the book onto disk. Finally, I want to thank Peg Bruno for her generous assistance in preparing the final manuscript.

J.E.C.

Author Biography

John E. Conklin, Professor of Sociology at Tufts University in Medford, Massachusetts, was born in Oswego, New York, in 1943, and was raised in Syracuse, New York. He is the father of four children—Christopher, Anne, Lydia, and Gillian—and is married to Sarah Belcher Conklin.

After earning a bachelor's degree from Cornell University in 1965, Professor Conklin attended Harvard University, completing his doctorate there in 1969. He then worked for a year at Harvard Law School's Center for Criminal Justice. He started teaching at Tufts University in 1970 and now offers courses in criminology and sociology of law.

Professor Conklin's first book, *Robbery and the Criminal Justice System* (1972), was based on data he gathered in Boston. He also wrote *The Impact of Crime* (1975), a study of community reactions to crime, and *"Illegal but Not Criminal": Business Crime in America* (1977). Two editions of *Sociology: An Introduction* were published in 1984 and 1987, and the first of six editions of *Criminology* appeared in 1981. Professor Conklin's most recent study is *Art Crime* (Praeger, 1994), an investigation of theft, forgery, and fraud in the art world. *New Perspectives in Criminology* (Allyn and Bacon, 1996), a reader Professor Conklin designed to supplement any criminology textbook, is a collection of papers published by leading criminologists during the 1990s.

PART I

INTRODUCTION TO CRIMINOLOGY

Chapter 1 introduces basic concepts used in the study of crime and delinquency. We see that crime is a social phenomenon rather than an intrinsic characteristic of behavior. The conceptual approach around which the book is organized is introduced, and an overview of later chapters is provided. We also look at the research strategies that criminologists use to study crime and delinquency.

Chapter 1
The Study of Crime

Watch an hour of television news tonight, and notice how many stories deal with crime. Murders will probably get the most coverage, but child abuse, domestic violence, fraud, and political corruption will probably be represented. Then look through the TV listings for the evening's "entertainment"; crime and violence will be featured. Pick up the newspaper and glance at the advertisements for the latest movies; at least a few will focus on crime. Chances are that several mysteries and suspense novels will be on the best-seller list as well. We can even buy trading cards depicting serial murderers and CD-ROM games that involve us in interactive murder mysteries. All of us are part of a vast audience for crime as entertainment. Crime stories offer escape, stimulation, relaxation, and the appeal of a "good-versus-evil situation where some sort of hero wins at the end through talent and, very importantly, morality" (Richard Meyers, cited in Pace, 1982: F9).

The mass media rapidly disperse crime news throughout the nation and inform even the residents of relatively crime-free areas of the extent of crime in the society. The media focus on attention-grabbing events, bringing the most sensational and bizarre crimes to public attention. As a result, people develop a distorted view of crime as inexplicably and unpredictably violent, even though simple theft, burglary, and commercial fraud are much more common than murder and rape (Schlesinger and Tumber, 1994: 184-185).

Because newspapers and television stations are businesses trying to make a profit, the crime news they present is designed to attract as big an audience as possible. The crimes that appeal most to the news media are those that are visible and spectacular, have sexual or political implications, can be presented in graphic—usually violent—terms, and seem to be the product of individual aberrations rather than social conditions (Chibnall, 1977). Newsworthiness is a product of a crime's seriousness, uniqueness, and salience; the characteristics of its victims and offenders; and the background and work environment of reporters and their sources (Chermak, 1995). The most newsworthy crime story of recent years, the O. J. Simpson case, is examined in the Crime and the Media box.

A systematic study of six weeks of prime-time television programs in the United States in 1981 found that crime was rampant, with violent crime twelve times as common on television as in real life, and murder—the most common crime on television—one hundred times as frequent. After murder, the next most common crimes on television were robbery, kidnapping, and aggravated assault. The crimes most often experienced by the public—theft, burglary, car theft, and public drunkenness—appeared much less often than violent crimes (Lichter and Lichter, 1983).

Not only does television distort the kinds of crime that are actually committed, but offenders are also portrayed inaccurately. Compared with suspects arrested in actual crimes, criminals on television tend to be older and more likely to be white and male (see Figure 1.1).

Television also distorts the consequences of crime. In real life, the chance of avoiding arrest for a serious crime is about four in five. On television, only 8 percent of offenders get away with their crimes. This distortion may deter crime by suggesting that crime does not pay, when in fact most real crimes do

CRIME AND THE MEDIA

Television and the Simpson Trial

The trial of O. J. Simpson on charges that he murdered his ex-wife Nicole Brown Simpson and her friend Ron Goldman was tailor-made for television: it involved a well-known celebrity charged with two brutal murders, and it was tried in the entertainment capital of the world. In January 1995, early in the trial, Cable News Network's audience was 700 percent above what it had been before the trial, and afternoon network audiences were up 20 percent. In all, 20 to 25 million people were watching the trial during the day and 35 million in the evening. Ninety percent of the nation watched as the jury acquitted Simpson on October 3, 1995; that audience of 150 million Americans was the largest in television history, although the percentage of the population watching was slightly less than watched President John Kennedy's funeral and the Apollo 11 landing.

The Simpson case attracted such enormous attention because it raised provocative questions. Could a black man accused of murdering two white people get a fair trial in a city where Rodney King had been brutally beaten by police officers? Could a wealthy celebrity win an acquittal by hiring the best available legal talent? Would the legal system continue to be ineffective in bringing to justice men with histories of abusing their spouses? Race, social class, and gender were all part of the protracted media discussions of the case and the public's fascination with it.

The race issue divided the public. A July 1994 *USA Today*-CNN-Gallup poll, conducted after Simpson was arrested but before his trial began, found that 74 percent of blacks, but only 35 percent of whites, thought that the criminal justice system treated blacks more harshly than whites. That poll revealed that only 24 percent of blacks thought that the charges against Simpson were definitely true or probably true; 68 percent of whites felt that way. The survey also found that 59 percent of blacks, but only 31 percent of whites, thought that the media had treated Simpson too harshly.

Another issue raised by the Simpson case was whether the wealthy could buy an acquittal by hiring the best legal talent. Much was made of the high-priced lawyers for the defense—Johnnie Cochran, Robert Shapiro, F. Lee Bailey, and others—who eventually cost Simpson an estimated $5 million in fees. An acquittal would have been less likely had he confronted the evidence in the case with a court-appointed public defender.

The gender issue was also raised in court and in media discussions. Simpson had a record of spousal abuse; one threat against his wife was even available on audiotape. Questions arose as to whether such abuse was a precursor of murder, with cases cited of murderers who had long histories of violence against their wives. The sister of Nicole Brown Simpson used the case as the basis for organizing a highly publicized campaign against domestic violence.

Sources: Based on Howard Manly and Adam Pertman, "Races See Simpson Differently," *Boston Globe*, July 10, 1994, pp. 1, 6–7; Brian McGrory, "For Many, Simpson TV Trial Is Irresistible," *Boston Globe*, January 28, 1995, pp. 1, 8; Renee Graham, "Viewership Put at Highest Ever," *Boston Globe*, October 4, 1995, p. 26.

FIGURE 1.1

Comparison of Offenders Portrayed on Television with Suspects Arrested by the Police, All Crimes, 1981

Source: Based on data from Linda S. Lichter and S. Robert Lichter, *Prime Time Crime: Criminals and Law Enforcers in TV Entertainment.* Washington, D.C.: The Media Institute, 1983, pp. 20, 23–27.

not result in arrest. Television also conveys the impression that private detectives and citizens solve more crimes than the police; actually, very few offenses are solved by people other than the police (Lichter and Lichter, 1983).

Media distortion of the reality of crime has important consequences. It generates anxiety among the public; people who watch a lot of television are more likely than people who watch less to see the world as violent, dangerous, and crime-ridden (Gerbner and Gross, 1976). Political leaders who do not want their constituents to be fearful of crime sometimes withhold or manipulate information about crime; this has long been the official policy in China, and in 1995 the mayor of New York City was accused of doing this. A study of crime news in *Time* magazine from 1953 to 1982 concluded that by focusing on violent rather than property crime, neglecting the role of unemployment in crime, and emphasizing crime by racial minorities, the magazine provided ideological support for the capitalist political economy (Barlow, Barlow, and Chiricos, 1995: 16). Even when corporate crimes resulting in the loss of lives are reported in the press, they are less apt to be treated as criminal behavior than as the consequence of lax enforcement of government regulations (Wright, Cullen, and Blankenship, 1995).

The way that crime is portrayed in the mass media differs significantly from what criminologists have learned about the patterns and causes of crime from their research. Sociologists, psychologists, economists, political scientists, biologists, and others who study crime in a systematic way gather empirical data to test their ideas and revise those ideas to fit new information. This book focuses on sociological research, but it also draws on material from other disciplines that study criminals and criminal behavior.

The Nature of Crime and Delinquency

Most people have an intuitive sense of what crime is, but social scientists try to define in precise terms the phenomena they study. By defining crime in an exact way, criminologists define the domain of their study. Definitions of crime serve another, more subtle function: they influence the kinds of causes of criminal behavior a criminologist will study. Let's look at several definitions of crime, see what they include and exclude, and consider how they influence the causes on which criminologists will focus their attention.

In their influential book *A General Theory of Crime* (1990: 15), Michael Gottfredson and Travis Hirschi define crimes as "acts of force or fraud undertaken in pursuit of self-interest." They explicitly avoid defining crime in terms of violating the criminal law, preferring as a definition one that focuses on "the nature of crime," which they describe in terms of selected research on what they call "ordinary crime." Ordinary or mundane crime is described as providing immediate and easy gratification of desires, few long-term benefits, little skill or planning, and pain for the victim. They exclude from their picture such highly organized crimes as Mafia domination of the garbage industry in the New York metropolitan area (Reuter, 1993) and a conspiracy in the electrical equipment industry to fix prices in violation of federal law (Geis, 1967). Gottfredson and Hirschi suggest that such highly structured crimes are rare and only seem to be highly organized because scholars or law-enforcement officials have imposed organization on what is really the impulsive behavior of individuals. Their definition of crime also seems to include too much; a student of mine suggested that boxing fit their definition, as would hockey and wrestling. Those sports are seen as involving the use of force in the pursuit of self-interest.

A very different definition of crime was developed in an essay by Herman and Julia Schwendinger (1975). They define crime as violations of "the historically determined rights of individuals." They suggest that their broad definition would incorporate most current violations of the criminal law, but it would reconstitute the study of crime by focusing attention on imperialistic war, racism, sexism, and poverty. They would treat as criminals those people who deny basic human rights to others through such practices. A problem with such a definition is that criminologists would disagree over what are basic human rights; for instance, are political leaders who allow poverty to persist by not redistributing income to be regarded as criminal, or might they be seen as criminal if they taxed the rich at such a high rate as to deprive them of their property? The Schwendingers' definition of crime implies that the causes of crime exist in the institutions of society, and more specifically in the institutions of capitalist economies. This definition allows them to develop a radical critique of capitalism and to encourage criminologists to become "guardians of human rights" rather than "defenders of order."

Most criminologists adopt legalistic definitions of crime quite different from those offered by the Schwendingers and by Gottfredson and Hirschi. This book will define **crime** as an act that violates the criminal law and is punishable by the state. Criminal **laws** are formalized or codified **norms**, which are rules that make explicit certain social expectations about what is appropriate behavior for particular people in specific situations. Crimes, which are violations of these codified norms, are treated as offenses against the state rather than acts against specific individuals. This definition has its origins in medieval Great Britain, where the king replaced formal vengeance by victim against offender with sanctions by the state. Thus, today a robbery is dealt with by the courts as *State* v. *Jones* rather than as *Smith* v. *Jones*. Smith as the victim of the robbery might sue Jones, the alleged robber, in civil court to recover money for damages caused during the holdup, but this rarely happens. Instead, the offense will be dealt with in criminal court, with a prosecutor or district attorney acting on behalf of the state in bringing charges against Jones. A person who is convicted of a crime is subjected to a **sanction,** a measure designed to ensure future conformity to the law and to punish past nonconformity.

In its ideal form, the criminal law is specific in nature, uniform in its application, dispassionate in its enforcement, and reflective of the culture's informal norms (Sutherland and Cressey, 1978: 5-8). Criminal law is a means to control behavior by allowing or prohibiting certain behaviors for particular individuals in specific situations. Thus, a police officer can use lethal force to stop a felon who poses a threat of serious harm to others, but a private citizen generally is not permitted to do so. The same act is treated differently because each individual occupies a different status. The law is also specific to the situation. A victim who fears for his or her life during a crime may use lethal force in self-protection and have the action treated as justifiable homicide. However, people generally are not allowed to use lethal force to prevent a simple theft.

This book treats crime in a legalistic way, beginning with the law's definition of crime and studying behavior that violates the law, rather than regarding the development of the law as the primary topic of study. Some criminologists have criticized this legalistic approach, claiming that it implies acceptance of the values of those who make the law (Becker, 1973; Platt, 1975). This is not necessarily the case, however, for it is possible to recognize the existence of a body of criminal law and examine the causes of behavior that violates that law, without at the same time giving one's moral support to that body of law or personally condemning behavior that violates it.

The Characteristics of Crime

Crime is behavior that is subject to legally defined punishment. The French sociologist Emile Durkheim (1895, 1933) asserted in the late nineteenth century that punishment is the defining characteristic of crime and that other characteristics—such as social harm—are corollaries rather than defining traits. Punishable behavior includes a myriad of actions, from forcible rape to price-fixing, from murder to pollution of the environment. Because crime includes so many diverse acts, it makes little sense to speak of "crime increasing" or "the typical criminal" without referring to specific crimes or specific criminals. However, many crimes have some characteristics in common.

Crime usually involves **criminal intent**, the willed or conscious desire to commit an act that violates a criminal law. Before the twelfth century, the law did not include the idea of a guilty mind that formed criminal intent; guilt was then based simply on the causing of injury. Over time, the idea of intent was gradually introduced into the law, partly as a result of the influence of Christian teachings about sin and moral blame. However, today, not all acts designated as crimes involve criminal intent. Some crimes arise from negligence or recklessness; for example, in 1995 two German executives were charged with murder and attempted murder for distributing blood products contaminated with the HIV virus that causes AIDS. Other crimes are strict liability offenses, meaning that there is no need to prove criminal intent in order to convict the defendant. One strict liability offense is statutory rape, or sexual intercourse with an individual below a legally defined age of consent; this is a crime regardless of whether the offender knows the age of the victim.

For most crimes, however, the law requires a causal connection among criminal intent, criminal conduct, and harm. For instance, an act that violates the law and causes harm may not be treated as a crime by the legal system if criminal intent is absent. This practice is based on the idea that punishment makes sense only if the violator of the law is responsible for his or her behavior. For intent to exist, an individual must have criminal capacity or be in control of his or her own behavior. Capacity is lacking in people who are too young to have criminal capacity (often defined as being under the age of seven) or are not legally adults (usually defined as being between the ages of seven and eighteen).

The law allows several excuses and justifications as defenses to criminal charges. **Excuses**, which deny criminal intent, include the insanity defense, which is examined in detail in Chapter 5. The excuse that one committed a crime because of drunkenness or the influence of drugs is an excuse that is less likely to exonerate a defendant than to reduce the seriousness of the charge for which he or she is found guilty. Ignorance of the law is an excuse that is accepted only under rare circumstances. Entrapment is the defense that one broke the law only because of illegal inducement by a law-enforcement agent.

A defense that the law allows a person to act in a particular way is called a **justification**. Self-defense against an offender threatening serious bodily injury is permitted if the potential victim uses no more force than necessary to prevent the harm. The defense of duress is the claim that another person coerced one into committing a crime; stealing a bicycle because someone forced you to at knifepoint is not a crime. The justification that one had to violate the law to avoid the threat of some greater harm from a nonhuman force is called the defense of necessity; stealing a car to escape an earthquake is an example.

Juvenile Delinquency

People who violate the law but are not legally adults—defined as those below the age of eighteen in many states—can be "adjudged delinquent" rather than convicted of a crime in juvenile court, an institution that is about a century old. These delinquents might have committed an act that would be a crime if done by an adult. The designation **juvenile delinquent** is also applied to those who commit **status offenses**, acts such as underage drinking, running away from home, or truancy, which are violations only because those who engage in them are below the age of majority.

Juvenile courts were originally designed as informal welfare agencies that offered counseling and therapy tailored to the needs of the individual offender. The offender's youth was thought to confer a kind of diminished capacity and to make the offender easier to reform than an adult criminal. A 1988 sur-

The juvenile justice system deals with acts that are crimes if committed by adults and with status offenses that are violations only because those who engage in them are below the age of majority.

vey in California found "overwhelming public support for a juvenile justice system, separate from the adult system, with rehabilitation as its primary goal" (Steinhart, 1988: 1).

Since the U.S. Supreme Court's decision *In re Gault* (1967), the juvenile court has become more formalized, more like "a scaled-down criminal court" (Feld, 1993: 197). Status offenders have increasingly been diverted from the juvenile court, but more punitive measures have come to characterize the treatment of serious juvenile offenders. Every state now specifies conditions under which juveniles can be prosecuted and punished as adults. In 1992, more than 10,000 juveniles were incarcerated in adult prisons. The "get tough" attitude toward juveniles that developed in the 1980s and persists today resulted from the perceptions that juvenile crime was increasing and that the juvenile justice system was treating too leniently young offenders such as the following:

- A twelve-year-old Florida boy was arrested for his fifty-seventh offense in 1993. Over the previous four years, he had been arrested twelve times for car theft, ten times for burglary, and three times for armed robbery.
- A nineteen-year-old New Jersey man sexually assaulted and murdered a six-year-old neighbor in 1994. State law required that his admission at the age of seventeen to sexually molesting two young girls and a boy could not be revealed to the public.
- Two boys who had killed a five-year-old boy by dropping him from a fourteen-story building when they were only ten and eleven were sentenced to Illinois juvenile penitentiaries in 1996.

Social Origins of the Criminal Law

Criminal law is a social phenomenon; behavior defined as crime in one society can occur in a different society and not be regarded as suitable for punishment there. We can see the social nature of the criminal law by looking at variations in the definition of theft in different societies. Most societies define theft as a crime, but there are significant differences in the way this behavior is treated. In Norway, petty theft from a relative with whom the thief lives is not treated as a crime. Thieves in Colombia are exempted from criminal sanctions if they can show that they or their family had a pressing need for food or clothing, that there was no legal way to meet that need, that no violence was used to perpetrate the theft, and that no more was taken than was necessary. The former Soviet Union distinguished the theft of private property from the theft of socialist property, a distinction based on state ownership of land and the means of production. In industrial societies, taking a neighbor's property for personal use is generally regarded as a crime, but in some tribal societies one is expected to take and use a neighbor's property in time of need. Understanding why one society permits such behavior while another condemns it as crime requires a careful study of the social structure, culture, history, and level of economic development of each society.

Theoretical Perspectives on Crime and the Criminal Law

Criminologists disagree on the origins of the criminal law and, as a result, disagree on the way they see crime. Conflict theorists claim that the law develops to benefit some groups to the detriment of others. Consensus theorists regard the law as a reflection of popular agreement on standards of behavior.

The Conflict Perspective   The **conflict perspective** sees the criminal law as closely intertwined with the distribution of political power and economic resources in a society (Gordon, 1973; Taylor, Walton, and Young, 1973, 1975a; MacLean, 1986). Conflict theorists argue that those who control power and wealth determine which kinds of behavior are defined as crime and which kinds are permitted (see the Cross-Cultural Perspective box). The criminal law thus reflects the will of the powerful and well-to-do, and behavior that threatens the interests of that elite—such as theft and violence by the poor—will be harshly sanctioned.

Marxist or radical criminology is a form of conflict theory that focuses on social class, defined by the relationship of a group to the means of production. This perspective claims that capitalists, who own and control the means of production, use the law to protect their property from those who threaten it, the lower and working classes. Crime by the wealthy and powerful is attributed to the greed generated by a capitalist economic system, and crime by the powerless is attributed to the need to violate the law in order to survive. Marxist and radical criminologists assert the relationship between capitalism and crime, but they offer little evidence that capitalism generates crime to a greater degree than alternative economic systems, such as socialism. Some capitalist systems, such as those of Japan and Switzerland, do not have high crime rates; and relatively high rates seemed to exist in the Soviet Union before its breakup. Indeed, after more than seventy years of Communist Party rule, Russia had a murder rate significantly higher than that of the United States. Even if some socialist or communist nations do have low crime rates, those rates might not be due to the greater amount of income equality or social justice in those countries, as Marxists suggest. Instead, those low rates might be due to the more oppressive social control that characterizes some of those totalitarian states, or the result of the low level of economic development of those countries.

Not all conflict theories are Marxist, but most such theories acknowledge that control of the economic system is an important way in which less powerful groups are dominated. Conflict theorists have also examined group differences other than social class, such as disputes over values and between racial, ethnic, and religious groups.

Left realism is a conflict theory that has shifted the emphasis from crime by the ruling class to the impact that crime by the lower and working class has on other members of the same class. Proposing crime-reduction strategies that are more concrete than the Marxist demand for a new social order to replace capitalism, left realists have called for closer attention to the actual circumstances of victims and offenders, the development of programs that

A CROSS-CULTURAL PERSPECTIVE

The Black Market in Peru

In Peru, the President and various governmental departments have used their power and resources to define many kinds of economic activity as illegal. Economic activity must meet the requirements of about 500,000 laws, executive orders, decrees, ministerial resolutions, and bureaucratic regulations. According to Mario Vargas Llosa, a Peruvian novelist, this "byzantine legal system seems designed to favor those already favored and to punish the rest by making them permanent outlaws" (p. 30). The multitude of laws has retarded economic development through legitimate channels, encouraged bribery of government officials in order to circumvent legal restrictions, and given rise to an extensive black market or "informal sector."

In 1983, a research institute in Peru tried an experiment to document the difficulty and cost of registering a small workshop, one with two sewing machines. The researchers decided to pay no bribes unless failure to do so would shut down the shop. Bureaucrats solicited bribes on ten occasions, but the researchers had to pay bribes only twice to keep the shop operating. To register the shop took them nearly a year, cost them about $1,200 in expenses and lost wages, and required the full-time labor of four workers. Clearly, anyone of modest means would be unable to comply with the legal requirements of registering such a shop, thereby undermining economic development through legitimate channels and forcing anyone who used those channels to commit the crime of bribery. In many cases, such shops simply operate illegally, without being registered, thus contributing to Peru's large and growing black market.

In Lima alone, the black market supports more than 400,000 people. Half of the population of that city lives in housing built by the black market, and 95 percent of public transportation there is provided by the "informal sector." Such black-market activity is essential to the Peruvian economy and seems to be a more productive way of accomplishing economic goals than the legitimate market.

Source: Based on Mario Vargas Llosa, "In Defense of the Black Market," *New York Times Magazine,* February 22, 1987, pp. 28–47.

---

increase "human capital" through job training and better wages, more citizen involvement in the fight against crime, a police force that is both more responsive to community needs and a more effective deterrent of crime, greater emphasis on rehabilitation, and less use of imprisonment (Lea and Young, 1984, 1986; Currie, 1985; Matthews, 1987; Matthews and Young, 1992; Lowman and MacLean, 1992).

Conflict theorists have contributed to the sociology of law by asking why some behavior is defined as crime and other behavior is not. They have shown that behavior that is especially common to powerless groups is more likely to be defined as criminal than behavior that is characteristic of the wealthy and the powerful (Turk, 1976). Thus, the criminal law does not reflect the values and interests of the whole society, but only those of the groups that are able to use the law to protect their own narrow interests. In tracing the development of criminal laws against vagrancy, drug use, theft, alcohol production and distribution, and antitrust violations, conflict theorists have shown that laws emerge from conflict among various interest groups, with victorious groups imposing their will on the losers through enactment and enforcement of laws. By looking at the process of law formation, conflict theorists have demonstrated that crime is behavior that is socially defined rather than intrinsically wrong (Quinney, 1970). However, the conventional crimes that have been the primary focus of modern criminology are widely supported by all segments of the population: there is little dispute over whether murder, rape, robbery, and even white-collar crime should be defined as criminal.

By focusing on crime by the wealthy and the powerful, conflict theorists have helped to redirect the attention of criminologists from conventional crime to white-collar crime and political corruption. However, this redirecting of attention to crime by the upper strata is not a unique contribution of conflict theory; Edwin Sutherland made the same point in the 1930s when he introduced the concept of white-collar crime, and most research on white-collar crime has been done by criminologists who do not identify themselves as conflict theorists.

Conflict theorists have focused on the way that laws are enforced as well as the way they are enacted. As Austin Turk (1969: 25) remarks, "Criminality is not a biological, psychological, or even behavioral phenomenon, but a social status defined by the way in which an individual is perceived, evaluated, and treated by legal authorities." Conflict theorists claim that the criminal justice system discriminates against those who are disadvantaged by class, race, ethnicity, and gender. They claim that the lower classes and minorities are more likely to be watched by the police, arrested in suspicious circumstances, held in jail rather than released on bail, tried in court, found guilty, and given harsh sentences (Chambliss, 1969; Reiman, 1995). These assertions of bias are testable and will be assessed in Chapter 13.

Some conflict theorists have argued that criminology should link the study of crime to the pursuit of social justice and the liberation of oppressed people (Schwendinger and Schwendinger, 1975). They deny the "objective" nature of criminal behavior and instead regard offenders as victims of oppression. Property crime, for instance, is seen as an effort to accumulate property as rapidly as possible, a goal highly valued in capitalist systems. These conflict theorists believe that criminology should be "normatively committed to the abolition of inequalities in wealth and power," rather than search for factors that distinguish offenders from nonoffenders or try to change people who violate the law (Taylor, Walton, and Young, 1975b: 44).

The Consensus Perspective   In contrast to the conflict perspective stands the **consensus perspective**, the position that the criminal law reflects broad agreement about which kinds of behavior should be punished by the state. Consensus theorists argue that the law represents shared values and norms held by all members of the society, rather than the norms and values of a particular group. Consensus is derived from discussion and compromise by elected lawmakers, rather than imposed on society by a group that controls political power or economic resources (Durkheim, 1895, 1933).

Consensus theorists see crime as behavior that exceeds a society's limits of tolerance. In this view, crime is behavior detrimental to the public interest, rather than behavior detrimental to the narrow interests of organized groups that are able to influence the law. For consensus theorists, the critical question is why some people violate the law, rather than why the law defines their behavior as criminal. These theorists propose that criminals are either inadequately socialized with dominant norms and values or are insufficiently integrated into conventional social institutions. Chapter 7 examines social control theory, which asserts that delinquents are free to violate dominant norms because they do not have strong attachments to such institutions as the family and the school. Processes of informal social control that induce conformity are also explored in Chapter 12.

Using the Conflict and Consensus Perspectives   The best way to view the criminal law is to examine the extent to which consensus and conflict are involved in the passage of laws, as well as the degree to which the public supports existing laws. Some laws reflect a widespread social consensus; for example, murder and rape are almost universally regarded as harmful acts that ought to be punished (Brown, 1952; Clifford, 1978). Other laws reflect the outcome of conflict among groups; for instance, an antitrust law in the United States was the result of a victory by small business owners, labor, and farmers over large corporations (Quinney, 1970). Sometimes, laws initiated through conflict are perpetuated through consensus; thus, the antitrust law is widely supported today.

The Social Construction of Crime

Crime is defined by the criminal law, but the social meaning given to crime varies from group to group and over time. In recent years, criminologists have studied the **social construction of crime**, the way that crime is interpreted or given meaning by groups with different interests they seek to promote by using their resources to gain ownership of an issue (Jenkins, 1994). Rather than assume that criminal laws are uniformly applied, this perspective proposes that laws are inconsistently applied; crime is less an objective property of behavior than a definition constructed through social interaction.

Gary LaFree (1989) used this perspective to examine official reactions to reports of sexual assault. Rather than focusing on the causes of sexual assault, he asked how the police and courts decided that a sexual assault constitutes a rape. He discovered that definitions of rape are constructed through social interaction and reflect stereotypes or typifications, which are shared ideas about the kinds of offenders, victims, and situations that characterize something called "rape." For example, he found that men accused of sexual assault are less apt to be convicted of rape if their victims had "bad reputations" and unconventional living arrangements, were chronic alcohol users, and did not report the assault promptly. None of these factors appears in legal definitions of rape, but all form part of the way that rape is socially constructed.

The abduction of children by strangers is another crime that has been examined in terms of its social construction. By merging perhaps 200–300 such abductions each year with millions of runaways and children taken by their noncustodial parents in violation of court orders, "claims makers" such as the mass media, politicians, law-enforcement agents, and child-advocacy groups exaggerate the problem of stranger abductions (Best, 1990; Finkelhor, Hotaling, and Sedlak, 1990; Kappeler, Blumberg, and Potter, 1996). Pictures of missing children are widely circulated, sensational cases are given front-page attention, and the sexual exploitation of missing children is highlighted. In this way, a tragic event—the abduction of a child by a stranger—that is only slightly more common than being struck dead by lightning is thrust to the fore of public consciousness and becomes a major crime problem.

Serial murder is another crime that has commanded great public attention in recent years. As with child abductions, this crime is a serious one, but one that has been exaggerated and distorted by various claims makers (Jenkins, 1994). The Federal Bureau of Investigation's (FBI) Behavioral Sciences Unit was influential in defining this problem during the 1980s, exag-

Aileen Wuornos, a prostitute sentenced to death for murder in Florida, was accused of killing seven men. Between 10 and 15 percent of all serial killers are women.

gerating the number of serial murderers active at any given moment and focusing on killers who wandered from state to state, even though most serial killers stay within their own metropolitan region (Hickey, 1997). This picture of serial murder served the FBI's interests by increasing its investigative resources and by redefining some murders as crimes requiring federal attention. Feminists cited serial murder as another example of men's domination of women, often linking serial murder to the influence of pornography. Some feminists even denied the existence of female serial killers, although 10 to 15 percent of serial killers are women. Certain religious groups tried to capture the serial murder problem by linking it to the rituals of satanic cults; lack of credible evidence and the FBI's resistance to this interpretation led to the failure of this attempted construction of the serial murder problem (Jenkins, 1994).

Crime is behavior that violates the criminal law, but groups with different ideological perspectives emphasize and distort crime stories to make rhetorical points supportive of their own positions (see the Crime and the Media box). Criminologists need to study criminal behavior, but they also must attend to the ways that crime issues are socially constructed by groups with various interests.

Criminology: The Study of Criminal Behavior

Criminology is a discipline that gathers and analyzes empirical data in order to explain violations of the criminal law and societal reactions to those violations. Rather than being organized around types of crimes—with a chapter devoted to violent crime, another to property crime, and still others to different kinds of offenses—this book is organized around concepts and theories that criminologists have developed and used to explain different kinds of crime. For instance, robbery and price-fixing are clearly different forms of behavior, but both offenses might be explained by the concept of relative deprivation: the idea that people commit crimes when they believe they have less than others with whom they compare themselves and when they think they are rightfully entitled to more than they have. Throughout the book, we explore in detail the needs and motivations of people who commit various kinds of crimes, the way they reduce their commitment to the law, the process by which they learn to commit crime, the way they select opportunities to commit crime, and the manner in which criminal activity is organized.

Needs and Motivations

The needs and motivations of people who engage in crime can be biological in origin, psychological in nature, or socially induced. Thus, a murder could be committed by one person because a brain tumor led to violence, by another person because of delusions about being persecuted by others, or by a member of a juvenile gang who is trying to impress his peers.

CRIME AND THE MEDIA

Crime on the Op-Ed Page

Theodore Sasson analyzed fifty-eight op-ed columns, the opinion pieces appearing opposite editorial pages, in six metropolitan newspapers in 1990 and 1991 to determine how the problem of street crime was "framed" or socially constructed. From this commentary on crime by political, journalistic, and academic elites, Sasson identified the following five themes or frames:

1. *Faulty System:* Crime is the result of a lenient and inefficient criminal justice system. The solution to the crime problem is for the system to "get tough."
2. *Social Breakdown:* Crime is a product of the breakdown of family and community. The solution is for citizens to unite to create traditional communities.
3. *Blocked Opportunities:* Crime is due to poverty and inequality. The solution is for the government to deal with the "root causes" of crime by creating jobs and reducing poverty.
4. *Media Violence:* Crime stems from violence in the media. The solution is for more government regulation of the media.
5. *Racist System:* The criminal justice system operates in a racist way. The solution is for blacks to organize to demand justice.

The dominant construction of the crime problem in the op-ed columns was in terms of a faulty criminal justice system and the breakdown of family and community. The *Faulty System* frame was advocated in 55 percent of the columns, with the subframe *Inefficiency* (failure to punish offenders swiftly and certainly, lack of adequate resources, and the need for new approaches to policing and sentencing) receiving more attention than the subframe *Leniency* (punishment being too lax). The *Social Breakdown* frame was supported in 36 percent of the columns, and the *Blocked Opportunities* frame was presented positively in 33 percent of the columns. The *Media Violence* and *Racist System* frames received little attention, being advocated in only 5 and 10 percent of the columns, respectively.

Sasson argues that the op-ed columns are important because they provide the general public "with ample *and diverse* resources for conjuring *Faulty System* and *Social Breakdown*" (p. 158), allowing them to make strong arguments for those constructions of the crime problem; resources for conjuring the *Blocked Opportunities* frame were more scarce. The op-ed pieces are also important because they are closely read by politicians and shape their perspectives on crime.

Source: Based on Theodore Sasson, *Crime Talk: How Citizens Construct a Social Problem.* New York: Aldine de Gruyter, 1995.

Reducing Commitment to the Law

Having certain needs, desires, or motivations is a necessary but not sufficient reason to commit a crime. Because all people to some extent learn that they should abide by the law, potential offenders must reduce their commitment to the law before they violate it. The critical question becomes, "Why, in a society in which such actions are widely known to be criminal and severely punishable, are they committed?" (Walker, 1974: 61–62). People who violate the law are often only weakly attached to groups and institutions that support the law, including parents, teachers, and peers. Being unconcerned about the opinion of others who are committed to a conventional way of life makes it easier to neutralize the constraints of the law. People also neutralize the influence of the law by using rationalizations to justify their violations; they might claim that coming from a broken home makes it acceptable for them to commit a crime.

Learning Skills to Commit Crime

Another factor critical to the perpetration of some crimes is the learning of certain skills. This learning may be from the general culture, the mass media, other criminals, or noncriminals who convey values conducive to crime. Safecrackers must learn how to blow a safe or pick a lock. Armed robbers have less to learn, because holding a pistol and demanding money require few specific skills. Some offenders use specialized skills that they have employed for legitimate purposes to commit crime; for example, an accountant might use his or her bookkeeping skills to embezzle funds from a company.

Opportunities to Violate the Law

Even given the need or desire to commit a crime, the reduction in commitment to the law, and the learning of the requisite skills, another factor is needed to commit a crime: opportunity. Crime is sometimes situational in nature; that is, people who might not otherwise think of breaking the law might commit a crime if they are confronted with a tempting opportunity to make an illicit gain with little risk. Other people systematically seek opportunities to commit profitable crimes, planning their offenses in advance and organizing a group of criminals to carry out illegal acts. Social change can increase opportunities for crime. For example, bank robberies have increased with the development of suburban branches that lack good security, and auto thefts have increased as the number of cars available to be stolen has grown.

Criminal Careers

When individual acts of crime by an offender accumulate over time, we speak of a **criminal career,** a sequence of criminal acts that can lead an offender to change his or her self-concept, behavior, and commitment to a life of crime.

Understanding criminal behavior requires knowledge of the factors that give rise to individual offenses, but it also requires detailed information about the way that those acts add up to criminal careers.

The Organization of Criminal Activity

Some criminal activity is organized; that is, at least two individuals associate with one another in an ongoing relationship that exists for the purpose of violating the law. Networks of this sort characterize organized crime syndicates, drug importers, art thieves, and juvenile gangs. Even conventional violent crime is sometimes organized, as the systematic rape of non-Serbian women in Bosnia has shown.

Reactions to Crime

Society responds to crime in many ways. Some of them are institutional; for instance, the criminal justice system responds by punishing those who are convicted of breaking the law. Other responses are less formal, such as the reaction of a bystander to a crime or community action against drug dealers.

Community Reactions to Crime   The social structure of a community influences its crime rate. Tightly knit neighborhoods are often able to keep crime down by maintaining informal social control. Public surveillance of the streets and willingness to call the police can deter potential offenders from violating the law or cause them to commit their offenses elsewhere. We will look at informal social control as one response to crime and as a factor involved in the causation of crime. We will also examine the social conditions conducive to bystander intervention in a crime and explore collective reactions to crime such as citizen patrols and community action groups.

The Criminal Justice System   A full understanding of crime requires attention to the criminal justice system: the police, the courts, and the prisons. What criminals do and how criminal careers develop are influenced by the agents of criminal justice; for instance, the exercise of police discretion influences who is arrested and who is not. The reactions of the criminal justice system to suspected offenders can push them into criminal careers or deter them from further crimes. We can also learn a lot about crime without limiting ourselves to the study of convicted offenders; for instance, we can learn much about robbery from police reports of robberies that do not lead to arrest.

Justifications for Punishment   The formal responses to crime by the criminal justice system are based on several justifications for punishment, each of which reflects ideas about why offenders should be punished. The first line of defense against crime is deterrence, the use of sanctions to prevent crime by raising the cost of crime to potential offenders. Incapacitation is a rationale for punishment that suggests that crime can be prevented if offenders are locked up for a period of time. Another rationale is retribution or just deserts, the idea that those who break the law should suffer in proportion to their blameworthiness and the seriousness of the harm they have produced. A fourth rationale for punishment is rehabilitation, the idea that convicted offenders should be reformed so they will not commit crime again. These four justifications for punishment are examined in Chapter 14.

Solving the Crime Problem

Conservatives, liberals, and radicals have proposed different ways to solve the crime problem, but in recent years most American political leaders have focused on reform of the criminal justice system as the best way to reduce crime. A second approach to crime reduction that has received less attention from politicians is situational crime prevention, the policy of making it more difficult for offenders to victimize people and property. A third approach, eradicating the causes of crime, has also received little attention from political leaders recently, but it could be the only effective way to reduce crime in the long run.

Ideally, criminology should begin with a description of criminal behavior, using crime statistics and interviews with offenders. It should then develop theories to explain the causes of crime, and finally derive policies from those descriptions and theories. Much criminological work does not take this form. It is either descriptive, nontheoretical, and lacking in policy analysis; or it is theoretical without empirical evidence or policy implications; or it prescribes policies but lacks supporting evidence and theoretical justification. The effort in this book is to integrate these three approaches—the descriptive, the theoretical, and the prescriptive.

Strategies of Criminological Research

The personal values of criminologists sometimes influence the kinds of crime they choose to study, yet they can still be relatively detached in their collection and interpretation of data. Stating a hypothesis and gathering data that might support or refute that hypothesis will increase objectivity, even if the selection of the problem for study (for example, robbery or white-collar crime) reflects personal values.

This section looks in detail at four research strategies employed by criminologists, giving an example of each. This will give the flavor of how social scientists go about the task of studying crime. Then several other strategies that researchers have used will be examined more briefly.

Comparative and Historical Research

One way to illuminate the problem of crime causation is to study violations of the law in other societies and at other times. This process offers insight into the relationship between crime and factors such as level of economic development and rate of urbanization. **Comparative research** can be used to evaluate whether a theory of crime developed in one society also explains crime in other societies, that is, whether the theory is universally true or limited in scope. The comparative approach also generates theory, for differences in crime from one society to another must fit a general theory of crime.

Comparative research of this sort is uncommon. Crime has been studied in countries other than the United States, but researchers rarely collect data simultaneously in different countries so that they can make direct comparisons. Methodological problems with crime statistics gathered by the police, the courts, or the prisons also make comparisons difficult. Comparative research is hampered, too, by geographic, political, and linguistic barriers, lack of funding, and the absence of a research tradition in some societies. Moreover, criminologists from one society sometimes approach the study of crime in another nation with an ethnocentric bias or a theoretical preference that distorts their interpretation of the data (Johnson and Barak-Glantz, 1983).

Similar in some ways to comparative research in contemporary societies is **historical research,** which examines the same society at different times and looks at the ways that crime has changed with economic and social development. Historical research often requires reliance on nonstatistical material, although researchers have sometimes used official statistics from the past or quantified material from historical documents. They have also used accounts by observers of the time, records of legislative hearings, narrative material from court files, and other documentary evidence.

Historical studies put contemporary crime into perspective, show how people have reacted to crime in the past, and suggest problems that may be encountered by nations now undergoing change. For example, one review of historical research concludes that the recent upsurge of violent crime in Western societies is a deviation from a decline in violence that has been going on for more than a century (Gurr, 1981). One historical study that illuminates the nature of crime in today's developing societies is J. J. Tobias's *Crime and Industrial Society in the 19th Century* (1967).

Tobias's Study of Crime in Nineteenth-Century England   J. J. Tobias's study of crime in industrializing England found that the crime statistics of that period were practically worthless for systematic study. As a result, he relied on parliamentary reports and contemporary accounts to piece together a picture of crime.

Tobias discovered that crime rates were high early in the nineteenth century because social institutions had failed to respond to a sizable increase in population; more specifically, the number of young people in the country had increased without a commensurate growth in employment opportunities. Migration from rural areas and small towns to larger towns and cities proved unsettling, and those larger communities provided ample opportunities for crime as well as an anonymity that reduced the risk of arrest.

During the nineteenth century, crime decreased as social conditions became more settled. Economic development increased job opportunities

Crime rates decreased in England during the nineteenth century, as social conditions became more settled. This engraving depicts the murder of a traveler by the notorious highwayman Richard Turpin; the crime occurred around 1840.

and raised incomes, and the government used its resources to introduce social services for the disadvantaged. The police and the courts also changed over the course of the century, from a system that had a low rate of detection and severe penalties for the few offenders who were convicted, to one that had more lenient sentences but a higher rate of detection. Tobias argues that this change enhanced the deterrent effect of the law and contributed to the decline in the crime rate.

It is difficult to support Tobias's interpretation of the historical changes with precise data, but he provides convincing documentary evidence of the social changes that accompanied the long-term decline in the crime rate. His conclusions are also consistent with evidence about the changing nature of crime in societies now undergoing social and economic development.

Biographies

A fruitful way to study the sources of criminal behavior and the development of criminal careers is to examine the experiences of a single offender. This

biographical method reveals the needs and motivations of the offender, the way that commitment to the law is reduced, the way that criminal skills are learned, the obstacles encountered in pursuing legitimate careers and illegitimate life styles, the pattern of criminal activity over a lifetime, and the consequences of contact with the criminal justice system (Rettig, Torres, and Garrett, 1977).

One problem with the biographical method is that the criminal who is studied may not be representative of other offenders. Separating an offender's experiences into those that are idiosyncratic and those that are common to other offenders is a difficult undertaking that requires more information than can be provided by one criminal's biography. The richness of the account of one offender's life sacrifices the representativeness provided by research on a sample of offenders, though the biographical method often yields hypotheses that can be tested on larger samples of offenders.

Another problem with the biographical method is that offenders may distort their experiences. They may do this because of faulty memories, because they view the past in light of their present circumstances, or because they want to glorify and romanticize themselves (Rettig, Torres, and Garrett, 1977). This problem of distortion can be minimized by double-checking the accuracy of an account with the offender at different times or by interviewing friends and relatives of the offender (Klockars, 1974).

An early example of the biographical technique is Edwin Sutherland's (1937) study of "Chic Conwell," a professional thief who recounted his life of crime in great detail. William Chambliss (King and Chambliss, 1984) used a similar approach to study "Harry King," a "box man" or safecracker. Another valuable biographical study is the story of a heroin addict and thief named Manny (Rettig, Torres, and Garrett, 1977). The biographical method has also been used to good advantage by Carl Klockars in *The Professional Fence* (1974) and by Darrell Steffensmeier in *The Fence* (1986).

Steffensmeier's Study of a Fence   Steffensmeier met his research subject "Sam Goodman" while Sam was serving time in prison for receiving stolen goods. He contacted this fence, who is an intermediary between thieves who steal property and members of the public who buy stolen goods, through the recommendations of several burglars Steffensmeier had been questioning as part of a different study.

In one chapter of *The Fence*, Sam tells how he became involved in criminal activity. He was self-reliant by the age of fifteen, working full-time and realizing that he was "out for a buck." His attraction to a fast life and hustling was reinforced by an uncle who led a similar life and had been in prison. From occasional petty theft, Sam graduated to burglary at age seventeen, being arrested and serving time in a juvenile reformatory. After his release, he worked full-time but continued to commit burglaries as part of a gang. Following his release from prison after another burglary conviction, he started to work for a furniture manufacturer. Eventually, he opened a secondhand furniture and antiques shop, though he continued to commit burglaries. Sam used his shop as a front to sell goods he had stolen. Other dealers began to pay him to upholster or doctor stolen goods for resale, and thieves began to bring him stolen merchandise. Sam's fencing operation grew after another prison term, and his burglaries became less frequent. Later he served time for receiving stolen goods, but after his release he seemed to become a legitimate dealer in secondhand goods and antiques, although he did fence on a small scale.

Steffensmeier's study of Sam Goodman offers rich insights into the crime of fencing. He details the network in which the fence is embedded, and the way that the fence interacts with thieves, criminal justice officials, antiques dealers and collectors, truckers, dockworkers, and competing fences. Steffensmeier looks at the rewards of fencing, including money, reputation in the criminal community, excitement, and a sense of mastery over one's life. He also provides insight into the ways that Sam justifies his fencing by claiming that fences are not the same as thieves, do little harm to the victims of theft, are much like legitimate businesspeople, and actually help other people.

Patterns of Crime

Another way to study crime is to look at it as a social phenomenon that has a specific form or structure. This study of **patterns of crime** often involves the use of police statistics to determine where crime is committed, who commits it, who is victimized, and what are the major dimensions of the criminal act. This kind of research examines the spatial distribution of crime in a city, the social background of offenders and victims, relationships between offenders and victims, and the social processes that lead to crime.

The patterns-of-crime approach assumes that police records can provide a comprehensive and valid description of crime and its participants. However, police statistics are not always representative of all the crime that occurs in a community. For instance, police records in Philadelphia, where this strategy has often been used, contain many details about those crimes that are reported to and recorded by the police, but there is evidence that a smaller proportion of all crimes that actually occur in Philadelphia are reported and recorded than is the case for other large American cities (Skogan, 1976b: 111–112). Thus, Philadelphia crime statistics might not reflect the actual nature of crime in that city very well.

Patterns-of-crime studies are useful in describing the criminal act and in providing information on the prior arrest records of offenders and victims. However, they usually do not deal with the issue of crime causation in much depth. They do not tell us much about how offenders reduce their commitment to the law, learn criminal skills, or find opportunities to commit crime. The failure to interview offenders is a major shortcoming of the patterns-of-crime approach. In crimes such as homicide, where a high proportion of offenders are caught and convicted, much could be learned from interviews that cannot be discovered in police reports.

The patterns-of-crime approach has been used extensively at the University of Pennsylvania's Center for Studies in Criminology and Criminal Law, where Marvin Wolfgang pioneered the approach in his *Patterns in*

Criminal Homicide (1958). Robbery and rape have also been studied using the same approach (Normandeau, 1968; Amir, 1971). A national study of four violent crimes in seventeen cities used a similar research strategy (Curtis, 1974).

Wolfgang's Study of Homicide   Wolfgang's pioneering investigation of homicide used police records from 1948 through 1952 in Philadelphia to analyze the race, sex, and age of homicide offenders and victims, the methods and weapons used to commit murder, the temporal and spatial patterns of homicide, the presence of alcohol in the offender and the victim at the time of the crime, the previous criminal records of offenders and victims, and the motives of offenders. He also explored the interpersonal relationships of offenders and victims, homicides committed during other crimes, and the extent to which victims contributed to their own murders. He looked at the solution of homicide cases by the police and at the court's disposition of charges against suspects.

One important finding that emerged from Wolfgang's research was that offenders and victims in homicide cases are often intimately associated with each other (see Figure 1.2A). About one-fourth of the homicides involved an offender and a victim who were relatives, and a similar number involved offenders and victims who were close friends. Homicides between strangers were relatively rare, accounting for only one-eighth of the cases. These findings focused criminologists' attention on the interpersonal dynamics of intimate relationships as a factor that can lead to lethal violence.

Another important conclusion was that homicides frequently occur in a context that includes the use of alcohol (see Figure 1.2B). Alcohol was absent in the homicide situation in only 36.4 percent of the cases. In 43.5 percent of the murders, both the offender and the victim had been drinking, in 9.2 percent of the cases only the victim had been drinking, and in 10.9 percent of the cases only the offender had been drinking.

Wolfgang's study of homicide provided other important findings. He found that most murders occurred between an offender and a victim of the same race; murders of whites by blacks or of blacks by whites were relatively rare (see Figure 1.2C). He also found that murder rates were highest among young black males, a finding he later used to support his theory of a subculture of violence.

The Cohort Study

One problem with some research techniques is the lack of a time dimension; that is, little attention is paid to the way a criminal career develops over time or the way crime rates increase or decrease. One strategy that introduces a time dimension follows a carefully defined group of people who are in a common situation over a period of time. Such a group is called a **cohort.** A cohort of all the individuals born in a given year will experience similar events over their lifetimes, even though they may be affected differently by those events.

FIGURE 1.2

Homicide in Philadelphia, 1948–1952, Selected Findings from Marvin Wolfgang's *Patterns in Criminal Homicide**

*Percentages may not total 100.0% because of rounding.

Source: Based on data from Marvin E. Wolfgang, *Patterns in Criminal Homicide.* Philadelphia: University of Pennsylvania Press, 1958, pp. 136, 207, 379.

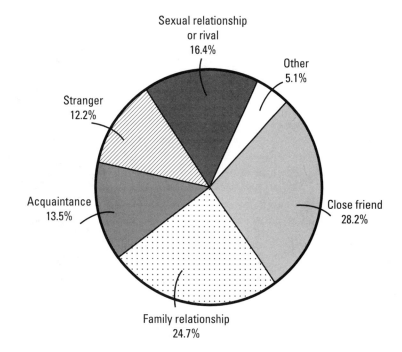

A. Victim/Offender Relationship

Sexual relationship or rival 16.4%

Other 5.1%

Stranger 12.2%

Acquaintance 13.5%

Close friend 28.2%

Family relationship 24.7%

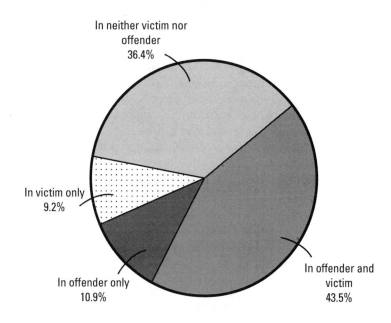

B. Presence of Alcohol

In neither victim nor offender 36.4%

In victim only 9.2%

In offender only 10.9%

In offender and victim 43.5%

FIGURE 1.2
continued

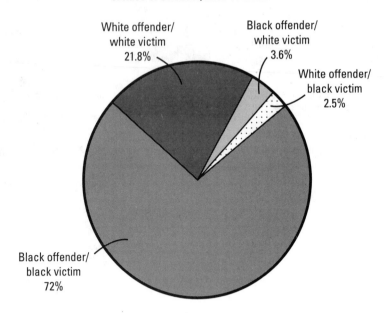

For instance, all people born in 1915 who lived until 1936 experienced the Great Depression during their adolescence, although some were exposed to abject poverty during that era and others were relatively insulated from its effects.

The ideal way to carry out a cohort study is to begin to collect data at an early age for the members of a cohort and then follow them through adolescence and into adulthood. Such a study could take twenty-five or more years to complete, if we assume that little crime is committed before the age of ten and that most offenders stop their criminal activities by the age of thirty-five. This kind of study would not have to rely solely on official records of delinquency or crime but could use questionnaires to measure violations of the law. Interviews could be conducted periodically to measure changes in an individual's social situation—for example, adjustment to school or family income—that might be associated with violation of the law. Some criminologists believe that such a long-term cohort study would yield information on the causes of criminal behavior and the development of criminal careers that we cannot get from other kinds of studies (Farrington, Ohlin, and Wilson, 1986; National Research Council, 1993).

Cohort studies do have several drawbacks. They are expensive to conduct, because they take so long to complete. A multicommunity cohort study of the biological, psychological, and social roots of violence proposed by the National Research Council would cost as much as $50 million, even though such a project "offers only a reasonable chance of breakthroughs in the understanding and control of violence" (National Research Council, 1993: 344). Pressure on academic researchers to publish scholarly work can inhibit them from undertaking cohort studies that will not yield data for years. In addition, interviewing cohort members on a regular basis could affect their normal process of growing up.

In spite of such difficulties, several cohort studies have been done. An important early one was the Cambridge-Somerville Youth Study (Powers and Witmer, 1951; McCord and McCord, 1959; McCord, 1978, 1981). Another major cohort study was carried out in England (West, 1969, 1982; West and Farrington, 1973, 1977), and a study of the relationship between juvenile delinquency and adult criminal careers was done in Wisconsin (Shannon, 1988). One cohort study that has received much attention is reported in Marvin Wolfgang, Robert Figlio, and Thorsten Sellin's *Delinquency in a Birth Cohort* (1972).

Wolfgang, Figlio, and Sellin's Cohort Study of Delinquency Wolfgang, Figlio, and Sellin studied a cohort of all males born in 1945 who lived in Philadelphia continuously from the age of ten (the first age at which there were a significant number of arrests) until the age of eighteen (the age at which juveniles became adults). The researchers studied only boys because of "the greater incidence, frequency, heterogeneity, seriousness, and persistency of male delinquency" (Wolfgang, Figlio, and Sellin, 1972: 30). Records kept by schools, draft boards, juvenile courts, and the police were examined for all 9,945 boys in the cohort. All police contacts that resulted in a written report about a delinquent act were examined. A study of the experiences of some of those boys as adults has also been done (Wolfgang, Thornberry, and Figlio, 1987).

Wolfgang, Figlio, and Sellin looked at the characteristics that distinguished boys who had had contact with the police from boys who had not. Thirty-five percent of the boys had at least one contact with the police as a juvenile, but a mere 6 percent of the boys accounted for 52 percent of all of the police contacts in the cohort. This suggests that a policy that could keep this small group of chronic offenders from engaging in delinquency would have a major impact on the overall rate of juvenile delinquency.

Blacks and lower-class boys were more apt to have police contacts than were whites and middle-class boys. In fact, the likelihood that a black middle-class boy would have contact with the police was the same as the chance that a white lower-class boy would have contact. The cohort technique permitted such conclusions because nonoffenders as well as offenders were included in the study. Conclusions of this sort would not be possible if the research design had included only people who had had contact with the police.

Because the cohort they studied included only boys whose contact with the police was examined during the relatively tranquil period from 1955 to 1962, Wolfgang and his colleagues later decided to study a second cohort. This cohort of 27,160 included both boys and girls who were born in 1958 and lived in Philadelphia from 1968 to 1975, a time of turmoil that included the Vietnam War, increased drug use, and social protest. In comparing the boys in the two cohorts, Wolfgang and his colleagues found that a similar percentage of each had had contact with the police, that in each cohort blacks were more likely than whites to have had police contacts, and that a relatively small proportion of each cohort accounted for most of the cohort's police contacts. The researchers did find, however, that the boys in the second cohort were much more likely to be involved in serious, costly offenses (Tracy, Wolfgang, and Figlio, 1985). Cohort studies can thus show how patterns of criminal and delinquent activity change over time.

Other Strategies of Criminological Research

Comparative and historical research, biographies, patterns-of-crime studies, and cohort studies are but a few of the many strategies that criminologists have used to study crime and the criminal justice system. Other strategies that have provided valuable information include the analysis of official and unofficial records, surveys, experiments, observation, and mathematical models and econometric techniques.

Official and Unofficial Records   The records of the police, the courts, and the correctional system have been used to study how the police arrest suspects, whether there is racial discrimination in sentencing convicted offenders, and how parole boards decide to release inmates.

Unofficial records of crime have also proved useful. For instance, department store records have been used to study shoplifting, a crime that often is not reported to the police by store managers (Cameron, 1964). In recent years, private security forces have patrolled private and public spaces to an increasing degree, and the records of those firms may prove to be an important source of information for criminologists in the future.

Surveys   **Surveys** are studies in which samples of people who are representative of a larger population are asked a series of prepared questions. In Chapter 2, we will see that surveys have been used to measure the extent of crime in two ways, by asking people about their experiences as victims of crime and by asking them about their own involvement in criminal activity. The Crime on Campus box shows how surveys have been used to measure rape among college and university students. Surveys have also been used to test theories of crime and delinquency, as we see in Chapter 7 when we examine Travis Hirschi's (1969) use of survey data to test social control theory.

Experiments   **Experiments** are controlled studies in which people are treated in different ways to determine the effects of that treatment on their attitudes and behavior. One experiment created a mock prison and assigned subjects to be inmates or guards; this study contributed to our understanding of the social structure of prisons (Zimbardo, 1972; Haney, Banks, and Zimbardo, 1973). Experiments have been used to evaluate the effectiveness of rehabilitation programs; one such study assessed the impact on inmates of group counseling (Kassebaum, Ward, and Wilner, 1971). A series of experi-

CRIME ON CAMPUS

Surveys of Rape among College Students

Compared with the larger society, college campuses have a high proportion of rapes that involve victims and offenders who know each other. A survey of thirty-two campuses found that 15.3 percent of female college students had been raped at least once and another 11.8 percent had been victims of attempted rape. In 84 percent of the cases, the women knew the men who attacked them, and 57 percent of the rapes occurred on dates (Warshaw, 1988). Neil Gilbert (1992) has questioned the validity of such high rates of rape, pointing out that about three-fourths of the women classified as victims by the survey researchers did not think that they had been raped; indeed, 42 percent of them reported having sex again with the alleged rapist.

This survey of thirty-two campuses also found that 6.3 percent of male college students reported that in the previous year they had committed an act that fit the legal definition of rape; another 5.3 percent admitted to attempting such an act. However, 84 percent of the males who admitted to these acts refused to label their behavior rape. According to psychologist Neil Malamuth, "When men are asked if there is any likelihood they would force a woman to have sex against her will if they could get away with it, about half say they would. But if you ask them if they would rape a woman if they knew they could get away with it, only about 15 percent say they would" (cited in Goleman, p. C1).

A 1979 study of high school and college men found that 43 percent said it was "acceptable" by a fifth date for a man to force sex on a woman and 39 percent said it was acceptable to do so if they had "spent a lot of money on her."

Gang rape seems disproportionately more common on college campuses than it is in the larger society. A study of twenty-three gang rapes found that in virtually all cases the victim was known by one or more of the rapists. The typical gang rape involved men who were members of a fraternity or of a basketball or football team. The men often claimed that their actions were acceptable because the victim was promiscuous, and they distinguished the victim from the more respectable women they dated. As the gang rape proceeded, the victim was increasingly defined by the rapists as a "whore" deserving of her fate.

Some rape victims have sued universities for failing to provide adequate protection from and information about the risk of victimization on campus and in university-owned facilities. In 1992, a jury awarded a rape victim $1.6 million because the University of Southern California had not provided sufficient security or information about crime near an off-campus dormitory where she was stalked and raped. Other civil suits have been brought against universities, but trials are rare and the terms of negotiated settlements are not usually revealed.

Sources: Based on Robin Warshaw, *I Never Called It Rape: The Ms. Report on Recognizing, Fighting and Surviving Date and Acquaintance Rape.* New York: Harper and Row, 1988; Daniel Goleman, "When the Rapist Is Not a Stranger: Studies Seek New Understanding," *New York Times*, August 29, 1989, pp. C1, C6; "University, Blamed in Rape, Is Told to Pay Victim," *New York Times*, March 29, 1992, p. 18; Neil Gilbert, "Realities and Mythologies of Rape," *Society* 29 (May/June 1992), 4–10.

ments conducted by Bibb Latané and John M. Darley (1970) focused on the question of why bystanders often fail to assist the victims of crime. Another experiment tested the impact on ex-convicts' criminal behavior when financial assistance was provided to them after their release from prison (Rossi, Berk, and Lenihan, 1980).

The National Institute of Justice favors experimentation as a research strategy. Some of the experiments it has funded were designed to refine criminal justice policies that had already been found effective in earlier experiments. Experiments sometimes show that the results of one policy do not differ from the results of alternative policies, an important finding that makes it possible to select the least expensive policy (Garner and Visher, 1988).

Observation   Another research method that has been used to study criminal behavior is **observation**, the careful and systematic watching of behavior. One difficulty in using this method is that criminals want to keep their offenses secret and wait to commit their crimes when no witnesses are present. Nevertheless, observation has been used fruitfully by criminologists. Francis Ianni (1972) examined the activities of an organized crime "family" for more than two years. Sociologists have often observed the behavior of juvenile gangs (Miller, 1974; Horowitz, 1983; Padilla, 1992). In another observational study, Patricia Adler (1993) spent six years investigating upper-level drug dealers and smugglers. Terry Williams (1989, 1992) used this method productively in his studies of teenage cocaine dealers and a crack house. Observational methods have also been used to examine interaction between the police and suspects (Piliavin and Briar, 1964; Reiss, 1971; Skolnick, 1975) and the operation of the courts, including the process of plea bargaining (Rosett and Cressey, 1976; Blumberg, 1979).

Mathematical Models and Econometric Techniques   An innovation in the study of crime is the use of mathematical models and econometric techniques. These abstract formulations of the relationships among variables are evaluated with data gathered from the police, the courts, and the prisons (Fox, 1981a, 1981b; Phillips and Votey, 1981). Such methods have been used to study the deterrent effect of punishment, including the death penalty, and to examine the relationship between crime and unemployment.

Combining Research Strategies   Criminologists sometimes combine several approaches in their study of crime, enabling them to maximize the advantages and minimize the disadvantages of each strategy. Information not found in police records, such as how crime is planned, can be uncovered in interviews with offenders. Material that cannot be gathered by interviewing offenders, such as the overall distribution of crime in a city, can be found in police records. Klockars (1974) relied mainly on the biographical method in his study of a professional fence, but he also examined police arrest records, observed a fence at work, and read historical documents on fencing.

Table 1.1 Some Strategies of Criminological Research

1. Comparative and historical research
2. Biographies
3. Patterns-of-crime approach
4. Cohort study
5. Analysis of official and unofficial records
6. Surveys
7. Experiments
8. Observation
9. Mathematical models and econometric techniques
10. Combining research strategies

Criminologists thus use a variety of research strategies to study criminal behavior and responses to it by the criminal justice system. Each strategy of research can provide useful information if properly used, but none by itself gives a complete picture of crime and the institutions that deal with it. As a result, the following chapters rely on research that has employed many different strategies to study crime.

Summary

Criminology is the systematic study of violations of the criminal law, a set of formal norms that define certain behaviors as legally punishable. Criminology also studies societal reactions to those violations of the law.

Crime includes a diversity of behavior, but most offenses are characterized by criminal intent that leads to behavior defined as socially harmful. People who are not thought capable of forming criminal intent, such as the legally insane, are not punished with criminal sanctions.

Crime and the criminal law are social phenomena, for behavior is socially defined as punishable rather than intrinsically criminal. This accounts for differences in the law from one society to another. Conflict theorists point to the criminal law as the social product of the domination of one group by another one that has more economic resources and political power. Consensus theorists see the law as the outcome of compromise and agreement among various groups.

This book looks at a variety of types of crime, examining them within a conceptual scheme that focuses first on needs and motivations to commit crime and then on the ways that offenders reduce their commitment to the law before violating it. Offenders learn criminal motives and skills before violating the law, and they must find the opportunities to commit crime. When these factors lead to multiple crimes by the same person over time, criminologists speak of a criminal career. The activities of offenders are sometimes structured in groups and organizations.

Reactions to crime can be informal or formal. Communities respond to crime with patrol groups and community organizations designed to improve the neighborhood, and bystanders might or might not respond to a crime they see in progress. The criminal justice system responds to a crime formally, and in doing so influences the behavior of offenders. Punishment has been justified as a way to prevent crime through threat (deterrence) or by locking up offenders (incapacitation), as a way to mete out deserved penalties (retribution), and as a way to reform offenders (rehabilitation).

Conservatives, liberals, and radicals have proposed different solutions to the crime problem. Over the past two decades, most American politicians have attacked the crime problem by trying to change the criminal justice system. Other approaches that would probably be more effective focus on situational crime prevention and the eradication of the causes of crime.

Criminologists use many research strategies. Some employ the comparative method, looking at crime in two or more societies to test or develop theories. Historical work is a kind of comparative research that compares the past with present, either explicitly or implicitly. Another useful strategy is the biographical approach. This method does not tell us how representative a particular offender is of all criminals, but it provides a richness of detail often missing from research based on official statistics or surveys. Another strategy is the patterns-of-crime approach, which uses police data to investigate the distribution of crime in time and space and to study offenders and victims. A very productive, but expensive and time-consuming, strategy is the cohort study. People who have a common characteristic—usually the same year of birth—are studied over time, allowing for the collection of data on criminal careers.

Many other research strategies have contributed to our knowledge of crime, as we will see in the following chapters. Unofficial records of crime, such as those kept on shoplifters by department stores, have been useful. Surveys that measure victimization and self-reported crime have enhanced our knowledge of the nature and extent of crime. Experiments have evaluated the effects on offenders of prison treatment programs and financial assistance. Social scientists have engaged in systematic observation of criminals and their behavior to uncover information that can be difficult to gather in other ways. Sociologists and economists have used mathematical models and econometric techniques to study crime. Often several of these strategies are used in combination.

Important Terms

biographical method	justification
cohort	juvenile delinquent
comparative research	law
conflict perspective	left realism
consensus perspective	Marxist or radical criminology
crime	norm
criminal career	observation
criminal intent	patterns of crime
criminology	sanction
excuse	social construction of crime
experiment	status offense
historical research	survey

Review Questions

1. What is crime? Why does the kind of behavior defined as crime differ from one society to another?

2. What is the difference between the conflict perspective and the consensus perspective? Which approach makes more sense when observing the development of the extensive black market in Peru?

3. Make a list of some of the research strategies that have been used to study crime. Then list in one column the advantages or strengths of each strategy. In a second column, list the disadvantages or weaknesses of each strategy.

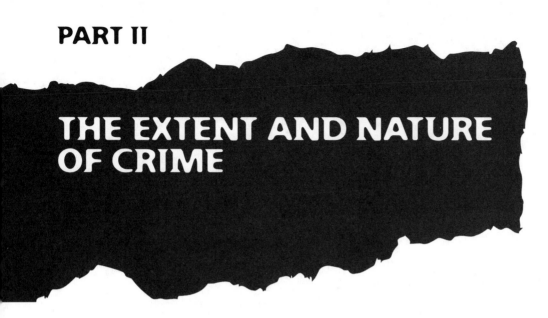

PART II

THE EXTENT AND NATURE OF CRIME

After tracing the development of modern criminology, **Chapter 2** examines three measures of crime. Official crime statistics provide information about crimes reported to the police and suspects arrested by the police. Victimization data gathered in surveys show that much crime is not reported to the police; these data can be used to construct a more complete picture. Crime is also measured by self-reports, questionnaires filled out by people who admit to their own violations of the law.

The characteristics and costs of conventional crime, white-collar crime, organized crime, and victimless crime are examined in **Chapter 3**. The extent and costliness of conventional crimes are described, as are the relationships between offenders and victims in those crimes. The financial costs, physical damage, and social harm of the various types of crime are also investigated.

Chapter 4 explores the variations in crime rates that theories of crime must explain. Cross-national and regional variations in rates are investigated, as are variations in rates by size of community. Temporal variations in crime rates, such as changes over the years, are explored. We examine male-female differences in both juvenile delinquency and adult crime, and the way that female involvement in crime and delinquency has changed in recent years. Variations in crime rates by age and race and the complex relationship between social class and crime are also examined.

CHAPTER 2
Measuring Crime

The scientific study of criminal behavior originated in Europe in the nineteenth century. Until then, there had been much speculation about crime, but it was abstract and not based on empirical research. Many early ideas about the causes of crime have proved inaccurate or incomplete, but the history of these ideas is important for understanding the emergence of modern criminology.

The Emergence of Modern Criminology

From 1500 until about 1750, philosophers who investigated the problem of crime usually proposed that people freely choose how to act. This assumption of free will implies that people are responsible for the consequences of their actions. Another implication is that people can be controlled through fear, especially the fear of pain. Punishment by the state, an institution based on a social contract among its citizens to live together in peace, is the primary means to instill fear and prevent criminal behavior.

Classical Criminology

These ideas were the basis of the **classical school** of criminology. This approach developed during the Enlightenment, an eighteenth-century movement in European thought that emphasized progress, individualism, the use of reason, the questioning of tradition, and the use of empirical data to test abstract ideas.

The major proponent of the classical approach was an Italian, Cesare Beccaria (1738–1794), who sharply criticized the criminal justice system, especially judges who imposed arbitrary and harsh punishments. Along with earlier philosophers, Beccaria believed that punishment was needed to prevent people from violating the law. He thought that people were motivated by pain and pleasure, that they exercised free will, and that rationality and responsibility characterized human action. According to Beccaria, fear of punishment would lead people to conform to the law.

Beccaria claimed that punishment should be based on the harm that the criminal act did to society, rather than on the harm incurred by the victim. Harm was to be judged by the consequences of the act rather than by the intentions of the offender. Marxist critics have argued that this approach contains a basic flaw: in capitalist societies, social harm is inevitably defined in a way that protects the interests of capitalists from interference by other classes (Taylor, Walton, and Young, 1973: 3).

Beccaria hoped that making punishment proportional to social harm would limit the arbitrary punishment meted out by judges. Implicit in his theory is the notion that similar crimes should be punished similarly, an idea violated by the judges of his time as well as those of today. This idea, basic to the theory of retribution or just deserts, suggests that an offender's characteristics and the circumstances of the crime should not be taken into account in meting out punishment.

Beccaria's ideas were the basis of the 1791 criminal code of France, but problems arose in implementing that code. The code ignored differences among offenders and differences in the circumstances of crimes. It treated first offenders and repeat offenders alike when they were convicted of similar offenses, and it gave no special attention to offenders who were minors, insane, or retarded.

The revised French criminal code of 1819 provided for somewhat more judicial discretion, allowing judges to consider the circumstances of the crime but not the offender's intent. The underlying assumption was that the idea of free will was valid, but that individual responsibility could be influenced by pathology, incompetence, or insanity. The notion of premeditation—the consideration of one's behavior prior to acting—developed as a measure of free will. Age, mental capacity, and the circumstances of the crime were accepted as factors that could mitigate punishment, for those factors were thought to reduce personal responsibility. This led to the use of testimony by experts to help the courts decide on the extent to which defendants could be held responsible and punished for their actions.

The idea implicit in the 1819 code was that sentences had different effects on different kinds of offenders. This was the beginning of the rehabilitation rationale for punishment, the idea that the goal of punishment is to change offenders so they will not commit crime again. Individual choice of behavior was the basis of the 1819 code, but choice was increasingly seen as influenced by social and psychological factors (Taylor, Walton, and Young, 1973: 9).

Cartography

Some European nations have been gathering official data on crime since the sixteenth century, but not until the nineteenth century did scholars start to use the statistics to understand crime. Their approach has been called **cartography,** because it involves the use of data to map or chart patterns of crime.

Important studies using this approach were published in 1833 by A. M. Guerry, a French lawyer, and in 1838 by A. Quetelet, a Belgian mathematician. These two cartographers worked independently, but they came to similar conclusions from their studies of national crime data. Both found that the annual total of crime recorded in a country remains fairly constant over time and that each kind of crime remains about the same proportion of the total over time. They concluded that officially recorded crime is "a regular feature of social activity" that is better explained by social conditions than by individual predispositions (Taylor, Walton, and Young, 1973: 37).

The cartographic approach was used to great advantage in a groundbreaking study of suicide by Emile Durkheim (1858–1917), one of the founders of sociology. In his writings on crime, Durkheim (1895, 1938) shared with Guerry and Quetelet the idea that crime is a normal feature of social life. He did not mean that crime was good or to be encouraged, but rather that crime exists in all societies and therefore must be studied in its relationship to the social structure. Durkheim did suggest that crime has some positive functions, or consequences, for society: it delineates what behavior is acceptable to the members of society, it draws official attention to the social conditions that cause crime, and it can create social solidarity in opposition to people who violate important social standards.

Positivism

Modern scientific criminology grew out of the work of three Italian students of crime—Cesare Lombroso, Enrico Ferri, and Raffaele Garofalo. They saw the proper course of criminology as "the systematic elimination of the free will 'metaphysics' of the classical school" (Taylor, Walton, and Young, 1973: 10). Rather than try to reduce crime by relying on the criminal justice system, as did the classical criminologists, they sought to learn the causes of crime and then eliminate the conditions that produce it. Modern criminology has been dominated by this perspective, but the criminal justice system has been dominated by classical thinking during the twentieth century.

This perspective, which is called **positivism**, relies on the scientific method, quantifying and measuring behavior and the social conditions associated with behavior. Positivists claim that scientific neutrality is possible in the study of crime, and that criminologists should focus on criminal behavior rather than on the criminal law. Positivists see themselves as relatively objective in their work, but critics allege that a positivist approach implicitly supports the existing legal system by adopting the state's definition of crime. However, positivists do have a legitimate claim to objectivity, for compared with the work done by scholars who argue that scientific neutrality is impossible, positivists have generally produced more reliable results—that is, results that different scholars would also get if they applied the same scientific methods to the same data.

Positivists claim that human behavior is subject to causal laws. This assertion that behavior is determined, or at least influenced, by forces outside the control of individuals contradicts the classical position that people are rational beings who exercise free will and determine their own behavior. Positivism sometimes goes too far in denying individual freedom to choose how to behave, but it is a method that lends itself well to the study of social, psychological, economic, political, and biological influences. Research using the positivist method fills the pages of the leading journals in criminology and is cited extensively throughout this book. This research has generated policy recommendations for reducing crime, such as strengthening the family and reducing income inequality, that are examined later in this book.

Cesare Lombroso   Cesare Lombroso (1835–1909) was the first influential proponent of the positivist approach to criminology. He has been called the "father of criminology" because he was able to direct the study of crime away from questions of free will and personal responsibility to a more scientific

Cesare Lombroso (1835–1909), the "father of criminology," used the positivist approach to study the causes of crime.

basis. Although Lombroso's ideas about the biological origins of crime have proved erroneous, and sometimes even ludicrous, his work marked an important turning point in criminology. By stressing measurable characteristics, even if they were the wrong ones, Lombroso made it possible to determine which factors are actually related to criminal behavior. In the early editions of his textbook on the criminal offender, Lombroso attributed crime primarily to biological factors, but in later editions of his book, his research led him to downplay the significance of those factors and give greater emphasis to insanity, poor education, and social background. This change in his views on crime causation is testimony to the positivist method, for by focusing on measurable factors Lombroso was able to test his ideas about the causes of crime and then modify his theory in light of new evidence.

Beyond Lombroso   Enrico Ferri (1856–1929) and Raffaele Garofalo (1852–1934) were two positivists who went beyond Lombroso in the study of the causes of crime. Ferri focused on causes such as climate, age, race, sex, psychology, population density, and political and economic conditions. His work has been criticized for failing to specify the relative importance of each factor in the causation of crime. Garofalo shared some of Lombroso's ideas on crime causation, but his work focused on psychological factors such as the lack of compassion among offenders. Positivism is not necessarily associated with any particular theory of crime, but is instead a method that can be used to assess the influence of many different factors on criminal behavior.

By 1900, the seeds of modern criminology had been sown. The emphasis on measurement, scientific neutrality, and the testing of hypotheses with empirical data was a major advance over earlier speculative work on crime. Even if the early positivists' explanations were often inaccurate or incomplete, they did provide criminologists with the methods to determine whether explanations are right or wrong. Recognizing that crime cannot easily be studied by direct observation, positivists try to develop indicators of crime that can be used to test theories and hypotheses. Positivists generate theories to explain their research findings and then test those theories with more research, modifying their explanations to fit new evidence. Before a theory supported by research can be developed, however, it is necessary to collect data on the dimensions of crime that must be explained by a theory. The rest of this chapter looks at several methods for gathering data on crime.

Official Crime Statistics

Criminologists often use measures of crime produced by law-enforcement agencies to study criminal behavior and offenders. Because students of crime frequently use statistics they do not collect, they must have a thorough knowledge of how those statistics are produced (Black, 1970). Changes in law-enforcement practices over time can alter the way that crime statistics are gathered. When this happens, a change in crime rates may reflect a change in enforcement activity rather than a real increase or decrease in the amount of criminal activity.

History of Crime Statistics in the United States

Support for a police-based system of crime statistics developed in 1926 and 1927 among police organizations (particularly the International Association of Chiefs of Police), philanthropic foundations (primarily the Laura Spelman Rockefeller Memorial Foundation), and social scientists (especially the Social Science Research Council). They saw crime statistics as a way to evaluate police performance, assess newspaper reports of crime waves, develop a scientific criminology, and control crime. In 1929, a manual for reporting crime statistics was distributed to police departments around the country and the collection of data began. The Federal Bureau of Investigation (FBI), which began compiling crime statistics in 1930, now publishes an annual volume, *Crime in the United States: Uniform Crime Reports.*

In 1931, Thorsten Sellin stated that "the value of a crime for index purposes decreases as the distance from the crime itself in terms of procedure increases" (p. 346). This view was widely shared and led the FBI to focus on crimes reported to and recorded by the police, rather than on data on arrested suspects, defendants in court, or prison inmates. The farther we move from the report of the crime, the more likely we are to get a distorted picture of it. For example, research shows that systematic distortion in the arresting of drug suspects does not allow us to measure trends in drug offenses with arrest data (DeFleur, 1975). This is because changes in arrests over time are related to changes in the perceived seriousness of drug law violations and changes in patterns of law enforcement (Sheley and Hanlon, 1978; Stoddart, 1982).

Ideally, national crime statistics should include police data on reported crimes and arrested suspects. Suspects could then be followed through the criminal justice system, and information would be recorded on the disposition of cases and the sentences meted out to convicted offenders. Maintaining such records will be costly and difficult, but it will give us a more complete picture of crime than we now have.

FBI Crime Statistics

The FBI has achieved nearly complete coverage of the country in its collection of data from the police. It now gathers statistics from over 16,000 city, county, and state law-enforcement agencies, which cover 95 percent of the country's population. Data are gathered either from state-level crime-reporting programs or directly from local police departments. What the FBI misses are crimes reported to agencies and institutions other than the police. For instance, statistics on crimes recorded by campus police forces sometimes fail to get into the FBI's reports (see the Crime on Campus box).

The FBI presents detailed data on eight crimes, the Part I offenses that together constitute the **crime index**. The FBI presents much less information on twenty-one Part II crimes. Table 2.1 defines the eight Part I and the twenty-one Part II crimes. The FBI justifies its presentation of more detail on the Part I offenses by claiming that those crimes

- are regarded by the public as very serious,
- are relatively frequent in occurrence, and
- often come to the attention of the police.

FBI data are gathered from law-enforcement agencies that cover 95 percent of the nation's population. These file cabinets in an FBI office are filled with fingerprinting data.

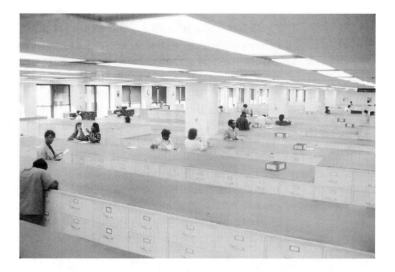

CRIME ON CAMPUS

Measuring the Problem

The extent of crime on the nation's campuses is unknown. The 1995 FBI crime report provides data on offenses known to the police for only 451 of the nation's more than 3,200 campuses. Most colleges and universities do not forward their crime statistics directly to the FBI, instead reporting them to the local police, who absorb the statistics into their overall figures before reporting them to the state crime-reporting system or the FBI.

College and university administrators fear that reporting campus crime might frighten off prospective students, potential donors, or job candidates, but this does not seem to have happened. Fear of damaging their school's reputation can lead administrators and campus police to underreport crime. Crimes that victimize students living off campus seem to be especially likely to be omitted from campus crime statistics.

The 1990 Federal Crime Awareness and Campus Security Act requires all colleges and universities receiving federal aid to disclose their security policies, publish campus crime statistics, and distribute annual safety reports to employees and prospective and current students. Students and employees are also supposed to be informed of crimes that might pose a threat to them. A 1992 provision requires colleges and universities to promote student and employee awareness of sex offenses and develop measures for reporting these offenses.

Violation of these regulations can lead to termination of federal funding, but no such actions have been taken. The U.S. Department of Education has not monitored compliance with the law, nor has it asked universities to send the information needed to report to Congress on campus crime.

Sources: Anne Matthews, "The Campus Crime Wave," *New York Times Magazine*, March 7, 1993, pp. 38–42, 47; Elizabeth Holland, "There's No Verdict Yet on Campus Crime," *New York Times*, January 7, 1996, Education section, pp. 21, 45.

Criticisms of FBI Statistics   Critics claim that the public may regard Part I offenses as serious because the FBI gives them the most attention. In other words, the FBI's choice of what to include in Part I conveys to the public a particular image of "the crime problem," one that for the most part consists of crimes against persons and property by people who have low incomes and who are members of minority groups (Reiman, 1995).

The FBI's crime report pays little attention to white-collar crime and fails to note that such crime inflicts much greater financial losses on the American public than do all the Part I crimes together (see Chapter 3). Of the eight Part I offenses, only arson is sometimes a white-collar crime. Embezzlement and fraud, which are Part II crimes, are sometimes white-collar offenses. White-collar crimes such as price-fixing and government corruption fit the FBI's criterion of being relatively frequent, but no mention is made of those offenses in its crime report. Local law-enforcement agencies rarely learn of white-collar

TABLE 2.1   Offenses in the FBI's Uniform Crime-Reporting System

Part I (Index) Offenses

Murder and nonnegligent manslaughter*: the willful killing of one human being by another.

Forcible rape: carnal knowledge of a female forcibly and against her will, including attempts.

Robbery: taking or attempting to take anything of value from another person by force or threat of force.

Aggravated assault: unlawful attack by one person upon another for the purpose of inflicting severe or aggravated bodily injury, usually accompanied by the use of a weapon.

Burglary-breaking or entering: unlawful entry of a structure to commit a felony or a theft.

Larceny-theft: unlawful taking, carrying, leading, or riding away of property from the possession of another; excluding motor vehicle theft, embezzlement, con games, and forgery.

Motor vehicle theft: theft or attempted theft of a motor vehicle.

Arson: willful or malicious burning, or attempt to burn, with or without intent to defraud, of a house, public building, motor vehicle or aircraft, or personal property of another.

Part II Offenses

Other assaults (simple): assaults and attempted assaults where no weapon is used and that do not result in serious injury to the victim.

Forgery and counterfeiting: making, altering, uttering, or possessing, with intent to defraud, anything false that is made to appear true.

Fraud: fraudulent conversion and obtaining money or property by false pretenses.

Embezzlement: misappropriation or misapplication of money or property entrusted to one's care, custody, or control.

Stolen property: buying, receiving, possessing: buying, receiving, and possessing stolen property, including attempts.

Vandalism: willful or malicious destruction, injury, disfigurement, or defacement of any public or private property, real or personal, without consent of the owner or persons having custody or control.

Weapons: carrying, possessing, etc.: all violations of regulations or statutes controlling the carrying, using, possessing, furnishing, and manufacturing of deadly weapons or silencers.

Prostitution and commercialized vice: sex offenses of a commercialized nature, such as prostitution, keeping a bawdy house, procuring, or transporting women for immoral purposes.

TABLE 2.1 continued

Part II Offenses

Sex offenses (except forcible rape, prostitution and commercialized vice): statutory rape and offenses against chastity, common decency, morals, and the like.

Drug abuse violations: state and local offenses relating to narcotic drugs, such as unlawful possession, sale, use, growing, and manufacturing of narcotic drugs.

Gambling: promoting, permitting, or engaging in illegal gambling.

Offenses against the family and children: nonsupport, neglect, desertion, or abuse of family and children.

Driving under the influence: driving or operating any vehicle or common carrier while drunk or under the influence of liquor or narcotics.

Liquor laws: state or local liquor law violations, except drunkenness and driving under the influence.

Drunkenness: drunkenness or intoxication, excluding driving under the influence.

Disorderly conduct: breach of the peace.

Vagrancy: vagabondage, begging, loitering, etc.

All other offenses: all violations of state or local laws, except the preceding offenses and traffic offenses.

Suspicion: no specific offense; suspect released without formal charges being placed.

Curfew and loitering laws (persons under age 18): offenses relating to violations of local curfew or loitering ordinances where such laws exist.

Runaways (persons under age 18): limited to juveniles taken into protective custody under provisions of local statutes.

*The FBI also includes manslaughter by negligence in the category "criminal homicide," but it omits manslaughter by negligence from the crime index.

Source: Adapted from Federal Bureau of Investigation, *Crime in the United States, 1995: Uniform Crime Reports.* Washington, D.C.: U.S. Government Printing Office, 1996, pp. 373–374.

crimes because of their complexity and because the public thinks that the police will not deal with such offenses. As a result, FBI crime reports convey the impression that white-collar crime is of little consequence in American society.

FBI reports are also deficient in failing to indicate the pervasive involvement of organized crime in criminal activities in the United States. Data on arrests for narcotics violations and gambling appear in the FBI's reports, but the statistics do not show gangsters' involvement in those offenses, nor are any data presented on loan sharking (usury), a major source of revenue for organized crime.

Crime Rates

The FBI Uniform Crime Report (UCR) gives the absolute number of crimes and the crime rates for the index offenses, except for arson for which data are incomplete. The FBI calculates national **crime rates** by dividing the number of reported crimes by the number of people in the country, and then expressing the result as a rate of crimes per 100,000 people. For instance, in 1995 there were 21,597 recorded cases of murder and nonnegligent manslaughter in the United States. The estimate of the nation's population in 1995 was 262,755,000. The murder rate per 100,000 is thus calculated as follows:

$$\frac{21,597}{262,755,000} \quad x \quad 100,000 \quad = \quad 8.2 \text{ per } 100,000$$

Expressing the crime rate in this way makes more sense than simply stating how many homicides occurred in 1995. For example, if the United States had 21,597 murders in a year in the past when its population was exactly half as large as its 1995 population, the murder rate in that earlier year would have been twice as high as it was in 1995, or 16.4 per 100,000 people.

Crime rates, rather than the absolute number of crimes, are the appropriate measure for comparing countries, states, or cities. In the following excerpt from an advice column in the *Boston Globe* (May 7, 1980, p. 86), the letter writer asks a question about rates in the correct way, but the newspaper provides an inappropriate response:

Q. I have to make a job choice between New York City and Houston. Can you tell me how the crime rates for these cities compare—V.P., Burlington [Mass.]

A. The latest available annual (1977) FBI major crime statistics for New York City and Houston are as follows: New York—1,553 murders; 3,899 rapes; 74,404 robberies; 42,056 assaults; 178,907 burglaries; 214,838 larcenies; and 94,420 vehicle thefts. Houston—376 murders; 965 rapes; 6,153 robberies; 1,810 assaults; 33,419 burglaries; 60,839 larcenies; and 13,726 motor vehicle thefts.

Here the newspaper gives the total number of crimes in each city, making it impossible for the letter writer to compare the crime rates of the cities without looking up their populations. The letter writer wanted to compare risks of victimization in the two cities, and crime rates are needed to do that. FBI reports do not give city-by-city crime rates, but the rates can be calculated by using census data on the populations of the cities and FBI data on numbers of crimes in the cities. Let us see what happens when we calculate murder rates for New York City and Houston:

	Number of Murders (1977)	Population (1977)	Murder Rate per 100,000 People (1977)
New York City	1,553	7,298,000	21.3
Houston	376	1,555,000	24.2

New York City had many more murders than Houston in 1977, but it also had a much larger population. When we calculate murder rates per 100,000 people—a measure of the risk that a person such as the letter writer will be killed in a given year—we find that the homicide rate per 100,000 people was actually higher in Houston (24.2) than in New York City (21.3). Based on the faulty answer by the *Boston Globe*, the letter writer might have moved to Houston, even though the risk of being murdered there was greater than it was in New York City.

Sociological criminology often focuses on crime rates. Rather than examining and explaining each and every criminal act, it makes more sense to look at rates of crime and seek explanations for variations in crime rates among different social groups. For instance, if poor people have a higher murder rate than well-to-do people, we might focus on blocked opportunities and frustrated ambitions as causes of murder. We might also suggest that policies that increase available jobs and reduce economic inequality could reduce the rate at which people kill others.

Prevalence and Incidence   The per capita crime rate can be disaggregated into two components: prevalence and incidence. **Prevalence** is the proportion of a population that commits crime in a given time; it is measured by dividing the number of offenders by the size of the population. **Incidence** is the frequency with which offenders commit crime, or the average number of offenses per offender; it is measured by dividing the number of offenses by the number of offenders. As the following formula shows, the crime rate is equal to the product of prevalence and incidence:

$$\text{Crime rate} = \frac{\text{Offenses}}{\text{Population}} = \frac{\text{Offenders}}{\text{Population}} \times \frac{\text{Offenses}}{\text{Offenders}}$$
$$\text{(Prevalence)} \qquad \text{(Incidence)}$$

Crimes of Violence   Calculating crime rates in terms of number of offenses per 100,000 people makes sense for murder, robbery, and aggravated assault because in these crimes of violence it is individuals who are at risk. The FBI rates for these and other index offenses are shown in Table 2.2.

According to the FBI's definition, forcible rape can only involve female victims. Because the FBI presents forcible rape statistics only for sexual assaults that involve women as victims, it makes no sense for it to present rates of forcible rape per 100,000 people in the country, because nearly half of the people in the denominator used to calculate the rate are men. For instance, in 1995 the FBI reported that there were 37.1 recorded rapes and attempted rapes per 100,000 people (men and women). The rate of rape would be better expressed by dividing the number of incidents (97,464) by the number of women in the country (134,441,000), a rate of 72.5 per 100,000 women. This rate provides a better idea of the risk of rape faced by women, although calculating the rate in this way means that it cannot be compared

TABLE 2.2   Rates of Crime per 100,000 People, United States, 1995

Crime	Rate per 100,000 people
Murder and nonnegligent manslaughter	8.2
Forcible rape	37.1
Robbery	220.9
Aggravated assault	418.3
Burglary	987.6
Larceny-theft	3,044.9
Motor vehicle theft	560.5
Arson	*
Crime index total	5,277.6**

* Sufficient data are not available to estimate crime rate.
** Total rate differs from sum of above rates because of rounding.

Source: Adapted from Federal Bureau of Investigation, *Crime in the United States, 1995: Uniform Crime Report.* Washington, D.C.: U.S. Government Printing Office, 1996, p. 59.

with rates of murder, assault, or robbery, which are calculated per 100,000 people (both men and women).

Property Crimes   Burglary, larceny, motor vehicle theft, and arson are crimes against property, even though it is people who own the stolen or burned property. The FBI calculates crime rates for these offenses by dividing the number of incidents by the number of people in the country and expressing the rates as offenses per 100,000 people. Rates calculated in terms of number of offenses per amount of property available to be stolen or burned would provide more useful information. For instance, rates of larceny might best be calculated in terms of dollars of property stolen as a proportion of the total gross national product (GNP) that is available to be stolen each year, rather than as the number of larceny incidents per 100,000 people. Rates of property crime per 100,000 people rise dramatically during economic development and increasing affluence, because the amount of property available to be stolen is growing (Clinard and Abbott, 1973; Shelley, 1981a).

The rate of thefts per number of motor vehicles in the country is a more meaningful statistic than the rate of motor vehicle thefts per 100,000 people. From 1963 to 1993, the rate of motor vehicle thefts per 100,000 people increased by 185 percent, while there was only a 67 percent increase in the rate of motor vehicle thefts per 100,000 registrations (a measure of the number of motor vehicles in the country). Using the per capita rate exaggerates the increase in the chance that a given car would be stolen, because over the thirty-year period motor vehicle registrations increased faster than the population.

Comparisons among countries should also take into consideration the number of cars available to be stolen. Table 2.3, which presents rates of car theft per 1,000 people and per 1,000 cars, shows that Italy and Spain have about the same rate of car theft per 1,000 people, but that Spain has nearly

Rates of motor vehicle thefts are best calculated in terms of thefts per number of vehicles available to be stolen, rather than in terms of thefts per number of people.

twice the rate of thefts per 1,000 cars; this is because there are more cars in Italy than in Spain.

The FBI Crime Index   In calculating an overall rate of Part I crimes, the FBI adds the reported number of seven crimes (omitting arson because of incomplete data) and divides by the number of people in the country to get a rate of index crimes per 100,000 people. In 1995 the crime index rate was 5,277.6 per 100,000 people.

The FBI does not attempt to weight the index crimes by their relative seriousness. Obviously a homicide is more serious than the theft of a quarter, but the FBI treats both the same in calculating the crime index rate. The FBI also treats all motor vehicle thefts as index crimes, even though many auto thefts are for joyriding rather than for resale of the car or its parts. A theft in which the car is shipped out of the country for resale would seem to be more serious than a theft in which teenagers abandon a car unharmed after it runs out of gasoline.

If the FBI systematically applied a measure of the relative seriousness of various crimes to police crime reports, the informational value of the crime index rate would be improved. However, a seriousness scale might magnify some of the problems with FBI statistics. Thus, weighting crimes would mean that robberies would count more than simple larcenies, but white-collar crimes would still be omitted from the overall crime rate. Nevertheless, some consideration of the relative seriousness of the different index crimes would provide better information than is now available from the crime index rate

TABLE 2.3 Thefts of Cars Recorded by the Police, 1987/1988

Country	Rate per 1,000 People	Rate per 1,000 Cars
Japan	.3	.7
Netherlands	1.6	3.8
Canada	3.4	6.9
Italy	3.6	6.9
Spain	3.7	12.7
France	4.3	9.3
United States	5.6	8.9
Sweden	7.0	16.8
England/Wales	7.6	20.3
Australia	7.7	13.4

Source: Based on Ronald V. Clarke and Patricia M. Harris, "Auto Theft and Its Prevention," in Michael Tonry, ed., *Crime and Justice: A Review of Research*, Vol. 16. Chicago: University of Chicago Press, 1992, p. 9. Reprinted by permission of The University of Chicago Press. © 1992 by The University of Chicago. All rights reserved.

(Wolfgang, 1968: 281). For instance, the overall crime index rate might remain the same for two consecutive years, even if a decline of 10,000 murders were offset by an increase of 10,000 larcenies from one year to the next. Clearly crime in the second year would be less serious because of the reduction in murders, but the FBI crime index rate would not reveal that change in the composition of the crime rate.

The problems that arise when crimes are added without weighting to form a single crime index were illustrated in a 1992 New York City Police Department report that startlingly showed that Seattle had a crime index rate 36 percent higher than New York's. Only when the individual crimes composing the index were examined was it apparent that the overall difference between the cities was primarily a result of Seattle's much higher rate of recorded larcenies, by far the most common crime in the index. New York had a murder rate more than three times as high as Seattle's and a robbery rate about two-and-a-half times as high; Seattle did have twice as high a rate of forcible rape (Bennet, 1992).

Gathering Crime Statistics

To ensure uniformity in the reporting of crime by local police departments and state reporting programs, the FBI circulates a *Uniform Crime Reporting Handbook* to tell the police how to record crimes. Still, crimes may be counted differently by local police departments. For instance, some departments may record an auto theft the instant a car is reported missing, and other departments may put such a report aside for a few hours to ensure the owner does not call back to say that someone in the family had just borrowed the car. The FBI is aware of the differences among police departments and cautions readers of its reports "against comparing statistical data of individual reporting units," in part because of different "administrative and investigative emphases of law enforcement" (Federal Bureau of Investigation, 1996: iv–v). However, if we cannot compare the crime rates of various communities, then we cannot add the crime rates of those different communities to get a national crime rate, and the FBI does that every year.

Sometimes multiple offenses are committed during the same crime incident. Thus, if an offender threatens a couple with a knife, forces them into their car, tells them to drive him somewhere, and then steals their money before riding off in their car, he has committed two simple assaults, two kidnappings, one auto theft, and one robbery. In this case, the FBI instructs police departments to count only the most serious offense, or one robbery. Some might consider kidnapping a more serious crime than robbery, but the FBI does not treat kidnapping as an index offense, probably because it occurs relatively infrequently. Information is lost because the FBI ignores some offenses and records only the most serious crime in a series of offenses, but recording each different violation of the law would overstate the extent of crime.

Crime Reporting   Because the police can cover only a limited territory and do not have easy access to private places, they must learn of many crimes directly from citizens, usually victims or witnesses. Sometimes people call the police switchboard to report a crime, and other times they report crimes to officers on the street or in patrol cars.

Some citizen complaints to the police are not officially recorded as crimes. One study found that only two-thirds of all complaints to the police produced an official crime report (Black, 1970). Another study found that most robberies that citizens report to interviewers in a survey are not reported to the police and recorded by the police as "founded" (or verified) crime incidents (Block and Block, 1980).

In contrast to **reactive police work** in which officers respond to a citizen's report of a crime, some police work is **proactive**, or the result of efforts by the police to discover and deal with crime on their own initiative (Reiss and Bordua, 1968; Reiss, 1971). Arrests for prostitution and narcotics offenses rarely result from complaints by the public but are typically the result of efforts by the police, especially the vice or narcotics squad. In crimes such as these, the number of recorded violations may tell us more about the size of the vice or narcotics squad than it does about the frequency with which such offenses occur. External pressure from political officials, the FBI, or crime commissions can also affect the level of proactive police work. Because the rate of arrests for vice offenses fluctuates wildly with changes in the social climate and changes in law-enforcement practices, the FBI does not include them in Part I of its UCR.

Reasons for Nonreporting   People fail to report crimes to the police for many reasons, the most significant of which have to do with the nature of the crime incident itself. Victims are least likely to report offenses

- that are attempted rather than completed,
- in which there is little or no financial loss or physical injury,
- that do not threaten their sense of personal security,
- that do not seem serious to them, and
- in which no firearm is used (Hindelang, 1976; Skogan, 1976b, 1984; Block and Block, 1980).

The effect of loss of property and extent of injury can be seen in the results of a survey that found that only 24 percent of robberies involving no loss and no injury were reported to the police, but that 72 percent of robberies with some loss of property and some injury were reported (Bureau of Justice Statistics, December 1985).

Many victims who do not report crimes to the police say they think there is little or nothing the police can do to catch the offender or retrieve the lost property. This view is supported by police statistics, which show that the police are least likely to arrest suspects in those crimes that the public feels the police can do little about (Skogan, 1976a: 547–549).

Some victims do not report crimes to the police because they believe the offense is not very important. This may occur, for instance, when an inexpensive item is stolen or when no real harm is done in an assault. The increased ownership of theft insurance—including automobile insurance—leads many victims to report crimes to the police even when they have little hope of recovering their property, because insurance companies often require notification of the police as proof that a theft has occurred before they will pay a claim.

Some crimes are not reported because the victim is afraid of what the police might discover if they investigate the crime. Thus, a drug dealer who is robbed by another dealer may not report the crime. Other victims do not report crimes because they do not want to cause trouble for the offender. A related reason is fear that the offender might take reprisals against the victim for reporting the crime, especially if the victim and offender are known to each other.

Victims are often unwilling to report crimes to the police because they see the offense as a private or personal matter. Rape victims may avoid the police because they feel stigmatized by the sexual attack or anticipate police insensitivity; a telephone survey of 4,008 women found that only one in six rape victims reported the crime to the police (Skorneck, 1992). Victims of assaults sometimes fail to report the crime because the attack was by a spouse or a parent. Police statistics in some developing countries significantly undercount assaults because there is a tradition in local villages of dealing with crime—especially assaults between people who know each other—in an informal way, rather than by bringing in the police (Clinard and Abbott, 1973: 219–228).

Some victims do not report crime to the police because they think that calling the police is too much trouble, especially if a suspect is later arrested and they have to testify in court. Witnesses, as well as victims, may not report crimes because of inconvenience. A study in which "shoplifters"—who were actually participants in an experiment—tried to gain the attention of other shoppers in order to determine how many shoppers would report their thefts found that only 28 percent of all shoppers said that they had seen the "crime." Of those who admitted to seeing the shoplifting, only 28 percent reported it to store personnel. Many of the witnesses said that reporting the crime would have been inconvenient or troublesome (Gelfand et al., 1973).

Cross-national surveys have found that crime reporting is not closely associated with attitudes toward the police; in other words, people who are hostile toward the police seem to be as likely to report crime as people who are friendly toward the police. In addition, demographic variables such as race and income do not seem to be closely related to whether a victim will report a crime. Females are slightly more likely than males to report crimes, and the elderly are more likely than younger people to report crimes (Skogan, 1984). Victims who are advised to call the police are also more likely to report crimes (Greenberg and Ruback, 1992). For the most part, however, it is the seriousness and type of the crime incident, rather than social characteristics or attitudes toward the police, that determine whether a victim or witness will report a crime (Gove, Hughes, and Geerken, 1985; Bennett and Wiegand, 1994).

Police Recording Practices   Aside from being incomplete because of nonreporting, police crime statistics have other problems (Chilton, 1968; Wolfgang, 1968; Weis, 1983). Because politicians and the public sometimes attribute rising crime rates to police ineffectiveness, the police might not record all of the crimes about which they learn.

The organization and guiding philosophy of a police department influences the accuracy of its crime statistics (Kitsuse and Cicourel, 1963). A legalistic department might see the failure to arrest a suspect as a weakness of the officer, but a service-oriented department would stress the solution of problems without formal arrest; the first department would probably record more interpersonal conflicts as crimes and produce more arrests (Wilson, 1968: 172–226). If a department assigns the collection of crime statistics to precinct captains and rewards them for low crime rates in their precincts, the captains will have an incentive to omit crimes from their official reports. With centralized crime reporting through a switchboard in headquarters, with greater professionalism, and with greater departmental resources, a police department will probably record crime more accurately and more completely, and thereby provide a more valid picture of the crime problem, even though this could mean a higher official crime rate than if some crimes were omitted (Skogan, 1976b: 110–114; McCleary, Nienstedt, and Erven, 1982).

Sometimes the police record a crime that is reported to them but classify it as a less serious crime than it really is. For instance, forcible rape might be classified as simple assault, and thefts in which force is used might be called larcenies rather than robberies. Recording crimes in this way reduces the rate of serious offenses but inflates the rate of minor ones. Because most public attention is focused on serious offenses, this would make the police look better to outsiders.

Political Use of Crime Statistics   Crime statistics have been used for political purposes at both the local and national levels (Seidman and Couzens, 1974; Cronin, Cronin, and Milakovich, 1981). The police are selective in the information about crime that they supply to the news media (see the Crime and the Media box). Rising crime rates are sometimes used to justify higher police salaries and increases in police personnel, although police chiefs often acknowledge that police efficiency cannot be evaluated by crime data or arrest statistics. J. Edgar Hoover was a master at using rising crime rates to argue for increased FBI appropriations from Congress. He also argued for more funds when crime rates dropped, claiming that the crime problem was finally being solved and that it was no time to reduce support for the fight against crime.

Politicians sometimes use rising crime rates to attack their opponents as "soft on crime." They claim that reductions in the crime rate during their time in office show that they have successfully battled crime, even if they cannot demonstrate exactly how they did so. An interesting twist on this argument was heard during Richard Nixon's administration, when he asserted that even though he had not actually reduced the crime rate during his first term in office, he had managed to reduce the rate at which crime rates were increasing. Public opinion polls after both the 1968 and 1972 elections showed that the crime issue was a major reason traditional Democrats voted for the Republican Nixon.

Clearance and Arrest Statistics   When the police are satisfied that they know who committed a crime, they classify the crime as "cleared" or solved. Most but not all cleared crimes lead to an arrest, and when someone is arrested the police provide information on the suspect to the FBI. In 1995, 21.2 percent of all index offenses were cleared by arrest; 45.4 percent of all violent crimes (murder, forcible rape, robbery, and aggravated assault) were cleared, but only 17.6 percent of all property crimes (burglary, larceny, auto theft, and arson) were cleared.

A study by the Police Foundation (Sherman and Glick, 1984) found that police departments define arrest in different ways, in spite of the FBI's efforts to standardize the definition. As a result, the probability that a citizen will end up with an arrest record depends on the jurisdiction in which the person is apprehended. Because of improper and inconsistent recording practices, the use of arrest data to evaluate police departments or to assess the characteristics of offenders is risky.

The FBI's National Crime Information Center (NCIC) has developed a system of centralized and computerized records of arrested suspects (Bureau of Justice Statistics, November 1986). Supporters justify this program in the name of more efficient crime fighting, but critics say that it threatens the privacy of Americans (Laudon, 1986). Studies have found that as many as three-fourths of the FBI's arrest records are inaccurate, incomplete, or ambiguous (Laudon, 1986) and that each day the FBI transmits at least 12,000 invalid or inaccurate reports on suspects wanted for arrest (internal FBI audits, cited in Burnham, 1985). Inaccurate records of this sort can keep people from getting

CRIME AND THE MEDIA

The Police and the News Media

Because newspaper and television reporters get more information about crime from the police than from any other source, the police have the power to provide information selectively and thereby influence public perceptions of crime and the police.

In his study of the news media in a midwestern city, Steven Chermak found that a major source of crime information was the police beat, an office in police headquarters staffed by reporters who monitored police scanners and had ready access to police documents. The police department's spokesperson, who met with reporters daily, decided which crimes were newsworthy and presented information in ways designed to protect the department's public image. The police determined "what information should be revealed and in what form, what details should be highlighted or discarded, and when the story should be released" (p. 19). Sometimes the police cut off media access to police documents or source contacts when they disliked the way the press was portraying the police or reporting a crime story.

Controlling the information supplied to the news media serves several purposes for the police. The release of information can influence the way an offender is punished; for example, the details of a gruesome murder might be provided as the offender is about to be sentenced, pressuring the judge to mete out a severe penalty. The police sometimes talk to reporters about an upcoming crackdown on drunk drivers or drug users in order to deter potential offenders. The police use the press to further their investigations, as by releasing a photograph of a suspect to elicit information from witnesses and victims. The police also use the press for public relations, hoping to create a positive image by spreading news about awards they have received or crime-fighting measures they have developed.

In exchange for serving the interests of the police, the media gain easy access to information about crime, making it possible to produce news stories efficiently and with little expenditure of resources. The press's dependence on the police for information can mute its criticism of the police; Chermak found that police effectiveness was evaluated in only 4 percent of all crime stories, and those stories tended to focus on a specific incident rather than on problems of the whole department.

Source: Based on Steven M. Chermak, *Victims in the News: Crime and the American News Media.* Boulder, Colo.: Westview, 1995, pp. 14–22, 30–31.

---

jobs or securing government benefits and might push some people deeper into a life of crime. Erroneous information also makes law enforcement less efficient and puts police officers at risk from people they stop without being aware they are wanted for crimes. Some critics claim that the FBI's national criminal history file has little effect on crime rates, because "well over 90 percent of violent street crime is committed by local criminals who are already known to cities' and states' computerized systems" (Laudon, 1981: A27).

Using FBI Data for Criminological Research

FBI crime data are of limited usefulness for criminologists, even though those data provide an indicator of the level of police activity in the nation. The statistics have also been used to get a reading on how crime rates have changed over time, but rising crime rates can result from more complete reporting and recording of crime as well as from increases in the actual amount of crime.

In the past, the FBI gathered only summaries of the number of crimes recorded by local police departments and then added the figures from those summary reports to produce the tables in its annual report. This limited the ability of criminologists to do additional analysis of the FBI's data. A 1985 report by a consulting firm suggested changes in FBI practices that would make UCR crime statistics more useful to criminologists. In addition to calling for more thorough auditing of crime statistics to ensure their accuracy and completeness, the report suggested that local police agencies submit short accounts of each crime incident to the national office. In 1989 the FBI began implementation of its National Incident-Based Reporting System (NIBRS), which collects information on the "incident, victim, property, offender, and arrestee" for each offense and arrest within twenty-two categories of crime (Federal Bureau of Investigation, 1996: 3).

Measuring Criminal Victimization

Crime rates can be calculated in several ways, and each kind of rate has both merits and drawbacks. Using official crime statistics, we can look at rates of recorded crime per 100,000 people, rates of recorded crime per number of available crime targets, rates of arrests for each kind of crime, and other rates based on crimes or suspects known to the police. Because many crimes are not reported to the police, or are not recorded by the police if they do learn of them, the rate at which people are victimized is likely to be greater than the rate of crime reported to the police.

History of Victimization Surveys

Apparently the first effort to measure crime by surveying members of households was carried out in 1720 in Denmark (Clinard, 1978: 222). However, the first large-scale, systematic effort to measure victimization by interviewing a cross section of a population was not conducted until 1966 in the United States (Ennis, 1967). This study of 10,000 American households by the National Opinion Research Center sought to determine how often people are victimized by crime. Since 1972, the federal Bureau of Justice Statistics (BJS) has done **victimization surveys** similar to the one carried out in 1966. Beginning with the 1992 survey, it has used a revised questionnaire aimed at jogging subjects' memories about crimes and uncovering more sexual crimes. The annual National Crime Victimization Survey (NCVS) now interviews national samples of 100,000 respondents age twelve and older in 50,000 households to measure both personal and household victimization rates. This survey is perhaps the most costly effort to gather crime data ever undertaken. Victimization surveys have also been used to measure crime in Great Britain, Canada, Australia, Germany, Denmark, the Netherlands, Switzerland, and other nations.

Comparing NCVS and FBI Data

The NCVS program measures crime in a somewhat different way than does the FBI's Uniform Crime Reports (UCR) data collection program. Consequently, the results of the two efforts to measure crime are not strictly comparable. The NCVS measures the offenses of rape, robbery from the person, aggravated and simple assault, household burglary, motor vehicle theft, and theft. It does not measure murder, kidnapping, or victimless crimes; and for reasons of economy it stopped collecting data on commercial burglary and commercial robbery in 1977. As a result, we cannot compare NCVS data on burglary and robbery with the FBI's UCR data on burglary and robbery, for the latter include burglaries and robberies of commercial establishments as well as of private households and individuals.

In recording crimes against the household, the NCVS and the FBI methods are the same; for instance, each counts one incident or one victimization for every burglary that is reported. However, the NCVS and FBI methods of dealing with crimes against the person differ. If a robbery has two victims, the FBI counts only one robbery incident, but the NCVS records two victimizations. NCVS data are oriented to victimizations and to individuals, whereas FBI data are oriented to crime incidents and to both organizational and individual victims.

The Dark Figure

Victimization surveys have uncovered a substantial **dark figure**, the number of crimes that actually occur but are not recorded by the police. The dark figure exists for many reasons, especially the failure of victims to report crimes and the failure of the police to record all reported crimes. Figure 2.1 shows the percentage of crimes uncovered in the 1994 NCVS survey that were reported and not reported to the police.

Figure 2.2, a hypothetical example that graphically depicts the dark figure, shows an actual total crime rate that is constant over time, as represented by the horizontal line parallel to the time axis. At time 1 (t_1), some of this total amount of crime is reported (the solid vertical line) and some of it is unreported (the dotted vertical line, which is the dark figure). By time 2 (t_2), the amount of reported crime has increased and the amount of unreported crime has decreased, but the actual total crime rate remains the same as at time 1. By time 3 (t_3), the official crime rate and the actual total crime rate are the same; in other words, at time 3, all crime that occurs is reported to and recorded by the police. Figure 2.2 shows how the official crime rate (the slanted

Type of Crime

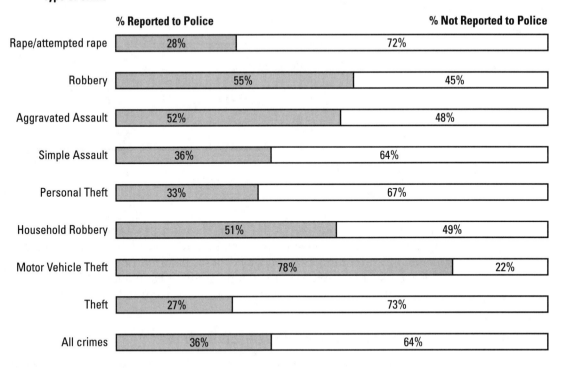

FIGURE 2.1

Percentages of Victimizations Reported and Not Reported to the Police, 1994

Source: Based on data from Craig Perkins and Patsy Klaus, *Criminal Victimization 1994.* Washington, D.C.: U.S. Department of Justice, April 1996, p. 3.

line) might increase over time without any increase in the actual total crime rate (the horizontal line). This would happen if people began to report crime that previously had not been reported or if the police began to record more of the crime reported to them. If this happens, official crime rates can rise without any increase in the actual total crime rate.

The dark figure has several important consequences. One is to keep cases, usually the least serious ones, out of the criminal justice system. As we have seen, victims are not as likely to report less serious crimes, and so those offenses that come to the attention of the police are likely to be completed crimes, to involve larger losses of property and greater personal injury, and to be committed with firearms (Skogan, 1984). Offenders who commit crimes that are not reported to the police cannot be brought to trial, reducing the deterrent effect of punishment. Police and court resources are sometimes allocated on the basis of how much crime is recorded in a community, and thus differences in crime reporting from one area to another could lead to a

FIGURE 2.2
Hypothetical Example of
Changes in Crime Rates
over Time

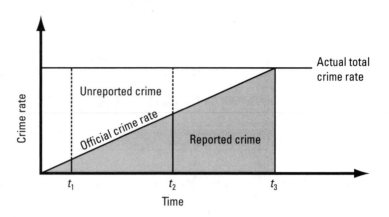

misallocation of resources. Victim compensation programs and insurance programs may also be affected by the failure to report and record crime, for benefits and premiums may be based on a distorted picture of how much crime occurs. FBI estimates of the financial costs of crime must also be inflated to account for crimes that are not reported or recorded.

Methodological Problems with Victimization Surveys

Victimization surveys are subject to several methodological problems. One problem is the issue of validity, or how well the surveys actually measure the amount of crime in a society. Forgetting can lead to underestimation of the amount of crime that has actually occurred, and it makes it difficult for subjects to tell interviewers exactly when they were victimized. Respondents may also refuse to tell interviewers about crimes for reasons similar to those that keep them from calling the police: the stigma of being victimized, unwillingness to confide in a stranger, and reluctance to take the time to give details of the crime.

Another problem is that victimization surveys can overestimate the amount of crime that occurs. Respondents might incorrectly interpret some experiences—such as the loss of a wallet—and report them as crimes. Overestimation of crime rates can also result if people report crimes that occurred before the period about which they are being questioned. This problem of "telescoping" might result from a faulty memory or from the respondent's wish to have something to talk about with the interviewer. The problem of telescoping can inflate victimization rates by as much as 20 percent, leading to estimates of crime rates that are higher than actual rates (Brantingham and Brantingham, 1984). Overreporting can also be encouraged by interviewers who prod respondents to remember crimes, both to keep the interview interesting and to ferret out the "hidden crime" on which the victimization survey is predicated.

Because of these and other methodological problems, the results of victimization surveys should not be regarded as "true" measures of crime. The surveys do measure some of the crime that is not reported to and recorded by the police. However, a comparison of victimization survey results and FBI UCR statistics concluded that "if one defines crime as criminal acts serious enough to be reacted to by both citizens and the police, then [the evidence indicates that] the UCR are at least as valid and probably more valid than the data from victimization surveys" (Gove, Hughes, and Geerken, 1985: 491).

Victimization surveys do not provide a complete and balanced picture of crime. They have not been used to measure white-collar crime, organized crime, or victimless crimes (Johnson and Wasielewski, 1982). They offer little or no information on offenders, as do FBI data on arrested suspects. To develop a full picture of crime, victimization surveys must be supplemented with other kinds of data.

Victimization surveys have been used primarily to look at the amount and distribution of crime rather than to test or develop theories of criminal behavior (see the Using Criminology box). These surveys have repeatedly shown that much crime is not reported and recorded, but they have added less to our understanding of the social processes that generate crime. As a result, they have contributed relatively little to the development of policies to reduce crime.

Measuring Crime by Self-Reports

Crime can be measured by police statistics or by questioning participants in the incident through a survey. Victimization surveys ask a cross section of the population about its experiences as victims of crime during a specific period. Another way to measure crime is to interview a cross section of the population, or a more limited sample such as high school students, about their involvement in crime and delinquency as offenders. **Self-report studies** reveal that much crime that respondents admit to in confidential interviews or on self-administered questionnaires never makes its way into police statistics.

History of Self-Report Studies

The first use of survey methods to gather self-reported information about involvement in crime and delinquency was Austin Porterfield's (1946) research that used this "self-disclosure" method to compare college students with delinquents who had been through the juvenile court. Porterfield found that both groups had been involved in delinquency in similar ways during their adolescence. In 1947, a self-report survey of adults discovered that 99 percent of a sample of "law-abiding" middle-class people admitted to at least one crime (Wallerstein and Wyle, 1947). These early studies showed that much self-reported crime is never detected by the police.

In 1957, James F. Short, Jr., and F. Ivan Nye (1957) developed a checklist of delinquent activities to be filled out anonymously by respondents. They found that delinquency was more evenly spread across social classes than

USING CRIMINOLOGY

The Risk of Victimization

In 1985, the Bureau of Justice Statistics of the U.S. Department of Justice began to use the results of its NCVS victimization surveys to calculate the risk of being the victim of a violent crime during a given year. The Bureau's Crime Risk Index can be used to compare the risks faced by different subgroups of the population (for example, whites and blacks, men and women, the young and the old, high- and low-income groups). It can also be used to compare the risk of being the victim of a violent crime with the risk of being in a fatal car accident or contracting a certain disease. The initial application of the Crime Risk Index found that each year 3 percent of Americans are victims of violent crime (defined as rape, robbery, and assault). The risk of victimization in a violent crime is higher for males than for females, higher for blacks than for whites, higher for those aged sixteen to twenty-four than for other age groups, and higher for low-income groups than for high-income groups.

In 1987, the Bureau of Justice Statistics began to use the NCVS data to calculate the risk of being a victim of a violent crime or a theft at some time during one's lifetime. This measure might be a better indicator of the costs of crime to individuals than are annual crime statistics, which an analyst at the Bureau said "provide a false sense of security." He added, "People are worried about the possibility that at some time in their lives they will be robbed or raped or assaulted, or their homes will be burglarized" (Koppel, p. 1).

The Bureau estimated that one in every 133 Americans will have his or her life ended by a murder. The percentage of people who will be victimized once or more during their lifetimes (starting at age twelve) are:

Rape and attempted rape	8%
Robbery and attempted robbery	30%
Assault and attempted assault	74%
Robbery or assault, resulting in injury	40%
Personal theft, including attempts	99%

Further analysis of the NCVS data allows even more refined calculations of risks. Thus, 11 percent of black women and 8 percent of white women will suffer a rape or an attempt during their lifetimes. Fifty-one percent of blacks but only 27 percent of whites will be victims of robbery or an attempt; 37 percent of males but only 22 percent of females will be victims of such a crime. Males are also more likely than females to be victims of an assault or an attempt, by 82 percent to 62 percent. Virtually everyone, regardless of sex or race, will be the victim of a personal theft or an attempt. During a twenty-year period, three-fourths of households will have a burglary, and one-fifth will have a car stolen.

These figures, based on victimization survey data from 1975 to 1984, must be updated regularly, for if crime rates change, then people's lifetime risks will also change.

Sources: Based on Bureau of Justice Statistics, *The Risk of Violent Crime.* Washington, D.C.: U.S. Department of Justice, May 1985; Herbert Koppel, *Lifetime Likelihood of Victimization.* Washington, D.C.: U.S. Department of Justice, March 1987.

---

was indicated by official crime statistics, which showed much more delinquency among the lower classes. Since this pioneering work, many researchers have used self-reports to test and refine theories of crime and delinquency and to provide a more complete picture of violation of the law than is given by official statistics. Table 2.4 shows six questions used by Travis Hirschi (1969) to gather self-report data on delinquency among California students and to test the social control theory of delinquency.

Self-report studies have also been conducted with groups of offenders other than those who engage in conventional crimes and delinquent acts. In 1976 the Internal Revenue Service (IRS) mailed questionnaires to 1,200 corporations to ask about their use of illegal bribes and "slush funds." Of the companies surveyed, 304 corporations did not respond, but among those that did, the IRS found 481 potentially illegal slush funds and 71 cases of apparent criminal fraud (Egan, 1978).

The Dark Figure

Self-report studies confirm the conclusion of victimization surveys that the dark figure, or hidden amount of crime, is large. These studies show that nearly everyone in the general population has broken the law at some time, even though most of the violations are petty. The general population falls on a continuum from highly criminal to completely noncriminal; it is not composed of two discrete groups of criminals and noncriminals. Researchers who compare a sample of convicted offenders with a "noncriminal" sample drawn from the general population usually fail to consider that many of these "noncriminals" have in fact engaged in crimes. Large numbers of people commit a few, often trivial, crimes; some commit a larger number; others commit quite a few crimes, including some serious ones; and a small proportion of the population commits many crimes, including large numbers of serious ones (Elmhorn, 1965). People who violate the law most often are the most likely to commit relatively serious crimes.

Methodological Problems with Self-Report Studies

Self-report studies have several methodological shortcomings that account for their failure to provide an ideal measure of crime. The questionnaires used in the studies sometimes lack validity; that is, they do not accurately measure the amount of crime that respondents have committed. Subjects might fabricate behavior to impress interviewers, or they might fail to mention some offenses out of fear that the information will be passed on to the police, in spite of guarantees of anonymity. Some studies have found that external control over lying helps to ensure the validity of self-report instruments (Clark and Tifft, 1966; Farrington, 1973).

Self-report studies have been criticized for using school or neighborhood samples that fail to include officially labeled, chronic delinquents. Critics question the assumption of many self-report researchers that "official delinquents are not different from adolescents located at various other points along the delinquency continuum" (Cernkovich, Giordano, and Pugh, 1985: 731). These critics urge researchers to locate and study more official delinquents, because data indicate that the factors explaining relatively minor transgressions are not necessarily the same factors accounting for the actions of chronic delinquent offenders.

TABLE 2.4 Survey Questions Measuring Self-Reported Delinquency

1. Have you ever taken little things (worth less than $2) that did not belong to you?
   A. No, never
   B. More than a year ago
   C. During the last year
   D. During the last year and more than a year ago

2. Have you ever taken things of some value (between $2 and $50) that did not belong to you?
   A. No, never
   B. More than a year ago
   C. During the last year
   D. During the last year and more than a year ago

3. Have you ever taken things of large value (worth over $50) that did not belong to you?
   A. No, never
   B. More than a year ago
   C. During the last year
   D. During the last year and more than a year ago

4. Have you ever taken a car for a ride without the owner's permission?
   A. No, never
   B. More than a year ago
   C. During the last year
   D. During the last year and more than a year ago

5. Have you ever banged up something that did not belong to you on purpose?
   A. No, never
   B. More than a year ago
   C. During the last year
   D. During the last year and more than a year ago

6. Not counting fights you may have had with a brother or sister, have you ever beaten up on anyone or hurt anyone on purpose?
   A. No, never
   B. More than a year ago
   C. During the last year
   D. During the last year and more than a year ago

Source: Adapted from Travis Hirschi, *Causes of Delinquency.* Berkeley, Calif.: University of California Press, 1969, p. 256.

Another problem with self-report studies is the way they have been carried out. The use of many different self-report questionnaires by researchers means that their results are often not comparable. Self-report studies would be much more useful if the same questionnaire were administered periodically to national samples. This would allow us to generalize about the amount of crime in the population as a whole and to look at changes in the amount of crime over time. We have accumulated some data of this sort on victimization

experiences, but we do not yet have such information on self-reported violations of the law. In fact, we know relatively little about self-reported crime by
adults, for the vast majority of self-report studies have been carried out on
samples of juveniles.

Self-report studies are also flawed in that they ignore certain kinds of
behavior. They rarely include questions that add to our knowledge of white-
collar crime or organized crime. The way questionnaires are written usually
makes it difficult to compare the results of self-report studies with official
crime statistics or with victimization survey data. This is partly a result of the
use of self-report questionnaires with juvenile samples, for it means that
respondents are asked about acts that would be crimes if they were adults as
well as about juvenile status offenses such as truancy and underage drinking.

Some self-report studies classify juveniles as delinquents if they admit to
one or more delinquent acts. Questionnaires that ask about large numbers of
acts are more likely to classify a high proportion of respondents as delinquents, even though many of them might be only minimally involved in trivial acts of delinquency (Reiss, 1975; Hindelang, Hirschi, and Weis, 1979). Self-
report studies should emphasize the frequency of delinquency and crime and
the seriousness of the acts, rather than whether an individual has ever
engaged in any act that violates the law.

Because of their methodological shortcomings, self-report studies cannot be employed to assess the efficiency of official crime statistics, even
though self-report studies do confirm that there is a large dark figure of crime.
They have proved useful, however, in telling us about the characteristics of
people who violate different kinds of laws with various degrees of frequency.
This information can be compared with official data on arrests, convictions,
and sentences to assess the fairness with which the criminal justice system
treats different kinds of people.

Because of the methodological problems with each of the three major
measures of crime, none provides us with a perfect measure of crime. When
all three measures agree on the extent and distribution of crime, we can have
some confidence in the conclusions. When the three measures disagree
about the extent and distribution of crime, as they sometimes do, it is difficult
to know which one to use. However, each measure can be employed to good
advantage by criminologists to answer certain kinds of questions. For
instance, victimization data and official crime statistics can be used to examine trends in crime rates. Self-report data cannot be used for that purpose,
but they can help us to understand the impact on delinquency of child-rearing methods and membership in peer groups, issues not dealt with by either
official statistics or victimization surveys. Used appropriately, each measure
can contribute to a fuller understanding of criminal behavior.

Summary

The classical school of criminology that developed in the eighteenth century
assumed free will and individual responsibility, sought to deter offenders from

crime by the threat of punishment, and emphasized punishment in proportion to the social harm caused by the criminal act. During the nineteenth century, cartographers such as Guerry and Quetelet looked for patterns of crime that appeared in official crime statistics. Positivists, reacting to the classical school's emphasis on free will, began late in the nineteenth century to use the scientific method to search for the causes of crime. Cesare Lombroso was the first to use empirical evidence to test hypotheses about why people violated the law, an approach that laid the groundwork for modern criminology.

Today criminologists use several statistical measures to study crime. Sometimes they use official statistics gathered by the police, the courts, or the prisons. The FBI's Uniform Crime Reports provide statistics on crimes known to the police throughout the United States. This report gives detailed information on eight Part I crimes that together constitute the crime index, and less detailed information on twenty-one Part II offenses. The report pays little attention to white-collar crime or organized crime and thus presents a distorted picture of the crime problem that emphasizes crimes committed by young males who are often poor and members of minority groups.

Official statistics are used to calculate crime rates, usually in terms of number of offenses per 100,000 people. This kind of rate makes sense for crimes in which people are victimized, but it makes less sense when property is the target. Careful thought should be given to the way crime rates are calculated and to the exact meaning of those rates.

Crimes come to the attention of the police when victims and witnesses report offenses and the police react, and when the police uncover crime on their own initiative through proactive work. Crimes are not reported to the police for many reasons: a sense that nothing can be done, a feeling that the offense is unimportant, a belief that the police do not want to be bothered, fear of reprisals, or definition of the crime as a private matter. The police might fail to record crimes, sometimes to keep crime rates down and make themselves look more effective. Official crime statistics have been used for political purposes at both the local and national levels.

A second important measure of crime is the victimization survey. A cross section of a population is questioned in detail about their experiences as victims of crime during a given period. This method was first used on a large-scale basis in the United States in 1966, and today it is employed as part of an ongoing federal effort to measure crime. Because the methods of the NCVS surveys differ from those used by the FBI to collect data, the two kinds of statistics cannot be compared easily. Victimization surveys have found a large dark figure, the amount of crime that occurs but does not make its way into police records. Because victimization surveys have methodological problems, they are not a "true" measure of how much crime there is, but they are important sources of information.

A third measure of crime is the self-report survey, a questionnaire administered anonymously to get respondents to tell about crimes they have committed. Self-report surveys were first used in the United States in 1946, and since then they have been used to measure the extent of crime and delinquency and to test theories of crime and delinquency. Self-report studies find a large dark figure, and sometimes they reach conclusions about who violates the law that differ from research based on official arrest data. Self-report studies have some problems: most have been done with adolescents, many have asked about involvement in trivial offenses, and there are some questions about how validly they measure crime and delinquency. Each of the three measures of crime has strengths and weaknesses, and, when used appropriately, each can contribute to a fuller understanding of criminal behavior.

Important Terms

cartography
classical school
crime index
crime rate
dark figure
incidence

positivism
prevalence
proactive police work
reactive police work
self-report study
victimization survey

Review Questions

1. What are the differences between positivism and the classical school of criminology? What policies might advocates of each approach recommend for reducing the crime rate?

2. What are the three major kinds of crime statistics used by criminologists? What are the advantages and disadvantages of each measure of crime? What kinds of questions about crime does each measure address most usefully?

3. In 1975, there were 464,973 robberies reported to the FBI. The estimated population of the United States in that year was 213,124,000. In 1995, there were 580,545 robberies, and the estimated population was 262,755,000. Calculate the rate of robberies per 100,000 people for each year. What do you conclude from your calculations?

Chapter 3
Crime and Its Costs

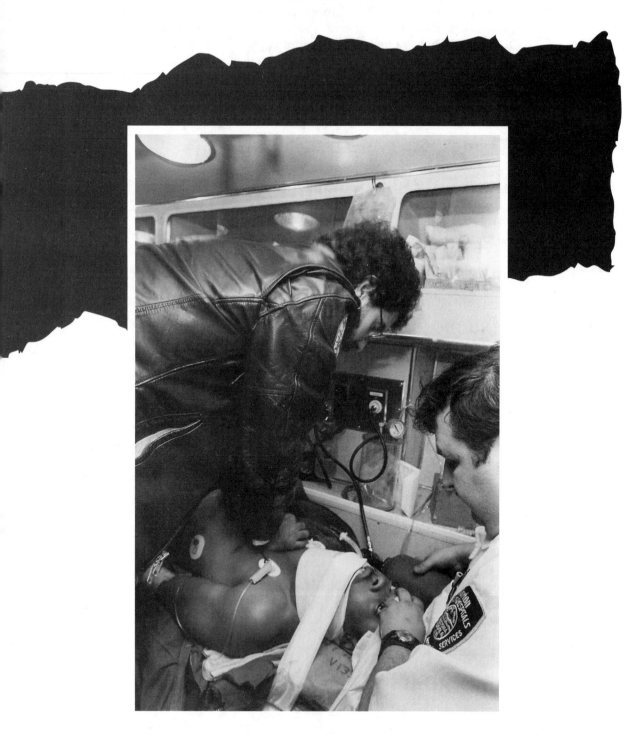

This chapter looks at the characteristics and costs of four major types of crime: conventional crime, white-collar crime, organized crime, and victimless crime. Conventional crimes are usually divided into two groups: crimes of violence (also called crimes against the person) and property crimes. Crimes of violence include murder, forcible rape, robbery, and assault. Major property crimes are burglary, larceny, motor vehicle theft, fraud, arson, and vandalism. There are a variety of white-collar crimes as well, including crimes by businesses such as deceptive advertising and antitrust violations, and crimes by employees against businesses such as embezzlement and expense account fraud. Organized or syndicated crime has traditionally been equated with the Mafia or La Cosa Nostra in the United States, but it has taken new forms in recent years. Victimless crimes, perhaps more accurately called "crimes without complainants," include drug use, gambling, prostitution, and pornography.

After looking at some of the characteristics of these crimes, their financial, physical, and social costs are explored. Estimates of the financial costs of crime, which often appear to be more precise than they really are, can be made only on the basis of assumptions about how much crime actually occurs. Even if we could measure exactly how much crime occurs, it would still be difficult to estimate the cost of each offense. For instance, if a robber beats up a person and steals $25, the victim loses the money but the robber has the use of that money. Placing a monetary figure on the physical and psychological harm to the victim is not easy. If the robber uses the $25 to buy heroin, we might count this expenditure as another cost of crime, even though counting both the initial theft of $25 and the use of that money for heroin might be seen as double counting. If the robber is then arrested, some part of the police budget will be allocated to the crime. The arraignment and trial cost money, and if the offender is convicted and imprisoned, there will be the additional costs of incarceration. The robber's family might have to receive welfare benefits during his or her imprisonment. The absent parent might create a family environment in which the children are more likely to get involved in delinquency. We can see that the initial loss of $25 in the robbery might be quite a small amount when compared with all of the other costs associated with the crime.

There are six distinct kinds of costs of crime (see Table 3.1). One is the **direct loss** of property. For example, arson destroys buildings, and vandalism ruins property. Both offenses reduce the stock of useful things in the world. We can also speak of direct losses from murder, although placing a monetary figure on lost lives is difficult.

A second kind of cost of crime is the **transfer of property.** The theft of a radio in a burglary and the theft of cash in a robbery transfer property from the rightful owner to the thief, and perhaps eventually to a fence and then to a new owner. The victim of the theft regards himself or herself as having lost the property, but from a societal perspective the property has been transferred from one person to another rather than made useless.

A third financial cost of crime arises from crimes of violence in which a victim is physically hurt. These **costs related to criminal violence** include the

TABLE 3.1   Kinds of Financial Costs of Crime

1. Direct loss
2. Transfer of property
3. Costs related to criminal violence
4. Illegal expenditures
5. Enforcement costs
6. Prevention and protection costs

loss of productivity by incapacitated victims, unemployment compensation paid to victims, fees paid for physical and psychological therapy for victims, and social security payments and funeral expenses associated with homicides.

Yet another type of cost of crime is the expenditure of money on illegal goods and services such as drugs, gambling, prostitution, and pornography. **Illegal expenditures** can be considered a cost of crime because they divert money from the legitimate economy and represent a loss of potential revenue for people who produce and supply legal goods and services. However, from another point of view, we might regard illegal expenditures as entertainment expenses, which are often paid for with income earned at a legitimate job. Some of these illegal expenditures do not victimize anyone; no direct and obvious harm to another person necessarily results from spending money on prostitution, illegal drugs, gambling, or pornography. Indeed, expenditures on legal goods such as cigarettes and alcohol may produce more obvious harm than do expenditures on some illegal goods and services.

Enforcement costs, a fifth kind of financial cost of crime, include the money spent by various criminal justice agencies. Employees of the agencies regard their salaries as legitimate payments for their work, but from another perspective crime diverts this money from other purposes. If enforcement costs are treated as a financial cost of crime, it follows that redefining some behavior that is now criminal as noncriminal would reduce the cost of crime. The costs of the American criminal justice system are examined in Chapter 13.

A sixth financial cost of crime involves **prevention and protection costs.** This includes the millions of dollars that people spend for alarm systems, spotlights, locks, bars, and other "target-hardening" devices, as well as the money they spend on insurance premiums to cover their losses through theft.

Conventional Crimes

Conventional crimes are often divided into violent crimes and property crimes; violent crimes are more feared, but property crimes are more common (see Figure 3.1). The distinction between violent crime and property crime is not always clear-cut. For instance, robbery is the theft of property from a person by force or threat of force, making it both a property crime and a crime of violence. Here we treat it as a crime of violence, because the use of force makes it a more serious crime than simple theft without violence. A second problem

FIGURE 3.1
Crime Index Offenses,
Percent Distribution, 1995

Source: Based on data from
Federal Bureau of Investigation,
Crime in the United States, 1995:
Uniform Crime Reports.
Washington, D.C.: U.S.
Government Printing Office,
1996, p. 8.

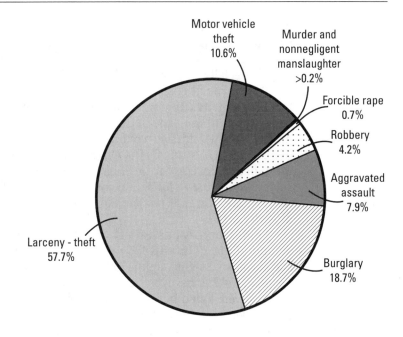

Motor vehicle theft 10.6%

Murder and nonnegligent manslaughter >0.2%

Forcible rape 0.7%

Robbery 4.2%

Aggravated assault 7.9%

Burglary 18.7%

Larceny - theft 57.7%

with the violent crime/property crime distinction is that one crime event can involve multiple offenses. Thus, after committing a forcible rape the offender may steal the victim's car to get away. Law-enforcement officials would count only the more serious offense, forcible rape, in recording the crime.

Crimes of Violence

The four major types of violent crime are murder, forcible rape, robbery, and assault.

Murder **Murder and nonnegligent manslaughter** are defined by the Federal Bureau of Investigation as the willful killing of a human being. The taking of another person's life may fall outside this definition if it is excusable, such as an accidental shooting of a playmate by a child, or if it is justifiable, such as a police officer's shooting of a dangerous offender who is about to hurt someone.

In 1995, 21,597 murders were reported to the FBI by local police departments. Because murders are usually reported to the police and because the FBI gathers data from most police departments in the country, the FBI's figure is a good estimate of the number of people actually murdered.

To get some perspective on the meaning of the number of murders that occur each year in the United States, it is instructive to compare the total with deaths that occur in other ways. In 1994, a year that the FBI reported 23,305 murders, there were 31,142 recorded suicides in the country, though the actual number may have been twice that figure. In that same year, 42,524 people died in traffic accidents, about half of them in crashes in which alcohol was present. Thus, more people commit suicide and more people die in car accidents than are murdered each year, although the death toll from murder is high, especially compared with murder rates in other industrial societies.

The financial costs of murder include medical expenses, funeral costs, lost productivity (the total wages the victim would have earned if he or she had lived until the expected age), the cost of welfare or social security payments to the victim's survivors, and such intangible costs as pain and emotional trauma. A study by the Office of Justice Programs (1996) estimates that the tangible costs of an average murder are $1,030,000 and the intangible costs are $1,910,000, for a total cost per murder of $2,940,000. That figure does not include criminal justice expenditures to arrest, prosecute, and punish offenders.

Murder occurs in a variety of circumstances. Of the 12,872 people murdered in Chicago from 1965 to 1981, 69 percent were killed in murders that started as arguments, fights, or brawls; 17 percent were slain in murders that began as robberies; 1 percent were killed in murders that followed rapes; 1 percent were killed in murders that developed from burglaries; fewer than 1 percent were victims of murders that began in some other way, such as a contract killing; and the remainder were murdered in unknown circumstances (Block, 1987: 3–4).

Murder typically involves an offender and a victim of the same race (see Figure 3.2A); this reflects racially based patterns of social interaction in the larger society. Most murders involve a male offender and a male victim; murders of females by males are the next most common type, although men kill other men nearly three times as often as they kill women (see Figure 3.2B).

Murder occurs more often between an offender and a victim who are known to each other than it does between strangers. In 1995, 12 percent of murders reported to the FBI involved an offender and a victim in the same family; 34 percent involved boyfriends, girlfriends, friends, acquaintances, neighbors, employers, or employees; 15 percent involved strangers; and in 39 percent of the cases the victim-offender relationship was not known to the police (Federal Bureau of Investigation, 1996: 19). Overall, murders between offenders and victims known to one another outnumbered murders between strangers by more than three to one. A study using data on murder cases disposed of in 1988 in the seventy-five largest counties in the United States found that 64 percent of the victims were killed by friends or acquaintances, 20 percent by strangers, and 16 percent by family members (see Figure 3.3) (Dawson and Langan, 1994). Table 3.2 compares the characteristics of murder in families to other kinds of murder.

The marital relationship is sometimes conducive to murder, as we can see in the Cross-Cultural Perspective box on pp. 78–79. In the United States, more husbands kill their wives than wives kill their husbands, but a substantial number of marital murders are committed by women (Wolfgang, 1958; Block and Christakos, 1995). In fact, the proportion of marital homicides committed by wives is much higher in the United States than it is in Canada, Great Britain, and Australia; the reason for the discrepancy is unclear (Wilson

FIGURE 3.2

Victim/Offender
Relationships by Race and
Sex, Murder and
Nonnegligent Manslaughter,
United States, 1995

Source: Based on data from
Federal Bureau of Investigation,
*Crime in the United States, 1995:
Uniform Crime Reports.*
Washington, D.C.: U.S.
Government Printing Office,
1996, p. 17.

A. Race of Offender/Race of Victim

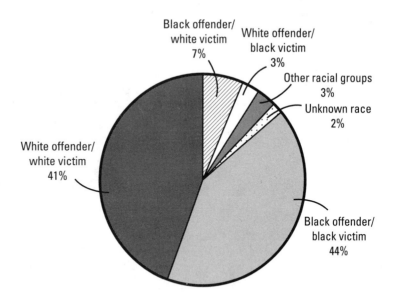

Black offender/
white victim
7%

White offender/
black victim
3%

Other racial groups
3%

Unknown race
2%

White offender/
white victim
41%

Black offender/
black victim
44%

B. Sex of Offender/Sex of Victim

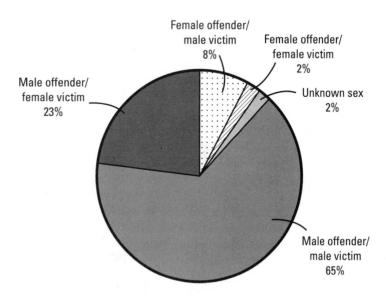

Female offender/
male victim
8%

Female offender/
female victim
2%

Male offender/
female victim
23%

Unknown sex
2%

Male offender/
male victim
65%

and Daly, 1992). FBI data for 1995 show that 1.3 percent of all homicide victims in the U.S. were husbands killed by their wives, and 3.7 percent of all victims were wives killed by their husbands (Federal Bureau of Investigation, 1996: 19). A national study of spouse murder cases disposed of in 1988 found that three-fifths of the defendants were husbands and two-fifths were wives.

FIGURE 3.3

Relationship of Murder
Victims and Defendants in 75
Largest Urban Counties, 1988

Source: Based on data from
John M. Dawson and Patrick A.
Langan, *Murder in Families.*
Washington, D.C.: U.S.
Department of Justice, July
1994, pp. 1–2.

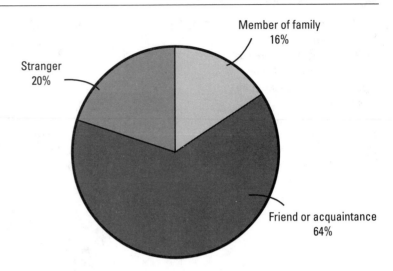

Stranger
20%

Member of family
16%

Friend or acquaintance
64%

Total number of victims 2,655

Wives were less likely to be convicted and were sentenced less severely than
husbands, apparently because wives were more often provoked by spouses
who had assaulted them (Langan and Dawson, 1995).

Forcible Rape   According to the FBI, **forcible rape** is "carnal knowledge of a
female forcibly and against her will" (Federal Bureau of Investigation, 1995:
23). However, some states now define forcible rape in sex-neutral terms, so
that a sexual assault on a male victim, typically by another male, is defined as
rape. Some states have also passed laws that distinguish among different
degrees of sexual assault, each carrying a different penalty according to the
degree of the offense as defined by the offender's intent, the nature of the sexual act, the amount of injury to the victim, and other circumstances of the
crime.

In 1995, there were 97,464 cases of forcible rape and attempted rape
reported to local police departments in the United States, but federal victimization surveys have found that many more incidents actually occur. The
revised NCVS questionnaire first used in 1992 asked respondents specifically
about rape and sexual assault, whereas earlier surveys had only asked about
any kind of assault. As a result, the number of reported sexual assaults
increased dramatically. Of the 433,000 sexual assaults reported in 1994,
316,000 were rapes and attempted rapes, three times the number reported by
the FBI for that year.

Rape always involves psychological damage to the victim, because by
definition it does not involve consent. Rape often involves physical harm as
well. A study of 646 reported rapes in Philadelphia found that 85 percent
involved some physical force by the offender. In 29 percent of the cases there
was roughness by the rapist; in 25 percent the rapist beat the woman "in a
nonbrutal fashion"; in 20 percent the offender beat the victim brutally; in 11

TABLE 3.2   Murder in Families Compared to Other Kinds of Murder

Compared to other murder victims, family murder **victims** were
More often:
      female
      under 12 or over 59 years old
      killed in the daytime
      killed in the victim's home
Less often:
      identified as alcohol users
      unemployed
      killed by a firearm
      armed
      killed by multiple offenders
      identified as having a criminal record

Compared to other murder defendants, family murder **defendants**
More often:
      were 30 or more years old
      had a history of mental illness
      committed a murder in the daytime
      committed a murder in the defendant's home
Less often:
      were identified as alcohol users
      were unemployed
      killed a victim of the same sex
      used a firearm
      had a criminal record

Source: Adapted from John M. Dawson and Patrick A. Langan, *Murder in Families.* Washington, D.C.: U.S. Department of Justice, July 1994, p. 2.

percent the offender choked the victim; and in only 15 percent of the rapes was no physical force used (Amir, 1971: 155). Another study found that 48 percent of rape victims were injured and 19 percent injured seriously enough to require medical attention (Hindelang, Gottfredson, and Garofalo, 1978). NCVS data from 1979 to 1986 indicate that 39 percent of rape victims were injured, about half of them seriously enough to warrant medical care (Harlow, 1989). A telephone survey of 4,008 women found that of those raped in 1990, 4 percent had suffered serious physical injuries, 24 percent had sustained minor injuries, and 70 percent had not been physically injured; degree of injury was unknown in 2 percent of the cases (Skorneck, 1992). Data from the NCVS study estimated that rape victims suffered economic losses of $33 million in 1992; this includes medical expenses and lost pay (Klaus, 1994). A report by the Office of Justice Programs (1996) estimates that the typical rape or sexual assault has tangible costs of $5,100 and intangible costs (such as

Dowry Murders in India

When Renu Puri married Rajesh Bhalla in 1980, the Bhallas demanded as dowry about $7,000 (85,000 rupees) worth of jewelry and gold, a $1,000 stereo system, an $800 Panasonic television, two gold Omega watches worth more than $200 apiece, a $300 silver tea service, electric fans, steam irons, and twenty-one silk saris for the Bhalla women. Renu's father was an airline engineer and her mother a school supervisor, and such lavishness strained their resources.... "Rajesh wanted to go to America to earn more money, but Renu refused to leave India," Mrs. Puri says. "That's how it started. Because she opposed him, he began demanding more dowry from us. He wanted a washing machine, and we gave him that. Then he demanded nine thousand rupees for a shopping trip to Hong Kong. He brought back a color TV and another 'music center,' and demanded that my husband pay the fourteen thousand rupees in customs duty for them. After that he tried to force Renu to make us transfer our property and home into his name, and when she wouldn't he began to beat her. He told her that she had ruined his life because she had kept him from going to America. Finally, he demanded a Toyota car. But how could we afford it? We had already given him everything we could."

In February of 1983 Renu's father received a phone call at his office. Renu, who had been a college beauty queen, lay in the hospital, charred almost beyond recognition. Rajesh had doused her with kerosene and set her on fire. She died about a week later. (Bordewich, p. 21)

This type of crime, called a dowry murder, has increased in recent years in India, though its exact extent is unclear, because many such crimes are not reported to the police or recorded by them as murders. In 1985 there were 999 registered cases of dowry deaths, in 1986 there were 1,319, in 1987 there were 1,786, and in 1992 there were 4,785. Feminists and social scientists believe that these numbers are but a small proportion of the actual numbers of dowry murders, but the police respond that many burning deaths of young wives are accidents or suicides, rather than homicides by husbands or by members of the husband's family. Rajesh Bhalla is now serving a life sentence for murder, but he is the exception; few dowry murderers are imprisoned, and most are not even prosecuted.

Traditionally, the dowry in India represented the daughter's share of the father's wealth, as only sons could inherit land. Since 1961, this practice has been illegal, and laws passed in 1983 and 1985 defined harassment over dowries as a crime. However, the definition of dowry in the law is still vague, and no effective way of enforcing the law has been developed.

A variety of social forces have given rise to dowry murders. Marriage in India has become increasingly commercialized, having never been based on romantic love, as in the West. Moral restraints exercised by caste and village have broken down with modernization and urbanization. Exposure to the high standard of living in industrialized nations has increased the materialism and acquisitiveness of India's middle class. Women

pain and emotional trauma suffered by the victim) of $81,400, for a total cost of $86,500 per rape or sexual assault.

Many forcible rapes are planned in detail, but some occur spontaneously. One study found that nearly three-fourths of rapes were planned, with offenders deliberately trying to force the victim into sex. Another one-ninth of the rapes were partially planned, with vague plans being hastily made after an encounter with a potential victim. About one-sixth of the rapes were

A CROSS-CULTURAL PERSPECTIVE

are subordinate in the Indian social structure, so that even their own parents tend to blame them for their marital problems, rather than blame their sons-in-law. In addition, lack of access to educational and employment opportunities makes it difficult for women to become economically independent of their husbands.

A dowry is seen by men with aspirations to upward mobility, particularly by those who are well educated but lack good job prospects, as a way to get the goods and the money necessary to enter the middle class. A dowry becomes for those men a "short-cut to importance" (Bordewich, p. 24), a way to acquire the money to start a business or build a house. The bride becomes a means by which a man can extort money and possessions from her parents, who yield to him because they fear for their daughter's safety or are concerned they will get a reputation for being stingy. When the bride's parents eventually refuse the husband's demands, he may beat or kill his wife.

Dowry murders are linked to the structure of the Indian family and to the culture's trait of avoiding psychological introspection. The husband's mother often sees the bride as an outsider to the family, and as a threat to alienate her son's affections. In a society that lacks the Western tradition of reflecting on one's feelings and motivations, husbands and their mothers tend to focus on the size of the dowry as the source of resentment and conflict within the family.

The presence in most Indian kitchens of kerosene for cooking offers husbands a handy means to commit murder and allows others to see the burning of the wife as an accident or a suicide. This means of death also fits with the traditional practice of *suttee*, in which Indian widows threw themselves on the burning funeral pyres of their deceased husbands.

Pressure from women's groups has produced some reforms in dealing with violence against wives. New laws require prosecution for harassment and mental torture as well as for physical abuse of women. Some cities now have special police units to handle crimes against women. In New Delhi, the police inspector automatically orders an autopsy in suspicious deaths in the home. In addition, an increasing number of parents are allowing their daughters to return home when they experience marital discord, in contrast to the traditional practice of demanding that married women adjust to their husband's family and never return to their parents' home.

Source: Based on Fergus M. Bordewich, "Dowry Murders," *The Atlantic Monthly*, 258 (July 1986), 21–27; Barbara Crossette, "India Studying 'Accidental' Deaths of Hindu Wives," *New York Times*, January 15, 1989, p. 10; Edward A. Gargan, "For Many Brides in India, a Dowry Buys Death," *New York Times*, December 30, 1993, p. A4.

"explosive," with the offender having no earlier intention of committing a rape but perpetrating one impulsively when an opportunity presented itself (Amir, 1971: 141).

Many forcible rapes involve strangers, but a surprisingly large number occur between offenders and victims who have close relationships. Three studies have found that the proportion of all rapes committed by total strangers to the victims ranges from 42 to 53 percent (Amir, 1971; Curtis, 1974; Timrots and Rand, 1987). Two of these studies found that 10 percent and 14 percent of the rapes occurred between an offender and a victim who had previously been intimately related, either as relatives, lovers, or close friends. The third study found that 4 percent of the rapes were committed by relatives. The telephone survey of 4,008 women produced quite different results: only 22 percent of rape victims had been attacked by strangers, 29 percent had been raped by nonrelatives known to the victim, and 46 percent had been assaulted by relatives, ex-husbands, or current or past boyfriends; relationships were unknown in the remaining 3 percent of the cases (Skorneck, 1992). Rape victims under the age of twelve are usually raped by family members or acquaintances, with the percentage of rapes by strangers increasing with the age of rape victims (*New York Times*, June 23, 1994).

One relationship between the rapist and the victim that has received considerable attention in recent years is the rape of women by their husbands or ex-husbands. According to one study, one-seventh of women who have ever been married have been the victims of rape or attempted rape by their husbands or ex-husbands (Russell, 1982). All states now permit the prosecution of a husband for the rape of his wife, but in some states the spouses must have been separated at the time of the attack for the case to be prosecuted as a rape. Rape in marriage is an underreported offense, and when it is reported the police often treat it as an assault, if they deal with it as a crime at all.

Robbery   **Robbery** is the theft of property from another person by force or threat of force. More severe penalties are usually meted out to robbers who are armed than to those who do not use weapons. Robberies involve both commercial and financial establishments (banks, stores, gas stations, and taxicabs) and noncommercial targets (people on the street and in residences). (See Figure 3.4.)

The FBI reported 580,545 cases of robbery in 1995. These robberies produced a total loss of $507 million. The National Crime Victimization Survey estimated that robbery victims lost $680 million in 1992 (Klaus, 1994). A report by the Office of Justice Programs (1996) estimates that a typical robbery or attempt with injury has tangible costs of $5,200 and intangible costs (such as the victim's pain and emotional trauma) of $13,800, for a total cost of $19,000 per robbery or attempt with injury. The FBI provides no information on the amount of harm suffered by robbery victims, but an NCVS study using data from 1979 to 1986 found that one-third of robbery victims were injured, half of them seriously enough to require medical care (Harlow, 1989).

Physical injuries during robberies are least common when an offender has a firearm, somewhat more common when a knife is used, and most likely when the offender uses no weapon at all (Conklin, 1972; Hindelang, Gottfredson, and Garofalo, 1978; Cook, 1987). Victims confronted by armed robbers are probably least likely to resist and thus least apt to be injured. Victims who believe they can overpower an unarmed robber are more likely to be injured while resisting.

Robberies sometimes lead to murders; these offenses are classified as murders rather than robberies. The FBI estimates that in 1995 there were 1,855 murders that had robbery as the motive. Thus, about one murder in eleven begins as a robbery. However, only one robbery in every 313 results in a murder.

FIGURE 3.4

Types of Robbery, as Percentages of All Reported Robberies, 1995

Source: Based on data from Federal Bureau of Investigation, *Crime in the United States, 1995: Uniform Crime Reports.* Washington, D.C.: U.S. Government Printing Office, 1996, p. 27.

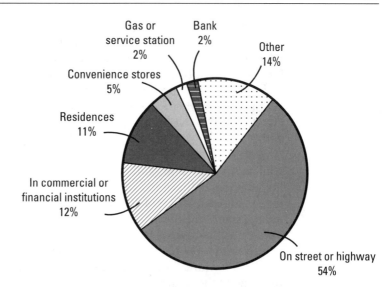

Gas or service station 2%

Bank 2%

Other 14%

Convenience stores 5%

Residences 11%

In commercial or financial institutions 12%

On street or highway 54%

Many robberies are planned only a few minutes before they occur, with offenders piecing together the elements of the crime by improvisation. One study found that more than 40 percent of juvenile robbers and 25 percent of adult robbers had not intended to commit the crime before it occurred (Feeney and Weir, 1973). One example of an unplanned robbery involved a man who usually planned his offenses with a partner well in advance. This man went into a liquor store to buy some beer, and when the clerk refused to sell to him because he was drunk, the man pulled a gun and demanded money. His partner outside in the car was taken by surprise because they had not planned the robbery; nevertheless, he ran into the store to help. After the robbery they drove away, but their license number was traced and they were arrested. When they had previously engaged in planned robberies, they had always stolen a car to avoid being traced (Conklin, 1972: 97).

Robbers and their victims rarely know one another. Because thieves have access to the property of people they know well, they do not need to use force to steal from them. They can simply take the property by stealth in a larceny. They might also explain their need for cash to those with whom they are close, and thus might be given or loaned the necessary money rather than having to steal it. Concern for people whom they know well can lead robbers to think that if they must use force to steal, they might as well use that force against strangers rather than against relatives or friends. Moreover, strangers are less likely to be able to identify robbers to the police. Thus, it is not surprising that more than three-fourths of all robbers are strangers to their victims (Curtis, 1974; Hindelang, 1976; Timrots and Rand, 1987).

Assault An **assault** is an unlawful attack by one person on another. The FBI distinguishes between **simple assault**, in which no weapon is used and no serious injury results, and **aggravated assault**, in which the purpose of the attack is to inflict severe bodily injury and a weapon is typically used.

In 1995, there were 1,099,179 cases of aggravated assault reported to local police departments. Many victims of this crime are permanently incapacitated. Others suffer injuries from which they eventually recover, but they often lose wages or jobs as a result of being hurt. An eight-city study found that 35 percent of aggravated assault victims were injured and 18 percent injured seriously enough to need medical attention (Hindelang, Gottfredson, and Garofalo, 1978). NCVS data from 1979 to 1986 show that 32 percent of aggravated assault victims were injured, nearly two-thirds of them seriously enough to require medical care (Harlow, 1989). The NCVS found that victims of all kinds of assaults suffered economic losses of $649 million in 1992; these losses were in the form of medical expenses and lost pay (Klaus, 1994). A recent report (Office of Justice Programs, 1996) estimates that the average assault or attempt has tangible costs of $1,550 and intangible costs of $7,800, for a total loss of $9,350.

The exact relationship between victims and offenders in assaults is difficult to determine, because many assaults occur within the family and are not reported to the police and perhaps not even to interviewers who conduct surveys about people's experiences as victims of crime. Fear of retaliation, embarrassment, and the desire to protect even abusive family members contribute to the underreporting of family violence. As a result, assaults between spouses and parental violence against children are more common than is suggested by crime statistics (Gelles and Straus, 1988).

In about one-fourth of the aggravated assaults reported to the police, the relationship between the victim and the offender is unknown. About one-seventh of aggravated assaults occur between members of the same family, and nearly one-third more involve lovers, friends, acquaintances, or neighbors. Another one-fifth of aggravated assaults occur between strangers, and one-tenth involve a criminal and a police officer (Curtis, 1974).

Aggravated assaults that are reported to interviewers in surveys of victimization experiences involve strangers 56 percent of the time, a much higher proportion than is the case with aggravated assaults reported to the police. Of the aggravated assaults reported to interviewers, 39 percent are by non-strangers such as relatives and acquaintances. In 5 percent of the cases, victim-offender relationships could not be determined (Timrots and Rand, 1987).

Crimes of violence such as murder, rape, robbery, and assault produce financial losses in the form of unpaid wages, hospitalization expenses, and the costs of therapeutic services. Based on victimization survey data for 1981, the Bureau of Justice Statistics (April 1984) estimated that the median medical expense incurred by victims of rape, robbery, and assault was $120; one-fourth of the victims had expenses of $375 or more. About two-thirds of the medical expenses resulting from these three violent crimes was due to assaults. A study that used FBI and NCVS data for murder, rape or sexual assault, robbery or attempt with injury, assault or attempt, and burglary or attempt estimated that each year the tangible costs of those offenses were $105 billion and that the intangible costs were $345 billion, for a total loss of $450 billion (Office of Justice Programs, 1996).

A study of 131 patients admitted to a San Francisco hospital with firearm injuries found that their average hospital costs were nearly $7,000 and that 86 percent of those costs were paid for by tax-supported government insurance programs. Extrapolating to the country as a whole, the researchers concluded that firearm injuries—the majority of which are inflicted by handguns—cost $429 million per year in hospital expenses and probably more than $1 billion if the costs of ambulance services, physicians' fees, follow-up care, and rehabilitation are added to hospital costs (Martin, Hunt, and Hulley, 1988). A much higher estimate of $63 billion lost due to firearm assault injuries and deaths was derived from estimates of the costs of medical and mental health care, emergency transportation, police services, insurance administration, lost productivity, pain and suffering, and reduced quality of life (Miller and Cohen, 1995).

Fear of Crime   Fear is a significant social cost of conventional crime, especially violent crime. People are most afraid of those crimes that occur least often, namely, murder, rape, and robbery. The public's "fear of crimes of violence is not a simple fear of injury or death or even of all crimes of violence, but, at bottom, a fear of strangers" (President's Commission on Law Enforcement and Administration of Justice, 1967: 52). This is true even though the chance of being killed by a stranger is much less than the chance of dying in a car accident or an accidental fall, and even though murder and aggravated assault are committed more often by people with whom the victim is acquainted than by strangers.

Fear of crime has socially harmful consequences. It makes people suspicious of strangers. It causes them to stay home, stay out of certain neighborhoods, move to safer communities, and even avoid traveling to other nations (see the Cross-Cultural Perspective box). They spend money on lights, locks, alarms, watchdogs, and other protective measures. In schools, fear of crime destroys the atmosphere necessary for learning, leads students to avoid dangerous places such as restrooms, and increases truancy. Chapter 12 examines in more detail the way that fear of crime affects community life.

Property Crimes

Property crimes involve either the theft or the destruction of property. Theft can take the form of burglary, larceny, motor vehicle theft, or fraud. Destruction of property occurs in the crimes of arson and vandalism.

Burglary   **Burglary** is unlawful entry of a building to commit a serious crime, usually the theft of property. A burglary might turn into a robbery if the burglar confronts the occupant of the building and uses force to steal, but most burglary involves no such confrontation. Burglary targets include both private residences and commercial establishments such as stores and offices.

In 1995, the 2,594,995 burglaries reported to the FBI produced estimated losses of $3.3 billion. Two-thirds of the reported burglaries were of residences (Federal Bureau of Investigation, 1996: 39). The NCVS study estimated that in

A CROSS-CULTURAL PERSPECTIVE

Fear of Crime and the German Economy

Fear of crime often has international repercussions. Caribbean islands have lost revenue from their tourist trade when violent crimes there have been publicized in the United States. Hijackings and terrorist bombs that destroy airplanes have, at least temporarily, reduced air travel to certain destinations.

A 1993 firebombing in Solingen, Germany, that killed five members of a Turkish family who had lived there for decades damaged German relations with Turkey, a NATO ally. This was just one of hundreds of violent attacks on foreigners and German Jews by neo-Nazis and militant nationalists that resulted in the loss of twenty-four lives in an eighteen-month period in 1992 and 1993. According to a German government agency, the number of such racist attacks declined from 2,277 in 1992 to 1,609 in 1993 and 860 in 1994.

This internationally reported violence aroused concern in Germany about possible damage to the nation's economy. Despite the refusal of the World Jewish Congress and other organizations to endorse a boycott of German exports or encourage travelers to avoid Germany, tourism officials in that country reported a decline in foreign visitors. The decline was greatest for Japanese, British, and American visitors to eastern Germany, but western Germany also reported fewer tourists.

German leaders worry that a continuation of the violence will exacerbate the fears of foreigners and diminish the attractiveness of their nation as a location for international expositions and trade shows, limit the market for the exports that the German economy so heavily depends on, and make the country less attractive to foreign investors. In these and other ways, fear of crime could further undermine the nation's economy, which ironically is seen as the source of the discontent being expressed in the violent attacks on foreigners and Jews. This violence has been concentrated in eastern Germany, where unemployment has been high since the demise of the Communist regime and reunification with western Germany.

Sources: Based on Stephen Kinzer, "Germans Fear a Cycle of Violence and Recession," *New York Times*, January 1, 1993, p. A3; Craig R. Whitney, "Bonn Suspects Neo-Nazi Arson as 5 Turks Die," *New York Times*, May 30, 1993, pp. 1, 9; Craig R. Whitney, "Germans Begin to Recognize Danger in Neo-Nazi Upsurge," *New York Times*, October 21, 1993, pp. A1, A10; "Germany Notes Fewer Hates Crimes," *New York Times*, July 7, 1995, p. 11.

1992 household burglaries alone accounted for losses of $4.0 billion (Klaus, 1994). The Office of Justice Programs (1996) estimates that the average burglary or attempt has tangible costs of $1,100 and intangible costs of $300, for a total of $1,400 per burglary.

Often a burglary is planned before the offender enters the building. Burglars examine the architecture of a building for ease of entry and escape. Often they first try to enter through an unlocked door, and only if that fails will they climb in through a window. They might seek a different target if they cannot make a quick entry. They look for alarm systems, occupants of the building, and nearby witnesses. Learning about police and security patrols in the area can also be a part of the planning of a burglary (Letkemann, 1973; Reppetto, 1974; Wright and Decker, 1994).

Although we might expect a prior relationship between burglars and their victims to be rare, because the burglars would have access to the victim's property or would be able to ask for a loan, a 1985 study found that 42 percent of burglaries were committed by a relative, an acquaintance, or someone whom the victim would recognize (cited in Greer, 1986).

Larceny   **Larceny**, or theft, is the "unlawful taking, carrying, leading, or riding away of property from the possession or constructive possession of another" (Federal Bureau of Investigation, 1996: 43). The FBI excludes from this category motor vehicle theft, embezzlement, confidence games, and forgery, although they are forms of theft. Larceny differs from robbery in that it does not involve force or the threat of force, and it differs from burglary in that it does not involve entry of a building.

The FBI recorded 8,000,631 larcenies in 1995. The average loss per larceny was $535, for a total loss of nearly $4.3 billion. Thefts from buildings were the most costly form of larceny, producing an average loss of $891 per offense. More than one-third of all recorded larcenies were of car parts, accessories, and contents. Figure 3.5 shows the other major forms of larceny (Federal Bureau of Investigation, 1996: 44).

The NCVS found that in 1992 crimes of personal theft produced losses of $2.7 billion; household larcenies cost an additional $1.8 billion (Klaus, 1994). The total loss of $4.5 billion from those forms of theft excludes some costly forms of larceny such as shoplifting.

Some larcenies are carefully planned in advance, and others are done on the spur of the moment. Shoplifting is carefully planned in advance by

FIGURE 3.5

Types of Larceny, as Percentages of All Reported Larcenies, 1995*

*Percentages do not total 100% because of rounding.

Source: Based on data from Federal Bureau of Investigation, *Crime in the United States, 1995: Uniform Crime Reports.* Washington, D.C.: U.S. Government Printing Office, 1996, p. 47.

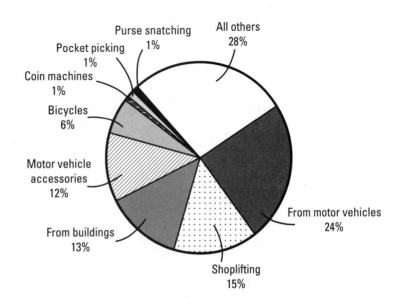

Purse snatching 1%
Pocket picking 1%
Coin machines 1%
Bicycles 6%
Motor vehicle accessories 12%
From buildings 13%
Shoplifting 15%
From motor vehicles 24%
All others 28%

"boosters," or professional thieves, and even amateur "snitches" who steal for personal use sometimes plan their thefts before entering a store (Cameron, 1964). Shoplifting often involves the intention to pick up certain merchandise, a plan to get out of the store, and a way to dispose of or use the stolen goods. Other thefts might not be planned; for instance, someone may be tempted to steal an unlocked bicycle or a coat left unattended in a movie theater.

There is little reason to expect that there will be a prior relationship between thieves and their victims. Indeed, one survey found that 90 percent of the victims of personal theft were complete strangers to the perpetrators of the crime (Hindelang, 1976: 12).

Motor Vehicle Theft   **Motor vehicle theft** is often distinguished from larceny, of which it is actually one form. The reason for this is that motor vehicle theft involves property of much greater value than is commonly stolen in other types of larceny, and often the car thief does not intend to deprive the owner of the property on a permanent basis. Most stolen vehicles are recovered, although the proportion that are never recovered has increased in recent years, apparently as the result of more thefts by professionals who strip vehicles of their parts, repaint and sell them, or even ship them to other countries for sale. The National Insurance Crime Bureau estimates that the number of stolen cars shipped abroad nearly doubled between 1990 and 1995, with about one-fourth of all cars stolen in 1995 being sent overseas, most often to Latin America, China, Eastern Europe, and the former Soviet Union (Onishi, 1995). Despite this trend, there are still at least twice as many thefts for joyriding and temporary use as there are by professionals (Clarke and Harris, 1992).

In 1995, the 1,472,732 motor vehicle thefts recorded by the FBI produced an estimated total loss of $7.6 billion, a figure comparable to the NCVS's estimate of $7.8 billion in losses from this crime in 1992 (Klaus, 1994). Three-fifths of the vehicles stolen in 1995 were recovered, and most of those that had been damaged by the thieves retained some market value. Seventy-eight percent of the stolen vehicles were automobiles, 16 percent were trucks or buses, and the remaining 6 percent were other types (Federal Bureau of Investigation, 1995: 50).

In 1992, newspapers throughout the United States were filled with stories of "carjackings," thefts of automobiles from drivers at traffic lights and stop signs, in parking garages, and in shopping center lots. Carjackers used firearms or caused minor accidents to get drivers to stop. Because the car is a second home for drivers, a private place in which they feel secure, this type of crime was very threatening. FBI officials were quick to point out that carjacking was not a new crime, even if it had increased in frequency, and that the FBI did not classify it as motor vehicle theft. Several carjackings have resulted in the death or kidnapping of the driver, but most carjackings are classified as robberies, because they involve the use or threat of force to steal property. In September 1992, the FBI added carjackings to the list of violent offenses investigated by its Operation Safe Streets task force. The following month a federal law was enacted to punish "robbery auto theft" with a minimum of fifteen years in prison, ten additional years if someone was hurt in the crime, and capital punishment if someone was killed. In at least one jurisdiction where this law applied, Puerto Rico, carjackings became less common, dropping from 8,669 in 1992 to 4,522 in 1993 (*New York Times,* September 16, 1992; *New York Times,* November 15, 1992; Terry, 1992; Navarro, 1994).

Arson   **Arson** is the willful or malicious burning of the building, motor vehicle, aircraft, or personal property of another person. It sometimes involves the intent to defraud an insurance company by filing a claim for the loss of one's own property through a deliberately set fire, though there are other motives for this crime. Revenge is one such motive, with Molotov cocktails or firebombs being used in gang-related attacks and drug-related disputes. Dozens of fires in 1995 and 1996 destroyed or damaged black churches in the South; some of the fires were racially motivated arsons.

According to one city planner, arson is forty times as common in the United States as in Japan, and the United States has "tallied the worst fire death rate in the industrialized world for decades" (McMillan, 1995: A17). The FBI does not estimate the total number of crimes of arson because of incomplete reporting, but this crime produced losses of at least $894 million in 1995. Of the reported cases, 53 percent involved structures (three-fifths of them residential), 26 percent targeted mobile property such as motor vehicles and trailers, and the remainder involved other kinds of property (Federal Bureau of Investigation, 1996: 54–55).

Fraud   **Fraud** is the crime of obtaining money or property by false pretenses. Facts are misrepresented and deception is employed to deceive victims by promising goods, services, or financial benefits that do not exist or are never intended to be provided (Titus, Heinzelmann, and Boyle, 1995). This crime is similar to larceny, but it does not involve the physical taking away of property in the possession of the owner. Fraud can involve false or deceptive advertising in which customers lose their money by purchasing inferior or misrepresented merchandise. Deceiving the government about one's true income and underpaying taxes is another form of fraud. Faking an accident or a theft and collecting from an insurance company for the nonexistent loss is another kind of fraud. Some types of fraud are white-collar crimes, but fraud is also committed by people who are not white-collar criminals (see the Crime on Campus box). Concern with welfare fraud led the New York City government to fingerprint recipients, but only forty-three cases of "double dipping" were found among 148,502 recipients; one interpretation was that welfare fraud had never been much of a problem, but another was that the threat of being caught scared off cheats (McLarin, 1995).

The IRS estimated that in 1995 it was owed $75 billion in delinquent taxes, although the General Accounting Office was unable to determine from its audit of the IRS whether that figure was reliable. Some unpaid taxes are the result of the "tax protester" movement, in which people file returns but omit the payment of taxes in protest of government policies. However, most of the underpayment of taxes is by individuals who fail to report all of their income

CRIME ON CAMPUS

Telephone Fraud

Telephone fraud costs long-distance companies over $500 million a year. Colleges, military bases, and prisons account for about $150 million of that amount, with colleges producing the largest losses.

Students make long-distance calls by using stolen telephone credit card or access numbers and unauthorized codes. Cards are stolen from student mailboxes, and numbers are obtained and sold by computer hackers. Recently, some students have tapped into corporations' switchboards to make illegal calls.

Telephone fraud seems to be especially common at the beginning and end of semesters. One expert on telephone fraud says, "College students, more than any other group in society except maybe prisoners, are prone to telephone fraud because they are generally away from home for the first time and they are lonely and probably short on cash" (p. B6).

Telephone companies have taken measures to reduce fraud. Electronic equipment now thwarts "blue boxes," which were first built by students in the early 1970s to produce computer tones that allowed them to connect into long-distance lines. Posters and leaflets have been distributed to warn students of the consequences of telephone fraud, the maximum sentence being fifteen years in prison and a $50,000 fine. Companies have obtained records from some colleges, allowing them to match illegal calls of which they have a record with the home addresses of students. Other colleges consider this information confidential and will not supply it to telephone companies.

Source: Based on Calvin Sims, "Phone Fraud: It's Still a Big Problem on Campus," *New York Times*, January 3, 1990, p. B6.

or exaggerate their deductions, or by corporations that do not comply with tax laws. Tax evasion seems to have increased over time because of a growing perception that there is little risk of being caught by IRS auditors; in recent years, the chance of an individual's tax return being audited has been less than 1 in 100. Over the past few years, the number of fraudulent refunds sent to taxpayers has increased as a result of more electronic filing of returns; a 1994 study estimated that such fraudulent refunds cost the government between $1 billion and $5 billion a year (Hershey, 1994).

When people who face a risk insure themselves against financial loss, an opportunity for fraud exists. An estimated 10 to 20 percent of all insurance claims are fraudulent, and 10 percent of the money spent on health care each year goes to pay fraudulent claims (Landis, 1982; Rosenthal, 1990). Some people pad their claims because they assume the insurance company will pay them less than they have lost, but other claims are more blatantly fraudulent, as the following example indicates:

There was a traveling salesman who started off his fraud career by claiming he had gotten sick after finding a fly in a candy bar. This was rapidly followed by a fly in a bottle of soda. Then he took to chipping the same two teeth on half a dozen candy bars. Most of these claims were denied, so the salesman began slipping and falling around his sales territory. After breaking the same pair of glasses in nine separate men's room accidents, he made the mistake of taking his forged optometrist's bill to the same agent who had paid him for breaking the glasses before. (Landis, 1982: D2)

Another clear-cut case of fraud involves "ghost riders," people who file claims for injuries they never suffered in bus or train accidents. A sting operation in New Jersey found that more than one hundred "passengers," physicians, attorneys, and police officers became involved in filing false claims for injuries allegedly sustained in six staged bus accidents. One accident involved a bus that was carrying fifteen passengers; another seventeen people at the scene who were videotaped jumping onto the bus claimed to be injured, and two people not even at the scene also filed claims. Doctors charged for treatments and office visits that never occurred; attorneys helped the "passengers" file claims; and police officers added names to the list of people injured in the accident (Kerr, 1993).

Arson-for-profit schemes are another source of insurance fraud. Building owners who find their neighborhoods deteriorating and taxes and repair costs rising sometimes burn down buildings. The building might be overinsured or even insured more than once, and then the insurance claim will exceed the real value of the property. Insurance companies contribute to the problem of fraud by not inspecting buildings before writing policies, by settling with arsonists if the cost of investigating the fire is too great compared with the size of the claim, and by failing to exercise their option of forcing owners to rebuild rather than collect the money (Brady, 1982).

"True identity fraud" starts with the theft of a social security number, credit cards, and personal checks, often in a purse snatching or other robbery. Because social security numbers are widely used for personal identification (for example, on drivers' licenses and college I.D.s), offenders can use them to gain computer access to information that permits them to use stolen credit cards, get money from bank machines, forge personal checks, and pass credit checks to open new charge accounts, rent apartments, or secure loans. The criminal abuse of credit cards also includes the manufacture of counterfeit cards and the alteration of stolen cards. Telemarketing fraud occurs when a caller announces the winning of a prize and asks for the "winner's" credit card number to verify the "winner's" identity, then uses that number for fraudulent purchases.

A study of fraud targeted at individuals found that it was very common and often quite costly, even though many fraud attempts failed. The only two personal characteristics strongly associated with victimization were age and education: younger people were victimized more often than older people, and more highly educated people were victimized more often than those with less education. There were no significant differences in victimization by income, race, or gender (Titus, Heinzelmann, and Boyle, 1995).

Vandalism   **Vandalism** is the willful or malicious destruction, injury, disfigurement, or defacement of property without consent of the owner. Breaking the windows in an abandoned building is an act of vandalism that has little social significance, but vandalizing an important painting in a museum can ruin property of great economic and cultural value.

The Costs of Property Crime   Reliable estimates of the costs of vandalism and fraud are not available, but the FBI estimates that total losses from robbery, burglary, larceny, motor vehicle theft, and arson were at least $16.6 billion in 1995. The 1992 National Crime Victimization Survey found the direct costs of robbery, assault, personal and household theft, burglary, and motor vehicle theft to be $17.6 billion. That figure is based on lost cash, lost or damaged property, medical expenses, and pay lost due to injury or crime-related activities (Klaus, 1994).

One study estimated the total cost of crime by adding direct out-of-pocket costs (such as stolen property, lost wages, medical expenses, mental health care costs, and legal fees) to the monetary values of pain, suffering, and fear that have been established by jury awards in personal injury accident cases. This study assigned dollar values to such intangibles as loss of quality of life for crime victims and loss of affection for the members of a murder victim's family. Money spent on police work was included, but correctional costs were not. This broad definition of the cost of crime yielded an estimated annual loss of $450 billion from index crimes, child abuse, and domestic violence; one-fourth of that amount was direct out-of-pocket losses (Cohen, Miller, and Wiersema, 1996).

White-Collar Crime

The concept of white-collar crime was first introduced by sociologist Edwin Sutherland in a speech before the American Sociological Society in 1939 and elaborated on by him in a book ten years later. To modify his definition slightly, **white-collar crime** is any illegal act, punishable by a criminal sanction, that is committed in the course of a legitimate occupation or pursuit by a corporation or by an otherwise respectable individual of high social standing (Edelhertz, 1970; Conklin, 1977).

An important aspect of this definition is that white-collar crime is punishable under the criminal law, even though it is often not actually punished as a crime but is instead ignored or dealt with by a regulatory agency or civil court. Another important aspect of the definition is that white-collar crime occurs in the course of legitimate activity; a corporate executive who murders his wife after an argument has not committed a white-collar crime. One problem with our definition of white-collar crime is that it does not make clear what "respectable" actually means. This term usually is interpreted to mean that the individual offender is held in high social regard, but some have taken it to mean that the white-collar offender has no previous convictions for conventional crimes or that the offender does not think of himself or herself as a criminal. Finally, white-collar criminals are of relatively high social standing, although Sutherland and other criminologists have sometimes treated as white-collar offenses certain crimes committed by people of relatively low status, such as fraud by people who repair cars.

Table 3.3 shows some of the many forms that white-collar crime takes. It includes actions by corporations, such as deceptive advertising or collusion to fix prices or divide a market. Embezzlement of the funds with which an employee is entrusted is a white-collar crime against a firm rather than by a company. Stock and securities fraud and theft are white-collar crimes. Tax fraud by companies or individuals in the course of their business activities can be seen as a white-collar crime. White-collar crime can result in losses to the public, stockholders, and competing companies, or it can involve losses to companies at the hands of their employees. Al Capone once referred to white-collar offenses collectively as "the legitimate rackets."

White-collar crime often involves elaborate planning. A price-fixing conspiracy among electrical equipment manufacturers that resulted in the conviction of companies and executives in 1961 required detailed planning. One conspirator described the techniques used by the offenders as follows: "It was considered discreet to not be too obvious and to minimize telephone calls, to use plain envelopes in mailing material to each other, not to be seen together on traveling, and so forth...not to leave wastepaper, of which there was a lot, strewn around a room when leaving" (cited in Geis, 1967: 143). Further evidence that the executives knew they were breaking the law is that they "hid behind a camouflage of fictitious names and conspiratorial codes," called their meeting roster the "Christmas card list," and referred to their gatherings as "choir practice" (Geis, 1967: 143). To ensure their anonymity, they used only public telephones and met at trade association meetings and at remote sites.

Most of the crimes that criminologists study as white-collar crime occur in the business world, but government corruption and police brutality also fit our definition of white-collar crime. The embezzlement of funds by public officials is a white-collar crime. Government officials (including police officers) who take bribes are committing crimes in the course of their legitimate occupations. We can also treat police brutality as a white-collar crime, even though it might be argued that police officers do not wear white collars and are of middle rather than high social status.

Is White-Collar Crime Different?

Sutherland's pioneering work on white-collar crime was important to criminology because it showed that people from other than the lower classes violate the law, even if they are rarely convicted in criminal court. In this way, Sutherland forced criminologists to reject the notion that crime is solely the product of pathological conditions common to poor people and to consider what factors might explain crime by both the poor and the well-to-do. (See the Crime and the Media box.)

TABLE 3.3 Major Types of White-Collar Crime

Crimes by Businesses

Deceptive advertising
Antitrust violations
Securities fraud
Mail and wire fraud
Tax fraud
Bribery of political officials
Unsafe workplace conditions
Production of dangerous products
Environmental law violations
Industrial espionage
"Sweetheart contracts" with union officers
False weights and measures by retailers
Misrepresentation of credit terms

Crimes by Employees against Businesses

Embezzlement and employee theft
Expense account fraud

Crimes by Government Employees

Police brutality
Bribe-taking by police officers and political officials
Embezzlement by political officials

Crimes by Professionals

Medical quackery
Health care fraud
Fraudulent damage claims by lawyers
Embezzlement by lawyers

Some sociologists have questioned whether white-collar crime really differs from conventional crime. Gottfredson and Hirschi (1990) claim that white-collar crime is indeed crime, because it involves the use of force or fraud for personal benefit; they assert that it is not the product of any unique causal processes and therefore needs no special theory to explain it. They say that all crime, including white-collar crime, offers the offender immediate benefits with little effort and is the result of acting impulsively rather than considering the long-term consequences of behavior. They cite evidence that criminals in general are versatile rather than specialized to support their claim that different types of offenders, such as white-collar criminals and conventional criminals, need not be distinguished from one another. According to Gottfredson and Hirschi, the characteristics that employers require of white-collar workers are usually associated with low rates of offending behavior, and therefore white-collar crime should be uncommon,

CRIME AND THE MEDIA

White-Collar Crime in the News

Because businesses support newspapers and television stations with the money they spend on advertisements and commercials, the news media might be expected to avoid white-collar crime stories that would alienate advertisers and sponsors. How do the media report white-collar crime, and what factors influence their reporting?

Steven Chermak's study of a newspaper and a television organization in a midwestern city found that white-collar crime was reported much less frequently than conventional crime, especially murder and other violent offenses. Eleven percent of crime stories in the newspaper, and only 5 percent of television crime stories, dealt with white-collar crime. In contrast, 39 percent of newspaper crime stories and 45 percent of television crime stories dealt with murder and other violent crimes.

Why did the newspaper pay more attention than the television station to white-collar crime? One reason is that the complexity of white-collar crime lends itself better to coverage in the printed media, where articles can go into whatever depth is necessary to explain an offense. Most newspapers also have a separate business section, where white-collar crimes can be covered in detail. Television news programs, on the other hand, cover crime news more superficially, rarely spending more than one minute on a story, a time too short to make sense of most white-collar crimes. In addition to their complexity, white-collar crimes have little visual appeal, lacking a specific victim and a definite crime scene, and so they are difficult for television to cover in a way that viewers will find interesting. Television is also unlikely to cover white-collar crimes because

white-collar crime is generally not a threat to the immediate safety of the audience. When a serial rapist strikes, the news report serves as an easily visualized warning. In television it is difficult to warn people about white-collar victimization because too much explanation is needed. (p. 120)

Source: Steven M. Chermak, *Victims in the News: Crime and the American News Media.* Boulder, Colo.: Westview, 1995, pp. 118–121.

---

which they argue it is. They point out that researchers who claim otherwise have usually compared rates of offending over several years by large corporations that have thousands of employees with rates of offending by individuals during a single year. In fact, we have little reliable data to indicate just how common white-collar crime really is.

A study by Weisburd et al. (1991) used presentence reports by probation officers who were advising federal judges on how to sentence offenders convicted of securities fraud, antitrust violations, bribery, bank embezzlement, postal and wire fraud, false claims and statements, credit- and lending-institution fraud, and tax fraud. A significant number of those crimes—especially credit fraud, false claims, and mail fraud—were committed by people without jobs or by employed people of low socioeconomic status, by people who did not have college degrees, and by people who did not own homes. The offenders were also more likely to be nonwhite and to be younger than previous studies of white-collar offenders had led the researchers to expect.

Many of the offenders in the Weisburd et al. study had prior criminal records, usually not for other white-collar offenses, suggesting that they did not meet Sutherland's criterion of respectability. They were less apt to have long or serious records than were conventional offenders, but they had more past involvement in criminal activity than would have been expected from previous research on white-collar crime. Indeed, they were about twice as likely to have a prior arrest record as the national population at large.

The researchers concluded that the typical white-collar offender convicted in federal court bears little resemblance to the wealthy and powerful offenders described in Sutherland's original study, even though that offender is higher in the class system than the typical conventional criminal. Most of the white-collar offenders were "average people in a financial jam who [saw] a way out through fraud" (Weisburd et al., 1991: 190). They turned to crime either to move up the ladder of success, especially when they encountered obstacles to further upward mobility, or to keep from falling in social standing. Weisburd et al. (1991: 45–46) were struck by the "banal, mundane quality of the vast majority of white-collar crimes," saying that the offenses involved no particular skills other than the ability to lie and cheat. Nevertheless, these crimes can be distinguished from conventional crimes in terms of the need for access to organizational resources to commit them and in terms of their financial impact on victims.

The Costs of White-Collar Crime

The 1996 report of the National Criminal Justice Commission estimated that the cost of white-collar crime was between $130 billion and $472 billion, seven to twenty-five times as much as the cost of all street crime (Donziger, 1996: 66). However, accurate measurement of losses from white-collar crime is not easy. Not only must direct losses to victims be calculated, but it is also necessary to determine how much prices rise as a result of passing on companies' losses to consumers. The ramifications of a single white-collar crime are often complex and hard to assess. For example, when a bribe is paid by a business executive to accomplish a particular objective, neither the bribe giver nor the recipient will necessarily feel that any loss has been incurred. However, there is a loss to the public from such transactions. For instance, the cost of a bribe paid by a construction firm to a city inspector will be passed on to the individual who has contracted to have the building erected, and the cost of the bribe might then be passed on to the building's tenants in higher rents. The fact that the tenants never learn of their losses does not make the bribe any less of a financial loss to them.

Perhaps half of the losses from white-collar crime are due to consumer fraud, illegal competition, and deceptive sales practices. Consumer fraud includes the sale of defective merchandise, the misrepresentation of interest terms, and the sale of unneeded or faulty home and auto repairs. Illegal competition costs billions of dollars each year, and introducing competition where it has been absent can save consumers much money. For example, an antitrust action against the manufacturer of the drug tetracycline reduced the price of that drug by 75 percent.

The sale of counterfeit merchandise is a deceptive practice that costs American companies $6 billion to $25 billion every year (Farnsworth, 1984; Jennings, 1989: 806). Fake designer clothing, purses, and cosmetics have inflicted substantial losses on couturier houses; products bearing the symbol of the designer firm but made with shoddy materials make customers unwilling to buy the original product. In 1995, an estimated $250 million worth of cassette tapes and compact disks, and an estimated $525 worth of computer software, were copied illegally in China (Faison, 1996). There is also a flourishing market in Russia for pirated audio and videocassettes, compact disks, computer software, and books; in 1994, American companies lost close to $1 billion in sales to Russians who sold illegally produced products (Specter, 1995). Figure 3.6 shows estimated losses from the piracy of American products for the five countries most involved in this practice.

Another business crime that is very expensive is stock fraud and securities theft. Securities are sometimes stolen by brokerage house employees, who may deliver the securities to members of organized crime in return for cancellation of the employees' debts that arose from gambling or borrowing from loan sharks. The gangsters then transport the securities out of the country and use them as collateral for loans from foreign banks.

One costly crime that occurs in the commercial sector is employee theft and embezzlement. Retailers lose in excess of $10 billion a year from "shrink-

Charles H. Keating, Jr., was sentenced to a ten-year prison term in 1992 after being convicted of eighteen counts of securities fraud related to the collapse of a savings and loan institution. Reimbursement of depositors who lost money when that institution collapsed has cost taxpayers $2.6 billion.

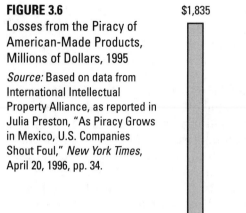

FIGURE 3.6

Losses from the Piracy of American-Made Products, Millions of Dollars, 1995

Source: Based on data from International Intellectual Property Alliance, as reported in Julia Preston, "As Piracy Grows in Mexico, U.S. Companies Shout Foul," *New York Times,* April 20, 1996, pp. 34.

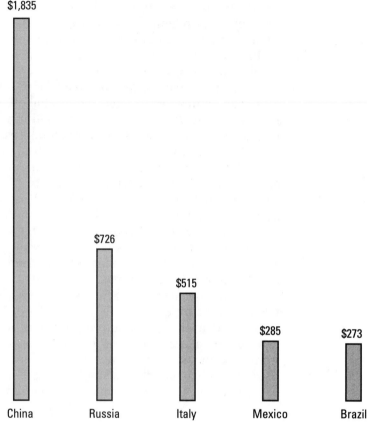

age," which includes employee theft, shoplifting, shoddy paperwork, misplaced goods, and vendor theft (Traub, 1996). In some urban stores, the percentage of merchandise lost through inventory shrinkage equals or exceeds profits. Crimes of this sort are costly for victimized companies; between 15 and 30 percent of all business failures are due to losses of this sort. Theft by employees and fraud by customers cost banks four to five times as much each year as do bank robberies.

White-collar crimes sometimes cause serious injuries to their victims, more often as a result of negligence than of intent. Air pollution and the dumping of toxic waste, which can violate the criminal law, cause respiratory ailments, cancer, and other diseases. Hazardous and often illegal working conditions result in many deaths and injuries every year. In 1985, three executives were found guilty, fined $10,000, and sentenced to twenty-five years in prison for murder in the cyanide poisoning death of an employee whose job involved the use of that chemical to recover silver from photographic film. In 1990, an appellate court overturned their convictions as "legally inconsistent."

Some of the millions of serious injuries that occur each year as a result of the use of consumer products can be attributed to criminal negligence or deceptive advertising by manufacturers. The Ford Motor Company was charged with reckless homicide for the deaths of three young women in Indiana in 1978; however, a jury acquitted Ford, finding that it had marketed a defective car but had not been reckless in its recall efforts (Kramer, 1982; Cullen, Maakestad, and Cavender, 1984, 1987).

White-collar crime can even involve the intentional taking of lives. For instance, in 1976, Don Bolles, a journalist who was investigating white-collar and organized crime in Phoenix, Arizona, was apparently killed by a "hit man" hired to keep illegal activities secret. In 1977, the hit man and a wealthy Phoenix contractor accused of hiring him were found guilty of murder, but their convictions were reversed by a higher court.

White-collar crime has major social costs in addition to the enormous financial losses and physical damage it inflicts on the public. The President's Commission on Law Enforcement and Administration of Justice (1967: 5) called white-collar offenses "the most threatening of all—not just because they are so expensive, but because of their corrosive effect on the moral standards by which American business is conducted." However, less than 1 percent of the material published by this commission dealt with white-collar crime. Possible indirect or secondary effects of white-collar crime include "(a) diminished faith in a free economy and in business leaders, (b) loss of confidence in political institutions, processes, and leaders, and (c) erosion of public morality" (Moore and Mills, 1990: 414). White-collar crime can reduce the public's willingness to invest in the stock market and engage in commercial transactions, and a capitalist economy that relies on public investment would thus be weakened. Illegal campaign contributions by large corporations can lead to public cynicism toward government; voters might believe that business is the "power behind the throne" and that politicians are corrupt. Bribes paid to officials of other nations can weaken foreign relations and diminish national prestige abroad. A company's interest in protecting its foreign investments can even lead to the rigging of elections or the overthrow of a democratically elected regime that is seen as hostile to American business. Business crime might also set an example of disobedience for the general public, with citizens who rarely see white-collar offenders prosecuted and sent to prison becoming cynical about the criminal justice system. A sense of injustice can develop when they or their friends are given long sentences for crimes that cost society much less than offenses committed by wealthy corporate executives or large multinational firms.

Despite these dire predictions, one study found that most of the victims who had lost money when a loan company collapsed due to criminal activity continued to have faith in the economic and political system; their longstanding faith in the established order was not easily shaken, and they blamed individuals rather than institutions for their losses (Shover, Fox, and Mills, 1994).

Organized Crime

Organized crime is criminal activity by an enduring structure or organization developed and devoted primarily to the pursuit of profits through illegal means. In the United States, organized crime traditionally has been equated with the Italian-American Mafia or La Cosa Nostra. In recent years, criminologists and law-enforcement agents have broadened their perspective on organized crime to include criminal enterprises run by Chinese, Japanese, Colombians, Vietnamese, Jamaicans, Russians, Nigerians, Israelis, and other ethnic groups.

Organized crime has the characteristics of a formal organization: a division of labor, coordination of activities through rules and codes, and an allocation of tasks in order to achieve certain goals (Cressey, 1969, 1972). The organization seeks profits from crime and tries to preserve itself in the face of external and internal threats. The structure of organized crime is explored in detail in Chapter 11.

The Costs of Organized Crime

In 1986, in a technical paper written for the President's Commission on Organized Crime, researchers at Wharton Econometric Forecasting Associates in Philadelphia concluded as follows:

> The effects of organized crime on the legitimate economy show up in higher prices for consumers when competition is suppressed, lower wages for workers when labor unions are controlled, and less safety when corners are cut on construction projects or toxic waste is not disposed of properly. (Fishman, Rodenrys, and Schink, 1986: 432)

The researchers stated that the taxes citizens pay

> must be higher by the amount of taxes not paid by these criminals to provide the government with needed revenues. Conversely, if taxes were paid on all income earned by the individuals associated with organized crime, the taxes paid by ordinary citizens could be reduced by this amount. (Fishman, Rodenrys, and Schink, 1986: 486)

From their study, the researchers estimated that organized crime reduces the nation's economic output by $18.2 billion per year, cuts employment by 414,000 jobs, raises consumer prices by 0.3 percent, and reduces per capita income by $77.

The activities of organized crime also have social costs. One essential element of organized crime is the corruption of public officials and police officers who allow gangsters to operate without interference (Cressey, 1969, 1972). Reports of corruption undermine faith in local, state, and even federal government. People might be unwilling to discuss political matters openly for fear that all officials are linked to organized crime. The influence of organized crime with elected officials can lead to public resignation and the belief that young people would be better off pursuing careers other than politics.

Victimless Crimes

A **victimless crime** is an offense that is consensual and lacks a complaining participant (Schur, 1965). It might be more accurate to refer to victimless crimes as crimes without complainants, because some observers question the idea that there is no victim of crimes such as drug use, gambling, prostitution, and pornography. What is important is that the offenses usually involve willing participants in activities that violate the law. Because no one complains to the police about being victimized, making arrests and prosecuting suspects is difficult.

Because the concept of victimization is a complex one, the kinds of behavior to be included in the category of victimless crime have been the subject of some disagreement (Schur and Bedau, 1974). When Schur first used the term "crimes without victims" in 1965, he focused on drug addiction, homosexuality, and abortion. Today, homosexual relations between consenting adults in private are legal in about half of the states. In 1973, abortion was legalized under most conditions by the U.S. Supreme Court in its decision in *Roe* v. *Wade*, although there is still a bitter debate about whether abortion should again be made illegal. What is called victimless crime varies over time as well as among individuals at any given time.

Estimates of the financial costs of victimless crimes are usually based on a calculation of the amount of money spent on goods and services such as illegal drugs, gambling, prostitution, or pornography. The assumption underlying the estimates is that if this money were not spent on illegal goods and services, it would be spent on legitimate goods and services.

Drug Use

The use of illegal drugs can be seen as a victimless crime in the sense that neither the user nor the seller is likely to report the crime to the police. Drugs do have ill effects on users, from physical deterioration to overdose deaths, but some sociologists see those effects more as the consequence of society's laws against drugs than as the result of the pharmacological effects of the drugs themselves. If the drugs were legally available, these sociologists argue, they would be much less expensive and the negative effects on users would be minimized. When drugs are illegal, they are expensive, and users need to spend much of their money on drugs. This, in turn, causes them to neglect food, shelter, and clothing, and such neglect leads to their physical deterioration.

The high cost of illegal drugs also leads users to commit crimes such as robbery, burglary, and larceny to get the money to pay for their drugs; those property crimes do have victims, even if drug use itself is victimless. Moreover, the high cost of illegal drugs leads some users to deal drugs, drawing into drug use some people who would otherwise not have engaged in such behavior. The illegal markets that develop to distribute drugs are dangerous settings; about one murder in ten in the United States in the early 1980s was related to a drug transaction, and that proportion was probably higher in large cities in the early 1990s (National Research Council, 1993: 187).

Illegal drug use has several costs: the money that users pay for the drugs, the revenue lost to the government because required taxes are not paid on those drugs, the expense of enforcing drug laws, losses from the property crimes committed by users to pay for their drugs, and murders that occur during drug transactions. The costs of these property crimes and murders are included in the costs of conventional crimes, but they can also be seen as by-products of drug offenses. In 1989, economists estimated the cost of illicit drug use in the United States to be over $60 billion a year, more than a 20 percent increase above the estimate for 1985. This cost includes the money spent on enforcing drug laws, losses due to absenteeism by drug-using workers, the artificial inflation of real estate values due to the infusion of money from the drug trade, and the medical costs of treating drug addicts, including intravenous drug users with AIDS and infants born dependent on drugs (Labaton, 1989).

Gambling

One argument for viewing illegal gambling as a victimless crime is that nearly every state now permits certain forms of legal gambling, such as on-track betting, off-track betting, and lotteries. If those forms of gambling are not defined as crimes, why then should betting with a bookie on sporting events and playing the numbers be treated as crimes? The variation from state to state in defining what kind of gambling is legal and what kind is illegal makes it clear that there is no national consensus on treating gambling as a crime.

It might be easier to make a case for an economic loss from illegal gambling than to make such a case for illegal drug use or prostitution. Gambling with a bookie produces a loss for the economy in those states that have lotteries or other forms of legalized gambling, if people who might bet legally use their money to bet in illegal ways. Funds are diverted from the state, which would have used that money for education or other social services. This can cause taxes to be higher, or services to be fewer, than would have been the case if the money had been gambled legally.

Another cost of illegal gambling is that money bet with a bookie who has links to organized crime can be used by gangsters to finance the importation of drugs or to engage in loan sharking. However, there is some evidence that many, perhaps most, bookies are not members of organized crime and that much money spent on illegal gambling does not make its way into the hands of gangsters (Reuter and Rubinstein, 1978; Reuter, 1983).

Pathological or compulsive gambling also has harmful consequences, including alcohol and drug abuse, health and emotional problems, family stress, and absence from work. Moreover, most pathological gamblers eventually engage in crimes such as check forgery, loan fraud, embezzlement and employee theft, confidence games, larceny, burglary, pimping and prostitution, selling drugs, and tax fraud in order to raise money with which to gamble or pay gambling debts (Lesieur, 1987, 1992).

Prostitution

The consensual transactions between prostitutes and their clients typically do not produce complainants, though clients who are robbed by prostitutes or their pimps, and prostitutes who are beaten by their customers, sometimes do turn to the police. In many cities, prostitution was once controlled by organized crime, but that is no longer the case. Individual prostitutes can be seen as engaging in a crime that has no victim, even though prostitution poses risks to both the prostitute and the client, such as the possibility of contracting venereal diseases or AIDS. Prostitutes who work for pimps are often the victims of physical abuse to "keep them in line," but the criminal offense of prostitution itself does not involve participants who define themselves as victims of a crime.

In estimating the costs of prostitution, as in estimating the costs of illegal drugs, some have assumed that money spent on illegal services is money that

Consensual transactions between prostitutes and their customers usually do not produce complaints to the police, but some customers are robbed by prostitutes or their pimps, and some prostitutes are beaten by their customers.

otherwise might have been spent on legitimate goods and services and so is lost to the economy. However, from another perspective, it is difficult to see how money spent for sex with a prostitute is any more of a financial loss than money spent to attend a movie or a baseball game.

Pornography

The distribution and sale of pornography is a criminal offense in certain jurisdictions and under certain circumstances, though the law is vague in defining such offenses. Usually, neither sellers nor purchasers of pornographic books, magazines, or movies define themselves as victims of a crime or complain to the police.

There have been some efforts in recent years to define pornography as a crime because the participants in the making of the pornography—the photographic models or the actors in a film—are victims. Federal law now defines as a crime any making or selling of pornography that involves a minor, on the assumption that younger people are coerced into the making of such pornography and can thus be seen as victims. An ordinance passed in Indianapolis, Indiana, in 1984, that defined pornography as material that discriminates against women through the portrayal of their subordination and humiliation, treated all women as victims of pornography. Later that year, a U.S. Court of Appeals ruled that the ordinance was unconstitutional because it infringed on freedom of speech and freedom of the press; that decision was subsequently affirmed by the Supreme Court.

Summary

Conventional crime, white-collar crime, organized crime, and victimless crime have enormous financial, physical, and social costs. Among the financial costs of crime are the direct loss of property and its transfer from an owner to a thief. Victims of criminal violence suffer lost wages and hospital expenses. Expenditures on illegal goods and services can be treated as a cost of crime because they divert money from the legitimate economy. Also important are the costs of enforcing the law and the money that people spend for prevention and protection.

Conventional crimes of violence include murder, forcible rape, robbery, and assault. Murder often occurs between an offender and a victim who were previously acquainted. Forcible rape, which has increasingly been defined in sex-neutral terms, often occurs between total strangers, but sometimes it involves a victim and an offender who are well known to one another.

Robbery involves force or threat of force to steal property and typically involves strangers. Most assaults involve a victim and an offender who are known to each other; assaults between people who are intimately associated are probably underreported to the police.

Conventional property crimes include burglary, larceny, motor vehicle theft, arson, fraud, and vandalism. Burglaries, which are often planned to some degree, involve unlawful entry of a building to commit a serious crime, usually a theft. Larceny or simple theft involves many varieties of behavior, including shoplifting and pickpocketing. Motor vehicle theft can involve professionals who sell the stolen car or its parts, or amateur joyriders who do not intend to deprive the owner of the car on a permanent basis. Other property crimes include arson, the deliberate burning of property; fraud, the obtaining of money or property by false pretenses; and vandalism, the willful destruction of property.

White-collar crime is an illegal act, punishable under the criminal law, that is committed in the course of a legitimate occupation or pursuit by a corporation or by an otherwise respectable individual of high social standing. Financial losses from illegal competition, deceptive advertising, product counterfeiting, stock fraud, price-fixing, and other offenses by "respectable" people are greater than total losses from robbery, burglary, larceny, motor vehicle theft, and arson. In addition, white-collar crimes injure their victims through pollution, unsafe working conditions, and defective products.

Organized crime is activity by an enduring organization developed and devoted primarily to the pursuit of profits through illegal means. Because of the great profits to be made, other ethnic groups have taken over some of the criminal enterprises that the predominantly Italian-American Mafia controlled in the past.

Victimless crimes, which are consensual offenses that lack complaining participants but which divert money from the legitimate economy, include illegal drug use, gambling, prostitution, and pornography. Drug use might be seen as harming users or as hurting the victims of theft by users who steal to buy drugs, but sociologists often argue that it is the law's definition of drugs as illegal, more than the drugs themselves, that produces such negative consequences. Gambling is legal in some forms in certain states, and illegal in other forms and in different states, leading many to question whether illegal gambling can be said to have a victim. Prostitutes can be victimized by pimps and clients, but their transactions with clients are usually offenses that involve no complainant. Federal law now defines pornography as a crime with a victim if it involves a minor, although most forms of pornography do not involve complaining participants and are rarely prosecuted as crimes.

Important Terms

aggravated assault
arson
assault
burglary
costs related to criminal violence
direct loss
enforcement costs
forcible rape
fraud
illegal expenditures
larceny

motor vehicle theft
murder and nonnegligent manslaughter
organized crime
prevention and protection costs
robbery
simple assault
transfer of property
vandalism
victimless crime
white-collar crime

Review Questions

1. What are the four major types of crime? What are the differences among them? What are their similarities?

2. What do sociologists mean by "victimless crimes"? Are people hurt in any way by these so-called victimless crimes? Is it useful to distinguish between victimless crimes and conventional crimes?

3. How would you calculate the financial costs of conventional crime, white-collar crime, organized crime, and victimless crime? Which kind of crime is the most costly in the United States? What physical harm does each type cause? What are the harmful social effects of each type?

CHAPTER 4
Dimensions of Crime

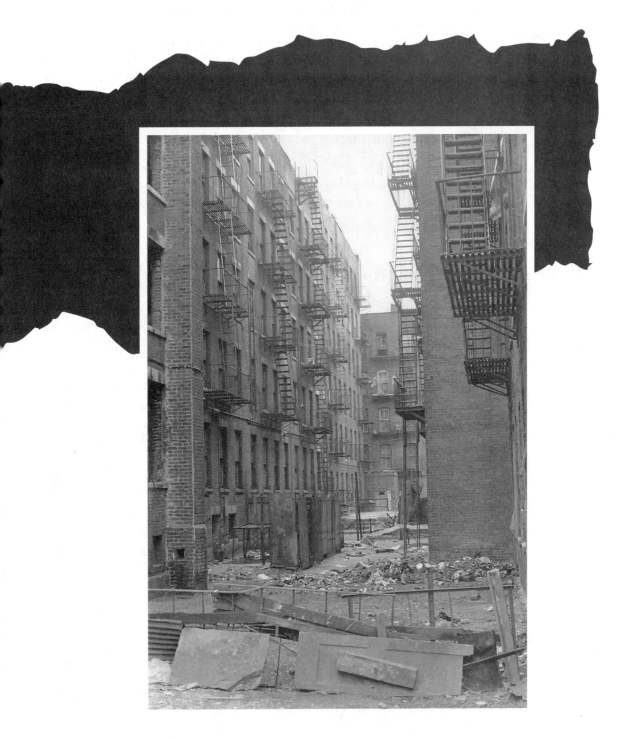

How does the crime rate of the United States compare with that of Japan? Is murder more common in some regions of the United States than in others? Is the risk of victimization greater in cities than in suburbs? Have crime rates increased in recent years? How does involvement in crime vary by sex, age, race, and social class? This chapter explores these variations by using data from the FBI Uniform Crime Reports, the Bureau of Justice Statistics victimization surveys, and self-report studies. Each type of data has flaws that should be kept in mind as the dimensions of crime are investigated.

Knowledge of how crime rates vary from society to society and from group to group point the way to a theory of crime causation. Statistical variations in crime rates are facts that criminologists' theories must explain, but the variations are not, by themselves, theories of crime. For instance, knowing that men commit more murder than women does not tell us why this difference exists, but it does tell us that a theory of crime should be able to account for this difference.

Cross-National Variations in Crime Rates

In the criminologist's ideal world, all nations would define crime and gather statistics in the same way. Comparison of crime rates in different countries would then facilitate the development of a general theory of crime. Unfortunately, this situation does not exist, nor is it ever likely to. There are significant cross-national variations in laws, the law-enforcement process, and the collection of crime data. In addition, many countries do not have complete and reliable crime statistics that are publicly available. For example, Soviet leader Josef Stalin prohibited the disclosure of crime statistics in 1933, and not until 1989 did the government make that information available, fearing that it would harm the nation's reputation and even contribute to the crime problem.

Crime rates usually rise as a nation develops economically, with property crime rates typically increasing faster than rates of violent crime. However, Japan's experience shows that social change is not inextricably linked to rising crime rates. In 1948, 1.6 million penal code offenses were recorded in Japan, but by 1973 that figure had dropped to 1.2 million, a decline of 25 percent. In 1986, 1.6 million crimes were recorded, an increase over the 1973 figure but the same as the number reported in 1948, despite significant population growth and urbanization over that time. From 1960 to 1987, Japan's homicide rate per 100,000 people dropped from 3.0 to 1.3; that same period saw increases in homicide rates in the United States from 5.1 to 8.3, in Great Britain from 1.3 to 5.5, and in West Germany from 2.2 to 4.3 (Hamilton and Sanders, 1992: 159). Japan's experience since the end of World War II shows that social change is not always accompanied by rising crime rates. Why social change leads to higher crime rates in some nations, but not in others, is explored later when we look at theories of crime causation. What is important here is that there are cross-national differences that need to be explained.

One offense for which some cross-national data exist is murder, but even this crime is not defined in the same way everywhere. For instance, laws differ in the role assigned to premeditation and responsibility. In addition, whether acts of war, civil insurrection, and political terrorism that result in death are recorded as murders or are treated as political acts differs from society to society and depends on who has the power to define criminal behavior. These and other problems make even murder difficult to examine cross-nationally.

Since 1975, the United Nations has gathered world-wide data on murder under the category of "homicide and injury purposely inflicted by other persons." It is this category that we use in Figure 4.1, where the rates per 100,000 people are given for selected nations reporting to the United Nations. Figure 4.1 does not include data for most African and Asian countries. In 1995, Russia had a murder rate of 16 per 100,000 and South Africa had what might have been the world's highest murder rate, 87.5 per 100,000. Some Latin American nations also report very high homicide rates, but deaths from political violence are sometimes counted as homicides in those countries, and there are problems with the validity of information reported by those countries; for example, Colombia's rate of 74.4 for 1990 was based on data of unknown completeness. The United States has a relatively high homicide rate, especially when compared to other advanced industrial societies.

Table 4.1 presents the 1984 rates of rape, robbery, burglary, and auto theft for selected countries. These rates must be compared with caution, because of differences among countries in definitions of crime and in the reporting and recording of crime. The table indicates that the United States has a significantly higher rate of rape and robbery than any other nation for which data are reported. Although the rates of burglary and auto theft in the United States are higher than the rates for some countries, they are lower than the rates for others. Thus, the United States has relatively high rates of violent crime, but its rates of at least two property offenses are not especially high.

Regional Variations in Crime Rates within the United States

The comparatively high murder rate of the United States leads us to ask what causes the differences between this country and other industrial societies. We can begin to zero in on an answer to this question by looking at variations in crime rates within the United States. One such variation is by region of the country.

In 1995, the murder rate for the United States was 8.2 per 100,000. However, there were significant variations in the rates for different regions (see Figure 4.2A). The rate for the Northeast was 6.2, the rate for the Midwest was 6.9, the rate for the West was 9.0, and the rate for the South was 9.8 (Federal Bureau of Investigation, 1996: 60–67). The homicide rate for the

Rate per 100,000

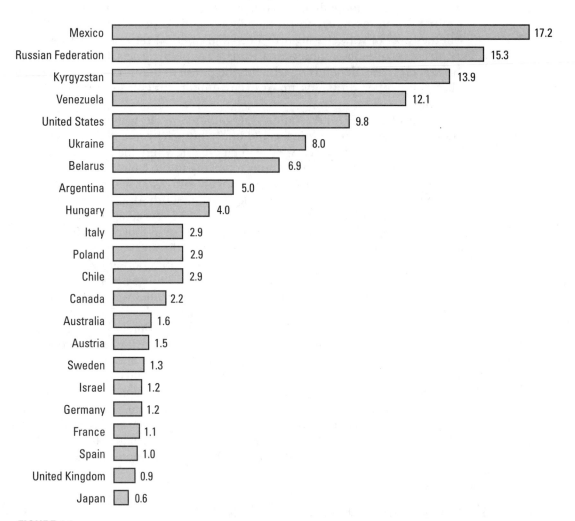

FIGURE 4.1

Homicide and Injury Purposely Inflicted by Others as a Cause of Death, Selected Countries, 1989–1992

Source: Based on data from United Nations, *Demographic Yearbook 1993.* New York: United Nations, 1995, pp. 484–503.

South had been about twice the rate for the rest of the nation until recently, when murder rates have become more similar for the different regions. Still, the murder rate in the South is now 32 percent higher than the rate for the rest of the country.

Several explanations have been offered for the South's high murder rate. Because both poverty and minority-group status are linked to murder, the South's high murder rate is partly a result of the relatively large amount of poverty and the relatively large proportion of blacks in that region. One study found that when murder rates are calculated separately for whites, blacks,

TABLE 4.1 Rape, Robbery, Burglary, and Auto Theft. Rates per 100,000 People, 1984

Country	Rape	Robbery	Burglary	Auto Theft
United States	35.7	205.4	1,263.7	437.1
Australia	13.8	83.6	1,754.3	584.7
Austria	5.3	29.8	805.8	16.9
Canada	NA	92.8	1,420.6	304.9
Chile	10.6	36.4	NA	7.6
Denmark	7.7	35.6	2,230.2	469.5
England/Wales*	2.7	44.6	1,639.7	656.6
France	5.2	105.6	809.8	483.4
Germany (FRG)	9.7	45.8	1,554.1	118.0
Greece	0.9	2.3	72.8	NA
Hungary	6.1	15.5	211.0	4.0
Indonesia	1.2	5.1	38.4	4.9
Japan	1.6	1.8	231.2	29.4
Spain	3.6	147.3	1,069.9	278.2
Sweden	11.9	44.1	1,708.8	460.0
Switzerland	5.8	24.2	276.8	NA
Venezuela	17.4	161.0	NA	85.9

*Data are for 1983.
NA = not available.

Source: International Police Organization (Interpol) data, as reported in Carol B. Kalish, *International Crime Rates.* Washington, D.C.: U.S. Department of Justice, May 1988, p. 3.

and other races, the rates for all three groups are highest in the West (O'Carroll and Mercy, 1989). However, a study that took into account regional differences in the metropolitan concentration of blacks and whites and the percentage of the white population that is Hispanic found that the homicide rate for non-Hispanic whites was highest in the South and that there was no clear regional variation in the homicide rates for blacks (Nelsen, Corzine, and Huff-Corzine, 1994).

Regional differences in homicide rates have also been explained by a "subculture of violence," a set of norms that allow violence to be an appropriate response to certain situations (Wolfgang and Ferracuti, 1967, 1982). Some claim that those norms are more widespread in the South than elsewhere. Attempts to explain regional variations in murder rates by this subculture-of-violence theory are explored later in the book, but what is important here is the existence of regional differences that a theory of crime causation must explain.

The West and the South had the overall highest rates of property crime in 1995 (Federal Bureau of Investigation, 1996: 60–67). Larceny rates were highest for the West, followed closely by the South. Burglary rates were highest in the South, followed by the West. The motor vehicle theft rate was significantly higher in the West than in the other regions. The total rates per 100,000 for the three property crimes were 5,312.3 for the West, 5,004.1 for the South,

FIGURE 4.2
Regional Variations in
Murder and Property Crime,*
Rates per 100,000 Population,
1995

*Rates are total number of larce-
nies, burglaries, and motor vehicle
thefts per 100,000 population.

Source: Based on data from
Federal Bureau of Investigation,
*Crime in the United States, 1995:
Uniform Crime Reports.*
Washington, D.C.: U.S.
Government Printing Office,
1996, pp. 60–67.

A. Regional Variations in Murder Rates per 100,000

Northeast	6.2
Midwest	6.9
West	9.0
South	9.8
United States	8.2

B. Regional Variations in Property Crime* per 100,000

Northeast	3,569.8
Midwest	4,163.5
West	5,312.3
South	5,004.1
United States	4,593.0

4,163.5 for the Midwest, and 3,569.8 for the Northeast. The rate for the country as a whole was 4,593.0 (see Figure 4.2B).

One possible explanation for the regional variations in rates of property
crime is that the relatively casual life style in the West and the South might be
conducive to theft. Warmer weather might mean that people are away from
their homes more often and leave their property unguarded, and this could
inflate property crime rates by creating more opportunities for theft. We can
speculate about the reasons for regional variations in crime rates, but theories of crime causation should make sense of such variations. This assumes,
of course, that the data that show such variations are valid measures of the
actual distribution of crime.

Variations in Crime Rates by Community

FBI data for 1995 show a general tendency for crime rates to increase with the
size of the community (see Figure 4.3). Crime rates are highest for cities of
more than 250,000 people, although the largest of those cities do not always

FIGURE 4.3

Variations in Crime Rates by Size of Community, 1995

Source: Based on data from Federal Bureau of Investigation, *Crime in the United States, 1995: Uniform Crime Reports.* Washington, D.C.: U.S. Government Printing Office, 1996, pp. 187–188.

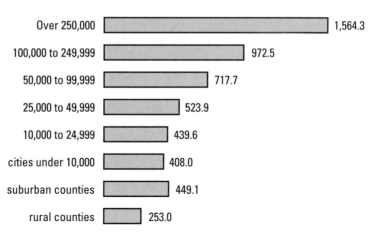

A. Violent Crimes

Over 250,000	1,564.3
100,000 to 249,999	972.5
50,000 to 99,999	717.7
25,000 to 49,999	523.9
10,000 to 24,999	439.6
cities under 10,000	408.0
suburban counties	449.1
rural counties	253.0

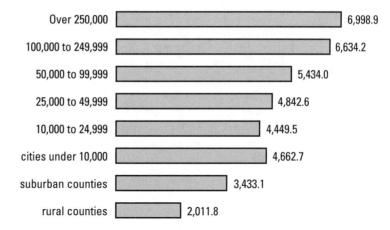

B. Property Crimes

Over 250,000	6,998.9
100,000 to 249,999	6,634.2
50,000 to 99,999	5,434.0
25,000 to 49,999	4,842.6
10,000 to 24,999	4,449.5
cities under 10,000	4,662.7
suburban counties	3,433.1
rural counties	2,011.8

have rates higher than the smaller cities in that category. An exception to the tendency for crime rates to increase with size of a community is that the murder rate in rural areas is higher than the rate in cities with populations of less than 50,000. Another exception is that rates of all index crimes but larceny and aggravated assault are higher in suburban counties than in towns with populations of less than 10,000.

Victimization survey data for 1990 indicate that rates of rape, robbery, assault, larceny from the person, burglary, household larceny, and car theft are higher in central cities than in suburban areas, and are higher in suburban areas than in rural areas (Bachman, 1992). In general, both official crime statistics and victimization surveys point in the same direction: conventional crime occurs at higher rates in larger communities, at least within the United States.

Social processes associated with large communities—such as the anonymity of the individual and the disruption of traditional social ties—

seem to be associated with more crime, but the growth in the size of cities has not always produced higher crime rates. Since the end of World War II, Japan has become more heavily urbanized, but its crime rate has not increased (Clifford, 1976). Switzerland was also able to keep its crime rate low while urbanizing, with a slow rate of urban growth making it possible to maintain social stability and avoid the disruption of traditional social ties (Clinard, 1978). Thus the association between community size and crime rates in the United States should direct our attention to social processes that have occurred with urban growth in this country, rather than lead us to assume that urbanization inevitably and by itself generates crime.

Crime within Metropolitan Areas

The first systematic examination of the distribution of crime within metropolitan areas was carried out in the 1920s in Chicago by Clifford Shaw and Henry McKay (1942, 1969). They followed Ernest Burgess in describing the metropolitan area as a series of identifiable concentric rings, depicted in Figure 4.4. In this **concentric-zone model** of the urban community, industry develops near the center of the city in order to be at the crossroads of transportation and communication. This may not be true of cities that developed after the mass ownership of cars and telephones, and in the future, cities may be located at the crossroads of electronic communications rather than at the crossroads of transportation. In Shaw and McKay's model, the central business district is at the center of the metropolis and is immediately surrounded by an area that is changing from a run-down residential area to one occupied by expanding business and industry. Beyond this are residential areas of increasing desirability and respectability.

Shaw and McKay found that rates of arrest for delinquency—as well as rates of adult crime, truancy, tuberculosis, infant mortality, and mental disorder—were highest in the center of the city and declined with increasing distance (see the Using Criminology box). Since Shaw and McKay completed their research, others have done work that supports their conclusion about the distribution of crime and delinquency in metropolitan areas (see, e.g., Short, 1969: xxv–liv). Rates of crime and delinquency are usually highest in areas characterized by low incomes, dilapidated and overcrowded housing, transiency, unemployment, broken families, and minority groups. These areas are most commonly in the center of large cities (Chilton, 1964; Turner, 1969; Miller, 1974). Evidence that the highest rates of crime and delinquency occur in the center of cities also comes from research carried out in Canada, Great Britain, Venezuela, Puerto Rico, Uganda, the Soviet Union, and other countries (Wallis and Maliphant, 1967; Grillo, 1970; Clinard and Abbott, 1973; Edwards, 1973; Jarvis and Messinger, 1974; Ferracuti, Dinitz, and Acosta, 1975; Shelley, 1981a, 1981b).

Looking at data for Chicago from 1900 to 1966, Shaw and McKay found that the delinquency rate for the members of any given racial or ethnic group was higher for members of the group who lived near the center of the city and lower for members who lived in neighborhoods more distant. For instance,

FIGURE 4.4

Shaw and McKay's
Concentric-Zone Model
of the City

Source: Reprinted from "The
Nature of Cities" by Chauncy D.
Harris and Edward L. Ullman in
volume 242 of *The Annals of The
American Academy of Political
and Social Science.* ©1945 by
The American Academy of
Political and Social Science.
All rights reserved.

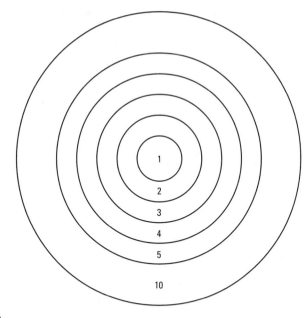

District

1. Central business district
2. Wholesale light manufacturing
3. Low-class residential
4. Medium-class residential
5. High-class residential
10. Commuter's zone

people of German ancestry who lived in the inner city had higher rates of arrest for delinquency than did German-Americans who lived in the suburbs. This suggests that it is the values and norms that are transmitted from generation to generation in an urban neighborhood, rather than the values and norms of any particular racial or ethnic group, that are conducive to violation of the law.

This conclusion is supported by Shaw and McKay's finding that the same urban neighborhoods generally had the highest rates of delinquency over the years, even when there was considerable change in the racial and ethnic composition of those communities. Areas with high delinquency rates were usually marked by rapid population turnover, socialization into patterns of crime and delinquency, and a lack of good jobs. A more recent study of the distribution of delinquency in Chicago found that Shaw and McKay's conclusion that rates remained the same despite racial and ethnic turnover fit the data for 1940 and 1950. From 1950 to 1970, however, changes in the racial and ethnic composition of a neighborhood were often accompanied by changes in delinquency rates. Rates of delinquency remained about the same when a neighborhood was able to maintain its stability in the face of a changing racial and ethnic composition, but in many neighborhoods racial and ethnic succession destabilized the community and led to an increased rate of delinquency (Bursik and Webb, 1982).

Shaw and McKay argued that the relationship between local rates of poverty and crime was mediated by neighborhood social organization,

USING CRIMINOLOGY

The Chicago Area Project

Research on the distribution of delinquency in Chicago led Clifford Shaw and Henry McKay to conclude the following:

> The consistency with which certain communities produce large numbers of delinquents, over a long period of time, focuses attention on the community as the basic unit for programs aimed at an understanding of the offender, treatment, or the prevention of violative behavior. Surely the processes of the community must be understood before programs, based on this understanding, can be brought into operation. Full recognition of the implications of the fact that a large proportion of young offenders come from a few areas should lead to further concentration on the neighborhood or the community as the appropriate units for social action. (p. 387)

To encourage efforts by residents of low-income areas to prevent delinquency and rehabilitate offenders, in 1932 the Institute for Juvenile Research and the Behavior Research Fund began the work of what came to be known as the Chicago Area Project. This private corporation had a board of directors composed of prominent citizens who sought to prevent delinquency. Funds and personnel for programs were provided by foundations, public and private agencies, and local residents and institutions.

The Chicago Area Project treated the neighborhood as the basic unit of operation. Activities and programs were developed in urban neighborhoods with populations from 10,000 to 50,000. The neighborhood orientation of the Chicago Area Project reflected Shaw and McKay's assumption that delinquency was the product of community conditions and therefore had to be dealt with as a local problem with local solutions.

Programs in each community were planned and implemented by a committee of local citizens, including members of churches, unions, business groups, athletic clubs, and other local organizations. This approach contrasts with the traditional practice of outsiders to the community running local programs. Though the funds for the Chicago Area Project's programs might have come from outside the community, the local committee

---

defined as the degree to which local institutions allow a community to cope with its problems. Recent work indicates that a community's control over crime and delinquency also depends on whether its institutions can attract resources from agencies outside the community that deal with health, welfare, education, and criminal justice (Moore, 1978; Bursik and Grasmick, 1993; Turk, 1993).

Rodney Stark's (1987) theory of the ecology of crime first identifies five characteristics of urban neighborhoods that have high rates of deviance: density, poverty, mixed use, transience, and dilapidation. Stark then develops a set of propositions about the ways that those five characteristics reduce social control and increase moral cynicism, opportunities for crime and deviance, and the motivation to deviate. These responses amplify the amount of crime and deviance in the neighborhood by attracting deviant people and activities to the area, driving out the least deviant people and activities, and further weakening social control. Residence in these "deviant places" is a cause of group differences in crime rates; for example, "high black crime rates are, in large measure, the result of *where* they live" (Stark, 1987: 905).

USING CRIMINOLOGY

assumed full leadership of the activities, thereby creating a sense of self-reliance in working toward common goals.

To the extent possible, the staff to carry out these programs was recruited from the neighborhood. Workers' ties to local organizations and residents helped promote social action programs. Local workers were also more aware than outsiders of the special strategies needed to make programs work in the community. Professionals from outside the community who worked with the local committee had to learn to translate their expertise into actions that would be effective in that particular community.

The programs developed by the local committees were designed to improve the community, and especially to enhance the well-being of local children. Activities included recreation, summer camping, scouting, handicrafts, and field trips. There were also programs designed to improve housing, sanitation, and the physical appearance of the neighborhood. Parent-teacher organiza-

tions were developed to improve the schools, and there were some efforts to increase job opportunities for local youths.

No systematic evaluation of the Chicago Area Project's impact on delinquency has been conducted. Annual committee reports document participation in the programs, tell of cases in which programs seemed to rehabilitate offenders, and show success in achieving goals such as building a new facility or gaining a concession from city government. Systematic evaluation of the Chicago Area Project is difficult because its philosophy of responding to local needs led to the implementation of different programs in different communities. The Chicago Area Project did increase local participation in programs designed to solve local problems, and it forced·outsiders to consider local needs before offering assistance.

Source: Based on Clifford R. Shaw and Henry D. McKay, *Juvenile Delinquency and Urban Areas*, rev. ed., with a new introduction by James F. Short, Jr. Chicago: University of Chicago Press, 1942, 1969.

The Geography of Crime   Geographers have provided a picture of crime in metropolitan areas by mapping the location of crimes, the residences of those who commit crimes, and the residences of victims (Georges-Abeyie and Harries, 1980; Brantingham and Brantingham, 1984). Often they use computer graphics to show the distribution of those elements in a metropolitan area.

Crimes of violence are often depicted as a triad of elements: the residences of the offender and of the victim, and the place where the crime occurs. However, many crimes of violence—especially homicide and aggravated assault—occur within the home, where much interaction takes place. As a result, sometimes the triad is a single point, with the residence of the victim and the offender also being the location of the crime.

Crimes against property are usually depicted as a dyad of elements: the residence of the offender and the place where the property is stolen (although larceny from a person may add the third element of the victim's residence). Most property offenses, as well as most crimes of violence, occur fairly close to the offender's home, with the number of crimes decreasing with greater distance from the criminal's place of residence. Offenders are familiar with their own neighborhoods and so can find targets there; they also know what risks they must avoid near home, even though they may run a greater risk of identification near home. Consequently, criminals' "journeys" or "trips" to the places where they commit their crimes are often short (P. Phillips, 1980; Brantingham and Brantingham, 1984). However, the dyads and triads of crime vary with the kind of offense committed and with the age and sex of the criminal.

Geographers have not mapped dyads and triads for white-collar crime. If they did, they would probably discover that the distance from the home of the offender to the location of the crime, which is usually the place of work, is considerably greater than is the case for most index crimes. Moreover, the places of residence of the victims of white-collar crimes are probably widely dispersed throughout the metropolitan area, and often throughout the nation or the world.

Chapter 9 explores the way that the routine activities approach explains the geographic distribution of crime in terms of the joint presence of motivated offenders, suitable targets, and a lack of guardianship.

Migration and Crime

Migration can lead to crime by disrupting the lives of people who move from small towns and rural areas to large cities, or from one country to another. Fear of crime can cause people to migrate from an urban neighborhood with a high crime rate to a safer suburban community, or from a nation with a high crime rate to a country with a lower one; if those who leave have low rates of committing crime, the neighborhood or country they leave might have its crime rate elevated by their departure.

Research on the relationship between migration and crime has produced mixed results. Studies carried out in Kuwait and several African and South American countries have found that migration is associated with high crime rates (Clinard and Abbott, 1973; Al-Thakeb, 1978; Shelley, 1981b). Migrants to cities in the former Soviet Union had higher crime rates than long-term residents of the same cities (Shelley, 1981b). Immigrants to England from Ireland have a higher crime rate than the native-born English, a difference attributed to the disruption of traditional controls by family and church, a high unemployment rate, and residence in high-crime areas (Radzinowicz and King, 1977: 26). Data from Japan show that the crime rate of young immigrants to Tokyo from the surrounding countryside is about one-and-a-half times as high as the rate for Tokyo residents who grew up there (Clifford, 1976: 114–115).

Research done in several European countries has yielded somewhat different conclusions. In some of those studies, the crime rates of natives and immigrants are similar, and in others the immigrants have somewhat lower rates than the natives. A study in western Germany concluded that aliens between fourteen and twenty-one had higher crime rates than their native-born counterparts, but the crime rate for all adult migrants was lower than the rate for native-born German adults (Albrecht, Pfeiffer, and Zapka, 1978). Other research from Europe, Australia, Canada, and the United States suggests that recent immigrants—whether permanent residents or "guest workers"—sometimes have crime rates lower than those of the native-born population (Savitz, 1960; Clinard, 1978; Shelley, 1981a).

During the first few decades of the twentieth century, there was a widespread feeling among native-born Americans that high crime rates were due to recent immigrants. In *Culture Conflict and Crime*, one of the first studies of the relationship between migration and crime, Thorsten Sellin (1938) showed that immigrants did not have crime rates higher than native-born Americans. In fact, for many crimes and for many nationalities, the immigrants' rates were lower. However, the rates for the offspring of the immigrants often approached the native-born rate. In other words, the crime rates of successive generations of the children of immigrants became more like the crime rates of the native-born. This indicates that crime is a learned behavior and that socialization into the dominant American culture is associated with rising crime rates for immigrant groups that had lower rates when they came to the country.

In 1980, about 125,000 refugees entered the United States from Cuba. Because some of those "Marielitos" had served time in Cuban prisons, the American press gave much attention to the crime they committed. Law-enforcement officials in many of the cities in which the Cuban refugees live have reported that they commit disproportionately large amounts of crime. However, a study of homicide in Dade County, Florida, found that the murder rate of the Cuban immigrants was no higher than the rate for blacks who were native to the county (Wilbanks, 1984).

The fact that immigrants sometimes have crime rates no higher than the rate for the native-born population is surprising, for there are several reasons to think the immigrants would have higher rates. Migrants are most often young males, a group particularly prone to crime in all societies. Moving often disrupts ties to family, friends, and community, and this weakens traditional controls over deviant behavior (Crutchfield, Geerken, and Gove, 1982; Tittle and Paternoster, 1988). The hostility and discrimination sometimes encountered by immigrants might also push them into crime. In addition, there is usually more affluence in the place to which migrants move than in the place from which they came, and this both provides more opportunities for crime and creates a sense of material deprivation conducive to crime. The relationship between migration and crime depends on several factors, including the crime rate of the migrants prior to moving, the crime rate of the native-born population, and the problems of adjustment encountered by the immigrants in their new home.

In both industrialized and developing capitalist societies, migration is usually uncontrolled. However, in some socialist societies, migration has been controlled. For instance, both China and the former Soviet Union developed policies to minimize the disruption that can occur with internal migration from rural areas and small towns to large cities.

Temporal Variations in Crime Rates

So far we have seen that crime rates vary by country, by region within a country, and by size of the community. In this section, we will see that crime rates also vary over time.

Seasonal Variations in Crime Rates

Some studies indicate that homicide is more common in some seasons than in others, but other research finds no such pattern. One comprehensive study concluded that "seasonal fluctuation, if it exists, may be too weak to affect practical policy or administrative decisions" (Block, 1984: 20). An investigation of homicide in Baltimore rejected the idea that there was a season for homicide, finding that it was somewhat more common in July, August, and December, but that month-to-month variations were not large enough to be statistically significant (Cheatwood, 1988).

FBI rates of rape fluctuate over the course of the year, peaking in August, diminishing steadily until December, and then rising again until the following August. In 1995, 9.9 percent of reported rapes occurred in August and only 6.8 percent in December (Federal Bureau of Investigation, 1996: 24). These variations probably reflect differences in the amount of social interaction that occurs in warm and cold weather.

Victimization data from 1973 through 1984 showed that some crimes fluctuate with the season. The offenses that exhibited the greatest degree of seasonal variation were household larceny, unlawful entry, and rape. Personal larceny with contact, personal larceny of less than $50 without contact, aggravated assault, and attempted forcible entry varied to a moderate degree with the season. Personal larceny of $50 or more without contact, motor vehicle theft, robbery, forcible entry, and simple assault showed little variation across seasons. The most common pattern of seasonal variation was for rates to be highest during the summer months and lowest in the winter months, but not all seasonal patterns were of this sort. The clearest exception to the general pattern was for personal larcenies of less than $50 without contact; rates for this offense were highest at the start of the school year from September to January and lowest in the summer months when school was out (Bureau of Justice Statistics, May 1988).

Seasonal variations are relatively small, but they must be explained by theories of crime. The Bureau of Justice Statistics (May 1988: 4) suggests the following approach:

> Individual behavior patterns change with the seasons and with them the opportunity for crime to occur. For example, people spend more time outside in the warmer weather, increasing the number of potential targets for street crime. Doors and windows in homes are more apt to be open or left unlocked at these times and thus provide easier access to intruders. More household articles are likely to be left outside, serving as invitations to theft. Patterns of economic activity may also be related to ebbs and flows of crime, especially the purchase of retail goods and services.

Annual Trends in Crime Rates

Figures 4.5 and 4.6 show fluctuations in rates of the FBI index crimes since 1933. Between 1933 and the early 1960s, rates were relatively stable, but they began to increase significantly around 1963. Since the mid-1970s, rates have declined in some years and increased in other years. Property crimes rates fell from 1991 to 1995, and violent crime rates dropped from 1992 to 1995. These FBI data must be interpreted cautiously, for changes in crime reporting and recording could account for some of the changes.

NCVS victimization rates changed little during the 1970s but declined somewhat from 1980 to 1991; redesign of the survey in 1992 made it impossible to compare victimization rates after that with rates for earlier years (Bastian, 1995: 6). Between 1973 and 1991, NCVS victimization rates sometimes declined while FBI rates increased. In general, both types of data suggest a greater stability or even a decline in crime rates in recent years. A theory of crime causation should be able to tell us why crime rates rise and fall over the years, but few theories have tried to do this.

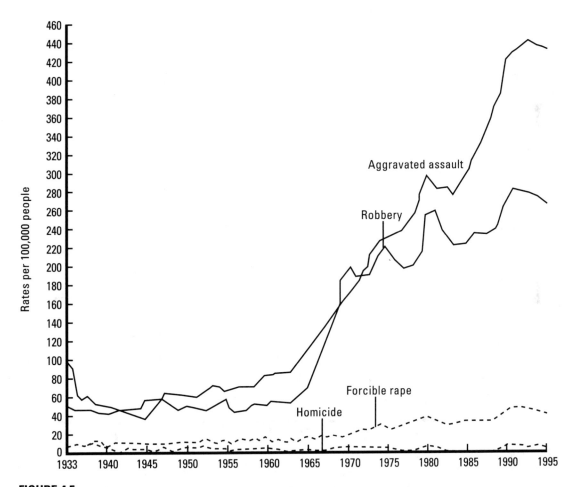

FIGURE 4.5

Trends in Crimes of Violence, Rates per 100,000, FBI Data, 1933–1995

Source: Data from FBI Uniform Crime Reports for 1966–1995 to bring up to date the figure presented in the President's Commission on Law Enforcement and Administration of Justice, *The Challenge of Crime in a Free Society.* Washington, D.C.: U.S. Government Printing Office, 1967, p. 23.

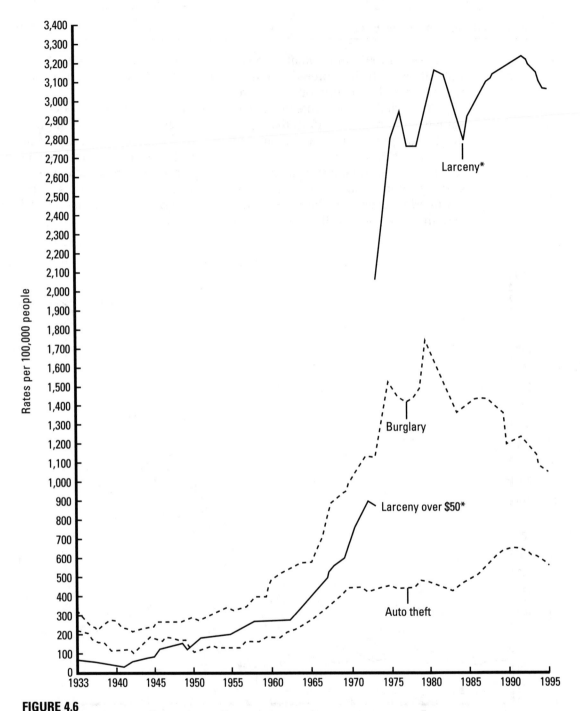

FIGURE 4.6

Trends in Crimes against Property, Rates per 100,000 People, FBI Data, 1933–1995

* Until 1972, the FBI counted only larcenies over $50 as index crimes. From 1973 to the present, it has counted all larcenies as index crimes.

Source: Data from FBI Uniform Crime Reports for 1966–1995 to bring up to date the figure presented in the President's Commission on Law Enforcement and Administration of Justice, *The Challenge of Crime in a Free Society.* Washington, D.C.: U.S. Government Printing Office, 1967, p. 23.

Variations in Crime Rates by Sex

Not everyone is equally likely to commit a crime or to be the victim of one. Offense rates and victimization rates vary with social characteristics such as sex, age, race, and social class.

Perhaps the best predictor of whether an individual will violate the law is sex: men commit much more crime than women in every society for which we have data. Even though male-female differences in crime rates vary from one society to another, over time, and from one offense to another, sex is a primary factor differentiating criminals from noncriminals. This could be partly a result of hormonal differences that make men more aggressive than women (see Chapter 5), but it is more likely the result of differences in the socialization of males and females. Boys and girls, and men and women, are taught to behave differently and play different roles. This socialization process, in combination with a social structure that assigns statuses to people on the basis of sex, leads to differences in personality, behavior, and opportunities that are linked to the large difference in crime rates between males and females.

Sex and Juvenile Delinquency

To examine male-female differences most fruitfully, we must look at juvenile delinquency and adult crime separately. Delinquency includes acts that are crimes when committed by adults, but it also includes juvenile status offenses (such as running away from home) that are prohibited only for those below a certain age. Because delinquency is defined so broadly, differences in expected behavior for boys and girls influence the way that each sex is treated by the juvenile justice system.

In 1995, the five offenses for which boys under the age of eighteen were most often arrested were larceny, drug abuse violations, simple assaults, disorderly conduct, and vandalism. For girls under eighteen, the top five offenses were larceny, running away from home, simple assaults, curfew and loitering law violations, and disorderly conduct (see Table 4.2, p. 122). The only Part I or Part II offense for which more girls than boys were arrested was running away. For all Part I and Part II offenses, there were three times as many boys as girls arrested. The ratio of male to female arrests varies with the offense, with boys being arrested about twice as often as girls for larceny, but nearly ten times as often for robbery.

FBI arrest data indicate that the percentage of all arrested suspects under eighteen who were female increased from 15.3 percent in 1963 to 25.5 percent in 1995, evidence that girls became more like boys in their rate of delinquency over that period. This trend also characterized the arrests of young people for major violent crimes (murder and nonnegligent manslaughter, robbery, and aggravated assault, with rape excluded because few females are arrested for that offense). In 1963, 7.9 percent of arrests for these three violent crimes were of females, but by 1995 the figure was up to 15.1 percent. However, most

TABLE 4.2   Five Most Common Offenses Arrested for, Males and Females
             under Eighteen Years Old, 1995

Males

Offense	Number of arrests
larceny	251,659
drug abuse violations	124,540
simple assaults	113,696
disorderly conduct	95,045
vandalism	88,989

Females

Offense	Number of arrests
larceny	120,911
running away from home	104,098
simple assaults	43,306
curfew and loitering law violations	33,039
disorderly conduct	30,957

Source: Federal Bureau of Investigation, *Crime in the United States, 1995: Uniform Crime Reports.*
Washington, D.C.: U.S. Government Printing Office, 1996, p. 217.

of the increase in the proportion of girls arrested for all crimes, and most of
the increase in the proportion of girls arrested for the three violent crimes,
occurred between 1963 and 1971. From 1971 to 1995, the proportion of all
arrested juveniles who were females did not change much, either for all
crimes or for the three major violent crimes.

Self-report studies indicate that when a girl commits an act that would be
a crime if committed by an adult, she is less likely than a boy to be reported
to the police or to be dealt with in court (Clark and Haurek, 1966; Gold, 1970;
Chesney-Lind, 1973). Boys who engage in conventional crimes are more likely to be arrested by the police and brought before a juvenile court, partly
because of the widely held opinions that girls are not as bad as boys and that
girls who violate the law are led into crime by bad male companions.

Some research reveals that for certain juvenile status offenses, girls are as
likely as—or even more likely than—boys to be arrested by the police and
brought into court (Clark and Haurek, 1966; Wise, 1967; Gold, 1970; Chesney-
Lind, 1973). A girl who runs away from home, drinks alcoholic beverages, or
has sexual relations is more likely to become involved with the legal system
than is a boy who does the same things, even though self-report studies suggest that female involvement in those acts is no greater than male involvement (Canter, 1982). This difference in treatment by the juvenile justice system is probably related to norms about appropriate gender-role behavior:
boys are expected to "raise hell" but girls are expected to be "well-behaved."
These expectations lead to more surveillance and control of adolescent girls

than of adolescent boys, and they result in more arrests and court appearances for girls than would be expected on the basis of sex differences in self-reported status offenses.

Sex and Crime

In addition to the male-female differential in juvenile arrests, there is a significant difference between the sexes in adult arrests. In 1995, four times as many men as women aged eighteen and over were arrested. This is a higher ratio than that for juveniles; in other words, adult crime is even more of a male phenomenon than juvenile delinquency.

For people of all ages, more males than females are arrested for each of the eight index crimes (see Figure 4.7). In 1995, males were at least 82 percent of all suspects arrested for every index crime except larceny; 67 percent of the suspects arrested for that crime were males. Despite the predominance of males among suspects arrested for index crimes, there have been important changes over recent decades in the proportion of women arrested for those offenses.

Trends in Arrests of Females   In 1963, women were 12 percent of all suspects arrested for index crimes, but by 1995 the proportion had risen to 24 percent; most of that increase occurred between 1963 and 1976. Most of the increase was due to the increased proportion of women arrested for larceny, by far the most common index crime for which arrests are made. In 1963, 19

FIGURE 4.7
Males and Females Arrested for Index Crimes, Percentages, 1995

Source: Based on data from Federal Bureau of Investigation, *Crime in the United States, 1995: Uniform Crime Reports.* Washington, D.C.: U.S. Government Printing Office, 1996, p. 225.

	%Males	%Females
Murder and nonnegligent manslaughter	90.5	9.5
Forcible rape	98.8	1.2
Robbery	90.7	9.3
Aggravated assault	82.3	17.7
Burglary	88.9	11.1
Larceny - theft	66.7	33.3
Motor vehicle theft	86.9	13.1
Arson	84.3	15.7
Crime index total	76.1	23.9

percent of larceny suspects were women, but by 1973 the proportion had climbed to 32 percent, a figure that did not change much thereafter. Without self-report data for women for 1963 and 1973, we cannot determine if the increase in the proportion of larceny suspects who were women reflects an actual increase in theft by women over that time. Perhaps the arrest practices of store detectives and the police changed during that period. One response to the big increase in FBI crime rates over that time may have been a decision to arrest thieves in 1973 who might have been warned and released in 1963.

From 1963 to 1995, there were increases in the proportions of suspects who were women for the crimes of robbery (from 5 to 9 percent), burglary (from 3 to 11 percent), and motor vehicle theft (from 4 to 13 percent). There was no marked change in the proportion of women arrested for aggravated assault over this time, and the proportion of women arrested for murder declined from 18 to 10 percent.

Women and White-Collar Crime   In one study of employee theft in a large retail organization, data gathered from personnel records, from files kept by the company's security force, and from interviews conducted with the firm's officials revealed that male employees committed more thefts and took more when they did steal than was true of female employees. Of 447 known dishonest workers, 56 percent were men, even though only 40 percent of the company's work force was male (Franklin, 1979). This study suggests that given similar on-the-job opportunities for theft, men commit crime more often than women, even though we would expect crime by women to increase somewhat as they gain more opportunities to steal on the job (Figueira-McDonough and Selo, 1980).

A study of white-collar offenders convicted in federal courts found that a surprisingly high 17.5 percent of them were female; there were nearly as many women as men convicted of bank embezzlement. The crimes committed by the women in the sample were, on the average, of less organizational complexity and had less impact on victims than was true of the offenses committed by men. However, women in the same positions as men seemed to inflict as much harm as men, suggesting that the reason for the overall lesser degree of harm inflicted by women was their lack of access to positions that provided access to the organizational resources needed to commit serious white-collar crimes (Weisburd et al., 1991). Unlike the study of employee theft, this research suggests that women commit as much and as serious white-collar crime as men when given the opportunity to do so.

Sex and Victimization

Victimization surveys find that men are much more likely than women to be the victims of robbery and assault, equally likely to be victims of nonviolent thefts, and much less likely to be the victims of rape and sexual assault (see Figure 4.8) (Perkins and Klaus, 1996). The NCVS victimization survey collects no data on homicide, but the FBI's UCR data for 1995 show that men are the victims of homicide more than three times as often as women.

FIGURE 4.8

Victimizations per 1,000 People Age Twelve and Older, by Sex, 1994

Source: Based on data from Craig Perkins and Patsy Klaus, *Criminal Victimization 1994.* Washington, D.C.: U.S. Department of Justice, April 1996, p. 4.

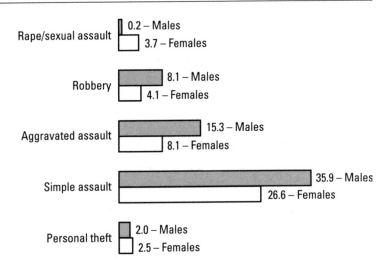

Variations in Crime Rates by Age

Most crimes are committed by relatively young people. In 1995, when the median age of the U.S. population was thirty-four, FBI data showed that 30.2 percent of people arrested for index crimes were under the age of eighteen and 54.7 percent were under the age of twenty-five. Suspects arrested for property crimes tended to be younger than those arrested for violent crimes (see Figure 4.9) (Federal Bureau of Investigation, 1996: 218–219).

Age-Specific Arrest Rates

Arrest data do not provide a perfect picture of how involvement in crime varies with age, because young offenders may be more or less likely than older offenders to be arrested for any given crime. However, arrest data do suggest that there are important age differences in criminal behavior.

Because the rates at which people are arrested vary with age, arrest rates for a whole society can mask important trends for different age groups. For instance, between 1985 and 1993, there was a dramatic increase in the arrest of juveniles for homicide, especially homicides committed with handguns (Blumstein, 1995). Over this time, the homicide arrest rate for people twenty-five and over declined by 20 percent, while the rate for eighteen-to-twenty-four-year-olds increased by 65 percent and the rate for fourteen-to-seventeen-year-olds rose by 165 percent (Fox, 1995).

Table 4.3 gives the **age-specific arrest rates**—or number of arrests per 100,000 people in each age category—for the crime of robbery for 1970, 1980, and 1990, three census years. We can see that in each year there is considerable variation in arrest rates among age groups. In 1970, the arrest rates rose to a peak at age eighteen and then declined with age. There was a similar pattern

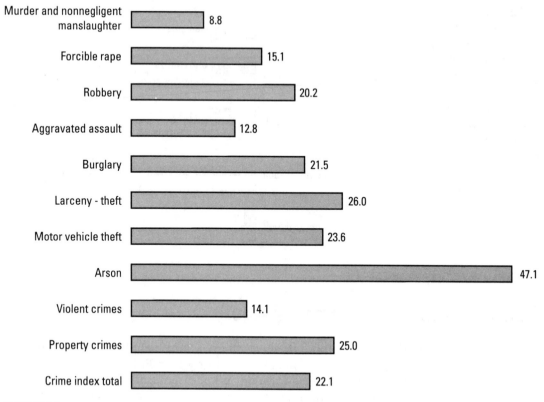

FIGURE 4.9

Percent of All Clearances Involving Arrests of Suspects under Eighteen Years Old, 1995

Source: Based on data from Federal Bureau of Investigation, *Crime in the United States, 1995: Uniform Crime Reports.* Washington, D.C.: U.S. Government Printing Office, 1996, p. 205.

in 1980 and 1990, except that the peak age for arrests was seventeen. In all three years, there was a precipitous decline in age-specific arrest rates after the mid-twenties.

Another important aspect of Table 4.3 is that the age-specific arrest rate for each group was considerably higher in 1980 than it was in 1970. This suggests more involvement in robbery by people of every age. The increase cannot be attributed to increasing rates of arrest by the police, because their clearance rate for robbery declined from 29.1 percent in 1970 to 23.8 percent in 1980. In other words, by 1980 a smaller proportion of all people who committed robbery was being arrested, but still the age-specific arrest rate had increased for every age group.

Table 4.3 reveals that the total robbery arrest rate dropped somewhat from 1980 to 1990, even though the clearance rate for robberies in 1990 was 24.3, slightly higher than in 1980. From 1980 to 1990, the age-specific robbery arrest rates decreased for all age groups up to twenty-three, but increased for

TABLE 4.3 Robbery Arrests per 100,000 People for Age Groups, 1970, 1980, and 1990

Number of Robbery Arrests per 100,000 People

Age Group	1970	1980	1990
Under 15	16.7	19.4	16.6
15	139.4	211.9	196.0
16	172.9	265.5	255.0
17	189.7	292.5	268.4
18	197.5	281.2	267.0
19	194.9	242.7	225.6
20	172.2	210.6	191.2
21	165.1	196.0	180.3
22	142.1	166.2	165.7
23	121.8	155.3	155.1
24	122.0	140.2	147.8
25–29	75.8	99.0	110.8
30–34	40.4	55.5	70.7
35–39	21.9	30.0	38.9
40–44	11.6	17.1	18.6
45–49	6.2	9.7	9.1
50 and over	1.5	2.2	1.6
All ages	43.1	61.6	54.8

Sources: Rates calculated from data in U.S. Department of Commerce, Bureau of the Census, *General Population Characteristics: United States Summary, 1970.* Washington, D.C.: U.S. Government Printing Office, 1972; Federal Bureau of Investigation, *Crime in the United States, 1970: Uniform Crime Reports.* Washington, D.C.: U.S. Government Printing Office, 1971; U.S. Department of Commerce, Bureau of the Census, *General Population Characteristics: United States Summary, 1980.* Washington, D.C.: U.S. Government Printing Office, 1983; Federal Bureau of Investigation, *Crime in the United States, 1980: Uniform Crime Reports.* Washington, D.C.: U.S. Government Printing Office, 1981; U.S. Department of Commerce, Bureau of the Census, *1990 Census of Population: General Population Characteristics: United States.* Washington, D.C.: U.S. Government Printing Office, November 1992; and Federal Bureau of Investigation, *Crime in the United States, 1990: Uniform Crime Reports.* Washington, D.C.: U.S. Government Printing Office, 1991.

all age groups between twenty-four and forty-four. The reason for this is not clear, but it might be due to the aging of a cohort that is especially prone to commit robbery.

Peak ages and age-specific arrest rates vary considerably from one offense to another. For all index crimes, 30.2 percent of the suspects arrested in 1995 were under eighteen, and their median age was twenty-three. For the four violent crimes, only 18.7 percent were under eighteen, and their median age was twenty-six. Suspects in violent crimes were generally older than suspects in property crimes, with 34.7 percent of them being under eighteen and their median age being twenty-one.

Age Distribution and Crime Rates

Because arrest rates differ by age group and because this seems to reflect a difference among age groups in actual involvement in criminal activity, a society can experience an increase or a decrease in its crime rate if the age distribution of its population changes. In other words, if the young have an especially high crime rate, a society with a large proportion of young people in its population at one time will have a higher overall crime rate than it would have at a different time when a smaller proportion of its population is young.

The post–World War II "baby boom" produced a significant increase in the proportion of the American population in the high-crime-rate years from fifteen to twenty-four in the 1960s; between 1960 and 1975, the size of that age group increased about six times as fast as the rest of the population. The dramatic increase in official crime rates during the 1960s is due in part to the increased proportion of the population in this high-crime-rate age group (President's Commission on Law Enforcement and Administration of Justice, 1967: 27–28). (See the Using Criminology box.)

Although changing age distribution explains some of the increase in index crime rates in the United States during the 1960s and 1970s, it does not explain most of it. Instead, there was an increase in the rate at which people of every age committed crime, as we can see in Table 4.3 for the crime of robbery. Looking at changes in the rate of violent index crimes from 1960 to 1970, for instance, we find that changes in the age distribution would have led us to expect a 40 to 50 percent increase in the rate of those offenses, but instead there was a 200 percent increase (Silberman, 1978: 31). The important theoretical question thus becomes what social changes, in addition to the change in the age distribution of the population, produced the increase in the crime rate.

Just as an increasingly youthful population can be expected to have rising crime rates, so too should an increasingly older population have declining crime rates. Recent research indicates that the decline in property crime rates

A society in which a high proportion of the population is between the ages of fifteen and twenty-four is likely to have a high overall crime rate, because that age group is especially likely to be involved in crime.

from 1980 to 1984 can be attributed largely to a change in the age structure of the population, with reductions in larceny and motor vehicle theft rates being the most influenced by the aging of the population (Cohen and Land, 1987; Steffensmeier and Harer, 1987). One study found that changes in violent crime rates were not explained by the changing age structure of the population (Steffensmeier and Harer, 1987), but another study concluded that the

USING CRIMINOLOGY

Can Curfews Stop Juvenile Crime?

"What if you've done your homework and you're a really good kid and you're out at a movie or something? It's, like, you're automatically guilty until you prove yourself innocent.... It's just so unfair and unconstitutional." (cited in Pertman, p. 1). This sixteen-year-old San Diego girl is reacting to her city's curfew law that requires her to be home by 10 P.M. during the week or face a $100 fine. Similar laws now exist in more than one thousand American communities, including three-fourths of the nation's 200 largest cities. Seventeen is the usual upper age limit for those restricted by curfews, but some cities set the age at fifteen or sixteen.

Curfews are aimed at curbing youth crime, particularly gang violence and drive-by shootings. Based on evidence that those under eighteen account for a disproportionate number of both offenders and victims, curfew laws seek to control potential offenders and protect potential victims by reducing opportunities for crime. These laws empower the police to disperse young people who congregate in public late at night and question youths who are on the street after curfew. They also provide parents with legal support for restricting their children's night-time activities.

Critics argue that curfew laws deny young people equal protection of the law, restrict their freedom of movement and association, are used in a racially discriminatory fashion, and intrude on the right of parents to raise their children as they wish. When the courts have ruled curfews invalid, however, it has not been on these grounds, but rather because the ordinances are too vague and broad. Ordinances that specify legitimate excuses for young people to be in public after curfew have been viewed favorably by the courts.

There is little research evaluating the impact of curfews on juvenile crime. Municipal officials claim that curfews have cut crime, but systematic evaluations by criminologists are lacking and some doubt that recent declines in crime rates can be attributed specifically to curfews. One study suggests that curfews might not be effective for the simple reason that only 17 percent of violent juvenile crime occurs during typical curfew hours.

Source: Based on William Ruefle and Kenneth Mike Reynolds, "Curfews and Delinquency in Major American Cities," *Crime and Delinquency* 41 (July 1995), 347–363; Howard N. Snyder, Melissa Sickmund, and Eileen Poe-Yamagata, *Juvenile Offenders and Victims: 1996 Update on Violence: Statistics Summary*. Pittsburgh, Penn.: National Center for Juvenile Justice, February 1996; Adam Pertman, "In by 10: Curfews for Minors Spur Debate," *Boston Globe*, January 17, 1996, pp. 1, 12.

decline in homicide rates during the early 1980s did reflect changes in the age structure over that period (Cohen and Land, 1987). Changes in the age structure of the population apparently contributed to a dip in crime rates after 1991, but a projected increase in the proportion of the population in the high-crime-rate age group will probably lead to higher crime rates by early in the twenty-first century (Blumstein, 1995).

Age and Victimization

Young people generally have higher rates of victimization than older people. In 1995, 24 percent of murder victims were between the ages of 9 and 21 (Federal Bureau of Investigation, 1996: 16). Victimization rates for rape and sexual assault, robbery, and aggravated and simple assault decline with increasing age; there is a similar but less pronounced decline in personal theft with age (Perkins and Klaus, 1996).

The NCVS has found that people sixty-five and above have lower victimization rates than any other group over the age of twelve. In contrast to violent crimes against younger victims, offenses against elderly victims are more likely to be committed by strangers, by armed offenders, by multiple offenders, and at or near the victims' homes. Elderly victims are also more likely than other victims to be injured by offenders (Bachman, October 1992). The characteristics of the crime incidents in which the elderly are involved might explain their high level of fear of crime, which exists despite their apparently low rates of actual victimization. There might also be a sense in which the elderly do have a high rate of victimization: they may be at risk less often than younger people because they do not usually go to work, they often live in age-segregated housing (including nursing homes), and they frequently stay indoors out of fear or infirmity. If victimization rates are calculated in terms of their time at risk, the elderly's victimization rate might actually be as high as or even higher than that of younger people (Lundquist and Duke, 1982; Stafford and Galle, 1984).

Variations in Crime Rates by Race

Variations in crime rates by racial and ethnic group reflect social, cultural, and economic differences among groups. In the past, some have suggested that such variations in crime rates are due to biological differences among racial and ethnic groups, but it is now well established that any biological differences among racial and ethnic groups are unimportant in explaining differences in crime rates. For instance, the crime rates of black Africans are considerably lower than the crime rates of black Americans, even though black Americans have racially intermixed with whites over the centuries and whites have crime rates lower than black Americans (Bohannan, 1960). Such variations in crime rates need to be explained by sociological theories of crime causation.

Race, Arrest Statistics, and Self-Report Studies

The FBI presents arrest data for whites, blacks, American Indian or Alaskan Natives, and Asian or Pacific Islanders. FBI data do not allow us to analyze differences in arrest rates for white ethnic groups such as Irish-Americans, Italian-Americans, Eastern Europeans, or Jews. However, sociological research has found the crime rates for Jews, Japanese-Americans, and Chinese-Americans are lower than rates for the total population, and crime rates for African-Americans and Mexican-Americans are higher than rates for the total population (Voss, 1963; Wolfgang, Figlio, and Sellin, 1972; Tracy, Wolfgang, and Figlio, 1985).

Ninety-eight percent of all arrests in 1995 for FBI index crimes were of whites or blacks. In that year, blacks were 12.6 percent of the U.S. population, but they accounted for 35.7 percent of arrests for index crimes. Blacks constituted 43.7 percent of arrests for crimes of violence and 32.6 percent of arrests for property crimes. For each index crime, blacks are arrested out of proportion to their numbers in the population. According to one estimate, the chance of ever being arrested for an index crime for blacks living in cities of more than 250,000 people is 51 out of 100, compared with a rate of 14 out of 100 for whites. Although there is a significant difference in the proportions of blacks and whites who have ever been arrested, there are similar patterns of offending among those members of both groups who have been arrested (Blumstein and Graddy, 1981–1982).

In Table 4.4, the rates of arrest per 100,000 people of the same race are given for whites and for blacks; the third column shows the ratios of blacks' arrest rates to whites' arrest rates. We can see that the likelihood of a black's being arrested for an index crime is much greater than the chance of a white's being arrested. Blacks are arrested between 4.2 and 10.1 times as often as whites for violent crimes, and between 2.1 and 4.3 times as often as whites for property crimes. Overall, blacks have an arrest rate for index crimes that is 3.8 times as great as the arrest rate for whites.

We must be wary of using FBI arrest data, for they can distort actual involvement in index crimes by blacks and whites if the police are more likely to arrest black suspects than they are to arrest white suspects. However, most criminologists agree that arrest statistics for blacks and whites reflect a real difference between the groups in their rates of committing crimes, and that the difference in arrests between the racial groups is not primarily a result of discriminatory arrest practices by the police. Later in the book, we examine racial discrimination by the police, the courts, and the prisons.

Some self-report research finds a higher frequency of all delinquent acts by blacks (Elliott and Ageton, 1980), but other studies find that blacks and whites report similar involvement in all delinquent acts (Williams and Gold, 1972; Tracy, 1987). Blacks and whites seem to be more similar in their self-reported involvement in relatively trivial delinquent acts, but blacks do seem to report serious offenses more often than whites (Williams and Gold, 1972; Hindelang, Hirschi, and Weis, 1979; Elliott and Ageton, 1980; Tracy, 1987).

TABLE 4.4　Rates of Arrest per 100,000 People, 1995

Crime	White Rate of Arrest per 100,000 People	Black Rate of Arrest per 100,000 People	Ratio of Black to White Rate
Murder	3.3	27.4	8.3
Forcible rape	6.8	33.9	5.0
Robbery	24.5	247.3	10.1
Aggravated assault	119.6	506.5	4.2
Burglary	89.6	272.8	3.0
Larceny	345.7	1,138.0	3.3
Motor vehicle theft	40.0	172.2	4.3
Arson	5.1	10.7	2.1
Total index crime	634.5	2,408.8	3.8

Sources: Arrest rates are calculated using Bureau of the Census data for 1995 on the number of whites (218,085,000) and blacks (33,141,000) and arrest data from Federal Bureau of Investigation, *Crime in the United States, 1995: Uniform Crime Reports.* Washington, D.C.: U.S. Government Printing Office, 1996, p. 226.

Race, Crime, and Background Variables

Differences in crime rates among racial and ethnic groups are a function of group differences in age, income, occupation, education, family background, place of residence, and other social characteristics, as well as a function of differences in opportunities to commit crime. This suggests that if blacks and whites of similar social backgrounds are compared, differences in crime rates between the groups will be reduced or eliminated. However, to suggest that people of different races but similar backgrounds will have the same crime rate is tantamount to suggesting that there are no cultural differences between the groups that result in different crime rates. More specifically, to argue that blacks and whites of similar backgrounds will have the same crime rate is to argue that centuries of discrimination have had no long-term effects on blacks that are conducive to criminal behavior.

Evidence suggests that blacks have higher crime rates than whites, even when individuals of similar backgrounds are compared, but that differences between the groups are reduced in comparisons of people of similar backgrounds. A study of murder in Philadelphia found that when blacks and whites with similar occupations were compared, blacks still committed homicide more often than whites (Wolfgang, 1958: 39). A study of rape in the same city found that blacks committed rape about four times as often as whites when people with similar occupations were compared (Amir, 1971: 69–72). Wolfgang, Figlio, and Sellin's (1972) cohort study revealed that 29 percent of the whites had had police contacts as juveniles, compared with 50 percent of the blacks. Even when blacks and whites of similar social class backgrounds were compared, blacks were more likely to have had police contacts. Thus, 53 percent of lower-class blacks had had police contacts as juveniles, compared with only 36 percent of lower-class whites; and 36 percent of higher-class blacks had had police contacts, compared with only 26 percent of higher-class whites. From those figures, we can see that blacks of the higher class were actually as likely as whites of the lower class to have had contact with the police. Blacks thus seem to have higher rates of crime and delinquency than whites of similar background, although black-white differences are reduced when people of similar backgrounds are compared (Green, 1970; Wolfgang, Figlio, and Sellin, 1972).

Race and Victimization

While acknowledging that the sources of high crime rates among blacks are in the larger society, African-American leaders in recent years have focused attention on the problem of black-on-black crime. Jesse Jackson has remarked, "I am rather convinced that the premier civil rights issue of this day is youth violence in general and black-on-black crime in particular. It's clear now that we must look inward to go onward" (cited in Rezendes, 1993: 1). Harvard Medical School professor Alvin Toussaint has commented,

> Yes, we can talk about the ongoing discrimination that affects our communities. But we also have to say to people: "You pulled that trigger. You committed that burglary. And you can't do it anymore because you're destroying your community." (cited in Rezendes, 1993: 4)

Blacks are disproportionately likely to be the victims of crime. In 1995, 48.8 percent of all homicide victims were black, although only 12.6 percent of the population was black. A recent study (MacKellar and Yanagishita, 1995: 6) found that homicide deaths for the period 1989-1991 varied by ethnic group as follows:

Rate per 100,000	
African-Americans	38.8
Hispanics	15.5
American Indians	11.7
Whites	5.7
Asian-Americans	5.5

Black males who live in cities have about a 5 percent chance of being murdered, and black males between fifteen and twenty-four are murdered at a rate seven times the rate for the rest of the population. In fact, murder is the primary cause of death for young black males. Some health officials have argued that murder among young black males should be considered a public health issue in much the same way that diseases are (Minsky, 1984; Foreman, 1987).

NCVS data in Figure 4.10 show that blacks have higher victimization rates than whites for rape and sexual assault, robbery, and aggravated assault and a lower victimization rate than whites for simple assault. Even though blacks, as a group, have a lower average income than whites, they are more likely than whites to be the victims of burglary, motor vehicle theft, and larceny (Perkins and Klaus, 1996).

Victim-Offender Relationships and Race

Researchers have found that violent crime typically involves a victim and an offender of the same race. A disproportionately high number of all murders involve a black offender and a black victim, and most other murders involve a white offender and a white victim. In 1995, only 12 percent of murders crossed racial lines; three-fifths of those cross-racial murders involved a black offender and a white victim. About three-fourths of forcible rapes involve an offender and a victim of the same race, with black rapist–white victim offenses being the most common kind of cross-racial rape. The majority of robberies involve

FIGURE 4.10

Victimizations Rates by Race, 1994

Source: Based on data from Craig Perkins and Patsy Klaus, *Criminal Victimization 1994*. Washington, D.C.; U.S. Department of Justice, April 1996, pp. 4–5.

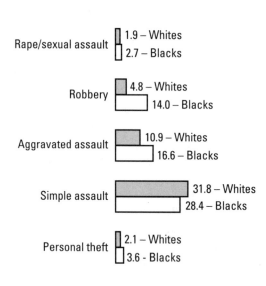

A. Rates per 1,000 People Age 12 or Older

Rape/sexual assault — 1.9 – Whites / 2.7 – Blacks

Robbery — 4.8 – Whites / 14.0 – Blacks

Aggravated assault — 10.9 – Whites / 16.6 – Blacks

Simple assault — 31.8 – Whites / 28.4 – Blacks

Personal theft — 2.1 – Whites / 3.6 - Blacks

B. Rates per 1,000 Households

Burglary — 51.7 – Whites / 70.8 – Blacks

Motor vehicle theft — 15.6 – Whites / 26.6 – Blacks

Theft — 234.6 – Whites / 243.8 – Blacks

a victim and an offender of the same race, but nearly two-fifths of white victims are robbed by black offenders (Wolfgang, 1958; Amir, 1971; Curtis, 1974; O'Brien, 1987; Whitaker, 1990; Federal Bureau of Investigation, 1996).

Hate crimes are offenses in which victims are singled out because of their race, ethnicity, religion, sexual preference, or disability. Assaults, vandalism, and intimidation against such victims are especially terrifying because the victims are aware that they were chosen because of their characteristics. Victims are often seriously injured, but they may be afraid to call the police. By evoking a more general fear in the targeted groups, hate crimes reinforce existing patterns of oppression.

In 1992, the U.S. Supreme Court ruled that the government could not prohibit speech, even hate speech, on the basis of its content, but the following year it held unanimously that it was constitutional to punish crimes motivated by bias more harshly than crimes not motivated by bias. In 1993, twenty-seven states had penalty-enhancement laws that punished hate crimes more severely than similar offenses not motivated by bias. Significant problems remain as to how to prove motivation in a hate crime, assess the precise role of "hate" in the offense, and determine whether provocation and mutual conflict preceded the crime (Morsch, 1991; Martin, 1995). The police construct hate crimes through their definition of situations and interpretation of the law, a process that requires them to consider the following:

> They must simultaneously protect the fundamental civil rights of citizens to be free from attacks based on their ethnic or other identity; allow for the constitutionally protected right of persons to express their opinions, including expressions of bigotry; and maintain order and peace in the larger community. (Martin, 1995: 322–323)

Hate crimes, such as this vandalism in a Jewish cemetery near Quebec City, are directed against victims chosen because of their race, ethnicity, religion, sexual preference, or disability.

In 1990, the federal government enacted a law to improve the collection of information on hate crimes. Police agencies serving three-fourths of the population provided the FBI with data on 7,947 hate crimes recorded in 1995. Race was the motivation in 61 percent of the crimes (three-fifths of the victims were blacks); religious bias was the motivation in 16 percent of the crimes (four-fifths of the victims were Jews); sexual orientation was the motivation in 13 percent of the cases (three-fourths of the victims were male homosexuals); and 10 percent of the crimes were motivated by the victim's ethnic or national origin (three-fifths of the victims were Hispanics) (*Boston Globe*, November 5, 1996).

Variations in Crime Rates by Social Class

When criminologists examine the relationship between crime and **social class**—which is defined as social standing based on economic resources, occupational prestige, political power, or life style—they usually look at conventional crimes such as murder, rape, robbery, and larceny. However, the most expensive crimes are white-collar crimes, and because these offenses are committed by middle- and upper-class people, we can conclude that the cost of crime is attributable primarily to violation of the law by the middle and upper classes, even though "the crime problem" defined by the FBI, the mass media, and the public usually refers to violations of the law most often committed by the lower and working classes.

Popular wisdom is that the lower and working classes engage in more crime, or at least more of the most serious conventional crime, than does the middle class. This view has existed for centuries and characterizes societies other than the United States. People act on their assumption that there is a relationship between crime and social class; they avoid slums after dark and expect to be safer when they move from the city to the suburbs.

FBI statistics include no information on the social class of arrested suspects, nor do victimization surveys provide us with that information, because victims could not be expected to judge in a reliable way the social class of the offender. There is, however, much research that has examined the relationship of social class to crime and delinquency. Unfortunately, that research does not lead to a simple conclusion.

Social Class and Adult Crime

When we look at official measures of crime produced by the police, the courts, or the prisons, we find "a small but consistent inverse correlation of social class with street crime" for adults (Hindelang, 1983: 180). For instance, one review of forty-six studies that used arrest data found consistently higher crime rates for lower-class adults (Braithwaite, 1979, 1981).

In the few studies that have been done of adult criminality using self-report questionnaires, researchers have found that the class-crime link is less strong in self-report data than in official data. The self-report studies conclude either that the lower class has a higher crime rate than other classes or that there are no significant differences by class; no self-report study of adults has found that the middle class has a higher crime rate than the lower class (Braithwaite, 1979).

Some have attributed the difference between the relatively strong association between social class and adult crime found in official statistics and the weak or nonexistent association found in self-report studies to class bias by the police and the courts. If the police are more likely to arrest a lower-class suspect than a middle-class suspect, arrest data would show that the lower class is more involved in crime, even though self-report studies might show little or no difference among the classes in criminal activity. However, a review of studies of adults that have used arrest data or self-report questionnaires concluded that class bias by the criminal justice system could not explain away the strong relationship between social class and crime found in studies using official statistics. The author concluded that "[l]ower-class adults commit those types of crime which are handled by the police at a higher rate than middle-class adults" (Braithwaite, 1979: 62).

Social Class and Juvenile Delinquency

One review of studies that have examined the link between social class and juvenile delinquency found that in forty-four of fifty-three studies that used official statistics, lower-class juveniles had higher rates of delinquency than middle-class juveniles (Braithwaite, 1979). Another review of the research found a "small but consistent inverse correlation of social class with street crime" by juveniles when official data were used (Hindelang, 1983: 180).

When self-report studies rather than official data are used to look at the link between social class and juvenile delinquency, the results are not clear. One review of the research found that self-report studies provide less support for a class-delinquency link than do arrest data, but that many self-report studies show higher delinquency rates for the lower class and that none finds higher rates for the middle class (Braithwaite, 1979). Another review of self-report studies of delinquency concluded as follows: "About half of the American studies support the hypothesis of an even smaller inverse relationship between various social-class indicators and reported illegal behavior [than is found in studies using official data], and half provide no support for the hypothesis" (Hindelang, 1983: 180). The class-delinquency relationship might be weaker in self-report studies than in research based on official data because the police are more likely to stop or arrest lower-class adolescents than they are to stop or arrest middle-class adolescents in the same circumstances.

Self-report studies suggest that class differences in delinquency are most pronounced for the most serious crimes, and smallest for the most trivial offenses. Serious and repetitive violations of the law seem to be most common among the lower classes (Reiss and Rhodes, 1961; Gold, 1970; Clelland and Carter, 1980; Elliott and Ageton, 1980; Braithwaite, 1981; Elliott and Huizinga, 1983).

Self-report studies that have looked at a broader range of delinquent acts, rather than only at the most serious ones, have sometimes concluded that there is little or no association between social class and delinquency. One review of the research found a weak-to-moderate relationship between class and official data on violations of the law, but almost no relationship between class and self-reported violations of the law (Tittle, Villemez, and Smith, 1978). Other self-report studies have also found no relationship between class and delinquency (Short and Nye, 1958; Dentler and Monroe, 1961; Akers, 1964; Krohn et al., 1980; Tittle and Meier, 1990). Several self-report studies of juvenile delinquency have even concluded that there is no relationship between social class and serious, repetitive violations of the law (Williams and Gold, 1972; Cernkovich, 1978a; Johnson, 1980; Krohn et al., 1980).

Contradictory evidence on the association between social class and self-reported delinquency also comes from the few studies that have compared the delinquency of people from the lowest class with that of all people of higher social standing. One self-report study that found no overall relationship between class and delinquency did find that boys from the lowest class were the most prone to delinquency. Of those boys whose fathers had been without a job and had received welfare assistance, 62 percent reported at least one delinquent act, compared with only 40 percent of the boys whose fathers had not been unemployed or on welfare (Hirschi, 1969: 72). However, another study found no significantly greater amount of self-reported delinquency—measured only by acts that would be crimes if committed by adults—among the underclass, a class that is below the poverty level, uneducated, often on welfare, and unemployed or working at low-prestige jobs (Johnson, 1980).

One researcher has suggested that there might be stronger evidence for a link between social class and juvenile delinquency in economically developing societies where people are categorized at birth into social groups with different perspectives on the world, where access to education is limited, and where social mobility is minimal. This view was supported by the author's research in South Korea. Using both official statistics and self-report data, he found that criminal behavior was confined largely to the lower class, and that the relationship between class and delinquency was strongest for the most serious offenses. The researcher concluded that in developing societies, "class remains an important factor in the explanation of crime and delinquency when educational opportunity is lacking" (Axenroth, 1983: 176).

Methodological Problems

Several methodological problems account for some of the inconsistency in the conclusions of the research that has examined the social class-delinquency relationship. One problem is how to measure the social class of adolescents. Rather than ask them about the class of their parents, as most researchers have done, it might make more sense to tap adolescents' job aspirations or expectations of future earnings. Another problem is that by gathering data from students who are in school on the day the survey is done, researchers miss truants and school dropouts, who may be especially prone to delinquency. In addition, self-report surveys sometimes increase the number of respondents who are classified as delinquents by asking about many relatively trivial acts.

Despite methodological problems, many self-report studies find higher rates of serious and repetitive delinquency among the lower classes, and none of those studies finds higher rates of serious and repetitive delinquency among the middle class. Official arrest data show even more consistent evidence for a class-delinquency link. Moreover, for adults, arrests show a strong class-crime association, and data from the few existing self-report studies of adults reveal an association between class and crime, although a somewhat weaker one than is found in studies using official data.

We will see later that many sociological theories of crime and delinquency are based on social class, even though the relationship between class and violation of the law is still somewhat unclear. The theories rarely consider that involvement in crime and delinquency can affect an individual's class standing by reducing job opportunities or by making upward social mobility difficult; unlike sex, age, and race, the variable of social class can be both a cause and an effect of crime and delinquency (Thornberry and Christenson, 1984). One review of eight theories of crime and delinquency concludes that none of them provides an adequate rationale for predicting an inverse or negative relationship between social class and crime without bringing in untested or unsupported assumptions about what the lower class is like (Tittle, 1983). Perhaps sociologists would be on firmer ground in looking for general social processes—such as ways of neutralizing the constraints of the law—that are sometimes correlated with class, rather than treating class itself as a cause of crime and delinquency.

Social Class and Victimization

A study of the medical records of homeless men, women, and children found that homicide was the leading cause of death, accounting for one-fourth of the deaths in the sample. The homicides often resulted from fights over the meager resources available to the homeless (Wright and Weber, 1987).

The NCVS does not use a single measure of social class, but it does gather data on indicators of class such as annual family income, education, employment status, and employment sector. Here we use annual family income as a measure of the social class of both individual victims and households. Victimization rates for rape and sexual assault, robbery, and aggravated assault decline with increasing income levels; rates of simple assault vary little with income level. Crimes of theft show less clear-cut patterns: personal theft shows no systematic variation with income, household theft rises with increasing income, burglary declines with increasing income, and motor vehicle theft varies little with income (Perkins and Klaus, 1996).

Summary

Rates of crime vary from one country to another; by region within a country; by size of a community; from one time to another; and by sex, age, race, and social class. Theories of crime causation should help us make sense of those variations.

Cross-national comparisons of crime rates are difficult because of differences among countries in their laws and their crime statistics. The United States has a high homicide rate compared with other industrial nations that report crime data to the United Nations. Within the United States, the South has a high homicide rate, and the West and the South have the highest rates of burglary and larceny.

Both FBI data and NCVS studies show that rates of index crimes are generally higher in larger communities. Shaw and McKay found that crime and delinquency are most common in neighborhoods closest to the center of the city. Geographers have mapped the residences of offenders and victims and the places where crimes occur, finding that most offenders commit crimes close to home. Immigrants frequently have crime rates no higher than, and sometimes lower than, native-born populations, in spite of perceptions by the native-born that the new arrivals are especially prone to crime.

NCVS studies show there are some seasonal fluctuations in crime rates that require explanation. FBI data show a large increase in crime rates beginning in the 1960s, with rates stabilizing and even declining in recent years. NCVS data show stable or declining crime rates since 1973.

In recent years, some kinds of juvenile delinquency have become more common among girls, but boys still outnumber girls in arrests. There is differential treatment of the sexes in the juvenile justice system, with girls less likely than boys to be processed formally if they commit acts that would be crimes when committed by adults, and girls more likely than boys to be processed formally if they commit status offenses such as running away from home.

Since 1963, there has been an increase in the proportion of females arrested for index crimes, with the greatest increase being for larceny. This may be because store detectives and the police have become more likely to treat female thieves formally rather than release them with a warning, because merchandising changes have made theft easier for women who shop, or because women have actually become more likely to steal.

In the United States, most people who commit index offenses are relatively young. Changes in the age distribution of a population over time can increase or decrease a society's overall crime rate. In general, victimization rates are higher for younger people than they are for older people, but the elderly may have a high victimization rate if we take into account their limited exposure to the risk of victimization.

Black Americans are arrested in numbers disproportionate to their numbers in the population, and this is more true for violent crimes than for property crimes. Arrest data seem to reflect a real difference between blacks and whites in their perpetration of index offenses, rather than police bias in the arrest of suspects of different racial groups. Self-report data also indicate that blacks are more likely than whites to commit serious offenses, but some self-report studies find that blacks and whites differ less in the rates at which they commit less serious crimes. Comparing blacks and whites of similar social backgrounds reduces the difference in their crime rates, but several studies have found that blacks have higher rates of involvement in crime even when people of the same backgrounds are compared. Blacks are more likely than whites to be the victims of violent crimes; blacks are also more likely to be the victims of most property crimes, even though they have a lower average income than whites. Violent crime most often occurs between an offender and a victim of the same race.

The relationship between social class and violation of the law is complex. In general, official arrest statistics show that lower-class adults commit more crimes than middle-class adults; the few self-report studies of adults find a similar but weaker association between social class and crime. Most studies of juvenile delinquency find an inverse relationship between social class and official measures of delinquency, but in some studies the relationship is not strong. Self-report studies of delinquency are mixed in their conclusions: some show an inverse relationship between social class and delinquency, and others find no relationship. Methodological problems with self-report studies make it difficult to unravel the exact relationship between social class and violation of the law, especially among adolescents. There is no clear-cut relationship between family income and victimization rates for property crimes, but rates of violent crimes decline with increasing income.

Important Terms

age-specific arrest rate   **hate crimes**
concentric-zone model   **social class**

Review Questions

1. Why do you think Japan has a lower crime rate than the United States?

2. What regional variations in rates of violent and property crime exist in the United States? How would you explain these variations?

3. Which kinds of communities in the United States have the highest crime rates? Why do you think this is the case?

4. What have been the trends in crime in the United States in recent decades? Why do you think crime rates have changed as they have in recent years?

5. Why are crime rates in the United States higher for men than for women, for younger people than older people, for blacks than whites, and for the lower class than the middle and upper classes?

6. What are hate crimes? What distinguishes these crimes from other crimes? Why did the federal government enact a law in 1990 to require the collection of official statistics on these crimes?

PART III

THE CAUSES OF CRIMINAL BEHAVIOR

Chapter 5 examines biological and psychological explanations of criminal behavior. We look at biological research on twins, adopted children, chromosomal abnormalities, and brain functioning that suggests that inherited factors may interact with psychological and social factors to cause crime. We also investigate research by psychologists on the link between intelligence and crime, the personality traits associated with criminal behavior, and the psychoanalytic perspective. Rules determining criminal responsibility, including the debate over the insanity defense, are also discussed.

Chapter 6 focuses on the socioeconomic sources of crime. Aspects of the economy and characteristics of corporations that are conducive to white-collar crime are investigated. Sources of income for organized crime are examined. In looking at conventional crime, we consider the impact of modernization, the relationship between unemployment and crime, and the way that a sense of being deprived can motivate people to violate the law. We look at several theories of delinquency: anomie, differential opportunity, reaction-formation, and lower-class culture as a generating milieu of delinquency. We consider the subculture-of-violence theory. Feminist theories of the relationship of gender and crime are also examined.

The ways that offenders neutralize the law and are free to violate it because of their weak attachments to conventional institutions are considered in **Chapter 7**. Techniques that people use to neutralize the hold that the law has over them are considered for embezzlement, crime by blacks, murder, and juvenile delinquency. Control theory is discussed, and evidence for this theory is assessed by looking at research on the family, the school, the peer group, religion, and migration.

Chapter 8 focuses on sources of learning to commit crime: the community, delinquent gangs and peer groups, the general culture, the mass media, sports, pornography, and correctional institutions. This chapter presents differential association theory and looks at evidence for that theory. This chapter also considers the labeling perspective, which proposes that crime and delinquency are the result of the effects of labeling on self-concepts, social opportunities and relationships, and membership in subcultures. Several reward-risk models of criminal behavior are also examined.

In **Chapter 9** we explore opportunities to commit crime and factors that facilitate criminal activity. We look at the way crime is linked to the routine activities in which people engage and at the way offenders choose their targets. We also examine the role of alcohol, drugs, and firearms in crime.

The cumulation of acts of crime into criminal careers is the subject of **Chapter 10**. Here we consider delinquent careers and the career patterns of adult offenders. We also look at the way career criminals eventually leave a life of crime for a conventional life.

The organization of criminal activity is examined in **Chapter 11**. Networks established for the purpose of violating the law are characteristic of organized crime syndicates, drug importers, art thieves, juvenile gangs, conventional violent offenders, and white-collar criminals. We look at the way that these ongoing relationships influence the form that criminal behavior takes.

Chapter 5
Biological and Psychological Explanations of Crime

Modern criminology began with the positivist approach of an Italian physician, Cesare Lombroso. His theories of crime causation have since been found deficient, but his emphasis on the collection of data to test hypotheses about criminals became the basis of modern criminology. Much criminological research is now conducted by sociologists, but biological and psychological approaches to the study of crime causation have been important in the past and continue to be so today.

Biological Explanations of Crime

Biological explanations of crime propose that offenders differ from nonoffenders in some physiological or anatomical way. The idea of a biologically unique criminal minimizes the role in crime causation of social conditions such as poverty and unemployment, and instead attributes crime to individual differences. One example of a biological explanation of criminal behavior can be seen in the movie *Frankenstein*, in which the monster apparently becomes destructive because Dr. Frankenstein's assistant stole an "abnormal" brain rather than a "normal" one to transplant into the monster's corpse.

Over the past two centuries, deviance in general and crime in particular have been seen increasingly in medical terms, being redefined over time as "sick" rather than "bad" behavior (Conrad and Schneider, 1980). This "medicalization" of deviance has given rise to an emphasis on rehabilitation and has led to a search for individual traits rather than social factors that will explain rule-breaking behavior. Some deviance—for instance, hyperactivity in children—has been explained in terms of biological factors, but the influence of the medical establishment has operated primarily through psychiatry, a branch of medicine that emphasizes psychological process more often than biological factors. The medicalization of deviance in modern society means we must look carefully at biological and psychological theories of crime, for those theories have played an important part in determining how the criminal justice system responds to criminals.

History of the Biological Perspective on Crime

The biological perspective on crime can be traced to about 1750, but this viewpoint was most dominant at the end of the nineteenth century and the beginning of the twentieth. With the rise of modern psychology and psychiatry in the early twentieth century, the biological perspective lost influence in criminology, although important work continues to be done by biological researchers.

Physiognomists and Phrenologists   Between 1750 and 1850, physiognomists and phrenologists tried to show links between criminal behavior and biological factors. Physiognomists studied facial features and sought a correlation between criminal behavior and characteristics such as the shape of the ears or the eyes. Phrenologists stressed the relationship between the external shape of the skull and an individual's propensity to engage in crime. They thought that studying the shape of the skull would allow them to tell which areas of a person's brain would dominate behavior and possibly lead to crime. Modern research indicates that certain areas of the brain do control particular types of behavior and that stimulating certain parts of the brain can incite violence, which might be socially defined as crime. However, phrenologists failed to understand the complexity of the brain and did not demonstrate any relationship between skull shape, behavioral control centers in the brain, and criminal behavior. Both phrenologists and physiognomists failed to test their theories in a methodologically sound way, but they did draw attention to the possibility that offenders and nonoffenders might differ in measurable ways.

Lombroso's Theory of the Atavism   Cesare Lombroso explored what he thought were the physically distinctive features of criminals. After examining the skull of a notorious Italian criminal, he observed:

> At the sight of that skull, I seemed to see all of a sudden, lighted up as a vast plain under a flaming sky, the problem of the nature of the criminal—an atavistic being who reproduces in his person the ferocious instincts of primitive humanity and the inferior animals. Thus were explained anatomically the enormous jaws, high cheek bones, prominent superciliary arches, solitary lines in the palms, extreme size of the orbits, handle-shaped or sensile ears found in criminals, savages and apes, insensibility to pain, extremely acute sight, tattooing, excessive idleness, love of orgies, and the irresistible craving of evil for its own sake, the desire not only to extinguish life in the victim, but to mutilate the corpse, tear its flesh and drink its blood. (Lombroso, 1911: xiv)

Lombroso theorized that criminals were **atavisms**, people "born out of time" who were similar to primitive people or lower animals in their biological makeup. This theory owed much to the influence of Darwinism at the end of the nineteenth century, but the idea that people could revert to an earlier stage of evolutionary development was not widely accepted even then.

Lombroso also erred in his ideas about what features could be inherited. For example, the tattoos he said were characteristic of criminals were obviously not inherited. Some of the features he thought were typical of offenders might have been the product of both inheritance and diet, with the latter being a function of income, education, and other social factors.

Lombroso made several important mistakes in testing his theory. He failed to select in a careful way a control group from the general population with which to compare criminals. In addition, many of the differences between criminals and noncriminals that he documented were small enough to have occurred by chance.

Lombroso's most important contributions to modern criminology were the application of measurement and the testing of hypotheses. As a result of this positivist method, his ideas on crime causation were revised, and he increasingly took social and environmental factors into account. In the final edition of his textbook on the criminal offender, Lombroso suggested that as few as one offender in three might be a born criminal. Other types were insane criminals and occasional offenders who were the products of a poor social environment. Nevertheless, the born offender remained at the center of Lombroso's work, and he never did systematic research on the social causes of criminal behavior.

Post-Lombrosian Researchers: Goring and Hooton   Several researchers built on Lombroso's ideas. The Englishman Charles Goring (1870–1919) sought to test Lombroso's theory that offenders had certain physical defects or anomalies. Goring found no significant differences between offenders and groups from the general population in skull shape, eye color, hair color, or various other physical traits. He did find what he thought was a real difference in height and weight, with offenders being shorter and lighter than nonoffenders. Still, Goring (1913: 173) concluded that "there is no such thing as a physical criminal type."

Earnest Hooton, an American anthropologist who worked on crime causation during the 1930s, criticized Goring's research. Hooton (1939) contended that criminals were the products of environmental influences on organically inferior people. However, he failed to provide a clear meaning for the idea of physical inferiority or how it might lead to criminal behavior. He offered no satisfactory evidence that "physical inferiority" was inherited rather than acquired. Moreover, Hooton's research contained important methodological problems; for instance, he did not compare offenders with a carefully chosen and random sample of nonoffenders.

Sheldon's Theory of Somatotypes   One biological theory that relies on psychological traits is William Sheldon's theory of **somatotypes** or body types. This theory focuses on differences among individuals in embryonic development and claims that people with different body types have different temperaments that affect their propensity to engage in crime and delinquency.

Sheldon, an American psychologist and physician, developed a rating scheme to classify bodies as one of three basic types. One study found that endomorphs, who are slow, "soft," and comfort-loving, exhibited no particular tendency to be delinquent, nor did ectomorphs, who are described as lean and fragile. However, mesomorphs, described as muscular, active, and aggressive, were twice as common among delinquents as they were among the general population (Glueck and Glueck, 1950, 1956). This association between mesomorphy and delinquency might result from a propensity by the police and the courts to label as delinquent those adolescents who are most muscular, active, and aggressive. A review of biological theories of crime concluded that "empirical research has revealed little evidence for the unique temperamental traits that Sheldon ascribed to the three somatotypes" (Pollock, Mednick, and Gabrielli, 1983: 309).

Modern Biological Research on Crime

The modern biological approach to the study of crime proposes that there is great variation among individuals in biological strengths and weaknesses, and that individuals with certain "vulnerabilities" have a greater risk of responding to stressful environmental conditions with antisocial behavior (Fishbein, 1996). Contemporary biologists and medical researchers have used various strategies to test the impact on crime and delinquency of physical traits and inherited characteristics.

Twin Studies One potentially rewarding approach to the study of biological influences on criminal behavior is the study of twins. Identical twins develop from a single female egg and have no hereditary differences. Fraternal twins develop from two eggs and do have hereditary differences. Researchers can thus look at the relative impact on crime of heredity and environment by comparing the criminality of identical twins with the criminality of fraternal twins of the same sex. Evidence for genetic factors would take the form of a higher **concordance rate**, or similarity of criminal behavior, between identical twins than between fraternal twins.

The results of twin studies done in the United States, Japan, and Europe between 1929 and 1962 are consistent with the idea that inherited factors influence criminal behavior. The concordance rates for identical twins were between 60 and 70 percent in these studies, but the concordance rates for fraternal twins were only 15 to 30 percent. However, because of methodological problems with the studies, they exaggerated the importance of genetics (Pollock, Mednick, and Gabrielli, 1983).

In what is perhaps the best twin study to date, Karl Christiansen (1974, 1977) examined all 3,586 pairs of twins born in one area of Denmark between 1881 and 1910. He found that if one identical twin had a criminal conviction, the other twin also had a conviction in 35 percent of the cases. The rate of concordance was only 12 percent for fraternal twins. Similar results were produced from a study of twins in Norway (Dalgaard and Kringlen, 1976). In a study in Ohio, a researcher found that concordance rates for self-reported delinquency were higher for identical twins than for fraternal twins (Rowe,

Studies of twins, such as England's notorious Kray brothers depicted here in the film "The Krays," find that identical twins are more similar in their criminal behavior than fraternal twins.

1983). In general, these studies yielded smaller differences in rates of concordance between identical twins and fraternal twins than early researchers had found; this was probably due to the poor methodology of the older studies.

Identical twins are more alike biologically than fraternal twins, and recent researchers acknowledge that because identical twins look more alike, they are probably more apt than fraternal twins to have similar environments when young and to receive similar treatment by parents, relatives, peers, and teachers. As a result, we would expect identical twins to be socialized in ways that are more alike than is true of fraternal twins, and thus similar behavior by identical twins cannot be attributed solely or even primarily to hereditary factors. A review of the research on twins concludes as follows:

> No definitive conclusions can be drawn from twin studies of aggressiveness or criminal behavior because no consistent pattern of genetic influence emerges. Nevertheless, twin studies of criminal and related behaviors fairly consistently provide some intriguing evidence for a genetic effect, and genetic influences warrant continued, but more rigorous, study. (Fishbein, 1990: 45)

Adoption Studies   An ideal method to test the relative importance of biological and environmental influences on crime would be to study identical and fraternal twins who are separated at birth and who never have contact again, and then compare their crime rates as adults. Because this situation is too rare to provide sizable samples for study, researchers have turned to other approaches. One that is promising is the study of adopted children, who are usually separated from their biological parents at a young age and often never see those parents again. Researchers have compared the criminality of adoptees with that of their biological parents and their adoptive parents. These studies are not without methodological problems, particularly in measuring subjects' involvement in crime and delinquency and in ensuring that subjects have a similar duration of biological parenting.

A study of all 14,427 adoptions that occurred in Denmark from 1924 to 1947 found that children who had biological parents with criminal convictions had a greater chance of themselves being involved in repetitive property crimes, but they had no greater propensity to engage in violent crimes. Among sons raised by adoptive parents, only 13.5 percent had a criminal conviction if neither their biological parents nor their adoptive parents had a criminal conviction. If their adoptive parents had been convicted of a crime but their biological parents had not, the proportion of the sons convicted of a crime rose slightly to 14.7 percent. However, if at least one of the biological parents had been convicted of a crime and the adoptive parents had not been, 20 percent of the sons had a conviction. If both the biological and the adoptive parents had criminal convictions, then 24.5 percent of the sons also had criminal convictions (see Figure 5.1). Similar results were found for female adoptees. This research is consistent with the theory that inherited factors influence criminal behavior, because the data indicate that the criminality of a child's biological parents is a better predictor of the child's criminality than is the criminality of the child's adoptive parents. However, the

% convicted   % not convicted

24.5	75.5

Biological and adoptive parents both convicted of crimes
(Number = 143)

20	80

Biological parents convicted of crimes, but adoptive parents not convicted
(Number = 1,226)

14.7	85.3

Biological parents not convicted of crimes, but adoptive parents convicted
(Number = 204)

13.5	86.5

Neither biological nor adoptive parents convicted of crimes
(Number = 2,492)

FIGURE 5.1

Percentage of Adopted Sons Convicted of Crimes, as Related to Whether Their Biological and Adoptive Parents Have Been Convicted of Crimes

Source: Based on Sarnoff A. Mednick, William F. Gabrielli, Jr., and Barry Hutchings, "Genetic Factors in the Etiology of Criminal Behavior," in Sarnoff A. Mednick, Terrie E. Moffitt, and Susan A. Stack, eds., *The Causes of Crime: New Biological Approaches.* Cambridge, Eng.: Cambridge University Press, 1987, p. 75.

researchers did not claim that the data proved that inherited traits cause crime. Instead, they cautiously concluded that inherited traits might lead some people who are raised in certain ways and who live in certain circumstances to become criminal more often than people in the same situation who lack the inherited traits (Pollock, Mednick, and Gabrielli, 1983; Mednick, Gabrielli, and Hutchings, 1987).

According to one review of adoption studies, the evidence on genetic involvement in crime causation is even stronger than those researchers asserted. This review states that the evidence provided by adoption studies approaches the limits of certainty in demonstrating a genetic influence on crime causation, with an adopted person's chance of being convicted of a serious crime more accurately predicted from knowledge of the criminal record of that person's biological parents than from knowledge of the criminal record of that person's adoptive parents. According to this observer,

to the degree that causal statements can ever be made with finality in science, the adoption studies carried out in the decade just past seem to be making the following, cautiously worded pronouncement about the involvement of genetics in criminal behavior possible: Significant amounts of the observed variation in human tendencies to behave criminally appear to be the result of some genetic factors, presumably operating on the functioning of the nervous system (at least for the variations observed in criminal behavior other than those describable as victimless and status offenses). (Ellis, 1982: 57)

Others have taken a more critical view of adoption studies. A reanalysis of the evidence from Denmark concluded that it pointed in the direction supporting the heredity-crime hypothesis, but that the magnitude of the association was "at best insubstantial" (Gottfredson and Hirschi, 1990: 56). An examination of thirty-eight previous studies found "a consistent and statistically significant association between various indices of heredity and crime," even though "the actual magnitude of the relationship was modest" (Walters, 1992: 604, 606). The studies that used the best methodology were the least likely to support the heredity-crime hypothesis. Support for this hypothesis was weaker in the adoption studies, which seem to be the purest way to investigate the influence of heredity on crime, than it was in either twin or family studies, which encounter more difficulty separating the effects of heredity from environmental influences.

The XYY Chromosome Complement   The possibility that abnormalities in the sex-determining chromosome could account for crime received much attention during the 1960s. There are twenty-three pairs of chromosomes in humans, one of which is the sex chromosome pair. The female usually has an XX pair, and the male normally has an XY pair. Beginning with the discovery of an **XYY chromosome complement** in some men in 1961, several unusual combinations have been found. During the 1960s there was speculation in the press and by some criminologists that men with the XYY complement might be prone to aggressive and violent crime. This idea apparently reflected the assumption that if the Y chromosome in the sex-determining pair makes a person a male, an extra Y should make that person a "supermale," hence more violent than the average male.

A cohort study in Denmark tested 4,139 tall men from a cohort of 31,436 men born in Copenhagen from 1944 to 1947 (Witkin et al., 1976). The reason that only tall men were studied is that earlier research had shown that XYY men are taller than average. This study found only twelve men with an XYY combination. The infrequency of this chromosome complement suggests that even if it is associated with criminal behavior, it would account for relatively little of the crime that is committed. This Danish study found that 42 percent of the twelve XYY men had been convicted of at least one crime, compared with only 9 percent of the XY group. In spite of the small number of men with the XYY combination, this difference was statistically significant; that is, the difference was very unlikely to have occurred by chance. However, the crimes for which the XYY men were convicted were not violent ones; there was no meaningful difference between the XYYs and the XYs in convictions for violent offenses.

The XYY men showed significantly lower levels of intelligence than the XY men, but both groups had attained similar educational levels. Comparing XYY men with XY men of similar intelligence, educational attainment, height, and social status, the researchers found that the XYY group was still more likely to have a criminal record. The researchers concluded that the XYY chromosome combination does not seem to predispose men to violent crime, but it might be tied to a higher-than-average likelihood of being detected for other kinds of crime (Witkin et al., 1976).

A follow-up to this study that used the same data found that differences in intelligence could not fully explain the excess criminality of the XYYs over the XYs. The XYYs were found to have different electroencephalogram (EEG) readings of brain activity and lower galvanic skin resistance (GSR) readings that measured arousability by noxious stimuli and rate of recovery after arousal (Volavka et al., 1977). In other words, the XYY combination might be linked to nonviolent crime through factors that are associated with brain functioning and the autonomic nervous system.

Sex Differences   Earlier we examined differences in crime rates between males and females. The fact that male and female crime rates differ to varying degrees from one society to another suggests that much of the sex difference in crime rates is due to social and cultural factors. However, the fact that men commit more crime than women in all societies suggests that some of the difference could be the result of biological differences between the sexes.

One review of research on differences in aggressiveness between males and females cites developmental studies that show that children under six do not seem to imitate the behavior of same-sexed adults (Maccoby and Jacklin, 1980; Mednick et al., 1982). However, most studies of children under six also reveal that boys are significantly more aggressive than girls; none of those studies finds more aggressiveness among girls. The data thus "suggest strongly that greater male aggressiveness is present in children before social learning can explain it. It is a likely hypothesis that greater aggressiveness in males is related to their higher levels of male sex hormones" (Mednick et al., 1982: 30). There is, however, little direct proof that male-female differences in aggressiveness are caused primarily by differences in sex hormones. One review of the research concluded as follows:

> Correlations between circulating testosterone levels and violence have been sought in a number of studies, which have employed different groups of subjects and different methods for quantifying levels of aggression and violence. These studies have ranged from the analysis of hostility questionnaires administered to normal male college students to the collection of histories of violent acts in male prisoners. Most have shown no relation between circulating testosterone and the behavioral measures, although a few intriguing studies have revealed higher testosterone levels in groups of especially violent persons, such as incarcerated rapist-murderers. (Rubin, 1987: 256–257)

A recent study pointed to the need to integrate biological and social factors in an explanation of crime, finding that testosterone had a moderately strong relationship with adult deviance, but primarily through the influence of testosterone on social integration and prior juvenile delinquent behavior (Booth and Osgood, 1993).

Compared to females, males have lower activity levels of monoamine oxidase (MAO), a neurologically active enzyme that is controlled by genetic and hormonal factors. Lower MAO activity levels are, in general, correlated with higher probabilities of criminal behavior and modestly associated with the following behavior patterns linked to criminality: extreme impulsiveness, childhood hyperactivity (attention deficit disorder), poor academic performance, sensation seeking, and recreational alcohol and drug use. Thus, sex differences in criminal behavior could be associated to some modest degree with sex differences in MAO activity levels (Ellis, 1991).

A few studies suggest that crime committed by women is more likely to occur in the four premenstrual days and the four days of menstruation than it is to occur at other times during the menstrual cycle (Shah and Roth, 1974; Ginsburg and Carter, 1987). In recent years, attention has been paid to **premenstrual syndrome (PMS),** a set of symptoms that includes tension, nervousness, irritability, fatigue, headaches, cramps, and depressed moods. PMS does not manifest itself in the same way in all women who suffer from it, and some doubt that it is a single condition. Even though PMS has been introduced in British courts as a factor to mitigate the sentences of some female offenders, the evidence for its association with crime is still unclear. Women experiencing PMS may simply be more likely to be arrested for crimes they commit during their premenstrual and menstrual days, perhaps because their reaction time is slower then or because they are more fatigued. Moreover, the changes associated with menstruation do not cause most women to commit crime, and women who do violate the law commit crimes at other times during their menstrual cycles (Shah and Roth, 1974; Fishbein, 1990).

Biochemical Factors and Temperament   There is growing evidence that some violent behavior is associated with defects in the neurotransmitters serotonin, dopamine, and norepinephrine. Serotonin reduces aggressiveness by inhibiting behavioral responses to emotional stimuli; violent and impulsive behavior seems to be more common among people with lower levels of serotonin. Dopamine and norepinephrine are excitatory neurotransmitters that counteract the inhibitory effects of serotonin, and so an imbalance in the activities of these neurotransmitters can produce mood disorders and aggressive behavior (Fishbein, 1996).

Some research suggests that a variant gene that influences the brain's response to dopamine might be linked to "novelty-seeking," a personality trait that predisposes people to be impulsive, quick-tempered, and excitable. Other research contradicts that conclusion (Angier, 1996a, 1996b). Whether novelty-seeking is linked to crime is not clear, but some sociological studies (for example, Katz, 1988) have emphasized the importance to criminals of the excitement generated by breaking the law.

Brain Dysfunctions, Learning Disabilities, and Conditionability   There is growing evidence that brain dysfunctions and neurological defects are more common among excessively violent people than among the general population (Fishbein and Thatcher, 1986). Many violent offenders seem to have defects in the frontal and temporal lobes of the brain that are associated with impaired self-control. The rate of epilepsy seems to be higher among delinquents than among nondelinquents, even though most epileptics are not delinquents. In spite of such evidence, researchers have been cautious in concluding that such abnormalities cause criminal behavior. One reason is that some studies, such as those examining the link between epilepsy and crime, reach contradictory conclusions (Pollock, Mednick, and Gabrielli, 1983). Another reason is that the cause-effect relationship is not clear. For example, physical abuse of a child can cause severe head injuries, including brain damage that leads to violent outbursts; but children who are the victims of such abuse may also learn to be violent by observing their parents' behavior.

Delinquents seem to be more likely than nondelinquents to have neurological problems (Fishbein and Thatcher, 1986). There is also some evidence that the parents of violent delinquents have more neurological problems than the parents of nonviolent delinquents, suggesting the possibility of a genetic factor associated with adolescent violence. Violent delinquency is not inherited behavior, but children can inherit a susceptibility to stress that could lead them to engage in violence in certain situations (Lewis et al., 1979). (See the Using Criminology box.)

Some delinquents and criminals produce abnormal EEG readings of brain activity (Mednick and Volavka, 1980; Mednick et al., 1981, 1982; Pollock, Mednick, and Gabrielli, 1983; Fishbein and Thatcher, 1986). Research suggests that the EEGs of criminals may be similar to those of normal people at younger ages, suggesting that antisocial behavior might be associated with, though not necessarily caused by, "brain immaturity" (Mednick et al., 1981, 1982; Fishbein, 1990).

There is good evidence that delinquency is associated with **learning disabilities**, which are "impairments in sensory and motor functioning which lead to deviant classroom performance, and are the product of some abnormal physical condition" (Holzman, 1979: 78). The causes of learning disabilities are not well understood, but they seem at least partly rooted in neurological dysfunction (Fishbein and Thatcher, 1986). Lead poisoning could be one cause of such problems (Denno, 1994). One learning disability is dyslexia, the failure to attain language skills commensurate with intellectual abilities. Another is aphasia, a problem of communicating verbally or understanding others' speech. A third learning disability is hyperactivity, or attention deficit disorder, which involves excessive inattentiveness and restlessness. One study found that hyperactive children were six times as likely to be arrested during adolescence as were children without that disorder, and that upper-class children who were hyperactive were as likely to be arrested as lower-class children who were hyperactive (Satterfield, 1987).

Hans Eysenck (1977; Eysenck and Gudjonsson, 1989) has proposed that criminals can be distinguished from noncriminals by the absence of conscience. Conscience is the product of conditioning, which depends on the sensitivity of the autonomic nervous system that a person has inherited (a biological influence) and on the quality of conditioning that a person receives during childhood (a social-environmental influence). Criminals, according to

USING CRIMINOLOGY

Neurological and Psychological Problems of Juveniles Condemned to Death

In November 1987, a study of fourteen death-row inmates who had been convicted of crimes committed when they were under the age of eighteen was presented to the United States Supreme Court. The inmates were all juveniles who had been condemned to death in the only four states that allowed Dorothy Otnow Lewis and her colleagues to carry out their research. The inmates had been convicted of murders committed when they were between the ages of fifteen years ten months and seventeen years ten months, with a mean age of sixteen years six months. There were an additional twenty-three inmates under sentence of death for crimes committed as juveniles in other states.

Lewis and her colleagues found that of their fourteen subjects,

- eight had suffered injuries to the central nervous system that were severe enough to result in hospitalization and/or an indentation of the cranium;
- nine had major neurological impairment;

- seven were psychotic or had been diagnosed as psychotic earlier in childhood, four had histories indicating severe mood disorders, and the other three experienced occasional paranoid ideation;
- only two subjects had IQ (intelligence quotient) levels above 90 (which is below average), and only three were reading at grade level;
- twelve had been brutally, physically abused, and five had been sodomized by older male relatives.

The researchers concluded that these handicaps were potential mitigating factors that might have been used to argue against imposition of the death penalty. However, the youths had little recognition of their vulnerabilities or the way they might have mitigated their punishment. Indeed, most of the juveniles tried to hide evidence of their problems, claiming that they were not crazy or retarded and concealing their parents' brutality toward them. Their parents also hid such evidence, sometimes pressuring their child's attorney

this theory, are less easily conditioned than other people. Because they have autonomic nervous systems that allow them to ignore pain and punishment with relative ease, they must be subjected to especially strong environmental stimuli in order to develop consciences that will inhibit criminal behavior (Shah and Roth, 1974; Mednick and Volavka, 1980; McCord, 1983; Ellis, 1987). These individuals recover more slowly when aroused by noxious stimuli and are aroused less easily by such stimuli. People with this physical makeup may also engage in risk-taking or thrill-seeking behavior, sometimes in the form of violent and impulsive crime, in order to compensate for the stimulation they otherwise lack. Some research indicates that the suboptimal arousal level of such individuals might be related to a deficiency of serotonin, a chemical that transmits signals from one brain cell to another (Ellis, 1987; Fishbein, 1990).

Some people might be more biologically predisposed than others to crime and delinquency, although many people who are predisposed that way still learn to conform to the law. Brain disorders, learning disabilities, and poor conditionability can predispose individuals to crime and delinquency,

USING CRIMINOLOGY

to keep such information secret. In only five of the fourteen cases were any pretrial evaluations of the youths carried out, and those evaluations were usually perfunctory and yielded inadequate data on the juveniles' neuropsychiatric and cognitive functioning.

Steven Pincus, an attorney who worked on this study, concluded as follows:

> This study demonstrates that people who are on death row for committing crimes as juveniles have major psychiatric problems, neurological problems, and educational and learning problems. The law says that if someone's capacity is diminished—and the capacities of these juveniles clearly are—that needs to be considered in any calculation of moral blameworthiness. (Cited in Bass, 1988: 53)

These findings were considered by the Supreme Court in reaching its June 1988 decision that it is unconstitutional to execute anyone convicted of a crime committed under the age of six-

teen, unless a state's law explicitly allows for the execution of such youthful offenders. The following year the Court considered the constitutionality of executing offenders who had committed their crimes when they were between the ages of sixteen and eighteen, the age range in which most of the researchers' subjects fell. In June 1989 the Court upheld state laws that permitted the execution of offenders who had committed their crimes between the ages of sixteen and eighteen, with the majority of the Court holding that there was no societal consensus that such executions were "cruel and unusual punishment" prohibited by the Eighth Amendment.

Sources: Based on Dorothy Otnow Lewis et al., "Neuropsychiatric, Psychoeducational, and Family Characteristics of 14 Juveniles Condemned to Death in the United States," *American Journal of Psychiatry* 145 (May 1988), 584–589; Alison Bass, "Head Injuries Found in Young Killers," *Boston Globe*, June 20, 1988, pp. 53, 55.

---

but those problems can also lead to rejection and stigmatization of people who seem unintelligent or unable to function socially. This rejection by itself could be conducive to violation of the law. Brain disorders, learning disabilities, and poor conditionability may also be reflected in poor academic performance and rejection by teachers, both of which can be conducive to delinquency. As Figure 5.2 shows, brain disorders, learning disabilities, and poor conditionability could directly lead to delinquency and crime, or they might increase the likelihood of delinquency and crime indirectly by leading to social rejection or academic failure.

Biology and Modern Criminology

There are several reasons that many modern criminologists have paid little attention to biological explanations of crime and delinquency. One is that relatively little research on crime and delinquency has been done by biologists and medical researchers. Some of their early work was based on a lack of understanding of the human brain and was marred by poor methodology. The political abuse of the biological approach in Nazi Germany also made this perspective suspect in the eyes of many criminologists. More recently, the technical nature of the language used by biological researchers has made it difficult

FIGURE 5.2
Possible Links of Brain Disorders, Learning Disabilities, and Poor Conditionability to Crime
and Delinquency

for those from other fields to understand their studies. As a result, many criminologists have ignored or prematurely dismissed biological studies of crime.

Some criminologists react hostilely to the biological perspective because
it is viewed as a threat to the ideology of welfare liberalism and social change
to which they adhere. Heredity appears unchangeable, and a theory that
stresses biological causes of crime seems to imply that efforts to reduce crime
through social change are misguided. Criticism of this sort led the National
Institutes of Health (NIH) to withdraw funding for a conference on the genetic
basis of criminal behavior that was to have been held at the University of
Maryland in October 1992. Opponents of the conference claimed that the
search for genetic sources of crime was thinly veiled racism and a way to
avoid looking at the impact of poverty and discrimination on crime. The NIH
believed that those planning the conference were too willing to accept the
idea that crime was genetically caused, and it feared that such research could
be used to single out for treatment people who were predisposed to violence.
Conference planners objected to the cancellation as a violation of academic
freedom and pointed out that the meeting would have considered ethical
issues involved in the study of the link between heredity and crime (Hilts,
1992). When the revamped conference was finally held in September 1995,
the meaning of biological research on violence received more attention than
did the content of that research, and participants agreed on the need for better funding of social programs to combat crime. There was discussion of possible genetic predispositions to crime, as well as the idea that individuals are
still responsible for their actions to a large degree, and no genetic solution to
the crime problem was proposed (Angier, 1995; Jeffery, 1996).

Another reason criminologists have paid little attention to biological
research in recent years is that this work does not seem to explain geographic,

temporal, and social variations in crime rates. Biological explanations do not help us understand why crime rates vary from one nation to another, from one region to another, or among communities of different sizes. Likewise, these theories do not seem to explain changes in crime rates over time, for there is no evidence that increases and decreases in crime rates are associated with changes in biological factors. Biological factors might account for some of the difference between the sexes in crimes of violence, but they do not seem to explain differences in property crimes. Biological research has not yet offered a good explanation of why crime rates peak in the late teens and early twenties and then decline with age. There is no evidence that biological differences among racial groups explain differences in crime rates among those groups; racial groups are socially defined categories rather than biologically distinguishable groupings. Finally, there seems to be no way for biological theories to account for social class differences in crime rates, for the factors on which biological researchers have focused are not associated with class standing in any obvious way.

Modern biological researchers do not dismiss nonbiological explanations of crime and delinquency, nor do they claim that all criminals and delinquents have physiological or anatomical disorders that cause them to violate the law. Indeed, biological criminologists often go only so far as to say that some physical factors are associated with a propensity to crime and delinquency, not that such factors cause people to violate the law. Thus, genetic factors are usually seen as interacting with the familial and social environment to increase the probability that a person will violate the law, rather than seen as operating alone to cause crime and delinquency (Mednick and Volavka, 1980; Rowe and Osgood, 1984; Fishbein, 1990; Denno, 1990; Walters, 1992).

One criticism of biological work on crime is that inherited traits are specific, but crime is a very broad concept. Thus, for biological researchers to make progress in their search for the causes of crime, they must focus on links between specific inheritable traits and specific kinds of criminal behavior. In a sense, there cannot be an inherited predisposition to violate a socially created law, but it is possible that certain inherited predispositions might be linked to behavior such as violence that is sometimes defined as crime.

Inherited traits can create a "range of potential" for behavior, even if they do not determine behavior; in other words, biological factors might limit the kind of behavior a person will engage in, even if the constraints are very broad. Often biological factors interact with social and environmental influences to make certain behavior more likely, as we can see in the following example from research on monkeys:

> It has been demonstrated that aggressive behavior can be evoked in free-ranging monkeys by stimulation of implanted intracerebral electrodes. However, such stimulation produces differing results depending upon the hierarchical structure of the monkey colony. Monkeys exhibit aggressive behavior with this stimulation when a submissive monkey is present as a target, but such responses are inhibited (despite the brain stimulation) in the presence of a dominant animal. (Shah and Roth, 1974: 106)

Research on humans suggests that the hierarchical structure of social relationships might influence an individual's propensity to homicide, but this research did not look at biological predispositions that might interact with the social context to produce violent behavior (Henry and Short, 1954).

Some criminologists have worked to develop an interdisciplinary approach that incorporates biological, psychological, and social factors (Jeffery, 1979; Mednick and Volavka, 1980; Ellis, 1982; Fishbein, 1996). One example is a longitudinal study of crime and delinquency that followed 987 black Philadelphia residents from birth through early adulthood (Denno, 1994). In looking at the correlates of gender differences in crime and delinquency in this sample, Deborah Denno concluded that

> biological factors (such as abnormal movements, left-foot and right-eye preference, and neurological abnormalities) are more significant predictors of crime among females; whereas environmental factors (such as lead intoxication, father's employment status, and number of household moves) are more significant predictors of crime among males. Indicators of family stability were important for both males and females—the lack of foster parents and father absence were important for females, and father's employment and household moves were important for males. (Denno, 1994: 117)

Overall, this Biosocial Study found that biological, psychological, and social factors interact in complex ways to generate crime and delinquency, with the data suggesting that

> delinquency is related to family instability and, most importantly, to a lack of behavioral control associated with neurological and later central nervous system disorders. It appears that attention deficit disorder and hyperactivity, which are part of disciplinary problems, are associated with the learning and behavioral disorders evidenced in some members of the Biosocial Study sample. These disorders would considerably inhibit the ability of young children to create social bonds even before the school experience. Academic failure would perpetuate misconduct and impede attempts at future social bonding. Indeed, a sizable amount of research shows that children who evidence attention deficit disorder and hyperactivity are significantly more likely to retain antisocial tendencies during adulthood, a time when most individuals start to show commitments to socially desirable behavior. (Denno, 1994: 119–120)

Psychological Explanations of Crime

The once-popular view that the criminal is biologically different was replaced during the twentieth century with the idea that the criminal is somehow psychologically abnormal. This view that offenders are "crazy" or "unbalanced" underlies the philosophy of rehabilitation that leads to the counseling of offenders by psychiatrists, psychologists, and social workers. The logic of this approach is that because only certain individuals commit crimes, something must distinguish them from those who do not break the law.

Mental Deficiency Theory

The mental deficiency theory of crime maintains that offenders either lack the intelligence to appreciate the reasons for the existence of the law and thus violate it, or are unable to control their actions if they are aware of the law. Nonoffenders are seen as intelligent enough to understand the law and control their actions.

IQ and Crime Intelligence, which is usually measured by IQ tests, has been linked to crime and delinquency by many researchers. Sometimes they claim that intelligence is inherited, but most modern researchers do not claim that intelligence is solely genetic in origin.

IQ tests have repeatedly been shown to contain cultural biases, in spite of efforts to develop unbiased tests. For instance, whites might average somewhat higher scores on IQ tests than blacks because those tests reflect the cultural biases of the whites who design the tests. As a result of such problems, critics claim that IQ tests measure social learning rather than native intelligence. The inadequacy of IQ tests is one reason to look at research on the link between intelligence and criminality with some skepticism.

Another reason for skepticism is the inadequate research design that some of the studies have employed. For example, researchers have administered IQ tests to prisoners and then compared the prisoners' IQs with those of a group from the general population. This kind of research encounters several methodological problems. First, prisoners are not necessarily representative of all people who violate the law; indeed, prisoners might be the least competent of all offenders. Thus, researchers are often comparing *prisoners* with the general population, not *criminals* with the general population. Second, the "general population" to which the prisoners are compared includes many people who have violated the law but who are not in prison at the time of the study. As a result, researchers often end up comparing those offenders who are imprisoned with a sample of the general population that is not in prison but includes some offenders. Such a research design does not allow us to say much about what distinguishes criminals from noncriminals. A better approach would be to administer IQ tests to a randomly chosen cross section of the nation's population (including prisoners), gather evidence on that sample's involvement in crime from official arrest records and self-report questionnaires, and then examine the relationship between IQ and both officially recorded and self-reported crime.

Evidence on IQ and Crime One study that employed a good research design to study the relationship between intelligence and delinquency concluded that if boys of the same class are compared, delinquents generally have lower IQs than nondelinquents. In other words, a lower-class delinquent usually has a lower IQ than a lower-class nondelinquent, and a middle-class delinquent generally has a lower IQ than a middle-class nondelinquent (Reiss and Rhodes, 1961). This study also found that lower-class boys are more likely to be delinquent than middle-class boys of the same level of intelligence. Thus, class affects delinquency (whether measured by self-reports or court records), and intelligence as measured by standardized IQ tests is also related to delinquency.

Hirschi and Hindelang (1977) claim that sociologists regularly ignore or deny the role of individual differences such as intelligence in the genesis of crime and delinquency because "kinds of people" theories are seen as nonsociological. Their systematic review of the research literature showed that there is a small but consistent and reliable difference of about nine points between the IQs of delinquents and the IQs of nondelinquents. Evidence for this difference came from studies carried out in diverse settings using different IQ tests and controlling for race and social class. They concluded that IQ is an important correlate of delinquency that seems to be as closely linked to delinquency as race and social class.

Several cohort studies have found an association between delinquency and IQ test scores. Wolfgang, Figlio, and Sellin (1972) found that the average IQ of boys who had been stopped by the police was 101, compared with an average of 108 for boys who had not been stopped. Looking at boys of the same race and social class, the researchers found that IQ scores were still three to five points lower for delinquents than for nondelinquents. An English cohort study (West, 1982) found that boys who were to become delinquent as teenagers scored an average of 95 on IQ tests at ages eight and ten, and boys who did not become delinquent during their teen years scored an average of 101 at ages eight and ten. This difference of six points showed that performance on IQ tests at a young age is a good predictor of future delinquency.

A cohort study carried out in New Zealand examined the relationship between scores on several neuropsychological tests and delinquency as measured by police, court, and self-report data (Moffitt, Lynam, and Silva, 1994). Test scores at age thirteen were not associated with delinquency that started in adolescence, but those scores did predict the early onset and subsequent persistence of male delinquency. As other studies have found (see Moffitt, 1993), verbal skills and verbal memory were the factors most strongly associated with delinquency. The researchers concluded as follows:

> Children who have difficulty expressing themselves and remembering information are significantly handicapped. Dysfunctional communication between a child and his parents, peers, and teachers may be one of the most critical risk factors for childhood conduct problems that grow into persistent antisocial behavior in young adulthood. (Moffitt, Lynam, and Silva, 1994: 296)

Interpreting Research on IQ and Crime   One criticism of the conclusion that delinquency is related to intelligence is that IQ test scores, which supposedly measure native intelligence, are significantly influenced by the social environment. By changing social conditions, IQ test scores can be raised by even more than the difference that researchers have found between delinquents and nondelinquents.

Hirschi and Hindelang point out that differences in IQ between delinquents and nondelinquents are consistent with some sociological theories of crime causation. If intelligence affects school performance and attitudes toward the school and its teachers, lower intelligence may be associated with a lower "stake in conformity," which can increase the chance that an adolescent will engage in delinquent behavior.

Another interpretation of the association between intelligence and delinquency is that instead of low intelligence producing trouble in school and thus generating delinquency, it may be that lower-class status is associated with both delinquency and trouble in school, and trouble in school may lead to a failure to learn. This failure to learn might then be reflected in lower IQ scores, which would produce correlations among class, IQ scores, and delinquency. Lack of motivation to do well in school might show up in the results of IQ tests, which can be seen as a measure of academic performance rather than of basic intelligence.

One structuralist interpretation of the evidence linking IQ and delinquency is that this association exists only because of specific responses by institutions such as the school to low levels of intelligence, low IQ test scores, and poor academic performance. Thus,

> the absence of access to desirable social roles plus premature and/or inappropriate negative labeling mutually reinforce one another and lead to alienation, a rejection of the rejectors. Alienation, in turn, leads to delinquent behavior. The behavior generated by institutional structures through opportunity and labeling may then feed back into the institutional structure, generating responses which reinforce that behavior. (Menard and Morse, 1984: 1349)

An empirical test of this theory with self-report data revealed that structural variables—access to desirable social roles, negative labeling, alienation, and delinquent peer-group association—explained significant amounts of both serious and nonserious delinquency, and that IQ, academic aptitude, and school performance added very little to the explanation of delinquency. The researchers concluded that IQ is not causally linked to delinquency, but is instead an individual characteristic that institutions may or may not reward. Consequently, it is "the institutional pattern of behavior that (a) is causally related to delinquent behavior and (b) must be altered if the frequency or type of aggregate delinquent behavior is to be reduced or changed" (Menard and Morse, 1984: 1374).

Another problem with determining the relationship between intelligence and violation of the law is that intelligence probably varies considerably among different types of offenders. Sex offenders such as child molesters seem to have lower-than-average IQ levels. Embezzlers probably have higher IQ levels than the general population, because they can embezzle funds only if they have attained a position of trust in the business world, and intelligence plays a role in achieving such a position. Intelligence influences an individual's social position and thus affects the opportunities that are available for crime.

Personality Characteristics

Many studies have tried to determine if any personality traits are more common among criminals than among the general population. A 1953 survey of 113 studies concluded that no personality traits were consistently and systematically linked to criminality (Schuessler and Cressey, 1953). Forty-two percent of the studies that were reviewed showed that the personality traits of offenders differed from those of the general population, but the differences were usually small, of questionable validity, and inconsistent with the results of other research. Studies of this sort might be more likely to reveal personality trait differences if specific types of offenders are compared with the general population. Thus a comparison of embezzlers with the general population might show embezzlers to have certain personality traits, and a comparison of bank robbers with the general population might show that bank robbers differ from the general population in personality traits, and probably differ from embezzlers as well.

Another review of studies of personality traits and criminality found that 81 percent of the ninety-four studies examined showed a statistically significant difference in personality traits between offenders and control groups (Waldo and Dinitz, 1967). Again the differences were small, even though they were greater than would have occurred by chance fluctuations in sampling. This review concluded that the role of personality in the genesis of criminal behavior remains unclear.

The Criminal Mind   Researchers have not yet found a "criminal personality," but some psychologists and psychiatrists persist in the search for personalities or personality traits that distinguish criminals from noncriminals. This was the thrust of a study by Samuel Yochelson and Stanton Samenow (1976, 1977). Samenow (1984: 5) has made the following claim:

> ... I shall draw a picture for you of the personality of the criminal just as the police artist draws a picture of his face from a description. I shall describe how criminals think, how they defend their crimes to others, and how they exploit programs that are developed to help them.

It seems unlikely that all criminals—from the corporate price-fixer to the sadistic rapist, from the professional burglar to the desperate addict, and from the organized crime boss to the juvenile shoplifter—would have the same personality, but that is the basis of Yochelson and Samenow's work.

In *The Criminal Personality*, Yochelson and Samenow (1976, 1977) report that in working with criminals they initially found that traditional psychiatric techniques were ineffective, and so they studied the psychology of the criminal in order to develop a workable treatment program. Their data come from interviews with 255 offenders, many institutionalized in St. Elizabeths Hospital in Washington, D.C., and the rest from referrals by the police or the correctional system. They did not compare their criminal subjects with a control group, nor were their subjects a representative sample of all offenders, so their conclusions are based on a flawed research design.

Yochelson and Samenow claim to have identified "thought patterns" that exist among all offenders, whether blacks from the ghetto or whites from the suburbs, whether grade-school dropouts or college graduates. As a result, they argue that the criminal personality is not the product of socioeconomic or other environmental factors. The fifty-two "errors of criminal thinking" that form the criminal personality include

- chronic lying,
- a view that other people's property is their own,
- unrelenting optimism,
- great energy,
- fear of injury or being insulted,
- intense anger,
- manipulativeness, and
- an inflexibly high self-image.

Without a control group, however, there is no way to show that those personality traits are more common among criminals than among the general population.

Treating the Criminal Personality Yochelson and Samenow then sought a way to treat people with this criminal personality. Traditional therapy seemed ineffective because the offenders were manipulative, mimicked psychiatric jargon, and faked insight into their problems. Job training did not work either, according to Samenow, who has said, "I'm all for job training, but if that's all you do, you'll simply have a criminal with job skills. And he'll use those skills to gain entry into new avenues of crime" (cited in Krost, 1982: 8).

Yochelson and Samenow developed a technique of confronting offenders with their flaws, subjecting their thoughts and actions to detailed examination, and forcing them to accept responsibility for their behavior. Much like the technique used by Alcoholics Anonymous, their approach was rigid in demanding full conformity to the rules and in being most effective for offenders who had hit "rock bottom" and saw their only options as prison, suicide, or change. By eliminating "criminal thinking" through this "exercise in self-disgust," Yochelson and Samenow hoped to create a morally responsible person.

Did their approach work? Samenow reports that of the 255 interviewed offenders, only thirty completed the 500 hours of therapy that the program required. Of the thirty, twenty showed improvement, although precise measures of their improvement are not provided. The kind of evidence offered by Yochelson and Samenow cannot tell us whether their method works. The twenty offenders who completed treatment might have changed even without the program. They are only a small part of the initial group of offenders and may not be representative of that group, much less of all criminals in society.

Cognition in Lifestyle Criminals Glenn Walters and Thomas White (1989; Walters, 1990) claim that "faulty, irrational thinking" characterizes "lifestyle criminals," offenders with a long-term involvement in law breaking. The thinking of these offenders is compared to that of adolescents: both groups emphasize self-gratification over responsibility and self-discipline. Walters and White's model proposes eight cognitive traits that are typical of lifestyle criminals:

1. *mollification:* the justification of criminal activity in terms of external forces that operate on the offender

2. *cutoff:* the elimination of such deterrents to crime as fear and anxiety

3. *entitlement:* a sense of privilege, with criminals viewing the world as existing for their own benefit and pleasure

4. *power orientation:* an emphasis on the dimension of strength and weakness in interpersonal relations

5. *sentimentality:* the expression of feelings in a fickle and self-serving manner that helps criminals feel better about themselves without genuinely caring for others

6. *superoptimism:* extreme self-confidence in their ability to get away with most things

7. *cognitive indolence:* laziness in exercising critical thinking, a tendency to be easily bored, and quick and easy acceptance of their own ideas

8. *discontinuity:* a tendency to be easily distracted by external events and an inability to carry out intentions over time.

Whether this model, which was developed from a study of incarcerated offenders, is applicable to all criminals can only be determined from a systematic study that compares the cognitive traits of the general population with the cognitive traits of a representative sample of offenders.

Self-Control and Crime   In *A General Theory of Crime*, sociologists Michael Gottfredson and Travis Hirschi (1990: 88) describe the personality trait of self-control as "the individual characteristic relevant to the commission of criminal acts." They argue as follows:

> In our view, lack of self-control does not require crime and can be counteracted by situational conditions or other properties of the individual. At the same time, we suggest that high self-control effectively reduces the possibility of crime—that is, those possessing it will be substantially less likely at all periods of life to engage in criminal acts. (Gottfredson and Hirschi, 1990: 89)

People lacking self-control are described as "impulsive, insensitive, physical (as opposed to mental), risk-taking, short sighted, and nonverbal, and they will tend therefore to engage in criminal and analogous acts" because they are less apt to consider the negative consequences of their actions (Gottfredson and Hirschi, 1990: 90). Gottfredson and Hirschi claim that these traits can be treated as a stable construct because they cluster together in the same people, are present at an early age, and persist over the life cycle.

Rather than providing direct evidence that offenders differ from the rest of the population in self-control, Gottfredson and Hirschi infer that criminals are low in self-control because of the nature of crime: it provides immediate gratification but little long-term benefit; is exciting and risky; and requires no special motivation, preparation, skill, or specialization. Their portrait of crime draws selectively from the research evidence, ignoring offenses such as

Michael Gottfredson and Travis Hirschi attribute criminal behavior, whether a white-collar offense or a street fight such as the one shown here, to the lack of self-control.

insider trading that would seem to contradict their theory. They assert that the low self-control they claim is common to all offenders, from juvenile delinquents to white-collar criminals, is the product of inadequate socialization, defined as the "absence of nurturance, discipline, or training" (Gottfredson and Hirschi, 1990: 95).

Research supports Gottfredson and Hirschi's contention that low self-control is linked to criminal behavior, but also finds that criminal opportunities and situational influences on the choice of behavior need to be incorporated into a complete theory of crime (Grasmick et al., 1993; Nagin and Paternoster, 1993). A study that confirmed that delinquency participation was associated with weak constraint (impulsivity or low self-control) also suggested that Gottfredson and Hirschi's theory was "simplistic psychologically" because it omitted another personality trait that was strongly associated with delinquency: negative emotionality, the tendency to experience fear, anxiety, and anger and to break down under stress (Caspi et al., 1994: 187).

Aggressiveness and Crime One personality trait sometimes associated with crime and delinquency is the inability to tolerate frustrating situations without resorting to aggression and violence. Frustration that arises from not being able to achieve a goal can lead to aggression that sometimes takes the form of crime, either against the frustrating object or against another object (displaced aggression). There is some evidence that children who are the most assertive, daring, prone to fight, quick to anger, and resistant to discipline are also the most likely to violate the law later in life (Radzinowicz and King, 1977: 89). A study done in Sweden that used teachers' ratings of boys' aggressiveness at ages ten and thirteen concluded that the most aggressive boys were the most likely to be involved in serious and repetitive crime by the age of twenty-six (Stattin and Magnusson, 1989).

Few psychologists now believe that aggression follows directly and simply from frustration. Even when frustration does lead to aggression, that aggression can be channeled into acceptable activities such as athletic or academic competition rather than criminal behavior. One psychologist (Megargee, 1982) identifies the following determinants of whether an individual will respond aggressively to a situation:

1. *Instigation to aggression:* the total of all internal factors motivating the person to commit an aggressive or violent act;

2. *Habit strength:* learned preferences for the use of aggressive behavior in a particular situation;

3. *Inhibitions against aggression:* learned preferences to avoid aggression against a certain target;

4. *Stimulus factors:* environmental influences facilitating or impeding aggressive behavior; and

5. *Competition:* making a choice among several responses to the situation so the individual's needs are met in the best way.

Even a model as complex as this does not incorporate influences on aggressive behavior such as genetic predisposition, endocrinological balance, the availability of weapons, and differences in political power and economic resources. Psychologists, biologists, and social scientists who have studied aggression in recent years have recognized that the causes of aggression and violence are very complex.

Children Who Kill   A study of homicidal behavior by children under the age of thirteen included a three-year-old who had held a knife to his mother's neck as she slept and a ten-year-old who had twice tried to kill his mother. The psychiatrist who did the study found that compared with nonhomicidal children who were also psychiatric patients, the homicidal children were more likely to have

- a history of psychomotor seizures,
- attempted suicide,
- fathers who had been violent to their mothers,
- fathers who had been homicidal, and
- mothers who had been hospitalized for psychiatric reasons (Lewis et al., 1983).

Another study found two kinds of murderers under the age of sixteen. One was the "nonempathic murderer" who was incapable of putting himself or herself in another person's place. Those children had histories of assaultive behavior, did not cope well with stress, and had spent their first year of life with little affection, either in an institution or with a mother who was not nurturing. One fifteen-year-old boy who killed a six-year-old girl said, "I didn't know the girl, so why should I have any feelings about what happened to her?" (Zenoff and Zients, 1979: 547). The second type of young killer was the "sexual-identity-conflict murderer." These were boys who carried weapons because they lacked physical confidence, often as a result of being taunted as effeminate. Their mothers were dominant, and their fathers absent or passive. Sometimes their parents actually encouraged them to commit crime. One thirteen-year-old boy who had his face rubbed in the mud by another boy was told by his parents to do whatever was necessary to defend himself; he then got a large knife and stabbed his tormentor in the heart (Zenoff and Zients, 1979).

Most children who commit murder have experienced severe rejection by one or both parents, and often they have no role model in the home from whom they can learn empathic behavior. The physical abuse that many of these young murderers have suffered can produce brain dysfunctions and neurological problems that are associated with violent behavior.

The Personalities of Rapists and Sexual Murderers One problem with studying the personality of the criminal is that different kinds of crime can be committed by people with very different personalities. Moreover, the same crime can be committed by people with several types of personalities. For instance, one study categorized 800 convicted rapists as follows:

1. *Exploitative rapists* (about 50 percent of all rapists): For them, rape is an impulsive and predatory act, with the victim seen only as an object for sexual gratification. The rape is often spur-of-the-moment, and it arises out of a social situation such as a casual date. These rapists tend to see active resistance by the victim as a sexual maneuver, and this often heightens their arousal.

2. *Compensatory rapists* (about 25 percent): They are obsessed with sexual fantasies and feel very inadequate. They have fantasies that their victims will enjoy the rape and perhaps even fall in love with them, but they also think that no woman would want to have sex with them.

3. *Displaced anger rapists* (about 20 percent): Rape expresses their displaced anger and rage. The victim represents to them a hated woman in their life, such as a mother or wife. Sex is a way of humiliating the victim, and physical resistance often increases the offender's anger.

4. *Sadistic rapists* (5 percent): Sexual feelings are linked to aggression for this type; he becomes more violent as he becomes more aroused. Often his crimes are premeditated, and they may involve a compulsive and ritualized fantasy (Prentky, Cohen, and Seghorn, 1985).

Knowing that the perpetrators of a single crime such as rape have very different personalities can be important in developing policies to treat criminals and counsel victims. Different kinds of rapists pose different threats to society, and they may respond to different kinds of treatment. Victims who are raped by different types of offenders can have quite different experiences, and counseling them might have to take different forms. In addition, advice to women about how to react to a rapist at the time of the crime—for instance, "resist at all costs" or "comply with the offender's demands"—often assumes a single kind of rapist, and knowledge that rapists have very different personalities should make advice-givers more cautious (Carter, Prentky, and Burgess, 1988).

Men who commit rape do seem to share certain attitudes and beliefs. One study found a strong association among three components of a Hypermasculinity Inventory (HMI): callous sexual attitudes, a belief that violence is manly, and an attitude that danger is exciting. Men scoring high on the HMI were likely to have a history of sexual aggression and become aroused when exposed to rape imagery (Mosher and Sirkin, 1984; Mosher and Anderson, 1986). The tendency to commit rape is also associated with younger age at first sexual intercourse, a large number of sex partners, a traditional view of gender roles, hostility toward women, a tendency to blame victims, peer-group norms supportive of sexual assault, and a strong belief in rape myths (such as, "when women say 'no' they really mean 'yes'"). These attitudes are most likely to lead to rape in the absence of a strong moral and legal framework, such as in a criminal subculture or during wartime (Archer, 1994b; Pollard, 1994).

A study by the FBI's Behavioral Science Unit of thirty-six convicted sexual murderers, twenty-nine of whom had killed multiple victims, provides insight into the social background and personality of those who kill in the context of power, sexuality, and brutality. The murderers had experienced numerous family problems when they were young: alcohol and drug abuse, psychiatric problems, criminal histories, sexual problems, abuse and neglect, negative parent-child interactions, poor discipline, lack of strong role models, and frequent changes of residence. To cope with their inadequate family life and their sense of personal failure, they retreated into a sexually violent fantasy world. Their fantasies, which drove their behavior, included themes of "dominance, revenge, violence, rape, molestation, power, control, torture, mutilation, inflicting pain on self/others, and death" (Ressler, Burgess, and Douglas, 1988: 74). Their personalities were characterized by "a sense of social isolation, preferences for autoerotic activities and fetishes, rebelliousness, aggression, chronic lying, and a sense of privilege or entitlement" (Ressler, Burgess, and Douglas, 1988: 73). Their lack of empathy made it possible for them to ignore the impact of their behavior on their victims and treat them as mere extensions of their own world who existed to gratify their desires.

The Psychopathic Personality   The psychopathic or antisocial personality is a cluster of personality traits thought to lead to criminal behavior. A **psychopath** (or sociopath) is an asocial, aggressive, highly impulsive person who feels little or no guilt for antisocial activity and who cannot form lasting bonds of affection with others. Psychopaths are asocial in the same way as infants: they have not learned to control their desires and impulses. They show poor judgment, do not learn easily from experience, are uncooperative, and are not easily influenced by social demands. They are narcissistic and interested only in gratifying their immediate impulses. They seek pleasure, variety, and excitement rather than security and stability. Because of their

Serial killer Ted Bundy was executed in 1989 in Florida for murdering two female college students, but the total number of his victims may have exceeded thirty. Bundy's social background and personality fit quite closely the FBI's Behavioral Science Unit's profile of sexual murderers.

impulsiveness, psychopaths' crimes seem purposeless to others. Because they are present-oriented, they rarely plan their crimes in much detail. When frustrated, they become furious and aggressive and are unable to sublimate or rechannel their impulses. They feel little anxiety or remorse after hurting other people. Psychoanalysts have described psychopaths as loners with a warped capacity for love, and as cold and compassionless people who treat others as a means to their goal of personal pleasure (McCord, 1983).

Experts estimate that 2 to 5 percent of the noncriminal population can be described as psychopaths, and that about 10 to 25 percent of convicted offenders fit this category. However, the term "psychopath" has been defined in many ways, and researchers often disagree on the incidence of this personality type (McCord, 1983).

Some evidence suggests that psychopaths and normal people respond similarly in learning tasks that are positively rewarded, but that normal people learn well and psychopaths learn poorly those tasks that are negatively reinforced. Psychopaths

> show signs of slower autonomic nervous system responses to punishment, and they differ significantly in pulse and heart rates. In general, research indicates that psychopaths are less fearful of punishment, are less anxious, respond more efficiently to stress, are less mature neurologically (that is, less able to learn from punishments), are more eager for excitement, and have a greater propensity for violence than nonpsychopaths. (McCord, 1983: 1315)

Some research indicates that psychopaths are physiologically insensitive, compared with nonpsychopaths. Psychopaths seem less able to learn from physical punishment, and they are less responsive to skin-conductivity stimuli. This may be a result of inherited traits, such as an adrenal gland deficiency in producing or releasing the hormone epinephrine. However, this relative insensitivity to pain could also result from socialization experiences while young or from being abused as a child (McCord, 1983). There is other evidence that psychopaths are more likely to have neuropsychological dysfunctions. For instance, one study found that in many right-handed psychopaths, language is controlled as much by the right hemisphere of the brain as by the left hemisphere, whereas in most right-handed people the control center of language is in the left hemisphere (Jutai, Hare, and Connolly, 1987; Hare and Jutai, 1988). Whether these and other differences between psychopaths and the general population are caused by heredity, accidents, physical abuse, childhood diseases, or environmental factors is unclear (McCord, 1983).

Most psychopaths have a childhood history of rejection, often severe rejection, by at least one parent. Many were institutionalized while young, and their parents frequently had a criminal record or a history of alcoholism, desertion, or neglect. One review of studies on the origins of the psychopathic personality concludes that

> (1) rejection, in combination with damage to such areas of the brain as the hypothalamus, results in psychopathy; and that (2) rejection, in the absence of neural disorder, can result in psychopathy if other influences in the environment (such as a criminal role model, differential association with criminals, or complete neglect) help direct the person in a criminal direction. (McCord, 1983: 1317)

A Critique of the Concept of the Psychopath   Some social scientists have criticized the use of the concept of the psychopathic personality to explain criminal behavior. One critic states that the psychopath is "in fact, *par excellence*, and without shame or qualification, the model of the circular process by which mental abnormality is inferred from antisocial behavior while antisocial behavior is explained by mental abnormality" (Wootton, 1959: 250). For example, let us take an individual who commits a "senseless" mass murder. The press and the psychologists quoted in the press might explain the murder by speculating that the killer has a psychopathic personality, assuming that anyone who would do such a thing must be asocial, impulsive, aggressive, and compassionless—characteristics of the psychopathic personality. The murderer might well be a psychopath, but the problem is that this term is sometimes used even when there is no information available about the offender's actual personality. Information that is independent of the act of murder is needed to assess the killer's personality; personality cannot be assumed from the act itself.

Another problem with the concept of the psychopathic personality is that different psychiatrists and psychologists often give quite different meanings to the term. This is one reason that anywhere from 10 to 25 percent of different samples of inmates have been classified as psychopaths. This variation could be a result of differences in the characteristics of the inmates of various correctional facilities, but it could also reflect differences among psychiatrists and psychologists in the meaning they give to the term "psychopath."

Personality Inventories   The Minnesota Multiphasic Personality Inventory (MMPI) is a personality test of 556 true-false items that have been carefully selected to distinguish average people from those who are suffering from certain forms of psychopathology. The MMPI includes ten clinical scales, three of which are especially important in distinguishing criminals and delinquents from the general population:

> *Psychopathic deviate scale:* conflict with authority and shallow personal attachments
>
> *Schizophrenia scale:* bizarre thought and affect, and withdrawal from personal contact
>
> *Hypomania scale:* unproductive hyperactivity.

Delinquents, especially those involved in the most serious offenses, score high on these three scales when compared with the general population, and so do prisoners when compared with the general population (Hathaway and Monachesi, 1953; Monachesi and Hathaway, 1967; Megargee and Bohn, 1979). In other words, delinquents and prisoners can be characterized as having personalities that include conflict with authority, shallow personal attachments, bizarre thought and affect, withdrawal from personal contact, and unproductive hyperactivity.

To James Q. Wilson and Richard J. Herrnstein (1985: 190), who have reviewed the research on the MMPI and crime, these results illustrate "vividly that institutionalized offenders have atypical personalities as compared to the general population" and that these three scales of the MMPI are "the major personality correlates of crime for adult criminals as well as juvenile delinquents." However, a closer look at what these scales are measuring makes this claim seem extravagant. "Conflict with authority" and "unproductive hyperactivity" can be seen as definitions of crime and delinquency rather than as personality traits that lead to crime and delinquency; these phrases describe actual behavior rather than personality traits. "Shallow personal attachments" and "withdrawal from personal contact" describe social interaction with others and fit well with a sociological theory of crime and delinquency called social control theory, which is examined in Chapter 7. Only the "bizarre thought and affect" of the Schizophrenia scale seem to be psychological constructs, and we might ask, "'Bizarre' from whose perspective? Those making and enforcing the law?"

In looking at research on crime that has used a second personality test, the California Psychological Inventory, Wilson and Herrnstein conclude that important parts of the "typical criminogenic personality" are lack of "conformity," lack of "value orientation," and lack of "social adjustment." This does not tell us much about the kind of personality apt to violate the law, because these "traits" are little more than ways of saying that an individual has engaged in behavior that violates social norms.

The Psychoanalytic Perspective

Another psychological approach to crime causation is the **psychoanalytic perspective** developed by Sigmund Freud (1930, 1962; 1933) and August Aichhorn (1935, 1951). Freud proposed three aspects to the personality. The "id" is composed of instincts and drives that need immediate gratification; it characterizes unsocialized and unrestrained individuals. The "superego" is social authority or conscience; it represents parental authority expressed in the individual as a continuing acceptance of cultural norms and values. The "ego" is the mediating force that tries to adjust the id drives with the demands of the superego by rechanneling and sublimating those drives. A state of "balanced conflict" exists among the three elements in healthy and integrated personalities.

The psychoanalytic approach sees people as antisocial by nature. Thus, a newborn baby needs to be socialized to avoid becoming a criminal (Aichhorn, 1935, 1951). All people are thought antisocial by nature, in contrast to Lombroso's view that some people are born criminals and others are born noncriminals. Lombroso, especially in his early work, focused on heredity as a cause of crime in some people, implying that external circumstances had a limited impact on behavior. By contrast, the psychoanalytic position is that external circumstances lead to the socialization of most people, and that those who become criminals do so because of inadequate socialization.

The id-ego-superego framework allows for the possibility of a "socialized criminal" (Aichhorn, 1935, 1951). If the social environment tolerates, supports, or even requires criminal behavior, a person may be socialized into a life of crime. Psychoanalysts imply that the superego is society's conscience, but in fact various social demands are placed on people. Individuals who are isolated from law-abiding influences and exposed to crime-generating ones can learn to conform to social demands that are contrary to the law.

Part of the socialization process involves the repression of instinctual drives by pushing them back into the unconscious. When those repressed instincts break through, crime can result. In such cases, offenders might not know why they have committed a crime. Some psychoanalysts claim that certain people commit crimes because of guilt developed in childhood. Crime then becomes a way to get the punishment they feel they deserve in order to atone for forbidden desires. This might be true of offenders who commit crimes carelessly and are easily arrested, but if this theory were generally true, we would expect offenders to be arrested far more often than they now are. Most offenders try to avoid arrest, and some who seem to be careless are probably incompetent or distracted rather than trying to atone for forbidden desires.

Neuroses and Crime   A neurosis is a functional disorder in which a person has some difficulty in coping with everyday life. Neurotics usually seem nervous, inhibited, and overconforming rather than aggressive, and so their disorders are probably not closely linked to crime. Neurosis has also been seen as an alternative to juvenile delinquency rather than a cause of it.

One neurosis that some people have associated with crime is the obsessive-compulsive neurosis, which can lead to certain nonaggressive crimes and to sexual perversions such as exhibitionism and fetishism. This neurosis has also been linked to kleptomania, a compulsive form of stealing sometimes thought to be caused by a desire for sexual excitement rather than financial gain. However, kleptomania seems to be a label that is applied to middle- and upper-class thieves who can afford a psychiatrist. The same behavior by a poor person would probably be labeled larceny. There is little evidence that kleptomania exists as a functional disease that can explain theft. For instance, one study of fifty-six shoplifters found almost no relationship between law-violating behavior and any neurosis or psychosis (Cameron, 1964). Shoplifters were understandably upset about being arrested, but there was no evidence of an obsessive-compulsive neurosis that led to theft. The fact that most shoplifters do not repeat the behavior after being caught once and the fact that shoplifting increases just before Christmas suggest that this form of theft is usually a way to stretch a budget and provide for material needs, rather than a form of behavior not under the shoplifter's conscious control (Robin, 1963).

Psychoses and Crime   A psychosis is a disorder characterized by a lack of contact with reality. Sometimes psychoses involve hallucinations that lead to irrational violence, but not all psychotics are dangerous. Definitions of psychoses are sometimes vague, but probably no more than 5 percent of all prison and jail inmates are psychotic (Strasburg, 1978: 68). It is not clear what proportion of the general population is psychotic, but if it does not differ much from the proportion of inmates who are psychotic, then psychosis is not associated with crime. Moreover, prisoners can be psychotic without their particular problem having caused them to violate the law. It is also possible that some prisoners become psychotic as a result of their prison experiences, and so their problem might not have existed prior to their violation of the law.

Because of methodological problems with previous studies that had found that former mental patients were more likely to be arrested than members of the general public, a recent study used both official arrest records and self-report measures of violent and criminal behavior to compare a sample of mental patients with a sample of people who had never been mental patients. Mental patients who exhibited psychotic symptoms were more likely than the nonpatients to engage in violent and illegal behavior, even though "the excess risk of violence posed by mental patients is modest compared to the effects of other factors" (Link, Andrews, and Cullen, 1992: 290).

The psychosis that has most often been linked to criminal behavior is **schizophrenia**, which involves disordered thought patterns characterized by fantasy, delusion, and incoherence. Paranoid schizophrenics have delusions of persecution; they are nervous and sensitive to interpersonal cues, act and speak primarily with reference to themselves, demand much of loved ones but criticize them for their lack of appreciation, and feel unfairly rejected by others. Schizophrenia is sometimes associated with acts of violence, including homicide, particularly against people who are thought to be threatening to the schizophrenic. One study of ninety-seven boys in a correctional school found that 82 percent of those who had engaged in serious violence such as murder or rape exhibited symptoms of paranoia, and only 17 percent of the less violent boys (who had engaged in fist fights, set fires, or threatened others) showed symptoms of paranoia. The violent boys also exhibited more neurological disorders and were more likely to have been physically abused by their parents (Lewis et al., 1979).

A Critique of the Psychoanalytic Perspective   Psychiatrists sometimes disagree about how to classify specific offenders in psychoanalytic terms, in part because those terms are not always precisely defined. Because many of the concepts of the psychoanalytic perspective are difficult to measure, hypotheses about the causes of crime are not easily tested. As a result, there is little systematic research that shows that neuroses and psychoses lead to specific kinds of crime.

Psychoanalytic work on crime often takes the form of case studies of offenders. In these studies, psychiatrists are usually aware that a crime has been committed before they begin to examine the patient. Through a process of "biographic reconstruction," psychiatrists "demonstrate" that certain traits and aspects of the patient's background led to the crime. These case studies do not constitute evidence for the psychoanalytic explanation of crime, because psychiatrists might well find a "dormant capacity for delinquency in any normal individual" (Rettig, Torres, and Garrett, 1977: 234).

A study of 257 indicted male defendants found that psychiatrists classified 154 of them as dangerous. There was little difference between the defendants classified as dangerous and those classified as nondangerous in social class background, past criminal behavior, or past hospitalization in a mental institution. The most important characteristic distinguishing the two groups was the current charge against the defendant, which was known to the psychiatrist before the defendant was questioned. Defendants charged with the most serious crimes were the most likely to be called dangerous by the psychiatrists, although few of the examining psychiatrists gave the current charge against the defendant as the reason for classifying the individual as dangerous. In other words, the psychiatrists seemed to take the crime with which the defendant was charged, classify the defendant as dangerous if it was a serious crime, and then construct an explanation of why that defendant was dangerous (Cocozza and Steadman, 1978).

Until we have evidence on the psychological characteristics of the general population, we cannot know whether criminals differ psychologically from other people. Proponents of the psychoanalytic perspective rarely gather evidence on the psychological state of the general population, because they are usually concerned with doing therapy rather than with testing theories. As a result, many of the ideas of the psychoanalytic perspective on crime remain untested.

Psychology and Variations in Crime Rates

Psychologists and psychiatrists have rarely tried to make sense of geographic, temporal, and social variations in crime rates. Thus we have no reason to believe that variations in crime rates from one society to another, from one region to another, or among communities of different sizes can be explained by differences among the residents of those places in intelligence, personality traits, or neuroses or psychoses. Similarly, we have no evidence that variations in crime rates over time are the result of changes in any of those psychological variables. For instance, it seems unlikely that the dramatic increase in the rate of index crimes in the United States during the late 1960s was caused by short-run changes in intelligence, personality, or neuroses or psychoses.

Whether psychological factors can explain variations in crime rates by sex, age, race, or social class is less clear. Males and females are socialized differently, and differences in personality traits that result from socialization might be linked to male-female differences in rates of crime and delinquency. Males and females also differ in the rate at which they suffer certain mental disorders; this might explain some of the sex difference in crime rates, but there is no strong evidence that this is the case. Intelligence does not seem to be a source of male-female differences in rates of crime and delinquency.

Differences in crime rates by age do not seem to be explained very well by psychological theories. Neither IQ test scores nor personality traits seem to change dramatically over the course of a lifetime for most people, but involvement in crime does vary significantly over the life cycle.

Differences in crime rates among racial groups do not seem to be easily explained by psychological theories either. On average, blacks score lower than whites on IQ tests, but those tests are widely regarded as biased against blacks because they are designed by whites. Moreover, the IQ scores of blacks can be raised significantly by education and by changing the social environment, suggesting that IQ scores are best seen as the product of the socially structured opportunities available to members of different racial groups.

Social class differences in crime rates are not explained well by psychological theories. IQ scores are lower on average for the lower classes, but this is probably due mainly to the poor quality of the schools that the lower classes attend. There may be class differences in personality traits or the frequency of neuroses and psychoses, but the differences have not been shown to explain class differences in rates of crime and delinquency.

Psychology and the Criminal Law

Psychological perspectives on crime have long been important in determining the legal responsibility of people who violate the law. Modern psychology questions the ability of some people to form criminal intent, a necessary element of most crimes, and the legal system sometimes relieves people of responsibility for their actions that violate the law if they cannot form criminal intent. The legal system's emphasis on the individual offender focuses attention on the psychology of the lawbreaker rather than on the social environment in which the offender lives. This serves to uphold the existing social system, because individuals rather than social conditions are blamed for crime.

Rules Determining Criminal Responsibility   One legal rule on criminal responsibility is the **M'Naghten rule**, which was originally spelled out in a case in Great Britain in 1843, well before the advent of modern psychology and psychiatry. The M'Naghten rule establishes a "right and wrong test." For defendants to prove a lack of criminal responsibility because of insanity, they have to demonstrate either (1) that at the time of the crime they were under a defect of reason so as to be unable to know the nature and the quality of the act, or (2) that if they were aware of the nature of the act, they did not know the act was wrong.

The M'Naghten rule raises difficult issues. It is concerned with the rational and cognitive elements of human thought, or what a defendant knows, rather than with human emotions and desires and with mental disorders. The law speaks of the "rational person," but it rarely consults modern behavioral science to determine what would be "rational" behavior for a particular person in a given situation. "Reasonable" often means what a judge thinks is reasonable in a situation, and what is reasonable for a judge earning over $75,000 may not be reasonable for an unemployed parent of five living in a slum.

One attempt to improve the criteria for determining criminal responsibility was made in a 1954 case in which the Court of Appeals for the District of Columbia held that defendants were not guilty if they could show their actions were products of a "mental disease or mental defect." This Durham rule is rarely used in the United States, for it is too general to provide jurors with much guidance for their deliberations.

The Model Penal Code drawn up by the American Law Institute in 1955 is the basis of a rule of criminal responsibility that is widely used today. This **Brawner rule** states that a person should be found not guilty "if at the time of such conduct as a result of mental disease or mental defect, he lacks substantial capacity either to appreciate the criminality of his conduct or to conform his conduct to the requirements of the law." This rule focuses on a defendant's understanding of his or her conduct, as well as on the defendant's ability to control that conduct.

The Insanity Defense Reform Act of 1984 dropped the idea of an inability to conform one's conduct to the requirements of the law, limiting the insanity defense to situations in which "the defendant, as a result of a severe mental disease or defect, was unable to appreciate the nature and quality or the wrongfulness of his acts" (cited in Simon and Aaronson, 1988: 22). This federal law was the product of a heated public debate that followed the attempted assassination of President Ronald Reagan.

The Hinckley Case and the Insanity Defense   On March 30, 1981, John Hinckley fired four shots at President Reagan in an assassination attempt he hoped would win him public attention and the love of actress Jodie Foster. Reagan and three others were wounded. Hinckley later pleaded not guilty by reason of insanity. Under federal law, the prosecutor had to prove beyond a reasonable doubt that Hinckley was sane; the defense attorney did not have to prove beyond a reasonable doubt that Hinckley was insane. More than a year after the shooting, Hinckley was found not guilty by reason of insanity and sentenced to an indefinite term in St. Elizabeths Hospital in Washington, D.C. The verdict caused a public outcry and much criticism by lawmakers, and led to a reevaluation of the insanity defense.

Critics of the Hinckley verdict point out that he purchased a gun, stalked the president, and knew what he was doing when he fired the shots, and that those things indicate that he had committed the crime intentionally. Some critics would not allow the insanity defense to be used if a crime were committed intentionally, even if the defendant's psychological condition meant that he or she was unable to control his or her behavior. Opponents of this view say it would reverse the development of the criminal law since the 1843 M'Naghten decision.

In the five years following Hinckley's 1982 acquittal, Congress and the legislatures of thirty-nine states made more than one hundred changes in their

In 1982, John Hinckley was found not guilty by reason of insanity for attempting to assassinate President Ronald Reagan. He was sentenced to an indefinite term of confinement in St. Elizabeths Hospital in Washington, D.C.

laws on the insanity defense, although one sociologist concludes that their impact has been negligible (Moran, 1991). A few states have abolished the insanity defense as a basis for acquittal, a reform that was allowed to stand by the U.S. Supreme Court in 1994. These changes do not seem to have significantly affected the number of defendants escaping conviction, and defendants still have a constitutional right to argue that they did not possess the mental capacity to form criminal intent to violate the law, a basis for an acquittal (Moran, 1991).

The Hinckley verdict led to other changes in the rules of criminal responsibility. Congress and ten states shifted the burden of proof from the prosecution to the defense, so that two-thirds of the states now require defendants to prove their insanity. Most insanity defenses are plea bargained (see Chapter 13), but in contested cases the side that has the burden of proof usually loses. Thus, if the Hinckley defense had had to prove him insane, rather than require the prosecution to show him to be sane, John Hinckley probably would have been convicted.

The Hinckley case caused eight states to adopt a verdict of "guilty but mentally ill." This did not replace the insanity defense, but instead added to it. If a defendant is found guilty but mentally ill, then the jury, the judge, or a board of mental-health professionals must determine whether the defendant should be sent to a prison or to a mental hospital. Such a verdict does not require the defendant to be given psychiatric care, nor does it mitigate punishment. Critics claim that the "guilty but mentally ill" verdict avoids the difficult question of whether the defendant is criminally responsible for violating the law, and that it is impractical and perhaps unconstitutional.

The Use of the Insanity Defense   Even total abolition of the insanity defense would have little impact on the crime rate, because it is used in less than 1 percent of all felony cases, and in fewer than one-fifth of those cases are defendants acquitted on the basis of insanity (Kenneth Appelbaum, cited in Bass, 1995: 4).

There is some evidence that the insanity defense has been used more often in recent years; for instance, in New York state the annual average number of successful insanity pleas increased from eight in the late 1960s to about one hundred in the early 1980s (Caplan, 1984). One reason for the increased use of the insanity defense is that there has been growing pressure to release mental patients after shorter periods in custody. The courts have expanded the civil rights of mental patients, and psychiatrists today prefer to return patients to the community rather than institutionalize them. The law now requires that patients be released unless they are still mentally ill and dangerous; John Hinckley must have a hearing for possible release every six months. However, psychiatrists cannot predict future dangerousness very well, and so vesting power in them to determine a release date seems to be asking too much of them. For example, a study of mental patients who had committed felonies found that 14 percent of those classified as dangerous by psychiatrists were rearrested for violent crimes within three years of their release, but 16 percent of those classified by psychiatrists as nondangerous were rearrested for violent crimes within three years (Cocozza and Steadman, 1978).

Another possible reason for the increased use of the insanity defense in recent years is the renewed use of the death penalty since 1977. If the alternative to an insanity plea is the risk of execution, then defendants charged with capital crimes will have a strong incentive to plead not guilty by reason of insanity. The link between the insanity plea and capital punishment can be seen in the experience of Great Britain, where the proportion of defendants found not guilty by reason of insanity declined noticeably after that country abolished capital punishment in 1965 (Wilson, 1983: 185).

Those who argue for abolition of the insanity defense sometimes claim that such a change would make it possible to imprison dangerous offenders for longer periods. However, few studies have compared the length of time spent in custody for convicted criminals with the length of time spent in custody for matched samples of defendants who are found not guilty by reason of insanity. What little research has been done is inconclusive as to whether those found insane spend more or less time in custody than those found guilty of similar charges. The studies do show that defendants initially charged with more serious crimes and then found insane spend more time in custody than defendants initially charged with less serious offenses and then found insane (Steadman, 1985).

The insanity defense will continue to be a source of controversy. Changes in the rules of criminal responsibility may redefine the conditions under which people who violate the law can be punished, but the insanity defense will probably continue to be raised in a very small proportion of all criminal cases, and so reforms in the rules of criminal responsibility are unlikely to have much effect on the crime rate.

Summary

Much criminological research today is done by sociologists, but biologists and psychologists have contributed in important ways to our understanding of criminal behavior.

Early biological theories of crime—such as the theories of the physiognomists and phrenologists, Lombroso's atavism theory, and Sheldon's somatotype theory—have little empirical support and do not receive much attention today, but they were significant in the development of criminology.

Modern biological research has produced important findings that might ultimately fit into a general theory of crime causation. Twin studies find that identical twins, who are genetically alike, are more similar in their criminal behavior than fraternal twins, who share fewer inherited traits. These findings have been explained by environmental influences as well as by inheritance. Adoption studies seem to provide evidence for an inherited propensity to crime, with criminality being better predicted from the criminality of an adopted person's biological parents than from the criminality of that person's adoptive parents. Research on the XYY chromosome complement suggests that this condition might be associated with a tendency to engage in nonviolent crimes. There is mixed evidence about the effects of sex hormones on behavior. Brain dysfunctions, learning disabilities, and poor conditionability seem to be correlated with involvement in crime and delinquency. Most biologists who study criminal behavior today are cautious in their conclusions, treating inherited predispositions to certain behavior as factors that interact with environmental influences. However, because biological explanations do not seem to make sense of geographic, temporal, and social variations in crime rates, many criminologists have not paid much attention to biologists' research on crime and delinquency.

One psychological approach to the study of crime and delinquency proposes that law violators have lower levels of intelligence than people who abide by the law. Research shows a small but consistent difference in IQ levels between delinquents and nondelinquents, even when class and race are taken into account. This research has been criticized because IQ scores can be changed by environmental factors, because IQ tests are culturally biased, and because structural factors determine what is made of IQ socially.

Researchers have not found a single criminal personality type, but efforts continue to identify such a cluster of traits. It is more likely that different kinds of offenders will have different personalities; in fact, research on rape finds that there are several personality types among men who commit that offense. Most psychologists now regard aggressiveness, which seems to be linked to some crimes, as the product of many interacting factors. The psychopathic personality, which has origins in both physiology and the environment, and especially in rejection by parents, seems to be linked to criminal behavior.

The psychoanalytic perspective sees crime as the result of inadequate socialization, although an individual could also become a criminal if socialized to conform to the demands of a group whose norms conflict with the law. Neuroses are not closely associated with criminal behavior, but some psychoses, particularly schizophrenia, might be linked to crimes of violence. The case-study approach used by psychoanalysts makes it difficult to test their theory of crime causation in a way that meets the requirements of scientific research.

There is little reason to think that psychological explanations can help us understand geographic or temporal variations in crime rates. Psychological factors might help explain variations in crime rates by sex, age, race, and social class, but there have been few systematic attempts to use psychological variables to make sense of those differences in crime rates.

Psychological perspectives on crime causation are used by the criminal justice system to determine if a defendant is criminally responsible. Several rules, most of them quite vague in their wording, have been used to determine if a defendant is not guilty by reason of insanity. The Hinckley verdict led to reform of the insanity defense rules. Acquittals because of insanity are rare, and, as a result, changes in the insanity defense are unlikely to have much effect on crime rates.

Important Terms

atavism
Brawner rule
concordance rate
learning disabilities
M'Naghten rule
premenstrual syndrome (PMS)

psychoanalytic perspective
psychopath
schizophrenia
somatotype
XYY chromosome complement

Review Questions

1. What are the major kinds of modern biological research on the causes of criminal behavior? What does that research tell us about the significance of biological factors as causes of crime?

2. Why have most modern criminologists paid less attention to biological research on the causes of crime than they have to the social causes of crime? What might be the advantages, or disadvantages, of an interdisciplinary approach to the study of the causes of crime?

3. How could biological factors explain variations in crime rates by nation, region, and size of community, over time, and by sex, age, race, and social class?

4. What is the relationship between intelligence (as measured by IQ tests) and criminal and delinquent behavior? Why might a less intelligent person be more likely to commit certain kinds of crime?

5. Is there a "criminal personality"? What personality traits might be common to all criminals, and why?

6. Is the idea of the psychopath useful in the study of crime? What types of criminals would be most likely to be psychopaths? What kinds of criminals would be least likely to be psychopaths?

7. How might psychoanalytic explanations of crime be tested more adequately than they have been so far? What kinds of criminals do you think would be most likely to be neurotic or psychotic?

8. How could psychological factors explain variations in crime rates by nation, region, and size of community, over time, and by sex, age, race, and social class?

9. What are the different insanity defense rules? What reforms have been made in the use of the insanity defense since the Hinckley verdict?

Chapter 6
Social and Economic Sources of Crime

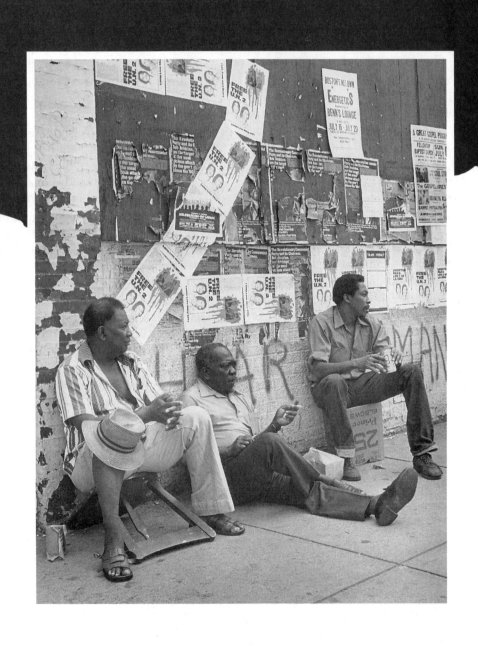

The traditional way to explain arson is to focus on the individual who sets fires. Seeing the arsonist as a deviant—perhaps a "pyromaniac" with severe psychological problems—leads nowhere in the prevention of arson, a crime that has destroyed major parts of our cities. A much better approach focuses on the social-structural causes of arson. There is an important link between legitimate institutions—particularly banks, real estate developers, and insurance companies—and arson-for-profit schemes by gangsters, professional arsonists, landlords, and corrupt political officials (Brady, 1983). Swiss insurance companies allow their clients to use the funds paid to cover losses due to fire only to rebuild the same structure on the same land, whereas American insurance companies provide their clients with a motive for arson by paying them cash to satisfy their claims. A cultural bias against regulating private residences means that American fire codes focus on public buildings rather than on the houses and apartment buildings where four-fifths of all fire-related deaths happen (McMillan, 1995). Knowledge of the socioeconomic sources of arson can be used to curb this crime through better regulation of banks, real estate developers, and insurance companies; more comprehensive fire codes; fixing legal responsibility for "accidental" fires on negligent people; citizen-action groups; arson-prediction methods; better communication between the community and the police; housing revitalization; and changes in environmental design (Brady, 1982; McMillan, 1995). Arson is better understood and more effectively controlled by paying attention to the socioeconomic context within which it occurs, rather than by studying the psychology of the individual offender.

This chapter looks at the social, economic, and cultural factors that are conducive to white-collar crime, organized crime, and conventional crime (especially juvenile delinquency). In the following chapter we examine the social and psychological processes by which people neutralize or weaken their commitment to the law. Then Chapter 8 explores the ways that people actually learn to commit crime.

Social and Economic Sources of White-Collar Crime

Several aspects of the social structure and economic system of the United States are conducive to white-collar crime. The American economy is based as much on the stimulation of new demands as on the fulfillment of existing demands. Competition in the business world creates pressure to increase consumer demand for products as well as pressure to capture existing markets. The result is advertising, which sometimes goes beyond "puffing one's wares" to fraud, a crime characterized by the intent to deceive. Some advertising is thus actually criminal. Advertising can also stimulate demand that leads to theft when that demand is not fulfilled. Advertising fuels consumption in the American economy, but by urging people to consume and maintain an expensive life style, it can also lead to larceny, robbery, and embezzlement.

Free Enterprise: Profits and Competition

The American ideology of free enterprise stresses two goals: the pursuit of profits and open competition among sellers. Each goal can be conducive to violation of the law by businesspeople.

The Pursuit of Profits   The emphasis on consumption and the use of advertising help create profits for firms. Some economists have suggested that companies seek a "satisfactory profit" rather than the maximum profit and that corporations have goals other than making a profit. However, profits are basic to the corporation, even if other considerations play some role in corporate decision making. (See the Crime on Campus box.)

In a study of sixty-four retired middle managers of large corporations, many of them cited the pressure to show profits and keep costs in line as the greatest pressure on middle management. About nine-tenths of the retired executives said that the various pressures on middle managers sometimes lead to unethical behavior; about four-fifths of the executives said that such pressures can lead to criminal acts (Clinard, 1983).

Firms seem most likely to violate the law to increase profits when the economy is unstable and their profits are declining. The drive for profits can lead to antitrust violations such as price-fixing, which is the illegal setting of prices by firms acting in collusion rather than depending on the free market to determine prices; this is an offense that the federal government explicitly states that it will prosecute. Profit-seeking can also push businesspeople into the arms of gangsters to secure capital for investment and expansion; this sometimes leads to the takeover of legitimate businesses by organized crime. Economically weak firms sometimes try to recoup their losses by "selling out to the insurance company"; that is, they hire a "torch" to burn down the plant in order to collect the fire insurance. Arson increases during recessions when firms are in financial difficulty. For instance, in 1986 Houston was regarded by insurance and fire officials as the worst place in the United States for arson, a consequence of unemployment, home foreclosures, bankruptcies, and business failures resulting from the near collapse of the gas and oil industry on which that city had depended.

One of the largest losses in any crime in history involved an attempt to create a profitable enterprise. The conspirators sought to make the Equity Funding Corporation of America "the largest, fastest growing, most successful financial institution in the world and in the process thereby to gain fame and fortune for themselves" (Parker, 1976: 122). Their fraud involved the writing of fake life insurance policies that were sold to other insurance companies at a discount, a practice known as reinsurance. What was peculiar about this massive fraud was not the extraordinarily large losses involved, but that the conspirators created a situation in which their firm would actually lose more money every year the fraud continued. Their crime created the illusion of making money while it was in fact losing money. The crime was apparently too complex for even its perpetrators to understand.

In 1986, indictments were returned against several Wall Street financiers for violating federal laws against "insider trading," the use of material and nonpublic information about a company to trade its stock. These investment analysts had sold or used inside information to speculate on the outcome of corporate mergers and takeovers. One of them, Ivan Boesky, was required to pay $100 million for his illegal use of such information, which had helped him accumulate nearly $2 billion in capital. He was also sentenced to a three-year

CRIME ON CAMPUS

The Abuse of Research Funds

Colleges and universities are nonprofit institutions, so they do not pursue profits in the way that businesses do. However, they do depend on outside sources of funds to erect and maintain buildings, pay for new and ongoing programs, provide financial assistance to students, and carry out research. A major source of outside funding for many institutions of higher learning is the federal government.

Colleges and universities build into the research grants they receive from the federal government money for "indirect costs" they incur in supporting research; these costs include building maintenance, overhead such as the cost of lighting and heating the space where research is done, and equipment needed to carry out the research. The "indirect cost recovery rate" can be as high as 88 percent of the money that goes directly to pay for the research.

In 1991, federal investigators reported that $14 million in research money had been misspent by twelve colleges and universities to pay for private club memberships, vacations, receptions, liquor, flowers, sculptures, chauffeurs, and other expenses not directly related to research. Stanford University received much negative publicity for its overcharges, which some members of Congress said could have amounted to $200 million over the previous decade. Included in Stanford's charges were part of the costs of a seventy-two-foot yacht, antiques for the president's home, and a retreat at Lake Tahoe for university trustees. Massachusetts Institute of Technology billed the government for jewelry, part of the salary of a cook at the president's house, and fees it had paid a lobbyist to try to convince a congressional committee to drop its probe of research fraud by an MIT employee. A trip to Grand Cayman Island and Florida by the wife of the president of the University of Pittsburgh was also charged to a research grant; the president reimbursed the government for the cost of the trip a week after a federal audit began.

Public reaction to the news of such expenditures was hostile, not only because of the mismanagement of taxpayers' money, but also because of the high and rising cost of tuition at the nation's colleges and universities. The federal government responded to the overcharges by reducing the indirect cost recovery rate; reductions in payments for research done at Stanford were estimated to cost the university as much as $20 million a year. Under pressure from both the public and the federal government, some universities agreed to repay money to the government or reduce their charges in the future. No criminal charges were filed against the colleges and universities.

Sources: Based on Michael K. Frisby, "U.S. Review Finds Colleges Misused $14m," *Boston Globe*, May 10, 1991, p. 3; Andrew Pollack, "U.S. Sharply Cuts Funds to Stanford as Result of Inquiry on Overcharging," *New York Times*, April 26, 1991, p. A10.

After Michael Milken pleaded guilty to violations of
securities laws, he was
heavily fined and sentenced
to a ten-year prison term,
although he was released
following twenty-two months
of confinement.

prison term, of which he served twenty-two months. In 1988, the investment firm of Drexel Burnham Lambert Inc. pleaded guilty to six felony counts relat-ed to securities fraud and agreed to pay a $650 million penalty. In 1990, Michael Milken, who built that firm, pleaded guilty to violations of securities laws; in addition to paying stiff fines, he was sentenced to ten years in prison, although he spent only twenty-two months there.

Many of those indicted in the insider trading cases were quite young; Milken was thirty-nine in 1986, when his "junk bond" empire began to col-lapse, and four people who pleaded guilty in one case were between twenty-three and twenty-seven. One executive of a brokerage house said that the young people coming to work on Wall Street in the 1980s "all want to do things faster, more aggressively, in terms of compensation, and that is their measure of success. They get here from the business schools with all sorts of knowledge about financial instruments, but less of a sense of what's right and what's wrong" (cited in Sterngold, 1986: 36).

In 1989, the American public began to learn of enormous losses due to fraud in the savings and loan industry. Even today, the total cost to taxpayers of bailing out the insolvent government-insured institutions is unclear; esti-mates range from $150 billion to $1 trillion. Criminal activity in the pursuit of profits in this newly deregulated industry was involved in about 80 percent of the insolvencies. Criminal behavior took the form of illegal risk-taking, loot-ing an institution's funds, and covering up fraud by manipulating an institu-tion's records (Calavita and Pontell, 1990). By early 1991, more than four hun-dred people had been convicted of fraud. In 1992, Charles H. Keating, Jr., was sentenced to a ten-year prison term for defrauding depositors into buying junk bonds.

Competition   The second element of free-enterprise ideology is open com-petition among firms, which is theoretically beneficial to the consuming pub-lic because it reduces profits to a "fair" level. However, competition can also lead firms to try to capture a larger share of the market through illegal acts such as false advertising or bribery. Individual firms do not seek to maximize competition for themselves and reduce their own profits to a "fair" level. Instead, they seek to reduce the strength of their competitors and maximize their own profits. To do this, they sometimes turn to price-fixing to drive competitors out of business, or try to get banks to charge competing firms a higher interest rate. Competition can also lead to the theft of new ideas through industrial espionage.

Competition in foreign markets sometimes involves businesses in the bribery of officials to secure contracts and establish plants. In recent years, the increased internationalization of trade, the rise of multinational corporations, and the growing interdependence of nations have generated concern about white-collar crime in the international arena. Competition among the corporations of the world sometimes leads to clearly illegal behavior such as assassinations, and sometimes into "gray" areas that involve unethical behavior that may not violate existing laws. Since the passage of the Foreign Corrupt Practices Act in 1977, firms based in the United States that pay bribes to foreign officials are in violation of American law; however, only ten cases were prosecuted under that law in its first decade of existence. Another unethical practice—the shipping to foreign buyers of products banned in the United States, such as carcinogenic Tris-treated infants' clothing—is not prosecuted as a crime in the United States. Competition and the search for new and profitable markets encourage behavior such as this, especially when the law does not cover the situation adequately or when the criminal justice system does not punish such actions.

A Comparative Note   The failure to look at white-collar crime in other societies can lead to an overemphasis on the competitive pursuit of profits in capitalist economies as a cause of white-collar crime. In fact, developing societies and socialist economies also experience white-collar crime. John Braithwaite (1988) has suggested some general causes of white-collar crime that apply to noncapitalist as well as capitalist economies. He says that white-collar crime is more likely to occur "when people in positions of responsibility are put under enormous performance pressures to achieve economic or cultural goals"; "in contexts with structural blockages to legitimate means of goal attainment"; and "in contexts in which illegitimate opportunities are more structurally available." White-collar crime "is less likely to occur when people in positions of responsibility are put under performance pressures to achieve economic and cultural goals by legitimate means only" (Braithwaite, 1988: 629–630). The goals these people seek to achieve may be profits, but they can also be state-imposed production quotas or success in a variety of other forms. The competitive pursuit of profits in capitalist economies is thus only one of many possible sources of white-collar crime.

Market Structure and Crime

Some white-collar crimes seem to be more likely to occur in certain market structures or economic circumstances (Leonard and Weber, 1970; Kramer,

1982). For example, seller concentration—a situation in which a large share of the market is controlled by a few leading producers—might be conducive to price-fixing, although research does not conclusively show that an industry's level of concentration is linked to its rate of antitrust violations (Coleman, 1994).

A small number of buyers or a great deal of wealth in the hands of a few buyers—called buyer concentration—can give buyers the power to demand bribes and kickbacks from sellers. When goods and services are in short supply, consumers might bribe those who control scarce resources in order to meet their needs.

Another aspect of market structure conducive to business crime is the price elasticity of demand. When demand is price-inelastic—that is, when there will be little reduction in the demand for a product if its price increases—firms may engage in price-fixing to increase profits. A slow rate of growth in demand in a given market can lead to business crimes such as false advertising.

Product differentiation, which is the ability to distinguish one's product from a competitor's product, can give rise to false or deceptive advertising. Sometimes the opposite situation, trying to make one's product seem as much like another product as possible, leads to crimes such as copyright or patent infringement. Consumer demand for designer clothing or designer cosmetics is conducive to the counterfeiting of those products.

Trust and Credit

Some business crimes stem from the economic system's reliance on trust and credit. Businesspeople have faith that others will fulfill their obligations honestly; when that trust is violated, crimes can occur. Robert Vesco exploited his business colleagues in Investors Overseas Services by looting about half a billion dollars from that international corporation. Employers sometimes violate the trust of employees and union leaders by engaging in illegal labor practices. Merchants abuse the trust of their customers when they misrepresent prices, engage in deceptive credit practices, or substitute inferior goods upon delivery. Corporate directors violate stockholders' trust when they fail to disclose information about illegal contributions to political candidates and bribes to foreign officials. The Trustee's Bankruptcy Report on the Equity Funding Corporation of America fraud case concluded that EFCA had violated the trust of other members of the insurance industry, saying that

> only someone with an exceedingly skeptical bent of mind would have ... inferred fraud. Such an inference would have been hostile to the presumption of good faith and honest-dealing which customarily prevails in American business practice. To the Trustee, that presumption, though sometimes grievously abused, is probably indispensable to a vigorous and productive economy. (cited in Parker, 1976: 166)

One trust relationship that is conducive to certain crimes is credit, which is given on the creditor's faith that the borrower will repay the money. Many crimes of credit abuse involve businesspeople defrauding one another.

Business credit fraud is sometimes planned in advance, with a new company established to defraud suppliers, or a legitimate business converted into a firm that abuses its creditors. Banks and corporations sometimes continue to extend credit to a firm even though that firm's shaky financial condition makes it unlikely that it will be able to repay its debts. One businessperson who aspired to wealth through fraudulent credit practices was Tony DeAngelis, who borrowed millions of dollars by using as collateral for his loans salad oil that he said was stored in large tanks. His creditors trusted him, but they failed to check on the existence of the salad oil. When the tanks were found to be empty, DeAngelis defaulted on the loans and his creditors lost millions of dollars.

Corporations and Crime

Various aspects of large corporations—such as their bureaucratic structure, their working conditions, and their use of rationality in decision making—are conducive to crime.

Bureaucratic Structure　Bureaucratic structure can be associated with the fragmentation of responsibility and the difficulty of pinpointing who made a particular decision. Supervisors often blame underlings for the company's violation of the law, and underlings claim that their supervisors encouraged them to break the law to meet corporate goals.

The division of tasks in a large corporation enhances bureaucratic efficiency but also makes it difficult to exercise control over business activities. The decentralization of General Electric in 1950 broke that large corporation into several relatively autonomous divisions, each of which was under pressure to show a profit. The need to stabilize profits at a high level led to price-fixing, an offense that was made easier by the company's fragmentation.

Corporate crimes can result from organizational defects such as poor information flow, lack of coordination, inaccurate promotional material, failure to deal with complaints after misleading advertisements, and failure to tell sales representatives all of the relevant facts about a product (Hopkins, 1980; Ermann and Lundman, 1982). The explosion of the space shuttle *Challenger* that killed seven astronauts in 1986 was caused by mechanical problems of which top-level managers at the National Aeronautics and Space Administration and Morton Thiokol were apparently aware, but they decided to go ahead with the launch because of a breakdown in communication with technical advisors and a willingness to accept risks that previously had been unacceptable (Boisjoly, Curtis, and Mellican, 1989). A study of fifteen Australian companies that had committed white-collar crimes involving organizational defects found that official sanctions led at least nine of the companies to make significant organizational changes to reduce the chance that the problem would recur (Hopkins, 1980).

Working Conditions　Employees of large corporations may find it easy to steal from the company if they have little loyalty to the firm. Crime against the employing firm is apparently less common in Japan, where workers traditionally remain with one company for their entire working lives, than it is in the United States, where job mobility is greater, and there is less loyalty to one's employer. In addition, when union-management conflict is necessary to increase wages and benefits, workers might believe that management is not concerned with their welfare and will make concessions only grudgingly. This attitude can be used to justify employees' crimes against the firm.

Dissatisfied workers who feel exploited or underpaid and executives who are frustrated by not being promoted or by an unsatisfactory salary might justify theft or embezzlement as the only way to gain the compensation they feel they deserve. Some observers believe that workers steal to increase their spendable incomes; the policy implication is that theft can be reduced by paying workers more (Jaspan, 1974). Another view is that because many jobs are dull, repetitive, lacking in prestige, or unchallenging, workers steal for job enrichment or to increase their self-esteem (Zeitlin, 1971). The impersonality of the work environment in large corporations and on plant assembly lines can generate a need to create a challenge that workers can meet, and this sometimes takes the form of crime against the company. Giving workers a vested interest in the company's success and integrating them into the firm might reduce employee theft (Hollinger and Clark, 1983).

Rational Decision Making   The rational decision making of large corporations can be conducive to business crime. Given a low risk of arrest, a small likelihood of being convicted in court, and a negligible chance of a meaningful criminal sanction, corporate executives may knowingly violate the law or enter "gray areas" where they are aware they might be breaking the law. It might be rational, if not moral or legal, for executives to break the law if their gains are great and their risks are small. Even if the company is convicted of a crime, it will probably gain more in profits than it loses in fines, and individual executives may gain more in promotion and salary than they lose from criminal sanctions.

In the 1970s, the Ford Motor Company calculated that it would be too costly for it to modify its cars and light trucks in a way that would prevent the fuel leakage that had caused serious burns and deaths. Ford estimated it would cost $137 million to make such modifications, but those changes would save the company only $49.5 million in repairs it would be required to make and civil damages it would be forced to pay to accident victims. The $49.5 million figure was arrived at on the basis of $700 in repairs per burned vehicle, $67,000 per serious burn injury, and $200,000 per burn death. Critics allege that on the basis of such calculations, Ford decided it would be too expensive initially to fix and later to recall the Pinto, which was involved in numerous serious accidents (Cullen, Maakestad, and Cavender, 1987).

Development of New Technology

Technology develops in a cumulative fashion, and new opportunities to violate the law often accompany breakthroughs in technology. The high-tech and computer industry has provided both new opportunities for crime and new techniques to commit traditional crimes such as embezzlement.

Computer crime, which is any violation of the law in which a computer is the target or the means, takes many forms, some of which are shown in Table 6.1. Computer crimes include the:

- introduction of unauthorized data into a system,
- manipulation of authorized data,
- creation of unauthorized files,
- unauthorized use of passwords or accounting ("hacking"),
- theft of hardware, software, or computer time, and
- use of the computer to support criminal enterprises.

"Shaving" is a crime in which someone programs a computer to round off each employee's paycheck down to the nearest ten cents and then to deposit the extra few pennies in the offender's account. One programmer made $300 a week with this scheme, an amount that was two-and-a-half times his regular

TABLE 6.1   Categories of Computer Crime

Internal Computer Crimes
Trojan horses
Logic bombs
Trap doors
Viruses

Telecommunications Crimes
Phone phreaking
Hacking
Illegal bulletin boards
Misuse of telephone systems

Computer Manipulation Crimes
Embezzlements
Frauds

Support of Criminal Enterprises
Data bases to support drug distributions
Data bases to keep records of client transactions
Money laundering

Hardware/Software Thefts
Software piracy
Thefts of computers
Thefts of microprocessor chips
Thefts of trade secrets

Source: Catherine H. Conly and J. Thomas McEwen, "Computer Crime," *NIJ Reports,* January/February 1990, p. 3.

salary. High-quality computer graphics have been employed to produce counterfeit checks, which might cost the economy as much as $1 billion a year.

Other criminal uses of computers are associated with developments in telecommunications technology. "Phone phreaking" is a form of fraud in which electronic signals are used to trick a telephone company into thinking that charges for long-distance calls are being paid for by the caller. In another form of telecommunications fraud, thieves use a device, available by mail order, to pick up radio waves and record private cellular codes from telephones in passing cars. They then use a personal computer with a chip etcher to reprogram microchips with the stolen codes. By inserting a reprogrammed chip into a cellular phone, they or others can charge calls to the owner of the phone from which the code was stolen. In 1996, two residents of Brooklyn were charged with the theft of 80,000 cellular phone numbers.

Several aspects of computer technology are conducive to crime. First, it is relatively easy for a knowledgeable computer programmer to hide a program or a modification within a larger program ("Trojan horses," "logic bombs," "trap doors," and "viruses"), or to destroy records and leave no trail of the crime. Second, computer software or programs are copied relatively easily, an act the courts have treated as copyright infringement. Third, the chips used in computer hardware are small but expensive and have been a target of thieves, who sell the chips to companies that cannot purchase enough in the legitimate market. Fourth, computers emit radio waves or "compromising emanations" that can be decoded with the proper equipment. The federal government calls this the "Tempest" problem and worries about electronic espionage that might reveal secret information in computerized files.

One important aspect of computer technology is electronic fund transfers (EFT), which include all payment systems that permit transactions or exchanges in which value is represented by electronic messages, rather than by paper such as currency or checks. **EFT crime** is any violation of the law that would not have occurred except for the presence of an EFT system. This includes crimes that involve automated teller machines (ATMs) and wire transfers from bank to bank by a company's computer. In 1993, thieves collected personal identification numbers (PINs) from bank cards by rolling a bogus ATM machine into a Connecticut shopping mall, and then used the numbers to withdraw at least $50,000 from the accounts of the unsuspecting users of the machine. In 1995, three thieves used a stolen bank card to make 724 withdrawals totaling $346,770 from the victim's account. There is no good source of data on the extent of EFT crime, but so far EFT crime seems to be a small proportion of all crimes involving financial institutions. However, EFT crime will probably increase as the number of financial transactions conducted electronically grows (Colton et al., 1982; Tien, Rich, and Cahn, April 1986).

Social and Economic Sources of Organized Crime

The tendency in American society to pass legislation that prohibits the consumption of widely demanded goods and services has produced vast profits for people who are willing to supply those goods and services. One example is Prohibition.

Prohibition and Organized Crime

Prior to the passage of the Eighteenth Amendment, which prohibited the manufacture, sale, and transportation of alcoholic beverages, there were gangsters in many American cities, but they were not well organized.

The efforts of religious, white, native-born Americans in small towns and rural areas to protect the dominance of their cultural values led to Prohibition in 1920. The consequence of making a widely demanded product illegal was that those willing to supply alcoholic beverages could charge higher prices than consumers had paid when those beverages were legal and in more plentiful supply. This source of great profits led to the organization of criminal gangs that distributed alcoholic beverages to meet the public's demand.

The Eighteenth Amendment was repealed during the Great Depression, partly for economic reasons. People needed the jobs that the liquor industry could provide, and the government hoped to raise more tax revenue from the legal sale of alcoholic beverages. Repeal was also a result of the unenforceability of the law and the public's reactions to the tactics used by the Prohibition Bureau. National prohibition became a thing of the past in 1933, but gangsters had become well organized as a result of this experiment in the legislation of morality.

Organized Crime after Prohibition

When Prohibition ended, gangs turned to other illegal enterprises for revenue. They became involved in prostitution, though they are not as involved in it today. Currently, the major sources of revenue for organized crime seem to be illegal drugs and loan sharking, and perhaps gambling. However, gangsters have shown ingenuity in making a profit from many different illegal activities, including bankruptcy fraud, the disposal of toxic wastes, and extortion.

Gambling   According to some scholars and most law-enforcement officers, many bookies work for, or are members of, organized crime "families." One sociologist with access to evidence gathered by law-enforcement agencies suggested that 95 percent of illegal gambling in the United States was controlled by organized crime in the late 1960s (Cressey, 1969). However, research in New York City, where the largest number of organized crime families in the country are located, indicates that organized crime does not have a firm control over gambling and that bookies operate in a competitive market rather than as agents of organized crime. Because the gambling business is unpredictable, bookies often turn to loan sharks, who do have ties to organized crime, in order to borrow money to keep their gambling operations afloat (Reuter, 1983). Bookies thus provide a source of income for organized crime not because their profits are channeled directly to gangsters, but because they pay high interest rates to loan sharks who are members of organized crime.

Loan Sharking   Loan sharks are a major source of income for organized crime. The interest rates on their loans are illegally high and well in excess of what borrowers pay to legitimate institutions. Loan sharks thrive on the difficulties that some people encounter in getting loans from legitimate institutions. Many borrowers from loan sharks are poor credit risks who are turned down by banks and finance companies. Other borrowers need money for purposes that legitimate institutions would disapprove, such as the repayment of gambling debts or the financing of a drug deal. Loan sharks are willing to lend money to such people with less financial information or collateral than legitimate institutions require.

Many who borrow from loan sharks have difficulty repaying their loans on time. When this happens, a loan shark may threaten violence against the borrower or the borrower's family. However, a study of loan sharking in New York City found that violence and intimidation were less common than some accounts suggest, because borrowers and lenders often have close ties and because borrowers usually repay their loans in the hope that they will be able to get money from the loan shark again (Reuter, 1983).

Illegal Drugs   The money lent by loan sharks who are linked to organized crime often comes from the profits made from the importation of illegal drugs. Laws against the sale and possession of drugs lead to high profits for those willing to take the risk of importing and distributing drugs. As a result, illegal drugs are far more costly to users in the United States than they would be if they were legal.

John Dombrink (1988: 63) has described organized crime's involvement in the drug business as follows:

> Heroin has for the longest time been viewed as an integral enterprise of traditional organized crime groups, despite protestations that narcotics trafficking was to be avoided, whereas the cocaine business has been operated by Cubans, and later Colombian "cocaine cowboys." Heroin has proven to be more hierarchically controlled, with careful attention to shielding important members of the organization from risk of detection and prosecution, and tributes paid to traditional crime families by leading heroin dealers…

Bankruptcy Fraud   Organized crime has sometimes taken advantage of the trust inherent in credit transactions in the business world to engage in bankruptcy fraud (DeFranco, 1973). In this crime, racketeers purchase a business that has a good credit rating or establish a "front business" with a name much like one of a respected firm. They stock up on merchandise bought on credit. They demand quick delivery, pay for initial orders with cash so as to establish good credit, and then buy to the limit on credit, excusing nonpayment because of the rapid expansion of their business or because it is the busy season of the year, the Christmas season being a favorite time for this crime. The goods they buy are appealing to consumers, can be purchased in volume, and are easy to transport and hard to trace. Office equipment, television sets, and toys are examples. The racketeers sell these goods as quickly as they can through discount houses and by mail order, then disappear and leave their creditors with unpaid bills. The widespread use of credit in the world of commerce makes it possible for gangsters to commit this kind of crime.

Disposal of Toxic Wastes   Organized crime has been adaptable in moving into newly profitable areas of illegal activity. For instance, the disposal of toxic waste material produced by industry has become difficult and expensive because of strict environmental protection laws. There is some evidence that garbage companies owned by organized crime have developed highly profitable, but dangerous and illegal, methods of waste disposal. One method involves mixing toxic materials with recycled fuel oil (Block and Scarpitti, 1985; Szasz, 1986).

Extortion   Organized crime has used its control of certain labor unions and the threat of violence to extort millions of dollars a year from industry. In New York City, concrete companies, some of which have ties to organized crime, overcharge construction companies about $50 million a year by threatening to withhold workers or slow down the delivery of concrete to construction companies that are working against deadlines. A U.S. Attorney estimates that such extortion has driven up construction costs in New York City by about 20 percent, an increase that is passed on to consumers in higher rents, higher taxes for public works projects, and higher prices for goods and services (Roberts, 1985).

A virtual monopoly over the waste-removal industry makes the cost of garbage collection in New York City about 50 percent higher than it would be without organized crime's involvement, according to one economist (Reuter, 1993). This monopoly was created and is maintained through the threat of violence against legitimate entrepreneurs seeking to enter the industry. For instance, according to an FBI official,

> some time ago a man... entered the refuse business in New York State, mortgaging his home to buy a few garbage trucks. Before long, sugar was found in the gas tanks.... Then someone tried to blow up a truck. One afternoon the phone rang, and a gruff voice described what the man's ten-year-old daughter was wearing that day. The voice warned that if the trucks were not sold, the girl would disappear. The business was shut down within hours. (Shenon, 1985: E4)

Organized Crime and the Economic System

The activities of organized crime are closely interwoven with the economic system. Illegal goods and services are supplied by gangsters at a high cost to consumers and at great profit to organized crime. Gangsters act as brokers who meet an unfulfilled public demand for illegal goods and services. Organized crime serves economic functions for some people; for example, loan sharks make money available to people who cannot borrow elsewhere. Gangsters in the United States, Japan, Russia, and elsewhere adopt the economic strategies and managerial skills of legitimate business to carry out their illegal profit-making ventures. (See the Cross-Cultural Perspective box.)

A CROSS-CULTURAL PERSPECTIVE

Japanese Corporations and the Yakuza

In Japan, about 90,000 gangsters known as *yakuza* belong to 3,300 groups, most of which are affiliated with three major syndicates. For years, these gangsters have amassed wealth in ways similar to those used by the Mafia in the United States: extortion, gambling, drug dealing, and prostitution. The yakuza have also been paid to use intimidation to collect debts, settle traffic accident disputes, force tenants from apartments, and break strikes. In the booming Japanese economy of the 1980s, the yakuza got involved in real estate development, the construction industry, and the stock market.

Japanese crime bosses now have access to corporate officials, financial institutions, and political leaders. In just a few years after his 1984 release from prison, one boss accumulated a fortune of more than $1 billion through speculating in real estate, stocks, and art. A major trucking company that some observers believe is a link among the yakuza, politicians, and financial institutions once loaned him $2.5 billion. That same man also borrowed more than $200 million from two of the nation's largest brokerage houses.

Linking organized crime and Japanese corporations are the *sokaiya*, professional extortionists who blackmail executives by offering to keep secret their knowledge of the executives' sexual indiscretions or information they have about the company's misuse of funds or failure to negotiate certain deals. The sokaiya, some of whom once worked as corporate accountants or journalists, often own stock in the company, making it easier to find out information about the company and giving them a reason to attend annual meetings.

The sokaiya exploit a Japanese cultural trait, the desire to avoid embarrassment. They intimidate executives by threatening to use violence, disrupt annual shareholders' meetings, and publicly share embarrassing information. After they have been paid off, they suppress even reasonable questions from shareholders at annual meetings, shouting down questioners and even threatening to assault them.

The sokaiya exist because corporate officials are willing to deal with them; one extortionist has said, "People like us are told we should not exist, but the fact is that some companies seek our help and trust us, or we wouldn't still be around" (p. F6). In fact, the sokaiya are such an integral part of Japanese business that a directory of them is published, listing their addresses, telephone numbers, syndicate affiliations, and methods of operation.

The number of sokaiya, nearly all of whom are members of the yakuza, has declined since 1982, when corporate payoffs were outlawed. Prior to passage of this law, there were an estimated 7,000 to 8,000 sokaiya; the number is now about 1,250. Their estimated annual earnings have declined from about $800 million to about $40 million, but as many as 300 companies still pay them to suppress information.

Sources: Based on James Sterngold, "Japan Takes on the Mob, and the Mob Fights Back," *New York Times*, June 15, 1992, pp. A1, A7; James Sterngold, "Corporate Japan's Unholy Allies," *New York Times*, December 6, 1992, pp. F1, F6.

Legitimate industries serve important functions for organized crime. For instance, banks "launder" or recirculate billions of dollars in illegal profits each year to make it seem that the money comes from legitimate investments. The Senate Permanent Investigating Subcommittee describes this process as follows:

These *yakuza* syndicate members are attending the funeral for one of their leaders in Tokyo.

A drug dealer gives a large amount of cash from drug sales to a "launderer" who dispatches "smurfs" to several banks to purchase money orders or cashier's checks.

The money orders or checks are then deposited in accounts which are usually fronts for criminal activity. The money from the accounts is then wired to overseas banks, where confidentiality laws prevent disclosures of information about the account's ownership or transactions.

The money can be sent back to the U.S. bank accounts controlled by the drug dealer, or it can be transferred to foreign bank accounts to purchase new drug shipments. (cited in *Boston Globe*, December 30, 1986: 10)

Increasingly, money laundering involves EFT crime, with home-banking computer programs being used to move money across international borders (Sanger, 1995). Perhaps the biggest money-laundering scheme was uncovered in 1991, when bank regulators in several nations closed the Bank of Commerce and Credit International (BCCI), which had served the money-laundering needs of the powerful Colombian drug cartel; in 1994, a court in the United Arab Emirates sentenced twelve former executives of that bank to prison. Organized crime is thus supported by the actions of financial institutions, as well as made possible by the failure of legitimate enterprises to meet certain public demands for goods and services.

Social and Economic Sources of Conventional Crime

Conventional crime is influenced by the economic system in many ways. Modernization affects the level of a society's crime rate and the kinds of crime it experiences. Changes in the value of goods create new opportunities for crime. Unemployment and crime are related to each other in complex ways. Cultures that encourage people to strive for material success can generate dissatisfaction, which is conducive to crime among the unsuccessful. Sociologists have sought to explain the impact of these and other socioeconomic factors on crime and delinquency.

Modernization and Crime

The process of economic development affects the amount and characteristics of crime in all societies. In general, high proportions of all of the crimes committed in economically developed societies are property crimes, because with prosperity there are many opportunities to steal. In less developed economies, property crimes usually make up a smaller proportion of all crimes, and violent crimes are relatively more common (Clinard and Abbott, 1973; Shelley, 1981a). The overall crime rate tends to rise with economic modernization, but some of that increase is probably due to the development of a professional police force that keeps better records. With economic development also come increases in the relative amounts of crime by juveniles and by women. In developing societies women rarely commit more than one-tenth of all crimes, but in economically advanced societies they are responsible for as much as one-fifth of all crimes (Shelley, 1981a: 141).

Some societies have avoided high and rising crime rates as they have modernized. High rates have been avoided where traditional group ties and cultural values have been maintained; Japan and some Middle Eastern nations are examples. Control over urbanization and migration can also reduce the rate at which crime increases. Harsh treatment of criminals—including long prison sentences or capital punishment—seems to have contained the crime problem in Stalin's Soviet Union and Franco's Spain. For years, eastern European nations limited the growth of crime by redistributing income and guaranteeing jobs. By contrast, crime has increased in advanced economic systems such as the United States, where everyone is urged to strive for material success in a system marked by great income inequality (Shelley, 1981a: 142).

Opportunity and the Economy

Property crime rates increase especially dramatically with economic development because of growing opportunities for theft. Within developed economies, fluctuations in the value of certain goods can create new opportunities for crime. For instance, the enormous increase in the market value of gold and silver during the 1970s changed the theft patterns of burglars, who began to leave behind televisions and stereos in favor of jewelry and silverware. Street criminals began to grab gold necklaces from women's necks, injuring and in a few cases even killing their victims. This increase in the theft of precious metals had several consequences: longer waiting lists for bank safe-deposit boxes; the updating of insurance policies; the establishment of refineries in the United States to melt down stolen jewelry, coins, and silverware; and advertisements by metal dealers to buy gold and silver with "no questions asked."

Unusual crimes have developed as the value of certain goods has increased. "Bee rustling"—the theft of beehives—became a problem as the cost of a bee colony climbed from $25 to $65 between 1975 and 1982; a truckload of one hundred hives could net thieves $6,500 for one night of work. Other items that have become the targets of thieves as price and demand have risen include endangered species of cacti (which can sell for up to $15,000 apiece); colonial tombstones (which fetch as much as $3,000 each); sports memorabilia (with a 1952 Mickey Mantle card valued at $10,000); car air bags (which sell for $200 to $600 on the black market); and laptop computers (of which 208,000 were stolen in 1995, a 40 percent increase over 1994).

Unemployment and Crime

Unemployment is related to crime in complex ways. Some crimes cannot occur unless a person is working; embezzlement and price-fixing are examples. In such cases, higher unemployment rates might reduce crime. Other offenders mix employment and crime by "moonlighting" in crime, by using a job as a front (as with a professional fence), or by using legitimate income as a stake for a crime (as in drug deals). For moonlighters, more unemployment might increase criminal activity, but for those who use a job as a front or use their income for a stake, unemployment might reduce crime. Some people, especially youths, alternate between employment and crime, and in those cases more unemployment might increase crime (Hagedorn, 1994). Finally, some offenders are committed to crime as a source of income. They would not work even if jobs were available, and so a higher unemployment rate would not affect their criminal activity (Thompson et al., 1981; Sviridoff and Thompson, 1983). Moreover, involvement in crime isolates offenders from the contacts typically used to secure good jobs (Hagan, 1993).

There might be a difference between people who are working or are temporarily unemployed, and people who have been out of work for a long time or who have stopped looking for jobs. The difference between having a job or not having a job at any given moment could be less significant (Votey and Phillips, 1974). Even more important than finding a job is keeping a job over time, for jobs bind people to legitimate institutions and give them a "stake in conformity" that they do not want to jeopardize by involvement in crime. Criminals tend to have poorer work records and higher rates of unemployment than nonoffenders, but some research indicates that more and better job opportunities could lead some offenders to select legitimate sources of income over illegal ones (Freeman, 1983: 106). People who hold unattractive jobs that are low paying, boring, and offer little room to advance may not think they stand to lose much if they are arrested (Cook, 1975; Orsagh and Witte, 1981). As a result, finding a good job to which a person can feel committed over time is probably more important than simply having some job.

People who are without jobs seem more likely to commit the kinds of crime that lead to imprisonment (Viscusi, 1986; Austin and Irwin, 1990). A 1991 survey found that one-third of state prison inmates had been unemployed during the month prior to being arrested for the offense for which they were incarcerated; that unemployment rate is much higher than the rate for the general population (Beck et al., 1993). In addition, offenders who are even slightly more successful at work commit fewer crimes than offenders who are less successful in the labor force (Petersilia, Greenwood, and Lavin, 1977). Some research indicates that unemployment rates prior to imprisonment are a strong predictor of which inmates will engage in crime at the highest rate after their release (Greenwood, 1982). An experimental study also concluded that employment in the postrelease period and the steadiness of that employment were associated with lower arrest rates (Rossi, Berk, and Lenihan, 1980).

Crime also occurs at work, with one-sixth of all fatal workplace injuries in 1994 being the result of 1,071 on-the-job homicides. Robberies accounted for three-fourths of those murders, and driving a cab was the riskiest job. Sudden loss of a job or conflict with a supervisor sometimes leads to violent crime against those thought to be responsible for the employee's problem. The typical offender is a middle-aged white male who fears losing a job, or has lost a job, in an economy that seems to offer few opportunities for a new job and that seems to him to offer advantages to younger workers, women, blacks, and foreigners. Workers who are predisposed to blame others rather than themselves for their problems and who lack the support of family and friends are especially likely to resort to violence against supervisors when they lose their jobs, especially if they have worked many years for the same company (Fox and Levin, 1993). One work setting that has generated much criminal violence is the U.S. Postal Service; between 1983 and 1995, twelve postal employees or former employees killed thirty-nine coworkers, supervisors, and customers in post offices. A 1994 congressional report attributed this violence to a "dysfunctional organizational culture" which it described as follows:

> Overall, we found that labor-management problems are long-standing and have multiple causes that are related to an autocratic management style, adversarial employee and union attitudes, and inappropriate and inadequate performance management systems. (cited in *New York Times*, October 28, 1994: A24)

One explanation of delinquency focuses on youths' lack of access to jobs that provide the income they need to participate in peer-group activities and to buy the clothes and other things that will win them the esteem of their friends. The exclusion of young people from adult work roles and the increased competition that youths have encountered from greater numbers of women in the work force deprive young people of income and make them financially dependent on their parents for longer periods of time (Phillips and Votey, 1981). Juvenile delinquency has been attributed to the "structural position of juveniles in an advanced capitalist economy" that excludes the young from good-paying jobs because of child labor laws, compulsory education, and minimum wage laws (Greenberg, 1977b: 220). Some delinquency is also situational; for example, among homeless youths in Toronto unemployment and problems of shelter led to prostitution, and problems of shelter and hunger led to serious theft (McCarthy and Hagan, 1992).

Research in New York City neighborhoods shows that persistent unemployment among adults limits the development of stable households and reduces job opportunities for young people in the community. These changes, in turn, weaken informal social control in the area, contributing to higher local crime rates. If legitimate jobs are not available or if they pay poorly, young people are more likely to turn to theft, the sale of drugs, or other crimes for income (McGahey, 1986).

Recent structural changes in the economy, such as the relocation of manufacturing to suburban areas or to Third World countries, threaten to create a permanent "underclass" of unemployed blacks. Discrimination in hiring and in pay in the retail industry also poses a formidable barrier to upward mobility for members of this underclass and reduces their attachment to the labor force (Auletta, 1982; Duster, 1987).

Despite some persuasive evidence for a link between unemployment and crime, aggregate national data show that fluctuations in the unemployment rate are no more than weakly related to the rate of index crimes (Gillespie, 1975; Orsagh and Witte, 1981: 1059). One review of the evidence concludes as follows: "There is a cyclical pattern to the crime rate, with crime rising over the cycle with unemployment—but only weakly, so that changes in crime rates are dominated by other factors" (Freeman, 1983: 106). Critics question the conclusion that unemployment and crime are not strongly associated, arguing that measures of unemployment are flawed, leaving out "discouraged workers" who are no longer seeking work and failing to measure the quality of the jobs that people are doing (Currie, 1985). Measures of crime are also imperfect (see Chapter 2).

Relative Deprivation and Crime

Even more important than poverty or unemployment as a cause of crime may be the way poor or unemployed people perceive their situation. Most poor and unemployed people are law-abiding, and the crime rates of the poor in many developing nations are lower than the crime rates of Americans, who have higher absolute standards of living. For instance, blacks in the United States have higher incomes, on the average, than black Africans, but black Americans have higher crime rates than black Africans.

What seems important, then, is people's relative standard of living. Resentment is probably more common among the poor in a wealthy nation than it is among people who have a lower absolute standard of living in a poor nation. Quetelet observed in the nineteenth century that the rural poor in Europe were generally honest, but that the urban poor who were nearer to great wealth and temptation were more prone to crime. Relative rather than absolute poverty was given as the reason for this difference (cited in Radzinowicz and King, 1977: 77). A study of fifty-two nations found that inequality generated by economic discrimination against certain groups, such as racial and ethnic minorities, is significantly and positively related to a society's homicide rate (Messner, 1989). Compared to other industrial societies, the United States has both a high rate of violent crime and great inequality in wealth and income; that inequality increased from 1968 to 1994, when it was greater than at any point since the end of World War II (Bradsher,

1995; Holmes, 1996). Growing income inequality within both black and white racial groups from 1957 to 1990 is associated with increases in the rate of homicide, robbery, and burglary arrests for each group over that time (LaFree and Drass, 1996). Crime rates are also highest in American cities where the difference between the income of the poor and the income of the rich is the greatest (Danziger and Wheeler, 1975; Blau and Blau, 1982; Sampson, 1985, 1986; Fowles and Merva, 1996).

The discrepancy between people's expectations and their capabilities can motivate them to violate the law. Expectations are the goods and conditions of life to which people think they are rightfully entitled, and capabilities are the goods and conditions of life they believe they can attain and maintain under the current social system (Gurr, 1970). The discrepancy between the two is called **relative deprivation.** Crime is probably most common when there is much relative deprivation with regard to deeply held goals such as material success. Crime also occurs when people think they have exhausted all constructive means to reach their goals and believe that legitimate opportunities to reduce their relative deprivation are unavailable to them. Crime is not, however, the only reaction to a sense of relative deprivation, for relative deprivation can also lead to political action, a social movement, suicide, or alcoholism. However, those who control political power often define the actions of the relatively deprived as crime, whether those actions are larceny, political protest, or terrorism.

Relative deprivation becomes greater when expectations increase or when capabilities decrease. A sudden drop in prosperity can reduce perceived capabilities, but relative deprivation more often increases because of a growth in expectations. In developing nations, the "demonstration effect" leads to a desire for a better standard of living among people who move to large cities where a wealthy life style can be observed firsthand. Capabilities usually do not rise as fast as expectations, and thus relative deprivation increases and crime rates rise.

People develop their ideas about what they are entitled to not only by comparing their own social position to that of others, but also by comparing their own efforts and contributions to those of others. A sense of equity exists when individuals believe that their own social position is in the same ratio to their efforts as are the social positions and efforts of others. The belief that others are getting more than they deserve relative to their efforts can lead to a **sense of inequity** that motivates people to violate the law for personal gain (Wilson and Herrnstein, 1985). An unexplored question is whether state lotteries, which produce millionaires on the basis of no more effort than the lucky selection of a few random numbers, increase a sense of inequity among the population at large.

Anomie, Strain, and Crime

In an important paper first published in 1938, Robert Merton (1968) related particular types of behavior to the social position of the people engaging in the behavior. Whereas Freud tried to explain deviance by the failure of the social structure to socialize people to control their natural impulses, Merton looked instead at social pressures that cause deviant or criminal behavior. For Merton, crime was rooted in the social system rather than intrinsic to the makeup of humans. He was not interested in explaining the behavior of each and every individual, but in explaining differences in rates of behavior for different groups and categories of people.

Goals and Means   Merton's theory is based on a distinction between culturally defined goals and the norms that regulate the means to achieve those goals.

Goals are the valued purposes and interests that a culture holds out as legitimate objectives for all members of society. For instance, American culture emphasizes equal opportunity for all to attain the goals of wealth and power. It encourages everyone to have the same high ambition and treats the failure to achieve cultural goals as an individual failing rather than as a flaw in the social system, a belief that protects the social system from criticism. The culture's emphasis on the measurement of individual worth by material success produces a society with a built-in incentive to achieve. This has helped the nation attain a high overall standard of living, but it has also generated relative deprivation and crime among those who do not achieve the goals of wealth and power.

The second factor in Merton's theory can be described as the institutionalized means to reach the cultural goals. Norms, which define acceptable ways to reach cultural goals, are derived from the values or preferences of a society, rather than from the pure technical efficiency of the means in reaching goals. Thus, robbing a bank might be the most technically efficient way for an uneducated and unskilled person to attain material well-being, but social and legal norms define this as an unacceptable way to achieve wealth. Instead, norms emphasize hard work at a socially approved occupation over a lifetime as the appropriate way to achieve financial well-being.

Anomie and Strain   Social equilibrium exists when satisfactions accrue to people who use the institutionalized means to reach the culturally approved goals. When there is a disjunction between means and goals, **anomie**, or normlessness, results. Such a disjunction often results from the socially structured incapacity of people to use the approved means to reach cultural goals. For example, racial discrimination in education and employment makes access to the institutionalized means of achieving success difficult for black Americans. Discrimination by social class is another socially structured incapacity; success might require a good education, which is less available to the poor, and "good manners," which are defined by the preferences of those who hold wealth and power. **Strain** is the frustration and sense of injustice that result from experiencing socially structured incapacities as low capabilities.

Socially structured incapacities might not produce anomie or strain in a society in which success goals are not held out to everyone. The relative significance of material well-being in comparison to other goals might be the same in most societies, but the absolute strength of the drive to attain material success is probably greater in the United States than elsewhere. This

American "fetishism of money" is spurred by the mass media (Taylor, Walton, and Young, 1973: 94). Television commercials urge consumers to spend money on goods and services that will bring them happiness. Sometimes the message to consume is more subtle. For instance, the large kitchens shown in television commercials for dish soap, scouring pads, and floor wax can be found in homes that only a small proportion of Americans can afford. Television viewers may vaguely sense being disadvantaged because the kitchens they see in television commercials are so much better than their own, and they may hope that someday they will be able to afford a home with such a kitchen.

Modes of Adaptation   Merton develops a paradigm of five **modes of adaptation** to the social structure. He looks at the ways that individuals in different social positions adapt to cultural goals and the institutionalized means to reach those goals. Table 6.2 indicates acceptance of a goal or means by a plus sign (+), rejection of a goal or means by a minus sign (–), and rejection of a goal or means and the substitution of a new goal or means by a plus-minus (±) sign.

Conformity   **Conformity** is by far the most common mode of adaptation to goals and means in a stable society. This pattern involves acceptance of cultural goals (such as material wealth) and acceptance of the institutionalized means to reach those goals (such as a legitimate occupation).

Innovation   **Innovation** is the mode of adaptation most relevant to the analysis of criminal behavior. Here the goal is accepted, but means are used that society regards as unacceptable. Innovation is especially common when the goal that is sought is charged with great emotion. Thus the strong emphasis on material wealth as a sign of individual worth in the United States produces a powerful emotional investment in that goal, leading to a readiness to resort to illegal means to attain it when acceptable means are unavailable. Shoplifting in department stores is closely related to the acquisitiveness of

TABLE 6.2   Merton's Five Modes of Adaptation

Modes of Adaptation	Goals	Means
I. Conformity	+	+
II. Innovation	+	–
III. Ritualism	–	+
IV. Retreatism	–	–
V. Rebellion	±	±

+ = acceptance
– = rejection
± = rejection of goals or means, and substitution of new goals or means

Source: Reprinted with the permission of The Free Press, a division of Simon & Schuster from *Social Theory and Social Structure*, Revised and Enlarged Edition by Robert K. Merton. Copyright © 1968, 1967 by Robert K. Merton.

American society and its emphasis on material symbols of success, with store goods being "dazzlingly arrayed before people who have been exhorted to desire them" (Cameron, 1964: 171).

Innovation occurs when businesspeople resort to embezzlement or price-fixing to attain material wealth for themselves or profits for their firms. Innovation also describes crimes such as tax fraud and larceny, which occur when the desire for more money or goods leads to violation of the law. The pressure to break the law might be greatest among the lowest classes, because they are most distant from the goal of financial security and because their access to institutionalized means to attain material success is the most limited. However, as we have seen, the relationship between social class and crime is not clear-cut, even though serious and repetitive index crimes seem to be most likely to be committed by people at the bottom of the stratification system. Merton's theory of the disjunction between goals and means is general enough to apply to property crimes committed by members of all social classes.

The rise of some big-city political machines in the nineteenth century grew out of efforts by Irish immigrants, who found industry and wealth controlled by native-born Americans, to gain power and status for themselves. When Italians arrived some time after the Irish, they found not only that wealth was controlled by the native-born and that political power was controlled by Irish-Americans, but also that society's need for unskilled labor was less than it had been in earlier years. With the stimulus of Prohibition, some Italian immigrants innovated by using criminal means to achieve wealth and power (Bell, 1962). Another view attributes the involvement of Italians in organized crime not to blocked opportunities to achieve wealth and power, but rather to a rational choice of crime as an easy and exciting way to get rich (Lupsha, 1981). Just as not all Irish-Americans became politicians, so not all Italian-Americans became gangsters, but in each case some members of an ethnic group innovated by using new means to reach societal goals. Irish-American politicians used acceptable and legal means, and Italian-American gangsters employed unacceptable and illegal means. In recent years, other racial and ethnic groups—including the Chinese, Vietnamese, Jamaicans, and Colombians—have also engaged in organized crime to achieve material success.

Ritualism   Merton's third mode of adaptation, **ritualism,** holds little significance for the study of crime. Ritualists accept society's norms about appropriate means to reach cultural goals; for example, they hold regular jobs that produce steady incomes. However, ritualists scale down or give up cultural goals. They keep working but relinquish the hope of achieving material success.

Retreatism   In **retreatism,** cultural goals are abandoned and institutionalized means are also rejected. Because retreatists, such as skid-row alcoholics and drug addicts, reject cultural goals and are unwilling to use accepted means to reach those goals, their behavior is often interpreted as a challenge to the goals most people hold, and so it may be defined as criminal, even if there is no identifiable victim of their actions.

Rebellion   The final mode of adaptation is **rebellion.** Here, a person seeks to create a new social structure that will more effectively allow people to meet what the rebel considers appropriate goals. Rebels attack the value system of the ruling class and seek to replace it with an "ideal universal concept of justice" (Schafer, 1974: 30). Rebels' goals include the humanitarian treatment of all members of society; they oppose the exploitation of some groups to further the narrow interests of the powerful and wealthy. Rebels have an "altruistic communal motivation" for crime, rather than an egoistic motivation, and their offenses are directed toward nonpersonal goals. They try to set an example for their followers and seek publicity for their crimes (see the Crime and the Media box). They pose a threat to lawmakers because they not only reject society's goals, but also propose to replace those goals with their own. Some acts of rebellion involve conventional crimes such as vandalism, burglary, arson, and murder. Other rebellious acts, such as treason and conspiracy to overthrow the government, are defined as crimes by those who control power in order to punish people who challenge the status quo. Crimes that are officially labeled "politically motivated" or "terrorist" are punished with prison sentences longer than those for nonpolitical offenses (Smith and Damphousse, 1996).

Critique of Anomie Theory　Merton's anomie theory is quite general, but it has stimulated important theoretical work on the values of different groups and the availability of legitimate and illegitimate means to reach cultural goals. The theory's assumption that everyone accepts the same cultural goals and that everyone is encouraged to achieve those goals does not describe many societies very well. Even in the United States, anomie theory seems to apply primarily to the goal of financial success and to crimes against property; it does not explain crimes of violence very well.

General Strain Theory　Robert Agnew has proposed and tested a **general strain theory** that expands on Merton's theory. In place of anomie theory's limited focus on the blockage of access to societal goals, especially those involving monetary success, Agnew (1992: 74) proposes that a general strain

The April 1995 bombing of a federal office building in Oklahoma City has been attributed to domestic terrorists with links to the paramilitary movement.

theory should focus on at least three measures of strain: "(1) the actual or anticipated failure to achieve positively valued goals, (2) the actual or anticipated removal of positively valued stimuli, and (3) the actual or anticipated presentation of negative stimuli." Agnew (1992: 74) suggests that criminologists should pay attention to such dimensions of strain as its "magnitude, recency, duration, and clustering of strainful events." He spells out several

CRIME AND THE MEDIA

Reporting Terrorism

Terrorists use or threaten violence against victims who have symbolic importance in order to produce psychological impact that will help them achieve their political objectives. They are less concerned with inflicting harm on the victims themselves than in invoking fear in those who identify with the victims. As a result, terrorists are often "media-motivated," scripting their violent acts to attract publicity that will threaten as large an audience as possible. This makes nations and even cities with prominent media organizations especially vulnerable to terrorism.

Terrorists choreograph their violence to enhance its newsworthiness, choosing a well-known victim, timing an act to coincide with an anniversary or widely watched event, or picking a location where news coverage will be more intensive. One terrorist describes this process as follows:

> We, we give the media what they need: newsworthy events. They cover us, explain our causes and thus, unknowingly, legitimize us…. You must understand: the media are very interested in our actions. They look for contacts with us, they try to get information from us and they are eager to report everything we do or say…. Take for example the news agencies—within a half an hour after calling them and briefing them, which we did quite often, you are in the headlines all over the world…. All you need is one phone call, a threat or a declaration. (p. 61)

The media play an important gatekeeping function in selectively reporting terrorist acts. Weimann and Winn found that the three major American television networks reported only 15, 17, and 18 percent of a large sample of terrorist acts, and that nine newspapers from around the world reported 22 to 33 percent of the events. For all twelve news media, a terrorist event was most likely to be reported if

- responsibility for the act was known,
- there were more injured victims and more fatalities,
- the mode of action was a hijacking,
- the target was an airline,
- the act occurred outside Latin America,
- the targets were British or Israeli, and
- the perpetrators were Irish or Palestinian.

Source: Based on Gabriel Weimann and Conrad Winn, *The Theater of Terror: Mass Media and International Terrorism.* New York: Longman, 1994.

cognitive, emotional, and behavioral adaptations to strain, some of which have received little attention from criminologists. Then he proposes a series of factors that determine whether an adolescent will cope with strain in a delinquent or nondelinquent fashion; these factors include temperament, intelligence, interpersonal skills, self-efficacy, association with delinquent peers, and conventional social support.

One test of general strain theory provided qualified support for the impact of strain on delinquency and drug use, and found that delinquent peers and self-efficacy conditioned the impact of strain on such behavior (Agnew and White, 1992). Another study found that delinquency helps adolescents minimize such negative emotional consequences of strain as anger, resentment, anxiety, and depression (Brezina, 1996).

Differential Opportunity and Delinquency

During the 1950s and 1960s, many cities in the United States experienced juvenile gang warfare, which involved assaults and sometimes murders. Not only did gang "rumbles" provide the basis for many newspaper, radio, and television reports, but they seeped into the popular culture in plays and movies such as *West Side Story*. During this era, criminologists focused their attention on juvenile delinquency, especially gang delinquency.

Opportunity and Gang Delinquency   One influential theory of gangs is Richard Cloward and Lloyd Ohlin's (1960) **differential opportunity theory**, which combines Merton's anomie theory with Sutherland's differential association theory (see Chapter 8).

Cloward and Ohlin follow Merton in emphasizing cultural goals and the means people use to reach those goals. According to Merton, innovation in the form of crime occurs when people lack access to the legitimate means to reach culturally approved goals and turn to illegitimate means to achieve those goals. Cloward and Ohlin add to this theory by suggesting that people's access to both legitimate and illegitimate means is socially structured. In other words, there is "differential opportunity" to reach cultural goals by legitimate means, but there is also "differential opportunity" to use illegitimate means to reach those goals.

Differential opportunity theory focuses on the discrepancy between what lower-class juveniles want and what is available to them. It assumes that "discrepancies between aspirations and legitimate chances of achievement increase as one descends in the class structure," with lower-class youths learning their goals from the larger culture but "unable to revise their aspirations downward" (Cloward and Ohlin, 1960: 86). Their lack of access to legitimate means to reach cultural goals produces intense frustration, and they search for illegitimate means to achieve cultural goals. This theory is much like Merton's except that Cloward and Ohlin go on to show that even illegitimate means are differentially distributed in the society.

Cloward and Ohlin claim that two kinds of opportunities are differentially distributed. First, there are differences in access to "learning structures," which are the "appropriate environments for the acquisition of the values and skills associated with the performance of a particular role" (Cloward and Ohlin, 1960: 148). Second, there are differences in access to "performance structures," or opportunities to join with others who share a similar problem of adjustment and opportunities to gain peer approval for one's behavior. In Cloward and Ohlin's theory, delinquents must not only learn certain values and skills, but they must also have support for the performance of delinquent behavior once they have acquired those values and skills. According to differential opportunity theory, the social structure of a community determines the access that lower-class youths will have to both learning and performance structures.

Critique of Differential Opportunity Theory   Like Merton, Cloward and Ohlin assume that people are socialized with the desire for cultural goals but confront obstacles to reaching those goals. Cloward and Ohlin offer no evidence that lower-class gang boys are socialized to want to reach those cultural goals, and no evidence that the discrepancy between goals and legitimate means is greater for lower-class gang members than for other lower-class youths. Like Merton, Cloward and Ohlin focus on social-structural factors such as institutionalized access to opportunities, rather than on individual decisions about how to act. A more complete theory might also look at the way people seek out or actually use opportunities to engage in crime and delinquency. In spite of its shortcomings, Cloward and Ohlin's theory has had a major influence on social policies, especially the Great Society programs of the mid-1960s, that have tried to reduce crime and delinquency by increasing the legitimate opportunities available to the lower classes.

Research on Illegitimate Opportunity Structures   A few criminologists have tried to identify the factors that determine access to illegitimate means to achieve goals. One study found that women's access to opportunities in the criminal underworld is blocked in various ways (Steffensmeier, 1983). Because women are excluded from criminal organizations and lack the contacts that would allow them to pursue criminal enterprises safely and profitably, they are less involved than men in most kinds of crime, and they tend to engage in criminal activity that is congruent with existing gender roles.

Research indicates that adolescents' use of illegitimate means depends on the resources available to them, such as money, a car, intelligence, and body type; these and other resources "provide the adolescent with the power and autonomy necessary to overcome the barriers to delinquency" (Agnew, 1990: 559). Access to such resources is most likely to lead to delinquent behavior among adolescents who are predisposed to delinquency, are high in perceived self-efficacy, and find themselves in situations in which the advantages of delinquency are high and its disadvantages are low.

Social Class, Values, and Delinquency

Closely related to Merton's and Cloward and Ohlin's social-structural theories of delinquency are social-psychological theories that emphasize social class differences in values and responses to blocked opportunities. Two important theories of this sort are Albert Cohen's (1955) reaction-formation theory and Walter Miller's (1958) theory of lower-class culture.

Reaction-Formation Theory   In *Delinquent Boys*, Albert Cohen (1955: 25) seeks to explain why a juvenile delinquent subculture that he characterizes as "nonutilitarian, malicious, and negativistic" is found among working-class male adolescents. His concern is only with certain kinds of delinquency: gang fights and vandalism, rather than profit-oriented theft.

Cohen describes dominant American values in much the same way Merton does: striving for success through hard work, deferring gratification, being ambitious, maintaining hope for the future, being self-reliant, respecting property, and controlling aggression. Cohen claims that working-class adolescent males pick up these values from their parents, who share middle-class values even though they are members of the working class. Adolescents also learn middle-class values from the mass media and from former members of the working class who have entered the middle class. The school is an important source of middle-class values such as discipline and self-reliance, and its teachers communicate middle-class values and often come from the middle class themselves. According to Cohen, working-class adolescents are at a disadvantage in school, because their background does not equip them for academic success in this middle-class setting. Because they are too young to form a family or to hold a job that pays well, working-class adolescents lack legitimate opportunities to achieve culturally approved goals.

Because they are emotionally attached to middle-class goals they cannot attain, these working-class boys must repudiate those goals. This produces a **reaction-formation**, in this case a reversal of middle-class values. For instance, the middle class favors the control of aggression, so the working-class male adolescent subculture awards prestige for the use of violence. The middle class reveres property, so the working-class gang values the senseless destruction of property. This reaction-formation, a psychological defense against the failure to achieve strongly held desires, seeks the exact opposite of middle-class values as a way of repudiating middle-class goals and validating the goals that replace them.

Cohen thus links a particular social class (the working class) to specific values (aggressiveness and destructiveness) that, in turn, lead to certain kinds of delinquency (gang fights and vandalism). The type of delinquency Cohen is interested in thus originates from a repudiation of middle-class values, rather than from conformity to working-class values.

Critique of Reaction-Formation Theory   Cohen's theory, like Merton's, requires a culture that encourages everyone to strive for the same goals, especially material success. The Cross-Cultural Perspective shows that Argentina is one society in which Cohen's theory does not work very well; little "non-utilitarian, malicious, and negativistic" working-class delinquency occurs there, apparently because the lowest classes are not socialized to seek middle-class goals.

Cohen's reaction-formation theory does not explain middle-class delinquency, nor does it explain why some delinquents turn away from violations of the law and leave gangs as they grow older, while other delinquents move on to become adult criminals. Cohen's emphasis on age explains why some males move out of delinquency as they gain access to other sources of prestige such as jobs and families, but his emphasis on social class does not tell us why most delinquents give up illegal behavior even though they remain members of the working class.

A CROSS-CULTURAL PERSPECTIVE

Delinquency in Argentina

To test the usefulness of Albert Cohen's reaction-formation theory, Lois DeFleur studied boys who had violated the law and appeared in court in Córdoba, Argentina, a city of 600,000 people.

Contrary to Cohen's theory that much theft by working-class adolescent males would be nonutilitarian, DeFleur found that Córdoban boys who appeared in court sold the stolen goods or personally used them in about 80 percent of their thefts. For these boys, stealing was a means to get money and goods, rather than a nonutilitarian activity.

DeFleur found little evidence that delinquency in Argentina was malicious, the second element in Cohen's theory. "Malicious jokes or tricks, senseless vandalism, and unprovoked assaults on others" were relatively uncommon among the Argentine boys.

DeFleur also found little evidence for the third element of Cohen's reaction-formation subculture, negativism. There was no clear evidence that the Argentine boys were expressing hostility toward people who had more property. They did envy them, wanted to have their possessions, and expressed scorn for people who worked hard, but they did not show open animosity toward the middle or upper classes, nor did they deliberately flout authority.

In sum, DeFleur found little evidence of a reaction-formation subculture in Córdoba. At most, there were scattered indicators of such a subculture, and even those occurred infrequently.

DeFleur did find juvenile street gangs in Córdoba. Most of them engaged in the theft of property, which was usually sold to adults. There were traditional neighborhood rivalries and gang fights, but fighting was not the gang's primary reason for existence. There was little drug use by gang members, for drugs were too expensive for these poor boys. The gangs in Córdoba represented an instrumental-theft subculture; theft was a way to pursue pleasure, not an end in itself, as it was in Cohen's reaction-formation theory.

Cohen's theory did not fit the experience of the Argentine boys very well because their culture does not emphasize status-striving for everyone. Latin American countries are more often characterized by a rigid social class structure that encourages people to keep to their inherited station in life. Cohen's theory, on the other hand, requires a strong commitment to achievement and upward mobility.

Source: Based on Lois B. DeFleur, *Delinquency in Argentina: A Study of Córdoba's Youth.* Pullman: Washington State University Press, 1970.

Lower-Class Culture Theory   Contrary to Cohen's theory that nonutilitarian, working-class male delinquency has its roots in the rejection of traditional middle-class values is the position of Walter Miller (1958). Miller proposes that gang delinquency in lower-class communities is a result of positive efforts by adolescents to achieve goals implicit in lower-class **focal concerns**, or areas of interest that elicit widespread, persistent attention and emotional involvement.

The focal concern of "trouble" refers to situations that bring unwelcome or complicating involvement with official authority. Issues of staying out of trouble and getting into trouble are of daily concern to the lower class, according to Miller. The lower class avoids illegal behavior, he says, in order to keep out of trouble, rather than because it is committed to a law-abiding way of life. The lower class seeks to avoid breaking the law, but at the same time may admire those who engage in crime and delinquency.

A second focal concern is "toughness," a concern with masculinity, physical prowess, bravery, and daring. A third is "smartness," the capacity to outwit or con others and avoid being duped oneself. Through clever verbal exchanges, lower-class youths can achieve prestige by demonstrating maximum use of their mental abilities and minimum use of their physical strength. There is an apparent contradiction here, for toughness can inhibit the display of smartness and smartness can inhibit the display of toughness; both, however, are of concern to the lower class, according to Miller.

Another focal concern of lower-class culture is "excitement," the concern with thrills, risks, and the avoidance of boredom. The life of the poor may be unstimulating because of the lack of money with which to pay for leisure goods and activities, and this could be a source of the lower class's interest in exciting activities. Indeed, an early study of teenage gangs concluded that avoidance of boredom was a major reason for gang delinquency (Thrasher, 1927, 1963). The search for excitement can also lead to gambling and the use of alcohol and illegal drugs.

Another focal concern of the lower class is "fate," an interest in luck, fortune, and jinxes. The poor often feel, and with some justification, that their lives are governed by external forces over which they have little or no control. Related to this concern with external control is a sixth focal concern, "autonomy," which is the desire to be one's own master, often expressed as "no one's going to push me around."

Critique of Lower-Class Culture Theory   Miller's theory might lead us to believe that all members of the lower class, even adults, will violate the law regularly, for the theory does not distinguish between offenders and nonoffenders from the lower class in terms of their focal concerns. Unlike Cohen, who examines the sources of the values and norms of working-class male adolescents, Miller does not explain the origins of lower-class focal concerns. Neither Miller nor Cohen explains variations in values and delinquency among racial and ethnic groups. For instance, a study in San Diego found that Mexican-American gangs were oriented to a local network of family and friends and emphasized the preservation of honor, whereas African-

American gangs were business-like enterprises that focused on making money through illegal means (Sanders, 1994).

An Evaluation of Delinquency Theories James F. Short, Jr., and Fred L. Strodtbeck (1965) have tested the theories of Cloward and Ohlin, Cohen, and Miller by gathering data from boys between sixteen and eighteen who belonged to gangs ("gang boys"), lower-class boys of the same age who did not belong to gangs ("lower-class boys"), and middle-class boys who did not belong to gangs ("middle-class boys"). They found little empirical support for any of the theories. The three groups evaluated middle-class values equally highly, and all of the groups evaluated middle-class values more highly than "nearly all other subcultural images, especially those that are unquestionably illegitimate" (Short and Strodtbeck, 1965: 59). Neither the gang boys nor the lower-class boys evaluated lower-class values significantly more highly than they did middle-class values. None of the theories would have predicted these results, suggesting that the theories are inaccurate or incomplete.

Short and Strodtbeck found that gang boys evaluated behavior in much the same way that nondelinquents of the lower class did and in much the same way that middle-class boys did. All three groups accepted what middle-class norms prescribed or recommended. There were, however, differences in their evaluation of things that middle-class values proscribed or prohibited. Goals approved by middle-class values were meaningful to all three groups, but the gang boys were more tolerant of theft and violence, which were proscribed by middle-class standards. The values of the gang boys thus allowed rather than required delinquent behavior. Boys became delinquent because they lacked commitment to conformity, rather than because they accepted norms that forced them to violate the law (Short and Strodtbeck, 1965: 72–76).

One way to interpret Short and Strodtbeck's finding that there was no difference between delinquents and nondelinquents in prescribed norms, but that there was a difference in proscribed norms, is to assume that the gang boys failed to condemn theft and violence because they had been improperly socialized. However, the fact that they shared many values with middle-class boys is evidence that they had been socialized in a way similar to middle-class boys. The gang boys' acceptance of behavior disapproved by middle-class values may better be seen as a difference in values rather than as a lack of values.

Delinquency and Values Social class by itself is not a cause of crime and delinquency. Instead, violation of the law is a result of factors associated with social class, such as values, goals, and socially structured opportunities. We might thus expect delinquents from all social classes to have certain values, goals, and opportunities in common, and also to differ from nondelinquents of all social classes in those factors.

One study that looked at lower-class, middle-class, and upper-class delinquency tried to explain youthful misbehavior in terms other than social class. The researcher found that commitment to values such as short-run pleasure seeking, thrills, excitement, trouble, toughness, conning, and the search for a "fast buck" was associated with self-reported involvement in delinquency; this was true for all social classes. This study also revealed less commitment to conventional value orientations such as hard work, delayed gratification, formal education, and various themes of the Protestant ethic among boys of all social classes who engaged in delinquency (Cernkovich, 1978c). This research suggests that social class is a less important predictor of delinquency than values, and that values are imperfectly correlated with social class.

Some people may violate the law because they are able to "stretch" values (Hyman, 1966). They may share values with the middle class and the law-abiding, but because they are weakly attached to family, school, and work, they believe they have little to lose from violating the law. They may thus be more flexible in interpreting social constraints on their behavior. For instance, one middle-class value is respect for property; a related norm is that property should not be stolen, damaged, or used without the owner's permission. This norm is adhered to by most people, but some people are able to stretch the norm by reinterpreting it to define a purse on an office desk as property that can be stolen because the owner was careless enough to leave it unattended. The stretching of norms to permit violation of the law probably occurs among members of all social classes, including poor people who shoplift and wealthy executives who engage in price-fixing.

Short and Strodtbeck (1965: 248–264) suggest a similar interpretation of their finding that all three groups of boys in their study supported prescribed middle-class values, but that gang boys held different attitudes toward acts proscribed by those values. They propose that some lower-class males might find it more practical to be deviant in certain circumstances, with situational pressures allowing those boys to neutralize norms prohibiting certain behavior. For instance, it may be rational for them to break the law if their behavior increases their prestige among their friends. Short and Strodtbeck argue that if there is a small chance of serious consequences such as arrest, and a great chance to gain prestige from fighting or theft, it makes sense for gang boys to violate the law. The payoff in social approval is immediate, but punishment is uncertain and remote in time.

The Subculture of Violence

One theory of the origin of violent crime that uses norms and values as explanatory variables is the **subculture-of-violence theory** developed by Marvin Wolfgang and Franco Ferracuti (1967, 1982). They state that the norms shared by a group of people sometimes define violence as an appropriate response to certain circumstances. These norms have a reality of their own and influence behavior, sometimes leading people to engage in violent crime in order to conform to others' expectations. Wolfgang and Ferracuti do not explore the historical and social-structural origins of these norms in detail, but they imply that the norms originate in the social conditions of certain countries, social classes, and racial and ethnic groups. This theory is a cultural explanation of violent crime rather than a social-structural explanation, and so it emphasizes norms, values, and beliefs rather than the social conditions that give rise to a subculture of violence.

A **subculture** is a patterned way of life similar in some ways to but different in others from the dominant culture of a society. It includes specific standards of behavior that are learned and transmitted from generation to generation. In a subculture of violence, the norms differ from those of the dominant culture in expectations about the use of violence or aggression as a response to threats, insults, or the display of a weapon. As a result, the more integrated into a subculture of violence an individual or a group is, the greater the likelihood that the individual or group will engage in violent crime. Violence in such a subculture is rarely accompanied by guilt, because violence is not considered wrong or deviant.

Evidence on the Subculture of Violence   Wolfgang's study of homicide in Philadelphia found evidence consistent with the subculture-of-violence theory. Forty-three percent of the homicide offenders had been arrested previously for crimes against the person, and about one-fourth of the homicide victims had been arrested for crimes against the person (Wolfgang, 1958: 178). Whites had a murder rate of 1.8 per 100,000, and white males between twenty and twenty-four had a rate of 8.2 per 100,000. Blacks, on the other hand, had a murder rate of 24.6 per 100,000, and black males between twenty and twenty-four had a homicide rate of 92.5 per 100,000 (Wolfgang, 1958: 33, 66). The homicide rate for young black males was thus much higher than the rate for any other group. Wolfgang and Ferracuti later interpreted these and other data—such as Colombia's pattern of *la violencia*, in which 280,000 people were killed from 1946 to 1958—as support for their theory that among certain groups and in certain nations there exist norms favoring the use of interpersonal violence.

There is other evidence that a subculture of violence might exist among black Americans. A study of fifty black offenders found that about 70 percent of them carried firearms because they anticipated attacks by others; this defensive posture could lead to crimes of violence (Schultz, 1962). There is also some evidence that blacks are more likely than whites to engage in angry fistfights, even though blacks do not report that they feel group support for this activity. The value that blacks place on "staying cool" leads to more talk about fighting than actual fighting (Erlanger, 1974). Evidence contradicting the idea that there is a subculture of violence among black Americans comes from a study that found that although whites commit fewer homicides than blacks, whites are more likely to report that they own firearms, are more likely to have been assaulted, and are more tolerant of assaultive behavior (Doerner, 1978).

Homicide in the South: Testing for a Subculture of Violence   Several criminologists have tried to explain regional variations in homicide rates by a subculture of violence (Hackney, 1969; Gastil, 1971; Loftin and Hill, 1974;

Erlanger, 1975; O'Connor and Lizotte, 1978; Messner, 1982, 1983a, 1983b; Dixon and Lizotte, 1987). In Chapter 4, we saw that although the South has a homicide rate higher than other regions, regional rates have become more similar in recent years, and the higher rate in the South is attributable in part to the demographic composition of its population.

One method used to test the effect of cultural values on the homicide rates of different regions is to isolate the effects of economic and social factors on homicide rates, and then attribute the remaining variation in regional homicide rates to cultural differences, such as the norms of a subculture of violence. The problem with this approach is that it includes no direct measure of regional variations in norms and values. As a result, if the measurement of economic and social factors is inadequate or incomplete, the residual effect of cultural factors will be exaggerated. One study concluded that the economic, educational, and racial composition of the states was relatively unimportant in explaining regional variations in homicide rates, and suggested that a subculture of violence explained such variations (Hackney, 1969). However, a later study that employed a more sophisticated measure of poverty found that poverty explained much of the state-by-state variation in homicide rates (Loftin and Hill, 1974). Thus an index that better measured poverty left a smaller residual variation in homicide rates that could be attributed to a subculture of violence.

One study found that the homicide rates of 204 metropolitan areas in the United States were influenced by the region in which the city was located and by its racial composition, even when factors such as poverty were controlled (Messner, 1983a). In other words, the higher homicide rates in the southern cities, and also in the cities with larger black populations, could not be accounted for by low income alone. However, this study, like most previous ones, provided no direct measure of subcultural values.

Another study used the results of a national survey to test for the existence of a southern subculture of violence. The researchers distinguished between "violent attitudes" (such as approving of a man who punches a protester or approving of a man who punches a drunk who has bumped into the man and his wife) and "defensive attitudes" (such as approving of a man who punches a burglar in his house or approving of a man who punches a stranger who has hit his child). The researchers concluded that the violent attitudes were not associated with a regional subculture of violence, after structural differences among regions were taken into account. Defensive violence was more widespread in the South, but the researchers argued that such defensive violence was not characteristic of a subculture of violence; they saw it instead as "a part of mainstream American cultural attitudes that regard violence in the protection of people and property as legitimate" (Dixon and Lizotte, 1987: 391). A critique of this study suggested that the greater willingness of Southerners to use defensive violence was in fact evidence of a subculture of violence, and that the questions measuring "violent attitudes" did not adequately characterize traditional southern attitudes toward the use of violence (Ellison and McCall, 1989). Dixon and Lizotte's study is an advance over previous research that had failed to measure attitudes toward violence in a direct way, but it raises another issue: exactly how do we define a subculture of violence, and what specific attitudes about when violence should be used will demonstrate the existence of such a subculture? The precise role of the subculture of violence in explaining regional variations in homicide rates is still unclear.

Critique of the Subculture-of-Violence Theory Some groups, regions, and countries do have high rates of criminal violence, but there is as yet no strong evidence supporting a role for the subculture of violence in the genesis of violent crime. This could be because the appropriate research design to test for this relationship has not been developed or implemented. Some researchers have inferred norms and attitudes supporting the use of violence from high rates of violent crime, and then explained those high rates of violent crime by the inferred norms and attitudes. This tautological approach provides no independent evidence that norms and attitudes supporting violence exist in groups, regions, or countries that have high rates of violent crime.

There is also no direct evidence that Southerners hold the values of a subculture of violence (Reed, 1971; Ball-Rokeach, 1973; Curtis, 1975; Dixon and Lizotte, 1987). More research on cultural differences among regions of the country might be done by carrying out surveys or by examining regional variations in preferences for art, literature, music, or sports (Messner, 1983a). Even if such regional variations were found, they might not explain differences in rates of violent crime, because violence might be more closely related to the nature of social interaction in a group than it is to the group's norms and values about when violence is appropriate (Ball-Rokeach, 1973).

Angry Aggression and Disputatiousness The failure to demonstrate conclusively that groups and regions with high rates of violent crime hold values that actually support violence has led some sociologists to suggest alternative explanations for violence. One theory proposes that "angry aggression" that sometimes takes the form of violent crime characterizes "the truly disadvantaged," William Julius Wilson's (1987) term for lower-class people who live in cities and experience discrimination and social isolation. Their low position exposes members of this social class to a high level of stress and limits the resources they have available for coping with the effects of that stress. The urban environment exposes the truly disadvantaged to stress, crowding, noise, and other conditions associated with a high level of arousal, which in turn is associated with a high probability of angry aggression. Racial and ethnic discrimination blocks opportunities and insults people, thereby heightening arousal and increasing angry aggression. Social isolation reinforces angry aggression by confining the truly disadvantaged to communities that have high rates of violent crime; living with the daily threat of crime exacerbates stress and angry aggression (Bernard, 1990). This theory does not propose that people value violence, but rather that certain social conditions heighten arousal, stress, and angry aggression, all of which are linked to high levels of violent crime for particular social classes, racial and ethnic groups, communities, and regions.

A similar theory proposes that differences in rates of violent crime may be explained by variations in "disputatiousness" (Luckenbill and Doyle, 1989). A dispute begins when a person defines a negative outcome of a social interaction as an injury for which the other person is to blame. After the negative outcome is defined as a grievance, the victim may demand reparation from the person who caused the injury. If that other person rejects the claim for reparation, the situation becomes a dispute. The person holding the grievance might react in a variety of ways, one of which is the use of force. Disputatiousness is the likelihood of defining an injury as a grievance and claiming reparation, and aggressiveness is the willingness to persevere and use force to resolve the dispute. When homicides occur, they are often the result of the use of force to resolve such interpersonal disputes (Luckenbill, 1977). Disputatiousness and aggressiveness could be concentrated among those groups, communities, and regions that have high levels of violence, but research to support that theory, as well as research to test the related theory of angry aggression, has not yet been done.

Gender, Crime, and Feminist Criminology

Explanations of the difference between men's and women's crime rates have long been part of criminology. Early theorists assumed innate differences between the sexes, portraying men as naturally more aggressive than women as a way of explaining why men commit so much more crime. Other criminologists have proposed that men commit more crime than women because they are socialized differently; that is, men are taught to be more aggressive, and women learn to be more passive. More recently, feminists have argued that **gender structure**—the institutional arrangements that treat men and women, and boys and girls, differently—is associated with differences between the sexes in crime. Gender structure involves a division of labor between men and women, males' domination of the power structure, and gendered differences in sexuality (Connell, 1993).

Kathleen Daly and Meda Chesney-Lind (1988: 504) describe feminist thought as having the following five characteristics:

- Gender is not a natural fact but a complex social, historical, and cultural product; it is related to, but not simply derived from, biological sex difference and reproductive capacities.
- Gender and gender relations order social life and social institutions in fundamental ways.
- Gender relations and constructs of masculinity and femininity are not symmetrical but are based on an organizing principle of men's superiority and social and political-economic dominance over women.
- Systems of knowledge reflect men's views of the natural and social world; the production of knowledge is gendered.
- Women should be at the center of intellectual inquiry, not peripheral, invisible, or appendages to men.

Feminist theories focus on gender, but they also incorporate race and social class into their explanations of behavior.

Daly and Chesney-Lind propose three major problems that gender poses for criminologists. The first is the **generalizability problem**, the question of whether theories of crime, most of which were developed to explain offending by men and tested on male subjects, can be applied to crime and delinquency by women. The second problem is the **gender ratio problem**, the issue of why males commit more crime than females. The third problem is sexism in theories of female crime and in the treatment of females by the juvenile and criminal justice systems. Daly and Chesney-Lind (1988: 517, 519) suggest that feminist criminologists should set aside the generalizability and gender ratio problems and "plunge more deeply into the social worlds of girls and women" in order to understand "crime at close range." In her study of sentencing in a New Haven, Connecticut, court, the results of which we examine in Chapter 13, Daly (1994) did this by using official documents to create narrative accounts of the same statutory offenses committed by matched pairs of men and women.

The Generalizability Problem

Most theories of crime and delinquency have been developed to explain males' violations of the law, and then been tested with data collected from boys or men. One explanation for this is that most criminologists have been men, and they have simply failed to acknowledge or be interested in law breaking by females. Daly and Chesney-Lind (1988: 506) believe that "criminologists should begin to appreciate that their discipline and its questions are a product of white, economically privileged men's experiences." A different explanation for criminology's neglect of women is that crime by females is less common, and less serious when it does occur, than crime by males. In 1995, 73 percent of suspects arrested for serious property crimes were males, 85 percent of those arrested for serious violent crimes were males, and 94 percent of prison inmates were males. These figures do not justify neglect of the female offender, but they do suggest that the crime problem, especially the serious violent crime problem, is primarily a male problem (Messerschmidt, 1993; Archer, 1994a; Newburn and Stanko, 1994).

Theories of crime have indeed paid little attention to the female offender, often speaking of criminals as if they are all males. This deficiency is common to both the privileged white men who have developed theories of crime in the past and some of today's feminists who propose theories of "male violence" with little effort to develop a general theory of violence (Archer, 1994a; Newburn and Stanko, 1994). For example, many feminists have treated serial murder as a prototypically male phenomenon, despite evidence that 10 to 15 percent of all serial killers are women (Jenkins, 1994).

Eileen Leonard (1982) has assessed influential theories of crime such as Merton's anomie theory and found that they typically neglect female offending and cannot explain it. Merton speaks of the learning of success goals, but his theory was developed at a time when striving for financial success was something boys were more likely than girls to learn from their parents, teach-

Even though only 6 percent of prisoners in the United States are women, criminologists need to study why some women commit crime and the special needs they have while incarcerated.

ers, peers, and the media. His theory would have been more complete if he had examined the goals that girls and women learned, and then looked at their modes of adaptation to disjunctions between those goals and the means available to attain them. Leonard also claims that Miller's theory of lower-class focal concerns does not explain gender differences in criminal behavior.

Travis Hirschi's social control theory, examined in Chapter 7, was tested only with the data for boys, even though he collected data from both boys and girls. Wolfgang, Figlio, and Sellin's first cohort study, discussed in Chapter 1, gathered data only from boys; but when a second cohort was studied, data were gathered for both boys and girls, allowing the researchers to test the generalizability of their results from the first study and determine if the same social processes were common to delinquency by boys and by girls.

The Gender Ratio Problem

Feminists have criticized criminologists for using the male offender as the point of comparison for assessing the female offender, claiming that the question traditionally asked about the female criminal was why she was not similar to the male criminal. The answer was often cast in sexist terms, portraying women as innately passive, unambitious, and well-suited to the domestic role. Today the gender ratio problem is commonly phrased as, "Why do so many more men than women commit crime, especially violent crime?" (Messerschmidt, 1993; Archer, 1994a; Newburn and Stanko, 1994).

Male-Female Convergence?   Freda Adler's *Sisters in Crime: The Rise of the New Female Criminal* (1975) looked at the gender ratio problem in terms of the changing position of women in society, arguing that the liberation of women from traditional gender roles and their greater participation in the labor force were opening up new opportunities to commit crime, and suggesting that this would eventually produce a convergence of male and female crime rates. As we saw in Chapter 4, this has not happened. Both male and female rates of crime have increased over time, but rates of violent crime have not converged, and the convergence of property crime rates (or, more specifically, larceny rates) seems to reflect differential treatment by law-enforcement agents (such as a greater tendency for stores to report shoplifting to the police, and a greater tendency by the police to arrest rather than warn thieves), instead of an increase in crime by women relative to men.

Has the feminist movement increased crime by women? Those most active in the feminist movement, white women of the middle- and upper-middle classes, are rarely arrested for index crimes; most crime by women is committed by poorer members of minority groups, and they are not well-represented among contemporary feminists. Moreover, research on delinquency by girls finds that violation of the law is not associated with feminist attitudes (Giordano, 1978); indeed, feminist attitudes seem to inhibit property offenses and violent crimes (James and Thornton, 1980).

Since the end of World War II, there has been a large increase in the proportion of women holding jobs outside the home. Some, but probably not most, of this increased involvement in the labor force is attributable to the feminist movement and the changes in gender roles that it has produced. Other social forces that have led more women to take jobs include rising rates of divorce and illegitimacy, an increase in average age at first marriage, and the perception that inflation has so eroded the family's buying power that two incomes are needed. Whatever the reasons for women's increased labor-force participation, women who hold jobs outside the home have more opportunities to commit crimes such as larceny and embezzlement. However, FBI data indicate that most arrests of females are not occupationally related; women are more likely to be arrested for passing bad checks, credit card or welfare fraud, and shoplifting, rather than for employee theft or embezzlement. One study concludes that the increase in theft by women is due less to the feminist movement or increased labor-force participation than it is to changes in merchandising—such as more self-service stores or more buying on credit—that make theft or fraud easier for shoppers, a traditional female role (Steffensmeier and Cobb, 1981).

Increased participation of women in the labor force might have a more subtle effect on the crime rate of females, increasing a sense of relative deprivation or entitlement among women who are not working outside the home, or among those who are being paid less than their male colleagues for the same work. If there is a widespread perception—accurate or not—that other women are doing well financially and being fulfilled by their jobs, then women who are not working may believe that they deserve more than they have. This sense of deprivation could also develop if women, whether in the labor force or not, compare their own position unfavorably with that of men. Feminism might have raised expectations faster than reality has changed, and thus produced frustration that has led to more crime by some women.

Gender Socialization

Male-female differences in crime, especially violent crime, are often explained in terms of differences in the way the sexes are socialized and the roles they play. Anne Campbell and Steven Muncer (1994; Campbell, 1993) reject biological explanations of sex differences in aggressiveness, claiming that men are more aggressive than women because they learn different attitudes toward aggressive behavior. Men are taught to regard aggression as a practical way to impose control over others and assume authority over the external world. Women, on the other hand, learn to regard aggression as a personal failure to control their impulses and therefore as something to avoid. This theory is consistent with some of the evidence on crime; for example, male serial killers frequently use sexual aggression to control their victims, and battered women who kill their husbands usually resort to violence only after a long period of trying to control their anger.

Feminist critics argue that some gender-socialization and gender-role explanations are simply elaborations on assumptions about innate differences between men and women, and that such explanations ignore the role of power and inequality between men and women and the way that social institutions such as the state, the family, the school, and the media construct and reinforce those differences. Gender-role theory also minimizes variability in the construction of gender by implying that there is a single way to be masculine or feminine. An emphasis on socialization also suggests that males and females passively accept what they are taught, rather than actively contribute to the construction of gender (Messerschmidt, 1993: 29–29).

Doing Gender

A concept that links socialization with social structure is **doing gender**, the idea that through their social behavior men develop and act out forms of masculinity, or masculinities, and that women develop and act out forms of femininity, or femininities. Ways of being masculine or feminine are learned through socialization, but they are also influenced by the situations in which people find themselves, the resources available to them, and by social structural factors such as the division of labor, the allocation of power, and cultural definitions of sexuality.

James Messerschmidt (1993) has explored the link between the masculinities that men enact and the crime they commit, showing that much crime by males involves behavior defined as masculine. Race, ethnicity, social class, and age determine the resources that boys and men have to construct masculinity; and the situations in which they find themselves (in school, on the street, at work, or in the family) influence the ways they enact masculinity. Lower-class black adolescents might enact masculinity by carrying a gun, and upper-middle-class white teens might enact masculinity by stealing hubcaps. Adult men of the upper-middle class enact masculine scripts by engaging in competitive business practices, which sometimes lead to white-collar crime, whereas adult men of the working class demonstrate their masculinity by drinking in bars, which can lead to fights. Masculine scripts of this sort both express and reinforce the division of labor between men and women, male dominance and power, and the norm of heterosexuality. As Messerschmidt (1993: 85) writes,

Crime by men is not simply an extension of the "male sex role." Rather, crime by men is a form of social practice invoked as a resource, when other resources are unavailable, for accomplishing masculinity. By analyzing masculinities, then, we can begin to understand the socially constructed differences among men and thus explain why men engage in different forms of crime.

Men are especially likely to enact masculine scripts when their manliness is in question and they need to establish their character. Murders and assaults by men are often efforts to reestablish a reputation after an argument, insult, or threat, particularly when there is an audience to the disrespect shown by another person (Archer, 1994b). Often men's violence against women is aimed at maintaining proprietary control over their wives or lovers, or at thwarting men who threaten that control (Polk, 1994). Men also enact masculine scripts to show others they are not feminine, indeed that they have contempt for women, when they engage in sexual assault, gay-bashing, and sexual harassment.

Most murders committed by men fit one of these scenarios, but relatively few murders by women do; for instance, women rarely kill their husbands or lovers to maintain proprietary control over them. One study of women who had committed murder found that most of them had killed men after long-term provocation and abuse (Kirkpatrick and Humphrey, 1989; see also Mann, 1996). Before resorting to lethal violence, the women usually had to define their situations as life-threatening or as seriously affecting their physical or emotional well-being. Nearly all of the women had violent upbringings, frequently seeing their parents fighting, sometimes with weapons. Many of the women had been beaten, tortured, or sexually abused as children. The women had typically lost someone close to them. Those losses produced an overpowering sense of aloneness, a resentment of others, and a feeling that the world was conspiring against them, which often caused the women to withdraw from social contacts and reject help offered by others. In such circumstances, repeated abuse by a husband or lover sometimes led to lethal violence. This kind of murder can be seen as a means of pursuing justice against a wrongdoer through self-help (Black, 1983). Some courts have accepted a "battered woman defense" as a justification for killing a violently abusive partner.

Power-Control Theory

John Hagan (1989: 145) and his colleagues have developed and tested **power-control theory**, which "asserts that the class structure of the family plays a significant role in explaining the social distribution of delinquent behavior through the social reproduction of gender relations." "Family class structure" is defined as "the configurations of power between spouses that derive from the positions these spouses occupy in their work inside and outside the home" (Hagan, 1989: 145). Also central to power-control theory is the idea of "social reproduction of gender relations," which refers to the "activities, institutions, and relationships that are involved in the maintenance and renewal of gender roles, in the family and elsewhere" (Hagan, 1989: 145).

Proposing that both the presence of power and the absence of control are conducive to deviance, power-control theory seeks to identify the family and social class relations most likely to lead to ordinary delinquency. The theory asks why male adolescents are more free than their female counterparts to deviate in ways defined by the state as delinquent. The answer, according to Hagan and his colleagues, lies in the greater control of girls' behavior by their parents. Both instrumental controls, such as supervision and surveillance, and relational controls, which involve ties of affiliation, are imposed more on daughters than on sons. This greater control of girls discourages them from taking risks, and because delinquency is a form of risk-taking, girls are less delinquent than boys.

Power-control theory links gender and social class differences in delinquency to the structure of the family, claiming that there are critical differences between patriarchal (male-dominated) families and families that are more egalitarian. In a patriarchal family, the husband works at a job outside the home in which he has authority over others, and the wife is not employed outside the home. In an egalitarian family, both the husband and the wife work outside the home at paying jobs in which they have authority over others. Power-control theory predicts that egalitarian families will treat their daughters more like their sons, being less controlling and more encouraging of risk-taking by their daughters. Patriarchal families, on the other hand, will control their daughters much more than their sons, and discourage their daughters from taking risks. In this way, patriarchal families prepare their daughters for an adult life centered around the home, and egalitarian families prepare their daughters for work outside the home.

Because delinquency is a form of risk-taking, power-control theory predicts that male-female differences in delinquency will be greater in patriarchal families, and in the lower and working classes where such families are most common. Male-female differences in delinquency will be less in egalitarian families, and in the middle and upper classes where those families are most common, because girls and boys in egalitarian families are both open to taking risks.

This complex theory has been subjected to several criticisms. Feminists object to the implication that participation in the labor force by mothers in egalitarian families is a cause of their daughters' delinquency, especially since female delinquency has not increased relative to male delinquency over a period when women's labor-force participation has increased significantly (Morash and Chesney-Lind, 1991). Others have argued that working at a paid job, even one with authority over others, does not necessarily translate into greater power in the home for women relative to their husbands; there is ample evidence that women working outside the home continue to do most of the domestic chores in the family, an indication of continuing patriarchy in two-worker households.

Power-control theory receives only mixed support from research studies. Work by Hagan and his colleagues in Toronto supports the theory's main points, but other studies have not supported the theory (Singer and Levine, 1988; Morash and Chesney-Lind, 1991; Jensen and Thompson, 1990; Jensen,

1993). Gary Jensen (1993) claims that power-control theory adds nothing important to Hirschi's social control theory (see Chapter 7) by introducing the concept of power, and that power-control theory weakens its explanatory value by omitting such normative variables as aspirations, commitments, and beliefs, which are included in social control theory.

Women as Victims, Women as Resisters

Feminist criminologists have focused on the victimization of women by violent men, particularly in domestic assaults and forcible rapes. Critics have argued that the portrayal of women as victims, or potential victims, and the need to protect them from male offenders, poses a risk to the liberation of women from traditional gender roles by implying that women are not capable of being independent and equal to men (Roiphe, 1993).

Most feminist scholars believe, on the contrary, that the study of male violence against women is liberating, in that it challenges patriarchal dominance by men and empowers women. Women are capable of acting on their own behalf, despite structural pressures to remain subordinate. Pressure from feminists has produced important changes in recent years: legal reforms have made it easier for rape victims to report their victimization, get help, and prosecute rapists; shelters have been established to house women who are leaving their abusive partners; and prisons have made changes to accommodate the gender-specific needs of female inmates.

Socioeconomic Factors and Variations in Crime Rates

The social, economic, and cultural factors examined in this chapter help to make sense of the variations in crime rates that we looked at in Chapter 4.

Cross-national variations in crime rates seem to be due to differences among countries in social structure, economy, and culture. For instance, some white-collar crimes are more likely to occur in certain kinds of economies; thus, price-fixing occurs in the American economy as businesspeople try to enhance profits, and bribery by consumers is more common in Russia, where goods and services are in short supply. The degree to which a society relies on laws to make widely desired goods and services illegal influences the development and strength of organized crime in the society. Variations in rates of conventional crime from one society to another are attributable in part to the level of economic development, the extent of relative deprivation, and the opportunities that are available to achieve culturally approved goals.

Regional variations in crime rates can also be explained by differences in social structure, economy, and culture. The subculture-of-violence theory proposes that regional variations in violent crime rates are a result of differences in norms and attitudes toward violence, but we lack strong supporting evidence for this theory.

Variations in crime rates by size of the community are also related to the factors examined in this chapter. For example, economic conditions in urban communities differ from economic conditions in small towns and rural areas, and those differences explain in part the higher crime rates of cities. In addition, the close proximity of people from different social classes in large communities can increase relative deprivation or a sense of inequity among the poor and lead to more conventional crime than occurs in the relatively more homogeneous small towns and rural areas.

Temporal variations in crime rates can be accounted for by changes in social structure, economy, and culture. Changes in market conditions can increase or decrease white-collar crime. Technological breakthroughs and a growing reliance on trust and credit create new opportunities for white-collar crime. The passage of laws prohibiting the consumption of widely desired goods and services results in more opportunities for organized crime; this happened during Prohibition, and again more recently with the development of strict controls on the disposal of toxic wastes. The modernization process leads to changes in rates of conventional crime, especially rates of property crime. Conventional crimes also increase or decrease as groups experience relative deprivation, anomie, and blocked opportunities.

Variations in crime rates by sex, age, race, and social class are also related to the social structure, the economy, the culture, and gender structure. For example, most white-collar crimes are committed by middle-aged or older white men of the middle or upper classes. The time needed to advance to the positions in which white-collar crime is committed means that white-collar offenders are usually middle-aged or older. White-collar offenders are usually white men, because discrimination by sex and race has closed many high-level corporate positions to women and minorities. As such discrimination is reduced, more white-collar crimes might be committed by women and minorities.

Anomie theory, differential opportunity theory, reaction-formation theory, and the theory that lower-class culture is a generating milieu of gang delinquency all account for the higher rates of serious and repetitive conventional crime among the lower and working classes. These theories help to account for the high rate of crime by young people, for young people are the most remote from the cultural goal of material success and are probably the most likely to encounter blocked opportunities. These theories also account for the high crime rates of blacks, who have had opportunities to achieve material success blocked by racial discrimination. The subculture-of-violence theory proposes that blacks' high rate of violent crime is due to a difference between their norms and attitudes toward violence and whites' norms and attitudes toward violence, but there is no compelling evidence that this is so. Many of the theories examined in this chapter do not do a good job of explaining the low crime rates of females and the high rates of males, but recently developed feminist theories have corrected this deficiency by showing how gender structure accounts for male-female differences in crime and delinquency.

We have not looked at all of the ways in which the social, economic, and cultural factors examined in this chapter can explain geographic, temporal, and social variations in rates of white-collar, organized, and conventional crime. From this brief discussion, however, we can see that social, economic, and cultural theories can be useful in explaining variations in crime rates.

Summary

This chapter has looked at the social and economic causes of white-collar crime, organized crime, and conventional crime (with an emphasis on juvenile delinquency).

American free-enterprise ideology emphasizes profit-seeking and competition. The pressure to make profits sometimes leads executives and corporations to violate the law; efforts to outperform competitors can lead to offenses such as false advertising. Certain market conditions are conducive to white-collar crime, and trust and credit are sometimes abused. Large corporations have characteristics such as bureaucratic structure, unsatisfactory working conditions, and rational decision making that facilitate white-collar crime and employee theft. As new technology develops, opportunities are created for crime; computer crime is a costly offense that has become more common in recent years.

Prohibition provided an opportunity for gangsters to become highly organized in their pursuit of profits. Since Prohibition ended in 1933, organized crime has turned to other sources of income, including gambling (according to some accounts), loan sharking, illegal drugs, bankruptcy fraud, the illegal disposal of toxic wastes, and extortion.

Conventional crimes, especially property crimes, increase with economic development. Modernization also brings increased participation in crime by juveniles and by women. New opportunities for crime develop as an economy modernizes, and changes in the value of certain goods (such as precious metals) can alter patterns of crime. Employment might be more important for the social ties it provides than for the income it produces, although the overall unemployment rate is not strongly associated with the overall crime rate. One source of criminal behavior is relative deprivation, a condition in which people believe they are entitled to more than they can achieve by the legitimate means available to them.

Anomie theory proposes that a disjunction between cultural goals and access to legitimate means to attain those goals can lead to certain kinds of crime. Innovation occurs among those who strongly pursue cultural goals with means that are not socially approved; examples include petty theft by the poor and price-fixing by corporate executives. Retreatists and rebels are often defined as criminals by those who control power.

Differential opportunity theory emphasizes access to both legitimate and illegitimate means to reach cultural goals, and claims that community social structure affects access to learning and performance structures.

Reaction-formation theory proposes that working-class male adolescents learn middle-class values, but, because they are not equipped to succeed in school and at work, they reject these values and create values opposite to them. Their new values support violence and the theft and destruction of property, and this leads to "nonutilitarian, malicious, and negativistic" behavior.

The theory that delinquents react against middle-class values differs from the theory that the lower class is a generating milieu for gang delinquency. In this lower-class culture theory, delinquency is seen as a kind of conformity to the values or focal concerns of the lower class: trouble, toughness, smartness, excitement, fate, and autonomy.

A study that evaluated differential opportunity theory, reaction-formation theory, and lower-class culture theory found little support for any of them. Instead, gang boys seemed to favor the goals of the middle class but did not feel bound to avoid deviance from middle-class norms. Delinquents seemed to be able to "stretch" values, and they often had more to gain in peer prestige from violating the law than they had to lose from such behavior.

The subculture-of-violence theory proposes that among certain groups and in certain areas there is a set of norms that support violent responses to certain situations. Some groups, such as urban blacks in the United States, and some regions, such as the South, do have high rates of criminal violence. However, there is no strong evidence that those groups and regions have distinctive norms and attitudes that support violence or that such norms and attitudes lead to violent crime.

Feminist theories claim that gender structure is associated with low rates of crime and delinquency by females and high rates by males. The way that gender is constructed by a society's institutions influences the way that men and women do gender; male crime, especially violent crime, is often a way of enacting scripts of masculinity. Power-control theory aims to explain differences in delinquency rates between boys and girls in patriarchal and egalitarian families.

The social, economic, and cultural factors examined in this chapter can be useful in explaining geographic, temporal, and social variations in different kinds of crime.

Important Terms

anomie	mode of adaptation
computer crime	power-control theory
conformity	reaction-formation
differential opportunity theory	rebellion
doing gender	relative deprivation
EFT crime	retreatism
focal concern	ritualism
gender ratio problem	sense of inequity
gender structure	strain
general strain theory	subculture
generalizability problem	subculture-of-violence theory
innovation	

Review Questions

1. What are the sources of white-collar crime in the United States? What policies can you suggest to reduce white-collar crime?

2. What are the major sources of income for organized crime in the United States? How do legitimate economic institutions contribute to organized crime?

3. What economic factors are conducive to conventional crime? What is the relationship between unemployment and conventional crime?

4. How does Robert Merton's anomie theory help us understand the sources of conventional crime? What are the shortcomings of the theory?

5. How do Richard Cloward and Lloyd Ohlin's, Albert Cohen's, and Walter Miller's theories of juvenile delinquency differ? Does research support one theory over the others?

6. What is subculture-of-violence theory? Does research support this theory as an explanation of violent crime?

7. How does gender structure explain the gender ratio problem? What is the generalizability problem? What does it mean to do gender and enact masculinities? How does power-control theory explain male-female differences in delinquency in patriarchal and egalitarian families?

Chapter 7
Social Control and Commitment to the Law

Because most people learn to abide by the law, or are at least aware that the law commands widespread respect, they can engage in crime or delinquency only after they have minimized their commitment to the law. People neutralize the power of the law by justifying their offenses to themselves and to others. People who are weakly attached to conventional institutions are already relatively free to violate the law. This chapter explores the ways that neutralization of the law and the absence of social control lead to crime and delinquency.

Neutralizing the Law

The theories of anomie, differential opportunity, reaction-formation, and lower-class culture all suggest that social forces push some juveniles into delinquency. A contrasting perspective is that delinquents exercise some free will, choosing to violate the law rather than being forced to do so by the social structure. According to this view, delinquents do not hold values that are diametrically opposed to dominant values, as reaction-formation theory suggests, nor are they members of delinquent subcultures that require them to violate the law, as differential opportunity theory and reaction-formation theory imply (Matza and Sykes, 1961; Matza, 1964).

Drift

David Matza (1964) proposes that some adolescents are in a state of **drift**, a condition of limbo between a conventional life style and a criminal life style with no strong attachment to either. Juveniles drift into delinquency in an almost accidental and unpredictable way through their exercise of personal choice. Becoming delinquent involves neither a compulsion to deviate nor the complete freedom to choose how to behave. Matza does not say why juveniles continue to engage in delinquency over time, nor does he indicate why they are drawn to delinquency in the first place. In other words, he does not specify the rewards of delinquent behavior.

In describing everyday delinquency rather than explaining its causes, Matza returns to the ideas of the classical school of criminology, particularly free will. He suggests that one motive for delinquency is existential in nature: adolescents need to "make things happen" to assure themselves of their existence and their mastery over the world. For some adolescents, delinquency involves less risk of failure, and more potential gains, than schoolwork or athletics.

Delinquent, Dominant, and Subterranean Values

Part of the attractiveness of delinquency for juveniles is that it has much in common with the leisure activities of the dominant classes. Rather than see society as split into various strata with distinct norms and values—as do Cloward and Ohlin, Cohen, and Miller—Matza and Sykes (1961) examine contradictions within the dominant value system. For example, the dominant value system exhorts people to work hard and defer gratification, but it also encourages them to seek excitement and go on occasional sprees. The search for adventure is best regarded not as a deviant value but as a **subterranean value** in the dominant value system. In other words, the value is subordinate or below the surface in the dominant value system and is sought by most people only occasionally and in appropriate circumstances. Delinquents can then be seen as people who act in accordance with subterranean values in inappropriate circumstances. For instance, vandalism is tolerated, within limits, on Halloween, but people who destroy property at other times will be labeled delinquent. Matza and Sykes (1961: 717) see the delinquent not as alien to society, but as "a disturbing reflection or a caricature" of society's values. The delinquent's "vocabulary is different, to be sure, but kicks, big-time spending, and rep [reputation] have immediate counterparts in the value system of the law-abiding" (Matza and Sykes, 1961: 717). The motivational thrust behind delinquent behavior is thus normal and derived directly from conventional morality.

Evidence that delinquents have a strong bond to dominant values is the fact that they often express respect for law-abiding citizens. If delinquents held values opposed to dominant ones, they probably would regard law-abiding behavior as incorrect or immoral. Their recognition of the moral validity of dominant values suggests an attachment to the larger culture, even if that bond is broken at times.

The fact that delinquents are selective in choosing targets for offenses is additional evidence that they recognize the dominant morality. Theft and violence are often directed against people who are held in low social regard, such as prostitutes, alcoholics, or other delinquents. This suggests that delinquents can distinguish acceptable victims from those who would elicit negative reactions from the larger society.

Techniques of Neutralization

Social norms that define expected or appropriate behavior for particular situations often lack specificity as to how and when they apply. In other words, norms have flexibility and act only as "qualified guides for action" (Sykes and Matza, 1957: 666). Thus, a norm that theft is wrong might be qualified so that theft is tolerated—or even actually encouraged—if one is hungry or needs to feed one's starving children, if the victim is another criminal, or if the theft is from a large and impersonal corporation.

Individuals can avoid moral blame and maintain self-esteem while violating the law if they tell themselves and others that they had no criminal intent or that their behavior was justified. People who accept the law as legitimate find it difficult to launch frontal assaults on dominant norms, and so they remove the constraints of the law by justifying their behavior in some way. These justifications, which Sykes and Matza call **techniques of neutral-**

ization, are tangential blows against dominant norms and help to render inoperative the social controls that would otherwise check law-violating behavior, enabling but not requiring people to break the law (Minor, 1981). These justifications make it possible for people to commit crime and delinquency without serious damage to their self-image. Deviance such as this has been described as apologetic rather than oppositional deviance (Sykes and Matza, 1957: 667).

The five techniques of neutralization that Sykes and Matza look at are used prior to violation of the law to allow an offender who otherwise accepts the moral validity of the law to break it. Rationalizations can also be used after the crime, but there is less need to justify a crime that has already been committed than to neutralize the law that would have kept the individual from committing the crime in the first place.

Denial of Responsibility   One technique of neutralization is the **denial of responsibility**, a refusal to be held personally accountable for one's actions. People sometimes claim that a criminal or delinquent act was an accident or assert that it was caused by factors beyond their control, such as a broken home, wayward friends, poverty, addiction, or drunkenness. Those who use this technique often feel acted upon by others and by the social environment, rather than in control of their own lives. Other people might avoid crime and delinquency because they accept personal responsibility for their actions. When asked why he had not become a criminal, one nonoffender said: "I was given a certain amount of responsibility and learned to become responsible, and accept the fact that I was accountable for my actions" (cited in Rogers, 1977: 91).

To the extent that the positivist approach to the explanation of criminal behavior has seeped into the popular culture, it may be used to deny responsibility. Sociological research that shows a link between violation of the law and factors such as poverty or minority-group membership can be used by delinquents and criminals to argue that those factors forced them to violate the law, thereby absolving them of personal responsibility for their actions. In recent years, some critics have argued that the United States has become "a nation of victims," with increasing numbers of people using an "abuse excuse" to support a claim that they should not be blamed for their actions (Sykes, 1992; Dershowitz, 1994). For example, the parents of a thief who was killed while driving a car that he had stolen from a parking lot sued the owner of the lot for failing to take measures to prevent the theft.

Walter Miller (1974) claims that the civil rights movement of the 1950s added a "justificatory vocabulary" to traditional explanations for gang activity and other kinds of juvenile delinquency. Gang behavior was not much different in the 1960s than it was in the early 1950s, before the civil rights movement, but in the 1960s gang members were more likely to attribute their behavior to "exploitation by the power structure, restitution for past injustices, and brutalization by the system" (Miller, 1974: 233). One example of this kind of justification for crime was black activist Eldridge Cleaver's "political" defense of his rapes of white women:

Rape was an insurrectionary act. It delighted me that I was defying and trampling upon the white man's law, upon his system of values, and that I was defiling his women—and this point, I believe, was the most satisfying to me because I was very resentful over the historical fact of how the white man had used the black woman. I felt I was getting revenge. (Cleaver, 1968: 14)

Denial of responsibility has also been used to justify white-collar crime and political corruption. In his final months in office, President Nixon blamed his advisors and tax lawyers for his problems. In his resignation speech, he blamed the press that had reported the Watergate incident and Congress that had forced him to leave office. Physicians caught defrauding the Medicaid program have blamed their patients' demands and bad advice from the welfare department for their violations (Jesilow, Pontell, and Geis, 1993). Corporate executives have asserted that their firms broke the law because their subordinates misunderstood orders or took the law into their own hands; subordinates have responded by claiming that their supervisors told them to violate the law for the good of the company or established goals that could be met only by breaking the law. What little information we have on the denial of responsibility by white-collar criminals is usually in the form of rationalizations after their offenses have been committed; we lack evidence that these justifications are used prior to violation of the law to make it possible for white-collar offenders to reduce their commitment to the law and commit crimes.

Denial of Injury   A second technique of neutralization is the **denial of injury**, the claim by offenders that no one will be hurt by their crimes, even if they technically violate the law. Nonoffenders sometimes say they do not break the law because they are able to perceive injury to others and because they are concerned about inflicting harm on others. In other words, sensitivity to others keeps some people away from crime and delinquency (Rogers, 1977). Those who violate the law are less sensitive to the effects that their behavior has on victims or regard their victims as objects or means to their own ends rather than as individuals who suffer when victimized.

Offenders sometimes contend that victims who lose money or have property damaged can afford the losses, or that they can recover their losses from their insurance companies. Offenders often see the losses incurred by insurance companies as unreal, even though policyholders pay higher premiums to offset the costs of claims paid by the insurance companies.

One instance of thieves' regarding their crimes as causing no real loss to anyone comes from a study of eighty-eight workers in a midwestern electronics assembly plant (Horning, 1970). Workers rationalized their theft as causing no injury by making a distinction among three kinds of property in the plant: property that belonged to the company, property that belonged to the employees, and property of uncertain ownership. Property classified as being of uncertain ownership was small, plentiful, inexpensive, and expendable, and the company did not regulate its flow within the plant. The property did belong to someone or to the company, but if workers could categorize it as being of uncertain ownership, they thought they were doing no injury if they stole it. Almost all workers reported pilfering goods from the plant, but few expressed any guilt at doing so, because work-group norms supported theft when it was confined to property of uncertain ownership and limited to what was needed for personal use. The conditions under which theft was tolerated were communicated to workers through "folktales" about thefts that had occurred in the past.

Delinquents use the denial-of-injury technique to justify their violations of the law. Car thieves say they are only "temporarily borrowing" cars, rather than permanently depriving owners of their cars. Gang fights are defined as private quarrels that are no one else's business. Sometimes delinquents and adult offenders actually claim that their crimes are socially useful, as by claiming that they are "Robin Hoods" who steal from the rich and give to the poor. For example, professional fences have justified their crimes as a way of redistributing property from wealthier neighborhoods to poorer ones (Klockars, 1974).

Criminals often say that it is appropriate to victimize certain targets, but that other targets should be avoided. The general public seems to think that theft from a large corporation is preferable to theft from the government, which in turn is better than theft from a small business (Smigel, 1956). People seem to believe that large corporations can afford losses because they are insured, are highly profitable, can raise prices to compensate for their losses, and cheat customers anyway. Large corporations are also unpopular because they are seen as impersonal, inefficient, and unresponsive to the best interests of their customers and clients (Smigel and Ross, 1970: 4). This "rip-off mentality" is evident in the following statement by a safecracker:

> We [professional thieves] would never beat the average working man or anything like that.... When I was a young kid learning, I stole anything. But later on I became a professional and started hanging around with professionals and learned from them that you didn't steal from a home or small place of business; you only stole from a big place that could afford the loss. (King and Chambliss, 1984: 13)

Denial of injury has also been used to justify white-collar crime. A Westinghouse executive responded as follows to a question from a congressional committee about whether he knew that his meetings with other executives to fix the prices of electrical equipment were illegal: "Illegal? Yes, but not criminal. I didn't find that out until I read the indictment.... I assumed that criminal action meant damaging someone, and we did not do that" (cited in Geis, 1967: 144). The executive was wrong; not only did the jail sentences served by some executives show quite clearly that harm had been done, but the fact that plaintiffs recovered millions of dollars in civil damages from the offending companies also indicated that financial harm had been done.

Denial of the Victim   A third technique of neutralization is the **denial of the victim**, the claim that a crime is justified as rightful retaliation against the victim. Offenders define victims rather than themselves as wrongdoers, and they use that attitude to justify their crimes.

The victimization of certain targets, such as prostitutes and shopkeepers who sell shoddy merchandise, is more likely to be socially accepted than the victimization of other targets, such as children and the elderly. Offenders sometimes appeal to widely held ideas about valued and disvalued people to justify their acts. Individuals who recognize that victims suffer, in spite of what those victims might have done to "deserve" victimization, are more likely to avoid criminal behavior. One nonoffender says, "If there is something I want, I work for it because I don't want to hurt anyone else by trying to obtain it by other means. I always try to remember that other people have feelings too" (cited in Rogers, 1977: 92). Offenders do not seem to share this view, but instead think it is acceptable to victimize certain people. For instance, con artists who engage in fraud and trickery justify their behavior by the complicity of their victims, who are seen as having "larceny in their hearts" (Maurer, 1974).

Rapists justify their crimes by saying that their victims "deserved" to be raped because they were sexually experienced, promiscuous, or had a bad reputation, and that such women are "public property" and have no right to reject them as sex partners (Hills, 1980: 67). Rapists also portray women as seductresses, claim that women mean "yes" when they say "no," contend that most women eventually relax and enjoy the sexual assault, assert that nice women don't get raped, and declare they are at most guilty of a minor wrongdoing (Scully and Marolla, 1984).

Condemnation of the Condemners   Another technique of neutralization is the **condemnation of the condemners,** the assertion that it is the motives and behavior of the people who are condemning the offender, rather than the motives and behavior of the offender, that should be condemned. Actions of the condemners, including police brutality and political corruption, are used to justify an offender's violation of the law. People who remain nonoffenders are able to concede the imperfection of the condemners without using it to justify their own violation of the law (Rogers, 1977: 96).

Many kinds of offenders justify their actions by condemning the condemners. Murderers and bank robbers compare the harsh punishments they receive with the lack of punishment for politicians who send young men to their deaths in pointless wars. Fences point out that some of their best customers are judges and police officers (Klockars, 1974). Political criminals and terrorists use the corrupt and self-serving nature of the political system to justify crimes aimed at changing that system (Schafer, 1974). Justifying his Medicaid fraud, one physician condemned the program in the following words:

> It's not related to reality, you know. It's done by people who are not medical people, who know nothing about the services being provided. One of the peculiarities that they do is that they make arbitrary decisions about things totally unrelated to the services you provide. They're constantly irritating and aggravating the doctors and their staff. (cited in Jesilow, Pontell, and Geis, 1993: 172)

Appeal to Higher Loyalties   The fifth technique of neutralization is the **appeal to higher loyalties,** an attempt to justify violation of the law by the demands of a group—such as a juvenile gang or a corporation—that is smaller than the whole society but that requires its members to conform to standards that might be incompatible with the law. Those who place loyalty to the larger social system and its laws above loyalty to individuals or a group are more likely to stay away from crime. One noncriminal expressed this as follows: "I am not a criminal … because I trust the system. I am willing to sacrifice for it. I believe in it" (cited in Rogers, 1977: 94).

Different types of offenders justify their violations of the law by appealing to higher loyalties. Juvenile delinquents rationalize their acts by peer pressure and the need not to let their friends down. Police officers justify graft and corruption by the need to remain loyal to fellow officers. Physicians sanctioned for committing Medicaid fraud cite the higher goals of serving their patients and adhering to professional standards (Jesilow, Pontell, and Geis, 1993). President Nixon's appeal to national security was an effort to justify the Watergate burglary and its cover-up by demands higher than the law. In a 1977 interview, he strongly implied that whatever the President did was not a crime because the President was above the law. Another use of loyalty to demands higher than the law was by an electrical company executive involved in a price-fixing conspiracy; he said, "I thought that we were more or less working on a survival basis in order to try to make enough to keep our plant and our employees" (cited in Geis, 1967: 144).

Other Techniques of Neutralization   Other techniques of neutralization are also used to justify crime and delinquency (see Table 7.1). A person who uses a "defense of necessity" may justify an act by saying it is required by the circumstances; this differs from the denial of responsibility in that the offender accepts responsibility for the act while claiming it was necessary. Stealing food to feed one's starving children might be justified as a necessary act for which an offender accepts full responsibility.

TABLE 7.1   Techniques of Neutralization

1. Denial of responsibility
2. Denial of injury
3. Denial of the victim
4. Condemnation of the condemners
5. Appeal to higher loyalties
6. Defense of necessity
7. Defense of the ledger
8. Denial of the justice or necessity of the law
9. Claim that "everybody is doing it"
10. Claim of entitlement

Another technique is the "defense of the ledger," which is used by offenders who claim that the good and evil they have done balance out favorably over time (Klockars, 1974; Minor, 1981). This technique was used by the lawyer for "junk bonds" dealer Michael Milken after Milken pleaded guilty to securities fraud and conspiracy, for which he was fined and imprisoned. The lawyer said,

> It is an enormous accomplishment for Michael to have been instrumental in finding the capital for hundreds of American corporations, which are generating jobs, providing a livelihood for hundreds of thousands of people. It is Michael's hope that in the long run history will see his violations in context and judge him not just on the basis of his lapses but on the basis of the contributions that he made to the economy and to the American people. (cited in Labaton, 1990: D1)

James William Coleman (1994: 201–213) has identified several additional techniques of neutralization. One is the claim that the law being violated is unnecessary or unjust. This argument can take the form of asserting that government interference in business affairs actually hurts the public, a variation on the condemnation-of-the-condemners theme. Another technique is the claim that "everybody else is doing it too." A version of this justification is that it is not fair to condemn one offender without condemning them all. An additional technique, which is sometimes used by employee thieves, is that the offender deserves the money or that the stolen property is a "morally justified addition to wages" or an "entitlement due from exploiting employers" (Mars, 1974: 224).

Evidence on Techniques of Neutralization

Several researchers have found that techniques of neutralization play an important role in the genesis of crime and delinquency, but some believe it is too early to assess the validity of neutralization theory as an explanation for violation of the law (Minor, 1981).

Embezzlement and the Techniques of Neutralization   From his study of imprisoned embezzlers, Donald Cressey concluded that people violate an employer's trust and embezzle funds when they face a nonshareable financial problem, become aware that they can solve that problem by turning the skills and opportunities of their job in a criminal direction, and can "apply to their own conduct in this situation verbalizations which enable them to adjust their conceptions of themselves as trusted persons with their conceptions of themselves as users of the entrusted funds or property" (Cressey, 1953, 1971: 30). These "verbalizations," which Sykes and Matza call techniques of neutralization, permit people to define the relationship between a nonshareable financial problem and an illegal solution to that problem in a way that makes embezzlement seem justifiable.

Cressey found that justifications were used either before or at the time of the crime; after the offense, there was no need for the verbalization.

Verbalizations were often applications of general cultural values to an offender's specific situation. For example, embezzlers said the following:

> "Some of our most respectable citizens got their start in life by using other people's money temporarily."
>
> "In the real estate business there is nothing wrong about using deposits before the deal is closed."
>
> "All people steal when they get in a tight spot." (Cressey, 1953, 1971: 96)

The vagueness of some business practices made it possible for embezzlers to say they were using the money "temporarily" and to claim that they were "only borrowing," even though they took the money without the owner's knowledge and rarely repaid it.

Whereas men typically cite nonshareable financial problems arising from business miscalculations, overspending, or gambling as reasons for embezzling funds, women are more likely to neutralize the law against embezzlement by citing their responsibilities as wives and mothers, such as keeping their family together or paying for the care of a sick relative (Zeitz, 1981; Daly, 1989).

Justifications for Crime by Blacks Another study that uncovered techniques of neutralization asked 150 black men between the ages of fifteen and thirty the following: "It is said that black men violate the criminal law more frequently than others. If this statement is true, are there any reasons you feel why such a higher violation rate exists?" (Davis, 1974: 74).

The men, who were approached on the street, said that the legal system lacked legitimacy for blacks and gave various reasons for a general "justification for no obligation" to the law by black men. More than four-fifths of the men thought that laws had been created by whites to control blacks, that blacks lacked equal access to participation in social institutions, and that unequal access to opportunities is unjust and indicative of hypocrisy about democratic ideals. At least two-thirds of the men said that racial discrimination had a long history and that whites had supported it over the centuries, that blacks were not obliged to obey the law because they had been forcibly brought to the country and had no choice in citizenship, and that blacks were not protected by the law in the same way that whites were.

For black men who find themselves in a state of drift and without a strong commitment to a conventional life style, these justifications can support involvement in crime. Crime by blacks can result from grievances about unjust conditions and a subsequent lowering of respect for the law and its enforcers, with illegal activity then being accepted as a solution to those grievances. This study did not test directly for the presence of Sykes and Matza's techniques of neutralization among black criminals, but it showed that one group of streetwise black men thought that crime by blacks was a result of the ease with which blacks can neutralize the constraints of the law.

Justifying Violence In a study of sex-related and robbery-related murders and execution-style homicides, several justifications for lethal violence were uncovered (Dietz, 1983). Street violence was justified by the need to protect oneself or one's property, the need to control others and keep them from using violence, the need to protect a reputation from personal affronts, and the need to ward off unprovoked attacks. In sex-related and robbery-related murders, offenders sometimes forced themselves to think of the victim as an object rather than as a person with feelings. The murderers also killed to prevent the victim from reporting the crime to the police and testifying in court. In execution-style homicides, "hit men" sometimes justified their crimes by saying that the victim "deserved to die" or by claiming that the murder was a "public service."

An analysis of National Youth Survey data found that few adolescents explicitly approved of violence or were indifferent to violence, but that many of them accepted neutralizations justifying the use of violence in certain situations. This study supported Sykes and Matza's contention that neutralizations precede delinquency: adolescents who accepted neutralizations were more likely to engage later in violent behavior, especially fighting with their peers. The impact of neutralization on violence was greatest for adolescents who disapproved of violence and associated with delinquent peers (Agnew, 1994).

Delinquency and Techniques of Neutralization   More evidence on the techniques of neutralization comes from a study of delinquency by Travis Hirschi (1969). Data were gathered in 1964 from interviews with California junior and senior high school students, and from school and police records. Self-reports were used to measure personal involvement in six delinquent acts: theft of property worth less than $2, theft of property worth $2 to $50, theft of property worth more than $50, auto theft, vandalism, and battery (beating someone up). The number of acts that a student admitted to formed an index of delinquency. Because few students had engaged in many delinquent acts, those who admitted to no acts were compared with those who admitted to one or more. It is questionable whether someone who has stolen only a pencil from a store should be classified as delinquent, or would be likely to be so classified by a judge, but this way of measuring delinquency was required by the data in order to explore relationships between self-reported delinquency and the acceptance of statements used to justify violation of the law.

Denial of Responsibility   Hirschi measured support for the denial-of-responsibility technique by asking students if they thought that criminals were to blame for their actions. Because few respondents—only 12 percent of the sample—said that criminals should not be held responsible for their actions, Hirschi could not use this question to measure support for this technique of neutralization.

Another indicator of support for the denial-of-responsibility technique was the following: "I can't seem to stay out of trouble no matter how hard I try." Students who agreed with this statement might be able to deny personal responsibility for their behavior and justify violation of the law. Thus, we might expect that those who agreed most strongly with this statement would be the most likely to report involvement in delinquent acts, and those who most strongly disagreed would be the least involved in delinquency. Hirschi's data show that this was the case. Sixty-three percent of the boys who strongly agreed with the statement admitted at least one delinquent act, but only 25 percent of those who strongly disagreed with the statement admitted at least one delinquent act. Those who expressed intermediate levels of agreement with the statement showed intermediate levels of self-reported delinquency (Hirschi, 1969: 207). The findings provide tentative support for a link between denial of responsibility and juvenile delinquency.

Hirschi's study was replicated by Michael Hindelang (1973), who gathered data from boys and girls in rural New York state in 1971. This study provided similar support for an association between this denial-of-responsibility item and self-reported delinquency.

Denial of Injury   Hirschi tested for the technique of neutralization called denial of injury with the following statement: "Most things that people call 'delinquency' don't really hurt anyone." Agreement with this statement would suggest greater ease in denying harm to potential victims of delinquent acts and should thus be associated with more involvement in delinquency. This was the case: 72 percent of those who strongly agreed with this statement reported at least one delinquent act, but only 31 percent of those who strongly disagreed with the statement reported a delinquent act (Hirschi, 1969: 208). Hindelang's (1973) replication of Hirschi's study found similar support for a link between this statement and self-reported delinquency.

Denial of the Victim   The item Hirschi used to measure denial of the victim was the following: "The man who leaves the keys in his car is as much to blame for its theft as the man who steals it." This particular item was not related to self-reported delinquency; the percentages who admitted at least one delinquent act were similar for those who agreed and those who disagreed with the statement (Hirschi, 1969: 210). Hindelang (1973) did not find support for this technique of neutralization either. Hirschi suggests that had he phrased the question as "The *sucker* who leaves the keys in his car…," he might have found an association between responses to this statement and self-reported delinquency. The item Hirschi did use might have said too little about the respondent's attitude toward the victim by referring to him simply as a man.

Condemnation of the Condemners   Condemnation of the condemners was measured by asking for responses to the following: "Policemen try to give all kids an even break." Agreement should be associated with low involvement in delinquency, because those who think the police are fair should be less able to justify violating the law. The evidence supports this: 35 percent of the boys who strongly agreed with the statement admitted a delinquent act, but 58 percent who strongly disagreed with the statement reported a delinquent act (Hirschi, 1969: 211). Hindelang (1973) also found an association between this statement and self-reported delinquency.

Appeal to Higher Loyalties   Hirschi could not test the technique of appealing to higher loyalties with the data he collected, nor did Hindelang ask about this technique.

Conclusion   Hirschi's and Hindelang's studies tentatively support a positive association between three techniques of neutralization and self-reported involvement in delinquent acts. Their work lends some support to Sykes and Matza's theoretical ideas but does not provide a definitive test for those ideas. For instance, Hirschi's and Hindelang's data do not allow them to conclude that the techniques of neutralization were used prior to committing the delinquent acts to make it possible for the boys and girls to neutralize the constraints of the law.

Critique of Neutralization Theory

Neutralization theory implies that people who are committed to a conventional life or who have not yet engaged in deviance will be the most likely to need to use techniques of neutralization. However, one study found that the techniques were used both by youths who disapproved of deviance and therefore needed to neutralize norms, and by youths who already approved of deviance and should therefore not have needed to use neutralization techniques. Moreover, the relationship between the acceptance of neutralizing excuses and subsequent deviant behavior existed only for people who had already committed that deviant act in the past, not for people who had never violated the norm before. This suggests that techniques of neutralization might develop and be used only after people commit an initial act of delinquency or crime, and that the techniques might not precede violation of the law as Sykes and Matza suggest (Minor, 1981).

Techniques of neutralization can be used after the law is violated, when other people call into question an individual's behavior and try to label that person a wrongdoer. At that point, techniques of neutralization might help people minimize their guilt and allow them to continue to see themselves as worthy citizens (Hamlin, 1988). The accounts that people give after the fact for violating the law might, however, reflect the reasoning they engaged in before breaking the law (Benson, 1985). More research is needed to determine whether techniques of neutralization precede violation of the law to make it possible, follow violation of the law to justify it to oneself and others, or both.

Neutralization of the law is a social-psychological process by which potential offenders justify crime or delinquency by employing general arguments about when such violations are acceptable. Neutralization theory can be criticized for ignoring aspects of the social structure that make it easy or difficult to justify violations of the law. These social-structural factors have been explored in social control theory, which proposes that people who are the most weakly attached to social institutions are the freest to violate the law.

Social Control Theory

The **social control theory** of delinquency developed by Travis Hirschi (1969) proposes that people who engage in delinquency are free of intimate attachments, aspirations, and moral beliefs that bind them to a conventional and law-abiding way of life. Delinquents are not forced into delinquency so much as they are free to commit delinquent acts because they lack ties to the conventional social order. Delinquency violates other people's expectations about appropriate behavior, so if people do not care about the opinions of others, they are free to deviate from norms. Most people have deviant impulses from time to time, but whether they act on those impulses depends on their attachments to others.

Delinquents believe in the conventional order even as they violate its norms; the critical factor is the extent to which they believe they should obey norms. Hirschi (1969: 198) says that "delinquency is not caused by beliefs that require delinquency but is rather made possible by the absence of (effective) beliefs that forbid delinquency." This position is similar to Matza's notion of drift: the delinquent is midway between crime and convention, between deviance and conformity. It is also consistent with Short and Strodtbeck's (1965) finding that gang boys support middle-class prescriptive norms but do not support some middle-class proscriptive norms. In sum, delinquents do not hold norms that require delinquency, but rather lack norms that strongly oppose such behavior. The absence of proscriptive norms is related to the lack of attachment to social institutions, and both leave some adolescents free to violate the law.

Social control theory does not make clear the motivations that give rise to violation of the law, but rather looks at the institutions that create barriers to the expression of deviant motivations. The desire to acquire material goods, the need for social approval, and association with other law violators can all push a person to violate the law. However, if a person experiencing those pressures to violate the law is also subject to social control that results from attachment to family, school, job, and friends, that control can counteract the pressure to break the law.

The Family

One institution that is basic to all societies is the family. It socializes the young and provides surveillance over their behavior. It also controls the behavior of people of all ages who value the good opinion of other family members.

Hirschi's research shows that delinquents are much less closely attached to their parents than nondelinquents are. The critical factor is not whether the parents are always physically present to supervise the behavior of the child, but whether the parents are "psychologically present" when the child faces a temptation to violate the law. If the parents are not present in the child's mind, he or she is free to commit a delinquent act without giving any thought to how the parents might react. Nonoffenders sometimes say that they abide by the law because they take their parents' feelings into account when deciding how to act (Rogers, 1977: 37–42). Nondelinquents are also more likely to say that their parents know where they are most of the time, and this acts as a check on their behavior. By contrast, delinquents are more likely to say that their parents do not know their whereabouts.

The closer a child's relationship with his or her parents, and the more intimate the communication with them, the less likely that child is to be delinquent. Relationships with mothers and fathers are of equal importance in controlling delinquency (Hirschi, 1969: 102; Rankin and Kern, 1994). Through attachment to a parent, children learn to care about parental expectations. Attachment to parents seems to be important for children of all classes and all racial and ethnic groups.

The School

A second important institution in controlling delinquency is the school. The most academically successful students are the least likely to be delinquent, for they are most attached to the school and its teachers. Adolescents are more likely to be delinquent if they do not care what their teachers think of them. Again, the expectations of "significant others" are important in controlling delinquency. As Hirschi (1969: 127) says, "Positive feelings toward controlling institutions and persons in authority are the first line of social control. Withdrawal of favorable sentiments toward such institutions and persons at the same time neutralizes their moral force."

Hirschi's research shows that students who are not much concerned with their teachers' opinions and who dislike school also have the weakest relationships with their parents. Those adolescents are the most likely to report that they have committed delinquent acts.

TABLE 7.2   Selected Questions Used by Travis Hirschi to Measure Attachments to Family, School, and Peer Group

Attachment to the Family*
1. Would you like to be the kind of person your father is?
    a. in every way
    b. in most ways
    c. in some ways
    d. in just a few ways
    e. not at all

2. Would your father stick by you if you got into really bad trouble?
    a. certainly
    b. probably
    c. maybe
    d. I doubt it.
    e. don't know

3. How are most decisions made between you and your father?
    a. He tells me what to do.
    b. We talk about it, but he decides.
    c. I decide, but I have to get his permission.
    d. We talk about it until we agree.
    e. I do what I want, but he wants me to consider his opinion.
    f. I do what I want.

TABLE 7.2 *continued*

Attachment to the School

1. In general, do you like or dislike school?
   a. like it
   b. like it and dislike it about equally
   c. dislike it

2. Do you care what teachers think of you?
   a. I care a lot.
   b. I care some.
   c. I don't care much.

3. During the last year, did you ever stay away from school just because you had other things you wanted to do?
   a. often
   b. a few times
   c. once or twice
   d. never

The Peer Group

1. Would you like to be the kind of person your best friends are?
   a. in most ways
   b. in a few ways
   c. not at all
   d. I have no best friends.

2. Would your best friends stick by you if you got into really bad trouble?
   a. certainly
   b. probably
   c. I doubt it.
   d. don't know
   e. I have no best friends.

3. Do the people you think of as your best friends also think of you as *their* best friend?
   a. All of them do.
   b. Most of them do.
   c. Some do.
   d. None do.
   e. don't know
   f. I have no best friends.

* Each of these questions also substituted "mother" for "father."

Source: Adapted from Travis Hirschi, *Causes of Delinquency.* Berkeley: University of California Press, 1969.

Students who are closely attached to their schools and teachers are likely to be academically successful and unlikely to be delinquent.

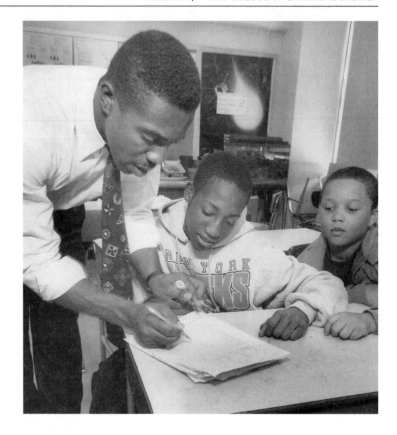

The Peer Group

The third type of attachment that is important in social control theory is relationships with the peer group. Hirschi finds that delinquents are more likely to have delinquent friends than nondelinquents are. However, the relationship between friendships and delinquency is less clear-cut than the commonly assumed pattern of poor family relationships leading to attachment to peers, which then leads to delinquency. Instead, Hirschi finds that adolescents who have weak relationships with their parents tend to have weak relationships with their peers, and those closest to their parents have the greatest number of close friends.

Attachment to peers does not necessarily produce attitudes conducive to delinquency, for the more adolescents respect the opinions of their friends, the less likely they are to be delinquent. Those who are more delinquent and more likely to have delinquent friends are also less likely to say their friends are worthy of respect. Contrary to the picture of the juvenile gang as a warm and supportive group similar to a family, Hirschi finds that delinquents do not have warm and intimate relationships with each other, or with anyone else for that matter.

Conventional Lines of Action and Adult Activities

Thus far, the picture that social control theory offers of the delinquent is of someone who lacks strong attachments to parents, teachers, or peers. Another link in the chain of circumstances leading to delinquency is an individual's aspirations to conventional lines of action, such as education and work. Adolescents who have such aspirations do not want to jeopardize their chances of success, and they would risk losing their "stake in conformity" by getting into trouble with the law.

Young people who do not aspire to conventional lines of action are more involved in adult activities during adolescence. Adult privileges without adult responsibilities might compensate for a bleak outlook on the future. Delinquents are more likely than nondelinquents to see their high school years and the years immediately after as the time in their lives when they will be the happiest. They are especially likely to engage in delinquency because their lack of orientation toward the future frees them from conventional pursuits such as education and a career.

As a measure of involvement in adult activities, Hirschi uses the age at which an individual began to smoke cigarettes and the number of "adult activities"—smoking, drinking, and dating—in which the person is involved. Each indicator shows a significant relationship to self-reported delinquency. Thus, adolescents who began smoking before they were thirteen were the most likely to admit a delinquent act; those who began to smoke between thirteen and fifteen were less likely to admit a delinquent act; those who started after fifteen were even less likely to report a delinquent act; and those who did not smoke at all were the least likely to report a delinquent act (Hirschi, 1969: 167). Involvement in the three adult activities was directly associated with a higher rate of self-reported delinquency. Boys who smoked, drank, and dated reported delinquent acts three times as often as boys who engaged in none of those activities (Hirschi, 1969: 168).

In conclusion, adolescents who have fewer attachments to family, school, peers, and conventional lines of action are more likely to engage in delinquency because they do not feel society's rules are binding on them and do not fear the disapproval of others. This perception can be seen as a "master technique of neutralization" supported by the specific techniques of neutralization examined earlier.

Evidence on Social Control Theory

Hirschi's study provides evidence that delinquency is associated with weak attachments to conventional institutions and lines of action. Other studies, too, support social control theory.

Comparing Delinquents and Nondelinquents A study of juvenile delinquency by LaMar Empey and Steven Lubeck (1971) found some support for social control theory. They used a group of boys who had been labeled delinquent in juvenile court and another group of boys who had not been so labeled. They combined the two groups and then looked at the factors that distinguished delinquents from nondelinquents.

Empey and Lubeck began their research with the theory that lower-class status reduces school achievement, which produces strain that leads to identification with peers, and this in turn draws boys into delinquency. Their analysis of the data led them to formulate a more complex explanation for delinquency. They found that lack of integration into institutions, particularly the family and the school, predicted delinquent behavior. Specifically, measures of strain—such as disharmony in the family and dropping out of school—were directly associated with peer identification, and peer identification was tied to delinquency.

The interrelationships of the critical variables related to delinquency in Empey and Lubeck's research are portrayed in Figure 7.1; a one-headed arrow means one-way causation, and a two-headed arrow means that variables have effects on each other. Hirschi's theory is diagrammed in simple terms in Figure 7.2; here four variables have direct effects on delinquency, but the four variables have no clearly specified causal relationships with each other. For instance, Hirschi finds that lack of family ties is correlated with weak ties to the school, but he does not claim that one directly causes the other. Hirschi's model can be described as follows: lack of attachment to parents, to the school, to peers, and to conventional lines of action each increases the likelihood of delinquency.

Empey and Lubeck's model is more complicated. Low achievement in school leads directly to delinquency, but it also has an indirect effect on delinquency by producing strain in school and in the family, which in turn leads to delinquency, and by increasing peer identification, which is associated with delinquency. Strain in school and in the family leads directly to delinquency and also leads indirectly to delinquency by increasing peer identification. In addition, strain is affected by a juvenile's involvement in delinquency; in other words, being arrested and taken to court produce problems for boys with their parents and teachers. Peer identification leads to delinquency, and involvement in delinquency affects identification with peers, both directly and indirectly, by producing strain in school and in the family. This model is a less satisfying one than Hirschi's model of direct, one-to-one relationships between causes and delinquency, but it is a more accurate reflection of the complex processes that lead to delinquency.

National Self-Report Surveys of Delinquency and Drug Use   Delbert Elliott, David Huizinga, and Suzanne Ageton (1985) employed self-report data from three National Youth Surveys conducted in 1977, 1978, and 1979 to develop a theoretical model that would explain delinquent behavior and drug use. This model, shown in Figure 7.3, reveals a complex pattern of interaction among variables that have both direct and indirect effects on delinquent behavior. However, this study has some methodological problems. The measures of bonds used by the researchers are measures of involvement with family, school, and peers rather than measures of direct attachments to others. Moreover, strain, which is distinguished in the model from bonding, is

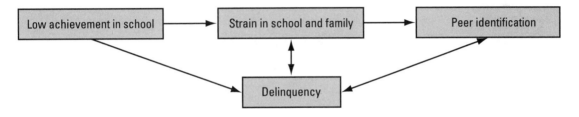

FIGURE 7.1
Empey and Lubeck's Model of Delinquency

Source: Reprinted with permission, from LaMar T. Empey and Steven G. Lubeck, with Ronald L. LaPorte, *Explaining Delinquency: Construction, Test, and Reformulation of a Sociological Theory.* Copyright © 1971 Jossey-Bass Inc., Publishers. First published by Lexington Books. All rights reserved.

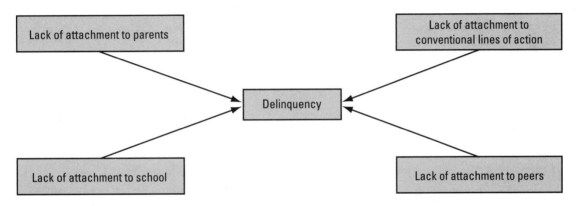

FIGURE 7.2
Hirschi's Model of Delinquency

Source: Based on Travis Hirschi, *Causes of Delinquency.* Berkeley: University of California Press, 1969.

measured in part by subjects' attitudes toward the importance of their bonds to parents and teachers.

This model indicates that delinquent behavior is directly affected by involvement with delinquent peers, contrary to Hirschi's conclusion that delinquents have weak peer ties. Delinquent behavior is also directly influenced by prior self-reported delinquency, suggesting a continuity of behavior over time and perhaps the impact of having been labeled delinquent in the past.

Weak conventional bonding means that individuals spend little time with their families and on academic concerns at school, and that they express relatively little commitment to conventional norms at home and at school. This weak conventional bonding leads to strong bonding to delinquent peers, which in turn leads to delinquent behavior. However, weak conventional

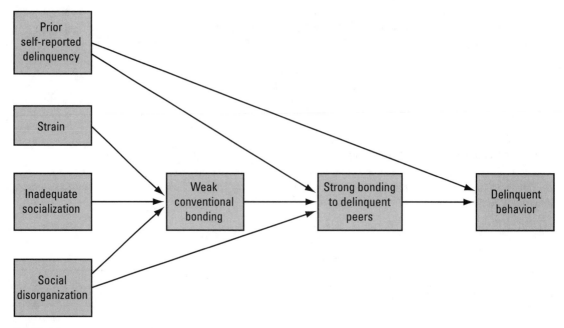

FIGURE 7.3

Elliott, Huizinga, and Ageton's Model of Delinquency

Source: Delbert S. Elliott, David Huizinga, and Suzanne S. Ageton, *Explaining Delinquency and Drug Use*, p. 146. Copyright © 1985 by Sage Publications, Inc. Reprinted by permission of Sage Publications, Inc.

bonding does not lead to delinquent behavior in a direct way, but only through its impact on attachment to delinquent peers.

The arrow from prior self-reported delinquency to strong bonding to delinquent peers shows that earlier involvement in delinquency makes it more likely that an adolescent will later associate with delinquent peers, who in turn influence the adolescent to become more involved in delinquent acts. The social disorganization of the community in which the adolescent lives might also influence attachments to delinquent peers, although there was no direct evidence of this.

Weak conventional bonding to family and to school is influenced by strain, inadequate socialization, and social disorganization of the community. Strain in the family was measured by the discrepancy between the subject's goals for family life—such as getting along with parents and holding their good opinion—and the subject's perceived realization of those goals. Similarly, strain in school was measured by the perceived discrepancy between academic goals—such as high grades and teachers' good opinions of the student—and the actual realization of those goals. Strain in the family and at school does not increase delinquent behavior directly, but instead leads to weak conventional bonding, which then produces strong bonding to delinquent peers, which in turn leads to delinquent behavior.

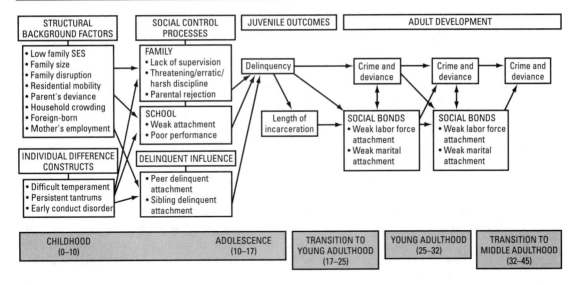

FIGURE 7.4

Sampson and Laub's Model of Delinquency and Crime over the Life Course

Source: Reprinted by permission of the publisher from *Crime in the Making: Pathways and Turning Points Through Life* by Robert J. Sampson and John H. Laub, Cambridge, Mass.: Harvard University Press. Copyright © 1993, by the President and Fellows of Harvard College.

This model suggests that a revised version of social control theory can explain delinquency, but that variables such as inadequate socialization and social disorganization that are not part of social control theory are also important parts of such an explanation.

Delinquency and Crime over the Life Course   In their reanalysis of Sheldon and Eleanor Glueck's (1950) data on 500 delinquent males and 500 nondelinquent males who were followed from childhood into their forties, Robert Sampson and John Laub (1993) examined structural background factors and social control processes that influence delinquency and crime over the life course. Figure 7.4 is the model that emerged from their study.

Family processes of social control were found to be critically important; "low levels of parental supervision, erratic, threatening, and harsh discipline, and weak parental attachment were strongly and directly related to delinquency" (Sampson and Laub, 1993: 247). Except for family size and household crowding, structural factors did not have consistent direct effects on delinquency. Structural factors such as family disruption and poverty indirectly influenced delinquency by affecting family and school processes of informal social control, which in turn affected delinquency. Thus, "families do not exist in isolation but instead are systematically embedded in social structural contexts" (Sampson and Laub, 1993: 96).

Attachment to school had a strong effect on delinquency, independent of family processes. Peer attachments were also positively related to delinquency regardless of family and school processes, although the effect of peer relations on delinquency was less important than the effect of either family or school processes.

Sampson and Laub found that individual characteristics such as temperament and early conduct disorder were linked to family and school processes as well as to delinquency, but those individual characteristics did not significantly diminish the strong impact on delinquency of family and school processes.

Traits such as low self-control that result from family and school processes can predispose individuals from an early age to become delinquent during adolescence and criminal during adulthood. However, antisocial behavior during childhood and adolescence can also lead to adult crime by weakening the social bonds that tie individuals to institutions such as the family and the labor force; those weakened bonds then contribute to subsequent violation of the law.

Social bonds during adulthood, such as marital attachment and job stability, by themselves have an effect on adult crime that is independent of any effects of childhood experiences. Adult experiences can thus counteract the negative effects of early childhood experiences; they can also lead adults with no previous history of delinquency to violate the law. Thus, "life-event transitions and adult social bonds can modify quite different childhood trajectories" (Sampson and Laub, 1993: 24).

Sampson and Laub's analysis confirmed their integrated theory of informal social control, which they derived in part from Hirschi's social control theory.

Delinquency and the Family   Not surprisingly, much research on crime and delinquency points to the crucial role of the family, the primary institution in the socialization and supervision of children.

Socialization   The way children are socialized by their parents is a major factor in the causation or prevention of crime and delinquency. A study that asked students why they had not become criminals found that many said that their parents had taught them right from wrong and had been models of hard work and honesty. The students said that their parents had taught them important values and that they themselves abided by the law because they believed in those values rather than because they feared punishment (Rogers, 1977: 36–45). Delinquents are more likely to say that their childhood experiences with their parents were unpleasant and that they rejected their parents as models while they were young (Medinnus, 1965). In general, crime and delinquency seem to be more common in societies where young people have less contact and less identification with their parents (Bacon, Child, and Barry, 1963).

Socialization by parents is most likely to reduce the chance that children will violate the law if

- parents clearly define their expectations,
- there is a close relationship between parents and their children,
- parents control their reactions toward their children's rebellious behavior, and
- parents reward the learning of expected behavior and withhold rewards for the failure to learn that behavior. (Toby, 1974)

People can also be socialized to break the law. They might learn values, norms, and skills from the members of a criminal or delinquent subculture. Few parents intentionally socialize their children to violate the law, but the failure to recognize their children's crime and delinquency as deviant and the use of ineffective methods of punishment can socialize children to break the law (Hirschi, 1983). A study of serious delinquents in Miami found that they had first been drunk at a mean age of 8.8, in four-fifths of the cases with an adult present, leading the researchers to conclude that "adults who gave children alcohol were also giving them a head start in a delinquent career, ...and this earlier start meant more serious drug/crime involvement [when they got older]" (Inciardi, Horowitz, and Pottieger, 1993: 136).

A study in which observations of the family environments of boys were compared with their subsequent juvenile delinquency and criminal behavior found that mothers were especially important in insulating boys against delinquency, but that fathers had a greater influence on the adult criminal behavior of their sons. Mothers who were self-confident, consistently non-punitive, affectionate, and provided leadership reduced the chances that their sons would become delinquent. High family expectations for the son had a similar effect. To the extent that these factors influenced adult criminality, they did so indirectly through their impact on juvenile delinquency. The father's interaction with the family was less strongly associated with juvenile delinquency but had a significant impact on adult criminal behavior, with the sons being more apt to engage in criminal behavior as adults if their fathers had undermined their mother's self-esteem, fought with the family, and been highly aggressive while their sons were young (McCord, 1991).

Discipline Careful observation of interaction between children and their parents has led researchers at the Oregon Social Learning Center to conclude that some parents are ineffective in disciplining their children, in that they fail to make penalties contingent on their children's behavior in a systematic and predictable way. (See the Using Criminology box.) Children are most likely to break the law and violate social conventions when parents care too little about their children to pay attention to their actions, when they fail to supervise their children, when they do not regard their children's misbehavior negatively, and when they fail to punish their children. The failure of parents to react consistently to deviant or criminal behavior leaves children with the belief that they cannot control what will happen to themselves by their own actions. Irritable parents who sometimes apply harsh penalties or even strike out violently at their children, but at other times "natter" at their children for similar behavior, make it seem to children that the punishment they suffer is not linked to their behavior in any predictable way (Patterson, 1980; West, 1982; Wells and Rankin, 1988; Larzelere and Patterson, 1990). Ineffective child-rearing is cited by Gottfredson and Hirschi (1990) as the major cause of low self-control, which they see as the source of criminal behavior.

The most effective parental style of discipline for reducing criminal or aggressive behavior is an "authoritative" approach, which combines a high degree of control over children with a great amount of support and encouragement. In contrast to this, an "authoritarian" style that combines tight control with a cold and detached parental attitude often leads children to withdraw from social contact. A "permissive" style that involves nurturing and encouragement, but a failure to control, often produces children who lack self-control (Baumrind, 1978; Wilson and Herrnstein, 1985). This permissive style was found to be common among the parents of delinquents in a longitudinal study done in England, with the researcher concluding:

> A particularly noticeable characteristic of parents of many of the delinquents in the study was carelessness or laxness in matters of supervision. They were less concerned than other parents to watch over or to know about their children's doings, whereabouts and companions, and they failed to enforce or to formulate fixed rules about such things as punctuality, manners, bedtime, television viewing or tidying up. (West, 1982: 57)

The way that parents discipline their children is quite likely learned from observing how they as children were disciplined by their own parents. This could explain why the children of parents with criminal records are especially likely to have criminal records themselves, for people discipline their own children in the way they were disciplined by their parents, and that style of discipline leads their children into crime just as it led them to violate the law.

Broken Homes   There has been much speculation and research on the broken home as a cause of delinquency and crime. Broken homes include those that are not structurally intact for various reasons: the death of a parent, divorce, desertion, separation, and illegitimacy (in which case the family was never completed). Broken homes could have an impact on delinquency in any of a variety of ways: by producing unstable habits and personalities in young children through inadequate socialization; by failing to provide children with ties to the conventional social order that would control their behavior; by producing stress and conflict that lead children to "act out"; and by offering fewer resources and opportunities to children and thus leaving them at a disadvantage in competing with others for a good education and a desirable job (Wells and Rankin, 1986). Because families can be "broken" in different ways and because families have many kinds of effects on children, it is not surprising that research on the relationship between broken families and delinquency is inconclusive.

In addition, many studies of this relationship have employed inadequate research designs. Because broken families are more common among the lower classes and among minority groups and because those groups have higher rates of officially recorded delinquency, researchers need to separate

USING CRIMINOLOGY

Holding Parents Responsible for Their Children's Behavior

A rising rate of juvenile crime and the widely held belief that a major source of that problem is inadequate supervision and discipline of children by their parents have led lawmakers across the United States to pass measures requiring parents to control their children's behavior more effectively.

Since 1903, when Colorado took the lead, most states have enacted laws that allow parents to be prosecuted for contributing to the delinquency of a minor. Today many states also hold parents liable for civil damages inflicted by their children. In addition, laws requiring children to attend school have been used to fine or even imprison the parents of truant children.

Since 1987, many measures have been implemented to hold parents responsible for a wide range of misbehavior by their children. In that year, the Detroit city council passed a Parental Responsibility Ordinance that imposed penalties on parents who failed to keep illegal firearms and drugs out of their homes, failed to keep their children from associating with known juvenile delinquents, or failed to supervise their children adequately and require them to attend school. Parents who violated this law could be required to undergo counseling or attend classes in parenting skills, fined up to $500, or jailed for up to ninety days. Another effort to force parents to supervise, protect, and maintain control of their children was the California Street Terrorism Enforcement and Protection Act, which was passed in 1988 to cope with street gangs.

As of 1996, about half of the states and many cities and towns had enacted parental responsibility measures. Idaho, Indiana, and New Hampshire require parents to pay some of the costs of detaining their children in state institutions. Parents in Louisiana can be fined up to $1,000 or imprisoned for up to six months for improperly supervising their children. Most of these recently enacted laws and ordinances have been used to force parents to participate in counseling or education programs.

Critics allege that these measures are useless, politically motivated "quick-fixes" aimed at a complex problem. Some find the laws intrusive or even unconstitutional and suggest that they might backfire by unfairly penalizing low-income parents who cannot afford to pay fines or by causing conflict within families. Supporters of these laws and ordinances claim that they can be a useful part of an overall strategy of forcing parents to pay more attention to the supervision and discipline of their children. The police chief of Silverton, Oregon, found his town's ordinance useful, saying, "The other day I brought a kid in here for shoplifting. What does the father do when he came in? He chews the kid out for getting caught. Not for what he did. Well, now I can cite him as well" (cited in Egan, 1995: B7).

Sources: Based on Ruth Bayard Smith, "Detroit Law Makes Parents Responsible for Their Children's Crimes," *Boston Globe*, May 31, 1987, p. 29; Timothy Egan, "If Juveniles Break Law, Town Is Charging the Parents, Too," *New York Times*, May 31, 1995, pp. A1, B7; Peter Applebome, "Holding Parents Responsible as Children's Misdeeds Rise," *New York Times*, April 10, 1996, pp. A1, D8.

the effects of class and minority-group membership on delinquency from the effects of family structure on delinquency. For instance, some research shows that among the middle class, neither officially recorded nor self-reported delinquency is associated with coming from a broken home (Grinnell and Chambers, 1979; Richards, Berk, and Foster, 1979). Researchers need to use self-report measures to determine if there are real differences in delinquency between adolescents from broken homes and those from intact homes, because adolescents from broken homes may be more likely to be arrested and found delinquent in court than are adolescents from intact homes (Nye, 1958; Hirschi, 1969).

The most carefully designed studies find a weak but consistent relationship between delinquency and broken homes, with delinquents slightly more likely than nondelinquents to come from broken homes (Hirschi, 1969; Hennessy, Richards, and Berk, 1978; van Voorhis et al., 1988; Wells and Rankin, 1991). Analysis of National Youth Survey data found that children who were strongly attached to both parents were less likely to commit delinquent acts than children who were strongly attached to only one parent, whether that one parent was in a broken home or in an intact one (Rankin and Kern, 1994).

One study of broken homes and delinquency found that different family contexts influence various kinds of delinquency in different ways. Running away, truancy, and motor vehicle theft were strongly associated with a specific kind of broken home, one in which both biological parents were absent. Vandalism and theft were more strongly associated with school and peer contexts than with family structure. In sum, certain kinds of broken families can generate particular kinds of delinquent acts (Rankin, 1983).

Broken homes have a greater impact on delinquency for some groups than for others. That impact is greater for blacks than for whites (Matsueda and Heimer, 1987). There is also evidence that broken homes have greater effects on girls and preadolescent boys than on adolescent boys (Toby, 1957; Austin, 1978). Compared with girls and preadolescent boys, adolescent boys are not especially well supervised by their parents, whether they live in an intact home or in a broken one. Thus, there is little difference between the delinquency rate of adolescent boys from broken families and the delinquency rate of adolescent boys from intact homes. However, the relative lack of supervision of adolescent boys is probably a cause of their high rate of involvement in delinquency, compared with girls and preadolescent boys. The difference between coming from a broken home or an intact family is more likely to be important for girls and preadolescent boys, because those two groups are usually better supervised in intact families than they are in broken ones. Consequently, delinquency among girls and preadolescent boys is more common among those who come from broken homes than among those from intact homes, at least according to some research. Other research does not support this conclusion; for instance, a national survey of adolescents failed to confirm this relationship between family structure and delinquency among girls. Broken homes did increase the rate of self-reported delinquency in this study, but in comparable ways for both boys and girls

(Canter, 1982). Earlier research may have found a sex differential in the impact of broken homes on delinquency because those studies used official data, which could reflect sex discrimination in the processing of adolescents by the police.

Contradictory findings about the relationship between broken families and delinquency might be partly a result of the use of different kinds of samples of adolescents. One researcher tentatively concluded that the relationship between delinquency and father-absence could be strongest for those groups that are the least tolerant of divorce, and that broken homes might make less difference for groups that are more accepting of divorce. If this were true, then researchers who study groups that are relatively tolerant of divorce—for instance, urban Protestants—would be likely to find less of an association between broken homes and delinquency than would researchers who use samples that are less tolerant of divorce. Future research should try to "specify the social characteristics of the children for whom the broken home has significant behavioral consequences" (Wilkinson, 1980: 39).

Separation of Children from Their Parents   One factor that might be related to delinquency is the early separation of children from their parents. Regular or prolonged separation from parents during the early years could make it harder for children to develop feelings for others later, and lack of empathy could be linked to delinquency and crime.

There is some evidence that delinquency is more common among the children of parents who both work outside the home (Austin, 1982). Hirschi (1969: 237–239) found that 37 percent of the boys whose mothers were housewives reported a delinquent act, 44 percent of the boys whose mothers worked part-time outside the home reported a delinquent act, and 50 percent of those whose mothers were employed full-time outside the home reported delinquency. An earlier study (Nye, 1958: 53–59) also found more delinquency among adolescents whose mothers worked outside the home. It is unclear whether there is a relationship between delinquency and mothers' working outside the home today, when 62 percent of American women with children under the age of six hold jobs.

Any negative effects on children of having both parents work outside the home might be attributable to a loss of supervision. However, conflict between a husband and wife could result from the wife's working outside the home, or the wife might take an outside job to escape from a problematic family situation, such as an alcoholic and unemployed husband. In these cases, intrafamily conflict related to working outside the home, rather than lack of supervision, could be the cause of delinquency. There is some reason to believe that interpersonal relationships in the family and the quality of care provided by the parents are more important influences on delinquency than whether both parents hold jobs outside the home (Currie, 1985).

Child Abuse   The abuse of children by their parents or by other caretakers can take the form of physical abuse, sexual abuse, emotional neglect, or other intentional maltreatment. Physically abused children are about twice as likely as children who are not abused to have trouble at school, be aggressive, and have difficulty with alcohol or drugs; three to four times as likely to violate the law and be arrested; and about ten times as likely as the general population to become abusing parents themselves (Gelles and Straus, 1988). The relationship between being treated harshly as a child and engaging in child or spouse abuse as an adult is mediated by the extent to which one's parents displayed an antisocial orientation (Simons et al., 1995). Being abused or neglected as a child is also a strong predictor of being arrested for alcohol or drug offenses as an adult, but does not predict arrests for those offenses during adolescence (Ireland and Widom, 1994).

One study compared the criminal records of a sample of people who had been officially reported to be victims of child abuse with the criminal records of a matched sample of people of similar social backgrounds for whom no official report of child abuse had been filed. Twenty-six percent of the abused children but only 17 percent of the control group were arrested as juveniles. By 1994, when nearly all of the subjects were at least twenty-six years old, 49 percent of the abused children and 38 percent of the control group had been arrested. Eighteen percent of the abused children and 14 percent of the control group had been arrested for violent crimes. Being abused thus increased the risk that a child would later engage in delinquency and crime (see Figure 7.5). Sexual abuse was no more predictive of being arrested as an adult than was physical abuse or neglect; the exception was being arrested as an adult for prostitution, which was more closely associated with childhood sexual abuse than with other forms of abuse (Widom, 1989, 1995, 1996).

Longitudinal research in Rochester, New York, found a significant relationship between maltreatment in early childhood and adolescent involvement in delinquency, whether measured by official records or self-reports. This relationship was especially strong for the most serious forms of delinquency; and it persisted when race and ethnicity, sex, social class, family structure, and mobility were controlled. The children who were most extensively maltreated exhibited the highest rates of delinquency (Smith and Thornberry, 1995).

A study that compared the officially recorded delinquent behavior of maltreated children, nonmaltreated schoolchildren, and nonmaltreated impoverished children concluded that the effect of maltreatment on juvenile delinquency has been exaggerated. The degree to which the maltreated children were more involved in delinquency than the other two samples was greatly diminished when children from the same demographic groups and family structures were compared. Moreover, most of the difference in delinquency between the maltreated children and the other two samples was due to the greater involvement of the maltreated children in status offenses. Maltreated children were no more involved in property or violent offenses than the schoolchildren or the impoverished children (Zingraff et al., 1993).

Family Cohesiveness   What seems most important in determining whether a child will become delinquent is family cohesiveness, the quality of interpersonal relationships in a family, communication between parents and children, and emotional support of the children by their parents (Hirschi, 1969;

Any arrest

Victims of child abuse	49%
Control group	38%

Any arrest as a juvenile

Victims of child abuse	26%
Control group	17%

Any arrest for a violent crime

Victims of child abuse	18%
Control group	14%

FIGURE 7.5
Arrests of Child Abuse Victims* and a Control Group**

  * Sample of 1,575 court cases of child abuse occurring from 1967 to 1971 in a midwestern county
** Sample of children with no official record of abuse, matched on age, sex, race, and social class

Source: Based on data from Cathy Spatz Widom, *The Cycle of Violence.* Washington, D.C.: U.S. Department of Justice, October 1992; Cathy Spatz Widom, *The Cycle of Violence Revisited.* Washington, D.C.: U.S. Department of Justice, February 1996.

Hindelang, 1973; Poole and Regoli, 1979; Wiatrowski, Griswold, and Roberts, 1981). A study of delinquency in three cultures found less family cohesiveness, less confiding in parents, and fewer stable home situations among delinquents than among nondelinquents (Rosenquist and Megargee, 1969). Higher levels of hostility within the family were found to be associated with more deviant behavior in a study done in Mexico (Meadow et al., 1981).

The quality of family relationships might be associated in different ways with various kinds of crime. For instance, one study found that adult males who as boys had frequently been exposed to conflict and aggression between their parents were especially likely to commit violent crimes such as murder, rape, and kidnapping. Men who as boys had lacked maternal affection and whose fathers had engaged in deviance were the most likely to be arrested for property crimes such as larceny, car theft, and burglary (McCord, 1979).

In explaining why Switzerland has relatively low rates of juvenile delinquency, Marshall Clinard (1978) focuses on the close ties and good communication between young people and adults. He suggests that Swiss adolescents often prefer interaction in mixed-age groups to interaction in peer groups, and that people of various ages often participate together in outdoor activities. Interaction of various age groups also occurs in the large Swiss army. In addition, many Swiss continue to live with their parents after they become young adults. Clinard attributes Switzerland's relatively small problem with youth crime to the culture's emphasis on harmony and compromise, which sustain close ties between people of different ages, both within and outside the family.

Men who as boys were exposed to conflict and aggression between their parents are especially likely to commit violent crimes such as murder, rape, and kidnapping.

The family is an especially important institution in generating or preventing delinquency and crime. The structure of the family is important, but what seems most critical is the quality of relationships among family members. Harmonious relationships between parents, and between parents and children, help to prevent delinquency and crime.

Delinquency and the School   Students with low levels of academic performance are especially likely to be delinquent, to commit serious and violent offenses, and to persist in delinquency (Maguin and Loeber, 1996). Poor academic performance in high school is a strong predictor of being arrested for crime as an adult (Polk, 1980).

When academic pressure is coupled with a high likelihood of failure, adolescents come to regard school as irrelevant to their future, ungratifying, and unrewarding. They see their grades as unimportant and spend less time on homework, factors that lower their academic achievement. Their ties to the school and its teachers then weaken, and they drift into delinquency (Hirschi, 1969: 170–183; Empey and Lubeck, 1971; Hindelang, 1973; Figueira-McDonough, 1987). Nondelinquents often mention their commitment to education and their respect for their teachers' good opinions as reasons for not turning to crime. They also say that education is important to their future and that they do not want to risk their stake in conformity by violating the law (Rogers, 1977: 52–53).

Evidence that weakened attachment to the school is linked to delinquency was uncovered in Wolfgang, Figlio, and Sellin's (1972: 66) cohort study. Boys with more contacts with the police were more likely than boys with fewer police contacts to have changed schools frequently, have lower IQs, have completed fewer grades, and have a lower overall level of achievement. Another study found that delinquency was more common among adolescents who were less bonded to the school, and that this was equally true for both blacks and whites. Even though school bonding was not a powerful predictor of delinquency, it played as significant a role in delinquency as family and peer factors (Cernkovich and Giordano, 1992). A study of drug use and serious delinquency in Miami concluded that

> most of the serious delinquents interviewed who were still in school have little if any attachment to school. Few consider high school graduation to be "*very* important," and they assign even less importance to good grades or teachers' opinions of them. They are often absent, and, when they are in school, they are usually high on drugs. Their high rates of suspensions/expulsions suggest that school personnel view them as troublemakers. And indeed many of them are. (Inciardi, Horowitz, and Pottieger, 1993: 146)

School Organization and Delinquency   Some research suggests that the organizational context of the school can influence the amount of delinquency by its students. A study in England concluded that the schools that did the best job of keeping rates of delinquency low were the ones that had a relatively high proportion of good students and the ones that combined firm but fair discipline with rewards for good academic performance. The presence of more students who found school rewarding seemed to set the tone for the whole student body in a way that kept delinquency rates down. Teachers who treated their students in the way that parents who were effective at discipline did—that is, by using an "authoritative" style of discipline—also seemed most likely to suppress delinquent behavior. For a school to keep delinquency down required parental involvement, a strong principal, and highly motivated and experienced teachers (Rutter et al., 1979).

Research in the United States has found less truancy, class cutting, verbal abuse of teachers, and student fighting in private and parochial schools than in public schools. Private and parochial schools are more likely than public ones to be characterized by clear goals, firm expectations, fair discipline, and rewards for work well done (Coleman, Hoffer, and Kilgore, 1982).

Delinquency and the Peer Group   Hirschi's conclusion that weaker peer-group ties are associated with higher rates of delinquency is challenged by other research, perhaps because Hirschi did not adequately distinguish ties to conventional peers from ties to delinquent ones. One national study found no relationship between attachment to peers and self-reported delinquency (Wiatrowski, Griswold, and Roberts, 1981), but other research has found that greater identification with peers is linked to higher rates of delinquency (Empey and Lubeck, 1971; Hindelang, 1973; Elliott and Voss, 1974; Elliott, Huizinga, and Ageton, 1985). This could be because the adolescent subculture is "oppositional" to the dominant, middle-class culture, and so closer ties to the peer group would be associated with more delinquency (Elliott and Voss, 1974).

A study that used National Youth Survey data for 1976 revealed a complex relationship between the peer group and delinquency. The degree to which adolescents associate with peers who engage in serious delinquency is not associated with the chance that they will be delinquent for those adolescents who are weakly attached to peers, spend little time with peers, and associate with peers who present few delinquent patterns. However, association with peers who engage in serious delinquency does increase the chance that adolescents will be delinquent if they report higher levels of attachment to peers, spend more time with peers, and associate with peers who present more delinquent patterns (Agnew, 1991a).

A longitudinal study done in Rochester, New York, found that association with delinquent peers increases delinquency, and that engaging in delinquency further increases association with delinquent peers. Delinquents associate with delinquent peers, increasing the chance of more delinquency; and nondelinquents associate with nondelinquent peers, increasing the chance of more conforming behavior (Thornberry et al., 1994: 74).

One effort to assess social control theory's contention that delinquents' friendships are exploitative rather than supportive questioned nearly a thousand twelve- to nineteen-year-olds living in a large metropolitan area. The researchers concluded that "youths who are very different in their levels of involvement in delinquency are nevertheless quite similar in the ways in which they view their friendship relations" (Giordano, Cernkovich, and Pugh, 1986: 1191). Social control theory's idea that individuals bring delinquent values to the group at the outset fits with the findings of these researchers, but they also conclude that after the group forms, mutual influence further strengthens patterns of delinquent behavior. The researchers contradict social control theory's assertion that delinquents lack attachments to their peers, finding instead that delinquents derive as many or more benefits from their friendships as other adolescents. This study suggests that the friendship patterns of adolescents, whether delinquent or not, are complex and multidimensional.

Peer Groups and Families Two researchers who looked carefully at the effects of parents and delinquent friends on self-reported delinquency concluded that both had independent effects on delinquency. However, the delinquent peer group had a greater effect on delinquent behavior for adolescents who had weaker family ties than it did on the behavior of adolescents who had more family support. Adolescents who had little support from their parents were more open to the influence of their delinquent peers, and adolescents who were wary of harming their good relationships with their parents were more likely to stay away from delinquent peers (Poole and Regoli, 1979).

A study of Chinese-Canadian adolescent gangs concluded that they had emerged as a consequence of poor family supervision and guidance.

Traditionally, the Chinese family in North America has been strong and able to insulate young people from trouble with the law, but in Canada during the 1970s this cohesive family unit was not as strong as it once was, and so young Chinese-Canadians turned to gangs. In part, this might have been an escape from family pressure to succeed in school, which created problems for recent immigrants who lacked the necessary language skills (Joe and Robinson, 1980).

In both the United States and France, adolescent marijuana users are more oriented to their peer group than are nonusers. Moreover, users in each country are less committed than nonusers to conventional institutions such as the school and the family (Kandel and Adler, 1982).

Delinquency and Religion   One bond that could prevent delinquency, but was not incorporated into social control theory, is membership in organized religion or a belief in religious precepts. Studies in Great Britain and Puerto Rico have found less delinquency among boys who attend church more often and express stronger religious interests (Belson, 1975; Ferracuti, Dinitz, and Acosta, 1975).

Religion is but one of a large set of influences on delinquent behavior, and one that interacts with the influence of the family, the school, and the peer group to inhibit or cause delinquency. A study that used religious salience (measured by strength of belief in the power of prayer) and religious orthodoxy as measures of religiosity found a weak to moderate relationship between religion and delinquency, but concluded that religion was not a significant predictor of delinquency when compared with other factors such as the family and the peer group (Elifson, Petersen, and Hadaway, 1983).

A review of research on the relationship between individual religiosity and criminality led Lee Ellis (1985: 511) to conclude there is "strong support and essentially no contradiction" for the following generalizations:

1. Among church members, frequent church attendees have lower crime rates than infrequent (or non-) attendees, especially in regard to victimless crimes.

2. Among church members, Jews have lower crime rates than Christians. Among Christians, Protestants have lower crime rates than Catholics.

3. Persons who believe in an afterlife with divine punishment for sins have somewhat lower crime rates than persons who lack such beliefs.

Despite these findings, Ellis (1985: 513) says that "no simple answer can be given to the question, do 'religious people' commit fewer crimes?" He concludes as follows:

> Overall, if one means by "religious" people who hold very orthodox religious beliefs, with the exception of a belief in immortality, there appears to be little or no association. If one means by "religious" being a member of an organized religious body, the answer markedly depends upon which religious body one is considering. And if, by "religious," one means attending church services frequently, there is manifestly a strong tendency for religious people to commit fewer crimes.

A recent study found that religious beliefs and values did not inhibit adult criminality, but that religious activities did have direct effects on a broad

People who engage in religious activities frequently have lower crime rates than people who engage in such activities infrequently or not at all.

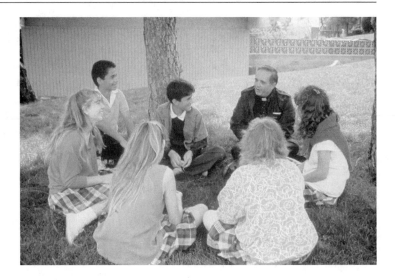

range of criminal behavior. Consistent with social control theory, regular involvement in religious activities exposed people to moral proscriptions and made real the threat of sanctions by enabling the "close monitoring and sanctioning of waywardness" (Evans et al., 1995: 210).

Migration and the Disruption of Social Bonds   Earlier in the book we saw that migration is sometimes associated with increases in crime rates for people who move. Increases are most likely to occur when migration from one nation to another or migration within a nation disrupts social bonds and weakens the informal control of behavior by family, school, peer group, religion, and community. The social integration of groups is sometimes undercut by population turnover and the arrival of newcomers and transients, a process that seems to have a greater impact on intentional crimes than on impulsive ones (Stark et al., 1983). Another study that found that the effects of geographic mobility varied with the type of crime in question concluded that "frequent potentially disruptive residential changes tend to undermine the individual's moral commitment to conventional norms that, in turn, increase the chances of offense" (Tittle and Paternoster, 1988: 324).

In developing nations, crime rates often increase as people become detached from traditional institutions through detribalization. One study found that Ugandans who left their villages and moved to the large city of Kampala, especially to its slum shantytowns, were likely to have high rates of crime unless they established new social bonds in the city. Migration caused crime rates to increase by weakening attachments to groups that had traditionally controlled deviant behavior (Clinard and Abbott, 1973).

Migration might not be disruptive if the receiving community contains groups into which immigrants can be integrated or if individuals move from one place to another in groups. People who move alone and lack social ties in their new community are especially likely to become involved in crime because there is little to control their behavior. In the study of Uganda, it was relatively unimportant for migrants to the city to maintain direct ties to their village; what was important was that they form attachments to relatives and other immigrants from their village in the city to which they had moved (Clinard and Abbott, 1973: 127). The ways that communities keep crime in check through a process of informal social control are examined in Chapter 12.

Social Bonds in Other Societies   One way to examine the usefulness of social control theory is to see whether it explains cross-national differences in rates of crime and delinquency. If social control theory is correct, we would expect the lowest rates to exist in societies characterized by close attachments to institutions. One effort to use social control theory in this way suggests that it can account for the relatively low rate of delinquency in India (see the Cross-Cultural Perspective box). A study of ten nations, which were characterized by less fear of crime than existed in the United States, found that those nations had been able to create or maintain effective institutions of social control, especially the family (Adler, 1983). Let us look briefly at the role of social bonds in several societies.

China   China, which apparently has a low rate of conventional crime, is characterized by strongly integrated groups. Chinese citizens learn an ideology of attachment to the country and to a version of communist ideology; they are thus subordinated to supraindividual concerns. The family is a strong institution that controls individual behavior, and young people spend much of their free time in state-run recreational facilities.

A study in Tianjin, China, confirmed that the family was a dominant institution that contributed to a low overall rate of delinquency. However, the strength of the family also meant that deviance within the family was strongly predictive of official delinquency status, suggesting that some families transmit deviance from generation to generation. Associating with delinquent peers also predicted delinquency status, contrary to the researchers' initial assumption that the influence of the family would overwhelm the influence of the peer group (Zhang and Messner, 1995).

The regimentation and lack of privacy in China have been compared to life in an army barracks (Butterfield, 1982). Two institutions that maintain social control by public scrutiny of behavior are the *danwei* (or workplace) and the street committee. All Chinese belong to a danwei through the school they attend or the office or factory in which they work. The danwei often provides housing, schooling, and medical care, and it must give permission to marry and to divorce. Ties to the danwei are so strong that the Chinese are more likely to be asked their danwei than their name if they travel to another community. The urban street committee is another institution that controls behavior, searching people's homes, recommending job assignments and housing changes, and even deciding who may have children. These and other institutions make the Chinese very sensitive to the expectations of others and help curb delinquency and crime.

Japan   The Japanese traditionally have had strong ties to their family, to the company for which they work, and to the community in which they live. Bonds to such tightly knit groups offer security and success to individuals and

A CROSS-CULTURAL PERSPECTIVE

Delinquency in India

In India, juvenile delinquency is relatively uncommon and not especially serious when it does occur. Why is delinquency relatively rare in India?

Part of the answer is that India's economy is a peasant or agrarian one, and in such an economy young people are not as superfluous as they are in advanced industrial economies. In postindustrial societies such as the United States, the absence of much need for unskilled labor means that young people must postpone their entry into the labor force. This often leads to an adolescent subculture that is sometimes supportive of delinquency. In contrast, a peasant economy makes use of unskilled labor, and children and adolescents are thus integrated into the social network of their community. In India, where many businesses are run by families, children are introduced into the economic system by their families at a young age.

Young Indians are integrated into their society to an even greater degree than their participation in the labor force would suggest. Indian society is organized in terms of role relationships that create for everyone a set of obligations to the family, the subcaste, and the community. People are expected to care for others, even distant relatives and employees. Agricultural workers and landowners have mutual obligations that extend beyond their worker/employer relationship, so that an

employer becomes almost a surrogate parent to the worker and is obliged to look after the employee's (and the employee's family's) welfare. The worker, in turn, has obligations to the employer (or provider) that are not due simply to economic dependence, but are defined by the work role itself. (p. 78)

Because all Indians are enmeshed in a complex network of social relationships, their deviance is of concern to many people. Indians learn at a young age what others expect of them and learn to conform to the expectations of those with whom they have relationships. There is a "psychological presence" not only of the child's parents, but also of an extended family network, a subcaste, and a community.

Indian culture defines young people as a part of the social structure, not as outsiders to it. Social activities are rarely segregated by age, adolescent hangouts are practically nonexistent, and there is no adolescent subculture conducive to juvenile delinquency.

Source: Based on Clayton A. Hartjen and S. Priyadarsini, *Delinquency in India: A Comparative Analysis.* New Brunswick, N.J.: Rutgers University Press, 1984.

---

ensure conformity by requiring the fulfillment of social responsibilities. The group nature of Japanese society is so strong that crime rates are low even in densely populated urban areas, where we might expect social bonds to break down and crime rates to be high (Clifford, 1976).

In Japan, individual behavior is guided by obligations to family, employer, neighborhood, and society, rather than by self-interest. Americans usually speak of their rights, but the Japanese more often think of the debts they owe to others. The social structure of Japan is similar in its group orientation to some communist nations such as China that also seem to have low crime rates; however, Japan provides striking evidence that crime is more a result of the social structure of a society than a product of its political and economic ideology. The capitalist society of Japan and the communist society of China seem to have low crime rates because both have created and maintained social bonds that tie people to groups and institutions.

During the 1980s, Japan experienced a rising rate of juvenile delinquency. Much of this delinquency occurred in the schools; some took the form of assaults against teachers. One explanation for this increase in delinquency was the breakdown of a traditional educational system that had once inculcated respect for authority. Japanese leftists claimed that the rising delinquency rate was a result of educational policies that favored the brightest students, neglected others, and created for all students "an examination-hell atmosphere from which violence is bound to erupt" (Chapman, 1983: 3). Competition for academic success led some students to feel ignored or discriminated against by teachers, weakening their bonds to teachers and the school and freeing them to engage in delinquent behavior.

Critique of Social Control Theory

One shortcoming of social control theory is that it does not identify the social-structural sources of motivations to break the law. Attachments to family, school, and peer group can keep people from violating the law even when other social forces—such as poverty—might impel them to engage in crime and delinquency. However, a complete theory of crime and delinquency needs to explain the way that social, economic, and cultural forces produce the motivation to break the law.

Social control theory would benefit from a more dynamic analysis of social interaction. Rather than describing attachments as they are at a given time, social control theory needs to examine the way that attachments change over time. For instance, the way that parents behave at one time affects their children's actions at a later time, but those actions by the children can in turn affect the way that their parents will treat them in the future.

One criticism of social control theory is that it fails to take into account possible reciprocal relationships between social bonds and delinquency, focusing instead on the way that weak attachments lead to delinquency (Agnew, 1985). One study found that weakened attachments to family and school caused delinquency, but also that delinquent behavior reduced the strength of bonds to family and school, which in turn increased delinquency (Thornberry et al., 1991). Another study found that parental attachment did affect delinquency, but that most of the relationship between school attachment and delinquency was due to the effect of delinquency on school attachment, rather than the effect of school attachment on delinquency (Liska and Reed, 1985).

Other research suggests that social control theory oversimplifies reality when it claims that low attachment, commitment, and belief create the freedom to violate social norms. Low attachment, commitment, and belief also increase anger and frustration, and anger and frustration act as sources of strain that generate delinquency. Moreover, this study shows that social control variables are associated with delinquency only for individuals motivated to engage in such behavior, namely those who are high in anger and frustration and those who associate with delinquent peers (Agnew, 1993).

Attachments to different institutions probably take on varying degrees of importance at different stages of the life cycle, and social control theory needs to identify more clearly the relative significance of bonds to different institutions for people of various ages (Agnew, 1991b). One study that did this found that the causal processes identified in Hirschi's social control theory are most applicable to youths in midadolescence (about age fifteen); attachments to parents and teachers and commitment to conventional lines of action are important "psychological anchors" to conformity for this age group. This study also found that the influence of delinquent peers was strongest for older adolescents (around age eighteen) (LaGrange and White, 1985). A different study found that the family's ability "to supervise and control developing youths is restricted by a lack of social and material resources in the communities where serious delinquency is concentrated" and concluded that because the family's impact on socialization wanes before adolescence, policy makers must look to schools, peers, and communities for ways to reduce delinquency (Fagan and Wexler, 1987: 664).

The way that bonds to different institutions interact with one another needs to be more fully delineated. Some researchers have examined the relationships among bonds to family, school, and peer group (Empey and Lubeck, 1971; Liska and Reed, 1985; Patterson and Dishion, 1985), but we need much more information on problems such as how relationships with parents affect attitudes toward school and work, how bonds to teachers during adolescence influence adult work history, and how attachments to family and job among adults are related to involvement in criminal behavior. For instance, a young father with strong bonds to a wife and children and a strong attachment to his career might experience conflict between his loyalty to his family and his loyalty to his job; this conflict could cause frustration that leads to violence in the home or theft at work. Social control theory needs elaboration, and researchers must investigate further the complex relationships among attachments to different institutions.

Techniques of Neutralization, Social Control Theory, and Variations in Crime Rates

We do not now have enough evidence on the distribution of the techniques of neutralization to know whether they can account for variations in crime rates. One country might have more crime than another because its culture includes beliefs that make it easier to neutralize the law and engage in crime and delinquency. Differences in access to techniques of neutralization could also help to explain variations in crime rates by region, by size of the community, or over time; however, we have no evidence that this is so. Similarly, socialization experiences and access to criminal subcultures could account for some of the variations in crime rates by sex, age, race, and social class; again we lack supporting evidence. Future research showing how techniques of neutralization vary from one society to another and within a society by region, community, and social group might help us explain differences in crime rates.

Social control theory does make sense of cross-national variations in crime rates, because nations that have lower crime rates seem to be characterized by stronger and more extensive bonds to family, peer group, school, community, and nation. We have little evidence that regional variations in crime rates in the United States can be explained by differences in the strength of attachments to such institutions. Variations in crime rates by size of the community might be accounted for by social control theory; attachment to community seems weaker in larger cities than in small towns and rural areas, with interpersonal relationships in large communities often being described as weak and segmented. We lack good evidence that fluctuations in crime rates over time parallel changes in social bonds to institutions such as the family, the school, the peer group, the community, and organized religion; however, some scholars have attributed increased crime rates to a reduced emphasis on obligations and responsibilities to others (Davies, 1983; Wilson, 1983).

Social control theory helps explain variations in crime rates by sex, age, race, and social class. Adolescent boys probably have high rates of delinquency because they are supervised less closely than girls and preadolescent boys, two groups that have relatively low delinquency rates. Age variations in crime rates can also be explained by social control theory. Adolescents are concerned with breaking away from their parents, and this creates pressure on parents to exert less control. Adults marry, have children, take jobs, and settle down in a community; these bonds help to account for the decline in crime rates with age. Blacks' high crime rates could be due in part to their weaker attachment to jobs, with the lack of promising jobs to which they can form strong attachments being a product of racial discrimination and the poor quality of education in many public schools. The higher rates of family dissolution and illegitimacy among blacks also suggest that differences in family relationships between blacks and whites might account for some of the differences in crime rates between the groups. Finally, social class differences in crime rates might exist because poorer families tend to be larger, more likely to be broken, and more likely to experience financial strain; these factors might be associated with reduced control over deviant behavior. In addition, lower-class students might feel that they cannot win the good opinion of their middle-class teachers, or believe that education will gain them little in improved job prospects even if they do form close attachments to their teachers.

We have little research that demonstrates that variations in crime rates among different groups, regions, and countries are directly due to variations in attachments to institutions. Social control theory is, however, compatible with some of these variations in crime rates, and more research might show that this theory can account for those variations.

Summary

Most people must neutralize the hold that the law has over them before they can violate the law. People who are in a state of drift and lack strong bonds to the conventional order are free to engage in delinquency and crime, but they are not forced to do so. The values of law violators have some things in common with the dominant value system, but delinquents and criminals act on subterranean themes in the dominant value system in inappropriate situations.

Techniques of neutralization, which are used to justify delinquency and crime prior to the deviant act, include the following: denial of responsibility, denial of injury, denial of the victim, condemnation of the condemners, and the appeal to higher loyalties. These and other techniques are used by many kinds of offenders—juvenile delinquents, professional criminals, and white-collar offenders.

Evidence that these techniques of neutralization are associated with violation of the law comes from a study of embezzlers, a survey of black men interviewed on the street, a study of sex-related and robbery-related murders and contract killings, and several studies of juvenile delinquency. However, we lack good evidence that offenders use these techniques prior to violating the law, and we do not know what aspects of the social structure make it easy or difficult to justify violations of the law.

Social control theory proposes that people engage in delinquency or crime when they are free of intimate attachments to the family, the school, and the peer group, and when the aspirations and moral beliefs that bind them to a conventional way of life are weak. The absence of a "psychological presence" of parents leaves adolescents free to violate the law without being afraid of how their parents will react. Close ties between adolescents and their parents inhibit delinquent behavior, as do strong ties to schools and their teachers. Adolescents who do not aspire to conventional lines of action such as education and work, but who want to engage in adult activities before assuming adult responsibilities, are especially likely to engage in delinquency.

Comparisons of delinquents and nondelinquents generally support social control theory, but the interrelationship of variables is more complex than Hirschi's initial formulation of the theory suggests. The way parents socialize their children, particularly the way they discipline them, is related to delinquency and crime. If relationships between parents and their children, and between the parents themselves, are characterized by conflict or poor communication, the children are more likely to become delinquents. The relationship between broken homes and delinquency is only weak to moderate, but it is stronger for some groups than for others. In general, more cohesive families seem able to insulate their children against trouble with the law.

Delinquents have weaker ties to schools and teachers than nondelinquents do. They also do less well in their academic work.

The relationship between the peer group and delinquency is not entirely clear, but most studies find that delinquents usually have delinquent friends. Whether those friends lead them into delinquency or whether they choose those friends after violating the law is unclear.

Some research indicates that there is less delinquency among adolescents who are more religious. Religion may also interact with the family, the peer group, and the school to curb delinquency.

Under some conditions, migration disrupts social bonds and increases criminality. This occurs when traditional social bonds are broken by moving and are not replaced by other attachments that inhibit criminality.

Social control theory has several shortcomings. It does not identify the social-structural sources of motivations to violate the law. It has not yet specified the relative importance of different kinds of attachments for people of various ages. Social control theory has also failed to spell out the way that attachments to different institutions interact with one another to prevent or cause crime and delinquency.

We do not yet have enough evidence on the distribution of the techniques of neutralization to account for geographic, temporal, and social variations in crime rates. Social control theory does seem capable of explaining those variations, with attachments to institutions being weakest in those countries and among those groups that have the highest crime rates.

Important Terms

appeal to higher loyalties

condemnation of the condemners

denial of injury

denial of responsibility

denial of the victim

drift

social control theory

subterranean value

technique of neutralization

Review Questions

1. How do juvenile delinquents neutralize the restraining influence of the law on their behavior? Do white-collar criminals use similar or different techniques of neutralization before committing crime?

2. What evidence is there that people who break the law use techniques of neutralization before engaging in crime and delinquency? How could researchers further test the significance of techniques of neutralization?

3. What bonds or attachments inhibit delinquent behavior, according to Travis Hirschi's social control theory? What evidence supports that theory? What are some of the theory's shortcomings?

4. Describe a family that would be especially likely to produce delinquent children. What government policies might reduce the number of families that produce delinquent children?

5. Have other societies been more successful than the United States in creating or maintaining social bonds that keep crime and delinquency to a minimum? What do the experiences of other societies tell us about how the United States might lower its crime rate?

6. How would social control theory explain variations in crime rates from one nation, region, or community to another, and across categories of sex, age, race, and social class?

Chapter 8
Learning to Commit Crime

C rime arises from needs that can be met by violating the law. Because most people are attached to the legal order, or at least know that the law commands widespread respect, they must justify their criminal acts and be relatively free of bonds to the legitimate social order before they can break the law. In addition to learning techniques for neutralizing the law, criminals must learn the skills and motives that are needed to violate the law. For instance, they learn how to recognize opportunities for crime, how to break into safes, how to reduce victim resistance, and how to find outlets for the property they steal. The degree to which such skills have to be learned varies from crime to crime. No particular skill is needed to steal an unattended purse, but finding a safe that contains a large amount of money, breaking into the building, and cracking the safe require considerable skill.

Sources of Learning to Commit Crime

Offenders learn motives and techniques for breaking the law from many sources, including the community, the peer group, the general culture, the mass media, sports, pornography, and correctional institutions.

The Community

Opportunities to learn to commit crime are associated with the social organization of a community. Learning about crime is easier when there are close ties and frequent interaction among people of different ages within a community (Cloward and Ohlin, 1960). Interaction between teenagers and adult criminals, as well as between teenage gang members and preteen nonmembers, provides opportunities to engage in criminal activities under the supervision of more experienced offenders. An unusual instance of this was reported in 1993 in Los Angeles, where two adults were implicated in 175 bank robberies carried out by teenagers whom they had enlisted and coached. The adults recruited boys as young as thirteen from gangs or from those who wanted to join gangs, provided them with automatic weapons and a stolen getaway car, and paid them with money or drugs. The supervisors remained a safe distance from the bank while the teenagers carried out the robbery, often firing their weapons before speeding away.

Local criminals sometimes act as role models for young people, as we can see from the following childhood memory of one of the robbers in the 1950 Brinks holdup:

> "When I was a kid, we all knew what a big-time crook was, and most of us looked up to them. I was always working to make money from the time I could walk. You wanted money because the parents were so poor. And I had all kinds of legitimate jobs, but they didn't pay nothing. But these racket guys would drive up in those big touring cars filled with pretty girls and all the money they wanted. I remember one of them giving us kids five bucks each just to stand and watch his car while he and the girl went to eat at a restaurant. Jesus, five bucks was almost as much as my father made in a week." (cited in Behn, 1977: 60)

Criminal role models are especially influential in communities that have high rates of poverty and unemployment, because in those neighborhoods there are few adults who have been successful in legitimate careers for young people to emulate.

The Peer Group

Learning to commit crime often occurs within groups or gangs, but many adolescents learn not to be delinquent from their peers. Those who are concerned with their reputation and believe they have an investment in abiding by the law cite the influence of their peers as a major reason for not violating the law (Rogers, 1977: 45–49). Adolescents who do not have a stake in conformity sometimes join gangs and learn criminal motives and skills from peers who encourage and reward violation of the law.

In gangs, adolescents gain respect for older criminals, develop specific skills such as car theft, learn to cooperate with other offenders, and become aware of fences, shady lawyers, bondsmen, and corrupt politicians and police officers (Rettig, Torres, and Garrett, 1977). One professional robber reports that he first got involved in an adult robbery gang because as an adolescent he had a reputation as a skilled car thief. Members of the gang approached him to steal a getaway car for a robbery, and he was gradually accepted into the gang on a permanent basis (Conklin, 1972).

A study of a New York City gang found that the integration of different age groups generates crime. This group of young adults provided a setting where even younger delinquents gathered. The younger boys were on trial by the older boys, who occasionally took them along to "case a job." Many of the gang's exploits were planned by an adult criminal who collected information on places to burglarize, planned the crimes, and contacted fences for the disposal of stolen goods. In such a highly integrated set of age groups, learning criminal motives and techniques is made easy for the gang members and for the young delinquents or "predelinquents" who interact with them (Bloch and Niederhoffer, 1958: 198–201).

The General Culture

People sometimes learn criminal motives from the general culture. For instance, the increase in violent crime after the end of wars is particularly dramatic in nations that were actively involved in the war, were victorious, and suffered large combat losses. The best explanation of this is that war makes violence legitimate, with people coming to believe that if their leaders can solve international disputes with violence, it is also a suitable means for resolving interpersonal differences (Archer and Gartner, 1976, 1984).

The techniques of neutralization examined in Chapter 7 are part of the general culture and are used to justify violations of the law. Embezzlers learn motives for their crimes from the general culture, justifying their offenses by the ambiguity that surrounds the ownership of money and property, and saying that they are only "borrowing the money temporarily" (Cressey, 1953, 1971).

Forcible rape is also closely linked to the values of the culture. Cultures that emphasize **machismo**—the demonstration of masculinity through the manipulation and exploitation of women—are likely to have more rape and other violence against women than are cultures that deemphasize differences between the sexes and provide men and women with the same opportunities (Hills, 1980; Schwendinger and Schwendinger, 1983). The Cross-Cultural Perspective illustrates this with an example from Brazil. One sociologist argues that rape and violence against women would be less common if

> our culture considered it masculine to be gentle and sensitive, to be responsive to the needs of others, to abhor violence, domination, and exploitation, to want sex only within a meaningful relationship, to be attracted by personality and character rather than by physical appearance, to value lasting rather than casual relationships ... (Russell, 1975: 264–265)

Conflict theorists claim that sexist values, and the economic inequality that often accompanies them, are the product of capitalism (Schwendinger and Schwendinger, 1983). Until we have better data on the incidence of rape in noncapitalist industrial societies, and until variations in rates of rape among different capitalist societies are explained, this hypothesis remains unproven.

The Mass Media

Today, the average American household has a television set turned on about seven hours a day. In looking at the consequences of such heavy television viewing, social scientists have focused on the large amount of violence that viewers see. A 1996 report found that violence—defined as "any overt depiction of the use of physical force or the credible threat of such force intended to physically harm an animate being or group of beings"—was included in 85 percent of premium cable channel shows, 59 percent of basic cable channel shows, and 44 percent of broadcast television channel shows (see Figure 8.1). Three-fourths of those who committed violent acts were not punished in the same scene, half of all victims of violence were not shown as being harmed, one-fourth of the violent incidents included a handgun, and only 4 percent of shows that contained violence also emphasized nonviolent means of resolving conflicts (Carter, 1996; Farhi, 1996).

The hypothesis that violence in the media might reduce real-life violence by releasing tensions is contradicted by most research. A recent review of the research literature confidently concluded that viewing violence in the mass media has the following major effects:

1. an *aggressor effect* of increased meanness, aggression, and even violence toward others;
2. a *victim effect* of increased fearfulness, mistrust, or "mean world syndrome," and self-protective behavior (such as carrying a gun, which ironically increases one's risk of becoming a victim of violence);
3. a *bystander effect* of increased desensitization, callousness, and behavioral apathy toward other victims of violence; and
4. an *appetite effect* of increased self-initiated behavior to further expose oneself to violent material. (Donnerstein, Slaby, and Eron, 1994: 240)

A CROSS-CULTURAL PERSPECTIVE

Machismo and Murder in Brazil

Brazilian culture traditionally has supported the use of violence by men against women who insult their dignity. Some men have killed their unfaithful wives and lovers, even though those men expect to have an unchallenged right to engage in sex with other women. Never a formal part of the Brazilian criminal code, the "legitimate defense of honor" has been used thousands of times to win acquittals for men who have killed their wives and lovers.

In a 1979 murder trial, Raul "Doca" Street, a forty-five-year-old man, was tried for shooting and killing Angela Diniz, his thirty-two-year-old lover, after she ordered him to move out of her expensive villa so that she could replace him with someone else. She also hit him in the face with a handbag. Street's attorney justified the killing by calling the victim "a luxurious Babylonian prostitute" and "a lascivious woman," claiming that his client had suffered "a violent moral aggression" and had murdered the victim out of "legitimate defense of his honor." Women who were present inside and outside the courtroom applauded the defendant and carried signs of support for him. A jury of five men and two women convicted Street of involuntary homicide, and he was given a two-year suspended sentence and allowed to go free.

Some observers claimed that this verdict and sentence increased the number of murders of women by "affronted" men. One feminist described the months following Street's trial as "a hunting season on women." Led by a small group of militant feminists, Brazilian women became increasingly angry over the murder of women in defense of "masculine honor." They demanded a retrial of

Street to show that women could not be killed merely for insulting a man's honor. Eventually, an appellate court declared that the verdict of involuntary homicide was invalid and ordered a new trial.

In the retrial, which ended in December 1981, Street was convicted and sentenced to fifteen years in prison. At the new trial, military police had to force an opening through five hundred angry feminist protesters. The atmosphere at the new trial was one of condemnation of machismo killings, rather than the supportive atmosphere of the first trial only two years earlier. Some Brazilians believe that the second verdict, and the protest over killing in defense of "masculine honor" that followed the first verdict, weakened this justification for murder. During the two weeks after the second verdict, three men who claimed that they had killed their wives to defend their honor were found guilty of murder.

Over the next decade, Brazilian women campaigned against the "legitimate defense of honor," and in 1991 the Brazilian Supreme Court finally outlawed the defense, ruling as follows:

> Homicide cannot be seen as a normal and legitimate way of reacting to adultery. Because in this kind of crime what is defended is not honor, but vanity, exaggerated self-importance and the pride of the lord who sees a woman as his personal property. (p. B16)

Sources: Based on Jim Brooke, "Feminism in Foreign Lands: Two Perspectives: Macho Killing in Brazil Spurs Protesters," *Boston Globe*, January 3, 1982, pp. A23, A24; James Brooke, "'Honor' Killing of Wives Is Outlawed in Brazil," *New York Times*, March 29, 1991, p. B16.

According to the authors,

scholars in the field of mass media overwhelmingly support the assumption of a strong relation between televised violence and aggressive behavior.... These analyses support a number of conclusions. First, there is a positive association between televised violence exposure and aggressive behavior over a wide range of ages and measures of aggressive behavior. Second, exposure to violent programming not

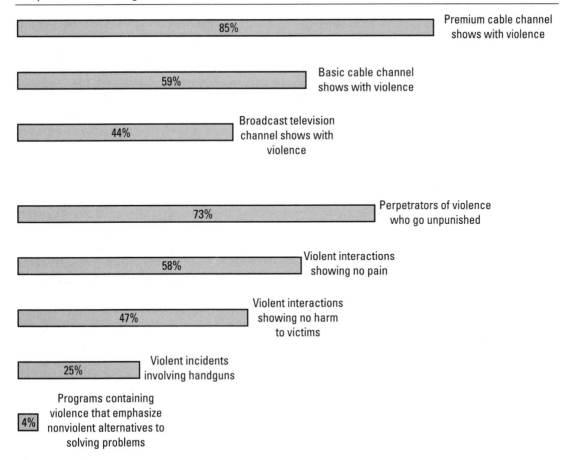

FIGURE 8.1

Violence on Television

Source: Based on data in Paul Farhi, "Researchers Link Psychological Harm to Violence on TV," *Boston Globe,* February 7, 1996, p. 3.

only increases aggressive behavior but is associated with lowered levels of prosocial behavior. (Donnerstein, Slaby, and Eron, 1994: 228)

One longitudinal study found that the exposure of young boys to televised violence was correlated with their aggressiveness at later ages, concluding as follows: "The greater was a boy's preference for violent television at age eight, the greater was his aggressiveness both at that time and ten years later" (Lefkowitz et al., 1977: 115–116). What the boys watched on television when they were eighteen was not related to their aggressiveness at that age, possibly because television violence was no longer realistic to them or perhaps because the modeling effect occurs only earlier in life. In response to methodological criticisms of this study, one of the researchers remarked:

Now, it could have been said that aggressive youngsters like violent programs to begin with. But because of the methodology we used to control the experiment, we were fairly certain this was a cause-and-effect relationship, with television viewing preceding the aggressive behavior. The highly aggressive youngsters who were watching nonviolent programs were significantly less aggressive by age eighteen than the youngsters who were not aggressive at eight but who had watched violent programs; they turned out to be more aggressive in the end. We later repeated the study, and found the same thing. Furthermore, the more violent the program, the more aggressive the children became. (Leonard Eron, cited in Bennetts, 1981: 25)

A follow-up study of the subjects at about age thirty found that "the violent programming they had watched was related to the seriousness of the crimes they committed, how aggressive they were to their spouses, and even to how aggressive their own kids were" (Leonard Eron, cited in Kolbert, 1994: D20).

The way that violence is portrayed in the media determines how much it will influence actual behavior (see the Crime and the Media box). Its influence is greatest if those who act aggressively are rewarded or fail to be punished, if the aggressive behavior is shown as justified, and if the violence is portrayed as similar to real life. Media violence is also more influential when it is motivated by a desire to inflict harm, seems to produce no pain or remorse, is unrelieved or uninterrupted, is not criticized, and leaves the viewer aroused or frustrated. The impact of media violence is also greatest when the viewer is predisposed to aggressive behavior and strongly identifies with the aggressor (Paik and Comstock, 1994; Donnerstein, Slaby, and Eron, 1994).

Media attention to real acts of violence can trigger additional violence in the general population. After the assassination of President John F. Kennedy in 1963, aggravated assaults and robberies increased throughout the country. Similar increases occurred in 1966 after two widely reported crimes: the murder of eight nurses by Richard Speck and the killing of fourteen people by Charles Whitman from a tower at the University of Texas (Berkowitz and Macaulay, 1971). One study found a noticeable increase in the homicide rate

Seven firebombing attacks on New York subway token booths occurred soon after the opening of the film "Money Train," which featured two similar crimes. Critics claimed the real-life arsonists were imitating the movie, which starred Wesley Snipes and Woody Harrelson (shown here).

after heavyweight championship boxing matches, and an especially great increase after those matches that were most heavily publicized (Phillips, 1983). News stories about violence that is rewarded, such as a championship fight, seem to be followed by a short-term increase in the homicide rate, but news accounts of violence that is punished, such as a murder for which the

CRIME AND THE MEDIA

The "Money Train" Controversy: Does Life Imitate Art?

In the film "Money Train," starring Wesley Snipes and Woody Harrelson as police officers who work as decoys in New York's subways to arrest robbers, a man twice sprays a flammable liquid into a token booth, then ignites it by throwing in a match. About 2 A.M. on November 26, 1995, four days after the film opened, a group of teenagers intent on committing a robbery sprayed a flammable liquid into a Brooklyn subway token booth and ignited it with a match. The booth exploded in flames, severely burning the attendant, who died two weeks later. There were six other similar incidents in New York subways in the month after the opening of "Money Train," but there was no evidence that the same people were involved. Between 1988 and the opening of the film, there were only eleven reported arson attacks on token booths, all of them minor.

Bob Dole, U.S. Senator from Kansas and presidential candidate, thought the subway attacks were directly attributable to "Money Train" and called for a boycott of the film. The president of the New York Transit Authority agreed with Dole, pointing out that Columbia Pictures, producers of the film, had consulted with his agency before making the film, and that the agency had objected to the scenes of the firebomb attacks on the token booths, fearing they might lead to actual crimes. The agency asked to have the scenes removed, or at least have the film show that there was a mechanism in the booths to extinguish fires. (Prior to the real-life attack, the mechanism had been immobilized by the attendant who was burned to death; apparently he did this so that his smoking of cigarettes would not trigger the mechanism.) The Transit Authority president was unsuccessful in his pleas for changes in the film.

Eventually, two eighteen-year-olds and a seventeen-year-old were arrested for the fatal attack, one of them reportedly confessing that he and four friends, all armed with handguns, had planned a robbery, and that one of them had firebombed the booth when the clerk refused to give up the money. According to the three suspects and the Brooklyn District Attorney, the crime had not been inspired by "Money Train," although the District Attorney could not comment on whether the suspects had seen the movie. Columbia Pictures also denied responsibility for the attacks, saying that the film was based on a series of firebombings of token booths that had occurred in New York in 1988.

Source: Based on Robert D. McFadden, "Token Clerk in Fire Attack Dies of Burns," *New York Times*, December 11, 1995, pp. B1, B4; Alan F. Kiepper, "What Does Hollywood Say Now?" *New York Times*, December 12, 1995, p. A27; Lynette Holloway, "Token Booth Fire Attack Seems Unrelated to Movie," *New York Times*, December 16, 1995, p. 26.

perpetrator is executed or imprisoned for life, seem to be followed by a short-term drop in the homicide rate. Apparently, the homicide rate is not affected by reports of violence that is neither punished nor rewarded (Phillips and Hensley, 1984).

Representatives of television networks frequently cite the small number of studies that find no association between media violence and aggressiveness, and point to the methodological flaws of the many studies that find such an association. Nevertheless, the networks continue to solicit billions of dollars from advertisers on the assumption that what people see on television does influence their behavior. In response to growing public concern about the effects of televised violence, the four major broadcast networks agreed in 1993 to run brief warnings about the violent content of upcoming shows. In 1996, a federal law mandated that within two years all new television sets would have to contain a violence- or V-chip that would allow viewers to screen out programs with violence, sexual content, or offensive language. In that same year, network executives bowed to pressure from the federal government and announced that a ratings system similar to the one used for movies would be introduced in 1997.

Even though media portrayal of violence is correlated with aggressive behavior, we lack conclusive proof that it is a major cause of crime and delinquency. Aggressiveness can be expressed in various ways, including athletics, and it does not necessarily lead to violation of the law. However, for some people in certain circumstances, media portrayals of violence might contribute to delinquency and crime. For example, social control theory suggests that people exposed to media violence would be especially likely to commit crime if they lacked attachments to conventional institutions and lines of action.

Sports

There is some evidence that sports can contribute to the aggressiveness of both athletes and spectators. High school and college athletes in combative sports such as football and hockey anger more easily than athletes in less combative sports such as swimming. In addition, athletes in combative sports become more aggressive during the course of the season and are more likely to remain more aggressive after the season ends (Russell, 1983; Goleman, 1985). By encouraging aggressiveness and male camaraderie, organized sports denigrate femininity and encourage attitudes conducive to sexual assault. A study of National Collegiate Athletic Association Division I varsity athletes found that they were significantly more likely than other male students to commit sexual assaults on campus (Bass, 1994). Because they are usually treated more leniently by the law and by their institutions than are students who are not athletes, athletes are not easily deterred from committing sexual assault, theft, and illegal drug use (Golden, 1995).

Watching sporting events can make spectators more aggressive. One study found that fans at an Army-Navy football game were more hostile after the game than before it, and that hostility increased whether the fan's preferred team won or lost, or even if the fan did not care who won the game. The largest increase in hostility occurred among fans of the winning team, apparently because they had seen aggression on the field rewarded with a victory. This study also found no increase in hostility among spectators at an Army-Navy gymnastics match—a nonaggressive sport—on the same weekend (Goldstein, 1986). Another study found that aggressiveness increased among spectators at hockey and wrestling matches, but not at swim meets, again suggesting that viewing aggression increases aggressiveness among spectators (Arms, Russell, and Sandilands, 1979).

Factors other than simple imitation of athletic aggressiveness also contribute to spectator aggressiveness. The anonymity and excitement of the event can weaken normal inhibitions against aggression, and the consumption of alcoholic beverages can have a similar effect. Spectator violence usually involves young males, a group especially prone to violent activity in other contexts. Factors such as nationalism, unemployment, general social unrest, and the cultural context also contribute to spectator violence, but the game itself builds up aggressiveness among spectators (Goldstein, 1983; Goleman, 1985).

Whether the increased aggressiveness of athletes and spectators leads to criminal behavior, and the exact conditions under which it does so, is not clear. Assaults by athletes on each other and assaults by fans against each other constitute crimes, even though they are not usually prosecuted as such. In 1985, thirty-nine people died when British fans at a soccer game in Belgium attacked an area of the stadium where Italian fans were sitting, resulting in the unexpected collapse of a section of the stands. Latin American soccer fans have assaulted referees who make unpopular decisions, and in 1994 fans murdered a Colombian national team player after he accidentally scored a goal for the opposing team. Sports do heighten aggressiveness, but the way the aggressiveness is channeled—whether into criminal assaults or into loud cheering and boisterousness—is less well understood.

Pornography

There is a widely held view that people who view or read pornography are more likely to commit sex offenses, because they learn to see such behavior as rewarding or because they are stimulated to act on their sexual fantasies. **Pornography** is material that is intended to arouse people sexually by portraying sexual matters in visual or verbal terms. **Obscene material** is material, often pornographic in nature, that has been declared illegal because it poses a threat to the state or to organized religion, violates common morality, has no redeeming social value, or appeals to prurient or lascivious interest.

Even though pornographic material arouses people sexually, not everyone responds to it in the same way. Those most likely to be sexually aroused by pornography are the young, the college educated, the religiously inactive, and the sexually experienced.

Exposure to pornography rarely causes major changes in the viewer's sexual behavior, except for short-term increases in masturbation or sexual intercourse with regular partners. No effects on sexual morality have been found, nor is there consistent evidence that nonviolent pornography causes sex crimes (Goldstein and Kant, 1973; Donnerstein, Linz, and Penrod, 1987). The 1986 Attorney General's Commission on Pornography concluded that aggressiveness is heightened by pornography that is either violent or degrading, adjectives the Commission asserted were descriptive of nearly all available pornography. The commission claimed that this increased aggressiveness led to sexual violence, but critics, including two members of the Commission, said that current social science research did not support that claim.

Contrary to what the Commission's conclusions suggest, the legalization of pornography in Denmark in 1966 actually preceded a decline in arrests for exhibitionism, voyeurism, child molesting, and physical indecency with adult women. Rates of rape and other serious offenses against adult women seemed unaffected by the legalization of pornography. Falling numbers of arrests do not necessarily prove that actual criminal behavior has declined; they could simply reflect greater police or public tolerance of the behavior. However, the data are consistent with the hypothesis that the legalization of pornography reduced sex crimes in Denmark; at the very least, they suggest that the legalization of pornography did not increase sex crimes (President's Commission on Obscenity and Pornography, 1970; Gagnon, 1974). Evidence from the United States, Sweden, and West Germany also supports the conclusion that the legalization or increased circulation of pornography does not increase, and can even decrease, rates of rape (Kutchinsky, 1988).

A study that looked at exposure to pornography among several groups—including the general population, regular users of pornography, child molesters, homosexuals, transsexuals, and rapists—found no clear-cut pattern of antisocial sexual activity following arousal by pornography. Erotic material was a factor in a few offenses, but sex crimes were more likely to be associated with lowered inhibitions due to alcohol consumption, rejection by wives or lovers, and interaction with peers who suggested sex crimes. Sex offenders rarely mentioned pornography as stimulating, but some of them reported being aroused by material depicting violence (Goldstein and Kant, 1973).

Several experiments have found that pornography combining sex with explicit violence against women increases aggressiveness toward females. Nonviolent erotic material does not have that effect (Donnerstein, Slaby, and Eron, 1994). However, these experiments used college students as subjects, and measured aggressiveness by the subjects' administration of electric shocks and by the subjects' responses to questionnaires. We cannot generalize from these studies and say that violent pornography increases actual sex offenses among the population at large. There is some evidence that men who are already angry have their level of aggressiveness increased by exposure to hard-core pornography, but this is not the same as showing that exposure to hard-core pornography causes sex crimes among the male population at large, or even among men who are already angry (Donnerstein, Linz, and Penrod, 1987).

Exposure to pornography can weaken condemnation of rape by both men and women. One experiment found that students who were exposed to more pornographic films recommended more lenient prison sentences for convicted rapists than did students who were exposed to less pornography. Those exposed to more pornography also became more tolerant of violent forms of pornography and less supportive of equality between the sexes (Zillmann and Bryant, 1984). However, other evidence suggests that exposure to pornography does not necessarily cause such attitudes, but might instead simply reinforce and strengthen attitudes that people already hold (Donnerstein, Linz, and Penrod, 1987).

Correctional Institutions

Prisons, jails, and juvenile detention centers are sometimes described as "schools of crime" where relatively inexperienced offenders are thrown into daily contact with skilled criminals. Conversations in those settings often focus on crime, spreading criminal motives and techniques from more experienced offenders to less knowledgeable inmates, possibly increasing criminal behavior by those inmates after they are released.

There are no reliable data on the extent to which this kind of learning actually takes place. Many offenders are quite skilled in crime before they are incarcerated. There seems to be no clear relationship between the length of time inmates are imprisoned and the likelihood that they will return to crime when released (von Hirsch, 1976: 113). Indeed, the longer inmates spend in prison, the less efficient and more out-of-practice they might become in the commission of crimes that require skill (Irwin, 1970: 147). Any learning of criminal motives and skills by inmates might thus be counterbalanced by the loss of efficiency that occurs with the passage of time.

To the extent that criminal motives and skills are learned in a penal institution, this seems to happen during an inmate's middle stage of confinement. Inmates are less likely to pick up skills when they are first incarcerated or when they are about to be released (Radzinowicz and King, 1977: 271–272). Whether inmates learn criminal motives and skills is also related to personal characteristics. For instance, inmates who have families and plan to go straight when released are probably less likely to learn criminal motives and skills than are inmates who have no family ties and are committed to a life of crime.

The prison experience can be conducive to the formation of motives to engage in crime, with deprivations of prison life such as lack of freedom and demeaning treatment causing resentment that is later used to justify crime (Sykes, 1958). Material deprivations and crowded living conditions lead to the exploitation of inmates by one another, and sometimes to assault, homicide, and homosexual rape. Because prisoners lack opportunities to make their own decisions and take responsibility for their own lives, they do not acquire the everyday skills needed to lead law-abiding lives once they are released, and this can push them back into crime after they leave prison (Kassebaum, Ward, and Wilner, 1971; Cordilia, 1983).

Offenders learn the motives and skills to commit crime from a variety of sources. One theory that emphasizes the process by which people learn to commit crime through interaction with others is differential association theory.

Differential Association Theory

Edwin Sutherland introduced **differential association theory** in the 1939 edition of his criminology textbook and modified the theory in 1947 (Sutherland, Cressey, and Luckenbill, 1992). This general theory aims to explain why crime rates are distributed as they are among various groups and why any given individual does or does not become a criminal.

Principles of Differential Association Theory

The first principle of differential association theory is that criminal behavior is *learned*, an assertion that rejects the possibility that individual pathology or biological factors cause crime. This principle also denies that criminal behavior is unique to or invented anew by individuals. This assumption is questionable, for some crimes—such as one kidnapper's attempt to have ransom money delivered through a computerized bank terminal—seem to be unique to the offender. Many aspects of an offender's behavior are learned from others—for example, the motives and justifications for the crime—but the criminal's specific actions might be the result of a combination of skills, ideas, and opportunities that are available only to that individual.

The second principle of differential association theory is that most learning of criminal behavior takes place in *face-to-face interaction* with other people. Differential association theory probably regards the mass media as unimportant in the causation of criminal behavior because the theory was developed before mass ownership of television. In 1994, 98 percent of all American households had television sets, 79 percent had videocassette recorders, and 62 percent had cable television. The pervasive role of the mass media in contemporary society would seem to require a modification of differential association theory to incorporate the effects of learning from that source (see the Crime and the Media box).

The third principle of the theory is that people learn from others both *the techniques of crime and the direction (legal or illegal) of motives, drives, and attitudes*. However, little or no skill is needed to commit some crimes; the murder of a spouse requires little skill, especially if a handgun is available, and many kinds of theft require little skill. Embezzlers have to learn "verbalizations" that allow them to use their accounting skills for illegal ends, but they do not need to learn specific techniques of embezzlement (Cressey, 1953, 1971: 147–151).

Differential association theory then proposes that *the direction of motives and drives is learned from definition of the law as favorable or unfavorable*. This assumes that people orient their actions toward the law; in other words, the law is not irrelevant to any individual who is deciding how to behave. Some situations are defined as favorable to violation of the law; for example, an unattended bicycle might be seen as a opportunity for theft. However, the same situation can also be defined as unfavorable to violation of the law, with the unattended bicycle being seen as a chance to alert the owner to the risk of theft. Some people define the situation in one way, and others define it dif-

CRIME AND THE MEDIA

The How-to-Commit-Crime Manual

First published in 1971, *The Anarchist Cookbook* has now sold more than 2 million copies. This book provides detailed instructions on the production of pipe bombs and LSD and was the first in a genre now enjoying great popularity: the how-to-commit-crime book. Available titles include *Homemade Grenade Launchers, The Ultimate Sniper, Successful Armed Robbery, 21 Techniques of Silent Killing,* and *The Ancient Art of Strangulation.* White-collar crime has not been neglected, with *How to Do Business Off the Books* and *Biz Op: How to Get Rich with Business Opportunity Frauds and Scams* selling briskly.

Three of the largest publishers of these books—Paladin Press, Delta Press, and Loompanics Unlimited—reported selling a total of 700,000 copies in 1993, twice what they sold in 1988. They advertise in *Soldier of Fortune* magazine, *The National Enquirer,* and gun magazines. The publishers claim that their customers, most of whom are young or middle-aged men, buy the books out of curiosity, but acknowledge that some criminals might use the material to carry out crimes. However, they argue, their books are not turning people into criminals; instead, people otherwise predisposed to crime are attracted to their books.

In 1996, the families of three murder victims sued Paladin Press, the publisher of *Hit Man: A Technical Manual for Independent Contractors,* for aiding and abetting James E. Perry, a hired killer who allegedly followed twenty-seven of the book's recommendations when he murdered a woman, her disabled son, and the son's nurse. Cases of this sort have proved difficult to win in the past.

Even if how-to-commit-crime books do not generate the motive to commit crime, they do make methods readily available that potential offenders can use to break the law and perhaps injure or kill more victims than they otherwise would have. Clearly, techniques of crime can be learned from the media as well as through face-to-face interaction.

Source: Based on J. Peder Zane, "You Too Can Be a Successful Criminal!" *New York Times,* July 24, 1994, p. E2; Mary Boyle, "Publisher Sued over Manual for Murder," *Boston Globe,* July 23, 1996, p. A3.

---

ferently. The way that the situation is defined depends on the favorable or unfavorable definitions of the law that an individual has learned in the past.

The primary proposition of differential association theory is that a person becomes delinquent or criminal because of *an EXCESS of definitions favorable to violation of the law OVER definitions unfavorable to violation of the law.* This principle stresses association with criminal or noncriminal definitions but does not require contact with criminal or noncriminal individuals. People can learn definitions favorable to violation of the law from law-abiding people, and they can learn definitions unfavorable to violation of the law from criminals. Parents might not violate the law but still verbally approve of theft for certain purposes (such as feeding a family) or in certain situations (such as from a large store). Parental approval of this sort will convey to children a definition favorable to violation of the law. On the other hand, a professional thief might convey to young thieves the need to avoid violence against the victims of theft. Some offenders even warn others away from behavior that they themselves engage in. For instance, heroin addicts often tell nonusers to stay away not only from heroin but also from marijuana, the drug with which many of them began.

Critical to differential association theory is the *ratio* of definitions favorable to violation of the law to definitions unfavorable. Any one individual holds both types of definitions. It is only when the definitions favorable to violation of the law exceed the definitions unfavorable that a person turns to crime or delinquency. There is an obvious difficulty in measuring these definitions of the law so that an exact ratio can be calculated for any given person.

Definitions of the law are a result of associations with criminal and noncriminal patterns that vary in *frequency, duration, priority, and intensity*. It is the nature of associations with criminal and noncriminal patterns, rather than the mere fact of those associations, that is important. Associations that are more frequent play a larger role in the balance between definitions favorable to violation of the law and definitions unfavorable to violation of the law. Associations that endure over the longest time are the most significant in determining criminal behavior. Associations that occur earlier in life—in childhood or in adolescence—are the most important in forming definitions of the law; this is called priority. Finally, the intensity of associations is important. This means that the prestige of the source of the definition of the law and the individual's emotional reactions to the source are significant in learning definitions of the law. Thus, a young child who learns a definition favorable to violation of the law from a parent who presents that definition frequently and over long stretches of time will be more influenced in the direction of violating the law than an adult who is exposed to a definition favorable to violation of the law by a passing acquaintance whom the adult sees infrequently and for short periods. (See the Using Criminology box, pp. 290–291.)

Critique of Differential Association Theory

The theory of differential association stresses the ratio of definitions favorable to violation of the law over definitions unfavorable to violation of the law. The theory might be mistaken in looking at definitions of the law in general, because individuals violate specific laws. Thus, a person might not need to hold an overall unfavorable view of the law before committing a crime; holding an unfavorable definition of one specific law could be enough.

Differential association theory examines the learning process by which people become criminals, but it does not explain why people have the associations they do. Because the theory does not tell us how the associations that expose people to different definitions of the law are distributed throughout the social structure, it does not fulfill its goal of explaining why crime rates vary among groups as they do.

Because differential association theory looks at the individual's perception of the situation, rather than at the actual situation itself, the theory is a social-psychological rather than a social-structural one. It is not, however, a purely psychological theory, because it does not consider personality traits and psychological variables to be important factors in crime causation.

One criticism of differential association theory is that it might describe how some people initially become involved in crime better than it explains why people continue in a criminal career. The direct rewards of crime—such as money, euphoria from illegal drugs, or prestige among peers—might be a sufficient cause of continued violation of the law.

Some critics argue that differential association theory is too general and imprecise to test easily or to verify fully. They claim that even if the concepts of the theory could be defined in measurable terms, an enormous amount of data would be needed to test the theory. Consider the difficulty of measuring not only all associations with criminal definitions, but also all associations with noncriminal definitions, from the time a person is conscious of the social environment. To test the theory, it would be necessary to measure how frequent all of those associations are, how long they last, how they vary in significance because of the person's age, and how the person reacts emotionally to the various sources of definitions. Although this measurement process cannot realistically be accomplished, others have found differential association theory useful, testing hypotheses derived from the theory and finding it has explanatory power (Orcutt, 1987).

Differential Identification Theory   Differential association theory has been criticized for holding an overly simplified view of the way that people choose models for their behavior. **Differential identification theory** proposes that the choice of models does not necessarily involve interaction with others in intimate personal groups, as differential association theory claims. Instead, differential identification theory argues that "a person pursues criminal behavior to the extent that he identifies himself with real or imaginary persons from whose perspective his criminal behavior seems acceptable" (Glaser, 1956: 440). Differential identification theory "allows for human choice, and stresses the importance of vocabularies of motives existing in the wider culture independently of direct intimate association" (Taylor, Walton, and Young, 1973: 129–130). Testing this theory would require the application of role theory to people who do and do not violate the law, which might be easier than testing differential association theory.

Differential Association-Reinforcement Theory   **Differential association-reinforcement theory** retains differential association theory's emphasis on learning from the people with whom an individual interacts, but it broadens the focus of Sutherland's theory by specifying the process of learning from other people and by examining the way that individuals learn from other sources (Burgess and Akers, 1966; Akers et al., 1979). Differential association-reinforcement theory proposes that people learn attitudes and techniques conducive to crime in both nonsocial and social situations from positive reinforcement (rewards) and negative reinforcement (punishments) that result

USING CRIMINOLOGY

Learning Not to Bully

Bullies, who are usually boys, torment their victims by being quick to use force in response to insults and threats, which are often imagined or exaggerated. This behavior is learned from others, especially parents, while young, but research suggests that bullies can be taught to interact with others in a nonaggressive way. These measures can keep bullies from growing up to be adults who commit violent crimes, including abuse of their spouses and children.

Many bullies have parents who use severe and inconsistent discipline and punish their children more in response to their own moods than in response to their children's behavior. When the parent is angry, the child will be punished, often for trivial things. When the parent is feeling good, the child will not be punished, even for violent or destructive behavior. This capricious behavior makes parents, and other people in general, seem unpredictable and threatening to the bully. The fear of not being in control is a source of the bully's need to dominate others. The parents also present the bully with a model of aggressiveness that he learns and applies in dealing with other children.

Most children gain self-control as they pass through kindergarten and first grade, but bullies become less self-controlled. Others learn to negotiate and compromise, but bullies learn to rely on

force. Bullies are more likely than other children to see ambiguous situations as threatening and to blame others for causing trouble, and bullies are more likely to justify an aggressive response to a perceived provocation.

Measures that have been taken to curb bullying include increased adult supervision, changes in the school environment, social-skills training for bullies' victims, and efforts to change bullies. Suggestions for dealing with bullies include the following:

1. Reasoning with bullies.
2. Praising and rewarding bullies' good behavior.
3. Deterring bullies through reprimand and punishment.
4. Encouraging children to report bullying and look out for one another.
5. Requiring bullies to make reparation to their victims, perhaps through agreements that they work out together.
6. Increasing bullies' empathy for their victims, and teaching bullies social skills for dealing with other children.

Psychologists have developed programs to teach bullies how to act differently. These early-intervention strategies, which focus on four- to

from their own behavior, whether that behavior is criminal or law-abiding. Thus, an absence of rewards for attending school or holding a menial job would make criminal behavior seem more attractive, as would the peer esteem that results from gang fighting. While agreeing that differential association with other people is an important source of learning criminal and delinquent behavior, this theory is actually a reward-risk theory of the sort that we examine later in this chapter.

Evidence on Differential Association Theory

There is some research that is consistent with differential association theory. Much of this research focuses on the relationship between delinquent behav-

USING CRIMINOLOGY

ten-year-olds, do not deal directly with personality traits produced by parental socialization, but instead involve efforts to teach bullies how to get their way by means of more peaceable action. One project takes groups of four or five bullies and shows them how to handle situations that frustrate and anger them. Bullies are shown how to respond to perceived insults and threats in a playful way, to count to ten before reacting, or simply to walk away. They participate in role-playing exercises that give them an opportunity to practice starting conversations with others or getting onto school buses when other children are taunting them. They are shown how to find friendly responses that will preserve their self-image and sense of worth, such as telling other children that they do not like to be teased. The bullies are taught to play with others cooperatively and to resolve conflicts without fighting. This requires them to spell out what is bothering them to others and to make agreements with others that will satisfy all parties.

A technique called "pair therapy" is based on evidence that aggressive children lack the skills needed for making and keeping friends. The method pairs highly aggressive boys with boys who are very withdrawn. The boys engage in activities they both enjoy, and gradually friendships develop. The boys are shown how to settle disagreements through negotiation rather than by fighting. They are taught that one person does not have to control the other to have a good time, and that both can get what they want.

Sources: Based on Daniel Goleman, "The Bully: New Research Depicts a Paranoid, Lifelong Loser," *New York Times*, April 7, 1987, pp. C1, C4; Daniel Goleman, "Taming Unruly Boys: Old Techniques and New Approaches," *New York Times*, February 1, 1990, p. B10; David P. Farrington, "Understanding and Preventing Bullying," in Michael Tonry, ed., *Crime and Justice: A Review of Research*, Vol. 17. Chicago: University of Chicago Press, 1993, pp. 381–458.

ior and patterns of interaction among adolescents, demonstrating that the associates of delinquents are other delinquents and that delinquency is often a group phenomenon.

Evidence against Differential Association Theory   Differential association theory does not explain all crimes. For instance, it is not consistent with some research on rural offenders and on landlords who violate rent-control regulations (Clinard, 1942; 1944; 1952, 1969). Some check forgers who operate alone apparently lack the associations with criminal patterns required by differential association theory (Lemert, 1953). Other crimes are evidently invented anew by offenders who have not experienced the learning process proposed in differential association theory.

Offenders who are not part of a criminal subculture or do not have ties to other criminals might lack exposure to the patterns and associations needed to learn criminal motives and skills. One study found that shoplifters often had no contact with a criminal subculture or with other criminal patterns. Few of those who were apprehended had prior convictions, most were "respectable" people who were employed or were housewives, many did not live in poor neighborhoods, most took inexpensive merchandise with little resale value, and many were ignorant of the arrest process (Cameron, 1964:

146–148). These characteristics suggest a lack of contact with a subculture that could have provided the shoplifters with criminal motives and techniques.

Professional Theft and Differential Association Theory   Evidence consistent with differential association theory comes from studies of professional thieves. Members of the subculture of professional thieves teach new recruits the skills that make expert theft possible, and immersion in the subculture isolates the thieves from noncriminal patterns (Sutherland, 1937; Maurer, 1955, 1964; 1974; Letkemann, 1973). The process of **tutelage** or instruction provides new thieves with knowledge of how to spot opportunities for theft and how to plan and carry out thefts. Burglars learn specific skills such as how to enter a building or how to open a safe. Robbers learn to interpret the body language of potential victims, to control victims, and to show self-confidence and mastery during the crime. Con artists learn to lie convincingly, to size up and manipulate victims, to display a winning personality, and to look respectable.

Experienced pickpockets teach novices to steal: "One thief turns out another. That is, he teaches him" (Maurer, 1955, 1964: 157). After learning that it is possible to steal from other people, pickpockets learn specific skills, practice them, and are evaluated by other thieves, refining their skills and eventually being accepted as professionals by other pickpockets. Novice pickpockets learn to look unobtrusive in public, be cautious, and use the opportunities with which they are presented. Manual dexterity is a source of professional pride for these thieves; they are expected to be able to take money from a victim if they can figure out where the victim is carrying his or her money. Pickpockets learn timing, speed, misdirection, concealment, rhythmic movement, and dexterity, blending those skills into a "single, almost instantaneous, and practically invisible act of theft" (Maurer, 1955, 1964: 41).

A study of professional thieves in a Canadian prison concluded that early involvement in juvenile delinquency is a prerequisite for an adult career as a professional criminal (Letkemann, 1973). As juveniles, the thieves learned such things as how to avoid attention when stealing and how the police would typically react to a certain crime. They usually progressed gradually from awkward juvenile theft, to some learning from other thieves while incarcerated, to trial and error with new forms of theft, and then to learning from skilled thieves and from personal experience. These professional thieves learned mechanical skills, social skills such as the management of victims, and organizational skills such as planning and executing a crime. They learned these things from other prisoners, from members of their gang, and from thieves they met in bars. In this way, safecrackers learned about different styles of safes and how to break into them, information that had to be continually updated.

Juvenile Delinquency and Differential Association Theory   Juvenile gangs stimulate and reinforce delinquency by supporting law-violating behavior and by offering protection from outsiders to gang members who break the law. A study of juvenile theft in Great Britain found that associating with other adolescents who had already stolen property was very important in leading boys to steal, especially if those associations began when a boy was quite young, continued over a long time, and involved boys who stole frequently (Belson, 1975). However, another study found that differential association theory's emphasis on priority is misplaced, because recent friendships have more impact on delinquency than do friendships formed earlier in life (Warr, 1993). Research also suggests that delinquent behavior is more strongly influenced by learning from direct observation of peers' behavior than it is by learning peers' attitudes (Warr and Stafford, 1991).

Much delinquency takes place in groups, although the extent to which this is true varies with the specific offense and with the age and sex of the offender (Erickson and Jensen, 1977; Giordano, 1978). Young shoplifters commonly steal in groups, learning attitudes and techniques from their peers, but as they get older they are more likely to steal by themselves (Cameron, 1964: 148–149).

One study found that the impact on delinquency of broken homes and attachments to parents and peers was better explained by differential association theory than by social control theory. Broken homes weaken parental supervision, which increases interaction with delinquent peers, exposure to definitions favorable to delinquency, and, eventually, delinquent behavior. Broken homes also contribute directly to an excess of definitions favorable to delinquency over definitions unfavorable to delinquency. Because this effect is much greater for blacks than for whites, broken homes have a larger impact on delinquency among blacks (Matsueda and Heimer, 1987).

Sexual Aggression and Differential Association Theory   One study found a strong association between sexual aggression by males and the presence of sexually aggressive friends. The researcher measured sexual aggression by self-reports, asking subjects the following:

> It has been noted that in the course of men's and women's sexual lives together, some men on occasion make physically forceful attempts at sexual activity which are disagreeable and offensive enough that the woman responds in an offended manner such as crying, fighting, screaming, pleading, etc. Have you ever engaged in such behavior? (Alder, 1985: 312–313)

The strongest predictor of this kind of sexual aggression, which includes forcible rape as well as lesser degrees of sexual assault, was the presence of sexually aggressive friends. The men who were most likely to report engaging in sexual aggression had sexually aggressive friends, had served in Vietnam, and held attitudes legitimating sexual aggression. These findings are consistent with the learning process described by differential association theory.

White-Collar Crime and Differential Association Theory   Differential association theory is useful in explaining white-collar crime, which results from the learning of cultural goals, such as material success, and the pursuit of those goals through illegal means. (See the Crime on Campus box.)

CRIME ON CAMPUS

Learning to Commit Tax Fraud

In 1992, ninety students at Hampton University in Virginia were investigated for suspicion of defrauding the Internal Revenue Service, tax-preparation businesses, and banks of a total of $230,000 by claiming false refunds through an electronic tax-return filing system. The fraud involved the application of techniques that the students had learned through interaction with one another.

Since 1986, the IRS has allowed taxpayers to file returns and ask for refunds electronically, then send documents supporting their returns later. Bank loans are made against the refunds that are due. This system creates an opportunity for taxpayers to file false returns and cash bank checks that are issued in anticipation of receiving their refunds from the IRS.

One Hampton University student accused of tax fraud said that she had learned from a friend that other students had easily made money this way and had not been caught. She learned of the scheme when she saw a stack of fraudulent wage statements in that student's apartment. False wage statements were prepared on word processors, using fictitious jobs at local businesses whose employer numbers were known to the students.

One student who was expelled from school, pleaded guilty to conspiracy to defraud the IRS, and was sentenced to eighteen months in prison said that he had learned how to commit the fraud from his roommate's brother. Other people learned of the scheme in conversations with that student, or with other students who had talked with him. Knowledge of how to commit tax fraud was thus spread through face-to-face interaction among the students, most of whom had never filed a tax return.

The students claimed $2,400 to $2,800 in tax refunds for each filed return, increasing their claims by taking tax credits for fictitious newborn children. Suspicion focused on the students when a tax-preparation agency they used noticed that a few of the students were filing returns under different names and that an exceptionally large number of babies seemed to have been born in 1991. A call to their "employers" found that the students had never worked there, and the IRS was alerted to the fraud. The students were easy to track down, because most of them had used their own names and social security numbers.

Source: Based on Mike Allen, "College Students Accused of Electronic Tax Fraud," *New York Times*, December 4, 1992, p. B20.

Because there is no enforceable code of business ethics to limit the pursuit of material success to legal means, definitions unfavorable to violation of the law are not readily learned in the world of business. Those who are most assimilated into a business organization seem to be the most likely to violate the law, and those new to the world of business are less apt to do so because they are more influenced by the definitions unfavorable to violation of the law that they bring with them from the outside world. A study of attitudes toward bribes and payoffs made by businesspeople to foreign officials found that experienced executives who were enrolled in business school programs were more tolerant of such bribes and payoffs than were undergraduate business students who lacked experience in the world of business (Jensen, 1976). This suggests that business experience is conducive to the learning of definitions supportive of bribes and payoffs. Whether these definitions lead to actual violation of the law depends on factors such as exposure to definitions unfavorable to violation of the law and the presence of opportunities to break the law.

Learning from superiors and colleagues in the company is probably a more important determinant of business crime than is the personality of the individual. A former head of the Securities and Exchange Commission's Division of Enforcement stated this bluntly: "Our largest corporations have trained some of our brightest young people to be dishonest" (Stanley Sporkin, cited in Kohlmeier, 1976: 53). Social pressure to violate the law was described as follows for the Equity Funding Corporation of America fraud: "Corporations can and do create a moral tone that powerfully influences the thinking, conduct, values, and even the personalities of the people who work for them. The tone is set by the men who run the company, and their corruption can quickly corrupt all else" (Blundell, 1976: 46).

Differential association theory fits much of what we know about white-collar crime. Businesspeople learn definitions favorable to violation of the law, such as loyalty to the corporation over loyalty to the law. In addition to techniques of neutralization that are conducive to violation of the law, the learning process involves the segregation of businesspeople from the law-abiding public, making them relatively immune to public criticism and limiting their exposure to definitions unfavorable to violation of the law. Ties to the law-abiding public are weakened and dependence on the corporation is strengthened by the common practice of regularly moving young executives from one region to another (Coleman, 1994).

Conclusion   Research on various forms of crime is consistent with differential association theory, but there is no direct proof of the theory as it is formally stated. In other words, there is no concrete evidence that different kinds of offenders initially became criminals because of an excess of definitions favorable to violation of the law over definitions unfavorable to violation of the law. To demonstrate this would involve a measurement task that might be impossible. It would also require comparisons of offenders with samples from the general population who did not become offenders.

The Labeling Perspective

Since Edwin Lemert's (1951) pioneering work on the labeling of deviant behavior, much attention has been directed to the way that individuals are affected by being treated as deviants. The labeling approach is a general perspective on deviance that has been applied to mental illness, homosexuality, and even stuttering. Because crime and delinquency are forms of deviant behavior, this perspective should help us understand some of the causes of law-violating behavior.

The **labeling perspective** assumes that people first violate a norm by chance or for unexplained reasons. This initial act of deviance, called **primary deviation,** sometimes elicits reactions from others. Those reactions often take the form of stereotyping and rejecting the deviant. For instance, one study suggests that offenders are treated more harshly in court if they fit the stereotype of a "normal primitive," an image of lower-class blacks and other minorities whose limited education, lack of job skills, orientation to the present, possession of weapons, and immaturity are thought to predispose them to violence (Swigert and Farrell, 1976, 1977). Another stereotype is of lower-class delinquents, who are thought to violate the law because of blocked opportunities, poor education, or other defects of the social structure. This contrasts with the stereotype of middle-class delinquents, who are said to violate the law because of a temporary lack of commitment to adult roles and values, a view that relies on social-psychological factors and social control theory (Cernkovich, 1978b). Ideas about why different types of people break the law influence the way those people will be treated by the criminal justice system.

Differences in norms about parental supervision of the sexual activity of sons and daughters can lead to the labeling of one sex but not the other as delinquent, even though the behavior of both sexes is the same. Many girls brought into juvenile court are there for reasons related to their "adult" sexual activities. By contrast, the boys with whom they were sexually involved are rarely labeled delinquent for the same behavior.

People who engage in socially disapproved behavior are disvalued as individuals. Their status as a deviant sometimes becomes a **master status;** that is, other aspects of their behavior are submerged in a social identity as a deviant. The labeling perspective directs attention away from the causes of primary deviation, or rule breaking, and focuses instead on the people and institutions that have the power to label behavior deviant. The processing of rule breakers by institutions such as prisons and mental hospitals keeps deviants at a distance from the rest of society. Deviant acts would occur even if there were no such institutions, but the deviant acts' "nature, distribution, social meaning, and implications and ramifications are significantly influenced by patterns of social reaction" (Schur, 1969: 115). The labeling perspective assumes that a major cause of continued deviant behavior is the way that people who initially violate norms are treated by lawmakers, police officers, judges, psychiatrists, and others who have the power to affix the label "deviant." Deviant behavior that is a product of this labeling process is called **secondary deviation.**

Labeling and Self-Concepts

One way the labeling of deviant behavior leads to secondary deviation is through the effects of the label on the self-concept of the person who has been labeled. People who violate the law and are arrested by the police and tried in court can have their conceptions of themselves altered and come to think of themselves as criminals or delinquents. Court appearances have been called "status-degradation ceremonies" in which people accused of violating the law are recast as unworthy persons (Garfinkel, 1956). These people then reject other people and become hostile to society in order to maintain their self-esteem. Being labeled criminal or delinquent in court can thus produce a self-fulfilling prophecy, so that people behave in ways consistent with their altered self-concepts. In other words, once they are labeled criminal by the police, the courts, and the prisons, people continue to behave as criminals.

The labeling perspective suggests that the first time youngsters engage in minor vandalism or petty theft, they think little of it. If they are arrested, brought to court, and treated as delinquents, they will come to think that they have done something drastically wrong and that perhaps they are unworthy people. As a result, they begin to associate with others who have also been labeled as troublemakers, and this leads them into more serious delinquency. A study of adolescent shoplifters found that those who had been exposed to the police by store officials were more likely to engage in subsequent shoplifting than were adolescent shoplifters who had not been subjected to the police (Klemke, 1978). This is consistent with the labeling perspective's assumption that processing a deviant will amplify or increase deviance.

Rather than engage in more deviance because of being labeled, some people who are labeled deviant react by changing their behavior to conform to social expectations. The fact that many juveniles who are arrested are apprehended only once can be interpreted to mean that the status-degradation ceremony that occurs in juvenile court persuades some of them to avoid delinquency in the future. This is probably most likely to occur for first-time offenders with the following characteristics:

They have a stake in conformity.

They are sensitive to others' evaluations of themselves.

They are labeled in private rather than in public.

They are not committed to a delinquent or criminal career.

They are able to remove the label with good behavior in the future. (Thorsell and Klemke, 1972)

Self-Concepts and Containment Theory   Self-concept plays an important role in the **containment theory** of crime and delinquency (Reckless, 1978). This theory proposes that people are insulated to various degrees against pressures to commit deviant acts by "external" and "internal" factors. External containment results from attachments to family, community, and other parts of the social structure. Internal containment is composed of the following "self" components:

1. A favorable image of self in relation to other persons, groups, and institutions.

Being arrested, brought to court, and treated as delinquents can cause young people to see themselves as unworthy and lead them to associate with others who are also labeled as troublemakers.

2. An awareness of being an inner directed, goal oriented person.
3. A high level of frustration tolerance.
4. Strongly internalized morals and ethics.
5. Well developed ego and superego. (Reckless, 1978: 189)

Greater strength of internal or external containment will reduce vulnerability to crime and delinquency, but "the inner containment is the more important in the mobile, industrialized settings of modern society" (Reckless, 1978: 189).

People who abide by the law see themselves as accountable for their actions. They feel good about themselves and behave accordingly, taking into account the hypothesized reactions of others before they act. This is much like what Hirschi calls the "psychological presence" of parents and authority figures. Noncriminals feel vulnerable if they deviate from the law, and they fear the loss of material rewards and the good opinion of others (Rogers, 1977: 64–68).

There is evidence that delinquents have poorer self-concepts than non-delinquents, and that delinquents are more likely to believe that they will break the law, not finish school, and be unsuccessful (Dinitz, Scarpitti, and Reckless, 1962; Jensen, 1973). Delinquents are less likely than nondelinquents to be committed to long-range goals, and they are more likely to strive beyond their means, be impulsive, have a short time perspective, and feel unable to control themselves (Dinitz, Scarpitti, and Reckless, 1962; Jensen, 1973; Reckless, 1973). One study concluded that self-rejection—as measured by self-derogation, perceived lack of socially desirable attributes, and perceived rejection by parents and teachers—had a strong direct effect on junior high school students' disposition to deviance, which was measured by disaffection from family, school, and the conventional community. That disposition to deviance in turn had a strong direct effect on deviant behavior, including many acts that might lead to being labeled delinquent (Kaplan, Martin, and Johnson, 1986).

Parents, teachers, and friends influence the part of the self that is a "reflected appraisal" of how significant others evaluate a rule violator. Previous delinquent behavior also affects self-concepts, directly as well as indirectly through its influence on parents' appraisals of the rule violator. Moreover, the self-concepts of rule violators have a major effect on their future delinquent behavior (Matsueda, 1992).

Not all research finds a strong relationship between self-concept and violation of the law (Farrell and Nelson, 1978). One study concluded that self-esteem has a negligible impact on subsequent delinquency, but that involvement in delinquency does lower subsequent self-esteem to some extent (McCarthy and Hoge, 1984). Another study found that delinquent behavior enhances self-esteem among youths with either very low or very high self-esteem, but that adolescents with normal levels of self-esteem do not have their self-esteem improved and can even have it hurt by involvement in delinquency (Wells, 1989).

Rejecting the Label   An individual's self-concept is a product of many influences. It is affected by the reactions of others, but it is also the result of choice and reflection by the individual. A label attached by the criminal justice system can alter a person's self-concept, but the individual can also reject or fight the label. Self-concepts are constructed in an active way: the opinions of others are considered and sometimes incorporated into the self-concept, but those opinions can also be rejected as inconsistent with a person's idea of himself or herself (Scimecca, 1977).

Conventional Criminals   Conventional offenders sometimes disavow the label "criminal." Professional fences see themselves as decent people who perform socially useful functions (Klockars, 1974: 151–161). Robbers claim that they are "not too dishonest" because they steal from their victims in a direct way, rather than sneaking around in a house at night to commit a burglary (Inciardi, 1975: 71–72). Many shoplifters disavow the label of criminal when first caught, but the threat of prosecution usually forces them to redefine themselves as offenders; this happens because they fear exposure and lack support for a noncriminal definition of self (Cameron, 1964: 159–170).

White-Collar Criminals   White-collar offenders often believe that because few of them are arrested, convicted, and imprisoned, they are not "real criminals." This view is shared by some law enforcers. The head of the Antitrust Division of the Department of Justice expressed this nicely in 1940:

> While civil penalties may be as severe in their financial effects as criminal penalties, yet they do not involve the stigma that attends indictment and conviction. Most of the defendants in antitrust cases are not criminals *in the usual sense*. There is no inherent reason why antitrust enforcement requires branding them as such. (cited in Sutherland, 1949, 1983: 54; emphasis added here)

White-collar criminals frequently see their offenses as "technical violations of government regulations" and are thus able to maintain a noncriminal self-concept, even when labeled criminal in court. A General Electric vice-president, who was on his way to jail after a conviction for price-fixing, said to the press: "All of you know that next Monday, in Philadelphia, I will start serving a thirty-day jail term, along with six other *businessmen*, for conduct which has been *interpreted* as being in conflict with the *complex* antitrust laws" (cited in Geis, 1974: 273; emphasis added here). This convicted offender has disavowed the label of criminal, something that is easiest for law violators who do not fit the stereotype of the typical criminal, and who are treated with leniency by the courts, and enjoy the support of their families, friends, and colleagues.

The Effects of Labeling on Self-Concepts Some research suggests that the effects of official labeling on the self-concepts of delinquents and criminals might not be as great as the labeling perspective proposes. One study found that labeling by law enforcers had no major effect on self-satisfaction, identification with other delinquents, or future commitment to delinquency (Hepburn, 1977). A cohort study found that a single delinquent experience often had a limited effect, and that being labeled once as a delinquent did not necessarily transform a person (Polk, 1980). Delinquents often express concern with the outcome of their cases, but their court appearances are not always obviously stigmatizing and frequently have no significant impact on their self-esteem (Mahoney, 1974).

The effects of labeling vary from individual to individual. One study found that the self-concepts of lower-class white delinquents are more influenced by a juvenile court appearance than are the self-concepts of other delinquents (Ageton and Elliott, 1973). Delinquents' self-concepts might be less influenced by official sanctions than by the frequency and seriousness of their illegal acts. In other words, their self-concepts could be grounded more in their actual behavior than in official reactions to that behavior, with the police and the courts validating or rubber-stamping their self-concepts rather than applying totally new labels.

Even if official labeling affects a person's self-concept, it does not necessarily increase that person's delinquent or criminal behavior, for there is no strong evidence that changes in self-concepts cause changes in law-violating behavior. Moreover, any effects that labeling has could fade over time. In sum, official labeling by the juvenile and criminal justice systems might not have the dramatic effects suggested by the labeling perspective. It is possible, however, that there are effects of labeling that are subtle and complex or that occur only over long periods, so researchers might not yet have uncovered all of the effects of stigmatizing people as criminals and delinquents.

Labeling and Opportunities

A second effect of labeling—in addition to its possible effects on self-concepts—is harm to the social relationships of people who are labeled by the criminal or juvenile justice system. Even if his or her self-concept does not change, a person may experience difficulty in relationships with parents, friends, teachers, or potential employers if those people react negatively to the label of delinquent or criminal.

One study of adolescent boys sought to determine if juvenile court intervention had reinforced their deviance by producing spoiled identities or by harming their relationships with people who viewed them with mistrust and suspicion because of their official status as delinquents (Foster, Dinitz, and Reckless, 1972). In general, the boys did not believe that their contact with the law had created major problems for them in their social relationships. They perceived no negative effects on their friends' attitudes toward them. Few of the boys thought that being in trouble with the law would cause them any special problems at school, because they would be protected by the secrecy of juvenile court records and by their ability to separate their out-of-school life from their role as student. The boys believed that their court experiences would not influence their parents' attitudes toward them, other than simply confirming attitudes that their parents already held. This conclusion is consistent with other research that finds that parent-child relationships are well established before court appearances and are not substantially influenced by those appearances (Mahoney, 1974).

The boys in this study thought that their contact with the courts might have some negative effects in two areas: their relationships with the police and their relationships with future employers. About half of the boys said that the police would be more likely to keep an eye on them because they had been to court, but they thought this problem could be solved by convincing the police that they had given up delinquency. Nearly half of the boys believed that future employers might hold their court appearances against them, but many thought that this liability would be unimportant if they avoided encounters with the law in the future. The boys also counted on the secrecy of juvenile court records to minimize their problems with future employers.

This study concluded that the labeling perspective overemphasizes the effects on the individual of stigmatization by the juvenile courts. Such labeling might actually close legitimate opportunities or harm social relationships, but the boys in this study did not generally perceive this to be the case. However, because nearly half of the boys had been involved with the juvenile justice system before, a study of the impact of their first court appearance might have found more dramatic effects on their social relationships.

Even though more than half of the boys in this study thought their appearance in juvenile court would not hurt them with future employers, there is evidence that job opportunities are lost when potential employers learn about a person's problems with the law (Erickson and Goodstadt, 1979). Even the knowledge that a job applicant has been acquitted of charges makes some employers less willing to offer that person a job (Schwartz and Skolnick, 1962). As a result, the law in the United States now prohibits employers from asking about arrests, limiting them to questions about actual criminal convictions. Until recently, juvenile court records were sealed or kept secret so that job opportunities would not be denied to those who had gotten into trouble at a young age. Many states are now loosening their rules on the confidentiality of juvenile records, especially for offenders who have committed serious crimes.

The labeling perspective has been extended beyond the study of how individual deviance is amplified by official labeling to look at the way that "criminal classes" are created and reproduced over time. An investigation of working-class crime in London from 1950 to 1980 concluded that the persistence of crime over generations can be explained by the imputation of deviance by people with the power to label others. Labeling made escape from a criminal class difficult because it limited the opportunities for succeeding generations to get ahead (Hagan and Palloni, 1990).

Labeling and Subcultures

In addition to the effects of labeling on self-concepts and social relationships, labeling people "delinquent" or "criminal" can push them into subcultures in which they learn criminal motives and skills in the way described by differential association theory. Learning from the subculture can affect an offender's self-concept, even if labeling by the police or the courts did not have that effect. Thus, a woman convicted of prostitution might be approached by a pimp, drug dealers, or gangsters who see her spoiled identity as making her vulnerable to exploitation. By pushing an offender into a subculture, labeling makes reintegration into society difficult and increases the probability that people will repeat their crimes.

Critique of the Labeling Perspective

Figure 8.2 shows the labeling perspective in schematic form. The perspective proposes that primary deviation, or rule breaking, sometimes leads to labeling of the rule breaker. This can affect the individual's self-concept and opportunities and drive the person into a subculture. In the subculture, the individual can experience a change in self-concept through differential association with deviant norms, values, and behavior patterns. In these ways, the labeling process increases secondary deviation.

The labeling perspective has some shortcomings. It does not tell us why some people engage in primary deviation and why others do not break rules or do so infrequently. The labeling perspective helps us understand what society makes of primary deviation, but it tells us little about rule breaking that is not socially labeled. The perspective fails to make clear the conditions under which labeling will alter self-concepts, restrict opportunities, hurt social relationships, and drive deviants into subcultures. It also does not specify when a label will be accepted by a rule breaker and when a deviant will reject or disavow a label. Moreover, there is little empirical evidence that labeling by the criminal justice system actually increases crime or delinquency. Experiences with the criminal justice system sometimes deter potential offenders, and some offenders who are labeled and then commit more crime might have committed more crime even if they had not been labeled. The labeling perspective is useful in directing our attention to social processes that might, under some circumstances and for some kinds of people, rein-

FIGURE 8.2
The Labeling Perspective

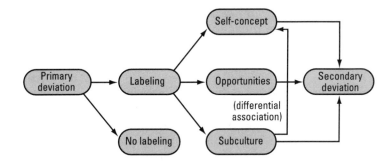

force tendencies to violate the law, but it is not a fully developed and empirically verified theory of crime and delinquency.

Rewards and Risks of Crime

Differential association theory claims that people turn to crime when their attitudes become supportive of crime—that is, when their definitions favorable to violation of the law outweigh their definitions unfavorable to violation of the law. The labeling perspective suggests that being processed by the criminal justice system changes self-concepts and social relationships and pushes people into criminal subcultures. A third approach sees criminal behavior as learned and reinforced through the intrinsic rewards and risks that it offers to offenders.

Reward-Risk Models of Criminal Behavior

One reward-risk model we have already looked at is differential association-reinforcement theory, which incorporates the ideas of Sutherland's differential association theory into a broader theory that proposes that people learn from rewards and punishments in both social and nonsocial situations. In recent years, several related reward-risk models have been proposed by political scientists, psychologists, economists, and sociologists.

Crime as Choice   In *Crime & Human Nature*, political scientist James Q. Wilson and psychologist Richard J. Herrnstein claim that people choose preferred courses of action and that their behavior is governed by its consequences. They argue that if the rewards (or benefits) of crime are great and its risks (or costs) small, and if the rewards (or benefits) of a noncriminal way of life are comparatively small and its risks (or costs) relatively great, people will choose to violate the law. Potential offenders thus consider the rewards and risks of criminal and noncriminal behavior before breaking the law. According to Wilson and Herrnstein (1985: 44), "The larger the ratio of net rewards of crime to the net rewards of noncrime, the greater the tendency to commit crime." Table 8.1 shows some of the many risks and rewards of criminal activity. Money is one of the rewards from property crimes, but many of the rewards from crime are noneconomic, including excitement and challenge, satisfaction in carrying out a difficult crime, prestige in the eyes of other offenders, and the chance to be one's own boss.

Wilson and Herrnstein argue that the impact of the rewards and risks of both crime and noncrime on the behavior of individuals is associated with several characteristics of those rewards and risks. Rewards and risks that are more certain will influence behavior more than rewards and risks that are less apt to be experienced. Rewards and risks that are experienced in the present will alter current behavior more than rewards and risks that will not be experienced for a long time. In addition, the more reinforcement (rewards and punishments) a person is receiving at any given time, the less impact any additional reward or punishment will have. Finally, people consider not only what they might gain from crime or noncrime, but also what others will gain from what are seen as comparable efforts.

The Rational-Choice Perspective The **rational-choice perspective** emphasizes offenders' strategic thinking, or the ways that they process information and evaluate opportunities and alternatives. It stresses calculated decision making, arguing that offenders choose how to act after determining the likely payoff from a particular kind of behavior. This perspective looks in detail at specific crimes, because different offenses meet different needs and

TABLE 8.1   Rewards and Risks of Theft

Rewards (or Benefits)
Money earned from crime
Freedom from taxation
Excitement of criminal activity
Satisfaction in a crime successfully carried out
Much leisure time
Reputation as a successful criminal
Free room and board if caught and imprisoned

Risks (or Costs)
Being caught and punished (lost freedom if imprisoned; lost money if fined)
Loss of benefits from legal work (paid vacation, social security, medical insurance)
Time to learn criminal skills
Costs of equipment to do the crime
Risk of injury while stealing (by police or by victim)
Work involved in casing a target and carrying out the crime
Anxiety about punishment
Stigma of being labeled a criminal

Source: Adapted from Gwynn Nettler, *Lying, Cheating, Stealing.* Cincinnati, Ohio: Anderson Publishing Company, 1982, p. 97. Reprinted with permission of the author and the publisher.

because there is considerable variation from one offense to another in the situational context of decision making and in the information that must be considered. This perspective focuses on the processes by which individuals initially decide to violate the law, choose to continue in a life of crime, and eventually opt to desist from crime. Not all people calculate rewards and risks in the same way; some of the many factors that affect the choices people make are age, marital status, group ties, social class background, opportunities for legitimate careers, attitude toward work, willingness to use violence, preferred life style, identity, and values (Shover, 1996).

The rationality of persistent property offenders is limited or socially bounded: they do not formally calculate the risks associated with theft, nor do they thoughtfully consider legitimate alternatives to crime. Instead, their decisions to commit crime are affected by lower- and working-class values such as autonomy, toughness, and excitement; by their lack of opportunities for legitimate careers; by their low aspirations; and by their desire to gain the respect of others (Shover, 1996). Their decisions to steal are made in the context of a life style characterized as "life as party," meaning that they seek the "enjoyment of 'good times' with minimal concern for obligations and commitments that are external to [their] immediate social setting" (Shover, 1996: 93).

Persistent property offenders believe they are unlikely to be arrested and think that if they are imprisoned it will be for a short time. They approach their first prison term with some fear, but soon learn they can survive incarceration, and even gain the respect of their peers for doing time. Young offenders typically see imprisonment as a temporary setback, vowing to be more careful the next time they commit crime. Conversations with other inmates change the way thieves calculate rewards and risks, making money a more important goal and teaching them the penalties they can expect for different offenses (Shover, 1996).

The Seductions of Crime   Some of the rewards and risks of crime cannot be easily incorporated into a perspective that treats offenders as reasoning decision makers. The rewards of challenge, excitement, and domination of victims are unlikely to enter into an offender's rational calculations about the payoff from a particular crime, nor are risks such as anxiety about being caught or the shame of being labeled an offender apt to be carefully weighed.

In *Seductions of Crime: Moral and Sensual Attractions in Doing Evil,* sociologist Jack Katz (1988) considers the subjective appeal of crime to offenders. He argues that people would not commit crime if they rationally considered its rewards and risks; for example, few robbers make much money from their crimes, and most of them end up in prison. Analyzing self-reports by his students, Katz found that shoplifting was valued more for the "sneaky thrills" it offered than for the property that was stolen. Describing the attraction of shoplifting and other crimes, Katz (1988: 312) writes:

> Follow vandals and amateur shoplifters as they duck into alleys and dressing rooms and you will be moved by their delight in deviance; observe them under arrest and you may be stunned by their shame. Watch their strutting street display and you

will be struck by the awesome fascination that symbols of evil hold for the young men who are linked in the groups we often call gangs. If we specify the opening moves in muggings and stickups, we describe an array of "games" or tricks that turn victims into fools before their pockets are turned out. The careers of persistent robbers show us, not the increasingly precise calculations and hedged risks of "professionals," but men for whom gambling and other vices are a way of life, who are "wise" in the cynical sense of the term, and who take pride in a defiant reputation as "bad."

Katz argues that offenders actively create the forces that impel them to break the law, saying that the

> causes of crime are constructed by the offenders themselves, but the causes they construct are the lures and pressures that they experience as independently moving them toward crime. By dissipating the proceeds of their crimes, stickup men, regardless of the social position from which they start, create an environment of pressures that guide them back toward crime. (Katz, 1988: 216)

Shoplifters sometimes endow the things they steal with a kind of magical power over themselves, as is suggested in the following recollection by a woman in her thirties:

> "A gold-plated compact that I had seen on a countertop kept playing on my mind. Heaven knows I didn't need it, and at $40 it was obviously overpriced. Still, there was something about the design that intrigued me. I went back to the counter and picked up the compact again. At that moment, I felt an overwhelming urge." (cited in Katz, 1988: 55)

This theft was sensually rewarding for the offender, even though her thinking cannot be described as rational decision making. In addition to providing immediate emotional rewards, thefts such as these are also influenced by factors to which Katz pays little attention, such as the age and gender of the thief, the strain resulting from lack of economic opportunities, and even the physical layout of department stores (McCarthy, 1995).

Reward-Risk Models and Self-Control   Reward-risk models that emphasize situational influences on criminal behavior might seem to be incompatible with theories that stress individual traits (for example, low self-control) that are established in childhood. A study by Daniel Nagin and Raymond Paternoster (1993) of college students' self-reported involvement in drunk driving, theft, and sexual assault found support for both kinds of theories and concluded that there was no incompatibility between them. All three forms of criminal behavior were strongly associated with low self-control, even after the researchers took into account prior behavior, situational aspects of the crime, and perceived rewards and risks of committing crime. The researchers also found support for reward-risk models: the intention to break the law was substantially influenced by the accessibility and vulnerability of the target, perceptions of the sanctions apt to result from breaking the law, and the pleasure derived from committing crime. The anticipated rewards from committing the crime turned out to be more important than the perceived costs of committing the crime in predicting the intention to break the law, apparently because rewards are more immediate and risks are more uncertain and remote in time.

Nagin and Paternoster concluded that there was support for both reward-risk models of criminal behavior and predispositional theories such as low self-control theory, and that both kinds of theories are needed to understand fully the sources of offending. They suggested that people with low self-control are oriented to the pursuit of pleasure in the present and lack commitment to conventional lines of action—such as education, a career, and lasting social relationships—that provide long-term rewards. As a consequence, they have little to lose when they break the law.

The Rewards and Risks of Crime

Before looking in detail at the rewards and risks of specific kinds of crime, we will consider the rewards and risks of crime in general.

Rewards   Many offenders find that the rewards of crime justify their violation of the law. Some of them believe that the income they derive from crime is more certain and more substantial than the income they could earn from the legitimate jobs that are available to them. However, even if all offenders were paid the amount they realize from their criminal activities, many of them would continue to violate the law because of the noneconomic rewards of crime.

One noneconomic reward of criminal behavior is the challenge of violating the law and getting away with it. This element of challenge is important in many computer crimes:

> A general characteristic of computer programmers is their fascination with challenges and desire to accept them. In fact, they face the great challenge of making computer systems do their bidding day in and day out. Telling a programmer that a computer system is safe from penetration is like waving a red flag in front of a bull. The challenge of an unauthorized act often overshadows the question of morality. (Parker, 1976: 47–48)

One example of this "electronic machismo" involved Robert Morris, the son of an important federal computer security official (Hafner and Markoff, 1991: 153). Attracted to the challenge of beating supposedly secure computer systems, Morris set in motion a "virus" that eventually slowed down or stopped 6,000 systems.

Another important noneconomic reward from crime is excitement. The author of a study of the criminal mind concludes that "thinking about the crime is exciting. Committing the crime is exciting. Even getting caught is exciting. Trying to figure out a way to beat the rap is exciting" (Stanton Samenow, cited in Serrill, 1978: 90). Excitement and relief from boredom often motivate juvenile delinquents to break the law (Belson, 1975;

Csikszentmihalyi and Larson, 1978). A study of adolescent shoplifters found that equal numbers stole for instrumental reasons (i.e., reasons related to the product of the crime, such as money) and for expressive reasons (i.e., reasons related to emotional needs fulfilled by committing the criminal act, such as excitement) (Klemke, 1978). Another study regards middle-class delinquency as a form of play, claiming that it serves needs similar to those served by other forms of leisure: adding interest to the daily routine, providing entertainment, learning new techniques and skills, and learning social rules (Richards, Berk, and Foster, 1979). Even white-collar criminals find breaking the law exciting; one insider trader describes his motivation as follows:

> Something deep inside me forced me to try to catch up to the pack of wheeler-dealers who always raced in front of me …. It was only in time that I came to view myself as an insider trading junkie. I was addicted to the excitement, the sense of victory. Some spouses use drugs, others have extramarital affairs, I secretly traded stocks. (Levine, 1991: 390)

What makes violating the law fun for some people? Perhaps breaking rules set by other people is satisfying because it gives the rule breaker a feeling of autonomy. Sometimes the physical activity involved in a criminal or delinquent act is intrinsically pleasing, or perhaps the consequences of the act are gratifying in some way. For instance, there might be an aesthetic element involved in vandalism, with vandals enjoying the visual, auditory, and tactile sensations resulting from their "creative conversion" of material things (Allen and Greenberger, 1978). The fun or "kicks" derived from crime are often short-lived, and this can lead to continued criminal activity. Some thieves claim that stealing is hard work with little thrill about it, and some say they are very tense while committing their crimes, but many offenders seem to be motivated by the challenge, excitement, and relief from boredom that they derive from criminal activity.

Some crime is motivated by a desire to preserve individual or collective honor. Trying to maintain one's self-image when insulted by another person can lead to homicide (Luckenbill, 1977). A study of Chicano gang violence found that preservation of the gang's collective honor and the self-esteem of its members often led to gang violence (Horowitz and Schwartz, 1974).

Repetitive property criminals report that they are motivated to steal by rewards in addition to money, but say that their desire for "quick, easy money" is the primary reason they commit crime. Rewards such as excitement, sense of accomplishment, peer respect, vengeance, and control over victims are usually latent by-products of their crimes rather than primary motivational factors (Tunnell, 1992).

Risks   The primary risk associated with crime is the threat of arrest, conviction, and imprisonment. Offenders often plan their crimes to minimize this risk, but most people who continue in crime for any significant amount of time are eventually arrested. They are turned in by informants, caught because the police happen to be near the scene of the crime, or are arrested because of police investigative work. The probability of arrest for any given crime is relatively low, with the overall clearance rate for index crimes in 1995 being only 21.2 percent, but the chance of being arrested for at least one crime if many crimes are committed is quite high. If an offender has an 80 percent chance of escaping arrest for a given offense, the chance of escaping any arrest if two such crimes are committed is only 64 percent, the chance of not being arrested at all if three offenses are committed is 51 percent, the chance of no arrest if ten offenses are committed is only 11 percent, and the chance of no arrest if the offender commits twenty crimes is only 1 percent (Glaser, 1978: 86–90). In other words, the chance of not being arrested for a single crime is quite high, but the chance of never being arrested over the course of a criminal career is quite small. As a result, most criminal careers are eventually interrupted by arrest.

Continued criminal activity might make offenders more expert, thereby minimizing their chance of being arrested, but with continued success many offenders become overconfident and careless. Because chance plays an important role in determining whether an offender will be arrested for a given crime, an offender's luck will eventually run out if he or she continues to break the law.

Conventional Property Crimes   The conventional property offenses of robbery, burglary, car theft, and arson involve many risks, but they also offer rewards in addition to money and excitement. Professional thieves mention satisfaction in a job well done, the leisure time between jobs, being their own boss, the nonroutine nature of theft, and the intrinsic satisfaction of stealing (Sutherland, 1937). For those who lack the education and skill to get a good job, the choice of property crime as a source of income might seem rational.

Robbery   A study of "casual robbers" in the United States found that they stole to buy drugs and clothing, to maintain or enhance their standing among their peers, and to create a more exciting life. Their "adventurous deviance" was more rewarding because it was risky, but they did try to keep their risks to a "manageable level" (Lejeune, 1977: 125).

Other robbers are more systematic in their crimes. For instance, two robbers who committed nearly two hundred crimes in an eighteen-month period decided to engage in robbery in a very calculating way. They had some money but lacked good job prospects and disliked the manual labor available to them. They wanted to make money quickly and decided on crime, which they saw as a business with risks and rewards like any other job. They spent four days in a public library doing research to find the best way to get money quickly and safely. After examining crime statistics, including the amounts stolen and the chances of arrest and conviction, they decided on armed robbery because it was direct and did not require them to convert property into cash. To reduce the risk of being injured by victims or the police, they carried firearms (Jackson, 1969: 20–21). Few offenders select their crimes in such a calculated fashion, but these robbers considered the rewards and risks of crime in a way that is consistent with the rational-choice perspective on crime.

Burglary   Few burglars commit their crimes primarily for excitement and thrills, although some mention those as secondary rewards. For most burglars, money is the primary motivating factor. They typically attribute their burglaries to a pressing financial need, which they define in terms of the streetlife value of "keeping the party going." Their proceeds are most likely to be spent on illegal drugs or status-enhancing clothes, although some of them report using their profits to pay for food, shelter, and clothing for their children. Many burglars claim that they would give up crime if they were offered a good job or if all of their financial needs were met, but those circumstances are unlikely to develop for most burglars (Reppetto, 1974; Cromwell, Olson, and Avary, 1991; Wright and Decker, 1994).

Car Theft   Car theft has multiple motives. Some thieves steal cars for joyriding—to have a good time and enjoy prestige in the eyes of their peers. Others steal cars for short-term transportation because of situational pressures for rapid mobility or the lack of other ways to get around. Some car thefts are for transportation over longer periods; these thieves keep stolen cars for personal use for a while. Cars are sometimes stolen to commit other crimes, such as burglaries and robberies, because stolen cars cannot be traced to the offenders. Amateur thieves strip cars of their tires or batteries, and well-organized professionals steal cars, repaint them, and ship them out of state or out of the country for sale.

Arson   There are also multiple motives for arson. Some arson is thought to be motivated by "pyromania"—a supposed psychological abnormality in which the arsonist or "firebug" derives pleasure from seeing things burn. Another motive for arson is revenge against rival gang members or the inhabitants or owners of a building. Others seek to profit from arson through fraud; landlords burn buildings they cannot rent or pay taxes on, and manufacturers suffering economic hardship "sell out to the insurance company" by burning a plant and collecting the insurance. Arsonists also burn buildings because others have paid them to and because they want to steal and sell copper tubing or plumbing from the abandoned building.

White-Collar Crime   For white-collar offenders, the risks are relatively small: few of them are convicted of a crime, and those who are usually are treated leniently by the courts. The instrumental nature of white-collar crime lends itself to a careful calculation of the costs and benefits of violating the law. For instance, in Chapter 6 we saw that in marketing the Pinto the Ford Motor Company carefully considered the costs it would incur in legal actions resulting from burn injuries and deaths and from burned vehicles. After determining that those costs were less than the cost of modifying the vehicles, Ford went ahead and produced dangerous automobiles (Cullen, Maakestad, and Cavender, 1987).

Drug Use   Drugs such as marijuana, cocaine, and heroin provide rewards in the form of physiological effects on users and profits for importers and dealers, but there are significant risks associated with drugs as well.

The Effects of Drugs   One study found that people who first try marijuana by themselves often experience no pleasurable effects (Becker, 1973). Those who use marijuana for the first time in the presence of experienced users get feedback from them about the proper way to smoke, how to perceive the drug's effects, and how to enjoy those effects. People who continue to use marijuana do so because they have found it rewarding.

Various addictive drugs are used by some physicians, especially anesthesiologists, who seek relief from the tension and exhaustion caused by their jobs. Drugs offer an escape, a way to relax, and a euphoria that allow them to maintain a sense of competence at their jobs. Doctors have easy access to drugs and are generally aware of the positive effects of the drugs, while minimizing the potential dangers of prolonged use (Winick, 1964).

Many heroin users are given the drug for free by friends and acquaintances the first time they use it; few first-time users have been looking for heroin on their own (Chein et al., 1964). The idea that it is usually strangers lurking around schoolyards who lure youths into heroin use is incorrect; peer influence is much more important in leading young people to try heroin (Hunt and Chambers, 1976; Hanson et al., 1985).

The effects of the first use of heroin are sufficiently strong for some people that they do not need to learn from others how to enjoy the effects of the drug; one book on heroin is titled *"It's So Good, Don't Even Try It Once"* (Smith and Gay, 1972). For many users, however, it is necessary to learn to experience the effects of heroin as pleasurable. One study found that 84 percent of a sample of regular heroin users described their first use of heroin in terms of euphoria and ecstasy, even though 38 percent of them reported that they were nauseated and 31 percent reported that they vomited after injecting the drug for the first time (Hanson et al., 1985: 80, 85).

Causes of Heroin Addiction   Scholars disagree about the causes of heroin addiction. A long-standing theory developed by Alfred Lindesmith (1938, 1968) holds that heroin addicts become hooked when they make a connection in their minds between the administration of the drug and the alleviation of withdrawal symptoms—such as sweating, nausea, trembling, and hallucinations—that occur when the amount of heroin in the body gets too low. Addicts crave heroin, but whether this craving is psychological or physiological, or some combination of the two, is not clear. Craving does occur in people who have been addicted but are no longer using heroin.

Research by McAuliffe and Gordon (1974) with street addicts in Baltimore concludes that addicts need a drug that staves off withdrawal pain but want a drug that produces euphoria. Whereas Lindesmith discounts the importance of the desire for euphoria, McAuliffe and Gordon present strong evidence that pleasurable sensations are the primary reason addicts use heroin. They find that nearly all addicts would like to get high every day, even though lack of money and commitment to a conventional life style—including a family and a legitimate job—keep some addicts from getting high more than two or three times a week.

A study based on interviews with 124 black inner-city men who were regular heroin users concluded that the search for euphoria is an important motivator for continued heroin use, but that it is not the sole reason, or even the primary one, for addiction. Instead, "heroin users seek calmness, stability, peace of mind, and even serenity, that fall short of transporting the user to

Heroin addicts crave euphoria and need a drug
that staves off withdrawal pain.

a euphoric state" (Hanson et al., 1985: 88). Many heroin users spend years trying to duplicate the euphoria of their first shot of the drug.

Heroin Use and Crime   The rewards of heroin use often produce addiction,
and in the United States addiction leads to crime because the sale, possession, and use of heroin are illegal.

Heroin use is associated with crime in other ways as well. State and federal laws prohibit the possession of "works," the hypodermic syringes used to
administer the drug intravenously. Some addicts have adapted to such laws
by gathering in "shooting galleries" where syringes are passed from one user
to another (Howard and Borges, 1972). This allows fewer addicts to possess
needles, and some users can thus avoid breaking the law against possession
of works. Shooting heroin in the presence of others also provides group support for drug use and protection against outsiders, and it gives users a chance
to observe addicts who are "on the skids" and thus get a realistic but depress-
ing view of their own future. Because heroin users know there is a good
chance of contracting AIDS or hepatitis from shared needles, those who share
needles are acting self-destructively, but the rewards of needle sharing—not
having to buy and carry works and the camaraderie of using heroin in a group
setting—make this activity a favored one for some users.

Heroin addicts also engage in crimes that are secondary to their addiction. Where heroin is illegal, the cost of the drug is far above what it would be
in an unrestricted market. One sociologist estimates that a heroin habit costing between $25 and $100 per day would cost no more than $1 a day if hero-

in were legally available (Glaser, 1978: 297). The cost of illegal heroin is so great that many addicts cannot support a habit on the income derived from legitimate work. McAuliffe and Gordon (1974) found that the average daily cost of a heroin habit was $40. To support such a habit with income from a legitimate job would require a net annual income of about $15,000. To have this much money left after taxes, social security payments, and other deductions would require a gross income of nearly $20,000. Fewer than half of the families in the United States were earning that much money when McAuliffe and Gordon did their research. A study of black inner-city men who were regular heroin users estimated the median daily cost of the drug at $25; even this lower figure requires more than $9,000 a year (Hanson et al., 1985). Because many heroin addicts come from less educated groups and disadvantaged minorities, they cannot rely exclusively on income earned at legitimate jobs to support their drug use, and so they turn to crime. There is also evidence that regular cocaine users earn much of their income illegally (Collins, Hubbard, and Rachal, 1985; Inciardi, Horowitz, and Pottieger, 1993).

Figure 8.3 shows the sources of income for male and female street addicts in a study carried out in Miami. We can see that criminal activities were mentioned by the largest number of addicts as a source of income; only about half as many mentioned legitimate jobs. Smaller numbers mentioned public assistance and family and friends as sources of income (Inciardi, 1979). In McAuliffe and Gordon's study, 96 percent of the addicts who got high every day committed crime to support their habits. Addicts' criminal activities include drug sales, pickpocketing, shoplifting, burglary, robbery, con games, gambling, and prostitution.

Between 50 and 80 percent of all heroin addicts engaged in crime before becoming addicted, suggesting that they experienced the rewards of crime even before starting to spend the proceeds of their crimes on heroin (Greenberg and Adler, 1974; McGlothlin, Anglin, and Wilson, 1978; Inciardi, 1979). However, addicts do increase their criminal activities greatly after becoming addicted (Anglin and Speckart, 1988; Chaiken and Chaiken, 1990).

Criminal activity declines when addicts enter treatment or kick their habits. However, their involvement in crime remains greater after treatment for addiction than it was before becoming addicted (Cushman, 1974; Stephens and Ellis, 1975). This suggests that the rewards of crime are still sought when crime is no longer necessary to support a drug habit; money previously spent on heroin might then be used for new clothes or a better apartment. At best, treatment programs moderate rather than eliminate addicts' involvement in crime.

Critique of Reward-Risk Models

Reward-risk models often fail to indicate exactly how potential offenders weigh the various benefits and costs of criminal and noncriminal behavior. For instance, how does an offender calculate the probability of arrest, or balance a small chance of a prison sentence against a high probability of making a small financial gain? Reward-risk models also seem to work better for some

FIGURE 8.3

Sources of Income for Drug
Use and General Economic
Needs among Active Street
Addicts in Miami, Florida*

* Figures add to more than 100%
because addicts mentioned
several sources of income.

Source: Based on data in
James A. Inciardi, "Heroin
Use and Street Crime,"
Crime and Delinquency 25
(July 1979), 341.

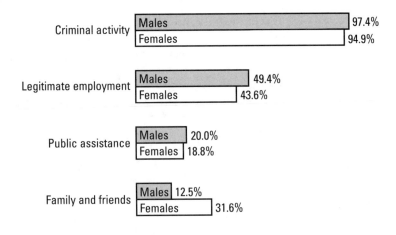

offenders (such as white-collar criminals) than for others (such as child molesters).

Reward-risk models have paid too little attention to the sources of people's methods of evaluating rewards and risks. For example, people who have little stake in conformity might think that a small financial gain is worth the risk of arrest. Others with a greater stake in conformity might think that even the possibility of a large financial gain is not worth a small risk of arrest. Reward-risk models need to spell out in detail the actual process of considering rewards and risks, the reasons that people balance rewards and risks differently, and the way that the social structure influences the assessment of rewards and risks.

Learning Theories and Variations in Crime Rates

The learning theories examined in this chapter suggest some ways that geographic variations in crime rates might be explained. If there are geographic differences in the definitions favorable and unfavorable to violation of the law to which people are exposed, differential association theory might explain variations in crime rates by nation, region, and size of the community. Geographic variations could also be due to cross-national, regional, or community differences in the groups that control power and label behavior criminal. For instance, the difference between the United States and Great Britain in rates of drug addiction and secondary crimes associated with addiction has been attributed to the definition of drug addiction as a crime in the United States and as a medical problem in Great Britain (Schur, 1962,

1965; Judson, 1974). Another possible explanation of geographic variations in crime rates is that people in different places might balance rewards against risks differently. For instance, if people living in one country have a low stake in conformity, they might be willing to take more risks to gain the rewards of crime than would be people elsewhere who have a greater stake in conformity. To date, however, we have little direct evidence that such cross-national, regional, or size-of-community variations in crime rates can be explained by the learning theories explored in this chapter.

Learning theories do not seem to explain temporal variations in crime rates very well. For differential association theory to explain changes in crime rates, it would have to tell us why an increasing or decreasing number of people have an excess of definitions favorable to violation of the law over definitions unfavorable to violation of the law. The theory does not make clear why that might happen and thus does not do a very good job of explaining changes in crime rates. Labeling theory would suggest that the kind of behavior defined or treated as criminal fluctuates over time as certain groups gain power or change their views about the kind of behavior that is threatening to them. However, there have been few efforts to use the labeling perspective to explain temporal variations in crime rates. Similarly, there have been few attempts to use reward-risk models to explain changes in crime rates, although the way people evaluate and balance rewards and risks might change over time in ways that would explain increases or decreases in crime rates.

Learning theories can make sense of variations in crime rates by sex, age, race, and social class. Differential association theory suggests that exposure to criminal and noncriminal definitions of the law varies by social group, with males, young people, minority groups, and the lower classes being the most likely to commit crime, because they are the most likely to be exposed to an excess of definitions favorable to violation of the law over definitions unfavorable to violation of the law. This explanation does not tell us why differences in definitions of the law are distributed in society in this way, nor is there much direct evidence that those groups actually differ in their exposure to definitions favorable and unfavorable to violation of the law. The labeling perspective suggests that one reason official crime rates are higher among certain groups is that those groups lack the power to define what kind of behavior will be treated as criminal. The high crimes rates of young people, minorities, and the lower classes could thus be explained by the tendency for crime to be defined by older people, dominant racial and ethnic groups, and the middle and upper classes. This approach would not explain the higher crime rate of males, because for the most part it has been men who have written and enforced criminal laws. Reward-risk models might explain variations in crime rates by suggesting that people with different characteristics evaluate the rewards and risks of criminal and noncriminal behavior differently, although there is little direct evidence that this is so.

In sum, learning theories might explain geographic, temporal, and social variations in crime rates, but there have been few explicit attempts to use those theories to make sense of such variations.

Summary

People learn skills and motives to commit crime from various sources. The social structure of some communities is conducive to learning criminal and delinquent behavior. Many delinquents become involved in violation of the law by learning from peers and from older adolescents in gangs. People also learn criminal motives and techniques from the general culture. Watching violence on television and viewing or participating in certain sports can increase aggressiveness, but whether they lead directly to criminal behavior is less certain. Exposure to pornographic material does not seem to cause sex offenses, but violent pornography could have this effect on people who are otherwise predisposed to commit such crimes. There is little solid evidence that correctional institutions act as "schools of crime," but some sociologists believe that interaction among inmates is a source of criminal motives and skills.

Differential association theory proposes that crime and delinquency are learned through face-to-face interaction. Techniques and motives are learned from definitions of the law in favorable or unfavorable terms. People violate the law when definitions favorable to violation of the law exceed definitions unfavorable to violation of the law. These definitions result from associations with criminal and noncriminal patterns that differ in frequency, duration, priority, and intensity. This theory is not easily tested, but some research is consistent with it.

Differential association theory fits much of what we know about white-collar crime, although the theory has not been rigorously tested. Business offenders might be exposed to definitions favorable to violation of the law within the company, and they can be isolated from definitions unfavorable to violation of the law. Research on juvenile delinquency is also consistent with differential association theory: much delinquency occurs in groups, and delinquents interact frequently with other delinquents. Professional thieves are often introduced to crime through tutelage by experienced thieves.

The labeling perspective proposes that some people who engage in primary deviation, or rule breaking, are labeled delinquent or criminal by institutions such as the police and the courts. This can change an individual's self-concept, close off opportunities, alter social relationships, and push people into subcultures. This leads to secondary deviation, or repeated rule breaking by those who see themselves as criminals or delinquents. There is mixed evidence about the actual effects of labeling on self-concepts, and changes in self-concepts do not necessarily lead to more violation of the law, but delinquents seem to have poorer self-concepts than nondelinquents. It is not clear that labeling closes off opportunities for all labeled deviants, but some adult offenders seem to have their job opportunities reduced. Labeling can push delinquents and criminals into a subculture, leading to a changed self-concept and more crime as a result of differential association with definitions favorable to violation of the law.

Crime offers offenders various rewards or benefits and produces certain risks or costs for them. In recent years, several reward-risk models have been developed by scholars in different disciplines. The major risk that most crime poses is the possibility of arrest and punishment. Rewards vary from crime to crime. Monetary gain is a primary reward, but challenge, excitement, and autonomy are other benefits derived from criminal activity. Some offenses, such as arson and car theft, provide different kinds of rewards to different offenders. Heroin addicts seem to be motivated by a desire for euphoria, but they also need the drug to prevent the pain of withdrawal. Reward-risk models focus attention on the factors that motivate offenders, but they can exaggerate the rationality of criminal activity. These models need to provide more details on the exact way that offenders consider the rewards and risks of crime, and they need to look at the influence of the social structure on the way that people balance rewards and risks.

Differential association theory, the labeling perspective, and reward-risk models might explain geographic, temporal, and social variations in crime rates, but so far there have been few explicit attempts by researchers to show how learning theories explain these variations.

Important Terms

containment theory
differential association-reinforcement
  theory
differential association theory
differential identification theory
labeling perspective
machismo

master status
obscene material
pornography
primary deviation
rational-choice perspective
secondary deviation
tutelage

Review Questions

1. What are the sources from which people learn to commit delinquency or crime? What sources other than those discussed at the beginning of this chapter can you identify? Which sources have the greatest impact on delinquents and criminals?

2. What are the principles of differential association theory? What are the advantages and shortcomings of the theory? For which kinds of criminal behavior does this theory work best? For which kinds does it work least well?

3. How does the labeling perspective suggest that official labeling affects crime and delinquency? What does this perspective contribute to our understand-

ing of law-violating behavior? What are the shortcomings of this perspective?

4. What are some of the reward-risk models of criminal behavior? What are the rewards and risks of different kinds of crime? How could crime be reduced by increasing the risks of criminal behavior or by increasing the rewards of noncriminal behavior?

5. How would the three theoretical perspectives examined in this chapter—differential association theory, the labeling perspective, and reward-risk models—explain variations in crime rates by country, region, size of community, sex, age, race, and social class?

Chapter 9
Opportunities and Facilitating Factors

Crime requires a social structure conducive to violation of the law, weakened commitment to the law through techniques of neutralization or detachment from conventional institutions, and the learning of criminal motives and skills. However, crime cannot be committed unless there are opportunities to break the law. The first section of this chapter looks at the way people's everyday behavior creates opportunities for crime. Then, the way that offenders select their targets is examined. The final section investigates three factors that are often associated with crime, even if they do not actually cause it: alcohol, drugs, and firearms. These facilitating factors increase the chance that a situation will lead to crime.

Routine Activities Theory

Routine activities theory sees crime as a function of people's everyday behavior. This approach focuses on three elements: motivated offenders, target suitability, and guardianship. Earlier chapters examined the factors that motivate offenders to commit crime. Target suitability refers to the form and value of property, the visibility and accessibility of targets, and the vulnerability of property and people to victimization. The third element is guardianship, the degree to which targets are protected from victimization. The routine activities approach proposes that crime occurs when motivated offenders are present near suitable targets that are not adequately protected. This approach can be used to explain crime rates, forecast trends in crime rates, understand the spatial distribution of crime, and plan future needs for criminal justice services and personnel (Cohen and Felson, 1979; Cohen and Cantor, 1981; Cohen, 1981; Messner and Tardiff, 1985; Felson, 1987).

The routine activities approach suggests that the presence of an abundance of goods that can be stolen will be associated with a high rate of property crime. In fact, economically developing societies do experience rising rates of theft (Clinard and Abbott, 1973). A study of Sweden's crime rates from 1950 to 1979 found that theft increased as more goods became available, and concluded that the increase was better explained by changes in opportunities for theft than by changes in income inequality (Stack, 1982).

Guardianship is measured by the extent to which people in the course of their daily behavior do, or do not, protect property and individuals from crime. Recent changes in patterns of behavior seem to have reduced guardianship, and thus increased crime rates. These changes include the following:

a large increase in the proportion of women holding jobs outside the home,

an increase in the proportion of all households that have only one person,

more recreational activity outside the home, and

more frequent and longer vacations.

According to routine activities theory, opportunities for burglaries should decrease if recreational activities become more home-centered.

On the other hand, we would expect crimes such as burglary to decrease if recreational activity became more home-centered, even though this might create more opportunities for interaction among intimates that could lead to violent crime.

The routine activities approach makes sense of the spatial distribution of crime. An analysis of more than 300,000 calls to the Minneapolis police department found that relatively few "hot spots" in the city accounted for most of the calls; 50.4 percent of the calls came from only 3.3 percent of the city's addresses and intersections (Sherman, Gartin, and Buerger, 1989). The hot spots in which motivated offenders, suitable targets, and inadequate guardianship converged to generate crime included a large discount store near a poor neighborhood, a large department store, convenience stores, bars, and a public housing apartment building. Another study found that crime was more common on residential blocks in Cleveland that had taverns and cocktail lounges; this effect on crime was greatest when the recreational liquor establishments were in areas characterized by anonymity and little guardianship (Roncek and Maier, 1991).

Routine activities theory can explain a wide variety of deviant actions by individuals as well as aggregate crime rates. Analysis of data from a national survey of eighteen- to twenty-six-year-olds found that criminal behavior, dangerous driving, illicit drug use, and heavy alcohol consumption were strongly associated with "time spent in unstructured socializing with peers in the absence of authority figures" (Osgood et al., 1996: 637). Lack of structure makes more time available for deviant behavior, the presence of peers makes deviance easier and more rewarding, and the absence of an authority figure reduces social control. Describing the routine activities of people with different characteristics, the researchers write that

> individuals in the most deviant structural condition—18-year-old males with D grade-point averages whose parents have graduate or professional degrees—typically go riding in a car for fun 110 times per year, visit informally with friends 200 times, go to 40 parties, and spend 170 evenings out for fun. In contrast, 26-year-old females who had A grades in high school and whose parents had grade school educations typically go riding in a car for fun 9 times, visit with friends informally 25 times, go to 6 parties, and spend 53 evenings out for fun. (Osgood et al., 1996: 652)

The researchers concluded that much of the relationship between deviant behavior and the variables of sex, age, and socioeconomic status was accounted for by such differences among groups in routine activities.

At first, researchers who used routine activities theory employed demographic variables such as sex, age, race, and social class as indicators of people's daily behavior. Lately, researchers such as Osgood et al. (1996) have used direct measures of people's life styles and behavior patterns, rather than assume how people with different social background characteristics will behave. One study that measured exposure to the risk of victimization with data on the nature and quantity of people's activities outside the home found that routine activities theory predicted variations in property crime rates better than it predicted variations in violent crime rates (Miethe, Stafford, and Long, 1987). However, an analysis of Canadian victimization data found that variations in violent crime were associated with lifestyle factors (Kennedy and Forde, 1990). In contrast to those studies, researchers who analyzed data from six Atlanta neighborhoods concluded that direct measures of routine activities were not strongly predictive of victimization; for instance, the amount of time that residents were away from their homes did not affect the chances that their homes would be targets of crime (Massey, Krohn, and Bonati, 1989).

A Critique of Routine Activities Theory

Recent research suggests that routine activities theory needs to be revised to incorporate additional variables associated with exposure to the risk of victimization. For instance, by limiting the communities in which people can live, the economic system and the housing market increase the proximity of some people to offenders and thus increase their exposure to the risk of victimization (Garofalo, 1987; Sampson and Lauritsen, 1990). The involvement of individuals in deviant behavior and violent crime also exposes them to a greater risk of victimization (Jensen and Brownfield, 1986; Sampson and Lauritsen, 1990; Lauritsen, Sampson, and Laub, 1991).

Terance Miethe and Robert Meier (1994) have developed a model that integrates routine activities theory with theories of victimization, criminal motivation, and social context. They propose that routine activities theory explains the production of opportunities for crime, that traditional theories identify the factors that motivate offenders, and that more attention should be paid to the situational context in which motivated offenders and criminal opportunities come together. Contextual factors that they find to be important in explaining crime rates and risks of victimization include a neighborhood's income level, unemployment rate, residential mobility, ethnic heterogeneity, and single-parent households.

Targets of Crime

The crime-generating process examined in previous chapters—the social-structural pressure to commit crime, the neutralization of the law, and the acquisition of criminal motives and skills—is necessary but not sufficient for the commission of crime; without an opportunity, there will be no crime.

There is a nearly unlimited number of targets for crime. What is important is the way these targets are perceived by potential offenders. A robber might see a bank with both a front and a rear entrance, a nearby expressway, and weak security as an excellent opportunity for a bank holdup; law-abiding citizens will view the same bank simply as a place to deposit and withdraw funds. One thief comments on the process of spotting opportunities for crime as follows:

> An underworld education makes a lot of difference to a man. In every way. Say you're a legitimate businessman and you're taking a ride in an automobile with a man that's a loser, that's been in the rackets for years. Like me…. I see an attractive young woman stepping out of a big restaurant. It's about one-thirty in the afternoon. She has a thick envelope under her arm and she's walking toward the bank. That doesn't mean anything to you. But to me it means she's bringing money to the bank. I'm gonna get back and check on her, see if she does that every day, it might be worth grabbing. As we ride along for eight or ten blocks, I've seen a half dozen things that are not legitimate and you have seen nothing but the ordinary street scenes. A man that's a thief, whenever he's moving around, will recognize a hundred opportunities to make a dollar. (Martin, 1952: 182–183)

The target selected by an offender depends in part on the specific skills the offender possesses. Some criminals specialize in or prefer one kind of offense, but most are quite versatile. Even experienced professional thieves usually "hustle" for crime opportunities rather than seek specific targets. They read newspapers, swap information with other thieves and fences, and keep their eyes open for crime targets. Specialization would force them to pass up lucrative opportunities.

Property Crimes

Thieves consider several factors in choosing targets for their crimes. The form of the property to be stolen is important, as is the value of that property. Target vulnerability and the likelihood of victim resistance are also considered.

Form of the Property   The form of the property to be stolen is important. If assets are in the form of computerized data, most thieves will have to avoid computers as targets for crime because they lack the necessary skills. However, assets in this form are vulnerable to theft by computer operators who have the necessary skills. Some observers have suggested reducing theft by eliminating cash and replacing it with computerized assets, thereby making property inaccessible to many thieves, at least until they develop computer skills.

Most thieves steal cash or property, with the property either being used personally or converted into cash. Conversion of stolen property into cash requires access to a fence, a receiver of stolen goods who pays the thief one-tenth to one-third of the retail value of the stolen merchandise. Young burglars often steal goods that they dispose of among their acquaintances, but older and more experienced burglars are more likely to steal goods that they convert into cash or drugs with fences (Reppetto, 1974: 20–21). Amateur shoplifters ("snitches") often take small, easily concealed goods for personal use. Professional shoplifters ("boosters") steal more expensive items and sell them to fences or to jewelry stores and clothing shops that are primarily legitimate retail outlets (Cameron, 1964).

The conversion of property into cash is time-consuming, an important consideration for offenders who require cash immediately, such as thieves who are heroin addicts looking for a fix. Selling stolen goods to a fence can be risky as well as inconvenient, because the police can trace stolen property back to the thief through the fence. For these reasons, some offenders prefer the direct theft of cash from victims and turn to robbery. Robbery has the important advantage over other forms of theft of providing offenders with immediately usable assets that cannot be traced back to them. Robbery also requires relatively little preparation in most cases, and there is an abundance of potential targets. Robbers often claim that burglary is more trouble than robbery because it involves entry into a house or building, a search for valuable goods, the physical labor of carrying the goods from the building, and the need to convert those goods into cash. Robbery is faster and more direct, and it provides readily usable assets, but it also involves the risks of violent confrontation with and identification by the victim.

Value of the Property   Thieves who commit robbery, burglary, and other types of theft consider which victims they can get the most money from with the least effort and risk. Pickpockets usually select their "marks" or victims by criteria such as sex (men being thought to carry more money), age (older people being thought to carry more money), and race (whites being thought to carry more money) (Maurer, 1955, 1964). For robbers, the holdup of a commercial establishment such as a supermarket or a bank will typically net more money than the robbery of an individual on the street. Burglars have to locate the money or valuable property once they enter a building, even if they have chosen a potentially lucrative target.

Offenders usually choose victims on the basis of general expectations about how much money or property they will get. Sometimes they are more systematic in calculating their profits in advance, especially if the crime involves elaborate planning and substantial risk. One gang of jewelry store robbers regularly sent its "straightest-looking" member into a store a few days before a planned crime in order to examine the jewelry and decide whether the robbery was worth the trouble and risk it would involve. The gang would then steal only the most valuable jewelry and fence it with a receiver of stolen goods in a different state. The members of the gang had a very good idea of how much they would gain from a particular holdup. Another robber secured information about the number of employees working for a firm and the approximate amount earned by each worker; his robbery of the company on payday netted him an amount very close to his estimate (Conklin, 1972).

The amount of money a given target will yield is often calculated in detail by professional thieves, who seek as large a "score" as possible while keeping risks to a minimum. By contrast, opportunistic thieves look for smaller gains and are less methodical in assessing what they will get from a theft. Still, even opportunists consider what they are likely to get from potential victims. They observe how expensively potential victims are dressed and watch to see who "flashes a large wad of bills." Sometimes they try to improve their odds of a large score by stealing on paydays and on days when welfare checks are delivered.

Vulnerability of Victims

A major factor that criminals consider in choosing targets is the vulnerability of their victims. Check forgers believe some stores are more willing to accept checks from strangers and are therefore easier to victimize. For instance, supermarkets are seen as easy "marks," but men's clothing stores are thought to be relatively invulnerable to check passing (Jackson, 1969). Shoplifting is also easier in certain stores. Stores that emphasize self-service seem to accept shoplifting as a cost of doing business. Managers may even think that if shoplifting is infrequent, their merchandise is not attractive enough or accessible enough to customers (Cameron, 1964: 17–19).

Opportunistic robbers—typically young, male members of minority groups who often operate in gangs—tend to choose victims who are elderly, female, and alone. In other words, they seek victims who are vulnerable because of their age, sex, or lack of company, even though these victims usually carry less money than other potential victims (Conklin, 1972: 89–91). Because opportunists often lack experience and skill in committing crime, they place greater emphasis on victim vulnerability and the minimization of risk than they do on the size of the score. In contrast, professional robbers have a broader conception of vulnerability; for them, a vulnerable target is one from which they can steal after planning and preparation. For example, the 1950 Brinks robbery was directed against a target that would be seen as invulnerable by most robbers, but careful observation by the thieves showed that the Brinks office lacked adequate security and was vulnerable to theft (Behn, 1977).

Obstacles to theft sometimes turn offenders away from particular targets. Exact-fare requirements on buses can reduce robberies of bus drivers but lead thieves to steal from the stores or newspaper stands that make change for bus riders. Since 1940, there has been an increase in bank security, including the installation of electronically controlled doors and cages, alarm systems, and closed circuit television. These measures have eliminated sneak theft from banks, a crime in which thieves go behind a counter, grab money from a till, and run from the bank (Inciardi, 1975: 15–19).

In a study of residential burglary by Thomas Reppetto (1974), nearly one hundred convicted burglars were shown slides of buildings and asked to pick the type of target from which they usually stole. They were then asked why they chose a particular building. The burglars emphasized easy access and the appearance of affluence in selecting targets. The type of information they most wanted before committing a burglary was whether there were occupants in the building; they also wanted to know if there was a burglar alarm and what valuables were available (see Figure 9.1). The importance of occupancy is shown by the fact that the more hours of the day a dwelling was unoccupied, the greater the chance it would be burglarized. Offenders learned whether anyone was home primarily by observing the dwelling, but sometimes they made telephone calls, questioned neighbors, or looked for signs of nonoccupancy such as piles of newspapers or mail. They learned if there were valuables to be stolen by peeping in windows and by tips from friends and fences.

A study of 105 active burglars in St. Louis found that even though they committed their crimes to meet what they defined as pressing financial needs, they were still cautious in assessing the costs and benefits of breaking into different buildings. Many of them had a target in mind before they felt a need for money. They learned of potential targets by knowing a dwelling's occupant, who was usually a casual acquaintance, neighbor, or drug dealer rather than a relative or friend; by observing a dwelling, its occupants, and their possessions for a time prior to the break-in; and, less commonly, by receiving inside information about a target from a "tipster," friend, or criminal associate (Wright and Decker, 1994).

Thieves try to minimize their risks by selecting targets that are not likely to be under police or neighborhood surveillance. They prefer targets that are isolated from the view of passersby, whether the police or private citizens. Even those who rob commercial establishments try to conceal themselves from public view during the crime, picking establishments that are set back from the street or positioning themselves inside the building so as to be invisible from the street. Lookouts are often stationed outside the building to report any threat of intrusion.

Robbers use nonverbal cues to assess the vulnerability of potential victims. A study that asked inmates who had been convicted of violent attacks on strangers to rate people who had been videotaped while walking on the street found that the people who were rated "easy to mug" by the inmates showed distinctive body movements that signaled that they would be good targets:

FIGURE 9.1

How Burglars Select Their Targets, Percentage of Burglars Giving Each Response

Source: Based on data from Thomas A. Reppetto, *Residential Crime.* Cambridge, Mass.: Ballinger, 1974, pp. 16, 105.

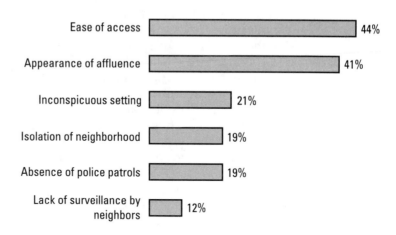

A. Reasons for Selecting a Particular Target

Ease of access — 44%

Appearance of affluence — 41%

Inconspicuous setting — 21%

Isolation of neighborhood — 19%

Absence of police patrols — 19%

Lack of surveillance by neighbors — 12%

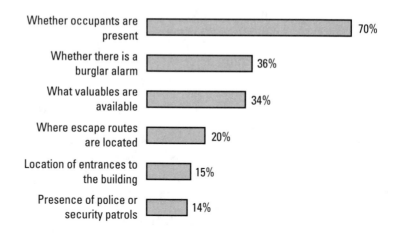

B. Information Wanted before Committing a Burglary

Whether occupants are present — 70%

Whether there is a burglar alarm — 36%

What valuables are available — 34%

Where escape routes are located — 20%

Location of entrances to the building — 15%

Presence of police or security patrols — 14%

Specifically, the most muggable people tended to take strides that were of unusual length, either too short or too long. Instead of walking heel to toe, they walked flat-footed. Instead of swinging their left arm while striding with their right foot, they moved their left arm and left foot, then right arm and right foot together. Instead of the usual figure 8-like sway of upper body and lower body, the most muggable people seemed to move their torsos at cross purposes to the bottom half of their bodies.

And instead of moving "posturally" (letting the movement start from within the body core), potential victims seemed to move "gesturally" (moving from one part of the body, an arm for instance, as though the movement started outside the body). Indeed, the most muggable people seemed to walk as though they were less in touch with their bodies. (study by Betty Grayson, described in Foreman, 1981: 20–21)

These movements were more important to offenders in choosing victims than were age and sex. Muggers read movement as an indicator of vulnerability, although they did not seem to do this consciously.

Serial murderers also select their victims on the basis of perceived vulnerability. They rarely kill people who are their equals in physical strength or intellect, instead choosing victims they see as weak, helpless, and easy to overpower and control. Most of the victims of serial murderers are either young women or children (Hickey, 1997).

Victim Proneness One measure of vulnerability is the frequency with which people are victimized repeatedly. There is a **victim proneness** among certain people because of their personal characteristics, social situation, physical location, or relationship to offenders (Nelson, 1980; Sparks, 1981). In a study of robbery in Boston, twenty-three of ninety victims who were held up in 1968 were robbed again during the next two-and-a-half years, even though the city's robbery rate suggested that only one or two of them would have been robbed again in that time if robberies were randomly distributed across the city's population (Conklin, 1972: 96–97). Whatever made these people vulnerable to robbery in the first place continued to make them vulnerable, and whatever measures they took to reduce their vulnerability seemed to have little effect.

Multiple victimization, or victim proneness, seems to be due to several factors, including:

1. *Precipitation or provocation:* The victim does or says something that causes an offender to violate the law;

2. *Instigation or perpetration:* The victim actively encourages a crime or takes criminal action against another person;

3. *Facilitation:* The victim places himself or herself at risk by deliberation, recklessness, or negligence;

4. *Vulnerability or invitation:* Some people are unusually susceptible because of personal attributes, social status, or entry into a risk-filled situation;

5. *Cooperation:* The victim is a party to a consensual crime such as gambling or prostitution;

6. *Attractiveness:* Affluence will often attract offenders, and

7. *Impunity:* Offenders can expect that the victim will not report the crime to the police or testify in court, perhaps because the victim is also breaking the law. (Sparks, 1981, 1982)

Victim Precipitation

Victim precipitation means that the person who suffers eventual harm from a crime plays a direct role in causing the crime to be perpetrated. One clear case of a victim-precipitated murder involved an incarcerated offender who reported that he had regularly used a knife to hold up drugstores because "a knife is quieter than a gun." A few months after the interview, he used a homemade knife to attack another inmate, who took the knife away and stabbed the attacker to death (Conklin, 1972).

Victims who act in particular ways with regard to potential offenders can create opportunities for crimes where none existed before. A man who enters a bar, picks an argument with another customer, and draws a knife in a sense contributes to his own murder if the other person responds by killing him with a handgun. This might not absolve the murderer of legal responsibility, but it could mitigate the punishment.

One definition of victim precipitation suggests that much information is needed to assess the role of the victim in the causation of a crime:

> Victim precipitation occurs when the offender's action in committing or beginning to commit a crime is initiated after and directly related to an action (be it physical or verbal, conscious or unconscious) on the part of the victim. The offender perceives the victim's behavior as a facilitating action (including temptation, invitation) to the commission of the crime. The action of the victim might be said to have triggered the offender's behavior. (R. A. Silverman, cited in Curtis, 1974: 96)

There is a continuum from deliberate provocation by the victim, to some involvement by the victim, to little or no victim contribution. The intent of the offender must be considered on a continuum from deliberate premeditation, to some intent, to none at all. Victim precipitation exists when offenders have little or no intent to commit a crime and victims clearly provoke them to commit a crime. Real-life situations are usually less clear-cut. Information on the interaction between the offender and the victim, and the state of mind of each, is difficult to get after a crime has been committed, especially if one participant is murdered. Witnesses might describe how the crime developed, but it is often difficult to gather data on the perceptions and expectations of the participants.

Murder   About one murder in four is victim-precipitated (Wolfgang, 1958: 254; Curtis, 1974: 82–84), although one study found that 38 percent of a sample of homicides were caused in part by the victim (Voss and Hepburn, 1968). Victims of victim-precipitated murders are especially likely to be male and black and to have prior criminal records. Female murderers are more likely than male murderers to be involved in victim-precipitated murders, because female murderers have often been provoked by their male victims.

In a study of interaction between offenders and victims prior to murder, about half of the seventy cases were found to involve prior hostility or physical violence between the offender and the victim (Luckenbill, 1977). Homicides were not usually one-sided events in which a passive victim was attacked by the murderer. In nearly two-thirds of the murders, the victim initiated the interchange, the offender stated an intent to harm the victim, and the offender then killed the victim. The interaction among the offender, the victim, and the audience to the murder can be analyzed in the following stages:

1. The offender first feels personally injured by the victim's behavior, which can be intentional or unwitting. This might include physical or verbal insults, gestures, or refusal to comply with the offender's wishes.

2. The offender then seeks to restore "face" by retaliating, expressing anger or contempt, or casting the victim as an unworthy person.

3. The victim next reacts to the offender's behavior by defining violence as the appropriate solution to the disagreement.

4. The offender interprets the victim's behavior as intentional noncompliance with his or her wishes.

5. Commitment to violence develops and actual violence is made more likely by the presence of weapons.

6. The offender "drops" the victim and then flees, voluntarily stays at the scene, or is involuntarily held at the scene by witnesses. (Luckenbill, 1977)

Another study looked at the interaction leading to 159 incidents of homicide and assault and found similar patterns of behavior. Physical violence typically followed an "identity attack," a failure to influence the antagonist, threats, and sometimes efforts at evasive action or mediation. Offenders retaliated in an effort to reestablish a favorable identity, and the situation escalated into assault or murder. Each individual responded to the other's actions and the implications of those actions for his or her well-being and honor. Consequently, it was difficult to classify violent crime as offender-precipitated or victim-precipitated. Victims often acted aggressively, but they attacked less often and were more likely to take evasive action than were the offenders. Efforts at mediation and evasion suggested that offenders and victims did not share norms supporting violence as the appropriate response to an identity attack (Felson and Steadman, 1983).

The interactional dynamics of homicides committed by single offenders differ from those committed by multiple offenders. Single-offender murders typically involve character disputes that evolve during a single interaction into a fatal confrontation. Multiple-offender homicides that are related to another felony are usually unplanned, often being the by-product of a robbery or burglary that "goes bad," rather than the result of a character dispute. Multiple-offender homicides that do not involve another felony usually develop over time from disputes over business or status; these murders are often planned, with a final decision to kill being made prior to the lethal interaction (Cheatwood, 1996).

Forcible Rape   The cultural stereotype that rape victims contribute to their own victimization reflects the mistaken belief that rape is primarily a sexual act rather than a violent crime, even though victims experience rape as violence rather than sex. The widely held view that some victims provoke rapists, and even enjoy the act, is used to defend rapists' actions as justifiable, excusable, or understandable. Violent pornography contributes to this view (Donnerstein, Linz, and Penrod, 1987).

The idea that rape is often a victim-precipitated crime overlooks an important difference between rape and homicide. In the events leading to a homicide, the lives of both the eventual victim and the eventual murderer are usually at risk. However, in a confrontation between a rapist and a woman, only the woman is at risk. Thus, most murders are symmetrical in terms of the risk of being killed, but rapes are asymmetrical in terms of risk.

Nevertheless, the view that rape victims precipitate their own victimization persists. Many people regard placing oneself in a risky situation—for instance, hitchhiking alone or telling dirty jokes in a bar—as a form of victim precipitation. A study of jurors in rape cases concluded that their decisions were frequently based on the reputation and social life of the victim. Jurors were especially likely to acquit defendants whose victims were sexually active, drank, or used drugs (LaFree, 1989). There are now "shield laws" to prevent defense attorneys from questioning rape victims about their sex lives, but attorneys have developed strategies to plant in jurors' minds the idea that a victim leads an unchaste and nontraditional life, and jurors seem to respond by "blaming the victim" for the crime and exonerating the defendant.

One researcher concluded from his study of rape in Philadelphia that 19 percent of the cases were victim-precipitated, in that the victim had actually agreed to have sexual relations with the offender—or had been thought to have agreed to this by the offender—but had retracted before the act, or had not reacted "strongly enough" when the suggestion of sex was first made by the offender. This researcher also categorized rapes as victim-precipitated if they were preceded by "risky situations marred with sexuality," such as a woman's using "indecent" language or gestures or behaving in a way that could be taken as an invitation to sexual relations (Amir, 1971). Application of this extremely broad definition of victim precipitation led the researcher to conclude that nearly one rape victim in five contributes to her own victimization, even though "contribution" here seems to encompass anything outside a very restricted range of puritanical behavior.

Using a different definition of victim precipitation of rape, a seventeen-city survey of violent crime found that only 4 percent of rapes were victim-precipitated, 83 percent were not, and 13 percent could not be classified easily or accurately (Curtis, 1974: 87–90). In this study, rape was defined as victim-precipitated if a female agreed to sexual relations and clearly invited them verbally or by gestures but then retracted before the act.

Crimes against Property Theft can be precipitated by property owners. Individuals who leave their homes vacant while on vacation, allow mail and newspapers to accumulate, and leave windows and doors open while away provide potential burglars with obvious signals that the dwelling is an easy target. People who leave car keys in the ignition facilitate car theft, because a thief does not even have to possess the skill to start the car without a key. Similarly, leaving property where it can easily be stolen encourages theft. A study of crime in Uganda found that immigrants to a large city from small villages brought with them a tradition of leaving property unguarded, thus encouraging theft. In the village, thieves could be observed and recognized, so the tradition of leaving property unguarded did not lead to theft there. In the city, similar informal controls were absent and the tradition frequently led to theft (Clinard and Abbott, 1973).

Offenders who lack a strong commitment to crime as a way of life might break the law when they happen upon easy opportunities to gain something with little risk. Sometimes they are drawn into crime because of victim precipitation. Thus, marginally committed offenders might steal unattended property, enter an empty house through an open window, or attack someone who insults them.

Facilitating Factors: Alcohol, Drugs, and Firearms

Three factors that often are present when crimes are committed, but do not actually cause crime, are alcohol, drugs, and firearms. The high frequency with which these factors are present during crimes suggests that they are **facilitating factors** that increase the chance that a situation will lead to criminal violence or theft.

Alcohol and Crime

Alcohol use and crime are strongly correlated with one another (Collins, 1981a, 1981b). A 1979 survey of state prison inmates found that nearly 30 percent of them said "they had drunk heavily just before they committed the offense for which they were convicted," and another 20 percent said they had been drinking but not heavily (Bureau of Justice Statistics, January 1983: 1). A 1991 survey found that 32 percent of state prison inmates had been under the influence of alcohol at the time of the offense for which they were incarcerated; 18 percent had been under the influence of only alcohol, and another 14 percent had been under the influence of both alcohol and drugs (Beck et al., 1993). Such self-reports can be questioned as to their validity, because inmates might try to diminish their personal responsibility for violating the law by blaming it on the effects of alcohol. Moreover, the percentage of inmates who report being under the influence of alcohol at the time of their offenses tells us little about the contribution of alcohol to crime unless we also know what percentage of the total population is under the influence of alcohol at any given time.

Alcohol is present in a significant proportion of homicides and assaults, and a smaller proportion of rapes, according to studies that have used official crime statistics. Researchers have found alcohol to be present in one-third to two-thirds of all murders (S. Greenberg, 1981). A survey of homicides in the seventy-five largest counties in the United States found that alcohol was present in 47 percent of the victims and 64 percent of the defendants (Dawson and Langan, 1994).

Alcohol also seems to play a role in various sex offenses. The Philadelphia study of forcible rape found that alcohol was present only in the victim in 10 percent of the cases, only in the offender in 3 percent of the cases, and in both the offender and the victim in 21 percent of the reported rapes (Amir, 1971: 98). A common pattern for incest is an unemployed man with an absent wife and an available daughter (or, less commonly, stepdaughter), along with a pattern of heavy drinking by the man (Gebhard et al., 1965). Physical and social isolation of the family and tension within the marriage are also conducive to incest. These conditions are especially likely to lead to incestuous behavior if the strong norms against it are neutralized by the heavy consumption of alcohol. Other sex offenses, such as child abuse and child molestation, are also associated with alcohol use (McCaghy, 1967, 1968). Most studies have found that alcohol is present in 40 percent or more of all sex offenses (S. Greenberg, 1981).

Explaining the Alcohol-Crime Relationship   Several explanations have been offered for the relationship between alcohol use and crime. (See the Crime on Campus box.) One explanation is that alcohol reduces inhibitions and triggers law-violating behavior in some people. The reduction of inhibitions from alcohol consumption is suggested by the results of a study of homicide in Philadelphia, which found that murders in which alcohol was present involved more violence and brutality than did murders in which neither the offender nor the victim had been drinking (Wolfgang, 1958). Another piece of evidence that is consistent with this disinhibition explanation comes from a study of robbery, which found that alcohol was present in 71 percent of the crimes committed on the spur of the moment, but in only 44 percent of the planned crimes (G. D. Wolcott, cited in Petersilia, Greenwood, and Lavin, 1977: 81).

A second explanation of why alcohol use is linked to crime is that people who are actively involved in a life of crime rely on alcohol to reduce their anxiety or build up their courage for crimes they plan to commit (Collins, 1981a, 1981b; Tunnell, 1992). However, the inmate survey found that heavy alcohol consumption was typical daily behavior for one inmate in five, not something they did only before committing a crime. Many offenders seem to be heavy

CRIME ON CAMPUS

The Role of Alcohol and Drugs

A 1989 survey of 1,857 students at colleges across the country found that since enrolling in college 8 percent had committed crimes and one-third had been victims of crimes but had never committed any. What was intriguing was the extent to which alcohol and drugs were associated with both criminal offending and criminal victimization.

Students who reported committing crimes were more likely than either victims or nonoffenders/nonvictims to be heavy users of drugs and alcohol. Those who reported committing multiple offenses reported heavier use of drugs and alcohol than offenders who reported committing a single offense. The six students who admitted to sex offenses were the heaviest drug and alcohol users.

The students who used alcohol and drugs the most had the greatest chance of being either an offender or a victim. Victims were heavier users of drugs and alcohol than nonvictims, and students who were victimized more than once reported heavier drug and alcohol use than those who were victimized just once.

Much of the alcohol use that occurs on campus is "binge drinking," defined in one study as five consecutive drinks for men or four consecutive drinks for women. A 1993 survey found that 50 percent of male students and 39 percent of female students had engaged in binge drinking at least once in the previous two weeks. Twenty-three percent of male students and 17 percent of female students had engaged in binge drinking three or more times in the previous two weeks. Binge drinking was most common on campuses in the Northeast and North Central regions, at residential rather than commuter schools, and in institutions that were not predominantly black and that were coeducational. Binge drinking was twice as common among the residents of fraternities (86 percent) and sororities (80 percent) as among students who were not members of fraternities (45 percent) and sororities (36 percent).

Source: Based on Carole R. Bausell, Charles E. Maloy, and Jan Mitchell Sherrill, *The Links among Drugs, Alcohol, and Campus Crime*. Towson, Md.: Campus Violence Prevention Center, Towson State University, January 1990; Henry Wechsler et al., "Health and Behavioral Consequences of Binge Drinking in College," *JAMA* (*Journal of the American Medical Association*) 272 (December 7, 1994), 1672–1677; William H. Honan, "Study Ties Binge Drinking to Fraternity House Life," *New York Times*, December 6, 1995, p. B16.

---

drinkers even when not engaging in crime, and so they probably do not drink just to build up their courage. It is more likely that they are problem drinkers who occasionally commit crimes when their inhibitions are reduced by alcohol.

A third explanation of the association between alcohol use and crime is that groups have norms about how people under the influence of alcohol should behave. Among some groups, drunkenness is seen as a "time out" from conventional demands. In this situation of relaxed behavioral standards, aggressive or even criminal behavior might be tolerated or expected. There is little research on differences among groups in their norms about "drunken comportment," but if such differences exist they would help explain why alcohol use and crime are associated with each other in different ways for different groups (MacAndrew and Edgerton, 1969).

We do not yet have enough research to tell us why alcohol use is associated with crime. More studies are needed to make clear "(1) the role of alcohol in the criminal situation, (2) the prevalence of alcoholism among criminals, and (3) the criminal history of alcoholics" (S. Greenberg, 1981: 106–107).

Drugs and Crime

Earlier in the book, we saw that many kinds of drug use are defined as crime, and that the need to support a drug habit can lead to secondary crimes. Drugs can also facilitate crime by reducing inhibitions or clouding a user's judgment, much as alcohol can facilitate crime.

The extent of drug use among criminals has grown in recent years. In 1974, 25 percent of a sample of state prison inmates reported that they were under the influence of an illegal drug at the time of the offense for which they were incarcerated. That figure increased to 32 percent in 1979 and to 35 percent in 1986 (Innes, 1988). In 1991, the figure dropped to 31 percent, with 11 percent of the inmates reporting that they were under the influence of marijuana at the time of their crime, 14 percent reporting that they were under the influence of cocaine or crack, and 6 percent reporting that they were under the influence of heroin or other opiates (Beck et al., 1993).

The Drug Use Forecasting program initiated by the National Institute of Justice in New York City in 1987 had expanded to twenty-three cities by 1994. This program uses voluntary and anonymous urine specimens from samples of arrestees to test for the presence of cocaine, opiates, marijuana, PCP, methadone, benzodiazepine (Valium), methaqualone, propoxyphene (Darvon), barbiturates, and amphetamines. In 1994, the median proportion of male arrestees testing positive for any drug was 66 percent for the twenty-three cities; the median proportion of male arrestees aged fifteen to twenty testing positive for any drug was 60 percent for the twenty-three cities; and the median proportion of female arrestees testing positive for any drug was 67 percent for the twenty-one cities that provided data on females (National Institute of Justice, November 1995).

Drug use is clearly associated with greater involvement in other criminal activities. According to the 1991 National Household Survey on Drug Abuse, there is a high correlation between drug use, especially cocaine use, and being booked for property and violent crimes (Harrison and Gfroerer, 1992). Heroin addicts in California prisons and jails report that they commit more than ten times as many thefts, robberies, and burglaries as nondrug-using inmates. Addicts in Baltimore commit four to six times as many crimes during periods of heavy drug use as they do when they are relatively drug-free. Drug users in New York City are at least as violent as their counterparts who do not use drugs (Graham, 1987).

Explaining the Drugs-Crime Relationship   The greater amount of drug use by offenders does not tell us the reason for the association between drug use and crime. Offenders might commit crime to secure the funds with which to purchase expensive drugs. They might have their crimes facilitated by the effects of the drugs; violence has been linked to the use of crack and PCP. However, drug users could be especially likely to be arrested because they are known by the police to be criminals, or because the drugs affect their behavior in ways that draw the attention of the police. Another explanation of the drugs-crime relationship is that both drug use and crime are part of a common life style or subculture to which street addicts commit themselves (Inciardi, Horowitz, and Pottieger, 1993).

Firearms and Crime

In 1992, handguns were used to murder 13 people in Australia, 33 in Great Britain, 36 in Sweden, 60 in Japan, 97 in Switzerland, 128 in Canada, and 13,220 in the United States (Herbert, 1994). Seventy-two percent of all murders in the United States in 1995 involved firearms, more than four-fifths of them handguns (see Figure 9.2) (Federal Bureau of Investigation, 1996: 17).

With more than 200 million firearms, a third of them handguns, in private hands in the United States, and two-fifths of all homes containing at least one firearm, there is a good chance that one will be present at the scene of a bitter argument or a fight. If a firearm is used during an altercation, murder is a likely result. Assaults with firearms are much more likely to result in death than assaults with a knife or without a weapon. According to one study, firearms assaults are fatal about 13 percent of the time, knife attacks are fatal about 3 percent of the time, and attacks with hands, fists, and feet are fatal only 1.7 percent of the time (Morris and Hawkins, 1970: 66). Other research finds that firearms assaults lead to death two to five times as often as attacks with knives (Wright, Rossi, and Daly, 1983: 198). Because guns are the most

FIGURE 9.2

Types of Weapons Used in Murders, 1995

Source: Based on data from Federal Bureau of Investigation, *Crime in the United States, 1995: Uniform Crime Reports.* Washington, D.C.: U.S. Government Printing Office, 1996, p. 17.

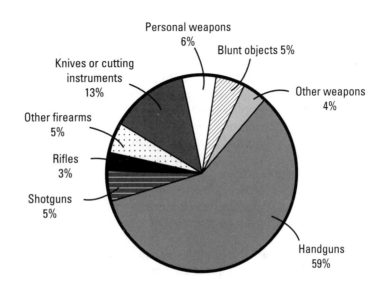

Personal weapons 6%
Blunt objects 5%
Knives or cutting instruments 13%
Other weapons 4%
Other firearms 5%
Rifles 3%
Shotguns 5%
Handguns 59%

These confiscated weapons are just a few of the
more than 200 million firearms in private hands in
the United States.

deadly weapon, their easy availability is associated with higher homicide
rates (Seitz, 1972; Fisher, 1976; Cook, 1983; Sloan et al., 1988; Eckholm, 1992).

Firearms violence in the United States increased dramatically from 1985
to 1994, with the increase being most pronounced among young people. The
number of murders by guns and the number of murders by means other than
guns committed by offenders aged ten to seventeen remained about the
same from 1976 to 1984; from 1985 to 1994, however, firearms homicides by
this age group tripled while non-gun homicides showed no increase (see
Figure 9.3). Alfred Blumstein (1995) attributes this increase in firearms violence by young people to the growth of the market in crack cocaine in the
mid-1980s, arguing that juveniles were recruited to make that growth possible and were provided with guns to protect themselves in the dangerous drug
trade. Gun ownership then diffused to young people who were not involved
in the drug trade, both for self-protection and for status-enhancement, with
the increased number of guns in the hands of young people leading to higher levels of violent crime.

Firearms are also used in rapes, aggravated assaults, burglaries, and robberies. The FBI does not report the use of firearms in rapes, but about one-fifth
of all rapists intimidate their victims with a weapon, although not necessarily
a firearm (Amir, 1971: 150; Beck et al., 1993). NCVS data reveal that one-tenth
of rape victimizations from 1973 to 1982 involved a firearm (Rand et al., 1986).
Those data also indicate that 11 percent of all assaults were committed with a
firearm; FBI data for 1995 show that 23 percent of all reported aggravated

Homicide victimizations

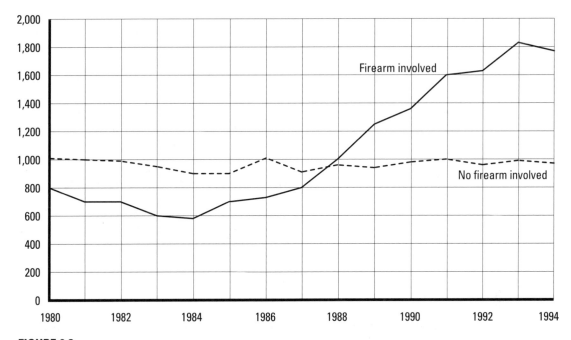

FIGURE 9.3

Trends in Juvenile Homicides Involving Firearms and Not Involving Firearms, 1980–1994

Source: Data from James Alan Fox, *Supplementary Homicide Reports 1976–1994,* as presented in Howard N. Snyder, Melissa Sickmund, and Eileen Poe-Yamagata, *Juvenile Offenders and Victims: 1996 Update on Violence.* Pittsburgh, Pa.: National Center for Juvenile Justice, February 1996, p. 3.

assaults involved firearms (Federal Bureau of Investigation, 1996: 32). Firearms also play a role in nonviolent crimes; one study found that 8 percent of burglars carried a firearm (Reppetto, 1974: 107).

Forty-one percent of all robberies reported to the police in 1995 were committed with a firearm (see Figure 9.4). Instead of using firearms to demonstrate their toughness and masculinity, robbers employ guns for instrumental purposes—to acquire money more easily and with less resistance, to protect themselves from armed victims, and to ensure a safe escape from the scene of the crime (Conklin, 1972; Sheley and Wright, 1995; Desroches, 1995). Paradoxically, the use of firearms by robbers might prevent violence, because victims are less likely to resist offenders who carry guns (Conklin, 1972; Block, 1977). When a victim does resist, the robber often increases the level of intimidation by cocking the pistol, holding it to the victim's head, or using it as a blunt instrument to hit the victim. Sometimes, of course, a firearm is used to shoot a victim, and then the robbery produces serious injury or death. Victims who resist armed robbers are about three times as likely to be injured seriously as victims who do not resist (Block, 1977, 1981).

FIGURE 9.4

Types of Weapons Used in
Robberies, 1995

Source: Based on data from
Federal Bureau of Investigation,
Crime in the United States, 1995:
Uniform Crime Reports.
Washington, D.C.: U.S.
Government Printing Office,
1996, p. 29.

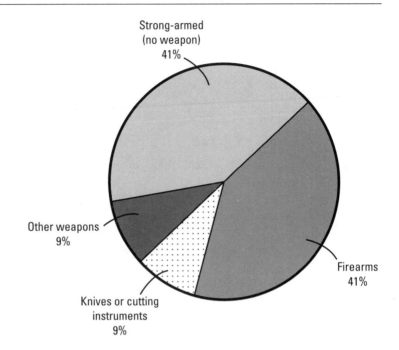

A 1991 survey found that 86 percent of a sample of male inmates of juvenile correctional facilities and 30 percent of a sample of male inner-city high school students had owned a gun at some time. The inmates and students rarely bought guns from retail outlets, but instead got them through purchase or trade from friends, family members, or street sources such as thieves and addicts. They preferred sophisticated firearms to small, cheap ones, saying that the characteristics they wanted in a gun were firepower, quality construction, difficulty in tracing the weapon, ease of shooting, and accuracy. Guns of this sort were readily available, usually for $100 or less. Those most likely to own firearms were drug dealers (not those who simply used drugs) and gang members, especially those who belonged to highly structured gangs. These drug dealers and gang members lived in a dangerous world in which they were visible to and threatened by others, so they saw firearms as necessary for survival. Those who committed the greatest number of crimes and the most serious ones usually carried firearms most of the time, not just when they were planning to commit crimes (Sheley and Wright, 1995; see also Wright and Rossi, 1986).

Explaining the Firearms-Crime Relationship   The relationship between firearms and crime is complex. The easy availability of firearms facilitates crime in several ways. Access to a gun can make the difference between wanting to hurt someone and actually committing a violent crime. The presence of a weapon during an argument can escalate the level of violence, producing a murder when an assault would have occurred if no firearm had been present. Firearms give some robbers and rapists the courage to commit crimes that they would otherwise have avoided. Tight restrictions on the ownership of firearms in Japan have been cited as one reason for that society's low rate of violent crime. On the other hand, Switzerland has widespread private ownership of firearms but no tradition of using guns to settle interpersonal disputes, and it has a low rate of criminal violence (Clinard, 1978). One assessment of research on the relationship between firearms and crime concluded that there was "little or no conclusive evidence to show that gun ownership among the larger population is, per se, an important cause of criminal violence" (Wright, Rossi, and Daly, 1983: 137).

Firearms might even deter potential offenders from crime. For example, a robber might think twice about holding up a store in which the owner had shot another thief the week before. Overall, however, there is little evidence that citizen ownership of firearms directly deters crime (Green, 1987; McDowall, Lizotte, and Wiersema, 1991). Gun ownership might have an indirect effect on crime by making people feel more secure and affecting their behavior in ways that keep crime rates low, for instance, by encouraging a storekeeper who feels safer to stay open at night, thereby providing informal control over nearby sidewalks and streets. On the other hand, firearms that people keep for self-protection are often stolen by burglars, who use them for illegal purposes or sell them to other criminals (Wright, Rossi, and Daly, 1983; Wright and Rossi, 1986; Green, 1987; Sheley and Wright, 1995).

Crime and firearms could also be related in another way. Crime generates fear, which can lead people to arm themselves. However, most firearms in private hands in the United States are not for self-defense against criminals, but for other purposes such as hunting, target shooting, or collecting; only 10 to 20 percent of all firearms are for self-defense (Wright, Rossi, and Daly, 1983). Fear of crime and victimization experiences do not seem to be strongly linked to firearms ownership, although a low level of citizen confidence in the ability of the criminal justice system to control crime is associated with more gun ownership (Young, McDowall, and Loftin, 1987).

How often do gun owners use their weapons against criminals? Victimization survey data indicate that victims use firearms to defend themselves against robberies and assaults about 55,000 times each year, and against burglaries about 25,000 times each year. There are also an uncounted number of incidents in which victims use firearms to protect themselves against domestic assaults (Cook, 1991). A 1993 national survey found that defensive gun use was much more prevalent than NCVS data indicated: civilians use firearms to protect themselves against crime 2.1 to 2.5 million times each year, with 1.5 to 1.9 million of the cases involving handguns. Three-fourths of those incidents occur in or near the home of the person using the gun; the crime being defended against is usually a burglary, an assault, or a robbery. The gun is only fired in one-fourth of the incidents, and an adversary is wounded in only 8 percent of the cases (Kleck and Gertz, 1995).

Firearms owned for protection against criminals are often used to inflict injury on innocent people. One study found that when the sex, age, and race of household members, their use of illicit drugs, and their history of domestic violence were taken into account, having a firearm in the home nearly tripled the chance that someone living there would be murdered. Half of the victims were killed following a dispute that involved a romantic triangle or some other type of altercation or quarrel; and three-fourths of them were killed by a relative or someone they knew (Kellermann et al., 1993). An example of this occurred in 1994, when a 53-year-old Louisiana man shot to death his 14-year-old daughter when she jumped out of a closet in their home and shouted "Boo!" as he and his wife returned home at 1 A.M. from visiting friends.

Gun Control and Crime Rates   There is mixed evidence as to whether crime can be reduced by controlling access to firearms. One study that compared five states with strong gun-control laws to five states with weak laws found that the states with the strong laws had lower homicide rates. In those states, a smaller proportion of the homicides that did occur were committed with firearms (Criminal Division, U.S. Department of Justice, 1968). Although this study suggests that strong gun-control laws might reduce the homicide rate, the results can also be interpreted to mean that the states that were able to pass strong gun-control legislation were the states in which people were more opposed to the use of firearms to begin with or were the states in which firearms were relatively unimportant to residents. Thus, both the low murder rate and the gun-control law could have been products of a nonviolent, anti-weapons attitude on the part of the state's residents. That attitude, rather than the law itself, might account for a low homicide rate.

One type of law aims to control the possession and use of firearms by the general public. The Bartley-Fox law was implemented in Massachusetts in 1975 to require a one-year jail sentence for anyone carrying an unlicensed firearm. One evaluation of the impact of this law found that it seemed to reduce the incidence of gun assaults, but it also produced a more than offsetting increase in assaults with weapons other than guns, apparently because people who avoided carrying firearms turned to other weapons to commit assaults. Gun robberies were reduced by the law, but armed robberies without firearms increased; however, the increase in robberies without firearms did not offset the decline in gun robberies. The law reduced homicides with firearms without any increase in nongun homicides. Thus, the Bartley-Fox law had some effect in reducing homicides and robberies with firearms. However, the researchers concluded that it was the publicity about the intent of the law, rather than the severity or certainty of the sanctions that were actually imposed, that produced this reduction in firearms crime; the researchers were unwilling to attribute the changes to the impact of the mandatory jail term (Pierce and Bowers, 1981). Another evaluation of this law concluded that

> although there is some evidence that the Massachusetts Bartley-Fox Amendment achieved at least an initial impact on gun-related crime, there is substantial reason to believe that long-range effects are not to be expected or will be considerably reduced in magnitude. In other words, there is some evidence that under some conditions gun-related crimes can be reduced through gun control legislation, but this outcome will be neither very common nor especially pronounced. (Wright, Rossi, and Daly, 1983: 308)

In 1980, New York state implemented a law similar to Bartley-Fox, except that in New York the mandatory sentence of one year was applied only to people who had been convicted of a crime in the previous five years. There is no evidence that this law has reduced street crime with firearms, and many who have been convicted under the law have not served the "mandatory" one year in jail. Indeed, the chance of being sentenced to a year or more in jail for illegal gun possession was the same in 1989 as it was in 1979, the year before the law went into effect (Roberts, 1990).

In 1976, Washington, D.C., implemented a law that prohibited civilians from buying, selling, transferring, or possessing handguns. Using monthly homicide data from 1968 through 1987 for the District of Columbia and for adjacent metropolitan areas, researchers determined that this ban on handguns reduced firearms homicides in Washington by 25 percent. There was no decline in homicides by other means in Washington, nor was there a decline in homicides in the adjacent metropolitan areas (Loftin et al., 1991).

A strategy tried by some states, including Michigan and Florida, requires judges to impose an additional prison term on offenders convicted of a serious crime in which they used a firearm. A study in Detroit found that crime rates declined after the implementation of a two-year mandatory additional penalty for the use of a firearm in a serious crime, but it concluded that the decline did not seem to be attributable to the new law. The decline began before the law was implemented, and unarmed violent crime as well as crime with firearms showed a decrease. The law's lack of impact was attributed to the fact that "offenders were not responsive to a mandatory two-year increment in sanctions for offenses which already carry maximum sentences much greater than two years" (Loftin, Heumann, and McDowall, 1983: 310). Thus, the law did not increase the perceived certainty or perceived severity of punishment in a significant way. The law would have affected rates of murder, robbery, and assault only if offenders who used weapons in those crimes placed relatively little value on the use of weapons, and this apparently was not the case. The fact that Detroit's population was heavily armed when the law was passed probably meant that offenders placed great value on being armed because of the high probability that they would encounter armed resistance from their victims (Loftin and McDowall, 1981; Loftin, Heumann, and McDowall, 1983).

A six-city study concluded that the announcement of mandatory sentence-enhancement laws for the criminal use of firearms reduced firearms homicides without at the same time increasing homicides with other weapons. Robberies and assaults did not decline as a result of such laws, although it was not clear if this was because there was no impact of the law on those crimes or because the data were too imprecise to measure the effects of the laws on those offenses (McDowall, Loftin, and Wiersema, 1992).

Research has not demonstrated that gun-control laws that require mandatory jail sentences for anyone carrying an unlicensed weapon or for anyone using a firearm in a serious crime have long-term effects on the use of firearms in crime. Sometimes "mandatory" penalties are not imposed. Either the police do not arrest everyone who carries an illegal firearm, or judges fail to impose the required sentence. Even if the criminal justice system imposed the mandatory penalty, it is not clear that felons would give up their firearms.

An experiment carried out in Kansas City, Missouri, offers evidence that aggressive police patrols aimed at taking guns away from people who illegally possess them can reduce crime. A special patrol specifically looked for opportunities to conduct legal searches of cars or pedestrians for illegal firearms; opportunities included curfew violations and traffic stops for driving a stolen car, using high-beam lights, or running a stop sign. This directed patrol, which concentrated on "hot spots" where many gun-related crimes had been reported, increased the number of gun seizures in the target area by 65 percent, while crimes committed with firearms there dropped by 49 percent. Neither gun seizures nor gun crimes changed much in a comparison area a few miles away where there was no patrol aimed at seizing firearms, and there was no apparent displacement of gun crimes from the area with the directed patrol to neighboring areas. Both homicides and drive-by shootings were significantly reduced in the target area, but did not decline in the comparison area (Sherman, January 1995).

The New York City Police Department also reports a decline in the carrying of firearms as a result of more aggressive police tactics, specifically, increased frisking of pedestrians who commit such minor infractions as playing a radio loudly or drinking alcoholic beverages in public. These tactics were cited as the reason for a 50 percent decline over two years in the percentage of people arrested for not paying subway fares who were also carrying loaded weapons (Krauss, 1995).

The Continuing Debate over Gun Control   Despite the uncertain effects of gun-control laws, most Americans support stronger laws than we now have. A 1994 Harris survey found that 70 percent of Americans said that the easy availability of handguns contributes to violence in the country. A 1995 Gallup poll revealed that 62 percent of Americans wanted stricter laws covering the sale of firearms; 24 percent thought the laws should remain the same, and only 12 percent thought they should be made less strict. That poll also found that 68 percent of Americans favored and 29 percent opposed a ban on assault rifles (Maguire and Pastore, 1995: 160, 191, 195).

Gun-control laws in the United States are relatively weak not because of lack of public support, but because of the power of the National Rifle Association (NRA). This well-financed organization of 3.5 million members can mobilize its supporters to write to members of Congress to oppose any gun-control legislation that is being considered. Many NRA members are "single-issue" voters who will vote against candidates who favor tougher gun-control laws. Because most voters who support tougher gun-control laws will not vote for or against candidates solely because of their stand on gun control, NRA members pose a more significant threat of lost votes to candidates, and thus many politicians vote against gun control out of fear of alienating the opponents of stronger gun-control laws.

Several lobbyist groups—such as the Center to Prevent Handgun Violence—now fight for stronger gun-control laws. However, these organizations are hampered by lack of funds, small memberships, and well-organized opposition from the NRA and the firearms industry. The efforts of these gun-control advocates have been strengthened by support from several police organizations for a ban on assault weapons.

The power of the NRA has eroded somewhat in recent years, as it has lost several important votes on state and federal legislation. In 1993, President Clinton signed into law the Brady bill, which imposes a five-day waiting period so that the backgrounds of prospective handgun buyers can be checked; and in 1994, a federal ban on many types of assault weapons was enacted. Despite such setbacks, the NRA remains influential; in 1996, it got Congress to eliminate funds used by the Centers for Disease Control and Prevention to record firearm-related homicides and suicides, a project the NRA claimed was a biased effort to support gun control. In that same year, the NRA successfully pressured Congress to eliminate a provision from an anti-terrorism bill that would have added chemical "taggants" to explosives to make it easier for law-enforcement agents to trace the materials used in bombs.

The NRA has been the center of controversy in the 1990s—for its aggressive efforts to reverse the ban on assault weapons, for its rumored links to anti-government paramilitary groups, and for calling federal law-enforcement agents "jack-booted government thugs," a comment that caused former President George Bush to resign from the organization. A 1995 survey found that only 47 percent of a national sample of 600 gun owners expressed overall agreement with the NRA's positions (*Boston Globe*, May 21, 1995).

The debate over gun control continues. Three-fourths of Americans think they have a constitutional right to own firearms, even though federal courts have consistently denied the existence of any such right for more than fifty years (Rezendes, 1995). The Second Amendment prefaces the phrase, "the right of the people to keep and bear arms, shall not be infringed" with the rationale for that right: "A well-regulated militia, being necessary to the security of a free state.... " The handguns involved in murders and robberies are not designed for military use, nor do their owners buy them for that purpose. Another argument against more gun control is that the criminal justice system cannot keep firearms out of the hands of potential offenders, and, even if it could, this might not produce any net reduction in violent crime (Kleck, 1991). In one survey, four-fifths of imprisoned felons thought they could get a firearm within a few days of being released from prison, even though the law prohibits convicted felons from acquiring firearms. That same study found that if cheap handguns were banned, the most serious felons would get a bigger gun or use a sawed-off shotgun rather than not carry a firearm (Wright and Rossi, 1986).

Gun-control advocates continue to hope that new or better-enforced laws will significantly reduce the crime rate, but research does not offer much support for that belief. An exception might be more aggressive police patrols that use existing laws to take illegal firearms from people before they commit crimes.

Summary

This chapter has looked at the way offenders seek suitable targets that are not protected by owners or bystanders. Opportunities for crime are a function of people's everyday behavior, according to routine activities theory.

Criminals consider various aspects of potential targets for crime: the form and value of property, and the vulnerability of victims. Some victims are more prone to victimization than others because they have characteristics or play roles that make them especially vulnerable.

Sometimes a victim precipitates an offense, contributing to his or her own victimization. Homicide victims are often the first to use abusive language or force in an interaction that culminates in murder. Rape victims sometimes enter risky situations, although this does not absolve rapists of legal responsibility for their crimes. Owners of property precipitate crimes by leaving their property unguarded and vulnerable to theft.

Alcohol and drugs sometimes facilitate crime. There is an association between alcohol use and crime, with many offenders being drunk or under the influence of alcohol when they violate the law. Similarly, many offenders are under the influence of illegal drugs when they engage in crime. More research is needed to determine the precise manner in which drugs and alcohol are associated with the commission of crime.

In the United States, many offenses are committed with firearms. Guns facilitate crimes such as murder and robbery. Assaults with firearms are more likely to produce death than are attacks with other weapons, and so the presence of a firearm makes murder a more likely outcome of an altercation. However, countries such as Switzerland have relatively low crime rates even though they have widespread ownership of firearms. There is little persuasive evidence that gun-control laws can significantly reduce crime. Mandatory penalties are often not applied, and additional penalties for the use of a firearm in a serious crime do not seem to deter most offenders. The debate over gun-control continues, with a majority of Americans favoring stronger laws.

Important Terms

facilitating factors
routine activities theory

victim precipitation
victim proneness

Review Questions

1. What is routine activities theory? What aspects of criminal behavior does it try to explain? What research supports routine activities theory? What modifications to the approach are needed to fit the findings of researchers?

2. How do the form and value of property and the characteristics of victims influence the way that property offenders select their targets?

3. What is victim precipitation? How does this concept help us to understand violent crime and property crime?

4. What are the three facilitating factors examined in this chapter? How would you explain the association between crime and each of the facilitating factors?

5. What does research tell us about the effectiveness of gun-control legislation in preventing crime? What kind of a gun-control law might reduce violent crime?

Chapter 10
Criminal Careers

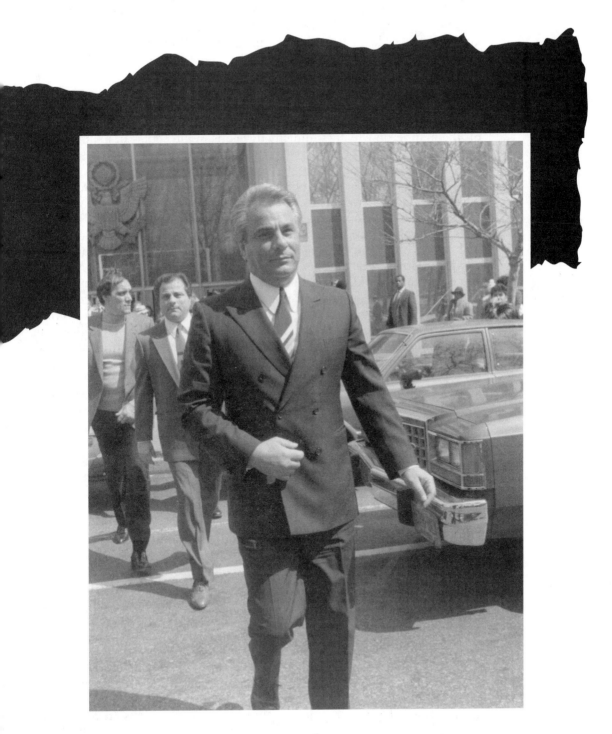

A career is a "sequence of movements from one position to another in an occupational system made by an individual who works in the system" (Becker, 1973: 24). A **criminal career** is not an "occupation" as we commonly understand that term, but a sequence of crimes over time can be analyzed much like a career in a legitimate occupation, for both involve skills, tasks, and commitment (Letkemann, 1973; Gibbs and Shelly, 1982). As long ago as 1893 it was recognized that "correct statistics of offenders can be developed only by a study of the total life histories of individuals" (Otto Kobner, cited in Petersilia, Greenwood, and Lavin, 1977: 2–3). Another student of crime noted in 1917 that the proper study of crime requires an examination of "the manner in which criminality develops in the course of a human lifetime" (Georg von Mayr, cited in Petersilia, Greenwood, and Lavin, 1977: 3).

Even though criminal careers are similar to legitimate careers in some ways, there are also important differences between them. Legitimate careers develop within stable contexts, such as a corporation or a law firm. Criminal careers usually develop in less formal contexts; for instance, robbers' and burglars' careers develop outside stable organizational settings. In addition, criminal careers often lack the well-defined sequence of stages and the pattern of upward mobility that frequently characterize legitimate careers. Although some legitimate workers do not experience these changes during their careers, and some offenders do gain in status over their lifetimes, there is probably less upward mobility in deviant careers than in legitimate ones. Careers in crime are less structured and perhaps more dependent on individual initiative in seeking out rewards than are legitimate careers. Moreover, criminal careers develop in secrecy from established authorities, whereas legitimate occupations have the support of social institutions (Luckenbill and Best, 1981).

Criminal careers can be studied by examining the autobiographies of individual offenders. These accounts reveal much about the subjective states and actual experiences of certain offenders, but they might not be representative of all criminals. Another approach is to develop conceptual typologies, or categorizations, of criminal careers. Arrest statistics have also been used to study the careers of offenders, but because relatively few crimes lead to arrest, the data might tell us more about contacts with the criminal justice system than about actual involvement in criminal behavior.

A heated debate has developed among criminologists about the importance of research on criminal careers. The position adopted by those who support such research is that different factors might explain the onset of criminal behavior, the persistence of that behavior over time, and desistance from that behavior; for example, lack of a legitimate job might push a person into crime, but access to such a job later in a criminal career might not lead that person out of crime (Blumstein, Farrington, and Moitra, 1985; Blumstein et al., 1986; Blumstein, Cohen, and Farrington, 1988). The opposing position is that research on criminal careers is of little or no value, because the tendency to engage in crime changes predictably over the life cycle, and thus criminal behavior at one time is highly correlated with criminal behavior at another time. Proponents of this position point to evidence that offenders neither specialize in crime nor commit increasingly serious crimes as they grow older (Gottfredson and Hirschi, 1988, 1990). In response, those who support criminal career research argue that some offenders do have long-term careers in crime, and that offenders differ among themselves and over time in the frequency with which they engage in crime. The little research that has been done to determine which of these two positions is better supported by data has so far proved inconclusive (Greenberg, 1991, 1992).

Knowledge of criminal careers has practical value. Understanding why offenders get involved in a life of crime can lead to policies that prevent criminal careers from developing. Knowing why career offenders "retire" from crime can generate programs that hasten their departure from crime. The fact that relatively few career criminals account for a large proportion of all of the crime that occurs suggests that the punishment and treatment of career offenders might have a significant impact on the crime rate.

Analyzing Criminal Careers

An analysis of criminal careers requires attention to the social conditions that influence the development of recurrent criminal activity (see the Cross-Cultural Perspective box). Labeling by the criminal justice system can affect an individual's life chances and make criminal behavior more likely. Criminal careers can be understood in terms of an individual's alternation between legitimate work and criminal activities. Attention must also be paid to the way that people are recruited into criminal careers, especially the way that involvement in juvenile delinquency is linked to adult criminal careers.

Career Contingencies

Criminal careers depend on various **contingencies**, or factors that determine movement from one criminal role to another, or from one crime to another (Becker, 1973). For instance, organized and professional crime primarily involves males, even though sex segregation in the underworld varies from one crime group to another. Women are at a disadvantage in being recruited into crime groups, in the criminal career paths available to them, and in their access to opportunities for learning criminal skills and gaining the rewards of crime. Gender-role socialization and patterns of parental surveillance of boys and girls also limit females' access to certain criminal careers (Hoffman-Bustamante, 1973; Steffensmeier, 1983).

One career contingency is apprehension for violating the law. People who break the law, are arrested by the police, and are convicted in court might later engage in crime because of the social contacts they make while incarcerated. Experience with the criminal justice system can also contribute to a criminal career by causing bitterness or by closing off job opportunities. However, offenders might commit more crimes if they were not arrested and convicted, because successful crimes could reinforce their law-violating behavior by providing them with rewards.

A CROSS-CULTURAL PERSPECTIVE

Serial Murder in Russia

Serial murderers, who have been the subject of much scholarly study and popular entertainment in the United States in recent years, have criminal careers in which they kill at least several victims over a period of time. These murderers seem to be especially common in the United States, but they also exist elsewhere. In 1992, the press reported that the "Canton Killer" had murdered and mutilated more than a half dozen young women in China. In that same year, a fifty-six-year-old Russian was convicted and sentenced to death for fifty-two murders; he was executed in February 1994.

Dubbed the "Forest Strip Killer" because of the place he had disposed of his victims' bodies, Andrei Chikatilo had once been a language teacher, office worker, and member of the Communist Party. He was married and raised two children during the twelve years that he raped, murdered, mutilated, and cannibalized his youthful victims, who included twenty-one boys, fourteen girls, and seventeen young women. Prior to committing his first murder in 1978, Chikatilo had sexually harassed children, leading to his dismissal from a teaching position. Over time, his murders became increasingly sadistic.

Chikatilo was constantly searching for vulnerable victims, and he always carried a knife and rope with him when away from home. He even took a job that allowed him to leave home without arousing suspicion. On his travels, he sought victims on trains, in railroad stations, at bus stops, and in isolated areas. Two-thirds of his victims have been described as drifters.

The obsession of the Soviet authorities with secrecy and the need to present a good face to their citizens and to the outside world allowed the murders to continue. Because the Soviets regarded crime as a capitalist phenomenon, Chikatilo's murders were not brought to public attention until five years after law-enforcement officials had learned of them. In an effort to stop the killings, another man was convicted and executed for the first of Chikatilo's murders. In 1984, Chikatilo was released after being detained for a murder, because blood and semen tests had proved inconclusive. He was not arrested again until 1990.

Source: Based on Serge Schmemann, "As Shrieks Fill Court, Killer in Russia Is Sentenced to Die," *New York Times,* October 16, 1992, p. A6.

Short-run rewards of peer prestige and money can create a "mobility trap" for juvenile delinquents, who gain immediate prestige and property at the cost of long-term upward mobility if they are expelled from school, are socially stigmatized, or become known to the police as offenders (Wiley, 1967). Evidence of this mobility trap comes from a study of Puerto Rican youths in a Chicago community (Padilla, 1992). Seeing no future for themselves in school or the kinds of jobs an education would lead to, they turned to gangs as an alternative source of income. Over time, car theft and drug dealing did not prove rewarding, but instead limited the youths' access to conventional jobs.

Russian serial killer Andrei Chikatilo was executed in 1994 for raping, torturing, and murdering fifty-two young victims over a period of twelve years.

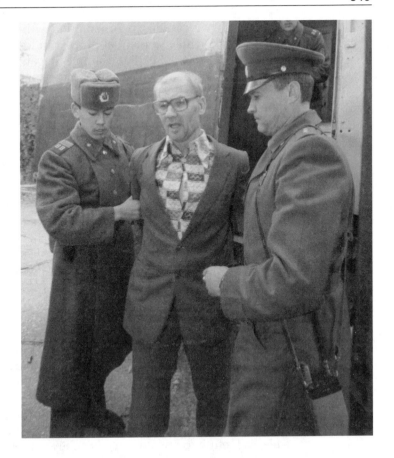

A study of month-to-month variations in the self-reported criminal behavior of convicted felons identified several "local life circumstances," or contingencies, that were associated with offending. During the months that the felons were using illegal drugs, their chances of committing a crime increased sixfold. Heavy consumption of alcoholic beverages also increased offending, especially property crimes. Living with a wife reduced criminal behavior, but living with a girlfriend was associated with higher levels of crime. Attending school significantly reduced involvement in crime. Working was weakly related to offending, decreasing assaults but unexpectedly increasing property crimes. These findings indicate that "local life circumstances can change criminal careers by modifying the likelihood of offending *at particular times*" (Horney, Osgood, and Marshall, 1995: 670; emphasis in original).

The Labeling Perspective

The labeling perspective focuses on the development of deviant careers, including careers in crime. People who break rules repeatedly and are labeled deviant by others sometimes organize their lives around deviant behavior.

What begins as casual experimentation with rule breaking becomes a deviant career, or "a whole sequential process in identity formation" (Rettig, Torres, and Garrett, 1977: 192). For example, negative labeling by parents and peers increases the chance that delinquents will continue in a delinquent career, apparently by affecting their perceptions of how other people see them (Matsueda, 1992; Smith and Brame, 1994).

Most people who break the law repeatedly are eventually arrested and convicted. As criminals say, "If you want to play, you have to pay," or "If you can't do the time, don't do the crime." Earlier in the book we saw that the chance of avoiding arrest for any given crime is good, but the chance of never being arrested if one commits many crimes is small. Offenders who are more skilled might go longer without an arrest, but eventually they "take a fall."

Because the legal system deals more harshly with some people than with others, it acts as a contingency that influences the development of delinquent and criminal careers. For instance, the police react to suspects on the basis of the seriousness of the offense, the individual's demeanor, the complainant's preferences, and the requirements of the police department (Piliavin and Briar, 1964; Black, 1980). The arrest, conviction, and imprisonment of an individual might be more likely if he or she is seen as a member of a criminal subculture who is likely to continue to commit serious crimes, rather than perceived as someone who violated the law because of poor judgment or situational pressures (Cloward and Ohlin, 1960: 12). Reactions to defendants by the criminal justice system might be based on valid assumptions about the likelihood that different kinds of people will continue in a life of crime, but these reactions also elicit patterned and persistent behavior. In other words, the label "criminal" can structure other people's responses to the offender; some people, for example, will refuse to hire an ex-convict. Responses of this sort then act as contingencies that influence the development of a criminal career.

The "Zigzag Path": Criminal Careers and Legitimate Pursuits

Criminal careers vary considerably. One study of thieves found that most followed a "zigzag path" back and forth between criminal and noncriminal pursuits (Glaser, 1974). Offenders would commit crimes, go to prison, try to get a job when released, and often return to crime later. Contacts with other criminals and the difficulty of finding a good job often made a return to crime the "path of least resistance" (Rettig, Torres, and Garrett, 1977: 4). The effects of situational factors such as peer influence and financial need were mediated in part by the ex-convict's commitment to a criminal career or commitment to a legitimate career, but tempting situations sometimes drew even those who were committed to a conventional way of life back into crime. People who are committed to a conventional way of life do engage in less crime than people who are committed to a criminal career, even if they do not stay away from crime altogether (McAuliffe and Gordon, 1974).

Success at crime can lead to continued criminal activities, and success in legitimate pursuits can lead to a continuation of those activities. Once people have engaged in crime and escaped arrest, they might think that the risk of negative consequences from crime is small and the rewards are great. Even if they are caught the first time, they may receive only a "slap on the wrist" in court and believe the chance of a harsh sanction is small. Serious failure in either criminal activities or legitimate pursuits can lead people to shift to the other form of behavior. Thus, losing a job might push a person into crime, and being arrested might lead someone else to look for a legitimate job (Glaser, 1974).

Recruitment into a Criminal Career

Recruitment into a criminal career often begins during adolescence, with early delinquency frequently being a prerequisite for an adult career in theft and violence. While still in their teens, future career offenders learn criminal skills and motives, what a criminal way of life involves, and how the police react to different crimes (Letkemann, 1973). Access to criminal careers seems to be greater in communities where there are close ties between adolescents and adult criminals who act as role models and communicate to the adolescents the values and skills necessary to commit crime. Access to criminal careers is also greater where there are stable relationships between people with conventional values and people with criminal values (Cloward and Ohlin, 1960). In such communities, a delinquent subculture is more likely to develop, and involvement in this subculture increases the likelihood of entry into an adult criminal career.

Adult offenders must also learn criminal skills and motives. For example, to move from various forms of hustling into a specialty as a professional fence, one career criminal had to acquire considerable knowledge about merchandise, including what he should pay for it and how much he could sell it for. This fence also needed "ability, energy, ingenuity, and certain persuasive skills," as well as a willingness to deceive both the buying public and the thieves who sold to him (Klockars, 1974: 177). To become a buyer of stolen goods required a modest amount of capital, the skill to purchase goods, the opportunity to buy goods for less than their retail price, a regular source of supply, a predictable demand for goods, and the ability to avoid arrest and imprisonment. The fence also needed a convincing front that would keep the police away but still attract customers looking for low prices.

Career criminals are recruited from various settings. Sutherland (1937) found that professional thieves had rarely been amateur thieves in slum areas, but instead came from legitimate occupations and severed their ties to the legitimate world after a period of unemployment. They spent time in bars and hotels where professional thieves gathered. Bartenders, taxi drivers, bellhops, and waiters who worked in the social world of the professional thief sometimes entered a life of crime by taking tangential roles in the commission of crime (Inciardi, 1975). Often they began by playing a small part in one crime and were called on later for more important roles in other offenses, gradually acquiring the skills and status of a professional thief. Others became career criminals by applying specific job skills to crime; for example, a printer might become a counterfeiter, or a locksmith might become a safecracker.

Typologies of Criminal Careers

One way to analyze criminal careers is to construct a **typology**—or set of categories—of offenders and their patterns of criminal activity. Such a typology is developed from criteria that a criminologist thinks are important in distinguishing one criminal career from another. This kind of typology assumes there is some specialization among offenders in the sorts of crime they commit.

One typology of "criminal role careers" was derived from information about the offense itself, the interactional setting of the behavior (alone or with others), the offender's self-concept and attitudes, and the pattern of crime over the offender's lifetime (Gibbons, 1992). Also taken into account were an offender's class and family background, peer-group associations, and contacts with law-enforcement agencies. The criminal role careers, twenty in the latest version of the typology, included "professional thieves," "naive check forgers," "embezzlers," "aggressive rapists," and "opiate addicts." However, because research shows that most offenders are versatile and do not specialize in a particular type of crime, many of them cannot be said to have a distinct kind of criminal role career (Hartjen and Gibbons, 1969; Shover, 1973; Petersilia, 1980).

Another way to develop a typology of offenders is to categorize them by the specific combinations of offenses they commit over time. A survey of nearly 2,200 adult male inmates in three states identified ten types of offenders by the combination of offenses they had committed. Chaiken and Chaiken (1984) found that these ten types differed in their rates of committing crime, their persistence in crime, and their personal characteristics. Table 10.1 shows these ten offender types and the kinds of crimes they committed. Chaiken and Chaiken gave the most attention to the first type, the violent predatory offender. This kind of offender engages in robbery, assault, and drug dealing, and sometimes burglary and other thefts. The violent predatory offender commits a disproportionate amount of all of the crime committed, is usually quite young, has been arrested frequently, began to commit crime at an early age, rarely has any family obligations, and has an irregular employment record. Violent predatory offenders are difficult to identify from official records, because they are young and the juvenile records that would indicate their heavy involvement in criminal activity are often unavailable to probation officers, prosecutors, judges, and researchers.

Delinquent Careers

Criminal careers can be studied by looking at lifetime patterns of delinquency and crime for a sample of individuals born in the same year. A cohort study of this sort was conducted by Wolfgang, Figlio, and Sellin (1972) in a project

TABLE 10.1 Ten Offender Types by Combinations of Offenses Committed

Group	Robbery	Assault[a]	Burglary	Theft,[b] Fraud, Forgery, Credit Card Crimes	Drug Deals	Percent of Study Sample[c]
Violent predators (robber-assaulter-dealers)	+	+	?	?	+	15
Robber-assaulters	+	+	?	?	0	8
Robber-dealers	+	0	?	?	+	9
Low-level robbers	+	0	?	?	0	12
Mere assaulters	0	+	0	0	0	5
Burglar-dealers	0	??	+	?	+	10
Low-level burglars	0	0	+	?	0	8
Property and drug offenders	0	??	0	+	+	6
Low-level property offenders	0	0	0	+	0	8
Drug dealers	0	0	0	0	+	6

Note: + = Group member commits this crime, by definition.

0 = Group member does not commit this crime, by definition.

? = Group member may or may not commit this crime. Analysis shows that nearly all members of the group do.

?? = Group member may or may not commit this crime. Most don't.

a Assault includes homicide arising out of assault or robbery.
b Theft includes auto theft.
c Percentages add to 87%. The remaining 13% did not report committing any of the crimes studied. Some serious crimes (e.g., rape, kidnap) were not included in the self-report survey. Respondents with missing data (150 out of 2,190) were excluded in calculation of percentages.

Source: Marcia R. Chaiken and Jan M. Chaiken, "Offender Types and Public Policy," *Crime and Delinquency,* Vol. 30, No. 2 (April 1984): 198. Copyright © 1984 by Sage Publications, Inc. Reprinted by permission of Sage Publications, Inc.

described in Chapter 1. They used school, police, court, and draft board records to study 9,945 males who were born in 1945 and lived in Philadelphia from their tenth through their eighteenth birthdays. Tracy, Wolfgang, and Figlio (1985) later replicated this study, using the same methods to study a cohort of 27,160 males and females who were born in 1958 and lived in Philadelphia from their tenth through their eighteenth birthdays. These Cohort I and II studies made it possible to examine past contacts with the juvenile justice system but did not allow the researchers to question individuals and administer self-report questionnaires to learn about offenses that never came to the attention of the police and the courts.

Chronic Offenders

Wolfgang, Figlio, and Sellin found that a relatively small proportion of the boys in Cohort I accounted for a large proportion of all of the cohort's contacts with the police that resulted in written reports. Table 10.2 shows the proportion of Cohort I that had no contact with the police (nondelinquents), the proportion that had one contact (one-time offenders), the proportion with two to four contacts (nonchronic offenders), and the proportion with five or more contacts (chronic offenders). Only 6.3 percent of the 9,945 boys were chronic offenders, but this group accounted for 51.9 percent of all of the cohort's contacts with the police. The nonchronic group accounted for 12.4 percent of the cohort, but 32.3 percent of all police contacts. If the nonchronic and chronic groups are combined into a category of "career delinquents"—that is, those with more than one police contact as a juvenile—the 18.7 percent of Cohort I classified as career delinquents accounted for 84.2 percent of all police contacts for the cohort. Thus there is a high concentration of police contacts among a relatively small proportion of the cohort.

Tracy, Wolfgang, and Figlio's Cohort II study confirmed the findings of the Cohort I study with regard to the concentration of police contacts among a small proportion of the total cohort. The 7.5 percent of Cohort II's boys who were classified as chronic offenders (five or more police contacts) accounted for 61 percent of all contacts with the police for the cohort. These chronic offenders accounted for 68 percent of all police contacts for FBI index offenses, including 73 percent of the cohort's robberies and 75 percent of the cohort's rapes.

A cohort study in Racine, Wisconsin, looked at the police contacts of both juveniles and young adults and found a similar concentration of police contacts among a small percentage of three different cohorts. Between 5 and 7 percent of each cohort accounted for more than half of all nontraffic contacts with the police, and about 20 percent of each cohort accounted for 80 percent of all nontraffic police contacts in the cohort. Moreover, 8 to 14 percent of each cohort accounted for all of the felony arrests in the cohort (Shannon, 1988: 122–128).

TABLE 10.2   Police Contacts among Members of Cohort I

Type of Offender	Percentage of Cohort	Percentage of All of Cohort's Police Contacts
Nondelinquents	65.1	0
One-time offenders	16.2	15.8
Nonchronic offenders	12.4	32.3
Chronic offenders	6.3	51.9

Source: Marvin E. Wolfgang, Robert M. Figlio, and Thorsten Sellin, *Delinquency in a Birth Cohort.* Chicago: University of Chicago Press, 1972, p. 89. Reprinted by permission of The University of Chicago Press. Copyright © 1972 by The University of Chicago. All rights reserved. (Adapted)

A cohort study in London found that 132 of 396 boys were convicted of an offense before the age of twenty-five. Of the 132, twenty-three were chronic offenders with six or more convictions. This group of chronic offenders, which was 6 percent of the cohort, accounted for about half of the convictions recorded for all youths in the cohort. These chronic offenders differed from the nonchronic offenders (one to five convictions) in that they "tended to be convicted at an early age, to come from low-income families, to be rated troublesome in their primary schools, to have low IQ and attainment, to be clumsy on psychomotor tests, and to have convicted older siblings" (Blumstein, Farrington, and Moitra, 1985: 196).

One of the few studies of chronic adult offenders examined arrests in California between 1974 and 1985 for people born in 1956. The 7 percent of the age cohort classified as chronic offenders (three or more arrests between ages eighteen and twenty-nine) accounted for 67 percent of the cohort's adult arrests. This again indicates a high concentration of arrests among a small proportion of a cohort, although the researcher concluded that the size of this chronic adult offender population in California was much larger than previously thought, about 29,000 chronic offenders in this one age cohort alone (Tillman, 1987).

Patterns of Delinquent Careers

Wolfgang, Figlio, and Sellin examined several issues related to delinquent careers. They discovered that boys who had one contact with the police and then had no more contacts usually had engaged in relatively trivial offenses the first time. However, boys with at least two police contacts were more likely to have been stopped the first time for a relatively serious offense that involved injury, theft, or damage.

Of the boys in Cohort I with at least one police contact, 53.6 percent were stopped a second time. Of those stopped a second time, 65.1 percent went on to a third contact with the police, and of those with three or more contacts, the chances of being stopped an additional time ranged from 70 to 80 percent. In other words, the likelihood of never again being stopped by the police for delinquency is greatest after the first contact; after a second contact, the chance of continuing in a delinquent career is greater. Another study found even higher "transition probabilities" among a sample of 1,591 adults arrested for violent crimes; the chance of being arrested again after any given arrest was about 80 percent, whatever the individual's prior arrest history (Miller, Dinitz, and Conrad, 1982).

Juveniles who are first stopped by the police at a very young age are more likely to have another police contact than are juveniles whose first contact with the police comes at a later age. Early age at first contact is also associated with a long career in crime and delinquency, a rapid development of that career, and involvement in serious offenses (Wolfgang, Figlio, and Sellin, 1972; Miller, Dinitz, and Conrad, 1982; Tracy, Wolfgang, and Figlio, 1985; Tontodonato, 1988; Loeber et al., 1991). Early contact with the police could indicate a serious behavioral problem that is conducive to a criminal career, or early police contact might subject individuals to a labeling experience in juvenile court that closes off legitimate opportunities, breaks conventional bonds, and pushes them into lives of crime. Recent research has not determined if past and future criminal behavior are correlated because prior participation alters individuals and their behavior, or because certain individual characteristics that have a stable association with criminal behavior persist over time (Nagin and Paternoster, 1991; Nagin and Farrington, 1992a, 1992b).

Most research on juvenile delinquents finds little tendency for them to specialize in certain types of offenses. The Philadelphia cohort studies found only "a weak propensity toward offense type specialization" (Wolfgang, Figlio, and Sellin, 1972: 249). Other cohort studies have also found no clear pattern of offense specialization among delinquent youths (Lab, 1984; Shelden, Horvath, and Tracy, 1989) and no marked tendency for offenses to escalate in seriousness over the course of delinquent careers (Datesman and Aickin, 1984). A study in Columbus, Ohio, of 1,222 boys and girls arrested at least once for a violent crime concluded that even violent juvenile offenders do not tend to specialize in the kinds of crime they commit, and that they do not progress from less serious to more serious offenses during their criminal careers (Hamparian et al., 1985). One study of nearly 70,000 juvenile offenders did find a "small but significant degree of specialization superimposed on a great deal of versatility," with about 20 percent of juveniles identifiable as specialists (Farrington, Snyder, and Finnegan, 1988: 483).

The Philadelphia Cohort I study found that the time between police contacts became compressed over the course of an individual's delinquent career. The average time from first contact to second contact was sixteen to eighteen months. However, the average time from second contact to third contact was only ten months, and the average time from the third to the fourth contact was only eight months. The interval continued to decrease with each additional police contact, so that the average time between contacts after the twelfth one was only about three months. A similar compression of time between police contacts as the criminal record lengthens has been found for adult offenders (Miller, Dinitz, and Conrad, 1982). It is unclear whether this compression results from increased criminal or delinquent activity once a career begins or whether it occurs because the police are more likely to arrest people they have come to think of as troublemakers.

Delbert Elliott (1994) used longitudinal data from the National Youth Survey to look at the careers of those reporting that they had committed serious violent offenses, defined as aggravated assaults, robberies, and rapes that involved injury or a weapon. Elliott found that the prevalence of such crimes was greater, the age of onset younger, and race differences smaller than indicated by studies based on official records. Compared to those studies, the NYS self-report study provided more evidence that careers escalate in terms of frequency, seriousness, and variety of offenses. The NYS study did support some of the conclusions of previous research based on official records: the general pattern of progression involved diversification rather than specialization in certain offenses; the proportion of all crimes reported in a given year that were serious violent offenses was small; serious violent offenders were less than 5 percent of the sample, but accounted for 83 percent of all index offenses reported by the sample; and early age of onset of serious violent offending predicted continuity of that behavior into adulthood (Elliott, 1994).

Juvenile Delinquency and Adult Criminal Careers

Wolfgang, Thornberry, and Figlio (1987) studied police contacts up to the age of thirty for a 10 percent sample of the original Philadelphia cohort of boys. The probability of being stopped by the police before age eighteen was .35; that is, thirty-five of every one hundred males in Cohort I had contact with the police as a juvenile. The probability of any contact with the police from age ten to age thirty for the 10 percent sample from the original cohort was .47. Thirty percent of the sample had a police contact between eighteen and thirty.

The likelihood of police contact as an adult for a person who had been stopped by the police as a juvenile was .51, but the probability of contact as an adult if a person had not been stopped as a juvenile was only .18. Thus, a male with a juvenile record was nearly three times as likely as a male without a juvenile record to have a police contact as an adult. In addition, those who had the largest number of contacts with the police as juveniles and those who were stopped for the most serious offenses as juveniles were the most likely to have long and serious adult criminal careers (Wolfgang, Thornberry, and Figlio, 1987). Data from the Cohort II study revealed that juvenile offenders who were most specialized by type of offense and who committed the most serious offenses were the most likely to become involved in crime as adults (Kempf, 1986, 1988).

The study of the 10 percent sample from the Cohort I study found that offenses committed as adults were, on the average, much more serious than offenses committed as juveniles. In addition, adult offenses escalated in seriousness over the course of a criminal career, although such escalation did not occur during the juvenile years (Wolfgang, Thornberry, and Figlio, 1987: 32).

The study of the Columbus, Ohio, cohort of 1,222 juveniles arrested for violent offenses found that 59 percent of them were arrested at least once for an adult felony by the time they reached their mid-twenties. The youthful violent offenders who were most likely to be arrested for a felony as an adult were male, had been arrested for an index violent offense as a youth, had first been arrested at age twelve or less, and had been committed to a state juvenile correctional facility (Hamparian et al., 1985). However, about two-fifths of this cohort of youthful violent offenders did not go on to be arrested for serious crimes as adults, although some probably committed offenses for which they were not arrested.

Using data on delinquent and nondelinquent males who were followed from childhood into their forties, Sampson and Laub (1993) found that whether a man engaged in crime was significantly influenced by his adult social bonds, regardless of any propensity to antisocial behavior that might have existed during his childhood and adolescence. Adult marital attachments and job stability can thus counteract, at least to a degree, the influence of childhood or adolescent experiences. In terms of the life-course perspective employed by Sampson and Laub, an event such as getting married or taking a job can be a "turning point" or "transition" that redirects an individual's long-term "trajectory" or line of development away from continued involvement in crime.

It is not too surprising that many juvenile offenders do not go on to commit crimes as adults, because often their delinquent acts would not be crimes if committed by adults. There is no reason to expect that a fifteen-year-old boy apprehended for underage drinking or skipping school will commit robbery or burglary as an adult, or even as an adolescent. Researchers have found weak or nonexistent relationships between such status offenses and serious acts of delinquency (LeBlanc and Biron, 1980; Rojek and Erickson, 1981–82, 1982; Kelley, 1983; Shelden, Horvath, and Tracy, 1989). Because juvenile delinquency includes status offenses as well as acts that would be crimes if committed by adults, juvenile delinquents cannot be seen simply as criminals who happen to be under the age at which people are legally treated as adults.

Even juvenile delinquents who do commit serious crimes often realize that when they become adults, the chance of a harsh punishment increases greatly. They might know that their juvenile records will usually be kept secret and that they will start with a clean slate when they reach adulthood. These considerations lead some juvenile offenders to avoid breaking the law when they become adults. Other juvenile offenders settle down when they become adults, taking full-time jobs, getting married, and having children. These changes take them away from the street life and the gangs that are conducive to criminal activities and reduce their motivation to engage in crime.

There is, nevertheless, a relationship between juvenile delinquency and adult criminal careers, both in the United States and in England (see the Cross-Cultural Perspective box). Some attribute this relationship less to the continuity of behavior over time than to the effects of the juvenile and criminal justice systems on young people (Wolfgang, Figlio, and Sellin, 1972; Shannon, 1982). This position has led some criminologists to support **radical nonintervention**, a policy of minimizing official reaction to delinquency to prevent the labeling that could drive juveniles into adult criminal careers (Schur, 1973; Shannon, 1982). A different view is that adolescent offenders who represent the most serious threats to society are the most likely to be labeled delinquent, and it is they who would be the most likely to go on to engage in crime as adults even without official intervention when they are young. To date, researchers have not provided persuasive evidence of whether the relationship between juvenile delinquency and adult criminal careers is a result of labeling, a result of continuity of behavior over time, or some combination of the two.

Adult Criminal Careers

One way to look at criminal careers is to examine the lifetime criminal and noncriminal experiences of a single type of offender. Petersilia, Greenwood, and Lavin (1977) used this approach to study forty-nine men who were serv-

A CROSS-CULTURAL PERSPECTIVE

Juvenile Delinquency and Adult Crime in England

An English cohort study that examined delinquent and criminal careers began with 411 boys who were eight and nine years old in 1961.

Each of the following factors was found to enhance the likelihood that a boy would later be arrested and convicted: low family income, large family size, criminal parents, poor child rearing, and low IQ level. Parents who had been convicted of crimes tended to have children who were also convicted of criminal and delinquent acts, but there was no evidence that the parents taught their children to violate the law or encouraged them to do so. Instead, criminal parents seemed to be poor at supervising their children, sometimes because of their own imprisonment, and they were therefore less likely to be "psychologically present" when their children found themselves in situations in which they were tempted to violate the law. There could also have been some police bias against children whose parents were known criminals, with the police being more likely to arrest rather than warn children who were caught violating the law.

Sixty-one percent of the boys who were convicted of delinquent acts were eventually convicted of crimes as adults, but only 13 percent of the boys who were not found delinquent went on to be convicted as adults. Some adult criminals had avoided any contact with the law as adolescents; in fact, nearly one-fourth of the adults who had two or more convictions had never been found delinquent. Boys who were convicted of delinquent acts at the earliest ages were the most likely to become persistent adult offenders. There was little specialization by type of offense by the age of twenty-one, although there was some continuity in aggressive behavior over time.

Source: Based on David P. Farrington, "Longitudinal Research on Crime and Delinquency," in Norval Morris and Michael Tonry, eds., *Crime and Justice: An Annual Review of Research,* Vol. 1. Chicago: University of Chicago Press, 1979, pp. 289–348.

ing sentences in a California prison for armed robbery and who had been in prison at least once before. They used self-reports of criminal activity as well as official data on arrests and convictions to trace the careers of these habitual offenders.

Career Patterns

The armed robbers had been incarcerated an average of half of their criminal careers, and they averaged about twenty years from their first self-reported offense until their current incarceration. Collectively, the forty-nine robbers reported 10,505 offenses over their careers, an average of 214 per offender. They had moved from crimes such as auto theft and burglary when they were juveniles to more serious offenses such as robbery when they became adults. The average age at first arrest was fifteen; 29 percent had begun significant criminal activity by twelve, 75 percent had started by fifteen, and 90 percent had started by eighteen. Over their careers, the average amount stolen in a crime was about $250, and their average annual income from crime was only a few thousand dollars.

There was no strong tendency toward crime specialization among these offenders; they often switched from one offense to another. They would continue one kind of crime as long as it proved successful and as long as they could find opportunities. Other studies support this finding of little specialization over the course of a criminal career (Blumstein and Cohen, 1980; Petersilia, 1980; Peterson and Braiker, 1981; Rojek and Erickson, 1982; Kempf, 1987; Britt, 1994). One study of thieves involved in commercial burglary and truck hijacking found considerable versatility in the choice of crimes (Gibbs and Shelly, 1982). A study of 1,591 offenders chosen because they had been arrested for a serious violent crime found that 93 percent of them showed "no discernible pattern of violence" in their arrest histories; few habitually violent offenders were found in the sample (Miller, Dinitz, and Conrad, 1982: 59).

The armed robbers were more likely to be arrested for any given crime as adults than they were as juveniles; arrest rates were calculated in terms of number of arrests per self-reported crime. Why they became less successful in avoiding arrest as their criminal careers progressed is not clear. Few of them believed they were watched more carefully by the police because of their prior record. They might have become careless over time, perhaps because their experience made them overly confident.

These robbers continued to commit crimes after their earlier releases from prison because they had difficulty getting good jobs, lacked financial resources, and continued to interact with other offenders. A criminal record can be an impediment to securing a good job, but even more important might be the offender's lack of job skills and experience. The jobs these career criminals found were often low-paying, menial jobs with little or no chance for advancement. The ex-convicts who managed to get good jobs had lower offense rates than the ex-convicts who found poor-paying jobs or no jobs at all.

Planning Crimes

Relatively few of the armed robbers did much planning of their crimes. One-fourth did no planning or preparation at all, about half did very little planning, and one-fourth planned their crimes to some extent. Planning was more common when the offenders were young adults or adults than when they were juveniles, but even planning by adults was quite limited. Offenders typically included in what plans they did make the location of the crime, the presence of police patrols, when money would be present, whether there was an alarm on the premises, where a getaway car would be stolen, what disguise (if any) to wear, and how to escape from the scene of the crime.

As the habitual armed robbers got older, they increasingly operated alone. This allowed them to keep the profits of their crimes for themselves and reduced the risk that a partner would be arrested and cooperate with the police. Some offenders used fences or drug dealers to meet certain needs, but in general they relied on others less as they got older.

Use of the Stolen Money

While the armed robbers were juveniles, their crimes tended to fulfill expressive needs, such as peer approval, revenge, hostility, excitement, and a sense of being grown up. Over the course of their criminal careers, financial needs became relatively more important (Petersilia, 1980). The increased importance of financial needs suggests that economic assistance or a job that pays well might draw some older criminals away from crime and into a conventional way of life.

In a survey of 624 male California inmates who were serving time for felonies, researchers discovered that 47 percent reported that economic distress was an important reason for their crimes; offenders who cited this reason reported fewer violent offenses than inmates who said they had other motivations for their crimes (Peterson and Braiker, 1981). Thirty-five percent of the felons reported that their desire for high times motivated them to commit crime; these offenders reported the most frequent commission of offenses. Finally, 14 percent of the inmates reported that bad temper was an important reason for their crimes, which were frequently violent. These three motivations for crime—economic distress, a desire for high times, and bad temper—were statistically unrelated to one another.

Intensive and Intermittent Career Criminals

Petersilia, Greenwood, and Lavin's research on armed robbers led them to distinguish between two kinds of career criminals: intensives and intermittents (see Table 10.3). **Intensive offenders** engage in criminal activity that begins at an early age and is sustained over time, consciously planned, persistent, skilled, and frequent. In contrast, **intermittent offenders** engage in irregular and opportunistic crimes with low payoffs and great risks and do not think of themselves as professional criminals. Intensive criminals see themselves as career criminals, have a specific goal for their crimes (such as supporting high living or a drug habit), and try to avoid arrest. Compared with the intermittent offender, the intensive criminal steals more money in each crime and is more likely to injure the victim. Intensives commit relatively serious crimes and engage in crime often; the intensives in this study admitted to an average of fifty-one crimes per year, compared with an average of only five self-reported offenses per year for the intermittent offenders (Petersilia, Greenwood, and Lavin, 1977).

The survey of 624 male felons in California prisons estimated that the average incoming prisoner had committed about fourteen serious crimes per year during the three years prior to his incarceration. However, this average conceals the fact that most inmates had committed few offenses, and a small number had committed many. More than half of the inmates had committed fewer than three offenses per year while on the street, but the most criminally active of the inmates accounted for more than sixty serious offenses per year (Peterson and Braiker, 1981). A study by a district attorney's office found that 6 percent of all suspects arrested in Manhattan for robbery, assault,

TABLE 10.3 A Comparison of Intensive and Intermittent Offenders

Intensives
begins crime at an early age
criminal behavior sustained and consciously directed
pre-crime planning
committed juvenile crimes alone
sees self as career criminal
committed profitable burglaries
unlikely to be well employed
more likely to injure victims
more violence in personal lives

Intermittents
starts crime at somewhat later age
criminal behavior irregular and opportunistic
little pre-crime planning
committed juvenile crimes with partners
does not see self as career criminal
committed unprofitable burglaries
likely to be better employed
less likely to injure victims
less violence in personal lives

Source: Based on Joan Petersilia, Peter W. Greenwood, and Marvin Lavin, *Criminal Careers of Habitual Felons.* Santa Monica, Calif.: Rand, 1977.

burglary, and rape in 1979 were responsible for nearly one-third of all crimes of that sort reported in that year. These intensive offenders averaged thirteen prior arrests and committed an average of thirty-four crimes per year (*New York Times,* April 9, 1981). In Chapter 14, we will see that the high rate of crime by intensive offenders has been the basis of programs that focus the criminal justice system's resources on the apprehension, conviction, and imprisonment of career criminals.

Leaving a Life of Crime

In Chapter 4, we saw that the rate of arrest for index offenses declines with age; only one-ninth of all suspects arrested in 1995 for index crimes were over the age of forty. Later we will see that programs to rehabilitate offenders have been, for the most part, ineffective. Criminals apparently "exit" or "retire" from criminal careers as they get older for reasons that have little to do with treatment programs.

The idea that criminals "burn out" or "mature out" of crime comes from studies of drug addicts. Heroin addicts are often young, and samples of addicts rarely include many older addicts. The absence of older heroin addicts cannot be accounted for solely by overdose deaths. Some addicts apparently stop using opiates, either on their own or as a result of an effective drug treatment program. Addicts who join such programs might already be "burned out" physically and mentally by the burdens of maintaining a habit and could thus be ready to stop using addictive drugs.

Exiting is the successful disengagement from a previous pattern of criminal behavior. If a criminal career is a "zigzag path" or alternation between criminal and noncriminal activities, what conditions or contingencies promote the change from criminal activities to noncriminal pursuits?

A Model of the Exiting Process

Neal Shover (1985, 1996) studied this exiting process through interviews with fifty ordinary property offenders. Most of these men had a high degree of identification with crime as a means of livelihood but had been unsuccessful at this pursuit, either making little money from their crimes or spending much time in prison. Figure 10.1 shows the theoretical model of the exiting process that Shover derived from his research.

As offenders get older, they experience both orientational change and interpersonal change. Change in orientation involves four elements:

1. *A new perspective on the self.* Offenders become more critical of their past behavior and more detached in evaluating how they behaved when younger.

2. *A growing awareness of time.* Offenders see time as a diminishing resource, viewing life in terms of the number of years they have left rather than in terms of how many years they have been alive. Offenders begin to plan how to use the rest of their lives. Sometimes this change is related to a fear of dying in prison.

3. *Changing aspirations and goals.* Offenders reduce their expectations of material well-being and assign greater priority to good relationships with others, a peaceful life, and a legitimate job.

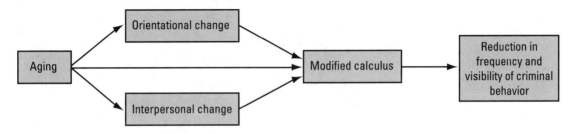

FIGURE 10.1
Shover's Model of the Exiting Process

Source: Neal Shover, *Aging Criminals.* Beverly Hills, Calif.: Sage Publications, 1985, p. 118. Reprinted by permission of the author.

4. *A growing sense of tiredness.* Offenders come to fear injury or death to a greater degree and become more wary of betrayal by crime partners. They feel they have slowed down relative to other offenders and inmates and must be careful of being victimized by them. Offenders also grow weary of fighting the more powerful criminal justice system.

In Shover's model, change in interpersonal relations is also important to the exiting process, with this change involving two components:

1. *Ties to another person.* Offenders seek mutually satisfying relationships with members of the opposite sex or with members of their family.

2. *Ties to a line of activity.* This typically involves finding a satisfying job, which provides direct rewards to offenders and reinforces their non-criminal identity. A job occupies their time, leaving little time for criminal activity.

According to Shover, these orientational and interpersonal changes lead to a "modified calculus," an alteration in the offender's balancing of the rewards and risks of criminal behavior. Persistent thieves increasingly see

Aging offenders develop new perspectives on themselves, see time as a diminishing resource, change their aspirations, become tired, form attachments to other people, and find satisfying jobs. This sixty-eight-year-old convict is being released after serving fifty-one years for a murder committed when he was seventeen.

crime as producing "only penury interspersed with modest criminal gains that are depleted quickly in sprees of partying, and repeated imprisonment" (Shover, 1996: 139). This changed calculus then leads either to a reduction in the frequency and visibility of criminal activity so as to keep risks to a minimum or to exiting from a criminal career altogether.

A study of previously incarcerated serious offenders by Shover and Thompson (1992) generally supported this model of exiting. Desistance from crime increased with age and education; it also increased as expectations for achieving friends, money, autonomy, and happiness through criminal behavior decreased. Desistance was not affected by income from legitimate work or by perceived risk of legal punishment.

Reasons for Leaving a Career as a Professional Thief

Evidence from biographical and autobiographical accounts of professional thieves suggests various motives for leaving a life of crime. Thieves might give up crime after they violate the code of the criminal subculture and are ostracized by other thieves; if they become inefficient as a result of fear, drugs, alcohol, or increasing age; if they can no longer find other thieves to work with them; or in rare cases if they make a "big score" (Sutherland, 1937: 24–25). Thieves might also leave a criminal career if a long prison term shocks them into reforming, if they take a legitimate job, or if they marry into the legitimate world (Inciardi, 1975: 73–74; Shover, 1983, 1985). Over time, thieves sometimes realize that the financial rewards of a legitimate job outweigh the financial rewards of crime, for few thieves ever make much money from crime (Petersilia, Greenwood, and Lavin, 1977: 71; Katz, 1988).

Whatever their reasons for retiring from crime, professional thieves who do so of their own volition and who still retain their skills at theft may be seen as "retired" professional thieves rather than as new members of the conventional world (Sutherland, 1937). Thieves who leave criminal careers do not always regret their past behavior, often reflecting nostalgically on the excitement and scores of the past. They sometimes retain a "latent criminal identity," an affinity for others who are involved in crime (Irwin, 1970: 202). Some former thieves do not break their bonds with criminals and never become fully integrated into the conventional world. Exiting from crime can thus be seen as a change in criminal identity from a manifest to a latent form.

Reasons for Leaving a Career as a Drug Dealer or Smuggler

In her in-depth study of upper-level drug dealers and smugglers, most of whom trafficked in marijuana and cocaine, Patricia Adler (1993) found that about 90 percent of those she had observed and interviewed had decided to get out of the business. Early in their criminal careers, they had seen their drug dealing as temporary. As they grew aware of the restrictions and sacrifices imposed by a deviant career, and as they tired of life as a fugitive, they decided to abandon this career. What had once been a novel form of activity had become routine, exhausting, dangerous, and isolating.

However, these drug dealers and smugglers were bound to their careers by the rewards of money, drugs, and sex; by their commitment to a deviant career; and by the difficulty of finding another way to earn a good income. As a consequence, they oscillated between a deviant career and a legitimate way of life, often for years after they had decided to leave the deviant career. They moved out of dealing and smuggling temporarily, and then back into the drug business, a process described as "phaseout and re-entries" (Adler and Adler, 1983: 201).

More than ten years after her initial fieldwork, Adler was able to locate thirteen of her original sample of sixty-five dealers and smugglers. All thirteen had left their careers in the drug trade. Their reintegration into conventional society, which was achieved by fits and starts and to varying degrees, was influenced by factors associated with their lives before, during, and after their involvement in dealing and smuggling. Predealing and presmuggling factors that influenced reintegration included the age at which they had first engaged in illicit behavior, the social class into which they had been born, and the legitimate interests and skills they had developed before entering deviant careers. Factors during the time they were involved in the drug trade that affected later reintegration into society included the extent to which they had continued to be involved in the legitimate occupational world, the relationships they had maintained with people not involved in crime, the entrepreneurial skills they had developed as dealers and smugglers, and the organizational sophistication of their illicit operations. Reintegration was also influenced by factors associated with their post-drug-trade lives, including their access to legitimate jobs, their relationships with people who could help them adjust to conventional society, and their adaptability to the organizational world (Adler, 1993).

Exiting and Theories of Crime Causation

The theories of crime causation examined in earlier chapters suggest why some offenders leave a life of crime. A complete theory of criminal behavior should be able to explain why some people break the law and others do not, and also why some people who engage in crime eventually disengage from a criminal career. In fact, the correlates of desistance from delinquency seem to be similar to the correlates of initial involvement in delinquency (Loeber et al., 1991). Here we look at some of the implications of different theories of crime causation for the process of exiting.

Differential Association Theory   Differential association theory would explain exiting by a change in a career criminal's ratio of definitions favorable to violation of the law over definitions unfavorable to violation of the law. In other words, just before leaving a criminal career, an offender should interact more with others who provide definitions that are not favorable to continued criminal activity or should interact less with people who are sources of definitions favorable to violation of the law.

There is no research that directly supports or refutes this explanation of exiting. However, this explanation is questionable, because many offenders probably decide to leave a criminal career while in prison, where their exposure to definitions favorable to violation of the law is great and where they are relatively isolated from definitions unfavorable to violation of the law. Some inmates might decide to exit because they are exposed to law-abiding values held by a correctional officer, a social worker, a visiting family member, or even another inmate who decides to go straight.

Another problem with using differential association theory to explain exiting is Sutherland's proposal that associations are more important if they occur early in life (the priority factor). This would suggest that an older career criminal would require very intense and frequent exposure to definitions unfavorable to violation of the law to change the ratio of definitions in a way that would lead to exiting. In a few cases, this might occur through religious conversion.

The Labeling Perspective   The labeling perspective offers a better explanation of why career criminals continue to commit crime than of why they abandon a life of crime. As criminal careers develop, the label "criminal" or "ex-convict" is more firmly affixed by the criminal justice system and the public. A criminal record, sometimes even an acquittal, signifies to the rest of the world a continuing intention to do social harm. There is little reason to change that label as long as an individual is involved in crime, and so we would not expect a change in the label to precede the abandonment of a criminal career. Even an offender who decides to terminate a life of crime faces continued labeling as an ex-convict and must deal with closed-off job opportunities and social contacts. More support from the criminal justice system and from the people with whom the ex-convict interacts would make exiting easier.

Exiting sometimes involves deviance-disavowal by an offender or the relabeling of an offender by others. One form of relabeling is **certification,** the social verification by the criminal justice system or by conventional people that an offender has been rehabilitated. Certification eases the transition from a criminal career to membership in the conventional social world (Meisenhelder, 1977).

Anomie and Differential Opportunity Theory   Theories that focus on anomie and differential opportunity would suggest that exiting is caused either by increased access to legitimate means to reach socially approved goals or by reduced aspirations. There is some evidence that changes in aspirations are associated with the decision to abandon a criminal career (Shover, 1983, 1985). Research indicates that securing a job that holds promise for career advancement is important to exiting, but this research fits better with control theory than with anomie or differential opportunity theory, because the bond to the conventional order provided by a job seems to be more important than the income produced by the job (Meisenhelder, 1977; Shover, 1983, 1985).

Social Control Theory   Social control theory suggests that a career criminal will "retire" when he or she forms bonds or attachments to conventional people and institutions. Just as adolescents who lack ties to family, school, peers, or a job are the most likely to become delinquents, so older offenders should be more likely to move out of crime when they form such conventional attachments.

Social control theory offers the most convincing explanation of the process of exiting. Exiting usually requires the acquisition of meaningful bonds to the conventional social order, a process opposite to the one that social control theory claims will generate delinquency. Thieves leave a life of crime as they form attachments to a life of conformity and develop a reluctance to give up those new bonds by risking further imprisonment. One important tie to the conventional order is a job that has the potential for advancement and that is perceived as meaningful and economically rewarding. A good job shifts a criminal's attention from the present to the future, and it provides a solid basis for the construction of a noncriminal identity. It also changes an individual's daily routine in ways that make crime less likely (Meisenhelder, 1977; Shover, 1983, 1985).

Good personal relationships with conventional people such as a spouse, a lover, children, or peers create bonds to the social order that an individual wants to protect. These people will then be "psychologically present" if the individual faces situations that offer a temptation to violate the law. Family members and lovers also provide a place of residence, food, and help in the development of everyday skills such as paying bills and scheduling time. Other bonds that can lead people away from crime include involvement in organized religion and activities such as sports and hobbies (Irwin, 1970). However, attachments of this sort are usually less important in the exiting process than ties to jobs and to other people. One recent study found that the quality and strength of two types of social bonds formed during adulthood, job stability and marital attachment, were strongly predictive of desistance from crime (Sampson and Laub, 1993).

Exiting and the Correctional System

Correctional treatment programs are designed to rehabilitate offenders, but some researchers have suggested that the conditions necessary for exiting are largely outside the control of the correctional system (Meisenhelder, 1977; Petersilia, 1980).

Some critics even claim that the correctional system impedes the process of exiting. In prison, inmates learn patterns of behavior opposite to the ones they need to leave a criminal career. They depend on the prison administration for their material needs, but after release they must rely on themselves to meet those needs. In prison their time is structured for them, and often they are idle; after release, they must learn to structure their time to keep themselves from drifting back into crime. Prison life is easier for inmates who do not spend much time thinking about their future, but outside prison they

Good personal relationships with conventional people such as a spouse, a lawyer, children, or peers create bonds to the social order that an individual wants to protect. These attachments make it easier for inmates to leave a life of crime.

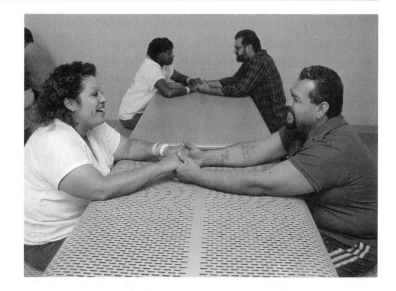

must develop personal goals. In sum, changes produced by prison often hinder offenders who might otherwise leave a life of crime (Cordilia, 1983).

In order to leave a life of crime, a released inmate must "keep out of the old bag," a way of life that involves the commission of felonies and a high likelihood of arrest and conviction (Irwin, 1970). The "old bag" offers excitement and glamour, but also physical danger and the risk of a return to prison. Some observers believe the only way to leave a criminal career is to stay away from all criminal behavior, a view similar to the claim by Alcoholics Anonymous that alcoholics cannot drink at all without risking a relapse.

An ex-convict's first few weeks on the street after release are especially critical. During that time, the individual must become reaccustomed to the outside world, which has a faster pace and less routinization than life in prison. Often a released offender feels like a foreign traveler during the first few weeks on the street (Irwin, 1970).

As the ex-convict develops bonds and as time passes, the motivation to stay away from crime increases. The longer the individual stays away from crime, the less the chance that he or she will return to crime. Conversely, the greater a person's past involvement in crime and the longer a person's criminal career, the less the chance of abandoning a life of crime (Kitchener, Schmidt, and Glaser, 1977; Glaser, 1979).

The successful termination of a criminal career seems to require detachment from other offenders and from a criminal subculture, and attachment to a conventional way of life that usually involves a family, law-abiding friends, and a job that holds promise for the future. The process by which offenders detach themselves from one way of life and become attached to another is not yet fully understood, but more research on this process could reveal as much about the causes of crime as do studies that focus on the way that people become involved in crime in the first place.

Summary

Individual acts of law breaking cumulate over time into a criminal career, which is both similar to and different from a legitimate career.

Certain contingencies influence the development of a criminal career. An individual's sex can close off access to some illegitimate occupations. Another important contingency is contact with the criminal justice system, which can influence the course of a criminal career through the labeling process. Offenders often alternate in a "zigzag path" between criminal activities and legitimate pursuits. Frequently they are recruited into criminal careers from a delinquent subculture or from occupations close to the underworld.

Typologies can be useful in developing theories to explain different patterns of criminal behavior. One potentially fruitful approach is to develop typologies that categorize offenders by the combination of crimes they commit over time.

Studies of delinquent careers find that a small number of offenders account for a very large proportion of all contacts with the police in any cohort. The chance of being stopped again by the police increases as the number of police contacts increases. People who have contact with the police while very young are especially likely to have further contacts. Delinquents show little inclination to specialize in one type of crime; this is true of adult career criminals as well. The time between police contacts becomes compressed as a delinquent career lengthens, indicating either increased delinquent activity or more attention to known offenders by the police. People who have police contacts as juveniles have a much greater chance of being stopped by the police as adults than do people who have no police contacts as juveniles. This could be because of the effects of labeling on young offenders, or it might be because of a continuity of law-violating behavior over time.

Most adult offenders do not plan their crimes in much detail. As they grow older, criminals increasingly commit their crimes for instrumental rather than expressive purposes. Intensive career criminals commit many more crimes than intermittent offenders do. These intensive offenders also engage in more planning and are more skilled and persistent in their criminal activity. As a result, they account for a disproportionately high percentage of all serious crimes.

Career criminals exit or retire from a life of crime for many reasons, but the exiting process usually involves a growing detachment from other offenders and a criminal subculture, and a growing attachment to a conventional way of life that includes a family and a job. Different theories of crime causation would explain exiting in different ways, but social control theory seems to make the most sense of the data we now have on the exiting process. The correctional system seems to play a relatively minor role in the process of exiting.

Important Terms

certification
contingency
criminal career
exiting

intensive offender
intermittent offender
radical nonintervention
typology

Review Questions

1. What is a criminal career? How does a criminal career differ from and how is it similar to a legitimate career? What contingencies influence the development of criminal careers? What is the "zigzag path" followed by some criminals?

2. What is a chronic offender? What background factors are associated with chronic offending?

3. What is the relationship between juvenile delinquency and adult crime?

4. What factors cause offenders to leave a life of crime? Does the correctional system play an important role in getting career criminals to "go straight"? How would differential association theory, the labeling perspective, anomie and differential opportunity theory, and social control theory explain the process of exiting a criminal career? Which theory explains exiting most convincingly?

Chapter 11
The Organization of Criminal Behavior

C rime is commonly regarded as the behavior of individuals, a view reinforced by crime statistics that emphasize the personal traits of arrested suspects. This individualistic perspective on crime permeates the criminal justice system: the insanity defense recognizes an offender's mental state as the basis for a not guilty finding, and treatment programs are person-oriented. Criminology has been heavily influenced by this attention to the individual offender: biological and psychological explanations, learning theories, and criminal career research all focus on the criminal behavior of individuals.

Because criminology in the United States has been embedded in sociology, a discipline that studies groups and organizations, the predominance of this individualistic orientation is surprising. This chapter looks at criminal behavior as a collective or socially structured activity, and examines the way that criminal groups and organizations develop, function, and persist.

Criminologists disagree about the extent to which criminal behavior is organized. Gottfredson and Hirschi claim that because criminals are low in self-control and pursue immediate pleasure, they are unlikely to participate in long-term, cooperative criminal enterprises. They argue that whatever organization is found among offenders is "imposed and maintained from without"; in other words, any apparently organized criminal activity is the result of "a post hoc interpretation by scholars or law-enforcement officials to account for a series of events that otherwise has no inherent structure or coherent purpose" (Gottfredson and Hirschi, 1990: 203).

Others disagree with Gottfredson and Hirschi, asserting that although not all criminal behavior is organized, some of it certainly is. Part of the disagreement about the extent to which criminal activity is organized is a result of different ideas about what it means for behavior to be "organized," so we first need to consider what sociologists mean when they speak of organization.

The Meaning of Organization

Social structure refers to recurrent, stable patterns of interaction among people. Within a system of patterned relationships that form a social structure are statuses (positions), roles (expected behaviors associated with those statuses), norms (standards of expected behavior), and sanctions (responses to violations of those norms). Social structure, which is the form or shape that social relationships take, can be distinguished from the actual people who are interacting at any given time. For instance, the organizational chart of a corporation, which describes the company's social structure, can be identical at two different times even if the actual people filling the statuses or positions in the corporation change.

One kind of social structure is a **group,** a set of relationships among people who interact on a face-to-face basis over time. Through communication among its members, a group develops common values, norms, and an identity or sense of "we-feeling." Members of a group are interdependent, being aware of and responding to one another; that is, a group is more than an

aggregate of people who happen to be in the same place at the same time but who do not interact much and have no sense of common identity. A group has a character of its own, apart from the behavior of its members, and it influences the behavior of its members, for example, by pressuring them to conform to shared norms. For this reason, studying groups that engage in crime, such as delinquent gangs or organized crime families, provides more knowledge about criminal behavior than just studying individual offenders.

Groups are characterized by **networks**, or ties among individual members. Networks exist among as well as within groups, with several juvenile gangs or several Mafia families sometimes tied to one another in a larger social structure. Loose networks also exist among the parties to a criminal transaction, such as the sale of illegal drugs or the fencing of a stolen painting. The participants in these transactions cannot be called a group or an organization, because they do not form a structure with durability and a shared sense of identity. However, the criminal activity itself is organized in the sense of being structured or patterned (Best and Luckenbill, 1994).

Primary groups, such as the family and the peer group, are small groups that have warm and personal relationships among their members. Members treat each other as whole people, rather than in terms of the specific roles they play, and they work together for shared goals. Primary groups are relatively permanent, and members who leave are not easily replaced. Whether juvenile gangs fit this image of a primary group has been debated by criminologists for years.

In contrast to primary groups, **secondary groups** are characterized by less emotional, less intimate attachments. Members who leave are replaced without much difficulty, and individuals are treated in terms of the roles they play for the group rather than as complete people. The group exists to achieve some common goal, but its members have other goals as well, and so their commitment to the group is less intense than that of the members of primary groups.

A large, complex secondary group that is deliberately created to achieve certain goals is called a **formal organization.** These organizations, which include corporations and universities, are characterized by a division of labor, which is a set of interrelated and specialized tasks coordinated with one another through clearly defined lines of authority and channels of communication. Members of formal organizations are treated impersonally in terms of the tasks they perform for the organization; from the point of view of the organization as a whole, they can usually be replaced with little difficulty. A **bureaucracy** is a formal organization that is rationally organized to pursue goals in an efficient manner. It has a complex division of labor, is rigidly hierarchical, relies on written records, requires specialization of its members, formally defines the expected behavior of its members, promotes them on the basis of how well they perform their assigned tasks, separates the world of work from the personal lives of its employees, and is not owned by those who work for the organization (Weber, 1979).

Some sociologists seem to have dismissed the idea that crime is organized behavior because it rarely, if ever, fits the image of a bureaucracy.

However, organizations of criminals do exist and can be described as varying along the following dimensions:

> "the *complexity* of their division of labor, including the number of members, the degree of stratification, and the degree of specialization of organizational roles"; "their *coordination* among organizational roles, including the degree to which rules, agreements, and codes regulating relationships are defined and enforced"; and "the *purposiveness* with which they specify, strive toward, and achieve their goals." (Best and Luckenbill, 1994: 11–12; emphasis added here)

Criminal organizations that are more complex, coordinated, and purposive offer their members a greater capacity for complex operations, more socialization into the ways of the organization, more elaborate services, and more security from external social control. Those who belong to the most highly developed criminal organizations are usually the most actively involved in crime themselves (Best and Luckenbill, 1994: 90).

Rather than being structured in complex, tightly coordinated, and highly purposive formal organizations, much criminal behavior is organized less formally in groups and networks in which offenders interact in predictable ways to carry out crime. This chapter investigates the extent to which juvenile delinquency, conventional crime, organized crime, and white-collar crime are organized activities.

Juvenile Gangs

The degree to which juvenile gangs are organized is a matter of dispute among criminologists. This disagreement stems in part from the different types of gangs that criminologists have studied: drug-dealing gangs seem to be more tightly organized than gangs that hang out on a street corner just to socialize. Because some juvenile gangs have become more tightly structured in recent years as they have entered the competitive and violent drug trade, recent studies would be more likely than older ones to conclude that gangs are highly organized. The site of a study can also affect the conclusions reached about gang organization; recent research indicates that few delinquents belong to gangs in Miami (Inciardi, Horowitz, and Pottieger, 1993: 154), but that many delinquents in San Diego do (Sanders, 1994).

The Unorganized Gang

Gottfredson and Hirschi (1990) claim that researchers have not produced convincing evidence that juvenile gangs have leaders and formal structures. They assert that "serious" studies have shown that male adolescent gang members cannot identify their leaders and resist efforts by others to do so. These gangs are unorganized, being no more than informal friendship networks, and their members neither like one another much nor feel very committed to the group. Participation in the gang is variable, and there are no rules of attendance. Moreover, much of the gang's activity is not truly group activity, but instead is simply the result of the presence of multiple adolescents in the same place at the same time; what seem to be groups are really aggregates. The presence of many adolescents in one place makes delinquent activity more likely, because there is safety in numbers, immunity from sanctions, and diffusion of responsibility. Gottfredson and Hirschi (1990: 207) conclude that "the reports of juveniles themselves are suspect as a source of information about the structure of gangs" and that "gangs are not structured in ways suggested by the classical image."

Lewis Yablonsky (1966) presents a similar picture of violent juvenile gangs. He suggests that because juvenile gangs engage in different activities, the degree to which a gang is organized will depend on the kind of behavior in which it specializes and the importance of group structure to that activity. **Social gangs** have a group identity, a relatively permanent structure, informal leadership based on popularity, and intimate interaction among members. **Delinquent gangs** have a "tight primary group structure" and are organized to carry out specific profitable crimes (Yablonsky, 1966: 145).

Yablonsky devotes most of his attention to the **violent gang**, a fighting gang that emerges spontaneously to defend a territory against rival gangs, often resorting to violence over trivial provocations. Leaders are described as self-appointed manipulators of younger members. Yablonsky characterizes the members of violent gangs as psychopaths who are unable to empathize with their victims or develop intimate bonds to others, including other gang members. Membership is fluid and participation is unpredictable; usually there is a small core of active members and a larger number of marginally involved participants. Gang members often speak of a large "pseudomembership" and an extensive network of allied gangs, but both are fictitious. Yablonsky (1966: 224) refers to violent gangs as "near groups" that are in a "partial state of organization"; they are more organized than collectivities such as mobs and crowds, but have less permanence and cohesion, a less well-defined division of labor, fewer shared norms, and less clearly defined role expectations than social gangs and delinquent gangs. Violent gangs do not need a tight organization to engage in episodic street fighting, whereas delinquent gangs that engage in systematic theft or drug trafficking require more structure to be successful.

William Sanders (1994) defines gangs in terms of their willingness to use deadly force to defend territory, attack other gangs, steal money, or engage in other group-related criminal activities. From his research in San Diego, Sanders concludes that gangs do not have strong leaders or hierarchical structures; instead, gang leadership is informal, derived from friendship cliques, and based on age, gender, and reputation. Gang cohesiveness is rooted not in hierarchical organization, but rather in loyalty to and identification with a neighborhood and its "homeboys." Sanders disputes Yablonsky's contention that gang members are incapable of forming intimate social bonds, but he supports Yablonsky's claim that the violent gang lacks a tight organizational structure. A study in St. Louis also found that violent gangs had loose organizational structures with diffuse goals, little solidarity, and few leaders.

Violence, which was usually an unstructured response to real or perceived violence by other gangs, served to unite members against a common enemy (Decker, 1996).

The Organized Gang

In his classic study *The Gang* (1927, 1963), Frederic Thrasher described gangs as coming together spontaneously at first, then becoming integrated through conflict with other gangs and with the community at large. These gangs have some of the features of formal organizations: an identity as a group, members' commitment, stability, exclusivity, and an internal structure with distinct statuses and roles. Two recent studies fit Thrasher's picture of the gang more closely than they do the image of the gang as an unorganized aggregate.

The Organization of Street Gangs   A study of thirty-seven street gangs in New York, Los Angeles, and Boston refutes the claim that juvenile gangs are no more than loosely structured collectivities. Instead, Martín Sánchez Jankowski (1991: 314) concludes that gangs

> are collectives in which the interaction of individuals, both leadership and rank and file, is organized and governed by a set of rules and roles. In short, they are organizations. Unlike other organizations, though, gangs function without a bureaucracy and this has tended to obscure their other organizational characteristics.... Ultimately, the fact that gangs have not been understood as organizations has crucially impaired our understanding of their behavior.

Gangs, as Jankowski sees them, are organized social systems that are closed to the public and keep much of their business secret from outsiders. However, because organizational survival is a major concern of gangs, they must deal with the external environment, gaining the support or at least avoiding the active antagonism of local residents and establishing links to local government, the criminal justice system, and the media. Concern for organizational survival also influences the gang's recruitment of new members, its provision of leadership, its development of rules to govern members' behavior, and its offering of incentives for members to continue to participate in the gang. Survival depends on the ability of the gang to meet its members' needs, which include entertainment, protection, and material well-being. Gangs allow their members to pursue personal goals, but they also try to bind them to the group through self-interest, moral incentives, and a code of behavior.

Gangs recruit members in several ways. Some use an approach similar to that of college fraternities, having a party or circulating information in the community to attract new members. Another recruiting strategy is to persuade local residents that they have an obligation to join the gang to help their community. Coercion is a third strategy, one used when a gang feels it has to increase in size rapidly; this happens when a gang expands its control to new territory, when it is defending itself against a rival gang's efforts to take over its territory, or when a new gang is formed.

According to Jankowski, to function efficiently gangs need formal leadership structures, defined roles for leaders and for rank and file members, and codes of behavior. One kind of leadership structure, which he labels "vertical/hierarchical," has three or four authority positions: a president, a vice president, a warlord, and sometimes a treasurer. Each officer has assigned duties and responsibilities; for instance, the president sets short-term goals, plans the gang's operations, and metes out rewards and punishments to members. This leadership structure is adopted by gangs that value control and efficiency in their efforts to amass material resources, gangs that are growing or taking over new territory, and gangs that need such a structure to compete successfully with other organizations, including the police.

The "horizontal/commission" type of leadership structure has several offices that are not ranked in a hierarchy; instead, officers are more or less equal in authority and share responsibilities. This leadership structure is found in gangs that are less concerned with accumulating material resources than with protecting their communities and families, and so there is not much need to maximize organizational efficiency. Cultural constraints, such as emphasis on family and unwillingness to submit to authority, make it difficult for some gangs to develop a vertical/hierarchical authority structure.

The third kind of authority structure identified by Jankowski is the "influential" model, an informal structure in which charismatic individuals influence gang activities even though they have no formal titles or offices. This structure is common in small gangs, in gangs whose members see participation as a transitional stage to adult roles that will soon take them away from the gang, and among people who object to a formalized authority structure. Members of this third type of gang see it as a way to build friendships they can rely on as adults; the influentials are those members who have traits that the others admire, such as loyalty to friends and community, fighting ability, and generosity.

All but one of the gangs studied by Jankowski had a cohesive organization that was the product of efforts to establish internal social control. One mechanism for establishing order was a code that defined appropriate behavior for fights among members, for interaction with women who were relatives and lovers of gang members, and for getting along in the gang's clubhouse. Some gangs had rules against heroin use, even though they tolerated the use of marijuana, cocaine, and alcohol. There were also rules about how changes in leadership were to be made, how certain behavior should be punished, and how leaders were to exercise power.

Jankowski suggests that some sociologists have downplayed the extent to which gangs have an organizational structure because they have observed gangs that were either in a pregang stage or in a state of dissolution. He accounts for his conclusion that gangs are more highly organized than others have found them to be by suggesting that recent changes in American society have forced gangs to become more structured. Contemporary gangs are more sophisticated than past ones because changes in the economy have reduced opportunities for youths from lower- and working-class backgrounds to find jobs that offer a promising career and upward social mobility. As a result, they increasingly rely on the organized criminal activities of gangs for income, often continuing to participate in the gang well into adulthood. Juvenile gangs have also become more highly organized in recent years because they have emulated adult crime groups such as Mafia families, at the same time that declining control of illegal markets by those Mafia families has opened new opportunities for juvenile gangs to establish profitable enterprises.

The Gang as a Business Enterprise   Felix Padilla's (1992) study of a Puerto Rican street gang in Chicago used biographical and observational methods to document the criminal activity of this group. Padilla (1992: 3) described the Diamonds as a "business establishment" that operated as a "street-level drug-dealing enterprise"; their business had "its own culture, logic, and systematic means of transmitting and reinforcing its fundamental business virtues."

The Diamonds began as a fighting gang that spent much time smoking marijuana; they did not become a drug-dealing operation until the late 1970s. A 1971 Illinois law that created harsh penalties for adult drug dealers led those dealers to turn to juveniles for help in distributing drugs, because those under the age of eighteen were not subject to the new sanctions. Eventually, the members of youth gangs recognized the money they could make by systematically organizing the drug trade in their neighborhoods. These enterprises were stimulated by the burgeoning demand for drugs, especially cocaine, during the 1970s. The Chicago drug trade flourished in the early 1980s with the development of an unusual organizational structure: a peaceful settlement that divided the city's gangs into two "gang nations" or alliances, with the expectation that disputes and violence would not occur among members of the same nation. This agreement was designed to reduce the gang violence that had been common during the 1970s, but the new structure also facilitated the development of stable enterprises that distributed illegal drugs, because it offered local gangs some security against competitors from outside their neighborhoods.

The Diamonds were a collective enterprise that had a distinctive ideology aimed at improving the well-being of its members: success was to be achieved not as individuals, as urged by the dominant American ideology, but rather through collective effort. Working in crews of three or more members protected the dealers against rival gangs, street criminals, and the police. The gang was supported by an ethnic community that provided a base of drug customers who were faithful to Diamond drug dealers, partly because the customers knew they could trust the dealers to provide high-quality drugs. Sometimes the Diamonds used a network of friends in the community to raise money to buy drugs to sell. Members of the community also helped gang members by refusing to provide information to the police. Belonging to the Diamonds thus offered members both a safe turf on which to sell drugs and a committed clientele.

The "hierarchical occupational structure" of the Diamonds was "an ordered arrangement of power, prestige, authority, and information" (Padilla, 1992: 111). The structure included a small number of drug suppliers and distributors, a larger number of cocaine and marijuana dealers, and several kinds of thieves. The suppliers and distributors (or "mainheads") were role models for those lower in the organization. There were few of them, and movement to that level in the gang was limited; those who did move up to that position usually had to organize a new section of the gang in a different territory. The mainheads bought large amounts of drugs and then hired other gang members to sell the drugs on the street. The street-level dealers either bought drugs from the suppliers with their own money or were "fronted" the drugs by the suppliers and sold the drugs at a small commission; these dealers regarded the gang as "their primary form of employment" (Padilla, 1992: 13). Newer and younger members of the Diamonds stole for profit, often being directed in their criminal activity by older members. They operated in crews of three or four, often targeting cars, and turned over much of what they got to the gang as a way of proving their commitment to the group.

Padilla's and Jankowski's studies indicate that present-day juvenile gangs are organized groups, even though they do not have the characteristics of a formal organization or a bureaucracy. Gangs are social structures in the sense that they have recognized leaders and identifiable if fluid memberships that interact over time. Gangs also have a sense of identity, as is evident in their having a name, wearing "colors," and spraying their turf with graffiti. In sociological terms, gangs are more than aggregates; they are groups that engage in organized activity.

Conventional Crime

Most conventional crimes are not committed by organized gangs of professional criminals, but those gangs do account for some of the largest losses due to robbery, burglary, larceny, and fraud. Networks of thieves and smugglers are often organized on a temporary basis to take advantage of a particularly lucrative opportunity; this is true for both the stolen-art trade and the illegal drug trade. Even conventional crimes of violence sometimes take an organized form.

Professional Theft

A **professional thief** is a skilled offender who is committed to crime as an occupation and thinks of himself or herself as a criminal. Professional crime is described by Mary McIntosh (1975: 12) as

> a relatively distinct occupational sphere [which] has its own patterning and continuity, whereas amateur activities, being only part-time, are much more influenced by a variety of circumstances, often peculiar to the individual criminal. Professional crime is thus distinguished not by its scale, or degree of turpitude or efficiency, but by its organisational differentiation from other activities.

Certain technical problems must be solved to engage in crime successfully, and organizations of professional criminals are designed for the efficient solution of those problems. According to McIntosh (1975: 24), the criminal underworld is an occupational community that serves the following functions for its members:

> It creates and develops the culture that establishes norms of working behaviour and appropriate work orientations; it provides people with contacts that help them in their careers, and referees who will vouch for their skills and character; it transmits information about new problems and techniques; it helps members in hard times; it offers congenial sociability to people whose hours of work, income, and even presence in the free world are irregular; it keeps trade secrets and does not betray members to outsiders.

Professional thieves sometimes work alone, but often they get together with other thieves to carry out specific crimes. The social organization of the underworld provides professional criminals with the contacts needed to find accomplices to help them carry out a particular criminal project. These networks of professional thieves, which are formed in high-crime communities and in bars and clubs, provide information about targets of theft and about fences who are willing to buy stolen goods at the best prices, and they offer some protection against arrest. Four kinds of organizations of professional thieves are picaresque, craft, project, and business organizations (McIntosh, 1975).

Picaresque Organization   A **picaresque organization** is a relatively permanent gang under the leadership of a single person, who sometimes relies on the support and advice of a few officers. Rank in this kind of organization determines a member's share of the profits, with shares decided before crimes are committed. This type of organization, which is characteristic of pirates and brigands, became less common after politically centralized states established control over the places where these criminals had traditionally found sanctuary.

Craft Organization   A **craft organization** develops "highly skilled routines for taking small amounts from a large number of victims" (McIntosh, 1975: 35). In these small and relatively permanent groups of two or three petty thieves or confidence tricksters, each member plays a well-defined role in the specific type of crime that the group commits. Pickpocketing, shoplifting, counterfeiting, and cheating at gambling produce profits that are shared equally among the members. Skills are often passed on by members of a subculture that has refined its techniques over the years. Typically, at least one member of the group acts as a lookout, and the person who actually steals the goods quickly passes them to an accomplice in order to avoid being apprehended with the loot.

Project Organization   A third type of criminal organization is the **project organization,** which brings together several criminals to commit one or a series of acts of robbery, burglary, fraud, or smuggling. Because these offenses are more lucrative than the kinds of crimes committed by craft organizations, their potential victims usually have taken measures to protect themselves against loss. These crimes are more complex and less routine than petty forms of theft, so they require skill, planning, and innovation.

Project crime does not usually involve a permanent organization of thieves, and those groups that do persist are usually in a state of flux, with thieves dropping out of "the life," moving, going to prison, or being replaced. A team assembled for a particular crime often breaks up after dividing the profits. Nevertheless, project organizations engage in structured criminal activity, even if the structure resembles a group more than a formal organization.

For any given project, specific tasks must be allocated to members of the group. Some individuals have specialties, such as defeating electronic security systems or breaking into safes, but most offenders are quite versatile. The 1950 Brinks robbery involved eleven thieves who had various skills, even though the crime probably could have been committed more efficiently with a smaller group (Behn, 1977). Even though the roles in a project organization might be interchangeable, it is necessary to coordinate the actions of the participants so that the group will function smoothly and carry out the tasks required for completion of the crime. Gangs of burglars often have one person act as a lookout while the others enter a building, break into a safe or otherwise locate valuable property, and carry the loot away. Often one member of a robbery gang is assigned to act as a "wheel man," stealing a car or license plates to enable the thieves to avoid identification; this person sometimes acts as a "peek man" or lookout for the gang, although other gang members might also perform that function (Conklin, 1972).

In project organizations, percentage shares or flat fees are determined before committing a crime. Some participants might be paid a flat fee for carrying out specific functions, such as stealing a getaway car or carrying messages. Tipsters who provide information about lucrative targets are often paid a flat fee; one robber who preyed on drug dealers because they were vulnerable and could not easily report their victimization to the police paid a tipster for guiding him to local dealers (Conklin, 1972). Flat fees and other expenses are deducted from the proceeds of the crime, and those who actually commit the theft divide the rest on some predetermined basis.

After completing a theft, offenders sometimes require the services of fences and fixers. They sell the stolen merchandise to a fence, who pays as little as possible for the goods and then profits from their resale (Klockars, 1974; Steffensmeier, 1986). Fences sometimes direct thieves toward particular targets or place orders for specific items (Walsh, 1977). Another part of the professional thieves' network is the fixer, sometimes a lawyer, who contacts victims, the police, or judges in an effort to have charges dismissed. Today this is apt to be done by offering to return the victim's property or compensate the victim for dropping charges; in the past, outright bribery of law-enforcement officials was more common (Sutherland, 1937; King and Chambliss, 1984).

One indicator of the group character of professional thieves, however they are organized, is their use of **argot** or cant, a specialized language that creates solidarity by differentiating them from outsiders (Maurer, 1955, 1964;

McIntosh, 1975). Argot is used when the offenders interact with other members of the underworld, but usually not when dealing with the straight world, because use of argot would then identify them as deviants. The argot that is used is closely linked to the kind of crime being committed. For instance, pickpockets in craft organizations use an elaborate argot in which different pockets and different means of taking wallets are given slang terms; the "stall" in the "whiz mob" picks out a "mark" and "steers" that potential victim into a position where the "tool" can take the wallet (Maurer, 1955, 1964).

The picture of professional thieves painted by "Chic Conwell," a thief interviewed by Edwin Sutherland (1937) in the 1930s, needs modification today. Conwell described thieving gangs as having an esprit de corps, or a "we-feeling" that provided the thieves with group support, and a code of behavior that required mutual aid, payment of debts to other thieves, and honest dealings with other thieves. This kind of loyalty seems a thing of the past, if it ever was common. One thief reports that there "is no loyalty among thieves today. There's no such thing at all. They have absolutely no loyalty. They'll beat one another to the money, you know, anything they can, they'll beat one another for their girls, or anything" (King and Chambliss, 1984: 78). The fact that groups of professional thieves are characterized by internal conflict and impermanence does not mean that they are not organized. The completion of individual crimes, or a series of offenses, often requires the development of a project organization, even if it does not persist for long.

Art Theft   Second only to the drug trade in profitability among international crimes, art theft is enormously costly; for example, an estimated $200 million worth of art was stolen from Boston's Isabella Stewart Gardner Museum on March 18, 1990. Most art theft is probably committed by project organizations, groups that are assembled to commit a specific theft and that use established networks to distribute the stolen art. However, one investigation of the black market in art regards it as more organized than this, describing it as "a tightly organized business operation which is all the more efficient for being excellently camouflaged within the honest trade" (Burnham, 1975: 37). History even provides examples of bureaucratically organized art theft. Napoleon Bonaparte looted art treasures throughout Europe, taking his director-general of museums on his campaigns, specifying what was to be stolen, and shipping the stolen treasures back to France. Adolf Hitler also engaged in systematic art theft, planning to use the stolen objects to turn his boyhood home in Austria into a pantheon of "Aryan" art. Hermann Goering used a government organization called Einsatzstab-Reichsleiter Rosenberg to loot art treasures, many of which became part of his personal collection, and Dr. Hans Posse used the Nazi party, the army, and the SS to steal art for the German state.

The way that art theft is organized is closely linked to the location of the objects to be stolen. Art in museums is easy to locate but difficult to steal, usually requiring elaborate planning by burglars and, occasionally, robbers. Works of art in private collections are more difficult to learn about; some thieves attend public exhibitions to determine who has loaned particularly valuable works, and others enlist the help of a domestic employee of a noted art collector.

Once valuable art is located, thieves must gain access to it. They might recruit into their gang a museum guard, an electronic security system specialist, an employee of the person who owns the art, or even a member of the owner's family. These insiders are either paid a flat fee or share in the profits of the theft in exchange for information about what art is available and how to steal it.

Most thieves have to find someone to buy the stolen art, which is often unique and well known, although several connoisseur-thieves have stolen art just to have it for themselves. Some art thieves work on commission, stealing objects that a dishonest collector or dealer orders in advance or expresses an interest in having. Other thieves have returned stolen art for a ransom. Thieves sometimes hire a restorer to alter a piece; this is often done with religious artifacts, antique furniture, and other objects not valued for their uniqueness. For paintings and sculptures, thieves might pay someone to fabricate bills of sale or letters attesting to the past presence of the piece in a well-known collection. They have also paid dishonest dealers or other thieves to buy the stolen art at an out-of-the-way country auction, thereby giving the object a history of having been legitimately sold in a public place.

Art thieves often move the stolen art out of the country after a theft, making it harder for law-enforcement agents to solve the crime. The international movement of stolen art involves highly developed criminal networks, with organized crime syndicates that distribute illegal drugs reportedly using the same networks to move stolen art; for instance, the movement of antiquities looted from the Turkish countryside to art galleries in Munich, Germany, involves an established network that is apparently engaged in drug trafficking as well. Less organized groups of thieves have paid diplomats, airline employees, and clergy to carry stolen art out of the country. Stolen art is moved by circuitous routes to countries where collectors have the money and the willingness to buy it and where local laws are protective of those who buy such art. Today, much stolen art ends up in Japan and Switzerland, where the law makes it difficult for victims of theft to retrieve works of art from people who have purchased them "in good faith" (Conklin, 1994).

One project organization moved a collection of recently uncovered Moche treasures from Peru to California, where they were sold to dealers and collectors. Antiquities dealer David Swetnam, who eventually served four months in a federal prison camp for his role in the smuggling of the antiquities, convinced his American backers to invest $80,000 in the purchase of the artifacts. He then contacted Fred Drew, a former American diplomat living in Lima, Peru, and a central player in a well-organized Peruvian network of grave looters, intermediaries, and dealers. Swetnam mailed Drew the money in a series of checks for less than $10,000 each, so as to avoid having to fill out currency transaction reports. Drew then purchased textiles, ceramics, and gold and silver pieces that the looters had taken from the Sipán tomb and sold to local dealers. Drew hired an expediter with reported ties to the Medellín drug cartel to ensure the safe export of the treasures from Peru to

England; the expediter was paid 5 percent of the value of the property, half of which he used to bribe customs officials. In England, an accomplice of Swetnam named Michael Kelly, who was both a British citizen and a resident of the United States, used the recent death of his father as a cover for shipping three trunkloads of the treasures to the United States; the shipments were accompanied by a letter claiming that the pieces had been collected by Kelly's father in the course of his travels around the world during the 1920s, prior to Peru's passage of a law prohibiting trade in its cultural property. In the United States, Swetnam created a convincing front as a well-to-do art dealer, living in a California mansion where his wife, formerly a maid there, was house-sitting for the owner. He entertained potential clients at cocktail parties and luncheons, conveying the impression that he owned the house. Eventually, this international smuggling network was broken up when Michael Kelly reported it to U.S. Customs agents (Nagin, 1990; Kirkpatrick, 1992).

Drug Smuggling and Dealing

Much drug smuggling and drug dealing is not carried out by highly structured and enduring organized crime gangs, such as Mafia families, but is instead engaged in by project organizations put together for a particular deal. Patricia Adler (1993) found that marijuana smugglers in southern California had to establish a relationship with a broker who would get the drug to them from the producers in the country in which it was grown, usually Mexico. Brokers sometimes supplied the marijuana producers with the equipment to harvest a crop, a place to cure it, and a place to package it. Cocaine smugglers had to establish ties to a foreign supplier, typically in Colombia; this was usually done through referrals in a more formal manner than that used by marijuana smugglers to establish ties to brokers, because cocaine suppliers operated more secretively and in a more organized fashion than marijuana brokers. Smugglers who brought the drugs into the United States by air had to hire a pilot; they also needed to recruit drivers to move the drugs to safe locations and partners to help distribute the drugs.

Adler characterizes the world of southern Californian drug smugglers and dealers as "a system of social organization which patterns the relationships of its members" (Adler, 1993: 63). She describes this world as a series of concentric circles (see Figure 11.1), with smaller circles representing closer relationships, and larger circles representing relationships that are less close. Interaction among partners was intense and involved mutual trust. One kind of partnership was the crew, a stable group of individuals who could perform the specific tasks necessary to smuggling drugs. The head of the crew provided emotional and financial support to the other members and settled differences among them. More common than crews were groups of dealers and smugglers that were less enduring but more flexible; often these groups engaged in several deals, then dissolved. Crews and groups had a division of labor in which specialists played certain roles, and their members agreed before a deal to some profit-sharing arrangement.

FIGURE 11.1

The Social Organization of Drug Smuggling and Dealing

Source: Patricia A. Adler and Peter Adler, "Relationships Between Dealers: The Social Organization of Illicit Drug Transactions," *Sociology and Social Research,* Vol. 67, No. 3 (1983), p. 265. Copyright, University of Southern California, 1983. All rights reserved. Reprinted with permission.

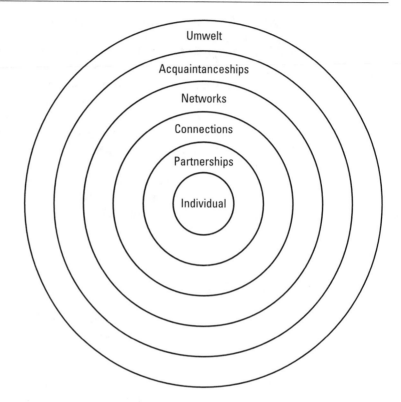

Connections in the drug world were important for carrying out drug transactions and often endured for some time. One kind of connection was a supplier; both dealers and smugglers tried to minimize the number of suppliers they used. A second connection was a circle of dealers who bought and sold similar quantities, often among themselves. Smugglers and dealers were also connected to their customers, but customers were less highly valued than suppliers because they were more numerous and easier to replace.

Less close than a dealer's or smuggler's relationships with partners and connections were their networks, acquaintanceships, and *umwelt.* Networks were made up of friends in the drug world with whom dealers and smugglers did not usually do business, but with whom they shared common interests and life styles. Members of networks offered one another advice and information, sometimes loaned each other money, and were used to check on the trustworthiness of someone who might become a business associate. Acquaintanceships were ties to people the dealers and smugglers knew socially but had no business dealings with; there was always a possibility of doing business in the future, but these relationships were primarily social in nature. The final circle of this organized social world was an umwelt, "a world of relationships that are based not on concrete knowledge but on reputation," that is, on knowledge of what others were doing and how trustworthy they were (Adler, 1993: 77).

Adler found that the illicit drug market in southern California was not monopolized by a criminal syndicate; instead, it involved competition among numerous enterprises of different degrees of organization and durability. Even though the drug market as a whole was not tightly organized, the activities of smugglers and dealers were structured in ways that made it possible for them to import and distribute drugs. Groups of smugglers and dealers had some degree of cohesion and a division of labor, and their members were committed to a life of crime; they were project organizations of professional criminals. These groups were more flexible and independent, and less centralized and formally structured, than organized crime groups or syndicates such as Mafia families. Groups of smugglers and dealers rarely lasted long enough to grow large; besides, greater size would have increased the chance of their being detected by the police. Rather than being regulated by corruption and violence, as are illegal markets dominated by organized crime groups, the world of dealers and smugglers was regulated informally by the allocation of prestige in the form of reputation. Instead of a formal organization, a peer subculture recruited and socialized new members of the drug trade, teaching them job skills, argot, the norms of the trade, and justifications for violating drug laws (Adler, 1993).

Violent Crime

Most violent crime is not highly organized, but there are exceptions; for example, Murder Incorporated was a gang of professional contract killers that operated in the 1930s and 1940s. Violence can even be bureaucratically organized, as was the case with the genocidal policies of the Nazis. The Cross-Cultural Perspective shows how the crime of forcible rape has been used as a conscious policy of terrorism.

Sometimes violent crime is socially structured in less formal ways, with individuals who share values and attitudes joining together to commit crime. Gang rape is committed by men who interact over time and share attitudes toward women that are conducive to sexual assault (Alder, 1985; Sanday, 1990). Some violent hate crimes are committed by white supremacist groups that are organized to carry out such acts. In these cases, there is more than simply an aggregate of individuals who are low in self-control; there is an identifiable group of interacting individuals who share common attitudes toward their victims and join together to commit crime on a systematic basis.

Organized Crime

The fourth kind of professional criminal organization identified by Mary McIntosh is the **business organization,** a permanent structure that profits from extortion and the provision of illegal goods and services. Here we follow common usage and refer to this kind of structure as organized crime, even though much criminal activity that is not called organized crime is still organized behavior. Organized crime is syndicated crime, the violation of the law on a large-scale basis by ongoing, tightly structured groups devoted to the

A CROSS-CULTURAL PERSPECTIVE

Rape in Bosnia

In 1996, a United Nations tribunal indicted eight Bosnian Serb military and police offi-cers for the rape of Muslim women. It was the first time that organized sexual assault by itself had ever been designated a war crime. All parties to the war in Bosnia engaged in sexual abuses, but the Bosnian Serbs were the primary offenders, raping an estimated 20,000 Muslim women in 1992 and 1993, after which reports of such assaults declined significantly.

The Serbs used rape as part of their policy of "ethnic cleansing," a practice that began when their troops established military command of an area. That command was then taken over by local auxiliary forces who knew the people in the area; they marked the homes of non-Serbians and ordered them to wear white armbands. Non-Serbians were then locked up, beaten, and raped or murdered. Following the rapes, officers arrived and offered residents the official documents they needed to move elsewhere, leaving the area free for Serbs to settle.

Concentration camps were built specifically for the purpose of sexually abusing women. There the victims were repeatedly raped, often by several men; they were also beaten, shot, and stabbed. Rapes were committed as sadistically as possible, often in front of members of the victim's family. Mothers and daughters were raped at the same time, and children as young as twelve were sexually assaulted. In some cases, soldiers forced Muslims to rape members of their own families. These assaults led to serious deterioration in the physical and psychological health of the victims; many suffered depression, and some attempted or committed suicide.

Rape victims who became pregnant often had to bear the children because they were locked up until it was too late to have abortions; many of these infants were aban-doned. Pregnant rape victims who were free to do so sought abortions at local hospi-tals, often quite late in their pregnancies. Some women were raped repeatedly until they became and stayed pregnant, with one rapist telling his victim, "Now you will bear a little Serb." The rape victims were treated with contempt by the authorities and even by members of their own families. The stigma of having been raped reduced the chance that these women would marry and have children in the future.

Sources: Based on Mladen Loncar, "Rape as 'Ethnic Cleansing,'" *New York Times,* January 10, 1993, p. 74; Marlise Simons, "For First Time, Court Defines Rape as War Crime," *New York Times,* June 28, 1996, pp. A1, A6.

pursuit of profit through criminal means. What distinguishes organized crime from other types of structured criminal activity are the durability and com-plexity of syndicates, which have some of the traits of formal organizations: a division of labor, a hierarchical authority structure, and coordination among various statuses. Members of organized crime groups are paid regularly or given a share of the organization's illegal profits. To remain successful, these groups must enjoy immunity from arrest, which they try to do through cor-ruption of law-enforcement agents. They must also thwart efforts by com-

Organized violent crime, including rape and murder, characterized the war in Bosnia. Here workers excavate the common grave of the Serbian victims of a 1995 massacre by Muslim and Croat forces.

petitors to take over their businesses, which they often accomplish through the use or threat of violence. Violence and demands for loyalty are used to ensure that members of the organization continue to work on its behalf.

McIntosh argues that barriers to entry into the four types of professional criminal activity are associated with the optimum size of the organization needed to carry out crime successfully. Entry into professional crime is harder when the optimum size of the firm is larger; for example, entry into syndicated crime is more difficult than entry into craft or project crime. This is because large-scale criminal organizations require more skill, specialization, training, and coordination, and creating such a structure is more difficult than putting together a craft or project group.

Gottfredson and Hirschi (1990) dispute the claim that a significant amount of crime is committed by rationally structured gangs that work together efficiently and competently over long periods of time. They argue that organized, long-term pursuit of goals by criminals is inconsistent with evidence that offenders lack self-control and are untrustworthy, unreliable, and uncooperative. What organizations do exist, they say, are ephemeral, with few lasting long enough to achieve their goals. Other scholars disagree, presenting evidence that organized crime groups do exist and do engage in profitable criminal activities over time.

The Mafia in the United States

Sociologists have reached different conclusions about the extent to which Italian-American Mafia crime families are organized, at both the local and the national levels. They have described these crime groups as formal organizations, as kinship structures, as patron-client relationships, and as business enterprises.

The Mafia as Formal Organization   Law-enforcement agents and some sociologists see Mafia families as rationally designed, highly structured formal organizations that operate much like modern bureaucracies. Entry into these organizations is tightly controlled, specific jobs are assigned to the members, and illegal profits are pursued in an efficient and systematic manner.

At the head of such a Mafia family, depicted in Figure 11.2, is a boss who has absolute authority over the other members. Below the boss in the hierarchy are an underboss who acts as chief deputy and assistant, a staff of counselors or advisors, lieutenants who act as buffers between the higher echelons and the lower-level workers, and soldiers who operate illegal and sometimes legitimate enterprises for the family. According to sociologist Donald Cressey (1972: 36, 38), for this organization to function there must be an enforcer who "makes arrangements for killing and injuring (physically, financially, or psychologically) members, and occasionally nonmembers"; a corrupter who "bribes, buys, intimidates, threatens, negotiates, and sweet-talks himself into a relationship with the police, public officials, and anyone else who might help 'family' members secure and maintain immunity from arrest, prosecution, and punishment"; and a corruptee who is a public official, usually not a member of the organized crime family, and who can wield influence on behalf of the organization's interests.

Many law-enforcement officials believe that Mafia families in the United States are organized in a national confederation led by a commission of powerful bosses. In 1986 in New York City, eight defendants were convicted of operating a national commission that decided what illegal enterprises to pursue, determined which families would control different criminal activities in particular geographic areas, and settled disputes among families. Some criminologists have made a strong case that the Mafia is not organized at the national level, pointing to internal inconsistencies in the testimony that gangsters have offered as proof of such organization (Hawkins, 1969), and citing research that has found no evidence that local crime groups are controlled by a national commission (Ianni, 1972; Chambliss, 1978).

The Mafia as Kinship Structure   Based on his participant-observation study of one organized crime family, Francis Ianni (1972: 9) concluded that Mafia families are "a form of social organization patterned by tradition and responsive to culture," a form more like a kinship structure than a formal organization. He found that a code of conduct governs the behavior of family members: be loyal to the larger family rather than to nuclear families within it, act like a man, do nothing to disgrace the family, and do not discuss family business with outsiders (Ianni, 1972: 139–148). Ianni (1972: 154) described the organizational structure of this crime family as follows:

1. The family operates as a social unit with social organization and business functions merged.

2. All leadership positions, down to the "middle management" level, are assigned on the basis of kinship.

3. The higher the position in the organization, the closer the kinship relationship.

FIGURE 11.2
A Mafia Family

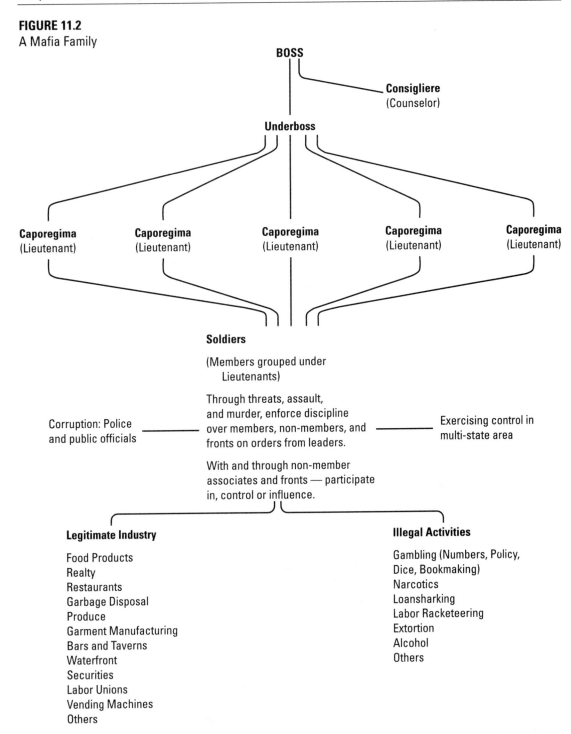

Source: President's Commission on Law Enforcement and Administration of Justice, *Organized Crime.* Washington, D.C.: U.S. Government Printing Office, 1967, p. 9.

4. Leadership positions in the family are assigned to a central group of fifteen family members, all of whom have close consanguineal or affinal relationships which are reinforced by fictive godparental relationships as well.

5. Members of this leadership group are assigned primarily to either legal or illegal enterprises, but not both.

6. Transfer of monies from illegal to legal and back into illegal activities takes place through individuals rather than companies and is part of the close kin-organization of the family.

In addition to claiming that individual crime families are organized around principles of kinship, Ianni also argues that Mafia families in different cities are linked together by intermarriage. He points out that of the more than sixty bosses participating in the 1957 meeting in Apalachin, New York, nearly half were related by blood or marriage, and many others were related by fictitious kin roles. Ianni (1972: 172) describes Italian-American crime families as "actually a number of lineages linked together into a composite clan," asserting that the universality of clan organization and its shared behavior has led some observers to conclude erroneously that there is a highly structured national or even international Mafia conspiracy. In fact, says Ianni (1972: 153), the various crime groups "have no structure apart from their functioning" and are not a nationally organized cartel.

The Mafia as Patron-Client Relationships   Joseph Albini (1971) regards Mafia families in the United States and Italy as hierarchical systems of power held together by a series of complex patron-client relationships among crime family members and between crime family members and people in legitimate society. Patrons look out for the best interests of their clients, and the clients repay their patrons with loyalty and service. Patron-client relationships are embedded in kinship networks, creating a complex structure for organized crime, but not one that can be described as a formal organization. Organized crime changes as the relative power of patrons changes and as new kinship ties are formed. This fluidity is functional for crime families, allowing them to adapt in ways that maintain organizational efficiency, meet new public demands for goods and services, and thwart law enforcement. In this patron-client model, influential crime family bosses who have been described as members of a national ruling commission are seen instead as powerful patrons who serve other members of organized crime, for instance, by intervening in disputes among family members.

The Mafia as Business Enterprise   Another view of organized crime is that all entrepreneurs develop organizations to carry out the tasks necessary to producing and marketing goods and services; what distinguishes organized crime from legitimate enterprises is simply the illegality of the goods and services in which it deals (Smith, 1978, 1980). Both illegal and legal enterprises must adapt to changes in the market to grow and to remain profitable, and both legal and illegal markets are characterized by competition and by alliances among entrepreneurs. (See the Cross-Cultural Perspective box.)

Economist Peter Reuter (1983) concluded that none of the three illegal markets in New York City that he studied—loan sharking, numbers betting, and bookmaking—was controlled by the Mafia, and that each was best characterized as a competitive market with many entrepreneurs. He suggested that an illegal monopoly would be vulnerable to attack by law enforcement,

A CROSS-CULTURAL PERSPECTIVE

The Russian Mafia

After the loss of power by the Communist Party and the breakup of the Soviet Union, social conditions in Russia were ripe for the emergence of organized crime. There was a strong public demand for goods and services that were in short supply. Relaxed economic regulations facilitated the bribery of officials and industrial managers. The Russian police had little public support and proved inadequate to the task of fighting organized crime. The legal system, designed for a socialist economy, could not deal with the complexities of the emerging free market. One gang member has described the Russian "mafia" as follows:

> "You know that in our country the government offers no structure or control. Without these things, a nation falls apart. The mafia is all that's holding the country together. We *do* provide structure, and when we take over a business, that business works. It's noble work. A young man of ambition, someone who wants to have an effect on this society: he'd have to be a moron to think the way to do it is to join the Parliament. If he's smart, he'll join the mafia." (cited in Solomon, p. 38)

There are about 5,600 separate gangs in Russia, with an average of twenty members each. Perhaps 4 percent of these gangsters operate abroad, primarily in the United States and Europe, and especially in South Brooklyn and in Berlin, Germany. The gangs in Russia, many of which are tightly structured and ethnically based, allocate spheres of influence among themselves. Legal authorities have been ineffective in reducing the number of these gangs; those that are broken up are quickly replaced with others.

These gangs have many illegal sources of income. According to a presidential commission, protection rackets are especially lucrative, with 70 to 80 percent of all private enterprises making payoffs to gangsters. Payoffs average between 10 and 20 percent of an enterprise's total revenue, or about half of its profits. The price of consumer goods increases when victims pass on the cost of payoffs to buyers. Russian gangsters also profit from illegal drugs, prostitution, gambling, money laundering, the smuggling of firearms and nuclear material, and the resale of any goods that are in short supply, including cars, food, furniture, clothing, and building supplies.

Violence by the "Mafiya" has been facilitated by an increase in the number of unregistered firearms available in Russia. Gangs have used lethal violence to curb competition from rival drug dealers and from legitimate businesspersons. Businesspersons who were also members of the Russian Parliament have been killed in disputes with gangsters, and the director of Moscow's largest television station was murdered in 1995, apparently by gangsters whose business interests would have been hurt by his plan to drop their commercials from his station. Such violence has reportedly dissuaded legitimate entrepreneurs from going into business, and experts estimate that gangsters now control about half of all free enterprise in Russia.

Sources: Based on Stephen Handelman, "Inside Russia's Gangster Economy," *New York Times Magazine,* January 24, 1993, pp. 12–15, 30–34, 40, 50; Andrew Solomon, "Young Russia's Defiant Decadence," *New York Times Magazine,* July 18, 1993, pp. 16–23, 37–42, 51; Fred Kaplan, "Underworld, Rife in Russian Firms, Infiltrates Politics," *Boston Globe,* May 9, 1994, pp. 1, 6.

and that the recent involvement of many law-enforcement agencies in the fight against organized crime has made it impossible to corrupt all of the agencies that would have to be neutralized for a single criminal enterprise to dominate an illegal market. Although Reuter presents a strong case that the three illegal markets in New York are not monopolized by the Mafia, various organized groups (including Mafia families) are involved in the business of supplying illegal goods and services there. Organized groups of criminals do exist within illegal markets that are not organized in the sense of being dominated by a single crime group such as the Mafia.

Whatever the basis of their organization, individual crime families seem to be highly structured. However, the strength of some crime groups, particularly Mafia families, has been weakened in recent years by enforcement of the Racketeer Influenced and Corrupt Organizations (RICO) Act (see the Using Criminology box).

Emerging Forms of Organized Crime

In recent years, ethnic and national groups other than Italian-Americans have developed organizations to pursue profits through illegal means (see Table 11.1). Much of this activity involves networks that buy illegal drugs in other countries, ship them to the United States, and distribute them to users; most prominent are the Colombians in the cocaine trade and the Chinese in the heroin trade. Drug trafficking is not the only source of profit for emerging organized crime groups; they have also been involved in extortion, gambling, prostitution, and the smuggling of illegal immigrants.

Organized crime is well entrenched in the Chinatowns of large American cities. Highly structured crime groups in these communities can be traced to the mid-1800s, when organizations known as tongs were formed to assist and protect immigrants from China. In addition to their legitimate functions, the tongs became involved in gambling and prostitution. During the 1970s, the tongs formed alliances with gangs of young immigrants who had recently come from Hong Kong. From their association with the tongs, the gangs receive protection, legal assistance, and respect in the community. In exchange, the tongs use the youth gangs for intimidation, for example, to guard their gambling establishments and houses of prostitution. The youth gangs also engage in extortion, "protecting" shop and restaurant owners from violence by the gangs themselves in exchange for weekly payoffs. They also rob people who frequent local gambling dens and massage parlors (Kifner, 1991).

One Chinese gang in New York that is involved in gun smuggling, the heroin trade, prostitution, gambling, and extortion also runs a lucrative trade in illegal immigrants, charging residents of China between $15,000 and $50,000 each to be smuggled into the United States. The criminal organizations responsible for this activity include Chinese gangs in the United States and Taiwanese businesspersons with connections in China, Hong Kong, New York, and elsewhere (Faison, 1993b). The organizers of the smuggling racket protect themselves from arrest by creating several levels between themselves and those who pilot the ships; when ships are intercepted, no one admits to any knowledge of who

USING CRIMINOLOGY

RICO and Organized Crime

In 1970, the federal government passed the Racketeer Influenced and Corrupt Organizations Act, commonly known as RICO. This law prohibits the operation of an enterprise that shows a pattern of racketeering and allows for the prosecution of all members of a criminal organization if any member commits two or more specified crimes as a part of that organization's work. Membership in such an organization is thus defined as a crime, allowing prosecutors to show in court how organized crime families are structured and how they go about their daily business.

RICO was not used regularly against organized crime until 1981, when the U.S. Supreme Court ruled that the law was not restricted to cases involving organized crime's infiltration of legitimate businesses, but could be used against any criminal racketeering scheme. RICO defines racketeering in broad terms and provides for the forfeiture of assets and for a twenty-year prison term.

The law has been used successfully to prosecute organized crime leaders in New York, Boston, Los Angeles, New Orleans, and Cleveland. Attorneys for organized crime figures have complained that the broad nature of RICO allows for the prosecution of many defendants for crimes committed by a few, and they have argued that charges brought under RICO are difficult to defend against. Business executives have criticized RICO for being too broadly written, claiming that this results in the use of that law to bring civil actions against legitimate corporations in fraud cases. These executives argue that such cases were not the original intent of RICO and that the law should be limited to traditional forms of racketeering such as loan sharking and illegal gambling. However, G. Robert Blakey, a law professor who wrote the law when he was on the Senate staff, disagrees: "The law addresses the crimes of organizations. If organizations act like racketeers, we should call them racketeers" (cited in Muro, 1989: A28).

Source: Based on William F. Doherty, "RICO—A Broad Tool for Prosecutors," *Boston Globe,* February 28, 1986, p. 9; Mark Muro, "Some Say RICO Is Reaching Too Far," *Boston Globe,* March 26, 1989, pp. A25, A28.

---

financed the trip. Efforts by law-enforcement agents to stop these ships have caused smugglers to change their routes and then turn to commercial airlines to move illegal immigrants into the country (Faison, 1993a).

For their passage to the United States, the illegal immigrants make an initial payment of at least $1,500, usually raising the money by selling personal and family possessions. Increased competition among smugglers has reduced the amount that needs to be paid in advance; having well-to-do relatives in the United States also keeps the initial payment to a minimum. The immigrants get forged passports and counseling when they arrive in the United States. Their relatives there sometimes pay the balance, but more often the immigrants themselves go to work for several years as indentured servants to pay off the balance. They work long hours at low wages in miserable conditions in restaurants, laundries, and garment factories; some

TABLE 11.1   A Comparison of Ethnic/International Organized Crime Factions

Ethnic Group	Origins	Exemplars	Notable Illicit Activities	North American Locales	Comments (Unique or Notable Characteristics)
Chinese (tongs, Triads, street gangs)	17th century China	Wo, 14 K	Gambling, extortion, drug trafficking, robbery, prostitution, murder, arms dealing, racketeering	California, New York	• Tongs and street gangs possess many of the characteristics we used to define organized crime groups
Japanese Yakuza	7th century Japan	Yamaguchi Gumi	Weapons trafficking (to Japan), methamphetamines trafficking (to Japan), murder, gambling, extortion, bookmaking	California, Hawaii	• All Yakuza gangs are highly structured/hierarchical • Legitimate activities include banking and real estate • Annual revenue estimated to be $32 billion
Colombian drug traffickers	Colombia has a long history of social banditry	Medellín and Cali cartels	Cocaine trafficking	New York area, Miami, Los Angeles, Houston	• Complex infrastructures employ about 24,000 according to one estimate • Criminal activities limited to those associated with the drug trade
Vietnamese gangs	Arrival of immigrants in U.S. in the 1970s	Born to Kill	Extortion, prostitution, auto theft, arson, gambling, armed robbery	Chicago, New Orleans, Houston, Washington, DC, Los Angeles, Boston	• Not a major problem compared to other ethnic organized crime groups • Closely linked to Chinese organized crime • Considered to be the most ruthless of Asian groups
Jamaican posses	Kingston, Jamaica. Came to U.S. in mid-1970s	Shower Posse, Spangler Posse	Cocaine (crack distribution), firearms trafficking, money laundering, fraud, robbery, kidnapping, murder, auto theft	New York, Miami, Los Angeles, San Francisco, Detroit, Philadelphia, Dallas, Washington, DC, Chicago, Houston	• One of the most violent organized crime groups in the country • 40 posses in the U.S. have 22,000 members • Control 30 to 40 percent of U.S. crack trade
Russian Mafia	Emigres arrived in large numbers in the 1970s	Odessa Malina, Organizatsiya	Marketing illegal goods (drugs, weapons, stolen cars), extortion, forgery, loan-sharking, racketeering, gasoline bootlegging (#1 activity)	New York, New Jersey, Philadelphia, Los Angeles, Chicago, Baltimore, Dallas, Cleveland, Phoenix, Toronto	• Perestroika reforms coupled with economic mayhem fueled a tremendous growth in new forms of organized crime

Source: Dennis J. Kenney and James O. Finckenauer, *Organized Crime in America.* Belmont, Calif.: Wadsworth, 1995, pp. 272–273. Copyright © 1995 by Wadsworth Publishing Company. Reprinted with permission.

These are some of the 250 illegal Chinese immigrants apprehended after a freighter smuggling them into the United States ran aground off New York City in 1993.

women have been forced to work as prostitutes in Chinatown brothels. To collect the balance of the fare, smugglers have threatened violence against the immigrants and their families, sometimes kidnapping the immigrants and releasing them only when their relatives pay a ransom for their release (Myers, 1993; Treaster, 1993).

There is evidence that Chinese Triads, highly organized secret societies that date to the seventeenth century, are a major force in the international heroin trade. One study of a drug ring uncovered a complex conspiracy in which each person had a designated task to carry out; some participants knew other members of the conspiracy, but some did not. Those involved in the drug ring were either members of Triads or had Triad connections, but the researcher found no evidence of any direct role played by a Triad organization in the operation of the drug ring. He concluded as follows:

> [D]ifferent structures appear to exist at the various levels of the heroin trade and include production, export, import, and local distribution. There is no denying that there is significant involvement of ethnic Chinese at all these stages or that distribution is facilitated by this common ethnicity, but there is no evidence supporting any overall organizational control or coordination. (Dobinson, 1993: 383)

To prove involvement by a criminal organization, Dobinson seems to require evidence of a higher level of control and coordination than is usually characteristic of either criminal enterprises or their legitimate counterparts. Highly organized multinational corporations buy raw materials from local producers, and they rely on independent stores around the world to sell their finished products; these corporations are still formal organizations, even if they do not control every stage of the process of production and distribution. In similar fashion, international drug traffickers often contract out the distribution of the drugs they import to local criminal groups rather than become involved in that risky enterprise themselves. Dobinson's research does provide evidence of structured criminal activity: an enduring group of individuals who coordinate the performance of the tasks necessary to make a profit through illegal means.

White-Collar Crime

Gottfredson and Hirschi's (1990) general theory of crime contends that white-collar crime is uncommon, simple in its techniques, condemned by business culture, and committed by people with characteristics similar to those of conventional offenders. Disagreeing with all aspects of this description, Gary Reed and Peter Cleary Yeager (1996: 377) show that white-collar offenders are not simply people with low self-control who pursue self-interest, but rather that their motivations and the opportunities they exploit are "socially constructed in a broad institutional context that emphasizes profit making and in organizational contexts that privilege success and survival." Much white-collar crime is condoned or even encouraged, rather than condemned, by business culture. This type of crime is frequently quite complex, impeding detection by law-enforcement agents. White-collar criminals often break the law on behalf of their company or work group, rather than pursue a narrow self-interest. There is also ample evidence that white-collar crime, especially corporate law breaking, is not rare.

Rather than investigating the actions of groups and organizations that engage in white-collar crime, researchers have usually focused on individual white-collar offenders who violate the law in an organizational setting by using organizational resources. Business enterprises established for criminal purposes would be classified as organized crime groups rather than white-collar offenders. Kitty Calavita and Henry Pontell (1993: 539) argue that much of the fraud committed in the savings and loan industry during the 1980s more closely resembled organized crime than white-collar crime, because the offenders sought personal gain through criminal conspiracies that were "premeditated, continuous, organized in networks, and shielded by connections to public officials."

White-collar criminals sometimes create structures within or across formal organizations in order to violate the law. Wayne Baker and Robert Faulkner's (1993) innovative analysis of three price-fixing conspiracies in the heavy electrical equipment industry during the 1950s found that the structure of illegal networks is driven by the need for concealment, unlike the structure of networks in legal business activities, which are driven by the need for efficiency. Illegal networks that have low information-processing requirements (i.e., relatively little need for data, knowledge, and intelligence with which to execute a sequence of tasks) tend to be decentralized, because they can be run acceptably, if not most efficiently, in that way. However, illegal networks that have high information-processing needs tend to be centralized, because face-to-face interaction among top executives is needed to carry out complex tasks and make difficult decisions in secret.

Deal-making in the securities industry also depends on "[c]omplex networks of relationships and information exchanges" (Reichman, 1993: 66). A central player in these networks is the investment banker, who mediates the flow of assets between sellers and buyers. Illegal insider trading occurs when people with access to nonpublic information that has value beyond a specific deal trade or tip others in their network to trade on the basis of that information. It is difficult to police insider trading because "the direct evidence of illegal trades is often embedded in sophisticated inter-organizational networks that lie beyond traditional means of surveillance and information access" (Reichman, 1993: 87).

Some kinds of white-collar crimes require more organization than others. In a study of white-collar offenders convicted in federal courts, Weisburd et al. (1991) found it useful to differentiate crimes by their degree of organizational complexity: offenses were rated as more complex if they were patterned, used organizational resources, involved more co-conspirators, and occurred over longer periods. The most complex crimes they studied were antitrust violations and securities fraud; the least complex were bank embezzlement, credit fraud, and tax fraud. Between those extremes in organizational complexity were mail fraud, false claims, and bribery. More research is needed to determine the extent to which white-collar offenders who engage in crimes of varying degrees of complexity develop group structures to enable themselves to break the law.

Summary

Criminologists have given less attention to organized criminal activity than they have to the behavior of individual offenders. Some have argued that crime is rarely committed by groups or organizations that endure over time. Crime by tightly structured bureaucracies is probably uncommon, but much crime is committed by criminals who belong to groups and organizations that have crime as their major purpose.

The extent to which a juvenile gang is organized depends on its purpose. One study found that violent or fighting gangs are not as highly structured as delinquent and social gangs. Gangs involved in the highly competitive drug trade are especially likely to be well organized. Research indicates that many juvenile gangs do have a structure: identifiable leaders, strategies for recruiting and socializing new members, defined statuses and roles, and codes of behavior.

Most conventional crime is probably not committed by groups and organizations, but some of it is. Professional thieves sometimes come together in project organizations, groups assembled to commit one or a series of crimes of robbery, burglary, fraud, or smuggling. These groups assign specific tasks to their members to carry out crimes smoothly, agreeing on the distribution of the proceeds before committing a crime. Project organizations sometimes pay nonmembers a flat fee to steal a car, carry messages, or point out lucrative targets. Art theft is a costly crime that is often done by project organizations, which are put together from international networks of thieves, smugglers, intermediaries, and dealers. Project organizations also smuggle and deal drugs, with crews and groups assembled for particular deals. Even violent crime is sometimes organized, with groups and even nations systematically murdering or raping designated victims.

Some criminologists argue that organized crime is not highly structured at the national level, and that it is even weaker at the local level than law-enforcement agents claim. Other criminologists assert that organized crime groups have a structure, but they have different ideas about the basis of that structure; organized crime has been seen as a formal organization, a kinship structure, and a set of patron-client relationships. Organized crime groups have also been analyzed as business enterprises that differ from legitimate ones only in the illegality of the goods and services in which they deal.

Little research has been done on the organizations and networks that exist among white-collar offenders. An organization established for the purpose of committing crime would be treated as organized crime rather than white-collar crime, but informal networks also develop among people who engage in such white-collar crimes as price-fixing and insider trading.

Important Terms

aggregate

argot

bureaucracy

business organization

craft organization

delinquent gang

formal organization

group

networks

picaresque organization

primary group

professional thief

project organization

secondary group

social gang

social structure

violent gang

Review Questions

1. What is social structure? What are aggregates, groups, formal organizations, and bureaucracies?

2. In what sense are juvenile gangs organized? What kinds of juvenile delinquency are most likely to give rise to an organized gang?

3. What are the four kinds of organizations of professional thieves in Mary McIntosh's

typology? To what extent can groups that engage in art theft and groups that engage in drug smuggling and dealing be characterized as project organizations?

4. What are the different views about the organizational basis of the American Mafia? What kind of evidence would support or refute each position?

PART IV

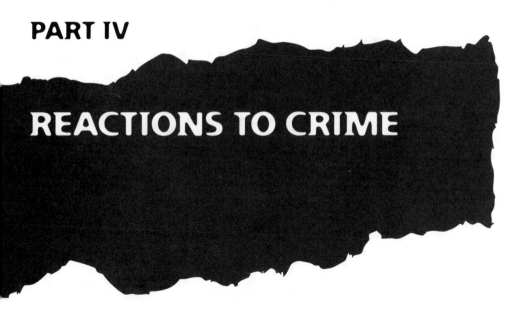

REACTIONS TO CRIME

Chapter 12 deals with community reactions to crime. We look at the fear of crime and at the informal social control of criminal behavior, including the way that architectural design might foster control and thereby curb crime. Bystander responses to crime and collective reactions such as urban patrol groups are also explored.

Chapter 13 provides an overview of the criminal justice system. We look at the history and organization of the police and the way officers do their job. We examine the criminal courts, including bail and plea bargaining. Disparities in sentences by race, social class, and sex are investigated. Prison conditions and parole are discussed. Finally, the changing role of the victim in the criminal justice system is explored.

Chapter 14 investigates four rationales for punishment: deterrence, incapacitation, retribution, and rehabilitation. We look at research on deterrence, the idea that the threat of punishment can keep people from breaking the law. Incapacitation is the idea that crime can be prevented simply by locking up offenders. Retribution or just deserts is the philosophy that punishment should inflict suffering on offenders commensurate with the harm they have inflicted on others. Rehabilitation, the idea that offenders can be treated in ways that will reform them and keep them away from crime in the future, is explored by looking at evaluations of program effectiveness.

Chapter 15 looks at the conservative, liberal, and radical approaches to the crime problem. It investigates crime and politics in the United States since the 1960s and explores three major strategies of reducing crime: reforming the criminal justice system, situational crime prevention, and dealing with the causes of crime.

Chapter 12
Community Reactions to Crime

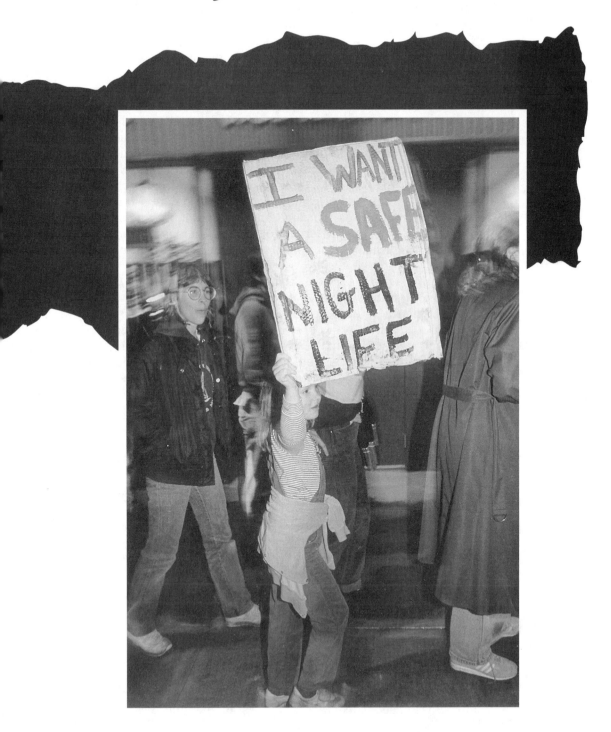

Toward the end of the last century, the French sociologist Emile Durkheim (1895, 1933: 73) defined crime as behavior that shocks the sentiments found in all "healthy" consciences. According to Durkheim, those sentiments are intensely held and specific to particular situations, and they are the basis of criminal codes. Crime is thus behavior that offends a shared sense of what is valued and worth pursuing, and punishment is a reaction to that behavior. Durkheim claimed that because people are brought together in their opposition to acts that violate the law, crime actually enhances social solidarity within a community.

One form of societal reaction to crime is **social control**, a process that brings about conformity to society's norms and laws. **Formal social control** includes efforts by the police, the courts, and correctional institutions to bring about conformity to the law; we examine those agents of the criminal justice system in Chapter 13. **Informal social control**, or the reactions of individuals and groups that bring about conformity to norms and laws, includes peer and community pressure, bystander intervention in a crime, and collective responses such as citizen patrol groups. There is reason to believe that the amount of formal social control varies inversely with the amount of informal social control; that is, the agents of the criminal justice system exercise more control when informal social control is weaker (Black, 1976: 107–111).

Donald Black (1983) has argued that some criminal behavior functions as a kind of informal social control, with both violent crime and property crime sometimes being the result of efforts to engage in self-help, correct injustice, and pursue justice against perceived wrongdoers. Murders in which people kill because they feel insulted by their victims, vandalism in which youths destroy school property because of hostility toward teachers who have hurt their self-esteem, and theft from stores that overcharge customers can be seen as efforts to correct serious wrongs perpetrated by others—that is, as efforts to exercise informal social control over unjust actions. Informal efforts to control crime sometimes violate the law; for instance, vigilante groups that lynch suspected offenders violate due process rights and break federal laws by denying others their civil rights.

Contrary to Durkheim's idea that responses to crime enhance community solidarity, one common reaction to crime, fear, seems more likely to undermine solidarity and thereby reduce informal social control. Before looking at the ways that individual and collective responses to crime might informally control law-violating behavior, the consequences of the fear of crime are examined.

Fear of Crime

Fear of crime became so widespread in the United States during the 1960s and 1970s that in 1978 the National Institute of Law Enforcement and Criminal Justice listed "fear" along with "crime" on its research agenda of problems in need of federal support. Noting the "unusual elevation of a psychological construct to the level of a major social problem," Rosenbaum and Heath (1990: 222) have characterized the period from 1968 to 1977 as the "war on crime" and the following decade as the "war on the fear of crime."

Individual property crimes have modest effects on fear, although they might have a large cumulative effect because they are relatively common. A relatively small percentage of American adults, perhaps 3 percent, are injured in crimes of violence during any given year. Why, then, is the fear of crime so pervasive?

Conversations with relatives, friends, and neighbors who have been victims of crime generate fear; this "vicarious victimization" seems to predict an individual's level of fear better than his or her own victimization experiences (Lavrakas, 1982). The mass media heighten fear, especially among heavy television viewers who live in high-crime areas and especially if the reported crime is gruesome, local, and without apparent motive (Rosenbaum and Heath, 1990). Fear of crime is also associated with weak ties to a community, a sense among residents that they cannot control what is happening in their neighborhood, a lack of powerful local organizations, the absence of knowledge about effective ways to prevent crime, and a perception of incivility ("signs of crime") in the area. These signs of crime include gangs of teenagers hanging out on street corners, drug addicts and prostitutes in doorways, abandoned and burned-out buildings, signs of vandalism such as graffiti and broken windows, and people urinating in public (Lewis and Salem, 1986; Skogan, 1986).

Changes in fear of crime do not always reflect changes in crime rates. Figure 12.1 shows that fear of walking alone at night increased from 1967 to 1975, a period over which violent crime rates nearly doubled. However, fear remained steady or even declined a bit from 1975 to 1993, despite a significant increase in violent crime rates over that time.

Fear is generated by "signs of crime" such as this van-dalized car on a street in the South Bronx.

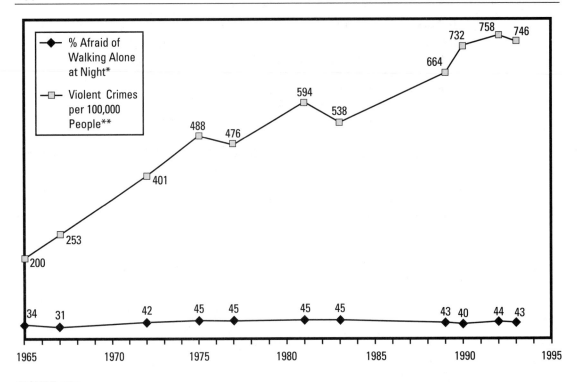

FIGURE 12.1

Fear of Walking Alone at Night and Rates of Violent Crime, 1965–1993

* Responses to Gallup Poll question: "Is there any area near where you live—that is, within a mile—where you would be afraid to walk alone at night?"

** Rates per 100,000 people for total violent crimes (murder and nonnegligent manslaughter, forcible rape, robbery, and aggravated assault) reported to the FBI.

Source: Based on data from Kathleen Maguire and Ann L. Pastore, eds., *Sourcebook of Criminal Justice Statistics—1994.* Washington, D.C.: Bureau of Justice Statistics, U.S. Department of Justice, 1995, pp. 167, 305.

Kenneth Ferraro (1995) has distinguished the fear of crime, which is emotional, from the perceived risk of crime, which involves a cognitive judgment. Using data from a national survey, he found that fear of crime was a product of the perceived risk of victimization, which in turn reflected actual risk as measured by official crime statistics. Ferraro found that women were more fearful than men, despite women's lower rates of victimization (except for rape); he attributed this to the effect that women's fear of rape had on their fear of other kinds of crime. Ferraro also showed that when gender and community of residence are taken into account, older people are no more fearful of crime than younger people, an assessment that reflects the elderly's relatively low rate of victimization. From his research, Ferraro concluded that fear of crime is, for the most part, based on realistic assessments of the risks that people have of becoming crime victims.

Consequences of the Fear of Crime

Fear of crime causes people to lock their doors and windows, install expensive alarm systems and bright lighting, engrave identification numbers on their possessions, enroll in self-defense classes, and buy firearms, watchdogs, electronic beepers, and cellular phones. A 1994 survey found that, as a result of their concerns about crime,

> 32 percent of Americans had carried a protective device such as mace or a whistle,
>
> 28 percent had bought a car alarm or car-locking device,
>
> 27 percent had purchased a gun, and
>
> 20 percent had installed a home security system (Maguire and Pastore, 1995: 173).

Money spent on protective measures might escalate to the point that it exceeds losses from the crimes those measures are intended to prevent.

Fear of being raped, robbed, and assaulted causes people to stay home rather than venture outdoors. When they do go out, they might do so only during daylight hours or might travel only in groups. At night, they use their cars to travel short distances or take cabs to avoid walking on unlit streets. Fear leads people to avoid certain neighborhoods, which then become even more deserted and dangerous. People may give up visiting the library, attending meetings, and using local parks. They forfeit income from overtime work that would require them to return home after dark.

A few people even respond to their fear of crime by moving to communities that seem safer. A 1980 Gallup poll found that crime was the leading reason given for dissatisfaction with cities: 24 percent of those who wanted to move from the city in which they lived cited crime as the reason, compared with 16 percent who mentioned overcrowding and 12 percent who mentioned the absence of job opportunities (Herbers, 1981). The high and rising rate of violent crime is a major reason that many white South Africans have moved abroad; one physician noted that at least 40 percent of his 1984 graduating class had emigrated (Daley, 1995).

Fear of rape restricts women's freedom of movement. Children and adolescents who are raped often stay out of school for some time; they may even transfer from schools to avoid questions and social discomfort. Adult rape victims often need outside help in homemaking and parenting, because of either physical injury or psychological distress. Some adult victims quit their jobs or stay away from work for a time in order to avoid having to talk about the rape (Burgess and Holmstrom, 1976; Gordon and Riger, 1989).

The fear of crime often becomes generalized to a fear of the streets, especially in communities that have high crime rates. As Jane Jacobs (1961: 30) has said, "When people say that a city, or part of it, is dangerous or is a jungle what they mean primarily is that they do not feel safe on the sidewalks." The public nature of the streets and sidewalks evokes a fear of strangers who are encountered there. As one observer notes: "The street is public, and the public display of tabooed behavior threatens to make it part of daily life. Openness gives such behavior an actuality and carries the threat of public acceptance and approval" (Rhodes, 1972: 36). (See the Using Criminology box.)

Fear and Trust   Social life, especially in large cities, requires a faith that others will abide by the law. Crime can reduce that trust, although some research finds that fear of crime is not strongly associated with mistrust and suspicion (Skogan, 1981). Even burglary, a relatively common nonviolent offense, can create mistrust. Imagine how the couple in the following incident felt:

> It was in Briarcliffe, N.Y., where a young couple went to dinner one evening at a local restaurant, and returned to find their car apparently stolen. After reporting it to the local police, they returned to their home and the next morning were surprised to see the car in the driveway, with an envelope on the windshield.
>
> "There was an emergency and we had to borrow the car," the note read. "Please excuse the inconvenience, but perhaps these two theater tickets will make up for it." The couple, surprised but pleased, told the police that their car had been returned, and the next Saturday used the theater tickets.
>
> When they returned that night, they found that their house had been completely looted. (Andelman, 1972: 49)

The burglars used the trust most people feel to their advantage; probably the victimized couple became less trusting of strangers and maybe even of their neighbors. This crime was not a violent one; the impact on interpersonal trust might well be even greater for victims of rape, robbery, or assault.

A dramatic example of the harmful effects of the fear of crime occurred in Atlanta, Georgia, several years ago. Between May 1979 and July 1981, twenty-nine young blacks disappeared; all but one were later found murdered. During this time, young blacks in the city were traumatized by their fear that they would be the next victim. Tests showed that children became less verbal and more withdrawn, a change that was greatest in the neighborhoods where the murder victims had lived. Children became more mistrustful of strangers; even interviewers had a difficult time approaching them. The children also suffered a decline in self-esteem and self-confidence. They became more hostile toward others, fought more at school, and carried weapons to defend themselves. Nightmares became more common. Fear of the dark, fear of school, fear of being left alone, and fear of being outdoors increased. Participation in sports and organized youth programs declined. Parents sometimes exacerbated these fears by being overprotective, an understandable response (Prugh, 1981; Rawls, 1981; Stuart, 1981). When Wayne B. Williams was arrested for some of the murders and eventually convicted of two of them, the murders stopped and tensions abated. Whether the reactions to the murders have had long-term effects on Atlanta's children can be determined only by follow-up studies.

One crime that did have long-term effects on the victims was a bizarre kidnapping in Chowchilla, California, in 1976. A school bus with twenty-six children was hijacked, and the children were buried underground in a truck trailer

USING CRIMINOLOGY

Reducing the Fear of Crime

Fear of crime has many harmful consequences, and policy makers have tried to develop programs to reduce it. In 1982, the National Institute of Justice awarded a grant to the Police Foundation to evaluate fear-reduction programs implemented by the police in Newark, New Jersey, and Houston, Texas. The police in those cities thought that by reducing fear they might prevent crime, and crime prevention was one of their primary tasks.

Careful evaluation of Newark's efforts to reduce fear found that the Coordinated Community Policing program was effective in reducing fear. The first component of this program was a storefront police community center that provided walk-in reporting of crimes, distribution of crime prevention and Operation I.D. information, recruitment for and holding of meetings of block watch groups and other local organizations, and coordination of the door-to-door activities of beat patrol officers. The second component of this program was a directed police-citizen contact program, which assigned officers to visit residents in order to elicit information about their fears, provide follow-up assistance and information, encourage citizens to become involved in block watch and neighborhood organizations, and distribute crime-prevention information.

Newark's Coordinated Community Policing program increased residents' satisfaction with their neighborhood and reduced their fear of personal victimization, their concern about property crime in the area, and their perceptions of social disorder problems and property crime in the community. The program created a sense among residents that they could improve things and increased police officers' sense that they were serving the public.

A fear-reduction program in Houston had similar effects. The Citizen Contact Patrol was designed to give residents the feeling that the police were present and involved in the community. Officers on routine car patrols stopped to get acquainted with citizens in their homes and businesses and tried to elicit the help of those citizens in defining local problems. This program reduced fear of personal victimization and perceptions of the amount of crime and social disorder in the community; it also increased satisfaction with the neighborhood as a safe place to live.

A second component of the Houston program was the Police Community Station, a storefront office to which citizens could come for information or to report crimes. It was designed to increase citizens' interaction with the police and enhance a sense of community; this was done through monthly meetings on topics of local interest. This station led to a reduced fear of personal victimization and to decreased perceptions of the amount of crime and social disorder in the area.

The third component of Houston's program was the Community Organizing Response Team (CORT), which worked to organize the community. Officers identified local residents who would host block meetings and who would meet with the police to discuss local problems. These organizations, which eventually were taken over by local residents, mounted such programs as a neighborhood clean-up campaign, identification of "safe houses" for helping children, a drug information meeting, and a program to get people to mark their household property with identification numbers. The CORT program did not reduce fear of crime, but it did lower the amount of crime and social disorder that residents perceived in the community.

Sources: Based on Hubert Williams and Antony M. Pate, "Returning to First Principles: Reducing the Fear of Crime in Newark," *Crime and Delinquency* 33 (January 1987), 53–70; Lee P. Brown and Mary Ann Wycoff, "Policing Houston: Reducing Fear and Improving Service," *Crime and Delinquency* 33 (January 1987), 71–89.

for sixteen hours; eventually, they dug their way out. Nearly five years later, those children, who were between five and fourteen when the kidnapping occurred, still showed effects. They experienced nightmares, feared ordinary things such as cars and dogs, and manifested an "on guard" mistrust of everyone. Some blamed themselves for their own victimization. They had distorted senses of time, thought, and perception. Adults experiencing stress of this sort often use denial as a defense mechanism, but the children did not. They faced the reality of the event and the threat that it posed for them. Most of them continued to fear another kidnapping, even five years later (Timnick, 1981).

One response to dramatic crimes against children has been the development of school programs, books, videocassettes, and records to teach children self-defense techniques and a wariness of strangers. Critics suggest that such efforts might exacerbate the insecurities felt by children and their parents and instill a deep-seated suspicion of all strangers. This suspicion of strangers can be seen in changes in Halloween trick-or-treating over the years, with many parents restricting their children's activities to school parties or ringing the doorbells of only people known to the parents. Despite the paucity of documented cases of harm to children on Halloween, fear of being given poisoned candy or an apple containing a razor blade persists.

Fear and Community Ties   One study of community responses to crime concluded that

> collectivities will unite and react to crime if there is a community able to identify itself as insiders and if an opposing group of outsiders (in a sociological rather than geographical sense) can be identified. [This perspective] does not argue that solidarity will be increased within a geographical area where there are few crosscutting ties and where individuals feel no sense of community. (Podolefsky and DuBow, 1981: 10)

The heterogeneity of many American communities and the high rate of geographic mobility of Americans mean that in many communities the conditions necessary for a unified response to crime do not exist.

Fear of crime can have severe consequences for a community, including

1. physical and psychological withdrawal from community life;
2. a weakening of the informal social control processes that inhibit crime and disorder;
3. a decline in the organizational life and mobilization capacity of the neighborhood;
4. deteriorating business conditions;
5. the importation and domestic production of delinquency and deviance; and
6. further dramatic changes in the composition of the population. (Skogan, 1986: 215)

These changes can, in turn, lead to even higher crime rates in the community.

Fear of crime generates suspicion and mistrust in homogeneous small towns as well as in heterogeneous urban communities. In his book *In Cold*

Blood, Truman Capote (1965) reports that a common reaction to the brutal murder of a family of four in Holcomb, Kansas, was suspicion of long-time friends and neighbors. A woman who owned a local café remarked:

> One old man sitting here that Sunday, he put his finger right on it, the reason nobody can sleep; he said, "All we've got out here are our friends. There isn't anything else." In a way, that's the worst part of the crime. What a terrible thing when neighbors can't look at each other without kind of wondering! Yes, it's a hard fact to live with, but if they ever do find out who done it, I'm sure it'll be a bigger surprise than the murders themselves. (cited in Capote, 1965: 70)

Others in the town concurred; for instance, the brother of one of the victims said, "When this is cleared up, I'll wager whoever did it was someone within ten miles of where we now stand" (cited in Capote, 1965: 88). When two outsiders to the community were apprehended, "the majority of Holcomb's population, having lived for seven weeks amid unwholesome rumors, general mistrust, and suspicion, appeared to feel disappointed at being told that the murderer was not someone among themselves" (Capote, 1965: 231). Many refused to believe that the two strangers had committed the murders. The café owner said, "Maybe they did it, these fellows. But there's more to it than that. Wait. Some day they'll get to the bottom, and when they do they'll find the one behind it. The one who wanted Clutter out of the way. The *brains*" (cited in Capote, 1965: 231; emphasis in the original).

These reactions do not indicate that people always unite in response to crime, even in homogeneous and closely knit communities where the offenders are outsiders. Instead, dramatic crimes and persistently high crime rates seem more likely to breed mistrust, insecurity, and weakened attachment to the community.

Informal Control of Crime

Because only 1 or 2 percent of all serious crimes are reported to the police and lead to arrest, conviction, and imprisonment, the formal sanctions of the criminal justice system are probably less important in controlling criminal behavior than are informal sanctions such as group censure and bystander intervention. Loss of esteem in the eyes of relatives and peers might be a more significant cost for an offender than a court's judgment that a crime has been committed. For instance, white-collar offenders are apparently affected more by accusation and indictment than by a criminal conviction. Concern for the good opinion of friends, relatives, and neighbors is a strong force controlling deviant behavior in Japan, where an internal "social policeman" induces conformity out of fear of losing face (Clifford, 1976).

Community and Informal Social Control

By creating fear and mistrust, crime weakens community solidarity and diminishes informal social control. This can, in turn, increase crime as interpersonal pressures on potential offenders to abide by the law are attenuated. One indicator of the effectiveness of a community's standards in controlling deviance is the proportion of all crimes in the community that are committed by local residents. In a study of crime in Honolulu, Andrew Lind (1930: 218) concluded: "An area capable of maintaining the strength of its prohibitions is likely also to discourage its wayward residents from attempting the violation of taboos within the boundaries of the district, although it may not succeed in entirely repressing the behavior." Similarly, riot activity during the 1960s was more common where there was no "extensive informal social interaction," and thus little informal control over potential rioters (Warren, 1969).

Mechanical and Organic Solidarity   Simple preindustrial societies, such as tribal groups, are characterized by more intimate relationships and more social integration than are modern industrial societies. In simple societies, primary groups such as the family and the peer group are relatively stronger than they are in complex societies. These simple societies are held together by what Durkheim (1895, 1933) called **mechanical solidarity**, a unity based on shared values and norms and on the similarity of functions performed by all members of the society. Children in these societies learn shared values and norms through face-to-face interaction; this socialization process perpetuates the collective conscience over generations.

In larger and more complex societies, primary groups are relatively weaker, and secondary groups such as corporations, labor unions, and schools become more important. Interpersonal relationships are less intimate, and people carry out very different tasks in their daily lives. Complex societies are integrated by **organic solidarity**, a unity based on an interdependence of functions, much as in a complex biological organism. In modern industrial societies, the collective conscience is less strong than it is in simple societies, and so legal institutions develop to control behavior. The overall severity of formal sanctions is less in complex societies, as normative diversity increases and some acts that are violations of the collective conscience in simpler societies are redefined as private matters (Durkheim, 1895, 1933; Green and Allen, 1981–82). However, legal sanctions are still invoked against people who violate intensely held values and norms.

Small Towns and Large Cities   Related to the idea that informal social control is stronger in simpler societies is the notion that informal control is greater in small towns than in larger cities. If informal social control is indeed stronger in small towns, it would help explain a fact discussed earlier in the book: crime rates, in general, are lower in smaller communities.

Evidence on the real nature of informal social control in small towns is mixed. A study of the Massachusetts Bay Colony in the seventeenth century found that the small size and cultural homogeneity of the community helped control deviant behavior by pressuring potential deviants to conform (Erikson, 1966: 169–170). Informal controls operate most effectively where people know each other well and interact on a regular basis, and small and homogeneous communities seem to be best suited to this kind of interaction.

In general, there is probably less informal social control in large cities than in small towns. The large size of the city means that residents have a difficult time distinguishing strangers from residents, and the heterogeneity of the city means that many neighborhoods include a variety of values and norms. Urban residents encounter many people on a day-to-day basis and have to screen out some of the input they receive in order to prevent "informational overload" (Milgram, 1970: 1462). The multitude of demands on city dwellers generates "norms of noninvolvement" that lead to mistrust of strangers, a desire for privacy, and withdrawal from social interaction (Milgram, 1970: 1463). Urban residents are more likely than the residents of small towns to deal with others in terms of the roles they play rather than on a personal basis. Thus, urban residents probably will be concerned only with paying for their groceries at a supermarket checkout counter, but small-town residents might ask the local grocer how his sick wife is feeling or how his children are doing in school.

A study of reactions to crime in cities, suburbs, small towns, and rural areas in Missouri found that large-city residents were the most likely to think that crime would occur in their community. Those people were also the most likely to say that their neighbors would not call the police about a burglary they witnessed. A majority of the residents of all communities believed their own community was safe, but city dwellers were the least likely to feel that way. When asked what made their own community safe, more residents of rural areas and small towns than residents of suburban and urban areas mentioned informal controls, such as a social network in the community that would lead bystanders to intervene in a crime. In comparison to the residents of small towns and rural areas, people in the suburbs and cities were more likely to say that crime in their community was kept in check by formal agents of control such as the police. Urban residents were thus the most likely to expect crime, and they relied more on formal than on informal means to control crime in their community (Boggs, 1971).

One study examined formal and informal social control in two Israeli communities (Schwartz, 1954). One community was a collective in which there was no formal mechanism to resolve legal disputes. The other community was a semiprivate settlement that had a judicial committee to handle legal disputes. According to the researcher, the collective did not need a legal committee because behavior was informally controlled through intense and frequent face-to-face interaction. The semiprivate settlement was characterized by considerably less interaction and less consensus; much everyday behavior was not visible to members of the community. Consequently, informal control was less effective in the semiprivate settlement, and formal control was needed. This study suggests that the structure of interpersonal relations is more important than size alone in determining the degree of informal control in a community. Intense and regular interaction, normative consensus, and surveillance of behavior are conducive to the informal control of behavior.

Differences among Urban Communities In developing nations, the process of migration from tribal villages to large cities sometimes reduces informal control over deviant behavior. For instance, in Liberia

the effectiveness of tribe and family as agents of social control has always depended upon the cohesiveness of the particular unit. In the urban areas, this cohesiveness increasingly gives way to individualism and the vacuum created by the decline
in family and tribal authority has only been filled by the impersonal sanctions of
the law. (Zarr, 1969: 194)

A comparison of two communities in the city of Kampala, Uganda, found
that the area with less crime had greater social solidarity, more interaction
among neighbors, more participation in local organizations, less geographic
mobility, and more stable family relationships (Clinard and Abbott, 1973:
149). There was also greater cultural homogeneity and more emphasis on
tribal and kinship ties in the community with the lower crime rate. These
conditions alleviated the anonymity that recent migrants to the city might
otherwise have felt. Crime in the community with the lower rate was also prevented by strong primary group ties among residents, which made strangers
to the area conspicuous.

Surveys carried out in England and Wales in 1982 and 1984 found that
communities with weaker social organization had higher rates of crime and
delinquency. One indicator of weak organization was the presence of unsu-
pervised teenage peer groups such as gangs; these groups were more common in communities that had higher rates of crime and delinquency. The
high-rate communities were also characterized by two other indicators of
weak social organization: sparse friendship networks and little participation
by residents in local organizations (Sampson and Groves, 1989).

A study of two neighborhoods in Cambridge, Massachusetts, supports
these conclusions. Although residents of the two communities were similar in
several ways, the community with the higher delinquency rate was less
socially integrated. Residents of the community that had the higher delinquency rate were more heterogeneous in religion and ethnicity, knew fewer
neighbors by name, thought they had less in common with their neighbors,
and liked the community less. They were no more tolerant of deviance than
were adults in the community that had less delinquency, but the residents of
the high-rate area were less likely to do something about delinquency if they
observed it. More adults in the area with the high delinquency rate said that
people ought to mind their own business and not interfere when the children
of their neighbors committed delinquent acts. This unwillingness to do
something about observed violations of the law creates "an atmosphere in
which delinquency can grow more easily.... [T]he lack of social integration
appears to have certain direct effects in a lowered level of social control of
delinquent and predelinquent activities" (Maccoby, Johnson, and Church,
1958: 49, 51). Here we see that the informal control of crime and delinquency
is greater in some urban neighborhoods than in others. The degree of informal control is thus related to the social structure and the nature of social relationships in a community, rather than to the absolute size of the community.

Feeling unsafe in an urban neighborhood means not having a sense of
security when in public places such as streets, sidewalks, and parks (Jacobs,
1961). Fear leads to the desertion of these public places, and so informal con-

trols that would check crime if people were there are weakened. The presence of people on the street creates surveillance of public places and attracts the attention of others to the streets, thereby reducing opportunities for crime. Fewer people on the street means less patronage of local businesses, which can cause shopkeepers to close early or move their businesses to other neighborhoods. A study of slum neighborhoods in Chicago found "impersonal domains" that were deserted and seen as dangerous at night, even though informal control over deviance was maintained in those areas during the day by businesspersons and their customers (Suttles, 1968: 36–37).

This evidence suggests a crime-generating cycle in which responses to crime actually increase the crime rate. In this model, fear of crime reduces interaction in public places, which decreases informal social control there; this leads to an increase in actual and perceived crime rates, which can further reduce interaction in public and begin the cycle anew. In contrast to this crime-generating model is a crime-reducing model suggested by routine activities theory. A study that used NCVS victimization data from twenty-six cities concluded that robbery increased fear, decreased interaction, and undermined community solidarity. However, instead of increasing crime in the neighborhood by reducing informal social control, the reduction in social interaction actually decreased crime, apparently by restricting opportunities to commit crime. By limiting people's daily activities to their homes, fear apparently kept the amount of crime lower than it would have been had people spent more time outside their homes (Liska and Warner, 1991).

Defensible Space and Informal Social Control

Informal control of criminal behavior can be enhanced through architectural design. Architect Oscar Newman (1972, 1973, 1996) claims that citizen involvement in crime prevention is needed and that it is possible to construct residential complexes that deter crime by creating **defensible space**. Defensible space involves the subdivision and design of housing to allow residents to distinguish stranger from neighbor. The design of housing can reinforce or create opportunities for surveillance of a building and its surrounding grounds by eliciting from residents a feeling of territoriality and a sense of proprietary interest in the protection of the community.

A survey of residents of New York City housing projects found that more than half felt unsafe. Newman (1973: 92) claimed that this sense of insecurity had important consequences: "Fear, in itself, can increase the risk of victimization through isolating neighbor from neighbor, witness from victim, making remote the possibility of mutual help and assuring the criminal a ready opportunity to operate unhampered and unimpeded." Project residents were less threatened by crime if they knew more of their neighbors, and they were more likely to know their neighbors in housing projects where architectural design facilitated interaction.

Housing design can enhance interaction and foster interest in nearby areas, thereby creating informal control over behavior. Crime might be reduced by making the interior spaces of large buildings more visible to people outside the buildings. Design can define private and semiprivate space near and within buildings. For example, the area enclosed by an L-shaped building often becomes the focus of surveillance and informal control by residents of the apartments that face the enclosed area, especially if the building is only a few stories high. Apartment clusters also create zones of influence by residents if shared areas are defined as private and are carefully watched. When children play in hallways or on playgrounds near a building, parents will watch those areas to protect their children from strangers. Filling the space around housing projects with play equipment, benches, or athletic facilities can attract people and attention, and keep children near home where they will be watched by their parents and neighbors.

Newman (1973: 59) states that residents of housing projects will feel safer if they can "see and be seen, hear and be heard, by day and night." Surveillance deters crime, and it reduces anxiety by creating an image of a safe environment. People who feel less anxious will spend more time in public places, thereby increasing surveillance and the informal control of behavior. Surveillance must be backed up with a willingness to intervene in a crime, either personally or by alerting the police, or mere observation will have little effect. If potential offenders believe that they will be seen committing a crime but will not be interfered with or reported to the police, they will not be affected much by surveillance. Only a real risk of apprehension can deter offenders. (See the Using Criminology box.)

The defensible space model is supported by research on public housing projects in the United States and Great Britain and by studies of residential blocks in the United States (Taylor and Harrell, May 1996: 8). Public housing sites with more defensible space characteristics have greater control by residents over outdoor areas and less fear and victimization among residents (Newman and Franck, 1982). Fear is lower in settings that offer few places for potential offenders to hide and that makes it easier for legitimate users to survey an area and escape if necessary (Fisher and Nasar, 1992).

Revising the Defensible Space Model   A flaw in Newman's defensible space model is that it pays attention to physical design features but slights or ignores social variables. For instance, the model ignores the demographic characteristics of the people who live in a housing area. Thus, a project that includes many teenagers and many elderly people probably will have a higher crime rate than a project limited to the elderly, whatever the defensible space design of each project. Newman's model also pays little attention to such social aspects of housing areas as neighborhood stability, residential mobility, employment rate, and racial integration. According to some critics, then, Newman's conception of defensible space lacks social reality (Taylor, Gottfredson, and Brower, 1980; Booth, 1981).

Another problem with the model is that the built environment can affect the crime rate either by encouraging residents to take action against potential offenders who violate the defensible space or by reducing opportunities for crime through controlled access or "target hardening" (for example, locks and

Schools and Defensible Space

Planners have begun to use the principles of defensible space to redesign the nation's schools in a way that will reduce crime and the fear of crime felt by students, teachers, and administrators.

Older schools were not built to maximize surveillance. They have long, winding corridors that are not easily observed from classrooms or by students, teachers, and administrators in the halls. Bathrooms are typically in remote places or at the ends of corridors, and so they become the loci of crime. Students fear going to the bathroom because they are afraid of being victimized by the troublemakers who control that space.

Today, architects and security experts are working with school district administrators to design safer schools. Floor layouts are simpler. Bathrooms are placed in central locations, where traffic to and from them can be observed by students and staff. Areas that were once used freely by all students, and therefore not under any specific group's control, are now allocated for "ownership" by particular groups. Each group then becomes responsible for maintaining order and keeping deviant behavior to a minimum in that part of the school.

Source: Based on "Crime Draws Some of the Lines in Blueprints for Schools," *New York Times,* March 6, 1991, p. B8.

bars on doors and windows). To test the idea of defensible space, it is necessary to separate those two processes. Moreover, if the design of a built environment impedes informal social control, the area might attract more police officers, thereby enhancing formal control. Researchers would then need to separate any crime-reduction effects of formal control from those that might result from the informal control generated by defensible space design (Gillis and Hagan, 1982).

Defensible space theory needs to take into account research on human territoriality. A revised model would pay more attention to barriers that deter access by unwanted outsiders, territorial markers that show that an area is cared for, and signs of incivility that indicate that social order in an area has disintegrated. This revised model would look at the way sociocultural characteristics affect territorial behavior; for instance, culturally homogeneous neighborhoods probably exert more territorial control than heterogeneous ones. A revised model would look not only at physical design, but also at the traits of people who might exercise territorial control and the ways that social networks are formed and affect territorial control (see Figure 12.2). In addition, defensible space theory needs to incorporate evidence on the ways that features of the physical environment affect the perceptions and behavior of offenders (Taylor and Gottfredson, 1986; Taylor and Harrell, May 1996).

FIGURE 12.2

A Revised Defensible Space Model

Source: Ralph B. Taylor and Adele V. Harrell, *Physical Environment and Crime.* Washington, D.C.: U.S. Department of Justice, May 1996, p. 7.

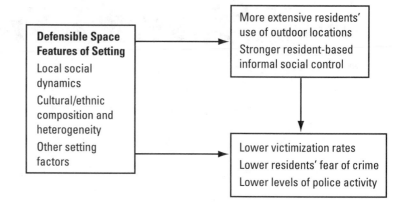

Individual Response to Crime

Informal control of crime depends not only on the surveillance of public places by the residents of a community, but also on the willingness of those people to take action if they see a crime in progress. The combination of cooperative surveillance and willingness to intervene has been called **protective neighboring** (Schneider and Schneider, 1978). Protective neighboring seems to be more common among people with higher incomes, among long-term residents of a community, and among homeowners. Just as crime and delinquency are less common among people who have a stake in conformity, so it seems that efforts to control crime and delinquency are also more common among people who have a stake in conformity. The Crime and the Media box looks at one effort to get more people involved in the fight against crime.

The most common action people take in response to a crime is to call the police to report it, but sometimes victims respond directly by taking action against offenders. A controversial case involving the right of victims to use deadly force against offenders occurred in 1984 in New York City, where Bernhard Goetz, a white man, shot four black youths on a subway, because he feared he was about to be robbed when one of the youths asked him for five dollars. Goetz was cleared of all attempted murder and assault charges in 1987, but he was convicted of the felony of illegal possession of a firearm. He was sentenced to one year in jail, but was released after eight months. Supporters of the jury's acquittal of Goetz on the most serious charges applauded its apparent willingness to allow potential crime victims to defend themselves against their attackers. Critics said that the jury's lenient treatment of Goetz opened the way for vigilante justice and posed a threat to young black men from whites who are afraid of crime. In 1996, a civil jury awarded $43 million to Darrell Cabey, who had been paralyzed and brain-damaged by one of Goetz's shots, but Goetz's financial situation makes it unlikely that Cabey will see much of that money.

CRIME AND THE MEDIA

Crime Stoppers

Crime Stoppers, a program started in Albuquerque, New Mexico, in 1976, unites the news media, law-enforcement agencies, and the community in an effort to reduce serious crime. "Dead-end" crimes that the police have been unable to solve are reported in the media, and citizens are encouraged to call in tips to help solve the crimes. Because of the fear of retaliation, callers are guaranteed anonymity. They are paid for their information if it leads to an arrest and an indictment. The tipster is given an identification number on the telephone and collects the reward at a prearranged place. Money for the rewards is donated by private businesses and individuals; some cities have raised funds through telethons and public appeals.

Crime Stoppers International claims that by the end of 1988 the program had resulted in the solution of 213,094 felonies, the recovery of $1,330,998,871 worth of narcotics and stolen property, the conviction of 43,839 defendants, and the payment of $17,023,467 in rewards. What is not clear is whether Crime Stoppers reduced the overall rate of crime in cities that had programs. Deterrent effects are probably limited, because the solved cases are only a small percentage of all serious offenses in those cities.

About two-thirds of the anonymous tips are from criminals and people associated with criminals, suggesting that Crime Stoppers might disrupt relationships between offenders and their accomplices, friends, and relatives by creating a fear among offenders that people close to them will turn them in for a reward.

The size of a reward is not related to a tipster's satisfaction with Crime Stoppers or to his or her willingness to participate in the program again. However, the payment of some reward seems essential to the program's success in getting people to report crimes. This raises the question of whether citizens should be paid to do their civic duty of reporting crime to the police. Another concern is whether the desire to collect reward money might entice some people to make false accusations or intrude on their neighbor's privacy.

Source: Based on Dennis P. Rosenbaum, Arthur J. Lurigio, and Paul J. Lavrakas, "Enhancing Citizen Participation and Solving Serious Crime: A National Evaluation of Crime Stoppers Programs," *Crime and Delinquency* 35 (July 1989), 401–420.

Bystander Responses to Crime

Occasionally, bystanders respond to a crime in progress by intervening. Such a response is probably least likely where fear of crime leads people to withdraw from social contacts, stay home at night, and avoid strangers. This kind of behavior minimizes the likelihood that anyone will be around to witness a crime. Fear also makes those people who are on the street more likely to adopt a self-protective stance and less likely to intervene personally in a crime.

The issue of bystander response to emergencies such as crime has been called the **Good Samaritan problem** (Ratcliffe, 1966). The crime that most

After shooting four young black men whom he thought were about to rob him, "subway vigilante" Bernhard Goetz was acquitted of attempted murder and assault charges, but convicted of illegal possession of a firearm. He served eight months in jail.

dramatically brought this problem to public attention was the 1964 murder of Kitty Genovese in Queens, New York. This crime occurred in a middle-class neighborhood that had a relatively low crime rate. A man attacked Kitty Genovese at about three o'clock in the morning when she was returning from work. She screamed, and lights went on in nearby apartments. People looked out and one witness shouted at the assailant to leave the woman alone. The assailant left but soon returned. Again lights went on and again the assailant left. When he returned a third time, he killed Miss Genovese. The three attacks took place over a period of about thirty-five minutes, and at least thirty-eight witnesses knew of the violence. When the witnesses were later asked about their failure to take action, some said they had been too tired to do anything and others said they had not wanted to get involved.

At first, social scientists were unable to provide a convincing explanation of the bystanders' failure to help the victim. Letters to the newspapers suggested printing the names of the nonresponsive witnesses. Others blamed the police, saying that New Yorkers were afraid of the police and were therefore unwilling to call them in an emergency. What was puzzling was that no help was forthcoming from a group as large as thirty-eight; had only one or two people observed the crime, it might have been possible to point the finger at a few heartless individuals. Many commentators concluded that something must be wrong with society as a whole; several gave apathy as the cause of the problem, concluding that people just no longer cared about their fellow citizens.

Reactions to Emergencies   How do people respond when faced with a crime or other emergency that requires action? Lawrence Zelic Freedman (1966) suggests that their initial response is often fear of being hurt and fear of reprisals. Often witnesses cannot fit the unusual event into any familiar category of past experience. The witnesses to the Genovese murder might have failed to take action because the crime seemed "totally incongruous in a respectable neighborhood," creating "a sense of unreality which inhibited rational action" (Milgram and Hollander, 1970: 208).

Before witnesses take action, they must clearly define the situation as an emergency that requires personal intervention. Emergency situations are often ambiguous to witnesses; several witnesses to the Genovese murder interpreted it as a "lovers' quarrel." Witnesses often fail to respond appropriately, denying to themselves that anything so unusual could be happening in their presence. What appears to be apathy might in fact be massive inhibition or paralysis of consciousness resulting from internal conflict. Freedman (1966: 175) claims that in response to emergencies,

> apathy and indifference are the least likely primary psychic vectors.... The sequence as I see it is, first, the intense emotional shock—characterized predominantly, but not exclusively, by anxiety; second, the cognitive perception and awareness of what has happened; third, an inertial paralysis of reaction, which as a non-act becomes in fact an act; and fourth, the self-awareness of one's own shock anxiety, non-involvement which is followed by a sense of guilt and intrapsychic and social self-justification.
>
> I do not assume that these things happen in such neat sequence. For all practical purposes they seem to occur simultaneously.

Witnesses sometimes justify their inaction by claiming that the victim and the offender must know one another, which might indeed be the case. Bystanders are more likely to intervene in assaults between strangers than to offer help when it seems that the assault involves a married couple (Shotland and Straw, 1976). Witnesses are also more likely to intervene if they believe that the victim is totally innocent and if they can identify in some way with the victim. On the other hand, witnesses find it easier to tolerate the victimization of people who occupy disvalued social statuses such as prostitutes and skid-row alcoholics. If a witness's identification with a victim is slight, the chance that the witness will assist the victim is probably low (Blumenthal et al., 1972).

Experimental Studies of Bystander Response   Social-psychological experiments have cast light on the reasons that witnesses to emergencies help under some conditions but not others. According to Bibb Latané and John Darley (1970), neither public apathy nor the absence of norms requiring assistance explains bystander nonresponse. In a series of experiments, they clarified the characteristics of situations that are conducive to bystander intervention. Personality traits that might plausibly influence helping behavior did not bear any relationship to such action. Situational determinants of bystander assistance were so strong that differences among the personalities of witnesses paled in significance as determinants of their behavior.

Before bystanders will intervene, they must make a series of decisions. A negative decision at any point means they will not help the victim. They must notice the situation and define it as an emergency. Then they must determine that they have a personal responsibility to do something; if they think the situation is none of their business, they will not help. Bystanders must also decide what kind of aid to offer—personal intervention, or calling the police or an ambulance. Finally, they must decide how to implement the course of action on which they have decided (Latané and Darley, 1970). The social context within which this decision-making process occurs will influence the outcome.

One reason for the public's condemnation of the nonresponsive bystanders in the Genovese murder was the failure of a large number of witnesses to help. The commonsense assumption is that if there are more people around, the chance that at least one will help should be greater. However, social-psychological research demonstrates that the presence of others at the scene of an emergency actually inhibits helping behavior. People might be embarrassed to help for fear that their assistance will turn out to be unwanted or unneeded. When no witness in a group of bystanders immediately offers help, others might assume their own interpretation of the situation as one requiring aid is wrong; if help were needed, would not someone already have offered it? People in groups take cues from others, and if no one helps they might reinterpret the event. This has been referred to as **pluralistic ignorance**: witnesses in a group fail to help because they interpret the failure of other witnesses to help as meaning that no help is needed (Latané and Darley, 1970).

Witnesses who are alone when they observe a crime or an accident are more likely to help than are witnesses who are in groups of two or more. Lone witnesses are more likely to seek information about the situation, to help the victim through their own efforts, and to report the situation to someone else who can provide assistance. A witness who is accompanied by another person is more likely to help a victim if that witness is personally acquainted with the second witness than if the second witness is a stranger; this is probably because personal knowledge breaks down pluralistic ignorance by making communication between witnesses more likely. However, pairs of witnesses who know one another are less likely to help victims than are witnesses who are alone. One reason for this is that there is no **diffusion of responsibility** when there is only one witness present (Latané and Darley, 1970). Diffusion of responsibility occurs in groups of witnesses because people can say to themselves that someone should act but that it need not be themselves, since other potential helpers are present. Especially when a victim's cries for help are not directed toward a specific bystander, people who witness an emergency can soothe their consciences by claiming that someone else should help or that others are equally responsible if no one helps. Indeed, the larger the group of bystanders, the more responsibility is diffused and the less likely it is that help will be offered.

One experiment that found that bystander intervention is more likely when responsibility is focused on a particular bystander was conducted on Jones Beach, Long Island. A "victim" placed a blanket near another bather, turned on a radio, and a short time later said to the bystander, "Excuse me, I'm going up the boardwalk for a few minutes. Would you watch my things?" This committed the bystander to watching the radio. Other bystanders were only asked for a match and were thus not committed to watching the radio. In a few minutes, a "thief"—who was actually part of the experiment—picked up the radio, which was playing loudly, and walked away with it. A third participant in the experiment observed the reactions of bystanders. Only four of the twenty uncommitted witnesses who later said they had noticed the theft tried to stop the thief, but nineteen of the twenty committed bystanders made an effort to stop the thief. Prior contact between the victim and the bystander had focused responsibility on the committed bystanders to take some action when the theft occurred (Moriarity, 1975).

Other aspects of the situation also affect the likelihood of bystander assistance to a victim. Familiarity with the location is important; help is probably more likely to be given if witnesses are in their own neighborhood than if they are in a strange neighborhood. Bystanders also consider the risks of providing help; they might be less willing to help if a weapon is present or if there are several offenders rather than one. Offering help might be a function of the other activities in which a witness is engaged at the time; for instance, help is probably more likely to be given if a witness is standing on the street doing nothing than if a witness is rushing to a doctor's appointment or a job interview (Darley and Batson, 1973).

Bystanders who are self-assured, feel good about themselves, or have specialized training in first aid, life saving, or medical and police techniques seem to be especially likely to help others. People who seek training in such skills could be more inclined to help to begin with, or they might learn an ethic of helping behavior as they learn those skills (Geis, 1981).

A study of thirty-two people who had intervened in actual crimes of violence or theft found that all but one were men, and that they tended to be above average in height and weight and were usually larger than the offenders they confronted (Geis, 1981). Perhaps size and sense of competence led more men than women to risk intervening when they encountered a crime in progress. However, an experiment at the University of Virginia staged a theft and found that three-fourths of female bystanders but only half of male bystanders tried to stop the theft (Austin, 1979). This experiment, which elicited promises from bystanders to watch the "victim's" goods, led the researcher to conclude that women might be more unwilling than men to break a promise, or that women might feel more empathy for victims than men do. These explanations would not tell us why nearly all of the bystanders who intervened in actual crimes in the first study were men.

Would Kitty Genovese Be Helped Today?   On the twenty-fifth anniversary of the Genovese murder, an article in the *New York Times* declared that "there are enough recent examples of people coming to each other's aid to argue that New Yorkers are not hard as rocks" (Martin, 1989: 29). The detective who led the Genovese investigation stated, "People are more willing to come forward now"; and Edward Koch, then mayor of the city, declared, "Today the likelihood of a crowd averting its eyes and not going to the defense of someone in trouble is much less likely" (cited in Martin, 1989: 29).

None of those optimistic assertions relies on any empirical evidence. Indeed, they ignore a wealth of research that suggests that a victim confronting the same situation faced by Kitty Genovese could expect no different response from onlookers today. In 1987 in Manchester, New Hampshire, a twenty-one-year-old mother of two, on her way home from a friend's party at 4 A.M., was grabbed by a man, dragged shrieking across the street, and then raped, beaten, choked, and robbed. An estimated two dozen people heard the attack, and at least three people witnessed the attack. The only person to call the police was a security guard and former Marine, a man who fit the profile of the kind of bystander most likely to take action. This man's statement after the rape should be taken with as much skepticism as the optimistic statements by New Yorkers that things have improved since the Genovese murder. He said, "The next time something like this happens, I think you'll see a lot more action" (cited in Hohler, 1987: 44).

Collective Response to Crime

People sometimes band together in a collective response to crime, working for a political candidate who promises "law and order," meeting to plan a crime-prevention program, or forming a civilian patrol group to perform tasks that they think the police are not doing adequately. Group action of this sort has been both condemned as a mob's taking the law into its own hands and praised as citizen involvement in crime prevention.

A Historical and Comparative Perspective

Collective response to crime has a long history. Ancient Roman plebeians engaged in community self-help when they threw alleged offenders from the Tarpeian rock. Early Germans raised a hue and cry, took up arms, blew horns, chased suspects, and occasionally lynched them. "People's police" sometimes had to be restrained from attacking innocent people in the former Soviet Union. In China, people informally police their communities, and Africans in tribal villages sometimes impose harsh punishment on suspected criminals. During the 1990s, vigilantism in response to an ineffectual criminal justice system has been reported in Great Britain, South Africa, Haiti, Venezuela, Colombia, and other countries. The Cross-Cultural Perspective box gives an example from urban Brazil.

Vigilante activity has occurred in the United States for more than two centuries. The first recorded movement was in the 1760s in South Carolina, where a group called the Regulators sought to bring order to communities in the Back Country. The Regulators apparently reduced crime, but they violated the due process rights of suspects. They elicited much hostility and eventually were disbanded when they began to mete out severe punishment, select victims rashly, and even supervise the morals and family life of law-abiding citizens.

Vigilante groups on the American frontier developed in response to a perceived lack of social order, rather than in response to specific crimes. Because the new frontier communities often lacked the resources to hire law-enforcement officials, were usually far from towns that could provide those officials, and were near open spaces to which suspects could flee, frontier vigilante groups sometimes developed as a way to establish social control over crime and bring stability to the community.

The leaders of many vigilante movements in the West were young men from the East who sought power and prestige and wanted to establish an orderly community in which they could pursue their ambitions. The rank-and-file

A CROSS-CULTURAL PERSPECTIVE

Lynchings in Brazil

Rising crime rates in the Brazilian cities of Rio de Janeiro and São Paulo have elicited a variety of public responses. In 1995, hundreds of thousands of Rio de Janeiro residents from all walks of life marched to protest the danger they faced from crime. Many well-to-do Brazilians have moved from houses to apartment complexes that are protected by armed guards, and those who continue to live in houses surround them with walls topped with sharp metal bars. Residents of some neighborhoods have hired guards to stand watch on street corners. More Brazilians are carrying weapons. People rarely wear jewelry or expensive clothes on the street, and they avoid places where they might be robbed or kidnapped. Most cars have alarms and secret locks, and drivers do not stop for red lights for fear of being robbed.

Perhaps the most dramatic response to Brazil's crime problem is citizen involvement in the lynching of suspected offenders. These lynchings are a response to the widely held view that the criminal justice system is ineffective in controlling crime. One lynching is described as follows:

Osvaldo Otavio Pires was brought handcuffed into Elio's bar in the Jardim Guanhambu slum on the outskirts of São Paulo at about 8 a.m. on April 2. Over 100 men, women and children had gathered in the small wooden building to await his arrival.

Mr. Pires, 33 years old, was thrust onto a bench facing the crowd and the handcuffs were removed. He was allowed to smoke a cigarette and drink a glass of rough liquor, but no one moved when he asked to see his two small children. Witnesses recalled that his hands were trembling.

Mr. Pires, long feared in Jardim Guanhambu, then heard an array of charges of armed assault brought by people filling the bar. After 20 minutes,

participants in the meeting later told reporters, a voice was heard to say, "All those in favor of death raise their hands." Dozens of arms were lifted; apparently no one objected.

Mr. Pires was pushed out of Elio's Bar and the crowd fell on him with sticks, poles and stones. Once he lay dead in the dusty street, the police were called. When they arrived, they took the names and addresses of 43 people who said they had joined in the lynching. No arrests were made. (Riding, p. 1)

Lynchings such as this have increased over time, and the nature of the crimes committed by lynching victims has also changed. One official remarks, "In the past, lynchings were restricted to heinous crimes—rapes of children or sadistic murders. Now a lynching can be sparked by the theft of a wallet" (cited in Brooke, p. 6). A study of fifty-six lynchings found that 58 percent of the victims had been suspected of theft and 18 percent of sexual assault. One-fourth of the victims were under the age of eighteen.

Lynchings in Brazil have been attributed not only to the fear of crime and an ineffective criminal justice system, but also to the nation's extraordinarily high rate of unemployment and underemployment, the low incomes of those who are working, the failure of the stagnant economy to offer people any hope, and the attention given to violence by the mass media.

Sources: Based on Alan Riding, "Brazilians Turn to Lynchings to Fight Soaring Crime Rate," *New York Times,* April 15, 1984, pp. 1, 12; James Brooke, "Lynching Increases in Brazil's Shantytowns," *New York Times,* November 3, 1991, p. 6; Diana Jean Schemo, "Rio Residents March and Samba to Protest Crime and Corruption," *New York Times,* November 29, 1995, p. A15.

members of those vigilante movements were often drawn from the middle classes, and the lower classes provided most of the targets of the movements.

Vigilante organizations in the West ranged in size from a dozen to as many as 8,000 participants; usually they had a few hundred members. Most groups lasted only a few weeks, but some endured for over a year. In nearly half of the recorded vigilante movements, there was at least one execution of an alleged offender, usually after a brief and formal—but extralegal—"trial."

Vigilantes traditionally espoused popular sovereignty, the right of the people to wield power in their own best interests (Brown, 1969). They also supported the idea that people had the right to revolt against established authority if it failed to maintain order. Vigilante groups sought to preserve and protect the life, liberty, and property of their members and the other residents of the community, and in this sense their extralegal efforts to preserve civil order were conservative (Little and Sheffield, 1983).

Some vigilante movements were socially constructive, dealing with specific problems of disorder and then disbanding; these movements usually represented the consensus of the community. By contrast, socially destructive vigilante movements encountered stiff opposition and produced community strife. Movements became socially destructive when they failed to exercise control over violent or sadistic members. The possibility that vigilante movements, including civilian patrol groups in today's cities, might become battlegrounds for personal and group conflicts rather than represent genuine community consensus is one reason to distrust such movements. Such consensus is difficult to establish in large and heterogeneous cities.

Urban Patrol Groups

Vigilante groups on the American frontier developed to provide social control of deviant behavior. Just as the western frontier was in transition from wilderness to settled territory, so can the transition from a small preindustrial city to a heavily industrialized urban center be understood as a kind of frontier. In Great Britain during the eighteenth and nineteenth centuries, urbanization and industrialization created a kind of frontier, a transition between social forms that left growing cities without effective law enforcement. Just as vigilante groups emerged in the American West, so did private "prosecution societies" develop in English cities. These prosecution societies sought to make the criminal justice system more accessible and more effective. They supported the rule of law and rarely meted out sentences on their own (Little and Sheffield, 1983).

Today more than 150 civilian patrol groups cover New York City's neighborhoods. The groups register with the local police, their members are given badges, and their leaders take a thirteen-week training program offered by the police academy. Patrol group members do not carry weapons; instead, they ride around in cars looking for disturbances or crimes in progress, then use radios or cellular phones to call the police (Kaplan, 1996).

One contemporary civilian patrol group that has received much attention is the Guardian Angels. Formed in 1978, this organization is made up primarily of young Hispanics and blacks who patrol subway stations and subway cars in groups in order to deter robbery, assault, and rape. Guardian Angels are trained in karate, resuscitation methods, and the legal requirements for arrests, although some members have been rushed into dangerous situations before being adequately trained. Curtis Sliwa, founder of the Angels, announced in 1992 that early in the group's existence he had fabricated six incidents to draw favorable public attention to his group and to counteract opposition from the police. By 1992, the Angels had been reduced to "little more than a security force for a block of midtown [Manhattan] restaurants, its membership and activities greatly exaggerated, its patrols, in their trademark red berets and T-shirts, converging only on highly publicized situations" (Gonzalez, 1992: B1).

There is little evidence that the Guardian Angels were ever very effective in preventing crime. Even when the streets seemed safer because of their presence, the Angels may simply have been displacing crime to other locations or to times when they were not around. One study in New York City found that Guardian Angel patrols apparently did not affect either the amount of crime on the subways or the level of fear felt by riders, nor did they change passengers' willingness to assist one another (Kenney, 1987). Another study found that the Guardian Angels in San Diego did not reduce violent crime but might have had a small impact on property offenses. Nevertheless, 60 percent of the citizens who knew that the group patrolled their neighborhood reported feeling safer as a result (Pennell et al., 1989).

Civilian patrol groups have been organized in New York, San Francisco, and Chicago to prevent hate crimes against gays and lesbians. In Chicago, the Pink Angels, an unarmed group that includes both homosexuals and heterosexuals, patrol the streets in neighborhoods where gays and lesbians live and radio the police for help when threatening situations develop.

Patrol groups face several problems (Marx and Archer, 1971, 1972). To sustain the interest of their members and the support of the community, they need to make the crisis to which they are responding continuously felt. They need a charismatic leader to inspire confidence in their members and in the residents of the community. Patrol groups need to be formally organized, and they require financial support. They have a better chance of survival if they have an ideology that states positive, specific goals; vague targets such as crime and disorder do not seem to sustain patrol groups for long. These groups are most effective in limited and well-defined settings, such as housing projects and rock concerts, where there are homogeneous populations separated from other people by clear boundaries. Even if all of these conditions are met, patrol groups face difficulties:

> Self-defense groups often lack a clear mandate from the groups they wish to serve and their legal position regarding the use of force and citizen arrests is ambiguous. They may have trouble defining their task. The tendency of the groups to lack the resources for recruiting, screening, and training appropriate manpower and for sustaining motivation beyond that which stems from a deeply felt crisis (along with the degree of autonomy some groups have) may contribute to ineffectiveness and

abuses. And even if internal problems are solved, the groups may face harassment from the police. (Marx and Archer, 1971: 68)

Urban patrol groups serve important symbolic and participatory functions for their members. They enhance the self-esteem and sense of power of those who are involved, leading patrol-group members as well as other community residents to think they can do something about crime. If people believe the patrols are effective in making the streets safer, even if they are not, people may be more willing to use the streets at night.

Patrol groups probably provide more structured surveillance of a community than is possible through informal observation by residents. The surveillance provided by patrol groups is likely to be more effective than unorganized surveillance in deterring crime, because the chance that a member of a patrol group will take direct action is greater than the chance that a private citizen will intervene personally or call the police. Patrol groups can thus create surveillance, stimulate interaction in public places, and help reduce crime by supporting formal control agents and by increasing informal control by community residents.

Neighborhood Watches

Crime-stopping groups such as Neighborhood or Block Watches, which are sponsored by law-enforcement officials in about 2,500 communities, "share information about local crime problems, exchange crime prevention tips, and make plans for engaging in surveillance ('watching') of the neighborhood and crime-reporting activities" (Rosenbaum, 1987: 104). A 1985 survey found that only 9 percent of Neighborhood Watch groups reported that informal surveillance of the streets was their sole activity. Other common activities included property engraving, household security surveys, crime tip hotlines, the improvement of street lighting, block parenting, and more general activities related to the community's physical environment (Garofalo and McLeod, 1989).

Unlike frontier vigilantes, Neighborhood Watch groups operate in a context in which there is already a fully developed system of law enforcement. They seek to supplement the police rather than to replace them, and they are usually sponsored by a local law-enforcement agency. These groups might improve police-community relations by providing opportunities for contacts between the police and law-abiding citizens. Police support for Neighborhood Watch groups acknowledges that the police cannot solve the crime problem by themselves, and this can foster a more realistic image of the police.

Research shows that Neighborhood Watch groups have had no more than modest success in reducing crime, with the crimes most likely to be prevented being residential burglaries and theft from the immediate vicinity of homes (Garofalo and McLeod, 1989). According to one review of the research, "neighborhood crime prevention programs have been unable to set in motion the social interaction, territoriality, surveillance, and other behaviors that theoretically are expected at the block or neighborhood level" (Rosenbaum, 1988: 375). Moreover, the difficulty encountered by

About 2,500 communities in the United States have Neighborhood or Block Watch groups that engage in such crime-fighting activities as street surveillance, property engraving, household safety surveys, and crime tip hotlines.

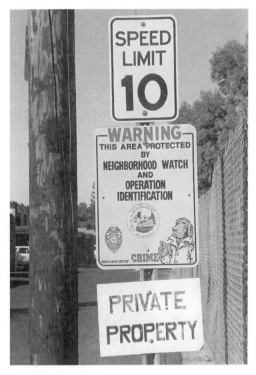

Neighborhood Watch groups in keeping their members involved over time suggests that sustained reductions in crime could be even harder to achieve than short-term reductions. Many of the groups' activities are one-time measures, such as engraving property and household security surveys, and the activity level of many groups is low, with 40 percent not even holding regularly scheduled meetings (Garofalo and McLeod, 1989).

In 1984, about one-fifth of American families lived in a community with a Neighborhood Watch program, and 38 percent of households in areas that had such programs participated in them (Bureau of Justice Statistics, March 1986). Dennis Rosenbaum (1987) doubts that participation can be expanded much, arguing that collective citizen action and the informal social control it might activate are difficult to implant in communities where they do not already exist. He finds little evidence that Neighborhood Watch meetings cause residents to engage in the neighborhood surveillance and bystander intervention that are needed to strengthen informal control and reduce crime, and he cites evidence that Neighborhood Watch meetings increase rather than decrease participants' fear of crime.

Community Crime-Prevention Strategies

In the mid-1980s, the appearance of crack, a new and powerful form of cocaine, aroused community action directed at changing the behavior of local drug dealers and users. In New York City, the leaders of black churches held all-night vigils as a part of their battle against crack. In Boston, drugs in general were the target of a group called Drop a Dime, which encouraged citizens to phone tips to its statewide hotline and report local drug problems to the police. Drop a Dime organizers set up block associations to swamp the police with complaints about drug problems, and they have sponsored prayer sessions and temporary occupancy of vacant buildings used by drug dealers to attract the attention of the police and the press.

Perhaps the most dramatic action against drug dealers has occurred in Detroit, Miami, and other cities where enraged citizens have burned down "crack houses." Objecting to the open sale of drugs from the curb and frightened by the gunfire of rival dealers, two residents of a previously quiet Detroit neighborhood burned down a crack house. In court the men admitted to setting the fire, but a jury quickly acquitted them. A local newspaper found that 87 percent of its readers thought the arson was justified (Wilkerson, 1988).

A study of thirty-six urban neighborhoods found that drug problems stimulate confrontational tactics by local residents rather than undermine organized community action. Contradicting some earlier research, this study found that confrontational responses to local drug problems were most common in high-crime-rate, poverty-stricken, and minority neighborhoods. The prior existence of block clubs and other broad-based community organizations was found to encourage confrontational responses (Skogan and Lurigio, 1992).

People who participate in patrol groups and other community efforts to fight crime are drawn to those organizations less by their fear of crime than by a general desire to improve neighborhood life (Lavrakas and Herz, 1982). Most community crime-prevention efforts develop from neighborhood organizations that have a general orientation toward revitalizing the community or providing services for local youths (Lewis and Salem, 1981, 1986). Neighborhood Watch and similar programs are most successful when they are part of multi-issue, general-purpose community groups rather than when they focus exclusively on crime. Few programs aimed specifically at reducing crime evolve into general community organizations that empower local citizens to effect neighborhood change (Lewis, Grant, and Rosenbaum, 1988; Garofalo and McLeod, 1989; Skogan, 1990).

One study of community crime-prevention efforts explicitly avoided the assumption that collective responses to crime are the result of fear of victimization, pointing out that similar levels of crime elicit very different responses in different communities. Every community studied by the researchers devoted some resources to fighting crime, and people everywhere believed that collective efforts could reduce crime. People did not see crime as a problem that could be isolated from other social problems, and so their crime-prevention efforts were usually part of a broad effort to improve the neighborhood. Some communities followed a "social problems" approach, dealing with general conditions that were seen as sources of crime, and others used "victimization-prevention" strategies, dealing more directly with crime by increasing surveillance or by developing protective measures. Instead of being linked to perceptions of the crime rate, participation in collective efforts to reduce crime was associated with the social and cultural context of a community—that is, with the family status, socioeconomic position, and race and ethnicity of the residents. Participation in community-wide efforts is most likely where residents are highly integrated into the community and tied to the area through home ownership and long-term residence (Podolefsky and DuBow, 1981).

The idea that crime-prevention organizations can be created in high-crime communities that need them but do not have them was tested in Chicago and Minneapolis. Although many residents of the neighborhoods in which block clubs and other crime-prevention measures were developed knew of and initially participated in the programs, the programs did not reduce fear of crime or increase crime reporting. The programs also failed to increase neighborhood solidarity, interaction among residents, watchfulness, or daily activities that might reduce crime. Because the programs in Chicago and Minneapolis were run by professionals, were highly visible, and got a good initial response, their lack of success cannot be attributed to a failure to implement the programs properly. It simply is difficult to get the residents of high-crime communities to participate in crime-prevention organizations, unless those organizations have emerged spontaneously from within the community and are concerned broadly with neighborhood improvement rather than narrowly with the reduction of crime (Skogan, 1990).

Summary

Fear can contribute to crime by undermining community solidarity and weakening informal social control. This fear, which is not always rationally related to the actual risk of victimization, causes people to stay home, restrict their travel when they do venture outdoors, and spend money on measures they hope will protect them from crime. By reducing interpersonal trust, fear can diminish the informal control of behavior in a community.

Informal control of crime is most effective when interaction is common and the surveillance of behavior is possible. Those conditions are probably more common in small towns than in large cities. In large cities, where crime rates are often high, people frequently assign the task of crime prevention to the formal control agents of the criminal justice system. There is, however, much variation among urban communities, with people most willing to play an active role in crime prevention in socially integrated and stable neighborhoods.

The defensible space model maintains that architectural design can increase citizen involvement in the crime-prevention process by encouraging people to exercise control over the territory in which they live. This process might reduce some kinds of crime in certain housing situations, but overall the evidence that defensible space can have a major impact on crime is not strong. A revised defensible space model that takes into account the social characteristics of residents and the way people form networks might describe more accurately the means by which informal control can check crime.

For informal social control to be effective in reducing crime, people must be willing to call the police or intervene in a crime. The Good Samaritan problem arises when witnesses fail to take action of this sort. Nonresponse to observed crimes is a product of the ambiguity of some crime situations, a sense of unreality when watching a crime in progress, pluralistic ignorance that results from thinking that if no one else is helping it must be because no help is needed, and a diffusion of responsibility among witnesses. Other factors that can affect the chance that a bystander will intervene include whether the person feels self-assured or is trained in offering assistance.

Collective action in response to crime has a long history, dating as far back as 1760 in the United States and even earlier elsewhere. Vigilante groups in the American West sought to create order in the absence of a criminal justice system, taking on responsibility for preserving life, liberty, and property from suspected criminals. Today, urban patrol groups operate in the context of a functioning, but often ineffective, criminal justice system. Citizen involvement in crime prevention is usually not a direct result of the fear of victimization, but is instead related to the characteristics of community residents and the presence of organizations broadly concerned with neighborhood improvement.

Important Terms

defensible space
diffusion of responsibility
formal social control
Good Samaritan problem
informal social control

mechanical solidarity
organic solidarity
pluralistic ignorance
protective neighboring
social control

Review Questions

1. How is fear of crime related to actual risk of victimization? What effects does fear of crime have on people's daily behavior, on their trust of others, and on community ties?

2. What are the differences between informal social control and formal social control? How do communities exercise informal control? In what kinds of communities is informal control most likely to be effective in keeping crime in check?

3. What is defensible space? How might buildings and communities designed to enhance defensible space reduce crime? Does research support the defensible space model?

4. Under what conditions will witnesses to a crime take action to help the victim? Under what conditions will they fail to act?

5. How do contemporary urban patrol groups differ from vigilantes in the American West? How effective do you think modern patrol groups are in keeping urban crime rates down?

6. What are Neighborhood or Block Watches? How might they reduce crime in a neighborhood? Can they be effective in high-crime-rate communities?

Chapter 13
The Criminal Justice System

Every modern society has a criminal justice system that exercises formal social control by meting out punishment to offenders. This system also shapes offenders' behavior. Labeling by the police, the courts, and the correctional system can contribute to the development of criminal careers, but arrest and conviction also keep people from violating the law by instilling in them a fear of punishment. A prison sentence might also reduce crime by cutting an offender's ties to accomplices, by causing criminal skills to grow rusty, or by pushing an inmate into treatment. On the other hand, a prison sentence could contribute to crime by creating a desire to strike back at society, by reducing ties to conventional people, or by exposing an offender to other criminals. Thus, the criminal justice system prevents crime under some circumstances but contributes to it under others.

This chapter examines three components of the criminal justice system—the police, the courts, and the prisons. The following chapter looks at the principles on which this system is based. One such principle is deterrence, the notion that the threat of sanctions can prevent crime by creating a fear of punishment in those who might break the law. A second principle is incapacitation, which assumes that crime can be prevented by locking up offenders. A third principle is retribution, the idea that offenders deserve to suffer for the harm they have caused and that their punishment should be in proportion to that harm. A fourth basis for the criminal justice system is rehabilitation, which proposes that criminal sanctions should aim to reform convicted offenders so they will stay away from crime in the future.

The effectiveness of the criminal justice system in meeting the goals of deterrence, incapacitation, retribution, and rehabilitation depends on coordination among the various agencies of law enforcement. Critics have claimed that the American criminal justice system is not really a system at all, in the sense of being a set of agencies that are coordinated with one another, seek the same goals, and try to implement a single policy to deal with crime. There are important linkages among the police, the courts, and the prisons, as we can see in Figure 13.1, but these agencies do not form a unified system. When we speak of a criminal justice system, we are talking about different law-enforcement agencies and the linkages among them, rather than about a single, well-integrated system.

The criminal justice system has been described as a funnel or sieve that sorts out cases. Only some of all crimes that are committed are reported to the police, and many of those that are reported do not produce an arrest. Arrested suspects sometimes have the charges against them dropped or are acquitted in court; of those who are convicted and sentenced, many are not sent to prison. The funnel or sieve effect that characterizes the criminal justice system is one of **case attrition**, with cases being sorted out as they proceed through the system and relatively few crimes ending with a perpetrator's conviction and imprisonment.

Data from the Offender-Based Transaction Statistics (OBTS) program for seven states for 1987 revealed that for every 100 felony arrests, there were eighty-one prosecutions, sixty convictions, and forty sentences of incarceration. Of those who were convicted, 21 percent were placed on probation,

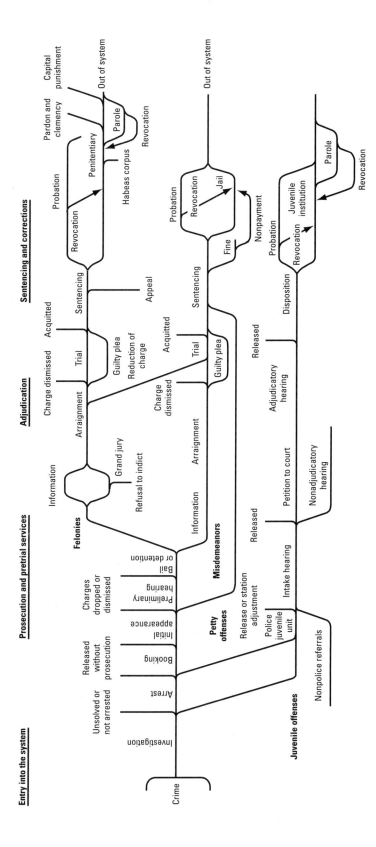

FIGURE 13.1

Case Attrition in the Criminal Justice System

Source: Bureau of Justice Statistics, *The American Response to Crime.* Washington, D.C.: U.S. Department of Justice, December 1983, pp. 2–3. Adapted from the President's Commission on Law Enforcement and Administration of Justice, *The Challenge of Crime in a Free Society.* Washington, D.C.: U.S. Government Printing Office, 1967.

14 percent were fined or given another penalty without incarceration, 45 percent were sentenced to a local jail (typically for less than one year), and 20 percent were sentenced to a state prison (Perez, 1990).

The cost of the American criminal justice system is enormous and has grown in recent years, primarily because of the system's increasing reliance on imprisonment. Imprisonment is an expensive form of punishment; the construction of each new maximum-security prison cell costs about $70,000, and the average annual maintenance cost for a prisoner is about $25,000. At the end of 1993, there were 909,080 Americans in state and federal prisons and another 459,804 in local jails. A total of 2,843,445 adults were on probation (court-ordered supervision), and 671,470 were on parole (supervised release from jail or prison). The lower cost of probation and parole has led some critics to argue for more use of these alternatives to incarceration.

In 1990, there were 1,798,000 employees of civil and criminal justice agencies throughout the country. Nearly half were police officers, with police departments accounting for 44 percent of all expenditures by the civil and criminal justice systems. Judicial and legal services accounted for 22 percent of the expenditures, and corrections for 34 percent of the total (see Figure 13.2). Most of these costs are incurred at the local rather than state or federal level; in 1992, 53.3 percent of the total was spent by local (city, town, or county) agencies, 32.3 percent by state agencies, and 14.4 percent by the federal government (Maguire and Pastore, 1995: 4–5).

FIGURE 13.2

Justice System Expenditures, 1992

Source: Based on data from Kathleen Maguire and Ann L. Pastore, *Sourcebook of Criminal Justice Statistics—1994.* Washington, D.C.: Bureau of Justice Statistics, U.S. Department of Justice, 1995, p. 3.

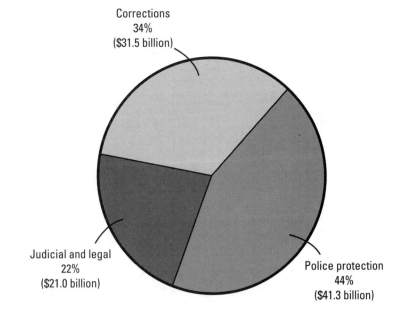

Corrections
34%
($31.5 billion)

Judicial and legal
22%
($21.0 billion)

Police protection
44%
($41.3 billion)

The Police

The police are the first formal line of defense against crime, for only if the police arrest suspects will the rest of the criminal justice system come into play in trying, convicting, and punishing offenders.

History of the Police

For centuries, societies have had some kind of a police force, an armed group of specialists who keep order and deal with violations of the law. The first modern police force was organized in London in 1829 by Sir Robert Peel, with officers nicknamed "bobbies" after their founder. This police force differed from earlier law-enforcement units in being full time, paid, uniformed, and organized for the city as a whole. Standards of literacy and character were established, and recruits were trained to perform their duties (Bayley, 1983).

Public police forces have existed in the United States since the seventeenth century, but it was only in Boston in 1837 that the first modern police force was organized along the same lines as London's department. By the 1870s nearly all large American cities had their own police force, which provided all citizens, rather than just wealthy ones, with criminal investigation services. Urbanization had weakened the informal social control provided by families and neighbors, and the police were needed as a formal means of controlling deviance. Another important factor in the rise of American police forces was the threat to the social order posed by mob violence in nineteenth-century cities (Bayley, 1983).

Marxist criminologists regard the police in a capitalist society as a tool used by the bourgeoisie to maintain a social order that is profitable to themselves and that exploits laborers (Harring, 1981, 1983; Spitzer, 1981). Marxists have shown how capitalists historically have used the police to quell collective action by organized labor. However, a study that used data from 1950 to 1980 found no relationship between inequality in the distribution of a city's income and the strength of a city's police force, a finding inconsistent with conflict theory (Greenberg, Kessler, and Loftin, 1985).

Marxist criminologists point to the unequal treatment by the police of suspects from disadvantaged social classes and racial and ethnic groups. Nevertheless, members of all social classes agree on the need to punish those crimes to which the police devote most of their attention: murder, rape, assault, and theft. Those crimes are the subject of police activity in socialist and communist societies as well as in capitalist ones. In addition, the criminal law is probably not the most important mechanism for maintaining the social order, nor is it a very effective tool for the dominant class to use in controlling all members of society (Sparks, 1980).

There is evidence that the criminal justice system responds to perceived threats to the social order. One study found that a city's expenditures on its police force can be predicted by the racial composition of the city's population and by the level of black mobilization activity in the city. Cities with larger black populations spend more on police salaries, operations, and capital expenditures than do cities with proportionally fewer blacks. In addition, cities with more political activity by blacks have higher rates of police capital expenditures. One explanation of these findings is that police expenditures increase when minorities are seen as a threat to the dominant racial group (Jackson and Carroll, 1981). Another study, using data from 1950 to 1980, found a moderate to strong relationship between a city's racial composition and the strength of its police force only in the South prior to 1970. This relationship was weak outside the South, except for the period from 1960 to 1970 (Greenberg, Kessler, and Loftin, 1985).

Organization of the Police

The police in the United States are organized at four levels. The first to develop were county sheriffs' departments, followed by municipal police departments. Next there were established state police departments, first in Texas and then in Massachusetts. Federal marshals, established in 1789, were the first federal police agency. Over time, the national government has expanded its policing activities, with the Bureau of Investigation—renamed the Federal Bureau of Investigation in 1935—being established in the Department of Justice in 1908 (Bayley, 1983).

Municipal police departments are organized hierarchically, with a police chief or superintendent at the top. Detectives and specialized investigative units—robbery, vice, and homicide, for instance—focus on solving crimes. One important aspect of police departments is that the individual at the lowest level of the hierarchy—the patrol officer on the street—has the most contact with the public and with criminal suspects, and also has a great deal of autonomy because superiors have difficulty in directly supervising the officer's activities. Within police departments, conflict and competition often develop between administrators concerned with efficiency and productivity, and officers on the street who must deal with the public and with suspects (Reuss-Ianni, 1983).

In their efforts to enforce the law and maintain order, the police in a democratic society are required to act in accordance with the legal rights of citizens and certain constraints on official behavior; these rights and constraints are spelled out in the Constitution, legislative enactments, and judicial decisions. As part of a bureaucracy, however, the police have an ideology that emphasizes order, efficiency, and initiative; these values are sometimes in conflict with the value of legality. Thus, "'law' and 'order' are frequently found to be in opposition, because law implies rational restraint upon the rules and procedures utilized to achieve order. Order under law, therefore, subordinates the ideal of conformity to the ideal of legality" (Skolnick, 1975: 9).

Police Abuses of Authority

The conflicting demands under which the police operate sometimes lead them to abuse their authority. For example, departmental pressure on officers to use their initiative and be efficient in solving cases can lead to the violation of due process rights, such as illegal seizure of evidence or coercion of a confession. Laws that define victimless crimes such as gambling, possession of drugs, or prostitution require the police to make arrests for consensual crimes in which the participants do not define themselves as victims; in such cases, the police sometimes find it easy to justify taking a bribe not to make an arrest. Stressful work conditions can increase police sensitivity to challenges to their authority and make brutality against citizens more likely. The camaraderie of the police subculture encourages retaliation against those who assault or kill fellow officers. Police abuses of their authority seem to be structurally induced, rather than the product of personality flaws in individual officers. Sometimes, entire departments systematically violate the law, as shown in the Cross-Cultural Perspective.

Periodically, police corruption scandals occur, frequently before elections and typically with the involvement of an activist press. Commissions are often established to document police corruption and bring charges against dishonest officers; action against those who pay bribes is less common. For a time, the department may be "cleaned up," as officers become wary of accepting bribes. Eventually, matters usually get back to "normal," with at least small favors for the police again becoming common.

The Working Personality of the Officer

Police officers develop a **working personality,** a distinctive approach to situations and events they encounter on the job (Skolnick, 1975). This working personality is a response to the danger of the job, the authority vested in the officer, and the need to appear efficient in the performance of assigned duties. The police learn to respond to "symbolic assailants," whose crimes threaten community standards and the police themselves. Officers learn how to do their jobs from the police subculture, which shares with the larger culture such values as conformity and authority, but which also includes specific values of its own such as suspiciousness and the need to maintain respect for the police at all costs. New recruits quickly learn the values and norms of this subculture; one study found that officers soon agreed that they might have to use force to gain citizen compliance and that respect in tough neighborhoods depends on the officer's willingness to use force (McNamara, 1967).

Suspiciousness Suspiciousness is a key component of the police officer's working personality. Officers learn to suspect that a crime is being committed or is about to be committed in situations to which other people would not give a second thought. What is not clear, even after many judicial decisions, is exactly when an officer's suspicion is a legal basis for searching a citizen or making an arrest.

Discretion A second important aspect of the working personality of the police officer is the exercise of **discretion,** the use of judgment to decide what

A CROSS-CULTURAL PERSPECTIVE

Police Corruption in Mexico

The police in Mexico are "symbols of corruption, abuse of power and in some cases outright criminality" (Riding, p. 12). One former officer was shot to death while resisting arrest after kidnapping and murdering an eleven-year-old boy. In 1995, the son of President Ernesto Zedillo was the victim of an attempted carjacking by three police officers.

The widespread corruption that permeates the Mexican police force has led to public cynicism, hostility, and fear. The police, who justify their acceptance of bribes by their low salaries, demand "mordidas" from drivers they accuse of violating traffic laws. They accept bribes from drug traffickers, offering them noninterference in the movement of narcotics and even carrying out killings for them. As one official notes, "With defenders of the law acting outside the law, the citizen doesn't stand a chance" (Riding, p. 12).

Elected in 1982, President Miguel de la Madrid dismissed 2,500 police officers for corruption or brutality in his first three years in office. He also introduced a training program for new police recruits to reduce their abuse of power. These reforms had little effect, and in 1984 the government announced a new five-year program to stop police abuses. During his successful campaign for the presidency in 1988, Carlos Salinas de Gortari pledged that he would no longer tolerate police abuses of authority and attacks on the dignity of citizens. The federal police force was reorganized under the control of civilians, anti-corruption and internal affairs units were established, and a new police unit was created to take calls from citizens seeking protection from federal agents.

Matters do not seem to have improved, but promises for reform continue. Elected in 1994, President Zedillo vowed to arrest anyone suspected of a crime; soon after, the brother of former President Salinas de Gortari was charged with involvement in a murder. Zedillo has promised to establish the rule of law, but critics doubt that the weak Mexican government and the public's attitude toward the police will make that possible.

Sources: Based on Alan Riding, "Criminals in Mexico: How Many Are Policemen?" *New York Times,* February 13, 1983, p. 12; Mark A. Uhlig, "Mexico to Combat Police Corruption," *New York Times,* June 5, 1991, p. A16; Anthony DePalma, "Mexico Lives by Virtual Law," *New York Times,* March 26, 1995, p. E3.

---

action to take. The police clearly possess delegated discretion, such as the power to decide when to give a traffic ticket. Unauthorized discretion is that which the police exercise but for which they do not have authority, such as making decisions on the basis of a suspect's race or sex (Skolnick, 1975).

The way the police exercise discretion helps define the outer limits of permissible behavior. They may regard some offenses as mere nuisances, and decide to warn an individual rather than make an arrest. They have less freedom in dealing with serious crimes and usually make arrests in those cases.

One decision that is difficult for a police officer to make is whether to use force against a citizen, a decision that must be made quickly and often under stressful and ambiguous circumstances. In *Tennessee* v. *Garner* (1985), the Supreme Court ruled that the police cannot use deadly force "unless it is necessary to prevent the escape and the officer has probable cause to believe that the suspect poses a significant threat of death or serious physical injury to the officer or others" (cited in Tennenbaum, 1994: 244). The use of deadly force to stop fleeing felons who are unarmed and nonviolent was thus declared unconstitutional. This decision significantly reduced police homicides by curtailing the use of deadly force against fleeing felons and by leading police departments to adopt guidelines that decreased other kinds of police shootings as well (Tennenbaum, 1994).

Another situation in which the police must exercise discretion is the "domestic dispute." The police traditionally have dealt with arguments or assaults between people who live together by making a judgment about the possible consequences of either arresting someone or trying to settle the dispute by mediating between the parties. An officer might judge that an arrest in a domestic disturbance will heighten conflict in the household over the long run, or the officer might believe that the complainant will not press charges in court. In such cases, the officer may not make an arrest. Officers may make an arrest if they think the conflict will flare up again as soon as they leave. Feminists have protested this use of police discretion, claiming that many wives are repeatedly abused by their husbands because the police are reluctant to make arrests. This is true, but so is the officer's contention that many women refuse to help in prosecuting their husbands, often out of fear, and that arrests can exacerbate tensions in the household. The following chapter examines research on the deterrent effects of different police responses to domestic violence.

In deciding whether to make an arrest, officers take into account a suspect's prior record, but they also assess the suspect's character by noting his or her group affiliations (including membership in a gang), age, race, hairstyle, dress, and demeanor. Demeanor includes how contrite the suspect is about the offense, how much respect he or she shows the officer, and how afraid of possible sanctions the suspect seems to be (Piliavin and Briar, 1964; Black, 1980).

One study found that an officer's decision to take a suspect into custody was influenced by the dispositional preferences of the victim, the race and demeanor of the suspect, the presence of bystanders, and the seriousness of the offense. Males and females were equally likely to be arrested, and antagonistic behavior by suspects of either sex increased the chance of arrest. Bystanders increased the probability of arrest, because the police thought that they needed to show others that they were in control of the situation. Arrest was less likely if the victim and the suspect knew one another, because this indicated that the victim would be less likely to help in prosecuting the suspect (Smith and Visher, 1981).

Recent research has called into question the assumption that demeanor independently affects the chance that a suspect will be arrested. Analyzing data collected in Dade County, Florida, David Klinger (1994) concluded that legally permissible displays of hostility do not, by themselves, increase the chance of arrest; instead, "hostile suspects are more likely to be arrested because they are more likely to commit crimes against and in the presence of the police, not because their demeanor connotes a lack of respect for authority" (Klinger, 1994: 489). Other studies are less conclusive. One found that the way demeanor is defined affects whether that demeanor predicts the likelihood of arrest (Lundman, 1994). Another found that active but legal resistance by a suspect increased the chance of arrest slightly but not in a statistically significant way (Mastrofski, Worden, and Snipes, 1995). Klinger's (1996) reanalysis of the Dade County data indicated that arrest might be more likely when a suspect displayed "extreme" hostility (Klinger, 1996). Another study concluded that hostile demeanor by suspects does indeed affect police behavior (Worden and Shepard, 1996).

Police discretion is, ideally, based on an officer's best judgment about the future course of a suspect's behavior and the likely effects of an arrest or a warning, but this judgment must be made within legal constraints. For instance, if an officer judges that one suspect is more likely than another suspect to commit more crime if not arrested and thus arrests the first suspect and only warns the second one, this decision involves illegal discrimination rather than delegated discretion if the only basis for the officer's decision is that the first suspect is black and the second one white.

Discretion and Racial Discrimination   There is mixed evidence on whether the police discriminate against minority groups. The complexity of this issue can be seen in a study based on data collected in 1965 and 1966 in Boston, Chicago, and Washington, D.C., by observers who rode in police cars and systematically observed police behavior (Black and Reiss, 1970; Black, 1980). The researchers found that the police were much more likely to arrest a black juvenile suspect than a white juvenile suspect. However, two factors other than racial discrimination seemed to explain this difference. One was that more of the black juveniles were stopped for serious crimes, and the police acted on the legal basis of seriousness of the offense in arresting more of the black suspects. Second, most complaints about black juveniles came from black adults, and they were more likely than white adults who complained to the police about white juveniles to demand that the police make an arrest, rather than merely warn the juvenile. In making arrest decisions, the police were thus responding to the seriousness of the crime and the preferences of the complainant, rather than to the race of the suspect.

Much research, especially that done outside the South in recent years, finds that the race of the suspect is a less important influence on the police arrest decision than are factors such as the seriousness of the offense, prior criminal record, demeanor, and the socioeconomic status of the neighborhood in which a police encounter occurs. However, even when the other variables are taken into account, some studies find that race remains as a factor that influences the disposition of a case. One study found that there was more evidence of racial bias by the police in deciding to send juvenile suspects to court than there was of racial bias in court decisions. This racial bias by the police increased the chance that a youth from a minority group would have a record, which could then contribute to a criminal career by affecting police actions and court decisions in the future (Dannefer and Schutt, 1982).

If the police discriminate by race, black offenders would stand a greater chance of being arrested than white offenders who committed the same offense. We can test this for the crime of robbery, which involves a face-to-face confrontation between offender and victim. If the police "overarrest" black robbers, the proportion of all arrested suspects who are blacks would be higher than the proportion of all robbers that victims report to be blacks. However, data from a study of robbery in Boston that are presented in Table 13.1 show that the police actually "underarrested" black robbers in comparison to white robbers. In the first six months of 1964, 55 percent of all robbers were blacks, according to victims, but only 44 percent of all suspects arrested for robbery were blacks, suggesting that black robbers had a smaller chance than white ones of being arrested for their crimes. The data for 1968 show a similar pattern. A study of robbery in 1974 in Milwaukee, Wisconsin, found that the percentage of all arrested robbery suspects who were blacks was about the same as the percentage of all robbers identified as blacks by victims (Pruitt and Wilson, 1983). Neither of these studies supports the contention that the police are more likely to arrest black suspects than white suspects, at least for the crime of robbery. A study that used victimization survey data and FBI arrest data concluded that there was "virtually no criminal justice selection bias for either rape or robbery but there [was] such bias for assault, especially aggravated assault" (Hindelang, 1978: 101).

The observational study of the police carried out in Boston, Chicago, and Washington, D.C., in the mid-1960s uncovered a significant amount of prejudice among the police, with about three-fourths of the officers classified as very prejudiced or considerably prejudiced against blacks on the basis of spontaneous comments and behavior. This study found that prejudice, an attitude, was not necessarily associated with discrimination, which is behavior. The observers saw forty-four cases of police assault on citizens during seven weeks of round-the-clock observation; in many of these assaults no suspect was arrested. They found a higher rate of undue force used against whites than against blacks. Black and white officers used violence with about

TABLE 13.1 Percentage of All Robbers in Boston Who Are Blacks

Percentage Who Are Blacks	1964*	1968*
By victim identifications	55%	66%
By arrest data	44%	53%

*Data are for the first six months of each year.

Source: Adapted from John E. Conklin, *Robbery and the Criminal Justice System*. Philadelphia: J. B. Lippincott Company, 1972, p. 33.

the same frequency, and usually against members of their own race, something that reflected the areas to which the officers were assigned. The police might have been less likely to use violence against blacks during this period because of the threat of urban riots, many of which occurred between 1965 and 1968. The civil rights gains of blacks might also have convinced some officers that police abuses would be reported and lead to trouble for them. In addition, officers might have adjusted their behavior in the presence of observers in order to avoid the appearance of discrimination, although they apparently did not adjust their verbal comments to avoid the impression of racial prejudice (Reiss, 1968, 1971).

One area in which the police possibly discriminate by race is in the shooting of civilians. However, a study of police shootings in Chicago between 1974 and 1978 found that if rates of being shot by the police were calculated for blacks, Hispanics, and whites by dividing the number of shooting victims of each group by the number of people of that group arrested for "forcible felonies"—defined as murders, rapes, robberies, assaults, and burglaries— then whites were actually somewhat more likely to be shot than blacks and Hispanics, although differences among the groups were small. Rates were calculated in this way to account for group differences in involvement in serious crimes, the situations that most often led to police shootings. This study suggests that the police are about equally likely to shoot whites, blacks, and Hispanics (Geller and Karales, 1981).

A study of police shootings in Memphis, Tennessee, found that the police were more likely to shoot blacks than whites, even if group differences in criminal activity were taken into account (Fyfe, 1981). This suggests that police discrimination against minorities in the use of force exists in some cities but not in others. Differences in the relative power of minorities, the organization of the municipal police department, and the department's administrative directives could account for such city-to-city variations in the use of force by the police against minorities (Fyfe, 1981; Waegel, 1984).

On March 3, 1991, three white Los Angeles police officers brutally beat Rodney King, a black man, in the presence of a white sergeant while twenty-three other law-enforcement officers watched. As many as twenty local residents witnessed the attack, and one of them recorded it with his new video camera. King, who had a criminal record, had been stopped after a high-speed car chase; some of the officers later said that King had resisted arrest and seemed to be reaching for a weapon. None of his behavior justified the violent response by the police: they kicked, bludgeoned, electrically shocked, and hog-tied him, then dragged him to the side of the road until an ambulance arrived. In a trial that took place in another county, four officers were acquitted of assault charges by a jury that had no black members. After the acquittals, a deadly riot broke out in Los Angeles, lasting from April 29 to May 2, 1992; fifty-two people were killed and more than $1 billion worth of property was damaged or destroyed. The officers who had been acquitted were then indicted on federal charges of violating King's civil rights. On April 17, 1993, two of them were acquitted and two were found guilty; the convicted officers were later sentenced to two-and-a-half years in prison.

Rodney King's lawyer displays a photo showing some of the injuries King sustained in a brutal 1991 beating by Los Angeles police officers.

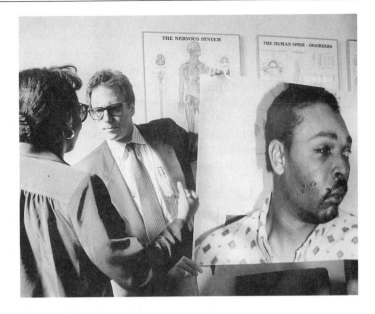

Sociologist Jerome Skolnick has commented on the King beating as follows: "It is highly unlikely that this is unrepresentative of Los Angeles police. Two people can go crazy, but if you have ten or twelve people watching them and not doing anything, this tells you that this is the normal thing for them" (cited in Mydans, 1991: B7). Skolnick and James Fyfe (1993) claim that such police brutality is partly the result of an attitude that officers learn on the job, namely that they are engaged in an all-out war on crime. Many officers see themselves as "ghetto gunslingers," outsiders to the communities they patrol, who must use force to maintain respect and enforce the law. Skolnick and Fyfe also fault some police administrators for being insulated from effective constraints on their power and reluctant to take strong action against brutal officers and their supervisors. Even though it is difficult to document police brutality, due to a code of silence among officers and because allegations of brutality are investigated by the police themselves, Skolnick and Fyfe believe that brutality has declined over the past fifty years, and even over the last two decades.

Discretion and Sex Discrimination   Research indicates that the police respond differently to male and female defendants. A study in a midwestern city found that from 1948 to 1976, police disposition of males and females became more similar for juvenile and adult misdemeanors and for adult felonies, but that males and females continued to be treated differently for juvenile status offenses and juvenile felonies. Overall, treatment of the sexes became more alike over time, but sex discrimination had not disappeared by the mid-1970s. Female status offenders were treated more leniently and paternalistically even in the 1970s (Krohn, Curry, and Nelson-Kilger, 1983).

A study that covered the period from 1934 to 1979 found that sex differentials in arrests had diminished in most offense categories, with the largest changes occurring in the 1960s and 1970s. Women showed the most significant increases in arrests for petty property crimes—such as larceny, fraud, and forgery—and for vagrancy and disorderly conduct, which were often related to prostitution. The researchers concluded that the narrowing of the sex differential had not yet produced a convergence of male and female arrests. This narrowing seemed to be due to changes in law-enforcement practices and changes in FBI statistical coverage of a larger part of the nation, as much as or even more than it was due to changes in actual behavior by men and women. The following factors accounted for the increases in arrests of females that had occurred:

1. A decline in chivalry and sympathy for female defendants;
2. A possible increase in the surveillance of women because of growing attention to crime by women;
3. Increased social and legal pressure to administer the law in a nondiscriminatory way;
4. Professionalization and bureaucratization of the police;
5. Improvements in police recording practices, including a greater likelihood of recording a suspect's sex; and
6. Changes in welfare agencies, which have led to more prosecution of crimes such as fraud and larceny. (Steffensmeier and Cobb, 1981)

The Clearance Rate

To measure their effectiveness in dealing with crime, the police use a **clearance rate**, the proportion of offenses that they solve to their satisfaction. Many cleared cases lead to arrest, prosecution, and conviction, but the police also classify as cleared some cases that do not produce an arrest. Sometimes an offender cannot be arrested because he or she is deceased, out of the country, or in prison in another state. For example, a man who kills his wife and then commits suicide would leave the police with no one to arrest for the murder, but they would still call the homicide cleared. In other cases, the police strongly believe they know who committed a crime but lack the evidence to make an arrest; often those crimes are classified as cleared.

There are problems with relying on clearance rates to measure the effectiveness of the police. Because the police themselves decide when a case is cleared, they can classify cases as cleared to make themselves look good. This might mean that the actual offender in a crime that is erroneously marked cleared will no longer be hunted by the police; such "false clearances" could reduce the deterrent effect of the law. Another difficulty with clearance rates is that a crime committed by several offenders will be marked cleared with the arrest of a single suspect, an action that exaggerates police effectiveness in apprehending criminals. Departmental pressure to clear cases can lead to illegal police actions to get suspects to do things for which they can be arrested. Critics see this as illegal entrapment, but supporters justify it by saying that only people predisposed to crime will be drawn into it.

The Boston robbery study paid close attention to the way the police cleared cases. The clearance rate for all robberies recorded by the police in the first six months of 1968 was 36 percent. Thirty-eight percent of all clearances resulted from an arrest at or near the scene of the crime, with the police interrupting the robbery or finding a suspect nearby. One-fifth of the clearances resulted directly from information supplied by the victim or a witness; this included giving the police the name or address of the robber and identifying a "mugshot." Nearly as many robberies were cleared by victim identification of a suspect in another case; 18 percent of the clearances resulted from victims' saying they were robbed by someone arrested on other charges whose photograph they were shown by the police or whom they picked out of a lineup. Another 18 percent of the clearances resulted from what might be called "multiple clearance by confession." This method, which did not use the victim as a check, involved suspects who confessed to similar offenses about which the police asked them. In cases of this sort, suspects know the police will not charge them with the additional crimes to which they confess, and might even be more lenient on the offense for which they were arrested, if they help the police clear their books. These multiple clearances by confession are used to make the department look more efficient at solving crimes. A final method by which robbery cases were solved was by a detective's investigation; this method accounted for only 6 percent of all clearances (Conklin, 1972).

The Role of the Detective in Clearing Cases   Detectives solve relatively few robberies because there is usually little they can do after a robber escapes from the scene of the crime. There is rarely any physical evidence, such as fingerprints, and victims' descriptions are often vague and unreliable. The few robberies that detectives do solve are usually the most serious ones, such as bank robberies and grocery store holdups.

One study of the role of detectives in solving crimes concluded that their efforts were as important as the investigative work of patrol officers in solving robberies and burglaries. Within the police department, robbery and burglary cases were divided into three categories:

1. cases that could not be solved with a reasonable amount of effort;
2. cases that are solved by circumstances, requiring only the arrest of a suspect and the development of the case for prosecution;
3. cases that could be solved with a reasonable amount of effort.

Many robberies and burglaries were not even assigned to detectives for investigation because there were few or no leads or because the case was solved by circumstances, but of those cases that were assigned to detectives, many were solved by investigation. The investigation process included interviews with witnesses and informants, discussions with other police officers, and an examination of the department's files. Interviews with victims produced few arrests (Eck, 1984).

A detective's decision to investigate a victim's complaint about the theft of property is affected by the characteristics of the victim and the crime. Detectives are most likely to spend time in a follow-up investigation if there is some evidence that might help them solve the crime. In burglary cases, victims living in well-to-do communities receive more attention from police investigators than victims living in poor communities. Minority-group members who are burglary victims are slightly less likely than white victims to receive favorable treatment by police investigators. Police activity in follow-up investigations of violent crimes is influenced by the willingness of the victim to aid in the prosecution of the case (Bynum, Cordner, and Greene, 1982).

A study of reported burglaries found that a southern sheriff's department was more likely to use evidence technicians to dust for fingerprints when entry into the building involved force or when the property that had been stolen was "a marker of the self." Jewelry, silver, and firearms were items that recalled the past or had special personal significance for victims, and the sheriff was more likely to make special investigative efforts when such property had been taken. Dusting for fingerprints rarely led to an arrest, but it helped to foster good public relations and restore the victim's peace of mind (Stenross, 1984).

The police are especially likely to investigate complaints about crimes that are serious, provide evidence, occur in well-to-do neighborhoods, have a victim who is willing to prosecute, and involve the loss of property with personal significance. As a result, police work introduces contingencies into an offender's career, with offenders who commit certain kinds of crime being especially likely to be arrested and processed by the courts.

Criminal Courts

In the United States, suspects are presumed to be innocent from the time they are arrested by the police until they are found guilty or innocent in court. As a consequence, they have a right to gain their release pending the disposition of charges against them. Usually, a district attorney prosecutes the defendant, a defense attorney helps the defendant get acquitted or secure the most lenient sentence possible, and a judge or jury decides guilt or innocence. Often a defendant pleads guilty in return for an agreed-on sentence that is less than the one that might result from a trial. Judges sometimes give very different sentences to offenders who have similar criminal records and have been convicted of similar offenses.

Bail

The Eighth Amendment states that "excessive bail shall not be required" of criminal defendants; even so, defendants in crimes that carry the death penalty are usually denied bail. **Bail** is designed to ensure that defendants will show up to face charges against them when their trial is scheduled, while allowing them to remain free until the trial takes place. To do this, an amount of money is set that must be deposited with the court before the defendant can be released. Because bail requires suspects to pay money, it discriminates against those who cannot afford their release, and so jails that hold suspects awaiting trial are usually filled with poor defendants.

A study conducted in Philadelphia concluded that defendants who were detained on bail—either because bail was denied or because they could not afford bail—differed from the average defendant entering the criminal justice system. Those who were detained on bail were more likely to be charged with serious crimes, more likely to have many prior arrests and convictions, more likely not to have shown up for trials in the past, and more likely to have been arrested when out on bail in the past. The defendants who were detained on bail thus seemed to be especially likely to commit new crimes ("bail crimes") if released, and especially likely to "default," or not show up for trial, if released. However, a significant number of the detained defendants, 13 percent of the total, were classified as "low risks" who might have been released with little threat of bail crime or default. The release of low-risk detainees would alleviate jail crowding (Goldkamp, 1983).

Defendants awaiting trial are released in several ways. Some are released on their own recognizance, a promise to appear for trial. Others gain their release by placing with the court an amount of cash equal to the bail set by the judge, or by giving the court something equal in value to the amount of bail, such as a savings account passbook or a real estate deed. Because most defendants have little money or property, a system of bail bondsmen has developed in the United States to help defendants gain their release.

Bail bondsmen write a bail bond, a kind of insurance policy, that guarantees the court that they will pay the full amount of the bail if the defendant fails to appear for trial as scheduled. In return for this guarantee, the bondsman charges the defendant a nonrefundable fee, usually 10 percent of the bail amount, to write the bond. Bondsmen make it easier for defendants to gain their release, but they do not seem to improve the chance that defendants will show up for trial and they cost defendants much money. They have also been involved in corrupt practices. As a result, several states have replaced bondsmen with a system that allows defendants to place a percentage of the amount of the bail with the court as a deposit, which is returned when their case is disposed of, even if they are found guilty.

Preventive Detention

Long delays from arrest until trial provide opportunities for defendants who are released on bail to commit crimes. Concern with such bail crimes has led to demands for **preventive detention**, a system that holds some defendants without bail. This system, which is common in Europe, was implemented in Washington, D.C., in 1971 but rarely used thereafter. Preventive detention was authorized for the federal court system in 1984. In about half of the states, judges are allowed to consider whether a defendant is dangerous to others in making a decision to release the defendant prior to trial. Even where preventive detention is not specifically authorized, judges often set very high bails for defendants they believe will endanger the safety of others or commit bail crimes. These defendants are held in jail when they cannot afford to make bail.

Critics claim that preventive detention violates the Eighth Amendment's right to have a reasonable bail set. In 1987 the U.S. Supreme Court rejected that argument, declaring preventive detention legal if a prosecutor could show that freeing a defendant would endanger the community. Another objection to preventive detention is that it imprisons people for acts they might commit if they were released, and accurately predicting the behavior of pretrial releasees is difficult (Angel et al., 1971; Fagan and Guggenheim, 1996).

Preventive detention could contribute to criminal careers, if defendants who are held in jail cannot consult with their attorneys and contact witnesses to develop a defense, or if defendants make a bad impression on judges or jurors when they arrive in court in jail clothes. Preventive detention could set in motion a cycle in which suspects thought to be dangerous are denied bail, are then more likely to be convicted as a result of being held in jail, and thus have a worse criminal record that is then used to hold them without bail the next time they are arrested. The denial of bail can also cause defendants to lose their jobs, force their families to go on welfare, sever their bonds to the conventional order, and even make criminal behavior by their children more likely.

Prosecutors

Prosecutors, or district attorneys, are usually lawyers who are elected officials. Often they see themselves as independent of public control, while still serving the public, and they regard themselves as lawyers whose behavior should reflect the standards of the legal profession. They bring charges against defendants and try to ensure that justice is done. They are concerned with all aspects of the case and interact with police officers, defense attorneys, judges, jurors, witnesses, victims, and defendants.

Prosecutors measure their success by a conviction rate, just as the police measure their effectiveness by a clearance rate. Some prosecutors blame the police when they fail to get convictions, claiming that the police are more concerned with clearing cases than with presenting cases that can produce convictions. In response, the police accuse prosecutors of being too willing to reduce charges from felonies to misdemeanors just to secure convictions, rather than using the resources of the district attorney's office to convict suspects on more serious charges. Prosecutors do screen cases brought by the police to find the ones that are the most likely to produce convictions. They are not necessarily concerned with getting judges to mete out the harshest possible sentences to convicted offenders, being more concerned with fairness than with getting the longest possible prison sentence or getting a conviction in a case in which the evidence does not warrant it (Neubauer, 1974; Stanko, 1981–82).

Defense Attorneys

The American criminal justice system is based on an adversary model or "fight theory" that assumes that the correct verdict will emerge if a prosecutor presents the best case against a defendant and a defense attorney presents the strongest case for the defendant. In fact, many more cases are settled by guilty pleas by defendants than by trials using this adversary model. Defense attorneys are an integral part of the court system, interacting cordially with prosecutors and judges, rather than behaving in an adversary manner; good relationships with other court personnel make plea bargaining easier and help defense attorneys get trial dates postponed when necessary. The close relationship of defense attorneys with other court personnel dilutes the adversary nature of the American criminal justice system, a system that seems designed to produce the most expeditious processing of cases (Blumberg, 1979).

At an arraignment, judges inform defendants of the charges against them and the maximum penalties for the crimes with which they are charged. The threat of a very long sentence, which few defendants actually receive, makes them eager to seek the advice of defense attorneys. Defense attorneys act as counselors who interpret the law for their clients and try to keep them out of court. The expertise of defense attorneys is important in getting defendants the lightest possible sentence—the "normal" penalty or "going rate"—in exchange for a guilty plea. When cases are tried before a judge or a jury, defense attorneys try to get their clients acquitted, convicted on the least serious charge, or sentenced as leniently as possible (Neubauer, 1974).

The Supreme Court decisions in *Gideon* v. *Wainwright* (1963) and *Argersinger* v. *Hamlin* (1972) guaranteed free counsel to any indigent defendant facing the threat of incarceration in a felony or misdemeanor case. Poor defendants are provided with legal counsel through public defender organizations or through the assignment of lawyers by the courts.

Judges

In lower criminal courts, where most criminal cases are first heard, one of the judge's primary functions is to ratify agreements between defense attorneys and prosecutors about the sentences that defendants will receive for pleading guilty. When cases go to trial, judges act either as decision makers or as supervisors of the proceedings when cases are tried before juries. Perhaps the most important function for the judge is the sentencing of convicted offenders.

Judges are supposed to sentence offenders on the basis of legal criteria: the nature of the crimes for which they have been convicted, and perhaps their criminal records. Criminologists are concerned that judges' sentences might be influenced by extralegal criteria such as race, sex, and age. The actual role of legal and extralegal criteria in determining sentences is examined later in this chapter.

Juries

The jury has been criticized as a group of amateurs who lack the legal training to make decisions that have major effects on defendants' lives. It has also been defended as an important democratic institution that involves the average citizen in the process of defining and meting out justice. However, no more than 5 percent of all felony cases that are prosecuted involve jury trials, as guilty pleas account for most convictions (Baldwin and McConville, 1980).

A landmark study of the American jury asked judges to fill out questionnaires about the jury trials over which they had presided. In about four-fifths of the cases on which data were collected, judges said that jurors had reached the same verdict they themselves would have reached. In the remaining cases, juries were much more likely to acquit defendants when judges said they would have convicted them, rather than to convict defendants whom the judges would have acquitted. The jurors seemed to require more proof to find guilt beyond a reasonable doubt than did the judges, and so juries can be said to be "defendant-friendly." The judges thought the juries performed quite well, considering the evidence carefully and taking longer to reach verdicts in cases the judges thought were the most difficult from a legal point of view (Kalven and Zeisel, 1966).

In contrast to this study's conclusion that juries are more lenient toward defendants than are judges, another study found that juries were significantly more likely than judges to convict defendants (Levine, 1983). This study of more than 58,000 felony trials concluded that since the 1950s there has been a growth in public conservatism regarding crime that accounts for the increasingly harsh treatment of defendants by juries. This researcher's methods differed from those of the earlier study, and so we must be cautious in attributing differences between the conclusions of the two studies to actual changes in jury behavior over time.

The American jury has been criticized as a group of amateurs who lack legal training, and praised as a democratic institution that involves citizens in the legal system.

Plea Bargaining

More than 85 percent of all felony convictions in American courts are the result of guilty pleas (Smith, 1986). **Plea bargaining** is an informal but structured process of negotiation in which a prosecutor and a defense attorney agree on a guilty plea and a sentence that the prosecutor will recommend to a judge. Because defendants can request trials or delays, which are costly and time-consuming for the court, prosecutors are often willing to agree to a reduced charge or a light sentence in exchange for a guilty plea. Because prosecutors have the power to go to trial and ask for a severe sentence, defendants are frequently willing to plead guilty and accept a penalty less than the one they might receive if convicted in a trial (Rosett and Cressey, 1976; Maynard, 1984).

One study found that judges sentenced defendants to longer terms if they asked for trials than if they pleaded guilty. Judges seemed to adopt the position that if a defendant took some of the court's time to have a trial, which is of course the defendant's legal right, then the judge would take some of the defendant's time by meting out a longer prison sentence (Uhlman and Walker, 1980). A second study confirmed that defendants who were convicted after trials received harsher sentences than defendants with similar characteristics who faced the same charges and pleaded guilty (LaFree, 1985). A third study concluded that although more defendants convicted after trials were incarcerated than was true for defendants who pleaded guilty, the difference was not evidence that plea bargaining was coercive. Instead, the difference in incarceration rates for the two groups was attributable to two factors: (1) some of the defendants who pleaded guilty would not have been convicted if they had gone to trial, and (2) cases in which pleas were negotiated had characteristics different from cases in which convictions followed trials (Smith, 1986: 966).

Plea bargaining has both critics and supporters. Critics claim that it induces innocent defendants to acquiesce to a guilty plea in order to get a more lenient sentence than they would if they demanded a trial and were found guilty by a judge or a jury. Critics also complain that plea bargaining goes on behind closed doors, therefore keeping the legal process from public view and making abuses more likely. In addition, some critics claim, a defendant cannot be sure that a judge will hand out an agreed-on sentence after the defendant pleads guilty in court. The sentences given out as a result of plea bargaining usually fall far short of maximum sentences so as to induce defendants to plead guilty. According to some critics, offenders are punished much less harshly than justice demands, thereby undermining the deterrent and incapacitating effects of punishment.

Supporters of plea bargaining argue that the criminal courts could not function if every defendant asked for a trial. Court resources would have to be multiplied many times to process all of the cases if plea bargaining were not used to resolve most charges. Supporters claim that plea bargaining does provide just sentences—that is, penalties proportional to the harm caused by offenders—even if those penalties fall short of the legal maximum. They point out that the actual penalties given out by the courts are much longer in the United States than in other Western democracies, and that plea bargaining keeps punishment from being even more severe than it already is (Rosett and Cressey, 1976).

Probation

One penalty that judges sometimes impose on convicted offenders is **probation**, a form of supervised release. Probation originated in the work of a Boston shoemaker named John Augustus, who in 1841 began to supervise offenders and report on them to the court. In 1878 Massachusetts became the first state to pass a probation law; today all states and the federal government provide probation for at least some kinds of offenders. Probation is much less expensive than incarceration, and as a result twice as many offenders are on probation as are in the nation's jails and prisons.

Probation is designed to offer convicted offenders treatment outside prison where they can maintain their ties to conventional society. Judges, with the help of probation officers who present them with presentence reports, try to select for probation those offenders who are the best risks to stay away from crime. In addition to providing probationers with services, this system aims to control behavior through surveillance by probation officers to whom offenders have to report regularly. However, many probation officers are so overburdened with cases that they have little time to supervise their clients or provide them with services. This problem has worsened in recent years as the number of drug-related crimes handled by the courts has increased.

Sentence Disparity

A major problem with American courts is **sentence disparity**, the difference in the criminal sanctions handed out to people who are convicted of similar offenses and who have similar criminal records. For instance, there is significant variation in sentences from one state to another, from one city to another, and from one judge to another in the same city. Here we examine research on the way that a defendant's race, social class, and sex influence sentencing.

Race and Sentencing   The fact that blacks constitute about half of all inmates in American jails and prisons, while being only 12.6 percent of the population, has led some critics of the criminal justice system to blame the imprisonment of so many blacks on racial discrimination by the judges who sentence offenders.

Much research has been done on racial discrimination in the sentencing of offenders, particularly for capital offenses, but the results are not conclusive. Two researchers have argued that it is the greater involvement of blacks in crime that explains most of the high proportion of inmates who are blacks. Using arrest data and victimization survey results, these researchers concluded that the participation of blacks in crime would produce a prison population that was about 43 percent blacks, rather than the 48 percent that it actually was (Blumstein, 1982; Langan, 1985; also, see Tonry, 1995). The 5 percent difference might be due to racial discrimination, but it could also be explained by legally relevant criteria for sentencing, such as prior criminal history or seriousness of the offense.

One review of the research on the role of race in sentencing showed that twenty-six studies discovered no racial discrimination, sixteen had mixed results, and fifteen found racial discrimination. However, thirteen of the fifteen studies that found discrimination did not compare blacks and whites who had similar prior criminal records. Of the twenty-four studies that did take prior criminal history into account, only two found evidence of racial discrimination (Kleck, 1981, 1985). When such legally relevant criteria as criminal record and seriousness of charge are taken into account, most research finds that race either disappears or greatly diminishes in importance as a factor influencing sentencing. This is especially true for studies carried out in recent years and outside the South.

A study of 11,553 offenders convicted in California in 1980 of assault, robbery, burglary, theft, forgery, and drug offenses concluded that race was not a factor in sentencing, once type of offense, prior record, and legal procedural variables (such as having a private attorney) were taken into account. This absence of racial discrimination was true for each of the six crimes, for the decision to imprison or place on probation a convicted offender, and for the decision about length of sentence (Klein, Turner, and Petersilia, 1988).

Some research does find evidence of racial discrimination (Thornberry, 1979; Christianson, 1981; Petersilia, 1983; Collins, 1987; Myers, 1989). A study that looked at the disposition of juvenile cases in Florida from 1979 to 1981 concluded that although the impact of race on sentencing was less than the impact of legally relevant criteria, blacks were "more likely to be recommended for formal processing, referred to court, adjudicated delinquent, and given harsher dispositions than comparable white offenders" (Bishop and Frazier, 1988: 258). Data from Florida for 1985 through 1987 confirmed that blacks referred for delinquent acts were treated more severely than whites, but that whites were treated more severely than blacks when referred for repeated status offenses (Bishop and Frazier, 1996). A study of the disposition of drug cases in Miami in 1971 found that discrimination was most likely to occur in ambiguous cases in which some aspects of the case (such as seriousness of the charge) pointed to harsh punishment and other aspects of the case (such as lack of prior criminal record) pointed to lenient punishment. When all aspects of the case clearly indicated that the offender should be treated either harshly or leniently, discrimination was less likely (Unnever and Hembroff, 1988).

Some research indicates that the role of race in sentencing is complex, varying with the type of crime, the race composition of the offender-victim dyad, and the relationship between the offender and the victim. One researcher found that judges handed out the harshest penalties to black men who had sexually assaulted white women and to black men who had sexually assaulted black women who were strangers. Penalties were most lenient when a sexual assault involved a white offender and a white victim and when a sexual assault involved a black offender and a black victim who was an acquaintance (Spohn, 1994).

Discrimination against racial and ethnic minorities sometimes takes subtle forms. A study of sentencing in California found that being white, black, or Hispanic did not directly affect sentences, but that judges emphasized different factors in sentencing the members of each group. For example, judges used the prior records of Hispanic defendants to justify longer sentences for them but were less likely to use the prior records of white and black defendants to justify longer sentences for them (Zatz, 1984, 1987).

The War on Drugs waged by the Reagan and Bush administrations led to the incarceration of many more blacks, despite the fact that there was little increase in the proportion of all suspects arrested for index crimes who were blacks. In 1979, 32 percent of suspects arrested for index crimes were blacks, and in 1992 the percentage was 35. Over that time, however, the proportion of offenders admitted to state and federal prisons who were blacks rose dramatically, from 39 percent to 54 percent. This increase was a direct result of more prison sentences for drug offenders; from 1980 to 1992, the proportion of state and federal prison inmates incarcerated for a drug crime rose from 8 percent to 26 percent (see Figure 13.3). The increased numbers of inmates serving time for drug offenses were disproportionately black; 22 percent of drug arrests in 1979 but 40 percent of drug arrests in 1992 were of blacks. Law professor Michael Tonry (1995: 49) demonstrates that blacks "are arrested and confined in numbers grossly out of line with their use or sale of drugs," and argues that the War on Drugs has been destructive to poverty-stricken black neighborhoods.

Discrimination against poor black women also characterizes the recent prosecution of drug offenders. Since 1987, increasing numbers of pregnant drug users have been prosecuted for crimes such as child abuse, endangering an unborn child, and even distributing drugs to a minor (the fetus). One study found that about 15 percent of both white and black women who were pregnant used illicit drugs, but black women were ten times as likely to be reported to the authorities as white women, and poor women were more likely to be reported than those with higher incomes (Kolata, 1990).

Recognizing that drug laws sometimes discriminate against blacks, a Minnesota judge in 1990 declared unconstitutional a state law that punished first-time users of crack cocaine with four years in prison but first-time users of powdered cocaine with probation. Lawmakers said they had singled out crack for harsher punishment because of its potency, cheapness, and devastating effects, but statistics for 1988 showed that 92 percent of all arrests for possession of crack were of blacks, whereas 85 percent of all arrests for possession of cocaine in powdered form were of whites (*New York Times,* December 29, 1990). In *United States* v. *Armstrong* (1996), the Supreme Court ruled that similar evidence in federal cases—blacks being 90 percent of convicted crack offenders but only 30 percent of powdered cocaine offenders—was not sufficient to prove racial discrimination; the Court said that a defen-

FIGURE 13.3

Percent of State and Federal Prisoners by Their Most Serious Offense, 1980–1993

Source: Allen J. Beck and Darrell K. Gilliard, *Prisoners in 1994.* Washington, D.C.: U.S. Department of Justice, August 1995, p. 10.

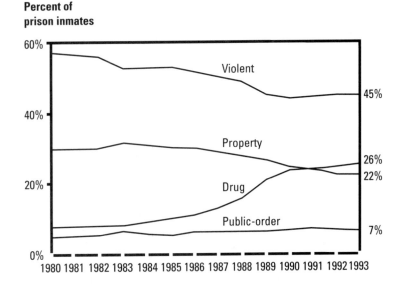

dant had to show that similarly situated defendants (e.g., whites charged with possession of crack) had been treated differently by the courts.

A useful distinction is between "direct" discrimination—in which race or ethnicity plays a part in the sentencing decision, even after taking into account seriousness of the crime and prior criminal record—and "organizational" discrimination, in which economically disadvantaged people are more likely to be convicted or get a long prison term because they cannot afford to be released on bail or hire a private attorney. Organizational or economic discrimination might not be based directly on race, but it affects the way blacks are treated by the criminal justice system, because they have lower incomes, on the average, than whites and are thus more affected by organizational discrimination (Lizotte, 1978; Unnever, 1982). Thus, some of what appears to be racial discrimination is actually a result of disadvantages more likely to be suffered by blacks, such as poverty, lack of job skills, unemployment, low levels of education, and residence in blighted urban areas. The relationship between direct discrimination and organizational discrimination is complex and has important consequences for social policy. Evidence of direct racial discrimination would require civil rights remedies, but evidence of organizational discrimination would point to the need for policies to alleviate the burden of poverty for people of all races.

Racial discrimination, whether direct or organizational, continues to be a factor in the disposition of noncapital cases, though legally relevant criteria have a much greater influence on the disposition of those cases. Research indicates that race plays an even more significant role in the disposition of cases involving the death penalty.

Race and Capital Punishment The major reason that the Supreme Court declared the states' death penalty laws unconstitutional in the 1972 case of

Furman v. *Georgia* was that the application of those laws had shown an excessive degree of arbitrariness, especially in the more frequent use of capital punishment for black defendants. Since 1972, three-fourths of the states have enacted new death penalty laws to satisfy criteria established by the Supreme Court, but those new laws have not eliminated racial discrimination in the use of the death penalty (Bowers and Pierce, 1980; Bowers, 1984). For example, a study using data from Florida for 1973 to 1977 found that the race of both the defendant and the victim influenced the classification of homicides by the police and by prosecutors in a way that increased the likelihood that the death penalty would be imposed on blacks (Radelet and Pierce, 1985).

Research has consistently found that the race of the victim is an important predictor of which homicides will result in the death penalty (Bowers, 1983, 1984; Paternoster, 1983; Gross and Mauro, 1988; Vito and Keil, 1988; Keil and Vito, 1989). A study of homicide in Florida in 1976 and 1977 found that people charged with killing white strangers were more likely to be indicted for first-degree murder (a capital offense) than were people accused of killing black strangers. Differences by race at the stage of bringing formal charges (indictment) thus accounted for the more frequent imposition of the death penalty on people who killed white strangers (Radelet, 1981). A study of homicides in eight states from 1976 to 1980 found that defendants were much more likely to receive the death penalty if their victims were white than if their victims were black, suggesting that the courts place greater value on the lives of whites than on the lives of blacks (Gross and Mauro, 1988). In the 1987 case of *McCleskey* v. *Kemp,* the Supreme Court upheld the constitutionality of the death penalty despite evidence that killers of whites are given the death penalty more often than killers of blacks.

Until 1977 forcible rape was a capital offense in some states, but in that year the Supreme Court ruled in *Coker* v. *Georgia* that the death penalty could not be imposed for rape. Before that decision, there was much racial discrimination in the administration of the death penalty for rape, with black males convicted of raping white females in the South especially likely to be executed (Kleck, 1981). One study finds that black men accused of raping white women still receive harsher penalties than either white men who rape white women or black men who rape black women; rapes of black women by white men rarely come to the attention of the courts. It thus appears to be the race of the victim, or a combination of the race of the victim and the race of the offender—rather than the race of the offender alone—that is most important in determining how convicted rapists will be sentenced (LaFree, 1980).

Much of the research on the death penalty that has found past discrimination in rape cases, and past and current discrimination in homicide cases, relies on data from the South. In part this is because all southern states, but only some nonsouthern states, now have the death penalty; and in part it is because southern states have meted out capital punishment much more often than those nonsouthern states that have death penalty laws. Since 1977, when executions were resumed after a ten-year hiatus, more than 90 percent of all executions have occurred in southern states. One study found that outside the South, black homicide defendants actually seem less likely than white ones to be sentenced to death and less likely to be executed if they are sentenced to death (Kleck, 1981).

Social Class and Sentencing   Some research supports conflict theory's contention that people of lower socioeconomic status fare worse in the criminal justice system than people of higher social standing. One study found social class bias in the court dispositions of juveniles charged with such status offenses as truancy and running away; for conventional offenses against person and property, the evidence of bias by social class was less clear-cut (Carter and Clelland, 1979). Another study found that juries' decisions were influenced by the socioeconomic status of the defendant (Adler, 1973). Research using data from Chicago courts found that length of sentence was influenced by a defendant's occupation; this unequal treatment was largely a result of poor defendants' inability to afford their pretrial release on bail and to pay for a private attorney, both of which made it less likely that they would mount a successful defense (Lizotte, 1978). Court-appointed lawyers are often overburdened with cases and cannot devote as much attention as private attorneys to the preparation of a defense.

Other researchers have found that social class has no strong and consistent impact on sentencing. A study of adult prisoners discovered that sentence severity was not associated with socioeconomic status, when prisoners with similar prior records and demographic characteristics were compared (Chiricos and Waldo, 1975). A review of research on discrimination in the criminal justice system concluded as follows: "Over 80 percent of both racial and socioeconomic studies fail to support differential processing hypotheses" (Williams, 1980: 222).

Sex and Sentencing   Traditionally, girls have been more likely than boys to be referred to the juvenile justice system for status offenses; they have also been more likely than boys to be formally processed, detained, and institutionalized for such offenses. For acts that would be crimes if committed by adults, boys have typically been treated more harshly than girls. However, some research published since 1980 has found little or no gender discrimination in the treatment of status offenders or in the treatment of delinquents accused of acts that would be crimes if committed by adults (Clarke and Koch, 1980; Teilman and Landry, 1981; Dannefer and Schutt, 1982; McCarthy and Smith, 1986). This research suggests that gender might be declining as a factor in the processing of juveniles, perhaps because of sociocultural or legal changes that have produced more egalitarian treatment of boys and girls. On the other hand, gender discrimination in the processing of young people might simply be taking a more subtle form. For example, there is evidence that girls and boys who are first-time status offenders are treated in a comparable manner, but that girls who are repeat status offenders are treated more harshly than boys who are repeat status offenders, indicating that female status offenders continue to be treated more protectively (Johnson and Scheuble, 1991; Bishop and Frazier, 1992).

Differential leniency toward women has been found in some research on the sentencing of conventional offenders (for example, see Parisi, 1982). Some criminologists claim that women who exhibit behavior that is socially defined as appropriate for women are especially likely to be treated leniently. Thus, older white women who are apologetic and submissive are less apt to be treated severely by the criminal justice system than women who are black, young, and hostile toward authorities. Similarly, women who are more economically dependent on their husbands might be treated more leniently than women who are economically independent, perhaps because judges think that the courts need to exert less formal social control over women who are controlled by the men on whom they depend economically (Kruttschnitt, 1982). Other factors might also explain the greater leniency toward women that some researchers have found. Judges might believe that women are only led into crime by men and are unlikely to violate the law on their own, or they might regard women as less dangerous or more easily rehabilitated than men (Steffensmeier, 1980).

Research on white-collar offenders convicted in federal courts found that although the decision to imprison and the sentence length depended for the most part on the harm caused by the crime and the blameworthiness of the offender, women were treated more leniently than men in the same situation. No sentence disparity by race was uncovered (Weisburd et al., 1991).

One review of the research on the differential treatment of men and women in the criminal justice system concluded that women were more likely than men to be released on their own recognizance (without bail), but that when bail was set there seemed to be no difference by sex in the amount at which it was set. Sex did not seem to make a difference in the decision to prosecute a defendant, nor were there differences by sex in the use of plea bargaining or in the likelihood of being convicted. At the sentencing stage, there was a small but consistent differential leniency toward female defendants, even when variables such as prior criminal history and the nature of the offense were taken into account (Nagel and Hagan, 1983). These findings of no differences by sex in prosecution, plea bargaining, or conviction, but a difference by sex in the sentencing of convicted offenders, were confirmed by a study in Dade County, Florida (Curran, 1983).

A study of sentencing in Pennsylvania concluded that "the primary determinants of judges' imprisonment decisions are the type or seriousness of the crime committed and the defendant's prior record, not the defendant's gender (or, for that matter, age, race, or other background/contextual variables)" (Steffensmeier, Kramer, and Streifel, 1993). Men were slightly more likely than women to be incarcerated, but interviews with judges indicated that this difference was usually either a result of the application of legally relevant criteria or a result of considerations that might not be legally relevant but that seemed justified, such as pregnancy, responsibility for the care of young children, or demonstration of remorse. There were negligible gender differences in the length of imposed sentences. The researchers suggested that they might have found more gender-neutrality in sentencing than earlier studies because over time the courts have become more bureaucratic and more concerned with equal application of the law, or perhaps because offense serious-ness and prior record were controlled more rigorously in their study.

Kathleen Daly's (1994) study of convicted felons in New Haven, Connecticut, found that women were less likely than men to be incarcerated and that women's terms of confinements were shorter than men's. However, a comparison of pairs of female and male felons matched by statutory offense, prior criminal record, age, race and ethnicity, and pretrial release sta-tus found that the women had committed less serious crimes and had been less centrally involved in the commission of the crimes. The researcher con-cluded that what initially appeared to be greater leniency in the sentencing of women was not due to gender bias, but was instead warranted by the nature of the crimes that the women had committed.

Perhaps because of a recent decline in differential leniency toward women, the percentage of female inmates in state and federal prisons increased from 3 percent in 1970 to 6.1 percent in 1995. During the 1980s, the total number of women in prison more than tripled, while the number of men more than doubled. Much of this increase was due to harsher penalties for drug offenders, a significant proportion of whom were women; the per-centage of women in prison for drug crimes rose from 12 percent in 1986 to 33 percent in 1991. Because most prisoners are men, insufficient attention has been paid to the development of programs to meet the needs of female inmates, including drug treatment, gynecological and obstetric care, and transportation so that children can visit their mothers.

Sex and Capital Punishment   In his concurring opinion in *Furman* v. *Georgia* (1972), Justice Thurgood Marshall suggested that women are treated more leniently than men in capital cases. Chivalrous treatment has been used to explain why the percentage of suspects arrested for murder and nonnegli-gent manslaughter who are women (14.3 percent for 1976–1987) is greater than either the percentage of death sentences given out to women (2 percent for 1976–1987) or the percentage of executed offenders who are women (less than 1 percent for 1976–1987).

Elizabeth Rapaport (1991) challenges this explanation. She shows that the death penalty is usually applied to offenders convicted of predatory mur-ders and felony murders (murders committed during the course of a rape, robbery, burglary, auto theft, or other felony). Only 6.2 percent of all suspects arrested for felony murders from 1976 through 1987 were women, much less than the 14.3 percent of all murder and nonnegligent manslaughter suspects who were women. Other characteristics of the murders most likely to result in a death sentence also reduce the chance that women who kill will receive the death penalty: females are less likely than males to kill strangers, to have a prior record of violence, and to kill multiple victims. Rapaport concludes that it is the kinds of murders that men and women commit and their records of criminal violence, rather than chivalrous treatment by the legal system, that account for the small percentage of death sentences for women. She also argues that by singling out predatory murders and murders of strangers as the crimes most deserving of capital punishment, and by treating as less seri-

Velma Barfield, shown here in her North Carolina prison cell, was executed in 1984 for having poisoned her boyfriend. She also confessed to murdering her mother, her nurse, and her cook. She is the only woman to have been executed since capital punishment resumed in 1977.

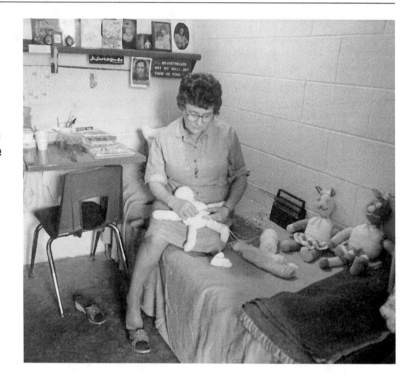

ous those murders that occur in domestic settings (the kind most apt to be committed by women, but also the type most likely to take the lives of women and children), the law reflects patriarchal values that attach more opprobrium to violence in the commercial sphere and between nonintimates than it does to violence in the domestic sphere.

The Prisons

No more than 1 or 2 percent of all serious crimes lead to the imprisonment of an offender, but most people who commit many crimes eventually end up in jail or prison. Prison sentences probably deter some people from crime, but the certainty of punishment is low in the present-day United States.

History of Prisons

For centuries, jails and prisons were places to hold people before they were punished for their crimes, rather than places of punishment for convicted offenders. People were locked up until they could be executed, pilloried, or subjected to other forms of suffering. Today, defendants are held in city or county jails until they are tried in court. Defendants who are found guilty in court are given a criminal sentence such as a fine, time on probation, a term in a state or federal prison or a local correctional institution, or the death penalty.

In the late eighteenth century, the Quakers in Philadelphia developed a use for prisons different from the earlier practice of holding people until they were punished. The Quakers believed that even the worst offenders could be saved, and they sought to do this by requiring offenders to serve long periods in total silence in prison, hoping this would lead prisoners to reflect on their mistakes and see the correct way to behave. These institutions were called penitentiaries, because the Quakers thought that inmates would grow penitent about their crimes while reflecting on their lives.

In the nineteenth century, prison reformers developed an institution at Auburn, New York, that used a different philosophy of punishment: put prisoners to work and teach them to become law-abiding by instilling in them the work ethic. Since then, inmates have often been put to work, although usually only for part of each day and often at menial and poorly paid tasks.

In contrast to the view that prisons originally had a humanitarian impulse behind them, a more recent view is that they were and continue to be weapons of class conflict, a tool used by the powerful and the wealthy to control the "dangerous classes" (Rothman, 1971; Foucault, 1978; Ignatieff, 1978).

The Prison Population

At the end of 1995, the number of prisoners in state and federal institutions was 1,078,357, the largest number in the history of the United States. According to a 1994 report by the Sentencing Project, there are 519 prisoners for every 100,000 people in the United States. Among the other fifty-one nations surveyed, only Russia had a higher rate (558). The rate per 100,000 for South Africa was 368, and most industrial societies had rates less than 100 (see Figure 13.4). Moreover, the use of incarceration has increased dramatically in the United States in recent years, with the number of state and federal inmates per capita nearly quadrupling from 1968 to 1993 (see Figure 13.5).

Critics suggest that the high rate of imprisonment in the United States means that the country is particularly punitive toward law violators. However, a comparison of the United States, England, Canada, and Germany concluded that the higher imprisonment rate in the United States was largely a result of the country's higher rate of crime, especially serious crime. In other words, the United States had more prisoners per capita than the other nations, but it also had more crime per capita than the other nations. The chance that a particular type of offender would be imprisoned was not much greater in the United States than in the three countries with which it was compared (Lynch, 1988).

An analysis of cross-national differences in imprisonment underscored the difficulty of making comparisons, showing that the usual comparison of jurisdictions in terms of number of inmates confined on a particular day or average number of prisoners over a whole year conceals cross-national variations in prison admissions, sentence lengths, pretrial detainments, and

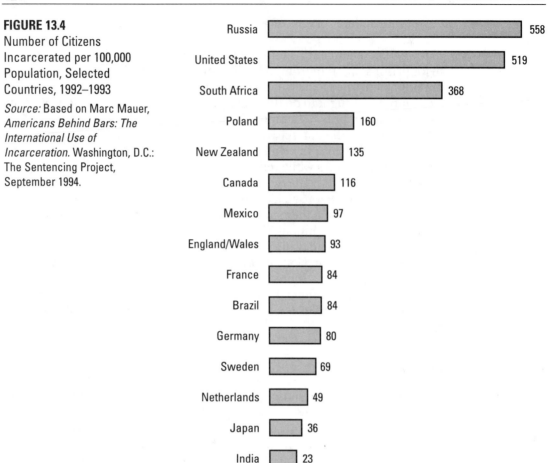

FIGURE 13.4
Number of Citizens Incarcerated per 100,000 Population, Selected Countries, 1992–1993

Source: Based on Marc Mauer, *Americans Behind Bars: The International Use of Incarceration.* Washington, D.C.: The Sentencing Project, September 1994.

parole revocations (Young and Brown, 1993). Typically, jurisdictions that have higher rates of prisoners per capita impose longer sentences rather than send more offenders to prison. Contrary to the above comparison of the United States, England, Canada, and Germany, this study found that cross-jurisdictional differences in prison populations were not primarily a result of differences in crime rates, nor were they mainly due to a nation's prison capacity or its unemployment rate. Cross-national differences in rates of imprisonment were instead associated with cultural differences in penal values, or public attitudes toward punishment. These penal values were, in turn, related to egalitarianism:

> Countries that have a highly individualistic and competitive ethos, premised on notions of meritocracy and equal opportunity, and have substantial gaps between rich and poor are likely to be comparatively severe in their penal outlook. Countries that have highly developed welfare systems and a less materialistic reward structure are likely to be comparatively mild. (Young and Brown, 1993: 41–42)

FIGURE 13.5
Number of State and Federal
Prisoners per 100,000
Population, United States,
1925–1993

Source: Kathleen Maguire and
Ann L. Pastore, *Sourcebook of
Criminal Justice Statistics—
1994.* Washington, D.C.: Bureau
of Justice Statistics, U.S.
Department of Justice, 1995,
p. 539.

**Number of sentenced prisoners
per 100,000 residents**

Prison Crowding

At the end of 1995, state prisons were operating at 114 to 125 percent of capacity, and federal prisons were operating at 126 percent of capacity (Gilliard and Beck, 1996). An inmate in Ohio has noted that state veterinary services standards recommend forty-three square feet of space for a calf that is more than five weeks old, but that he had only thirty-two feet of living space in his cell. Crowding creates unpleasant living conditions for inmates: lack of privacy, arguments and fights over the use of limited space, and the threat of sexual assaults (Gaes, 1985).

Why are prisons so crowded? One reason is a long-term increase in crime rates, arrests, and commitments to prison. From 1957 to 1984, arrests for serious crimes increased by 385 percent, but the state prison population grew by only 165 percent, and state prison capacity increased by only 79 percent (Schlesinger, 1987). Thus, the growth in prison capacity did not keep pace with the increase in the number of offenders sentenced to prison, resulting in more crowded conditions. In addition, the failure of prison capacity to keep pace with the number of offenders convicted in court probably led judges to place some offenders on probation rather than send them to prison, and this could have reduced the deterrent and incapacitative effects of punishment.

Some of the increase in prison crowding in recent years is due to an especially large age cohort of men in their twenties, the group with the highest imprisonment rate in the population. Other reasons for prison crowding include tougher public attitudes toward crime, mandatory minimum sentences, laws that give judges less discretion in sentencing, and restrictions on parole release (Blumstein, 1983). A national campaign against drugs has also contributed to prison crowding; from 1986 to 1991, the total number of state prison inmates serving time for drug offenses more than tripled, and the proportion of all inmates serving time for drug offenses rose from 8.6 to 21.3 percent (Beck et al., 1993).

Steps have been taken to alleviate crowded jail and prison conditions. The states have built new prisons and expanded existing ones. Some criminologists oppose the construction of new facilities, claiming that the new prisons will be filled to capacity in short order as judges send more people to prison and parole boards keep inmates behind bars longer. These critics call for shorter prison terms, or no prison sentences at all for less serious offenders, as the way to reduce crowding. Research is inconclusive as to whether building more prison cells will result in a larger prison population rather than reduce crowding (Abt Associates, Inc., 1980; Blumstein, Cohen, and Gooding, 1983).

Because of the high cost of building and maintaining prisons, state governments have increasingly turned to other ways of alleviating crowding. Some have moved away from the use of mandatory sentences; Florida adopted such a policy in 1993. Others have released inmates who do not have mandatory minimum sentences before they have completed their sentences. States have also looked for ways to punish offenders outside prison walls. Southern states, which have higher incarceration rates than the rest of the nation, have turned to such programs as confining convicts to their homes, allowing them out only to work at jobs or perform community service; electronic monitoring of offenders on probation or parole; community work centers, which house inmates who work for no pay at city or county jobs; extensive drug testing; and intensive probation supervision, in which offenders see probation workers five times a week. (See the Using Criminology box.) Foundations, labor unions, and other private groups have become more involved in developing these and similar programs for punishing and treating offenders outside prisons. If alternative sanctions can be devised that ensure public safety, satisfy a sense of justice, and are inexpensive, prison crowding might be alleviated. This will happen only if these sanctions are used for offenders who otherwise would have been incarcerated, rather than for offenders who would have been placed on probation in the absence of alternative sanctions.

Parole

Both prison crowding and the high cost of incarceration can be reduced by releasing inmates before they complete their full sentences. They can then be supervised on the street and sent back to prison if they violate the conditions of their release. This system is called **parole**.

State parole boards meet regularly to review inmates' progress toward rehabilitation and to determine whether they can be safely released if certain conditions are met. Parole board decisions cause anxiety and bitterness in prisoners, who often see the decisions as arbitrary and in violation of their due process rights. One study found that the most annoying thing to inmates about serving time in prison was never knowing when they would be released; 52 percent mentioned this problem, and only 12 percent mentioned

USING CRIMINOLOGY

Felons on Probation

In the past, most offenders placed on probation had been convicted of relatively minor crimes, but now judges are sentencing an increasing number of serious offenders to probation because there is little room in prison. These felony probationers may pose a danger to the public.

To assess the extent of that risk, researchers at the Rand Corporation followed 1,672 felony probationers for forty months after their sentencing and concluded that they did indeed "present a serious threat to public safety" (Petersilia et al., p. 381). During the follow-up period, 65 percent were arrested again, 51 percent were convicted of a new crime, 18 percent were reconvicted of a serious violent crime, and 34 percent were reincarcerated. More than three-fourths of the new charges filed against the felony probationers involved the kinds of crimes most threatening to the public: burglary, theft, robbery, and other violent offenses.

The researchers concluded that the poor performance of the felony probationers demonstrated the need for a new type of punishment that is more stringent than probation (which gives offenders their freedom) and less harsh than imprisonment (which takes away their freedom). Their proposed Intensive Supervision Program (ISP) involved "intensive monitoring and supervision; real constraints on movement and action; employment; added requirements of community service, education, counseling, and therapy programs; and mechanisms for immediately punishing probationers who commit infractions" (Petersilia et al., p. 384). Such a program might "force offenders to be gainfully employed, functioning members of a community, and this might help them break old habits and establish new and more positive lifestyles" (Petersilia et al., p. 386).

Intensive Supervision Programs have been widely implemented since the mid-1980s. Joan Petersilia and Susan Turner's (1993) evaluation of fourteen such programs found that they have not done a very good job of increasing participation in treatment. Closer surveillance of participants' behavior has increased technical violations and commitments to prison and jail. Participation in ISPs has not reduced the frequency or seriousness of new arrests. The programs have been less costly than incarceration, but more expensive than the routine probation programs to which most participants would have been assigned in the absence of ISPs.

Sources: Based on Joan Petersilia et al., "Executive Summary of Rand's Study, 'Granting Felons Probation: Public Risks and Alternatives,'" *Crime and Delinquency* 31 (July 1985), 379–392; Joan Petersilia and Susan Turner, "Intensive Probation and Parole," in Michael Tonry, ed., *Crime and Justice: A Review of Research,* Vol. 17. Chicago: University of Chicago Press, 1993, pp. 281–335.

the next most commonly voiced complaint, being treated like a child by the prison staff (Kassebaum, Ward, and Wilner, 1971: 31).

If a parole board decides to release an inmate, it specifies the conditions of release, which typically include a steady job, staying away from known offenders, and avoiding the use of alcohol and illegal drugs. The parolee is required to meet regularly, perhaps once or twice a month, with a parole officer to discuss problems of adjustment and signs of progress. Parole officers frequently know about violations of parole conditions but usually do not send inmates back to prison for minor infractions. Instead, parole officers "save" those infractions so that if a major one occurs, such as arrest for a new crime, their decision to revoke parole and send the parolee back to prison can be justified with a list of infractions.

Not all inmates who leave prison are paroled. Some "wrap up" their sentence, that is, complete their full sentence in prison. The use of parole has been restricted in response to criticisms that the granting of parole is arbitrary and violates due process rights and that the behavior of parolees is difficult to predict and monitor. The federal prison system and some states have abolished parole, and other states have limited its use through sentencing reforms. Even where parole is used, inmates must serve a minimum part of their sentence before they are eligible for release.

The Victim in the Criminal Justice System

The American criminal justice system includes procedural rights designed to protect defendants against the power of the state. Some people complain that this emphasis on defendants' rights neglects "victims' rights," or what those who are victimized are entitled to. Critics also complain about the slowness of the legal process, which costs victims and witnesses time and money to sit in court hallways awaiting trials.

In recent years, more attention has been paid to the victims of crime. State systems of compensation and restitution have been developed to repay victims for their losses. District attorneys have come to realize that cases cannot be prosecuted successfully without cooperative victims and witnesses. Judges have increasingly considered the impact of crimes on victims before sentencing offenders, and parole boards sometimes listen to victims before releasing inmates. More than forty states now have laws that give certain rights to crime victims, and at least thirteen states have amended their constitutions to allow victims a greater role in the prosecution of defendants. One scholar concludes that "what the 'victims' movement,' however defined, has achieved within a short space of time can only be described as remarkable, and there are few signs of a waning of enthusiasm" (Maguire, 1991: 420).

Compensation

Compensation is a system by which a state repays victims for their financial losses or physical injuries. Under this system, it is not necessary to arrest and convict an offender for a victim to be compensated, nor does a convicted offender have to be financially solvent for the victim to be repaid for his or her losses. Most states now provide compensation for victims, but many programs are not well-funded or well-publicized.

Compensation has been justified in several ways. Some say that the state has an obligation to protect the welfare and safety of its citizens, and that when it fails to prevent crime, it should pay victims for their losses. Another rationale for compensation is that it prevents victims from becoming angry at the criminal justice system and alienated from the political system (Schafer, 1968; Stookey, 1981). Even though compensation programs are aimed at improving public attitudes toward the criminal justice system and the government, research indicates that many victims who have sought compensation are disenchanted with the criminal justice system. Indeed, administrative obstacles to securing compensation and the inadequate rewards provided to victims seem to engender more discontent toward the legal system among applicants for compensation than exists among people who do not apply for compensation (Elias, 1983, 1984).

Compensation programs must deal with the problem of the victim's contribution to the crime. Victims sometimes precipitate a crime or contribute to their own victimization, and in such cases the state might choose not to compensate the victim. For instance, someone who first uses force against another person and then ends up badly injured in a fight might not be compensated if the state compensation board found that the crime would not have occurred without the victim's initiating actions.

Restitution

A system of **restitution** requires offenders to make monetary payments or provide services, either to the victim or to the community at large. Relatively few criminal courts have used restitution extensively, but growing concern for victims' rights has led some judges to require offenders to repay victims for their losses.

Some claim that restitution makes offenders take responsibility for their behavior and thus helps rehabilitate them (Deming, 1976). Others claim that offenders who repay their victims might stop feeling guilty for their crimes if they believe they have corrected their wrongs, and this could make it more likely that they will continue to commit crime. Restitution might improve crime reporting if victims thought they would be repaid for their losses. Moreover, by easing public hostility toward offenders, restitution could reduce the isolation of offenders from conventional society and make it easier to reintegrate them into society after they are released from prison. Restitution would also lighten the burden on taxpayers if it replaced a system of state compensation (Barnett, 1977; Bridges, Gandy, and Jorgenson, 1979).

The Changing Role of the Victim

Many states have implemented programs to help the victims of crime, including compensating them for their losses and requiring offenders to make restitution. Victims have been given a greater voice in the sentencing of offenders, although offenders are usually allowed to respond to victims' statements. In some jurisdictions, victims must be notified of hearings and trials and informed when an inmate is being considered for parole or escapes from prison.

District attorneys have started to pay more attention to the role of the victim in the criminal justice system. They can help to deal with a victim's fear of retaliation by the offender, frustration with delays in court, and intimidation by a defense attorney's cross examination. District attorneys can also impress on victims and witnesses the importance of testifying in court. In some jurisdictions, victims have even been included in plea bargaining conferences with the district attorney, the defense attorney, and the defendant (Heinz and Kerstetter, 1981). One study found that victim-witness programs in prosecutors' offices contributed in an important way to keeping victims informed about the progress and outcome of cases, and that crime victims expressed more satisfaction with the criminal justice system when they knew the outcome of a case and thought they had influenced that outcome (Forst and Hernon, 1985).

Few judges learn directly from victims about the impact crime has had on their psychological well-being, physical condition, and financial situation. Usually, judges learn about this only from presentence reports prepared by probation officers, who draw on secondhand information from police reports, medical records, and victims' discussions with prosecutors. As a result, some courts have introduced **victim impact statements**, detailed written reports based on interviews with victims about the effects of crime on them (Forst and Hernon, 1985). One study of sexual assault cases found that victim impact statements had little influence on the sentences that judges imposed, beyond the effects one would expect from legally relevant variables such as seriousness of the crime and prior criminal record. This study suggested, however, that often there was agreement between the sentences recommended by victims and the actual sentences. This could produce a "placebo" effect in which victims are satisfied with the outcome of a case because they believe they have influenced the sentence, even if the sentence would have been the same without their recommendation (Walsh, 1986). A second study also found that legally relevant factors explained most of the variation in sentences, but concluded that victim impact statements influenced the sentences that judges handed out by improving their knowledge of the harm suffered by victims (Erez and Tontodonato, 1990). In 1991, the U.S. Supreme Court reversed a ruling it had made only four years earlier and permitted jurors to use victim impact statements to help them determine whether convicted murderers should be sentenced to death.

Today, nearly all states permit victims to appear at parole board hearings or file written statements with parole boards, in order to make known their wishes about whether a prisoner should be released. Many victims do not make their wishes known, either fearing retaliation or not wanting to dredge up unpleasant memories about the crimes committed against them.

Those who oppose the use of victim testimony to parole boards and victim impact statements in court fear that those reforms might introduce public pressure or vengeance into proceedings that should be dispassionate. They claim that poor and uneducated offenders might be punished more severely if they are confronted with articulate victims who demand long sentences. These critics assert that sentencing and parole should be based on an offender's threat to society and behavior while in prison, not on a victim's wishes.

Supporters of these reforms argue that they draw the victim into the criminal justice system, thereby providing a new perspective to criminal justice administrators. They also point to the greater satisfaction with the criminal justice system among victims who believe that their wishes have been taken into consideration in assigning punishment, arguing that satisfied victims are more likely to report crimes and aid in the prosecution of defendants in the future, and that this could help to deter crime.

Summary

The criminal justice system aims to dispense justice and reduce the crime rate. In doing so, it also influences the development of criminal careers. This system has been described as a funnel or sieve that sorts out cases as they pass from the police through the courts and to the prisons.

The police were first formally organized at the municipal level in the nineteenth century. They are organized so that the most important contacts with the public and with suspects are by patrol officers, who are not easily supervised by administrators. The working personality of the police officer includes a demand for respect, suspiciousness, and the exercise of delegated and unauthorized discretion. The exercise of discretion is influenced by the officer's perception of the likely consequences of an arrest or a warning, by the community in which an offense occurs, by a suspect's demeanor, and sometimes by race and sex.

The police measure their effectiveness with a clearance rate, the proportion of offenses they solve to their satisfaction. Sometimes they inflate clearance rates by encouraging suspects to confess to multiple offenses.

Suspects who are arrested by the police have the right to have bail set at a reasonable level, but this system discriminates against the poor. Preventive detention has been proposed as a way to reduce "bail crimes," offenses committed between the time of release and the disposition of the original charge.

Prosecutors, who bring criminal charges against defendants on behalf of the state, measure their effectiveness by conviction rates. Defense attorneys try to get their clients acquitted, or at least get them the lightest possible sentences. Because many defendants are poor, defense attorneys are often appointed and paid for by the state. Prosecutors and defense attorneys theoretically engage in a "fight" or adversary process, out of which the truth is supposed to emerge. In practice, they more often engage in plea bargaining over guilt and an appropriate sentence in order to save the time and resources of the court. Judges then usually ratify the negotiated plea and sentence, treating defendants more leniently for speeding up the processing of cases. Judges preside over trials, but their most important function is the sentencing of convicted offenders. Juries also try cases, but no more than 5 percent of all felony cases are disposed of in this way. Convicted offenders are sentenced in a variety of ways, one of which is probation, a form of supervised release.

One problem with the courts is sentence disparity. Legal criteria are usually the basis of judges' sentences, but race sometimes plays a role in the sentencing of offenders. This can be due to direct racial discrimination, but often it is a result of organizational or economic discrimination that affects minorities more because of their lower incomes. Criminal justice procedures rather than direct racial discrimination account for most of the disparity in sentences among racial and ethnic groups, but in capital cases murderers who kill blacks are punished less severely than murderers who kill whites. Some research indicates that defendants of low socioeconomic standing fare worse in the criminal justice system than those of higher standing. The sex of a defendant can also make a difference, with women sometimes treated more leniently than men, although the sex differential in sentencing has diminished over time.

Prisons in the United States are crowded. Not everyone agrees that building more prisons is the best solution to this problem, because judges might simply imprison more offenders if there were more cells. Prisoners are sometimes released on parole prior to the expiration of their sentence; they are then supervised in the community to help them become rehabilitated.

Victims are playing an increasingly important role in the criminal justice system. Compensation programs and penalties of restitution are designed to repay victims for their financial losses and physical suffering. Some victims now testify in court about the sentence they believe is appropriate for an offender, and some of them appear before parole boards to say whether they think an offender should be released. The criminal justice system might function more efficiently if it counseled victims and tried to incorporate them more into the system.

Important Terms

bail	preventive detention
case attrition	probation
clearance rate	restitution
compensation	sentence disparity
discretion	victim impact statement
parole	working personality
plea bargaining	

Review Questions

1. Why do the police sometimes use excessive force? How is this abuse of power related to the officer's "working personality"? To what extent do the police discriminate on the basis of race and gender?

2. What purpose does bail serve in the American criminal justice system? What is preventive detention?

3. What is plea bargaining, and why is it so common in U.S. courts? Who participates in negotiating a guilty plea and a sentence for a defendant?

4. What is sentence disparity? To what extent does it characterize the sentencing of blacks in both capital and noncapital crimes? To what extent does it exist for members of different social classes? To what extent does it exist for males and females, both in juvenile court and in criminal court?

5. What is the recent trend regarding the number of prisoners in the United States? What accounts for this trend? How is it associated with prison crowding?

6. In what ways have victims been increasingly incorporated into the criminal justice system? What are the advantages and disadvantages of this increased role for victims?

Chapter 14
Deterrence, Incapacitation, Retribution, and Rehabilitation

Why does every modern society have a criminal justice system? One answer is that the threat of punishment dissuades potential offenders from violating the law. Another is that locking criminals up keeps them from victimizing more people. Yet another response is that those who break the law deserve to be punished. Others believe that the primary function of the criminal justice system is to reform offenders through treatment. This chapter explores these rationales for punishment and looks at research by criminologists bearing on each justification.

Deterrence

Crime has increased dramatically in Eastern Europe since the demise of Communism. A senior Polish police official remarks, "Now that Poland has a government that the people support, you might think there would be less crime. But for some people, freedom means greater freedom from moral responsibility. Not everyone feels this way, but there is a segment that is easily tempted by crime" (cited in Greenhouse, 1990: 20). The domestic policy adviser to the president of the former nation of Czechoslovakia observes, "People lost what was a major commodity here. Fear of the police" (cited in *New York Times*, December 18, 1991: A21).

Deterrence is the inhibition of criminal activity by state-imposed penalties. When people perceive the threat of punishment to be weakened, as has occurred in Eastern Europe, we would expect crime rates to rise. Deterrence is a utilitarian rationale for punishment—that is, it is based on the idea that punishment should be used to prevent crime.

Specific deterrence means that individuals who are punished for a particular crime will not commit that crime again because their risk-reward calculations have been altered by the punishment. They have learned that the risk is greater than they thought, and so the rewards become relatively less attractive, leading them to avoid crime in the future.

General deterrence is the inhibition of the desire to engage in crime among the general population through the punishment of certain offenders. Most research focuses on general deterrence rather than on specific deterrence. One report even defines deterrence as the inhibiting effects of sanctions on the criminal activity of people other than the punished offender (Blumstein, Cohen, and Nagin, 1978: 3).

The **marginal deterrent effect** of punishment is the extent to which crime rates respond to incremental changes in the threat of sanctions (Nagin, 1978). Increasing the rate at which the police arrest offenders from 0 to 100 percent would undoubtedly deter many criminals, but increasing the arrest rate from 20 to 22 percent would probably have little or no impact. Similarly, most research indicates that murder is not deterred by executing offenders rather than imprisoning them for life.

Philosophers such as Cesare Beccaria (1738–1794) and Jeremy Bentham (1748–1832) argued that the punishment of criminal acts can deter potential offenders by making the negative consequences of crime greater than its rewards. Writing in the eighteenth century, Beccaria (1764, 1963: 42) stated that the goal of crime prevention should be pursued with punishments "which will make the strongest and most lasting impression on the minds of men, and inflict the least torment on the body of the criminal." He believed that punishment should be as certain as possible and as harsh as necessary to deter potential offenders, but that "all beyond this is superfluous and for that reason tyrannical" (Beccaria, 1764, 1963: 43). For Beccaria, punishment should be consistent with the principle of retribution or just deserts, a principle examined later in this chapter.

For much of the twentieth century, the notion of deterrence was ignored or held in disrepute by social scientists, because positivists focused on individual and social pathologies as causes of crime. Beginning with an influential paper published by the Norwegian law professor Johannes Andenaes in 1952, there has been a rebirth of interest in deterrence.

Assumptions about Behavior

The deterrence model assumes that people engage in an act only after carefully and rationally considering its costs (or risks) and its benefits (or rewards). Punishment supposedly induces compliance with the law, because people fear punishment and do not want to risk their stake in conformity. In the deterrence model, the rationale for punishment is to affect future behavior, rather than to inflict pain that offenders might deserve because of their past actions; the latter is the retribution or just deserts rationale for punishment.

The deterrence model assumes free will or voluntarism, suggesting that people choose how to behave, even if they are limited in their choices by social, psychological, and biological factors. However, not all behavior is governed by careful consideration of costs and benefits; much of it is unplanned or habitual. Internalized values and beliefs, sometimes referred to as "conscience," also guide behavior. Other behavior is avoided because people lack the skill or opportunity to commit an act.

Rational choice is involved in some criminal behavior. Some offenders try to minimize risks by planning their crimes, and they select targets according to what they hope to gain. Even the most rational offenders, however, often lack good information on the actual risks of arrest and conviction, and on what they might gain from a particular crime. Moreover, many offenders act on impulse.

Deterrence and Other Effects of Penalties

A criminal penalty might act as a negative inducement that discourages people from engaging in behavior that violates the law, but deterrence is not the only effect of punishment. The very existence of a criminal penalty indicates moral condemnation of the behavior and a corresponding support for other values; people learn these attitudes through socialization and formal education. The law has an "eye-opener effect," directing attention to punished acts and inviting reflection on the reason those acts are condemned (Andenaes, 1974). The actual punishment of offenders makes credible the threat of a sanction and helps convince people that the government is serious in its effort to deter crime. Punishment also keeps people in line by convincing them that those who violate the law will gain no advantage over those who abide by the law.

One analysis suggests that three distinct forces operate independently and have additive effects on keeping crime in check:

1. Moral commitment, or internalized legal norms;
2. Social disapproval, or fear of informal sanctions by peers; and
3. Threat of legal punishment, or fear of physical and material deprivation from legally imposed sanctions. (Grasmick and Green, 1980)

Usually, only the third factor is called deterrence.

These factors interact with one another. Subjective appraisals of social disapproval and the threat of punishment affect criminal behavior, but involvement in crime can alter perceptions of social disapproval and the threat of punishment. Criminal activity can show an offender that the consequences of breaking the law are not serious, lead an offender to a moral reassessment of norms, or provide the opportunity for an offender to learn an accomplice's values (D. Greenberg, 1981). Testing the effects of the three inhibiting factors thus requires a model like the one depicted in Figure 14.1. Research that tested a model like this found that internalized normative constraints, or moral commitment, was the best predictor of later delinquency. Perceptions of the threat of both informal and formal sanctions added significantly to the model's ability to explain subsequent delinquency. There was also evidence that the threat of sanctions might compensate for weak internalized constraints in inhibiting delinquency (Bishop, 1984). Another study concluded that informal threats such as social disapproval and moral commitment inhibit drunken driving more effectively than the threat of formal sanctions (Green, 1989a, 1989b). A third study found that the perceived certainty of punishment deterred marijuana use, but that peer behavior was an even more important influence on that behavior (Paternoster, 1988: 176).

Deterrence and the Criminal Act

William Chambliss (1969: 360–372) suggests that some crimes are more easily deterred than others. Instrumental or goal-oriented behavior, such as theft, is more easily deterred than expressive behavior that results from the inner needs of an offender, such as a violent outburst that leads to murder. The distinction between instrumental and expressive acts is not always easy to make; for instance, a juvenile gang member might commit a robbery in order to feel a sense of mastery over others (an expressive need), rather than to acquire property (an instrumental goal). Chambliss also links deterrence to the

FIGURE 14.1
A Model of Crime-Inhibiting
Factors

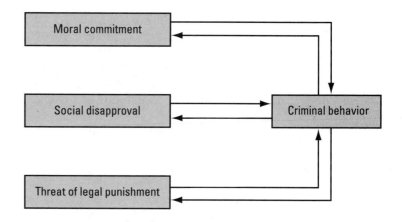

offender's commitment to a life of crime: offenders who are highly committed to a life of crime are more difficult to deter than offenders who are not committed to crime as a way of life. Table 14.1 indicates that the kind of offender least apt to be deterred from crime is one with a high commitment to crime as a way of life and whose offenses result from expressive needs. On the other hand, instrumental crimes by offenders who are not highly committed to a life of crime are the easiest to deter because these offenders are likely to consider the possible rewards and risks of committing a crime.

Deterrence and Conventional Crime   Some conventional offenders, such as robbers and burglars, commit crimes without carefully assessing risks; doing so might reduce their confidence in being able to carry out the crime and might keep them from committing the crime at all. Risk-taking can even make breaking the law exciting and thus rewarding to the offender. Offenders might assess risks differently from the way that the general population does. One robber describes his feelings prior to his first mugging as follows: "I was scared, but it was exciting. You see, the whole thing, I was scared and excited. And I knew, you know, I had a fifty-fifty chance of either getting away or getting caught. But I figured that was the chance I was going to take. I wanted to get the money" (cited in Lejeune, 1977: 129). This robber clearly overestimated the chance that he would be caught, which was probably no more than one in eight. Most people would not commit a robbery if they thought the chance of being arrested was one in two, but some robbers will take that risk.

 Kenneth Tunnell has found that harsher penalties are unlikely to deter persistent property offenders because they focus on the rewards they expect from their crimes but rarely give much thought to the risks they are taking. To the extent that they think about the chance of being arrested, chronic property offenders underestimate the length of time they will serve in prison. They are not much threatened by the possibility of imprisonment, especially if they have already served time and know they can easily survive in prison (Tunnell, 1992; Shover, 1996). Young minority-group members from urban ghettos might even

TABLE 14.1   Chambliss's Typology of Crime Deterrence

Commitment to Crime as a Way of Life	Type of Criminal Act	
	Instrumental	Expressive
High	Professional thief Booster[a] Some check forgers Some murderers	Most drug addicts Some murderers Some sex offenders
Low	Snitch[b] Parking-law violator White-collar criminal Some murderers	Most murderers Some drug addicts Most sex offenders

[a] A booster is a professional shoplifter.
[b] A snitch is an amateur shoplifter.

Source: From *Crime and the Legal Process* by William J. Chambliss. Copyright © 1969 McGraw-Hill Book Company. Used with the permission of The McGraw-Hill Companies.

regard prison as a "shelter from the storm" where they are provided with a place to live, food, clothing, medical care, remedial education, and job training, things to which they lack access in the outside world (Butterfield, 1992).

Deterrence and White-Collar Crime   Because white-collar criminals usually have little commitment to crime as a way of life, and typically engage in instrumental acts, some sociologists have suggested that their crimes should be easy to deter (Conklin, 1977; Braithwaite and Geis, 1982). Charles Moore (1987) suggests that although individual white-collar offenders might be deterred by the threat of punishment, corporate offenders are not easily deterred.

Several retired middle-level executives in one study cited the threat of government sanctions as a major deterrent to illegal corporate behavior, singling out the effects of legal action against antitrust violators (Clinard, 1983). In one case, when the government filed a complaint for price-fixing against bakery companies for colluding on prices, and when civil suits for treble damages were threatened, price-fixing stopped and the price of bread dropped (Block, Nold, and Sidak, 1981).

A study of white-collar offenders convicted in federal courts found no specific deterrent effect of incarceration over a 126-month follow-up period. Imprisonment might have adversely affected the personal lives or job opportunities of white-collar offenders, but it had no marginal deterrent effect over the experience of arrest, conviction, and a sentence other than prison (Weisburd, Waring, and Chayet, 1995).

Deterrence and the Sanctioning Process

People have imperfect knowledge of the maximum penalties for various crimes, but their perceptions of the severity of sanctions, the certainty with which they will be administered, and the promptness of punishment influence their choice of behavior.

Severity of Punishment   Criminal behavior can be deterred by harsher sanctions, but there is not enough research on marginal deterrence to know how much crime is prevented by a specific increase in punishment. There does seem to be a diminishing return from increased punishment at certain levels; a twenty-year prison term deters more crime than a $10 fine, but it is not clear that a twenty-five-year sentence deters more crime than a twenty-year sentence. Harsh penalties are costly, and sometimes they backfire; in early nineteenth-century Great Britain, where over two hundred crimes could be punished with the death penalty, juries often acquitted defendants rather than send them to the gallows for relatively trivial offenses.

Research in Chicago showed that juvenile delinquents who were punished more harshly were arrested less often after they were punished. The "suppression effect"—the drop in arrest rates after punishment—was greatest for juveniles who were treated most severely. For instance, offenders who were removed from their community and incarcerated for an indefinite time on an involuntary basis and with custodial supervision showed a greater drop in their rate of arrest after release than did juveniles who were removed from the community for a specified period and placed in a noncustodial and voluntary program. The mildest penalties—supervision and probation—did not significantly reduce arrest rates (Murray and Cox, 1979).

A study that looked at police contacts for a cohort of males in Racine, Wisconsin, found that arrest was more likely than release without arrest to deter future criminal conduct, ending the criminal careers of novice offenders and reducing crime by experienced offenders (Smith and Gartin, 1989).

Research on adult arrestees discovered that their perceptions of the severity of punishment increased after their experiences with the criminal justice system, and that harsher penalties raised their perceptions of severity more than lighter penalties. Nevertheless, a heightened sense of the severity of sanctions does not necessarily lead an individual to avoid criminal behavior; it can also produce a sense of injustice that leads to more crime (Apospori and Alpert, 1993).

An examination of corporations that had been charged with serious antitrust violations found that the severity of formal sanctions had a greater deterrent effect on repeat offending than did either the certainty or the promptness with which the sanctions were applied. However, the deterrent impact of sanctions was a less important influence on corporate behavior than the motivations and opportunities for offending, the culture and structure of the firm, and the climate of the industry and the general economy (Simpson and Koper, 1992).

Certainty of Punishment Perhaps more important than the maximum statutory penalty for a crime or the length of the sentences actually meted out is the certainty of some punishment for the crime. For example, one study revealed that residential burglars' decisions to commit crime were more influenced by perceived risk of arrest than by the severity of a threatened sanction (Decker, Wright, and Logie, 1993). Two centuries ago, Cesare Beccaria (1764, 1963: 58) wrote, "The certainty of a punishment, even if it be moderate, will always make a stronger impression than the fear of another which is more terrible but combined with the hope of impunity." Thus, a 100 percent chance of a one-year prison term might deter more crime than a 5 percent chance of a twenty-year sentence. The consequences of 0 percent certainty are shown in the Cross-Cultural Perspective box.

The exact combination of certainty and severity that will maximize deterrence is unknown. A certain sentence of a $10 fine or a day in jail will probably deter few robbers, because they will think that crime pays if the costs are that low. Similarly, the low certainty of any punishment for white-collar crime probably limits the deterrent effect of even those laws that permit harsh penalties; according to one estimate, a convicted antitrust violator is less likely to be imprisoned than someone who violates a migratory bird law (Yoder, 1978). However, a 5 percent chance of being executed would probably deter instrumental crimes by people with little commitment to crime as a way of life; thus, the effect of a very severe penalty would offset the low certainty of punishment.

In 1973, New York state increased the severity of penalties for major drug dealers, who were to be sentenced to a minimum of fifteen years and a maximum of life in prison. This law did not curtail heroin trafficking in New York City, nor did it reduce property crimes associated with heroin addiction (Joint Committee on New York Drug Law Evaluation, 1978). Although the law

A CROSS-CULTURAL PERSPECTIVE

Deterring Italy's AIDS Gang

In 1995, a gang of three Italian bank robbers demonstrated the consequences of 0 percent certainty of punishment. The members of the gang, all of whom had AIDS, took advantage of a 1993 law that prohibited the incarceration of offenders who were in the terminal stages of a disease. The gang held up five banks and netted over $40,000.

The robbers were repeatedly caught for their crimes, in part because they wore no masks and did not try to avoid security cameras, but they could only be held under house arrest, from which they easily escaped. When apprehended, they announced that they would continue their crime spree until the government offered them understanding and a pension, saying that they had to rob banks in order to eat.

Source: Based on "No Jail Can Hold Italy's 'AIDS Gang,'" *Boston Globe,* August 10, 1995, p. 2.

increased the severity of sanctions, it left several ways for defendants to avoid the penalties. As a result, the law did not increase certainty of punishment, and many defendants avoided severe sanctions through plea bargaining. Those who were unable to plea bargain to their satisfaction demanded trials, causing a backlog in the courts that delayed punishment, which can also reduce the deterrent effect of punishment (Wilson, 1983).

It is not clear that certainty of punishment can easily be increased. Doing so would require better citizen reporting of crime, more complete recording of offenses by the police, higher arrest rates, higher rates of prosecution, or higher conviction rates. These changes cannot be made without greater expenditures, reorganization of law-enforcement agencies, or infringement on defendants' constitutional rights.

Promptness of Punishment   The promptness with which sanctions are administered can also affect criminal behavior. If an offender is punished soon after committing a crime, both the specific deterrence of that individual and the general deterrence of the public might be greater than if the offender is not punished until years later. The closer in time a negative reinforcement (or legal sanction) is to a crime, the more likely it is that the behavior that elicited the negative reinforcement will be avoided.

Types of Punishment   Little is known about the relative deterrent effects of imprisonment, restitution, fines, probation, and other sanctions. Marginal deterrence is often examined by focusing on the reduction of crime that results from using more of one type of penalty, rather than from using a different kind of penalty.

An experiment sponsored by the Police Foundation in Minneapolis in 1981 and 1982 tested the impact of three different sanctions on men accused of domestic violence: arrest, mediation or advice, and ordering the man to leave the home for eight hours. Officers chose one of these methods at random to deal with "moderate" domestic violence, a simple assault that did not produce severe or life-threatening injury. Suspects were followed up for six months to determine if violence recurred; both official data and victims' reports were used. The results suggested that arrests deter moderate domestic assaults. Only 10 percent of the arrested men were involved in a new official report of domestic violence within six months, compared to 19 percent of those receiving mediation or advice and 24 percent of those who had been ordered from the home. Victim self-reports also indicated that arrest was a more effective deterrent than either mediation or being ordered from the home (Sherman and Berk, 1984; Berk and Newton, 1985).

The heavily publicized Minneapolis Domestic Violence Experiment led most urban police departments to implement mandatory or preferred arrest policies for domestic assaults. These policies were also developed in response to pressure by feminist groups, a growing interest in crime victims, police concern with the violence they suffered while investigating domestic assaults, and successful lawsuits against municipal governments for police failure to protect the victims of domestic violence.

Because the conclusion that arrest was an effective deterrent of domestic violence was based on a single experiment, the National Institute of Justice (NIJ) funded six replications of the Minneapolis study to determine if that conclusion held for other jurisdictions as well. These replications called into question the generalizability of the Minneapolis experiment's findings, concluding that arrest had no greater long-term deterrent effect on domestic violence than mediation or separation (Dunford, Huizinga, and Elliott, 1990; Sherman et al., 1991; Sherman, 1992b, 1992c; Hirschel and Hutchison, 1992). Critics have suggested that the authors of the original study failed to disseminate the generally negative results of the replication studies with as much enthusiasm as they promoted the original finding that arrest deters domestic assault (Binder and Meeker, 1993).

The exact combination of severity, certainty, promptness, and type of sanction that will maximize deterrence for different kinds of crimes is not known, but these factors are important influences on the effectiveness of punishment in reducing crime.

Deterrence and the Criminal Justice System

Scholars studying deterrence have traditionally focused on the circumstances under which the threat of punishment deters crime. More recently, economists have raised the problem of **simultaneity**: sanctions might reduce crime, but the crime rate also affects the sanctions meted out by the criminal justice system. An inverse relationship between crime rates and the certainty of punishment—that is, lower crime rates when punishment is more certain—might exist because the threat of sanctions reduces crime, but it could also exist because a high crime rate reduces the certainty of sanctions, for example, by overburdening the police or the courts. Thus, the crime rate could affect the certainty of punishment as much as the certainty of punishment affects the crime rate (Blumstein, Cohen, and Nagin, 1978). This simultaneity of causation should be kept in mind when considering the possibility that criminal sanctions deter crime.

Deterrence and the Police   Do cities with larger police forces have less crime? How is the risk of arrest associated with the crime rate? Which police tactics are most likely to reduce crime? These are important questions for researchers, because the American people and their lawmakers often turn to the police to deal with crime.

Deterrence and Size of the Police Force   There is little evidence that increasing the resources or the numbers of the police will significantly reduce crime. Researchers have found that within the range of police officers per capita that exists in the United States, increasing or decreasing the number of officers in a city has no marginal deterrent effect on its crime rate (President's Commission on Law Enforcement and Administration of Justice, 1967: 96, 106; Loftin and McDowall, 1982; Greenberg, Kessler, and Loftin, 1983).

Large variations in the number of police officers per capita may affect crime rates in certain situations. Police saturation of an area sometimes occurs for a short time, and it can reduce crime, but this policy is not feasible over the long run (Sherman, 1986). A study of eighteen police crackdowns—sudden increases in the numbers of officers, sanctions, or threats of arrest—found that fifteen showed an initial deterrent effect, although this effect usually decreased after a short time. Five studies found that the deterrent effect continued even after the police crackdown ended. The evidence of an initial deterrent effect that usually decreases quickly and a residual deterrent effect in some cases suggests that police crackdowns might be most effective if they are of limited duration and are rotated from area to area (Sherman, 1990).

At the other end of the spectrum, the presence of very few police officers might cause crime rates to rise. Several American cities have experienced widespread looting during blackouts, a time when the resources of the police are overtaxed. When the Nazis arrested the Danish police in 1944, rates of robbery, burglary, and larceny rose dramatically despite harsher penalties for offenders who were caught and convicted (Andenaes, 1974). On the other hand, a study of eleven cities that have had police strikes found little evidence that the strikes significantly affected crime rates (Pfuhl, 1983).

Deterrence and Risk of Arrest   Politicians and the public commonly assume that the police deter crime through arrest, even though the rate at which the police solve crimes is quite low. The figures in Figure 14.2, the percentage of index crimes cleared by arrest in 1995, overestimate the chance that an offender will be arrested, because many crimes are not reported to or recorded by the police. Even though arrest rates are higher for violent crimes than for property crimes, violent offenses are probably harder to deter because they are often expressive in nature and occur in private settings to which the police have little access. Crimes against property are probably more likely to involve some consideration of risks and rewards, but they are solved infrequently and are thus not easily be deterred.

Can the police deter crime by increasing the risk of arrest? Some researchers have found a inverse relationship between clearance rates and crime rates; in other words, the more crimes the police solve, the fewer crimes of that sort there are (Tittle and Rowe, 1974; Logan, 1975; Wilson and Boland, 1976; Yu and Liska, 1993). Another study found no consistent evidence that higher clearance rates reduce crime rates (Greenberg and Kessler, 1982).

Deterrence and Police Patrol Tactics   Police patrol cars increase the area that the police can cover, and increased mobility enhances the likelihood that officers will be at or near the scene of a crime when it occurs. However, patrol cars isolate the police from the public, cutting off a source of information that can be used to maintain order, prevent crime, and arrest suspects.

One study that sought to determine whether police patrol has a deterrent effect was conducted in Kansas City, Missouri, in 1972 and 1973 (Kelling et al., 1974). The number of patrol cars was doubled in five areas of the city, the number remained the same in five areas, and in five areas all patrol cars were taken off duty and reassigned to other areas (although they did answer calls for

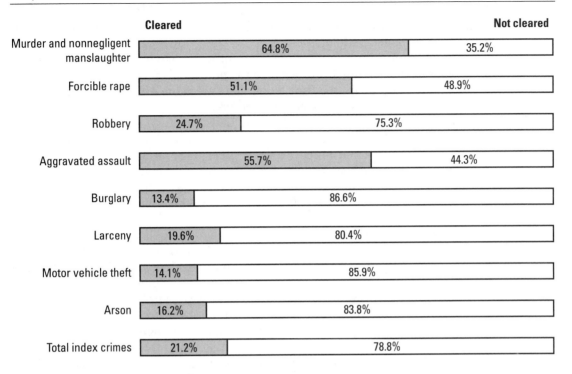

FIGURE 14.2

Clearance Rates of FBI Index Crimes, 1995

Source: Based on data from Federal Bureau of Investigation, *Crime in the United States, 1995: Uniform Crime Reports.* Washington, D.C.: U.S. Government Printing Office, 1996, p. 199.

help). The fifteen areas were matched by crime rate, characteristics of residents, and number of calls to the police. This experiment found that changes in police patrol practices in the fifteen areas had "little value in preventing crime or making citizens feel safe" (McNamara, 1974: iii). There were no significant differences among the areas in rates of offenses reported to the police, rates of crime reported in victimization surveys, citizen fear of crime, or citizen satisfaction with the police. One critic thought these negative results were unsurprising, because crime is concentrated in certain "hot spots," whereas patrol cars are widely dispersed, and so there is little chance that the police will encounter crime while on routine patrol (Sherman, 1992a).

The Kansas City experiment found no evidence of a **displacement effect**, a change in the pattern of crime without a reduction in the total amount of crime that occurs because criminals try to avoid punishment. Crime can be displaced from one target to another, one area to another, or one kind of offense to another (for instance, a burglary instead of a robbery). Displacement also refers to changes in a criminal's tactics and changes in the times at which crimes are committed (Hakim and Rengert, 1981; Barr and Pease, 1990). Visible police patrols could alter patterns of crime, but the

Kansas City study found no evidence of such displacement as a result of variations in police patrol tactics.

There is, however, evidence from other research that the police sometimes displace crime from one area to another where there are fewer officers or patrol cars, or from a time when there are more officers around to a time when the police are less likely to be present (Reppetto, 1974: 87–88). In a report on crime-reduction efforts in New York City, precinct captains and headquarters commanders claimed that robberies had decreased as a result of police efforts, but officers on the street were more likely to believe that patrol tactics had merely displaced robberies. One community relations officer remarked, "As long as there are haves and have nots, we're never going to deter crime. We're just going to push it from one area to another" (cited in Farber, 1982: B6).

Most research on the deterrent effects of the police has looked at clearance rates or at the number of officers on patrol. Even more important may be what the police do while on patrol. An experiment in San Diego found that robbery, burglary, theft, auto theft, assault, sex crimes, malicious mischief, and disturbances were reduced by an aggressive patrol strategy that included field interrogations (Boydstun, 1975). These "street stops" apparently changed perceived risks of apprehension, even though they did not increase the actual number of arrests. Another study found that proactive policing of disorderly conduct and driving under the influence of alcohol was associated with lower rates of robbery (Sampson and Cohen, 1988). These studies have been used to develop the "zero-tolerance" policy described in the Using Criminology box.

Many law-enforcement experts now advocate **community policing**, an approach based on the idea that officers in patrol cars are too isolated from the community and that there needs to be more contact between the police and the people they serve. Community policing involves foot patrols, decentralized police operations, storefront stations, participation in community organizations, crime newsletters, and contacts with people in their homes and places of work (Skogan, 1990; Bratton and Kelling, 1993; see the Using Criminology box on p. 409). Critics allege that community policing might increase corruption and lead officers to take sides in local conflicts. So far, there is little evidence that community policing reduces crime, but it does seem to reduce the fear of crime (Skogan, 1990).

Deterrence and the Courts   There is an inverse relationship between crime rates and the risk of conviction: lower crime rates are associated with higher conviction rates (Blumstein, Cohen, and Nagin, 1978). The issue of simultaneity again arises: a lower risk of conviction might increase the crime rate, but a higher crime rate can make convictions less likely. A high crime rate would reduce the risk of conviction if prosecutors drop cases because they lack the resources to bring all suspects to trial or if they lose cases because of hasty preparation. A high crime rate could also increase reliance on plea bargaining in order to ease the court's workload; this might produce more guilty pleas but fewer convictions on the most serious charges.

USING CRIMINOLOGY

Deterring Crime through "Zero-Tolerance" Policing

A new strategy of policing employed in Houston and New York is based on the assumption that attention by the police to even minor offenses can reduce serious crimes. This "zero-tolerance" policing is derived from a 1982 article by James Q. Wilson that argued that if social order in a community is allowed to deteriorate even a little, more decay and higher rates of serious crime will follow.

Periodic neighborhood sweeps that arrest people for truancy, jaywalking, vandalism, drunkenness, urinating in public, and double parking have, according to the advocates of zero-tolerance policing, reduced serious crimes. This is accomplished in part by letting local gangs know that the police are paying attention to them and will take steps to control even minor forms of misbehavior.

The assumption that those who commit minor offenses will also commit serious crimes proved correct in New York City in 1996 when fingerprints at the scene of a murder were used to arrest John Royster for killing a woman who owned a dry cleaning shop. Royster's fingerprints were in the police computer because a few months earlier he had been apprehended for jumping a subway turnstile without paying. When he was arrested, he confessed to the murder and three other brutal assaults.

Not everyone supports zero-tolerance policing. Critics claim that communities inhabited by the poor and by minorities are those most often targeted by the police, who harass and intimidate the disadvantaged for doing what others do with impunity.

Sources: Based on Brian McGrory, "'Zero-Tolerance' Policing in Houston: No Crime Too Small," *Boston Globe*, January 2, 1996, pp. 1, 4; Fred Kaplan, "In Suspect's Arrest, a Win for NYC," *Boston Globe*, June 16, 1996, p. 16.

Deterrence and the Prisons Crime rates are inversely related to the risk of imprisonment, with crime being more common when there is less threat of incarceration. Research is less supportive of an inverse relationship between crime rates and the actual amount of time served in prison: crime is not consistently more common when prison terms are shorter (Blumstein, Cohen, and Nagin, 1978). The problem of simultaneity plagues much of this research: it is unclear if the risk of imprisonment affects crimes rates, if crime rates influence the risk of imprisonment, or if both are true.

One strategy that has been tried as a deterrent to delinquency is a "shock sentence," with offenders being given "a taste of the bars" to keep them from further wrongdoing. The Massachusetts Department of Youth Services once sentenced some juvenile offenders to thirty to sixty days of confinement, in the hope that their experience with "hard time" would break their pattern of delinquent activity. One study found that a shock sentence followed by probation had no apparent marginal deterrent effect over regular probation (Parisi, 1981).

Community policing is based
on the idea that crime will be
deterred more effectively if
there is more contact
between the police and
the people they serve.

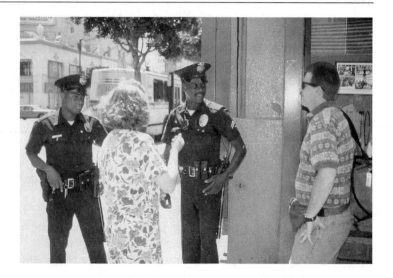

   "Scared Straight" is a program that brings young people into prison to listen to inmates talk about the unpleasantness of prison life; violence and
homosexual rape are described in graphic terms to scare the young people
away from a life of crime. This program, formally named the Juvenile
Awareness Project, was initiated at Rahway State Prison in New Jersey in 1976
and was the basis of a television documentary broadcast nationally in 1979
and shown again with a follow-up report in 1987. The show claimed that the
program kept more than 80 percent of its participants from getting into trouble with the law again. However, a systematic evaluation found that youths
who had participated in the program were actually arrested more often than
those who had not (Finckenauer, 1982). A second evaluation concluded that
delinquent behavior by those who had participated in the program remained
relatively constant after participation, but that the delinquent behavior of
those who had not participated increased significantly, suggesting that the
program might keep participants from becoming more delinquent.
Nevertheless, this second evaluation found that 85 percent of the participants
continued to commit delinquent acts after the program (Langer, 1979).
   An approach now popular with politicians and the public is the **boot
camp**, a military-style program designed to scare offenders away from crime
by subjecting them to harsh discipline, rigorous exercise, and strenuous
work. Some camps provide drug treatment, educational programs, and vocational training, but the emphasis is on deterrence rather than rehabilitation.
In 1993, thirty states had boot camp programs, using them mostly for young
adults convicted of nonviolent crimes who had never been incarcerated
before; the average stay in a boot camp was 107 days. There is no evidence
that boot camps keep their graduates from returning to crime, nor do they
reduce prison crowding or cut prison costs. Indeed, the use of boot camps for
offenders who would otherwise have been placed on probation can actually
increase correctional costs (Morash and Rucker, 1990; MacKenzie, 1993).

Deterrence and Capital Punishment   In 1994, 74 percent of Americans favored the death penalty for convicted murderers, 20 percent opposed it, and 6 percent answered "don't know." Support for capital punishment was greater among men than women, among whites than blacks, among people with higher rather than lower incomes, and among Republicans rather than Democrats (Maguire and Pastore, 1995: 183).

There is a direct association between support for the death penalty and the belief that it is a deterrent, but it is not clear that people support the death penalty just because they believe it deters crime. A study of northern Californians found that most based their support for or opposition to the death penalty on symbolic or ideological grounds, rather than on a set of reasoned beliefs. Nearly all of the 59 percent of the sample who supported the death penalty believed it was a better deterrent than life imprisonment, but two-thirds of those supporters said they would favor capital punishment even if it had no deterrent effect. Nearly all of the 31 percent of the sample who opposed the death penalty believed it had no marginal deterrent effect over life imprisonment, but three-fourths of them said they would continue to oppose the death penalty even if it proved to be a much better deterrent than life imprisonment (Ellsworth and Ross, 1983).

Scholars have done much research on the deterrent effect of capital punishment. Some have compared the homicide rates of states that have the death penalty with the homicide rates of states that do not have the death penalty. Others have examined the murder rates in a state before and after its abolition of capital punishment to determine if that change affected its murder rates. Another method has been to look at murder rates in an area just before and just after executions to see if executions affect the murder rate. Most research has found no evidence that either death penalty laws or actual executions deter

Boot camps try to scare offenders away from crime by subjecting them to a military-style program of harsh discipline, rigorous exercise, and strenuous work.

homicide. One cross-national study found that abolition of the death penalty was followed by a drop in the murder rate more often than by the increase that deterrence theory predicts (Archer, Gartner, and Beittel, 1983).

A few studies have found that capital punishment deters homicide. One frequently cited paper that used econometric techniques estimated that each execution deters as many as eight homicides (Ehrlich, 1975). A second econometric study estimated that each execution prevents up to eighteen murders (Layson, 1985). Critics argue that the methodological shortcomings of these studies invalidate their conclusions (Blumstein, Cohen, and Nagin, 1978; Knorr, 1979; Fox and Radelet, 1989). Two studies have found that well-publicized executions produce short-term reductions in homicides (Phillips, 1980; Stack, 1987); other research has found no evidence of such short-term reductions (McFarland, 1983; Peterson and Bailey, 1988; Bailey and Peterson, 1989). Most researchers agree that there is no long-term reduction in homicides after even highly publicized executions (Zeisel, 1982; Bailey and Peterson, 1989; Bailey, 1990; Peterson and Bailey, 1991).

Most research is consistent with the conclusion that capital punishment does not deter those crimes for which it has been used in the United States—forcible rape (until 1977) and homicide. There are reasons for the absence of a deterrent effect. Rapists and murderers do not usually reflect much on the consequences of their behavior before acting. Murder often occurs between people who are intimately involved with one another, and the emotion that characterizes such relationships can interfere with a careful assessment of the costs of violating the law. Lack of prompt punishment also reduces any general deterrent effect that the death penalty might have; the average time from imposition of a death sentence to actual execution has been eight years for murderers executed since 1977. Another consideration is that because capital punishment statutes apply only to specific kinds of murder (for example, felony murders, premeditated murders, extremely brutal slayings, and murders of police or correctional officers), those laws are unlikely to deter all types of murder.

Capital punishment in the United States also lacks certainty, with most murderers not sentenced to death and most who are sentenced to death never executed. From 1977 through 1994, the FBI recorded 386,307 murders and nonnegligent manslaughters and 376,360 arrests for those crimes. During that time, 4,557 people were admitted to prison under sentence of death and 257 were executed. Two-fifths of those sentenced to death were removed from Death Row by being retried or resentenced, having their death sentence commuted, or dying before they were executed (Stephan and Snell, 1996). The Cross-Cultural Perspective indicates that certainty of execution is greater in China than in the United States.

Incapacitation

Incapacitation is the custodial control of convicted offenders so that they cannot commit crimes that affect the general public (van Dine, Conrad, and

A CROSS-CULTURAL PERSPECTIVE

Capital Punishment in China

Beginning a crackdown on crime in August 1983, the Chinese government executed 10,000 to 20,000 offenders over the next two-and-a-half years. About 2,000 executions a year were carried out over the following decade. In April 1996, the government began a "Strike Hard" crackdown in response to a growth in serious crime, which was increasingly committed with firearms and by organized gangs. In just two months, tens of thousands were arrested and more than one thousand executed. (Compare these figures with the number of executions in the United States, shown in Figure 14.3.)

In China, execution follows conviction in short order, sometimes by only a few weeks, and there are few legal safeguards against conviction of the innocent. Offenders appear at public "sentencing rallies," where they carry banners telling of their crimes. Their executions, which are carried out in public with a bullet to the back of the head, are designed to deter crime by creating a general fear of punishment. To instill fear of the death penalty, the government has even executed criminals who were descendants of national heroes and who had been Communist Party leaders.

Fifty crimes are now capital offenses in China, including murder, rape, robbery, burglary, bribing the police, distributing pornography, enticing women into prostitution, embezzlement, "hooliganism," and drug trafficking. Most of those put to death have been convicted of murder, rape, or robbery, but an increasing number are being executed for drug dealing; thirty-five drug traffickers were executed at a single public sentencing rally on October 26, 1991, and twenty-one more were put to death at a similar rally on June 26, 1992.

Sources: John F. Burns, "When Peking Fights Crime, News Is on the Wall," *New York Times*, January 28, 1986, p. A2; Nicholas D. Kristof, "Law and Order in China Means More Executions," *New York Times*, January 15, 1991, p. 42; Patrick E. Tyler, "Crime (and Punishment) Rages Anew in China," *New York Times*, July 11, 1996, pp. A1, A8.

Dinitz, 1979: 125). Incapacitation assumes that offenders will commit a certain number of crimes over a given time if they remain in society, and that those crimes can be prevented by incarcerating the offenders for that time. According to Figure 14.4, the public believes that the main purpose of prisons is incapacitation.

James Q. Wilson (1983) argues that incapacitation will work if three assumptions are correct:

1. Some offenders are repeaters.
2. Offenders who are taken off the street are not immediately and completely replaced by other offenders.
3. Prison does not increase crime by changing inmates in ways that offset the reduction of crime from incapacitation.

**Number of
executions**

FIGURE 14.3

Number of Persons Executed in the United States, 1930–1995

Source: James J. Stephan and Tracy L. Snell, *Capital Punishment 1994.* Washington, D.C.: U.S. Department of Justice, February 1996, p. 2. Updated with number for 1995.

Wilson suggests that the first assumption is clearly correct. The second one is plausible for certain offenses: replacement occurs in organized crime families, and to some extent among prostitutes, drug dealers, and white-collar offenders; it is less likely for offenders who engage in domestic violence and conventional crime. Wilson acknowledges that the third assumption is debatable, but suggests that the "schooling" effect of prison probably does not outweigh its incapacitating effect.

Estimating the impact of incapacitation on crime rates is difficult. Because we do not know how many offenses different criminals will commit in a given period of time, it is hard to determine how much crime will be prevented by locking up offenders. Offenders who are at the end of their criminal careers might have stopped committing crime soon even if they had not been imprisoned; for them, incarceration will have little incapacitating effect.

Selective Incapacitation

Selective incapacitation is a policy that aims to separate high-risk offenders from low-risk ones, and hold only those who are the most likely to be dangerous if released.

FIGURE 14.4

Public Attitudes toward the
Main Purpose of Prisons,
1994

Source: Based on data provided
by The Wirthlin Group, in
Kathleen Maguire and Ann L.
Pastore, *Sourcebook of Criminal
Justice Statistics—1994.*
Washington, D.C.: Bureau of
Justice Statistics, U.S.
Department of Justice, 1995,
p. 177.

Question: "What do you feel is the main purpose of prisons? Is it to
keep criminals out of society [incapacitation], to punish criminals
[punishment], or to rehabilitate criminals (rehabilitation]?"

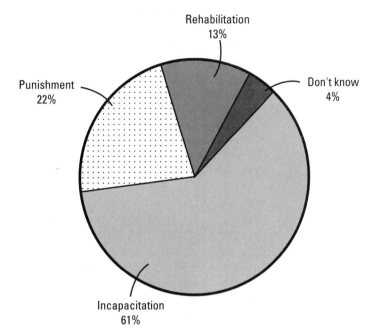

Rehabilitation
13%

Don't know
4%

Punishment
22%

Incapacitation
61%

Peter Greenwood (1982, 1984) has devised a system that would separate offenders who should get "incapacitating" prison sentences from those who can be released or placed in alternative programs. Using interviews with incarcerated robbers and burglars, he discovered that the offenders who had committed the most crimes had the following characteristics:

1. An earlier conviction for the same offense;
2. Imprisonment for more than half of the two years prior to the current arrest;
3. A conviction before the age of sixteen;
4. Previous commitment to a juvenile institution;
5. Use of heroin or barbiturates during the previous two years;
6. Use of heroin or barbiturates as a juvenile; and
7. Unemployment for half or more of the preceding two years.

Robbers who had four or more of these characteristics had committed an average of thirty-one robberies per year while on the street, compared with an average of only two robberies per year for those who fit one or none of the criteria. Greenwood's seven-item scale also predicted self-reported offending by a sample of New Orleans inmates (Miranne and Geerken, 1991).

Greenwood claimed that implementation of his system of selective incapacitation would allocate the limited amount of prison space more efficiently and reduce crime rates. Other researchers have found that the crime-
reduction potential of his system is less than he suggested, and that the
prison population would have to increase dramatically to achieve even a
modest reduction in crime (Visher, 1986; Bernard and Ritti, 1991).

Critics claim that many errors would be made if Greenwood's scale were
used to predict which offenders should be incapacitated; many of those
locked up would not have returned to crime if they had been released (Cohen,
1983a, 1983b; von Hirsch, 1984; Decker and Salert, 1986). Greenwood's
response to this criticism is that judges and parole boards now decide on sentences and release dates on the basis of their best guesses about future behavior, and a selective incapacitation policy would simply allow them to use
available data efficiently to make their decisions (Greenwood, 1982, 1984).

One objection to selective incapacitation is that penalties should reflect
the seriousness of an offender's crime rather than his or her prior record, and
Greenwood's system does not base punishment on the amount of harm done
(von Hirsch, 1984). Critics have also opposed selective incapacitation systems
that use predictive criteria over which offenders have no control. Of
Greenwood's seven criteria, only unemployment might be seen as a factor
over which offenders have little or no control, as in times of high unemployment; however, it could also be argued that unemployment often reflects voluntary behavior by offenders.

Career Criminal Programs

District attorneys' offices around the country have established units to prosecute career criminals who repeatedly commit felonies. These programs concentrate resources on suspects who have prior records of serious crimes in
order to incapacitate them as quickly and for as long as possible. To do this,
career criminal programs encourage cooperation between prosecutors and
the police, screen defendants for priority prosecution, assign experienced
lawyers to top-priority cases, reduce the caseloads of prosecutors assigned to
top-priority cases, have the same prosecutor stay with a case until it is disposed of, assign all cases involving a defendant to the same prosecutor, have
a senior prosecutor monitor the progress of top-priority cases, and minimize
plea negotiation (Chaiken and Chaiken, 1991).

Career criminal programs have increased conviction rates, incarceration
rates, and the length of sentences by modest amounts. A New York state program that focused on offenders who had at least one prior felony conviction
and who were currently charged with a major crime convicted more than 95
percent of the defendants; nearly four-fifths of those who were convicted
were sentenced on the highest charge they faced (Fowler, 1981). The federal-
ly sponsored Habitual Serious and Violent Juvenile Offender Program, initiated at thirteen locations in 1984, focused on young people who had prior convictions for serious offenses and who were charged with homicides,

robberies, forcible sex offenses, assaults, or burglaries. Experienced prosecutors paid special attention to cases involving those youths, and victims and witnesses were offered special assistance. The program succeeded in prosecuting cases differently from the way they had been handled before, and correctional commitments increased at all sites (Cronin et al., 1988; Office of Juvenile Justice and Delinquency Prevention, 1988).

"Three Strikes and You're Out"

In 1994 California enacted a "three strikes and you're out" law that required the incarceration of offenders for twenty-five years to life for a third felony conviction, and required that a penalty be double the prescribed one for a second felony conviction. California, the thirteen states that have similar laws, and other states that are considering such legislation hope that incapacitating career felons will reduce the crime rate. The "three strikes" approach is widely supported, with 86 percent of a national sample questioned in 1994 favoring the policy and only 12 percent opposing it (Maguire and Pastore, 1995: 176).

Critics of California's law allege that it will cost taxpayers billions of dollars to lock up additional offenders, and that rising correctional costs might lead to reduced funding of educational and environmental programs (Greenwood et al., 1994). Three-strikes laws have also encouraged some offenders who are facing a third felony conviction to use violence against the police to avoid arrest. California and Washington report that defendants facing a third felony conviction have refused to negotiate pleas that would result in long prison sentences, resulting in court backlogs as more trials are required. Jails have filled up with defendants awaiting trial under the three-strikes law, and inmates serving time for misdemeanors have been released to make space for them. Many of those incarcerated under three-strikes laws are older offenders who are apt to be near the end of their criminal careers; locking these and other offenders up for life will inevitably lead to high health care costs for correctional systems. So far, many more second- and third-strike convictions have been for nonviolent crimes (such as drug possession and burglary) than for serious violent offenses (such as murder and rape). The long-term impact of three-strikes laws is unclear; one California court ruled that judges had the right to ignore prior convictions in sentencing defendants, and some victims and witnesses have refused to testify and some juries have refused to convict because of the long prison terms that defendants would face if convicted.

Retribution

In 1996 two boys, ages twelve and thirteen, were sent to Illinois's maximum-security juvenile prison for murdering a five-year-old boy by dropping him from a fourteen-story building two years earlier. The boys must remain in state custody for at least five years, but they have to be released when they turn twenty-one. Also in 1996, a federal judge sentenced the former treasurer of the nation's Episcopal Church to a five-year prison term for stealing $2.2 million from the church. The prison sentence, which exceeded federal standards for this type of crime and offender, was accompanied by a judicial order that the fifty-two-year-old woman repay embezzled funds to the church.

How much punishment do offenders deserve for their crimes? (See the Crime on Campus box.) **Retribution** or **just deserts** theory proposes that offenders should be punished because they deserve to suffer for the harm they have caused, and that their punishment should be proportional to that harm and to their own blameworthiness. This theory assumes that offenders freely choose to break the law and know that punishment might result from their actions. Retribution is oriented toward behavior that offenders have already engaged in, rather than toward their future conduct or the conduct of potential offenders. Retributivists suggest that offenders should be punished because they have gained an advantage over others by their crimes, and only punishment can restore a balance among all citizens.

Retribution differs from **vengeance**, which is private and personal and not imposed by an established authority such as the state. In contrast, retribution requires an authority with the acknowledged right to sanction convicted offenders (Armstrong, 1971). Whereas vengeance is motivated by the desire to be gratified or compensated for a loss, retribution is justified by the need to enforce the law and maintain social order (van den Haag, 1975).

Retribution is commonly associated with *lex talionis*, the principle of "an eye for an eye, a tooth for a tooth," which was expressed in the Code of Hammurabi in the eighteenth century B.C. To take this rule literally, a person who blinded another person would be blinded in return. Being made to pay a small fine would be an unjustly lenient sentence, and execution would be an unjustly severe penalty. Retributivists claim that offenders should be punished because they deserve to suffer, but they should be punished only in direct proportion to the harm they have caused. The idea of making punishment proportional to the seriousness of the crime makes mercy possible, "because to be merciful is to let someone off for all or part of a penalty which he is recognized as having deserved" (Armstrong, 1971: 36).

Critics argue that retribution is simply a justification for harsher sanctions, perhaps to shore up a faltering capitalist economy (Reiman and Headlee, 1981; Reiman, 1982). Others point out that just deserts theorists have not supported harsh penalties in recent years, and that their work has not been directed at strengthening a troubled capitalist system (Greenberg and Humphries, 1982).

Retribution theory claims that people who violate the law are blameworthy and deserve moral disapproval for their acts. This disapproval is seen as the basis for punishment, even if the punishment does not serve a socially useful function such as deterring people from crime or rehabilitating offenders. This contrasts with the deterrence perspective, which aims to control crime by punishing offenders so that they or others will not commit crime in the future. The principle of retribution also differs from the rehabilitation

CRIME ON CAMPUS

Just Deserts for Student Offenders?

The system used by colleges and universities to punish students who break the law has been described as "a kind of parallel judicial universe where offenses as serious as arson and rape can be disposed of discreetly under the same student conduct codes that forbid sneaking into a university dance without a ticket" (p. 1).

Victimized students have the right to file charges with the local police departments and pursue justice through the courts. Most campus police forces have arrest power and can refer suspects to the district attorney or to university administrators, but many crimes are not reported to the campus police. Instead, dormitory residents and administrators who learn of crimes encourage victims to pursue justice through a disciplinary system that "tries" cases before a committee of students, faculty, and administrators. This permits the school to avoid publicity and maintain its reputation, and it leads to swifter action than the courts can offer. Because universities lack the power to fine or incarcerate offenders, the most severe sanction students face is expulsion from school. Campus justice might be swifter and more certain than that provided by the legal system, but administrative sanctions are usually less severe than those handed out by the courts.

Source: Based on Nina Bernstein, "With Colleges Holding Court, Discretion Vies with Fairness," *New York Times*, May 5, 1996, pp. 1, 16.

---

perspective, which seeks to reform criminals so they will not again make the incorrect decision to break the law.

If the only goal of punishment were to deter people from crime, innocent people might be punished, as long as the public believed they were actually guilty. A very severe penalty administered with certainty could also have a strong deterrent effect; for example, a thirty-year prison term for petty theft might deter stealing. The usual objection to punishing the innocent and to very harsh penalties is that those penalties are unjust. This idea of the "justness" of penalties is the essence of the retribution rationale.

If rehabilitation were the only goal of punishment, people identified as potentially dangerous might be imprisoned and treated even before they were convicted of a crime. If there were no effective treatment for serial killers, the rehabilitation rationale would require that they not be imprisoned at all. If there were an effective treatment method that could fully reform a petty thief with a thirty-year prison sentence, such a penalty might be justified in terms of rehabilitation. The usual objection to penalties such as these is that they are fundamentally unjust. Indeed, if there were general agreement that a six-month prison term is a just penalty for petty theft, keeping a petty thief locked up for even one month longer would seem improper to retributivists, even if the thief were rehabilitated by the extra month in prison and other people considering theft were deterred by that extra month (von Hirsch, 1976).

Retributivists assert that deterrence and rehabilitation are secondary or derivative goals of punishment; the primary justification for punishment is that offenders deserve to be punished in proportion to the harm they have inflicted on the victim and on society. Others suggest that deterrence and rehabilitation should play a part in determining sentences; one philosopher says that "a modified retributive theory is perfectly possible, one which only uses retributive considerations to fix some sort of upper limit to penalties and then looks to other factors to decide how much and what sort of pain shall be inflicted" (Armstrong, 1971: 38–39). A just deserts model might set an upper limit, a lower limit, or a range of penalties, with considerations of deterrence, incapacitation, and rehabilitation determining where within those limits the actual punishment falls (Morris, 1981; Wilson, 1983). Strict retributivists disagree with this approach, claiming that penalties should be proportional to the seriousness of the current offense, and that other considerations should not play a role in determining punishment (von Hirsch, 1981, 1985).

A System of Just Deserts

A workable system of retribution or just deserts would require the rank ordering of crimes by their relative seriousness and the rank ordering of punishments by their relative unpleasantness. Seriousness of crimes and unpleasantness of penalties are not objective facts, so these rankings have to be based on subjective evaluations. Researchers would then need to link these two scales so that crimes of specific degrees of seriousness would be associated with penalties of certain levels of severity.

The Seriousness of Crimes   A scale that ranks offenses by seriousness might be based on the amount of harm caused by a crime and on the blameworthiness of the offender, with harmfulness and blameworthiness combined into a single measure of the seriousness of the crime (Bedau, 1977):

Seriousness = Harmfulness + Blameworthiness

Research has been done to develop scales that measure harmfulness and blameworthiness, but less work has been done to combine harmfulness and blameworthiness into a single scale of seriousness.

Harmfulness of Crimes   Thorsten Sellin and Marvin Wolfgang's (1964) pioneering study found widespread agreement about how crimes should be ranked. They showed that various components of a crime, such as amount of injury to the victim and amount of monetary loss, could be assigned scores, with a summary score then derived for the offense. This made it possible to rank crimes by their harmfulness and to state how much more serious one crime was than another.

Table 14.2 shows the values assigned to the various elements of a crime incident. A robbery in which the victim suffered minor injuries and lost $300 when verbally threatened would have an overall score of 6, the sum of 1 point for minor injury, 3 for the theft of $300, and 2 for verbal intimidation in connection with a theft. A robbery in which there was no injury to the victim but a loss of $5 as a result of verbal intimidation would receive a score of 3, the total of 0 points for no injury, 1 for the loss of $5, and 2 for verbal intimidation in connection with the theft. We can thus say that the first robbery was twice as serious as the second one.

Sellin and Wolfgang's scoring system allows for a more meaningful measurement of crime than is possible by just counting the number of incidents. The difference between a bank robbery in which a guard is seriously injured by an armed offender who steals $10,000 and a schoolyard robbery in which a child gives up lunch money because of a verbal threat would not show up in the FBI's UCR statistics, because each event would be counted as one robbery. Sellin and Wolfgang's scoring system would emphasize the difference between the incidents. The bank robbery would be scored 16, the sum of 4 points for the use of a weapon in connection with the theft, 7 for injury to the guard, and 5 for the theft of $10,000. The schoolyard robbery would be scored

TABLE 14.2 Seriousness Scores for Elements of Crimes

Elements of the Crime	Score Value
Minor injury to victim	1
Victim treated and discharged	4
Victim hospitalized	7
Victim killed	26
Victim of forcible sexual intercourse	10
Intimidated by weapon, add	2
Intimidation of persons in connection with theft, etc. (Other than in connection with forcible sex acts):	
Physical or verbal only	2
By weapon	4
Forcible entry of premises	1
Value of property stolen and/or damaged:	
Under $10	1
$10–$250	2
$251–$2,000	3
$2,001–$9,000	4
$9,001–$30,000	5
$30,001–$80,000	6
Over $80,000	7
Theft of motor vehicle (recovered, undamaged)	2

Source: Thorsten Sellin and Marvin E. Wolfgang, *The Measurement of Delinquency.* New York: John Wiley, 1964, p. 298. Reprinted by permission of Marvin E. Wolfgang.

3, the sum of 1 point for the theft of less than $10 and 2 for verbal intimidation connected with the theft.

The National Survey of Crime Severity, conducted in 1977, asked people to rank 204 illegal acts (Wolfgang et al., 1985). Table 14.3 shows the average severity scores for some of these offenses. There was significant agreement on the ranking of the crimes by people with different social characteristics, although victims assigned somewhat higher severity scores than nonvictims, blacks and other minorities assigned lower severity scores than whites, and older people ranked thefts with large losses as more severe than did younger respondents. In ranking crimes, people took into account the ability of victims to protect themselves, the amount of injury and loss, the relationship of the offender to the victim, and the kind of business from which property was stolen (Bureau of Justice Statistics, October 1983).

Research that yielded a seriousness ranking of crimes similar to the one produced by the National Survey of Crime Severity employed data on victim injury rates, jury awards in personal injury cases, crime-related death rates, estimates of the financial value of life, and out-of-pocket expenses borne by crime victims. This research concluded that violent crimes were relatively more costly to victims than the national survey indicated (Cohen, 1988).

There is considerable cross-cultural consensus on the ranking of crimes. A study of India, Indonesia, Iran, Italy (Sardinia), Yugoslavia, and the United States found substantial agreement on the perceived harmfulness of various deviant acts and on the amount and type of punishment thought to be appropriate for each act (Newman, 1976). Other research shows that offense rankings are similar in the United States, Canada, Norway, Finland, Sweden, Denmark, the Netherlands, Great Britain, and Kuwait (Scott and Al-Thakeb, 1977; Kvålseth, 1980; Evans and Scott, 1984).

Blameworthiness of Offenders   One form of retribution theory claims that penalties should be imposed only for the harm caused by the crime; this position would ignore the offender's blameworthiness. Another form of retribution theory holds that because offenders should be punished as they deserve, their blameworthiness must be considered in determining their sentences (von Hirsch, 1992).

Blameworthiness can be measured in different ways. One is to consider motivation or mental state: did the offender act intentionally or negligently? Another way is to look at the circumstances of the crime; an offender who is involved in a victim-precipitated crime or who is an unwilling or peripheral participant in a crime might be treated as less blameworthy than someone who, alone, plans and carries out a crime. Offenders could also be regarded as more blameworthy if they victimize strangers rather than intimates or if their victims are respectable (Blum-West and Hembroff, 1982; Hembroff, 1987; Hamilton and Sanders, 1988).

Blameworthiness is usually measured by the number and seriousness of an individual's prior convictions, the assumption being that a crime is more serious if an offender has committed other crimes in the past. This use of prior arrests or convictions to indicate blameworthiness can lead to "a cyclic reconfirmation of criminality" (Farrell and Swigert, 1978: 451). More specifi-

TABLE 14.3   Public Ranking of Severity of Crimes

Severity Score	Offense
72.1	A person plants a bomb in a public building. The bomb explodes and twenty people are killed.
52.8	A man forcibly rapes a woman. As a result of physical injuries, she dies.
43.2	A person robs a victim at gunpoint. The victim struggles and is shot to death.
39.2	A man stabs his wife. As a result, she dies.
33.8	A person runs a narcotics ring.
27.9	A woman stabs her husband. As a result, he dies.
24.9	A person intentionally sets fire to a building, causing $100,000 worth of damage.
22.9	A parent beats his young child with his fists. The child requires hospitalization.
15.9	A teenage boy beats his mother with his fists. The mother requires hospitalization.
14.1	A doctor cheats on claims he makes to a federal health insurance plan for patient services.
13.9	A legislator takes a bribe from a company to vote for a law favoring the company.
13.0	A factory knowingly gets rid of its waste in a way that pollutes the water supply of a city.
10.3	A person operates a store where he knowingly sells stolen property.
9.6	A person breaks into a home and steals $1,000.
9.4	A public official takes $1,000 of public money for his own use.
9.2	Several large companies illegally fix the retail prices of their products.
7.9	A teenage boy beats his father with his fists. The father requires hospitalization.
7.5	A person, armed with a lead pipe, robs a victim of $10. No physical harm occurs.
7.4	A person illegally gets monthly welfare checks.
7.3	A person breaks into a department store and steals merchandise worth $1,000.
6.2	An employee embezzles $1,000 from his employer.
4.9	A person snatches a handbag containing $10 from a victim on the street.
4.6	A person carries a gun illegally.
4.5	A person cheats on his federal income tax return.
3.6	A person knowingly passes a bad check.
2.2	A person steals $10 worth of merchandise from the counter of a department store.
2.1	A woman engages in prostitution.
1.1	A person takes bets on the numbers.
0.9	A person under sixteen years old runs away from home.

Source: Adapted from Marvin E. Wolfgang et al., *The National Survey of Crime Severity.* Washington, D.C.: U.S. Department of Justice, June 1985, pp. vi–x.

cally, research showing that lower-class suspects are more likely than middle-class suspects to be arrested, convicted, and severely punished for the same crime suggests that the use of prior records to indicate blameworthiness and determine penalties can lock lower-class offenders into criminal careers.

The Unpleasantness of Penalties A retributive system of punishment requires data on how people perceive the relative severity of penalties. For example, how do people perceive the relative unpleasantness of a sentence to a state prison, a term in a county jail, a fine, and probation? We also need to know the perceived unpleasantness of an increment of a particular kind of penalty; for instance, do people think that a ten-year prison sentence is twice as severe as a five-year sentence?

There is general agreement on how unpleasant criminal sanctions are. Probation is undesirable because it imposes restrictions on offenders; they are required to report regularly to probation officers, and their mobility and privacy are restricted. Fines are disagreeable because they deprive offenders of property; they are a relatively lenient form of punishment because they do not disrupt ties to family and job as imprisonment does, but they do discriminate against people who cannot afford to pay. Imprisonment deprives offenders of freedom of movement and contacts with the outside world. Restraint on freedom of movement is subject to many gradations, with the amount of time and the institution in which an offender is confined indicating the severity of the penalty.

Little research has been done on the equivalence of different penalties. One study had people rate the severity of various penalties in comparison with a standard of one year in jail (Erickson and Gibbs, 1979). The researchers then developed a series of scales that allowed them to equate a particular jail sentence with a specific prison sentence, probationary period, or fine. For instance, one year in a local jail was perceived as equivalent to six months in a state prison, 7.8 years on probation, or a fine of about $3,000. The researchers suggested that eventually it might be possible to convert different penalties into a common quantitative measure of perceived severity. Such a measure could be used to compare judges and jurisdictions in terms of the severity of penalties given. It might also be used to have convicted offenders choose from a list of equivalent penalties.

Linking Penalties to Crimes Developing a scale that measures the seriousness of crimes or the unpleasantness of penalties is easier than determining how severe a penalty should be administered to a person who commits an offense of a certain degree of seriousness. A pioneering effort to do this was a proposal by the Committee for the Study of Incarceration that four sentence levels be used for offenders convicted of crimes of varying degrees of seriousness (as measured by the harmfulness of the offense and the number and seriousness of the offender's prior convictions). The committee recommended that minor offenses be punished with warning-and-release or intermittent confinement (for example, for a few Saturdays); intermediate-level offenses usually should be punished with intermittent confinement; serious offenses (lower range) should be punished with jail or prison terms of less than eighteen months; and serious offenses (upper range) should be punished with incarceration for one-and-a-half to three years. There would be no prison sentences over five years, except for certain murders and a few cases involving exceptional circumstances. Fines were avoided because of the difficulty of equalizing fines for people with different incomes (von Hirsch, 1976).

The recommendations of the Committee for the Study of Incarceration were not derived from research. Studies that first develop a scale ranking penalties by severity and a scale ranking offenses by seriousness, and then ask people to propose specific penalties for different crimes, would be a better basis for a system of just deserts. Efforts to link crimes and penalties in this way have encountered obstacles; some research has found a close match between perceived seriousness of crimes and perceived severity of penalties, but other research has found no straightforward relationship between the two variables (Hamilton and Rotkin, 1976; Blumstein and Cohen, 1980; Hamilton and Rytina, 1980; Samuel and Moulds, 1986). One study found that in recommending penalties, whites are more likely to consider a crime's seriousness, whereas blacks are more likely to consider an offender's characteristics and the circumstances of the crime (Miller, Rossi, and Simpson, 1986).

When the public is asked to recommend sentences in the way that judges do—that is, by taking into account the circumstances of the crime, the characteristics of the offender, the kinds of sanctions available, and the cost of sentencing alternatives—its recommendations for punishment approximate those of judges (Thomson and Ragona, 1987). People are most punitive toward offenders who appear to have committed their crimes intentionally, seem unrepentant, and have committed crimes before; these offenders are seen as especially likely to repeat their crimes, because they do not acknowledge the moral validity of the law.

Retribution and the Criminal Justice System

Considerations of just deserts have always played an important role in the American criminal justice system, but that role has increased in recent years as research has cast doubt on the effectiveness of treatment.

Retribution and the Police   One way to determine the goals of the police is to look at their organization and their use of resources. Police departments include detectives and squads that specialize in the investigation of the most serious offenses (e.g., homicide), and they allocate more resources to the investigation of crimes that rank high on the scale of seriousness. Retributive considerations also influence the way the police respond to apprehended suspects, with arrest and prosecution more likely than release if the offense is a harmful one and the suspect has a criminal record and thus seems blameworthy.

Retribution and the Courts   Retribution is a consideration in district attorneys' decisions about how to prosecute defendants and in judges' decisions about how to sentence convicted offenders, and it has been the impetus for recent changes in the handling of juvenile offenders.

Prosecutors' Decision Making   Prosecutors assume that the defendants against whom they bring charges are guilty and should be punished appropriately by the criminal justice system. To save the court's time and ensure a conviction, prosecutors pressure defendants to plead guilty. Because the plea to which a district attorney will agree is based on the harmfulness of the offense and the defendant's criminal record, offenders are usually punished according to the principle of just deserts.

One study of prosecutors' attitudes toward different offenses produced unexpected results. Prosecutors thought that white-collar crime was very serious, equivalent to offenses such as kidnapping and rape and more serious than the theft of a similar amount of money by a conventional offender. The amount of money stolen in a crime was not seen as an important consideration in determining the seriousness of an offense, because the amount of money available to be stolen was a matter of chance. In addition, whether an assault victim died was seen as partly due to chance, and so manslaughter was viewed as only slightly more serious than aggravated assault (Roth, 1978). These considerations are not written into the criminal code, but prosecutors use them to determine appropriate penalties.

In contrast to this study, another survey found that most prosecutors did not regard white-collar crime as a serious problem, even though they believed that tougher penalties could deter it. They said that they were more likely to act against white-collar offenders if their crimes involved substantial harm and a large number of victims, had been committed deliberately or negligently, had victims who wanted to prosecute, and had not been dealt with by other agencies (Benson, Cullen, and Maakestad, 1990).

The relatively lenient treatment of white-collar criminals is not primarily due to lack of prosecutors' support for tough penalties or their empathy for high-status offenders. Instead, leniency is a function of the difficulty of detecting and prosecuting white-collar crimes (Shapiro, 1990). Prosecutors claim, with justification, that public pressure to enforce drug laws has drained away resources that they might have used to deal with white-collar crimes (Benson, Cullen, and Maakestad, 1990).

Judges' Decision Making   In considering how much punishment a convicted offender deserves, judges are primarily influenced by the crime that has been committed and the offender's prior record, although extralegal factors such as race, income, sex, and age can affect sentencing (Clarke and Koch, 1976; Cohen and Kluegel, 1978). One review of sentencing concluded that only 7 to 10 percent of all sentences in the United States reflect "arbitrary or idiosyncratic judicial behavior"; most sentences can be predicted from legal factors such as harmfulness of the crime and blameworthiness of the offender (Silberman, 1978: 292). As court personnel have become more professional and the courts more bureaucratized, these legal factors have become even more important in the sentencing of offenders (Pruitt and Wilson, 1983).

Until the 1970s, the **indeterminate sentence** was the most widely used penalty in the United States. Under this system, state legislators established long maximum sentences for different crimes, and judges could impose any penalty up to the maximum. Sentences were often a range of years to be served in prison, such as five to ten years. Actual release dates were set by parole boards, based on the board's view that an inmate had been rehabilitated.

Since the mid-1970s, concern with the discretion that indeterminate sentencing allows judges, and evidence that rehabilitation does not seem to work, have led to sentencing reforms. The federal government and some states have adopted **determinate sentences**: an offense of a certain degree of harmfulness committed by someone with a particular prior record is expected to carry a specified sentence, unless extraordinary circumstances justify a departure from that sentence. One way to establish such a system is to have a sentencing commission write detailed guidelines that define appropriate sanctions for given offenses and offenders. Crimes are fitted into given categories that have narrow ranges of prescribed penalties. A judge sentences from within that range, and the inmate cannot be released until the sentence has been served, although time off for good behavior in prison can reduce the sentence a bit. Judges can give sentences outside the prescribed range only if they spell out in writing the reasons for the unusual sentence. Defendants can appeal sentences above the upper limit, and prosecutors can appeal sentences under the lower limit.

The vast majority of sentences handed out by judges in states with determinate sentencing laws have fallen within the ranges specified by the guidelines. Most sentences that depart from the guidelines have been less severe than the mandated penalties. Sentences outside the prescribed ranges have usually been a function of prior criminal history and offense type and severity; but women, whites, and those who plead guilty have been especially likely to be favored by mitigating departures. Nevertheless, state determinate sentencing laws have reduced disparities in sentences by gender, race, and urban-rural residence. Determinate sentencing reforms have produced these changes without increasing prison populations, but they have had no apparent impact on crime rates (Stolzenberg and D'Alessio, 1994; Marvell, 1995; Marvell and Moody, 1996; Kramer and Ulmer, 1996).

Sentencing guidelines implemented in the federal courts in 1987 were aimed at reducing sentence disparity, enhancing deterrence by increasing the certainty of punishment, and creating greater proportionality between the seriousness of crimes and the severity of sanctions. The federal guidelines work as follows:

1. Crimes are classified into forty-three offense levels, each of which has a range of prison sentences in terms of months (see Table 14.4). For example, level 43 crimes (which include first-degree murder and aircraft hijacking resulting in death) receive life in prison; level 25 offenses

(which include the production of pornography through sexual exploitation of a minor) are given sentences of 57 to 137 months; level 17 crimes (which include burglary of a residence) receive sentences of 24 to 63 months; and level 8 offenses (which include insider trading) receive sentences of 0 to 24 months). The score on the 43-point scale is determined by taking a "base offense level" and adjusting it upward or downward according to the circumstances of the crime, such as amount of financial loss and use of a weapon.

2. Federal judges then place the offender in one of six criminal history categories, based on points assigned for prior sentences (especially imprisonment) and whether the current offense was committed while under another sentence or within two years of release from prison.

3. Judges next consult a grid (Table 14.4) that is six columns by forty-three rows. Each of the 258 cells contains a range of sentences (for example, 37 to 46 months in prison for an offender convicted of a level 17 offense who scores in category IV in criminal history points). The range can be disregarded only in very limited circumstances. The four lettered zones correspond to instructions about appropriate penalties; for example, probation is authorized for Zone A and for Zone B under specified conditions. The guidelines eliminate parole, with time served equaling the full sentence minus time off for good behavior while in prison (Tonry, 1993).

More flexible sentencing guidelines that use fewer offense categories have been successful in several states, but the federal system is widely regarded as a failure. Judges claim that the system forces them to dispense unreasonably harsh penalties, especially to the drug offenders who have been crowding the federal prisons in recent years. Judges have complained that the sentencing guidelines take away their discretion and give it to prosecutors, who influence sentences by the seriousness of the charges they bring against defendants. Court backlogs have been attributed to the guidelines, which discourage plea bargaining because the sentence is based on actual offense behavior rather than on the crime to which a defendant pleads guilty. The guidelines have been attacked for being too complex and too mechanistic, leading to excessively severe penalties that do not take into account such offender characteristics as family ties and employment record. Defenders of the sentencing guidelines claim that hostile reactions by federal judges are a result of the limitations placed on their exercise of discretion and the requirement that they give out more severe penalties than they have in the past (Margolick, 1992; Tonry, 1993).

Juvenile Justice Considerations of just deserts have led to reforms in the handling of juvenile offenders in recent years, because of the growing belief that there is a lack of proportionality between the harm caused by juvenile offenders and their blameworthiness, on the one hand, and the way that they are treated by the juvenile justice system, on the other hand. Those who support harsher penalties for young offenders claim that the juvenile justice sys-

TABLE 14.4 United States Sentencing Guidelines, 1995

SENTENCING TABLE (in months of imprisonment)

	Offense Level	Criminal History Category (Criminal History Points)					
		I (0 or 1)	**II** (2 or 3)	**III** (4, 5, 6)	**IV** (7, 8, 9)	**V** (10, 11, 12)	**VI** (13 or more)
Zone A	1	0–6	0–6	0–6	0–6	0–6	0–6
	2	0–6	0–6	0–6	0–6	0–6	1–7
	3	0–6	0–6	0–6	0–6	2–8	3–9
	4	0–6	0–6	0–6	2–8	4–10	6–12
	5	0–6	0–6	1–7	4–10	6–12	9–15
	6	0–6	1–7	2–8	6–12	9–15	12–18
	7	0–6	2–8	4–10	8–14	12–18	15–21
	8	0–6	4–10	6–12	10–16	15–21	18–24
Zone B	9	4–10	6–12	8–14	12–18	18–24	21–27
	10	6–12	8–14	10–16	15–21	21–27	24–30
Zone C	11	8–14	10–16	12–18	18–24	24–30	27–33
	12	10–16	12–18	15–21	21–27	27–33	30–37
	13	12–18	15–21	18–24	24–30	30–37	33–41
	14	15–21	18–24	21–27	27–33	33–41	37–46
	15	18–24	21–27	24–30	30–37	37–46	41–51
	16	21–27	24–30	27–33	33–41	41–51	46–57
	17	24–30	27–33	30–37	37–46	46–57	51–63
	18	27–33	30–37	33–41	41–51	51–63	57–71
	19	30–37	33–41	37–46	46–57	57–71	63–78
	20	33–41	37–46	41–51	51–63	63–78	70–87
	21	37–46	41–51	46–57	57–71	70–87	77–96
	22	41–51	46–57	51–63	63–78	77–96	84–105
	23	46–57	51–63	57–71	70–87	84–105	92–115
	24	51–63	57–71	63–78	77–96	92–115	100–125
	25	57–71	63–78	70–87	84–105	100–125	110–137
	26	63–78	70–87	78–97	92–115	110–137	120–150
	27	70–87	78–97	87–108	100–125	120–150	130–162
Zone D	28	78–97	87–108	97–121	110–137	130–162	140–175
	29	87–108	97–121	108–135	121–151	140–175	151–188
	30	97–121	108–135	121–151	135–168	151–188	168–210
	31	108–135	121–151	135–168	151–188	168–210	188–235
	32	121–151	135–168	151–188	168–210	188–235	210–262
	33	135–168	151–188	168–210	188–235	210–262	235–293
	34	151–188	168–210	188–235	210–262	235–293	262–327
	35	168–210	188–235	210–262	235–293	262–327	292–365
	36	188–235	210–262	235–293	262–327	292–365	324–405
	37	210–262	235–293	262–327	292–365	324–405	360–life
	38	235–293	262–327	292–365	324–405	360–life	360–life
	39	262–327	292–365	324–405	360–life	360–life	360–life
	40	292–365	324–405	360–life	360–life	360–life	360–life
	41	324–405	360–life	360–life	360–life	360–life	360–life
	42	360–life	360–life	360–life	360–life	360–life	360–life
	43	life	life	life	life	life	life

Source: United States Sentencing Commission, *Guidelines Manual.* Washington, D.C.: United States Sentencing Commission, November 1995, p. 272.

tem created a century ago to deal with truants and petty thieves is no longer adequate for dealing with today's young murderers and drug traffickers.

Now all states allow or require some juveniles accused of serious crimes to be tried in criminal court as adults, where they can be punished more severely than in juvenile court. However, even states that use specific criteria to identify "dangerous" juveniles for treatment as adults "single out many juveniles whose records do not appear to be very serious and fail to identify many juveniles whose records are characterized by violent, frequent, and persistent delinquent activity" (Osbun and Rode, 1984: 199). One study concluded that there was no evidence that juveniles remanded to adult criminal court were the most dangerous and intractable delinquents, nor was there evidence that trying juveniles as adults enhanced public safety (Bortner, 1986). There is some evidence that incarcerating juveniles in adult prisons leads them to commit more frequent and more serious crimes and return to crime more quickly after release than is true of offenders who are sentenced to juvenile institutions (Bishop and Frazier, cited in Butterfield, 1996).

Some states no longer require the records of juvenile court proceedings to remain "sealed" or secret, so those who frequently break the law as juveniles will no longer be dealt with as first-time offenders when they are arrested as adults. Criminal justice agencies and some employers now have greater access to juvenile records. The impact of juvenile records on sentencing is not yet clear, but one study concluded that even where such records are available, they do not always affect sentencing: a prior juvenile record had little impact if there was a clear predisposition for or against incarceration; it influenced the sentence only when the decision was less clear-cut (Greenwood, 1986).

Retribution and the Prisons   The blameworthiness of the offender and the harmfulness of the crime largely determine the kind of institution to which an offender is sent, with maximum-, medium-, and minimum-security institutions limiting prisoners' freedom of movement and isolating them from the outside world to varying degrees. In the mid-1990s, considerations of just deserts were the basis for reforms in several states that were aimed at making prison life harder for inmates; Alabama briefly revived the chain gang, and other states took away televisions and radios, stereos and computers, weight-lifting equipment, and basketball courts.

Because sentences in some states cover a range of years—for example, five to ten years for a robbery—the decision about how long an inmate stays in prison is made by the parole board rather than the court. Decisions about when prisoners are to be released are predictable to a large degree from the harmfulness of the offense for which they have been imprisoned, their prior criminal record, and their conduct while in prison. In other words, the decision about how much of a court-imposed sentence is actually served is based largely on retributive considerations, even though the decision is supposed to be based on whether an inmate has been rehabilitated.

Retribution and Capital Punishment   As we saw earlier in this chapter, public support for the death penalty is based partly on the belief that it is a deterrent, although many supporters say they would favor it even if it had no deterrent effect. Rather than focusing on the utility of the death penalty, many people believe that justice requires that people who commit certain heinous crimes be deprived of their own lives.

The death penalty has been both supported and opposed on religious grounds. The Roman Catholic Church has traditionally accepted the right of the state to execute people convicted of serious crimes, but in recent years the death penalty has been redefined as inconsistent with Catholic theology because execution lacks utility and dignity, fails to contribute to the common good, and discriminates against the poor and minorities (Beristain, 1977). In asking for clemency for people under the sentence of death, Pope John Paul II in 1983 criticized capital punishment, the first pope to do so. Catholic bishops in the United States have also voiced their opposition to the death penalty. Protestant leaders in the United States have opposed capital punishment since 1957, denying that the state has the right to execute offenders and seeing capital punishment as "a contradiction of both the values of our Christian traditions and the principles of humane government" (cited in Franklin, 1982: 30).

Opponents of the death penalty claim that even if certain offenders deserve to die, a civilized society should not execute them. They argue that it is immoral for the state to take a human life as a form of punishment, and that doing so "cheapens the value of human life" and might even encourage others to kill.

Those who favor capital punishment do not always agree about when it is appropriate to put offenders to death. Few Americans would support capital punishment for thieves, but thieves were executed in eighteenth- and nineteenth-century England. Likewise, there is little support in the United States for using the death penalty for economic crimes such as currency violations and profiteering, but more than sixty Iraqis were executed for those offenses in 1992. On the other hand, many Americans would favor the death penalty for someone who brutally murdered several children or assassinated the president.

The Eighth Amendment to the Constitution prohibits "cruel and unusual punishment," and although the Supreme Court has never ruled that capital punishment by itself is cruel and unusual, it has ruled that the death penalty is cruel and unusual punishment for the crime of forcible rape (*Coker* v. *Georgia* [1977]). In *Furman* v. *Georgia* (1972), the Supreme Court struck down the states' death penalty statutes because they had been administered in an excessively arbitrary way. Four years later the Court approved a new kind of law that it thought would be fairer: a defendant's guilt or innocence would be determined in a criminal trial, and then in a separate proceeding a judge or a jury would consider the death penalty as a possible sentence. Looking at the harmfulness of the offense and the blameworthiness of the defendant, a judge or jury could choose the death penalty only if there were aggravating circumstances defined by state law, and if there were no mitigating circumstances counteracting those aggravating factors. The introduction of specific aggravating and mitigating factors was an attempt to be fair to defendants while retaining the principle of retribution.

The American public strongly supports capital punishment, but there is little articulate support for the death penalty in the intellectual community. Two exceptions are Walter Berns (1979) and Ernest van den Haag (1975), both of whom have argued that the death penalty is a deserved and appropriate penalty for some crimes. They believe that justice requires capital punishment, which reinforces the moral order and is a reasonable expression of community outrage at the violation of important values. For example, one man remarked that the execution of his brother's killer nine years after the murder "was an extraordinary relief. I don't know how to explain it. It relieved the grief. This has been an overriding obsession for all of us" (cited in Joyce, 1984: A18). Opponents of the death penalty point out that retribution simply requires a punishment proportional to the crime, not any specific form of punishment such as the death penalty (Bedau, 1980).

Those seeking to abolish the death penalty argue that when an error is made and an innocent person is executed, there is no way to rectify the error as there is with other penalties. One study documented twenty-five cases since 1900 in which Americans have been wrongfully executed (Radelet, Bedau, and Putnam, 1994). Because this study did not examine every execution, and because it is difficult to reconstruct cases years later, possibly more innocent people were executed. Some opponents of capital punishment assert that the execution of even one innocent person is reason enough to abolish the death penalty. Those who favor capital punishment claim that recent developments in the procedural rights of defendants have greatly reduced the chance of such errors, but the evidence does not support that contention (Radelet, Bedau, and Putnam, 1994). Proponents of capital punishment also argue that if there have been only a few mistakes in the more than 7,000 executions since 1900, then the criminal justice system is quite reliable. A 1995 national survey found that three-fourths of those who support capital punishment would continue to do so even if one in every 100 people sentenced to death were actually innocent (Maguire and Pastore, 1995: 184).

Support for and opposition to the death penalty are based to a large extent on considerations of just deserts. Even if there were irrefutable evidence that the death penalty does or does not deter crime, the ultimate decision about its use would be based on values concerning the sanctity of human life and the requirements of justice.

Rehabilitation

Rehabilitation is the restoration of criminals to a law-abiding way of life through treatment. More specifically, rehabilitation is the result of any planned intervention focused on the offender that reduces criminal activity, whether that reduction is achieved by changes in personality, abilities, attitudes, values, or behavior. Excluded from rehabilitation are the effects of fear and intimidation—or specific deterrence—and the maturational effects that cause older offenders to stop committing crime (Sechrest, White, and Brown, 1979: 20–21).

One early approach to rehabilitation was that of the Quakers, who recommended silence and reflection, and the isolation of inmates in their own cells, where they worked, ate, and read the Bible; this method was implemented in a prison established at Cherry Hill in Philadelphia in 1829. A different approach was used in the New York state prison at Auburn in the 1820s, where inmates slept alone in their cells, but silently worked, ate, and worshipped together during the day. Post–Civil War reformers suggested giving offenders the incentive of early release to motivate them to reform, and the indeterminate sentence was introduced. Progressives of the early twentieth century supported indeterminate sentences, presentence reports that judges could use to individualize sentences, treatment in the community rather than in prison, and parole release for offenders who seemed likely to stay away from crime. The positivist approach of the newly developing behavioral sciences, especially sociology and psychology, supported this therapeutic model by focusing on the causes of crime (Cullen and Gilbert, 1982). Rehabilitation was the dominant perspective in the American criminal justice system from the 1920s to the 1970s, when attacks on the therapeutic model led to a search for alternative ways of dealing with offenders.

The rehabilitation model assumes that the causes of human behavior can be identified by scientific study, and that treatment based on knowledge of those causes should be aimed at changing the offender's behavior "in the interests of his own happiness, health, and satisfaction and in the interest of social defense" (Allen, 1971: 318). The principle underlying rehabilitation is to return "the offender to society not with the negative vacuum of punishment-induced fear but with the affirmative and constructive equipment—physical, mental and moral—for law-abidingness" (Wiehofen, 1971: 261).

Inmates are not required to join treatment programs, but prison programs are not truly voluntary. To be paroled, inmates must convince a board that they are rehabilitated. To do so, they often enlist in treatment programs to create a favorable impression with the board; joining too few programs can be taken as evidence that the inmate does not want to reform.

Seeing rehabilitation as a required function of punishment, the courts have guaranteed inmates access to treatment programs. Because inmates sometimes feel degraded and dehumanized when treatment is forced on them, some have argued that they should also have the right to refuse treatment (Kittrie, 1971). As one ex-convict said,

> The whole point of the psychological diagnosis is to get [the inmate] to go for the fact that he's "sick," yet the statement he's sick deprives him of his integrity as a person.
>   Most prisoners I know would rather be thought bad than mad. They say society may have a right to punish them, but not a hunting license to remold them in its own sick image. (cited in Mitford, 1973: 104)

The deterrence perspective regards offenders and potential offenders as rational decision makers who will stay away from crime if the threat of punishment is great enough; those who commit crime presumably think the threat of punishment is outweighed by the rewards of crime. The rehabilitation perspective, on the other hand, sees those who violate the law as defective and in need of treatment, rather than as rational decision makers who knowingly take risks when they break the law.

In contrast to the rehabilitation perspective, retribution theory proposes that if penalties are specific and just, offenders can retain their dignity while paying for their crimes. Retribution does not necessarily lead to harsher penalties than rehabilitation; indeed, the rehabilitation model can lead to longer sentences, which are justified by the need to cure inmates.

Rehabilitation and the Criminal Justice System

The belief that offenders' behavior can and should be changed has had a significant impact on American criminal justice, especially in the three decades following World War II.

Rehabilitation and the Police   Rehabilitation is not generally considered a police function, because the police deal with people suspected, rather than convicted, of breaking the law, and it would seem to violate the legal principle that suspects are to be presumed innocent until proved guilty if the police were to try to rehabilitate suspects. Nevertheless, the rehabilitation perspective influences the way the police deal with suspects. In exercising discretion, an officer might think that one suspect will avoid crime in the future if subjected to the shock of arrest and a court appearance, and believe that another suspect will be most likely to stay away from crime if sent home to his or her family.

The police are most likely to consider the possibility of rehabilitation in dealing with juveniles. They might not arrest a young suspect if he or she will enroll in a counseling or training program. Sometimes the police work out an informal agreement with juvenile troublemakers and their parents or guardians to report to the police regularly, attend school, make restitution, and maintain a neat personal appearance. Measures such as these can spare the juvenile the legal stigma of court appearance and institutionalization.

Rehabilitation and the Courts   **Pretrial diversion** programs allow a district attorney to recommend to a judge that a criminal proceeding be suspended while a suspect participates in treatment. Pretrial diversion can keep suspects from acquiring criminal records and criminal identities, although one study concluded there was not enough evidence that court appearances had labeling effects to justify creating diversion programs on that basis alone (Mahoney, 1974). If a suspect is not arrested again while enrolled in a diversion program and seems to be profiting from the program, the judge at the suggestion of the district attorney can "file" the case—that is, not charge the suspect and eventually dismiss the case.

Juvenile courts use pretrial diversion on the assumption that the labeling effects of a court appearance might do more harm than good to young people. One study that looked at status offenders—juveniles charged with acts that would not be crimes if committed by adults—found no difference in the likelihood of rearrest for those processed formally by the juvenile courts and those placed in diversion programs. The data supported neither labeling theory's contention that diversion is better nor deterrence theory's claim that court processing will keep status offenders from getting into trouble again (Rausch, 1983). Another study also concluded that diversion had no significant effects on status offenders' behavior or attitudes, but warned that competition among community-based programs for diverted juveniles could "widen the net" of the juvenile justice system and lead to the processing of more juveniles (Rojek and Erickson, 1981–82). Some scholars have concluded that diversion is indeed more promising than other juvenile correctional programs, and that widening the net does not seem to harm juveniles (Binder and Geis, 1984; Lab and Whitehead, 1988).

The sentences to which district attorneys and judges agree in exchange for guilty pleas are partly a product of their beliefs about the kinds of sentences that are most likely to rehabilitate offenders. Some criminologists regard plea bargaining as an essential first step in the rehabilitation process, because it forces defendants to take responsibility for their actions (Casper, 1978). Others claim that plea bargaining makes defendants cynical about the criminal justice system and thereby impedes their rehabilitation.

Judges' sentencing decisions depend on their beliefs about rehabilitation, as well as on their beliefs about just deserts and deterrence. Judges weigh the likely effects on an offender of paying a fine, making restitution, or spending some time on probation. They consider the potential benefits of the various treatment programs available in the community and in correctional institutions. In reality, judges usually have few sentencing alternatives, because prisons do not differ much in their treatment programs, and many offenders cannot be fined or placed on probation because the law prohibits it or because the judge's or the public's sense of just deserts would not allow it.

Rehabilitation and the Prisons   Although indeterminate sentencing was based on the humanitarian belief that inmates should be released as soon as they are cured, indeterminate sentences have lengthened the time served by prisoners. In 1900, the inmates at Indiana State Prison, sentenced under the recently introduced indeterminate-sentence system, served an average of six months and twenty-three days more than inmates committed to the same institution for the same crimes in 1890, when a system of definite sentences was in effect (Mitford, 1973: 84). The time served by inmates also increased when the California correctional system introduced rehabilitation (American Friends Service Committee, 1971: 91). Indeterminate sentences can also lead to the incarceration of more offenders, because it is assumed that they are being helped. The principle of rehabilitation thus acts as a "highly efficient control mechanism," even though its original justification was humanitarian (Irwin, 1974: 975).

A parole board determines when an offender serving an indeterminate sentence is ready to be released, deciding how much of a sentence is to be served behind bars and how much is to be served in the community under the supervision of a parole officer. In deciding when to release an inmate, a parole board considers the offense for which the offender was sent to prison, the inmate's criminal record, the number of disciplinary reports filed against the inmate while incarcerated, and the treatment programs in which the inmate has participated. Participation in treatment programs and number of disciplinary reports indicate the extent to which an offender is rehabilitated; the original offense and the criminal record are retributive considerations.

The conditions of parole are designed to help rehabilitate the released offender: stay away from known criminals, hold a steady job, support a family, and avoid the use of alcohol and drugs. However, the heavy caseload of most parole officers means that ex-convicts get little assistance in developing a law-abiding way of life and avoiding a return to crime. Parole has been described as "surveillance and control, not casework and counseling" (Kassebaum, Ward, and Wilner, 1971: 3).

Types of Treatment

Treatment programs aimed at rehabilitating offenders take many forms. Some deal with individuals and others with groups. Some seek to alter personality and others only to change behavior. Some equip offenders with vocational skills or educational credentials, and others try to cure drug addiction or alcoholism.

Individual Therapy, Casework, and Social-Skills Training   **Individual therapy** carried out by psychiatrists, psychologists, or psychiatric social workers is based on the assumption that offenders are emotionally troubled people who need to solve the psychological problems that have caused them to commit crime. Psychotherapy is unlikely to be effective because most therapists manipulate and control verbal behavior rather than try to change overt actions directly. Another problem is that because psychotherapy is usually done inside the prison, rather than in the environment in which crime actually occurs, any beneficial effects that it has may not carry over to behavior in the outside world. Moreover, few prisons today provide therapy that is intensive enough to have much impact on inmates.

In some prisons, social workers provide inmates with counseling that is intended less to help them understand their motivations than to help them cope with the specific problems they face. This **casework** approach is oriented toward getting inmates to realize they can change, showing them how to solve problems of daily living, teaching them how to adapt to reality, and informing them of community resources that can help them to reform.

Social-skills training programs use methods such as role-playing and modeling to help offenders take the perspective of other people, exercise greater self-control, negotiate solutions to interpersonal problems, and develop moral reasoning.

Group Counseling   **Group counseling** allows several inmates to be treated at the same time and at low cost, especially if correctional officers are used as group leaders. Groups are also led by psychotherapists and by people who have been specially trained in guided-group interaction. Inmates in these groups discuss their feelings and attitudes in an effort to create mutual acceptance and support. However, in correctional systems that use parole, inmates might conceal their true feelings rather than risk revealing feelings that could be used against them in a parole hearing.

Family Intervention   Some programs, especially those focused on juvenile offenders, treat the whole family rather than just the individual who has broken the law. Some **family intervention** programs seek to improve communication and the expression of feelings, but others try to change patterns of behavior within the family and alter the way that parents manage their children.

Education and Work Programs   Many prisons offer educational programs that help inmates work toward a high-school equivalency degree or take courses for college credit. Some correctional systems make it possible for inmates to leave prison on a daily basis to take courses outside.

Prisons put inmates to work producing goods for sale to outsiders or maintaining the institution, but these jobs rarely provide skills that can be used to find attractive employment after release. Work-release programs try to ease reentry into society by allowing inmates to be released during the day to work at jobs outside the prison.

Prisons offer inmates educational programs and training in work-related skills. Here inmates in a privately run prison are learning computer skills.

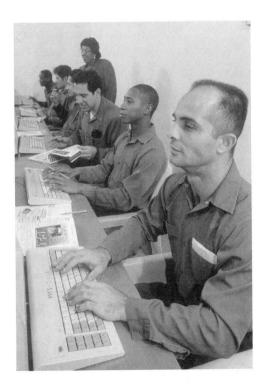

Behavior Modification   **Behavior modification** or behavior therapy tries to shape conduct by rewarding desirable actions (for example, with money) and punishing undesirable ones (for example, by withdrawing institutional privileges). This form of treatment does not regard criminal behavior as a symptom of underlying personality flaws that must be corrected, but sees it instead as a problem that has to be dealt with directly.

A major question about behavior modification is whether changes produced in inmates will persist after they are released. A review of twenty-four treatment programs of this sort concluded that virtually all of them succeeded in modifying the behavior of the institutionalized offenders, most of whom were juveniles. Only four programs followed offenders after release, and only one found a lasting and significant effect of the program (Ross and McKay, 1978). There is thus little reason to believe that behavior modification programs within institutions can significantly change how offenders will act after they are released.

Milieu Therapy   **Milieu therapy** is a treatment method that introduces the idea of rehabilitation into all aspects of an institution, including relations between inmates and staff. This treatment method employs casework and group counseling, stresses inmate responsibility and self-determination, and creates a warm and supportive climate for change.

Does Rehabilitation Work?

It would be surprising if treatment programs were effective in rehabilitating inmates, because most of them are poorly funded, inadequately staffed, and available to a limited number of inmates. The skills learned in prison industries are often inapplicable to the outside world; for instance, there is little demand for the skill of manufacturing license plates, because many states manufacture all license plates in their prisons.

Recidivism Rates   The extent to which offenders are helped by a treatment program is often measured by a **recidivism rate**. This rate is calculated by taking the percentage of offenders who, during a specific period of time after their treatment has ended, are arrested and convicted of new offenses or have their punishment made more restrictive because they have failed to meet the conditions of a less restrictive sentence. The recidivism rate of inmates released from prison is often calculated by adding the number of releasees who are arrested for new crimes and the number who are sent back to prison because their parole is revoked, and dividing that number of "failures" by the total number of released inmates. Thus, if one hundred inmates are released from prison, and within three years eighteen of them are back in prison because they have been convicted of new crimes, and another thirty-three are back in prison because their parole has been revoked for a suspected new crime or for violation of parole conditions, the recidivism rate would be 51 percent for the three-year period.

Recidivism rates vary from study to study. In some jurisdictions, parole is revoked quickly, and so those communities have high recidivism rates. Where parole officers are more tolerant of violations of parole conditions, recidivism rates are lower. The length of the follow-up period affects the recidivism rate; the longer the period after release, the higher the recidivism rate. One study (Kitchener, Schmidt, and Glaser, 1977) found the following percentages of federal ex-convicts returned to prison as parole violators or with new sentences for serious crimes:

Years after Release	Recidivism Rate
1	15%
2	34%
5	51%
10	59%
18	63%

A study that used data from eleven states found that 19 percent of inmates were back in prison within a year of their release, 33 percent were back within two years, and 41 percent were back within three years (Beck and Shipley, 1989).

A major problem in using rearrest data to measure recidivism is that many crimes that ex-convicts commit are not reported to the police or do not lead to an arrest if they are reported. For instance, a study of convicted rapists and child molesters found that they admitted to two to five times as many sex offenses as they had been arrested for. Because of the low rate of reporting sex offenses to the police and the difficulty of making arrests for such crimes, recidivism rates are poor measures of the degree to which sex offenders have been rehabilitated (Groth, Longo, and McFadin, 1982).

Other Measures of Treatment Effectiveness   In addition to recidivism rates, the effectiveness of treatment has also been measured by changes in personality, attitude, and behavior, including the way that ex-convicts function in the community, on the job, in school, and within the family (Lipton, Martinson, and Wilks, 1975: 12–14).

Rather than designate ex-convicts as "successes" or "failures" on the basis of whether they remain crime-free after release, it might be better to measure the degree to which a program reduces arrest rates. A program could be considered a partial success if it lengthens the time from release until the time ex-convicts commit new crimes; a program whose graduates remain crime-free for two years but then return to crime would be regarded as more successful than a program whose graduates return to crime within a month of their release. A reasonable goal for a rehabilitation program is to reduce the number and seriousness of the crimes committed by its participants, even if they are not kept from criminal activity altogether.

Experimental Design and Treatment Effectiveness   Inmates released from prison might not return to crime because they are deterred by the fear of more punishment, because they have matured while in prison, or because they have been rehabilitated. The proper way to isolate the effect of treatment from the other effects of imprisonment is to assign inmates randomly to a group that receives treatment (an experimental group) or to a group that does not receive treatment (a control group). If treatment is effective, those in the experimental group will show a lower recidivism rate (or some other kind of improvement) than those in the control group. The difference between the groups can be attributed to treatment, because chance determined the group to which an inmate was assigned, and the inmates in both groups presumably had similar experiences in prison except for their exposure or lack of exposure to treatment. Experiments of this sort are expensive and difficult to implement, but the failure to carry out well-designed evaluation research means that treatment programs that are both costly and ineffective will continue (Sechrest, White, and Brown, 1979).

The Amenability Issue   Complicating research on rehabilitation is the possibility that certain kinds of offenders are suited to treatment of a particular sort, with other types of offenders not benefiting from the same treatment. This **amenability issue** might arise in evaluating a treatment program in which 50 percent of the participants avoided recidivism and 50 percent returned to prison. Those who did not return to prison might have been amenable to the treatment they received, and those who returned to prison might not have been amenable to the same treatment. Randomization in the evaluation of treatment programs avoids some of this difficulty but leaves unanswered the question of whether inmates with specific characteristics might be matched to particular treatment methods to produce higher rates of success. More research is needed on which kinds of offenders are best suited to different forms of treatment (Sechrest, White, and Brown, 1979).

The Effectiveness of Treatment Methods   Lipton, Martinson, and Wilks (1975) systematically examined 231 treatment programs conducted between 1945 and 1967 that could be evaluated by social science methods. Each program used an independent measure of participants' improvement and a comparison of an experimental group of treated offenders with a control group of untreated ones. Martinson (1974: 25) has summarized the findings of this review as follows: "With few and isolated exceptions, the rehabilitative efforts that have been reported so far have had no appreciable effect on recidivism." He wrote that the data reviewed

are the best available and give us very little reason to hope that we have in fact found a sure way of reducing recidivism through rehabilitation. This is not to say that we found no instances of success or partial success; it is only to say that these instances have been isolated, producing no clear pattern to indicate the efficacy of any particular method of treatment. And neither is this to say that factors *outside* the realm of rehabilitation may not be working to reduce recidivism—factors such as the tendency for recidivism to be lower in offenders over the age of 30; it is only to say that such factors seem to have little connection with any of the treatment methods now at our disposal. (Martinson, 1974: 49)

Lipton, Martinson, and Wilks uncovered little evidence that treatment programs that prepared inmates for life outside prison through education, vocational training, or the development of social skills had any appreciable impact on recidivism rates. There was little evidence that individual or group counseling reduced recidivism, nor was there any evidence that milieu therapy worked. Existing evidence also failed to show that recidivism was affected by either length of sentence or type of institution in which a sentence was served.

Other evaluations of treatment programs have reached conclusions similar to those of Lipton, Martinson, and Wilks. An examination of one hundred programs found that rehabilitative effects were "slight, inconsistent, and of questionable reliability" (Bailey, 1966: 157; see also Robison and Smith, 1971; Greenberg, 1977a). An updating of Lipton, Martinson, and Wilks's study carried out for the National Academy of Sciences also concluded that nothing yet tried had been proved effective, and that the earlier survey might even have been too generous in assessing the benefits of treatment programs (Sechrest, White, and Brown, 1979). An assessment of the research on juvenile treatment programs found that of forty-eight studies that compared experimental and control groups and tested the statistical significance of their findings, only fifteen showed that the experimental group fared better than the control group. The authors concluded as follows: "Based on these statistics, it is hard to reaffirm rehabilitation" (Lab and Whitehead, 1988: 77).

Why Is Rehabilitation Ineffective? Defenders of the rehabilitation perspective claim that the apparent ineffectiveness of treatment is the result of a failure to implement programs properly, but critics suggest that the rehabilitation perspective has intrinsic problems. Martinson (1974: 49) proposes that

> treatment programs are based on a theory of crime as a "disease"—that is to say, as something foreign and abnormal in the individual which can presumably be cured. This theory may well be flawed, in that it overlooks—indeed, denies—both the normality of crime in society and the personal normality of a very large proportion of offenders, criminals who are merely responding to the facts and conditions of our society.

An effective method of rehabilitation requires an empirically supported theory of crime causation. Instead, today's treatment methods are often based on vague or untested assumptions about why individuals commit crimes. As Kassebaum, Ward, and Wilner (1971: 320) remarked in their study of group counseling,

> The most fundamental requirement for further research on the effectiveness of prison and parole programs would seem to us to be a frank recognition that psychological treatment programs involve assumptions about the causes of crime, the

informal and formal organization of the prison and parole, and the nature of the postrelease experience, all of *which may be quite unrealistic when applied to actual existing conditions.* (emphasis in the original)

One assessment of prison treatment programs found that not only were there low rates of participation in work, vocational training, mental health programs, drug and alcohol treatment, and parent counseling programs, but the programs that were available reinforced the gender inequality that existed in the world outside prison. Men in prison were rarely offered parental training that might induce them to take greater responsibility for their children. Incarcerated women worked at the low-paying, menial jobs available to women in the larger society: cleaning, cooking, and secretarial work. Neither women nor men had access to programs that would help them find financially rewarding jobs after they were released (Morash, Haarr, and Rucker, 1994).

Reaffirming Rehabilitation

Some criminologists seek to reaffirm rehabilitation, pointing out that critics who have concluded that treatment is ineffective have actually uncovered programs that have positive results (Cullen and Gilbert, 1982; Andrews et al., 1990a, 1990b; Palmer, 1994). For instance, Lipton, Martinson, and Wilks found that about half of the sixty-five programs in their sample that had used the best research designs had achieved positive results (Palmer, 1975). In a follow-up study of more recent treatment programs, Martinson (1979) concluded that some treatment programs lower recidivism rates under certain circumstances. A review of ninety-five correctional programs carried out between 1973 and 1978 found that some had beneficial results under certain conditions; family intervention strategies were especially effective. An examination of about four hundred experimental studies of juvenile treatment programs found that about two-thirds of them benefited the experimental group and about one-third benefited the control group, although the differences between the groups were not always statistically significant (Lipsey, 1991).

One evaluation of treatment programs defined "appropriate correctional service" as that which focuses on high-risk offenders and criminogenic needs, and that matches clients' needs and learning styles to types of treatment. The authors concluded that appropriate treatment reduces recidivism rates by about 50 percent and that there is "a reasonably solid clinical and research basis for the political reaffirmation of rehabilitation" (Andrews et al., 1990a: 384). A critique of this study claimed that the concepts of "risk," "need," and "responsivity" to appropriate treatment had been defined in ways that served to confirm the researchers' pro-rehabilitation views (Lab and Whitehead, 1990).

Criminologists seeking to reaffirm rehabilitation claim that critics of the treatment approach use especially rigorous methodological standards in evaluating programs, and are thus led to conclude that nothing works (Gottfredson, 1979). One "treatment destruction technique," or way of making even positive results seem questionable, is to raise alternative explanations for positive findings, thereby casting doubt on the conclusion that the program itself had a beneficial effect. Another method of attacking positive results is to show that the criterion of success is inadequate. Parole revocation, for example, might be criticized as a criterion of success by arguing that the decision to revoke parole is highly arbitrary and thus an unreliable measure of an ex-convict's readjustment to society. Yet another treatment destruction technique is to claim that even if a program seems to work, it might not work for everyone. Methodological criticisms such as these are valid, but those seeking to reaffirm rehabilitation assert that the application of such high standards minimizes the beneficial effects that treatment programs have and makes it unlikely that any program will ever be declared an unqualified success.

According to Ted Palmer (1991), there was little faith in rehabilitation from 1975 to 1981, but increasing evidence that treatment was effective weakened this pessimism in the early and mid-1980s, a time when "skeptics" claimed that there was little evidence of treatment effectiveness, but "sanguines" argued that some programs worked for certain kinds of offenders. Skeptics and sanguines agreed that effective treatment required the use of multiple approaches at the same time, frequent contact, and the matching of offenders to appropriate treatment methods. Palmer claimed that

> by 1989–1990 the emerging picture or perhaps new implicit consensus among many skeptics, sanguines, and others was that "something" apparently works, although no generic method or approach … especially shines. Stated differently, several methods seem promising, but none have been shown to usually produce major reductions when applied broadly to typical composite samples of offenders. (Palmer, 1991: 340)

From his analysis of previous research on the effectiveness of correctional intervention, particularly programs aimed at juveniles, Palmer (1994: xviii) discovered that some forms of treatment programs have substantial positive effects, although no single type of program was "simultaneously very successful and widely applicable." The most effective approaches were behavior therapy, cognitive or cognitive-behavioral (social-skills) training, life-skills or skill-oriented (education and vocational) programs, family intervention, and multimodal programs. Ineffective methods included individual and group counseling, diversion, confrontation (such as the Scared Straight program), and area-wide delinquency-prevention programs. Palmer claimed that a multiple-intervention strategy is most likely to reduce recidivism and improve adjustment, and he called for more systematic evaluation of such programs, especially with experimental methods.

"Doing Less"

Even if treatment programs fail to reduce recidivism, they do not seem to make offenders any worse, leading Martinson (1974: 48) to conclude that "if

we can't do more for (and to) offenders, at least we can safely do less."
Alternatives to imprisonment are less expensive; for instance, it costs ten
times as much to imprison offenders as to have them on parole or probation.
Sanctions other than incarceration are less onerous for offenders and their
families, and might even benefit society. For instance, punishing offenders by
requiring them to work for a charitable agency would let them atone for their
crimes, subject them to a regular work routine, satisfy the public's demand for
just deserts, provide society with a useful service, permit surveillance by probation or parole officers, and be less expensive than imprisonment (Brown,
1977). In order to reduce prison crowding and the high cost of incarceration,
some states have introduced community corrections or expanded their use of
probation and parole.

Reintegrating the Offender into Society

Criminals in the United States are usually stigmatized and cast out of society
for violating the law, and little effort is made to reintegrate them after they are
punished. In Japan, on the other hand, efforts are made to reintegrate offenders into social networks after sanctions have been applied. The difference
between the societies is a result of an American cultural attitude that regards
criminals as enemies of society, and a Japanese attitude that emphasizes role
obligations and social solidarity (Hamilton and Sanders, 1992). John
Braithwaite (1989) suggests that crime might be reduced in the United States
by using an approach similar to Japan's. Instead of ostracizing criminals, he
proposes a process of **reintegrative shaming** that would follow expressions of
community disapproval of the offender's behavior with gestures of reacceptance by the larger law-abiding community. This process "communicates
respect for the person as well as disapproval of that person's deed"
(Braithwaite, 1995: 193–194). China's *bang-jiao* is an example of such a neighborhood-based effort aimed at rehabilitating young offenders by accepting
them back into the community and providing them with support and services (Zhang et al., 1996).

Reintegration of the offender is important, but it is necessary to consider
the kind of community into which the offender is being reintegrated.
Community-based correctional institutions and work- and education-release
programs can help offenders maintain ties to a community that is characterized by crime-generating conditions rather than by positive social forces.
What is really needed are programs in the community that help offenders
develop a stake in conformity and form conventional social bonds.

More attention should be given to the adjustment problems faced by ex-
convicts. On leaving prison, they have to support themselves financially, cope
with parole restrictions, and stay away from their former life of crime (Irwin,
1970). They want to gratify their desires and meet certain goals when they
leave prison, but their lack of resources and unfamiliarity with the outside
world often make this difficult. Providing ex-convicts with a place to live and
new clothing can ease their transition from prison to the outside society. An

important aspect of this transition is finding and keeping a job that offers hope for future advancement. One thief describes the following predicament faced by many ex-convicts: "During the last month [since release from prison] I have had at least forty invitations from thieves to go out stealing with them, but I have not had a single suggestion from a legitimate person about how I could make some money honestly" (cited in Sutherland, 1937: 188). Providing ex-convicts with good jobs when unemployment rates are high can be difficult, particularly if honest, unemployed workers think that ex-convicts have an advantage over them. Motivating ex-convicts to search for work and keep a job can be a problem, because their lack of job skills means that only unrewarding jobs are available to them and because they often have unrealistically high expectations.

The Future of Rehabilitation

Some former advocates of rehabilitation have abandoned it, while others seek to reaffirm it. Critics argue that treatment has not been proved effective, but defenders of rehabilitation point to programs that have had positive results. Critics claim that the indeterminate sentence and the ineffectiveness of treatment programs have lengthened sentences and extended the criminal justice system's control over more offenders. Defenders assert that rehabilitation is the most humane justification for punishment and the only one that "obligates the state to care for an offender's needs or welfare" (Cullen and Gilbert, 1982: 247).

Diminished faith in rehabilitation has led some criminologists, lawmakers, and citizens to argue that until treatment is shown to be effective, punishment should be based on the principle of just deserts (McCorkle, 1993; Logan and Gaes, 1993). They argue that offenders found guilty of crimes serious enough to warrant imprisonment should be incarcerated for fixed terms under humane conditions. Voluntary treatment could be provided for inmates, with the clear understanding that participation will not affect the length of the sentence or the conditions of release. Until recently, most treatment had been provided under a system of indeterminate sentences, with participation affecting the time and terms of release, so it is uncertain whether treatment under a just deserts system can be more effective than it has been so far. Treatment might be more effective under a just deserts system because programs would be populated only with inmates who sincerely wanted to change.

Despite efforts by some criminologists to reaffirm rehabilitation, this justification for punishment has become less dominant in the American criminal justice system since the mid-1970s, as lawmakers have introduced sentencing reforms based on retribution, incapacitation, and deterrence. Parole has been restricted or eliminated, weakening inmates' motivation to participate in treatment programs. Efforts to rehabilitate offenders will continue, but they are being given less attention by correctional systems than they once were.

Summary

Deterrence is the utilitarian philosophy that criminal activity can be inhibited by state-imposed punishment. This model assumes that offenders rationally consider the risks and rewards of crime before acting. Sometimes this assumption is correct, but not all offenders act with deliberation.

Specific deterrence is the impact of a penalty on the offender who is punished, and general deterrence is the effect of penalties on the behavior of the general public. Marginal deterrence refers to the greater impact of one penalty rather than another on criminal behavior.

Instrumental acts are probably easier to deter than expressive crimes, and offenders who are not committed to crime as a way of life are easier to deter than those with a commitment to crime. Severity of punishment is probably less important in deterring crime than certainty of punishment, and punishment is a more effective deterrent if administered promptly. The type of sanction also influences the degree to which criminal behavior will be deterred.

The impact of the police, the courts, and the prisons on crime rates is difficult to determine, because of the problem of simultaneity; that is, crime rates affect the way that the criminal justice system functions, just as the actions of the criminal justice system influence crime rates. The size of a police force does not have much effect on a city's crime rate, but what the police do while on patrol can affect the crime rate. It is not clear whether higher probabilities of conviction and imprisonment deter more crime, or whether more crime affects the chances of conviction and imprisonment.

There is little reliable evidence that capital punishment deters the crimes for which it has been used. The low certainty of this very severe penalty and the lack of promptness with which it is administered suggest that capital punishment is unlikely to prevent crime.

Incapacitation is the policy of locking up offenders to prevent them from committing crimes that affect the general public. Selective incapacitation is a system of predictive restraint that uses past behavior to imprison those convicted offenders who seem most likely to commit more crime if allowed to go free. Career criminal programs that concentrate the resources of district attorneys' offices on convicted felons have had modest impacts on crime. A currently popular form of incapacitation is the "three strikes and you're out" policy.

Retribution or just deserts theory claims that only the guilty should be punished, and their penalties should be proportional to the harm caused by their crimes and their blameworthiness. A system of just deserts would include a scale to measure the seriousness of crimes and a scale to rank the severity of punishments; seriousness is determined both by the harmfulness of the act and the blameworthiness of the offender. People generally agree on the ranking of crimes by seriousness and on the ranking of penalties by severity, but there is little research that links the two scales.

Retribution plays an important role in the American criminal justice system. The police show that they consider some offenses to be more serious than others in the way they allocate their resources. Prosecutors take into consideration the harmfulness of the crime and the blameworthiness of the defendant in negotiating guilty pleas and deciding which cases to prosecute with the greatest vigor. Judges use just deserts considerations in deciding how to sentence offenders. The federal government and some states have enacted determinate sentencing guidelines since the mid-1970s as a way of curbing judicial discretion. Retribution has been introduced into the juvenile justice system in recent years, with juveniles accused of certain crimes now tried as adults. The harmfulness of a crime and the blameworthiness of an offender influence the length of a sentence and the kind of prison to which an offender is sent.

The death penalty is often supported or opposed on grounds of just deserts. Religious beliefs are used both to support and oppose the death penalty. Some people do not think the state should execute anyone, and others disagree about which crimes warrant capital punishment.

The idea that punishment should rehabilitate offenders was dominant in the American criminal justice system from the 1920s until the mid-1970s, when considerations of just deserts, incapacitation, and deterrence became relatively more important. The police exercise discretion in part on the basis of ideas about what kind of response is most likely to keep a suspect away from crime in the future. In court, pretrial diversion is sometimes used to prevent labeling, which could push defendants into a life of crime. Plea bargaining and sentencing are influenced by ideas about what kind of punishment is most likely to reform an offender. Indeterminate sentences and parole are products of the idea that offenders should be released only when they are rehabilitated.

Treatment programs include individual therapy, casework, social-skills training, group counseling, family intervention, education and work programs, behavior modification, and milieu therapy. Efforts to measure the success of such programs often employ recidivism rates; other criteria of success include indicators of improved offender functioning in the community, in the family, or at a job. Research on rehabilitation is complicated by the amenability issue, the idea that some kinds of offenders are suited only to certain types of treatment. Evaluations using experimental and control groups have not proved that any type of treatment consistently reduces criminal behavior, but some programs have had positive results. Even if the impact of treatment is unclear, we could do less to and for offenders without increasing the crime rate. Reintegration of offenders into the community is important, but attention must be paid to the kind of community into which offenders are being reintegrated. Rehabilitation will continue to be an important part of the American criminal justice system, but it is now a less influential perspective than it once was.

Important Terms

amenability issue
behavior modification
boot camp
casework
community policing
determinate sentence
deterrence
displacement effect
family intervention
general deterrence
group counseling
incapacitation
indeterminate sentence
individual therapy

just deserts
lex talionis
marginal deterrent effect
milieu therapy
pretrial diversion
recidivism rate
rehabilitation
reintegrative shaming
retribution
selective incapacitation
simultaneity
social-skills training
specific deterrence
vengeance

Review Questions

1. What assumptions does the deterrence model make about human behavior? What is meant by specific, general, and marginal deterrence? How important are severity, certainty, promptness, and type of punishment in deterring criminal behavior?

2. Do the police deter crime? How important are size of the police force, risk of arrest, and patrol tactics in deterring crime?

3. What are selective incapacitation, career criminal programs, and "three strikes and you're out" laws? Are these policies likely to reduce crime?

4. What is retribution? How are the seriousness of crimes and the unpleasantness of penalties measured? How can scales measuring seriousness of crimes and unpleasantness of penalties be linked?

5. How does the idea of retribution influence the police, the courts, and the prisons?

6. Which influences attitudes toward capital punishment more, a desire to deter murder or a desire for retribution? Does the death penalty deter murder?

7. What is rehabilitation? What assumptions does it make about offenders? How does this perspective influence the performance of the police, the courts, and the prisons?

8. How effective have treatment programs been in rehabilitating offenders? What is a recidivism rate? What other measures of program effectiveness have been used?

Chapter 15
Solving the Crime Problem

Many solutions to the crime problem have been proposed, but few have reduced crime in any significant way. As a result, there is widespread pessimism about the possibility of solving the problem. Perhaps we know too little about the causes of crime to design effective crime-reduction programs, or maybe we simply have not yet developed and implemented the correct policies. This chapter looks at three ideological positions and their proposals for reducing crime, then traces the politics of crime in the United States since the mid-1960s. Finally, three strategies for solving the crime problem are examined: reforming the criminal justice system, minimizing the opportunities for crime, and dealing with the causes of crime.

Ideological Approaches to Solving the Crime Problem

Three general ideological orientations toward the crime problem are the conservative approach, the liberal approach, and the radical approach. Each position includes a set of general beliefs and assumptions about the causes of crime and the appropriate ways to reduce it. The assumptions of each perspective underlie the policies proposed by its adherents, even though those assumptions are not always made explicit.

The Conservative Approach

The **conservative approach** seeks to preserve the status quo from criminals, who are seen as challengers to the social order. Conservatives worry about the high costs of crime and the criminal justice system. They focus on conventional crimes such as the FBI's index offenses; white-collar crime and government corruption are ignored, denied, or even justified.

Conventional crime is attributed to the lower and working classes, who are thought to be improperly socialized or irresponsible. Crime is said to be caused by the defective family structure of the poor and by the failure of those families to inculcate in children the values appropriate to a law-abiding life. Conservatives' concern with the permissiveness and immorality of groups that have high rates of conventional crime has a long history, going back at least to nineteenth-century Paris, where crime was attributed to the "dangerous classes," a term synonymous with the lower and working classes (Chevalier, 1973).

The conservative solution to the crime problem is to encourage "adherence to the legitimate directives of constituted authority" (Miller, 1973: 144). The means to do this include the improvement of family life, better discipline, more self-control, and harsher and more certain penalties. Because conservatives are ideologically opposed to the intrusion of the government into the home, even into homes that produce criminals, they rarely give much attention to programs to strengthen the family or teach parents better ways to instill law-abiding values in their children. Conservatives speak of "family values," but their proposals for reducing crime stress deterrence, incapacitation, and just deserts, and encourage the criminal justice system to mete out certain, severe, prompt, and just penalties. Conservatives call for a larger, more efficient, and less restrained police force; a higher conviction rate in court; less use of probation and parole; longer prison sentences; and more capital punishment. Conservatives are often willing to abridge the procedural rights of defendants, and indeed the rights of the entire population, in order to increase the chances of arrest, conviction, and punishment.

The Liberal Approach

The **liberal approach** holds that crime can be reduced by policies that attack its underlying causes. Liberals claim that people are the products of the social and economic system in which they live. Inequality of income and power and the lack of opportunities for certain groups increase the probability that more members of disadvantaged groups will engage in behavior defined as criminal by those who hold power.

Liberals believe society can be reformed in ways that will reduce the crime rate, but they reject the idea that a full-scale revolution is required. They point to white-collar crime and government corruption as evidence that members of all social classes break the law, but they focus on conventional crimes by the lower and working classes, which they attribute to poverty, discrimination, and oppression. They propose that educational and vocational training, welfare assistance, job opportunities, anti-discrimination laws, and community organization can reduce crime. Liberals usually believe that the primary function of criminal penalties should be the rehabilitation of offenders.

The Radical Approach

A third perspective on the crime problem is the **radical approach**. This viewpoint focuses on crime by both the underprivileged and the privileged, and attributes crime by both to the conditions of a capitalist society. Radicals point to evidence—such as some self-report studies—indicating that crime is more evenly distributed among the classes than is suggested by official crime statistics. Differences in crime rates among various groups are then attributed to the differential handling of groups by the criminal justice system, rather than to actual differences in their criminal behavior. The crime problem is regarded as a socially defined product of selective crime recording, media attention, and differential treatment by the criminal justice system.

The radical approach focuses more on white-collar crime and political corruption than do the conservative and liberal approaches. Conventional criminals are seen as victims of a capitalist system, rather than as offenders against society. Radicals shift attention from the criminal offender to the social and economic system that defines certain behavior as criminal and pushes people into crime by failing to meet their needs. The radical perspective emphasizes justice rather than crime, and looks at the negative implications of values such as competition and material success.

Radicals offer few specific solutions to the crime problem, other than calling for the construction of a new and fundamentally different social system, one vaguely described as communist or socialist. Whether such a society has ever existed, now exists, or can be created in the future is open to question; radicals rarely describe in detail the alternative society that might keep crime to a minimum.

Attitudes toward the Causes and Prevention of Crime

What do Americans believe are the causes of crime, and how to they think crime can be reduced? Can their attitudes be characterized as conservative, liberal, or radical?

Figure 15.1 shows the results of a 1993 Gallup poll that asked a national sample to evaluate the importance of several causes of crime. Republicans were more likely than Democrats to cite a decline in the influence of religion and the lack of moral training in the home as critical causes of crime, themes common to the conservative approach. The related factor of fathers absent from the homes of children was mentioned by only slightly more Republicans than Democrats. Democrats were much more likely than Republicans to see as critical causes of crime the availability of guns, the lack of good jobs for young people, and racism in American society. The latter two themes are commonly cited by both liberals and radicals. There was little disagreement between Republicans and Democrats on the importance of drugs, television violence, and schools as causes of crime.

When asked whether government funds should be spent on prevention, punishment, law enforcement, or rehabilitation, Americans favor prevention and are least supportive of rehabilitation. Figure 15.2, based on a national survey conducted in 1994, indicates that Republicans and Democrats differ in their proposed solutions to the crime problem: Republicans are relatively more likely to favor punishment, and Democrats are more disposed to prevention and rehabilitation.

There is substantial agreement between Republicans and Democrats on the causes of crime and the best ways to reduce it, but Republicans are more likely to emphasize the conservative approach and Democrats to prefer the liberal approach. Many Americans see as causes of crime some of the factors identified as important by radicals (for example, racism and lack of jobs for young people), but there is no evidence that significant numbers of Americans favor the solutions usually offered by radicals.

The Politics of Crime

Since the 1960s, crime has been a major political issue, often used most effectively by "law-and-order" politicians who have adopted a conservative approach.

Question: "Next, I'm going to read some reasons that have been given as the causes of crime in this country. While some people view all of these as important causes of crime, we'd like to know which factors you think are the most important. As I read each item, please tell me whether you think it is a critical factor, a very important factor, a somewhat important factor, or not an important factor."

Percent Responding "A Critical Factor"

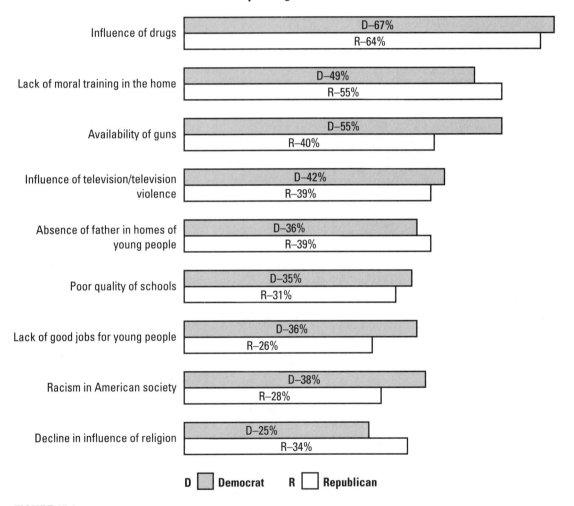

FIGURE 15.1

Attitudes toward the Causes of Crime, 1993

Source: Based on Gallup poll data, in Kathleen Maguire and Ann L. Pastore, *Sourcebook of Criminal Justice Statistics—1994*. Washington, D.C.: Bureau of Justice Statistics, U.S. Department of Justice, 1995, pp. 158–159.

Question: "In order to fight crime, the government can spend money in four different areas. The first is prevention, such as community education and youth programs. The second is enforcement, such as more police officers and tougher laws. The third is punishment, such as better courts and bigger jails, and the fourth is rehabilitation, such as education and work programs for former criminals. If the government could spend money in only one of these four areas to try to reduce crime in this country, do you feel the money should be spent on prevention, punishment, enforcement, or rehabilitation?"

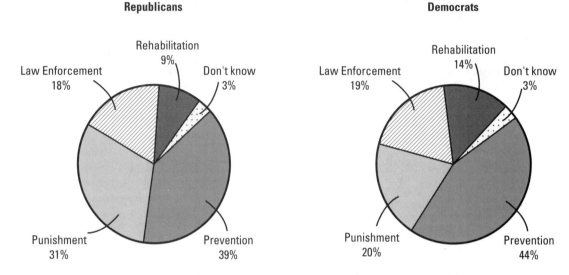

FIGURE 15.2

Attitudes toward Government Spending to Reduce Crime, 1994

Source: Based on data provided by The Wirthlin Group, in Kathleen Maguire and Ann L. Pastore, *Sourcebook of Criminal Justice Statistics—1994.* Washington, D.C.: Bureau of Justice Statistics, U.S. Department of Justice, 1995, p. 171.

The President's Commission on Law Enforcement and Administration of Justice

Index crime rates began to rise dramatically in the mid-1960s. One of the earliest political reactions to this increase was President Lyndon Johnson's 1965 appointment of the President's Commission on Law Enforcement and Administration of Justice. President Johnson asked the Commission to "deepen our understanding of the causes of crime and of how society should respond to the challenge of the present levels of crime" (President's Commission on Law Enforcement and Administration of Justice, 1967: 2). The seventeen volumes published by the Commission in 1967 included many proposals to deal with crime, but little new information about the causes of crime. Because most of the Commission's members were lawyers, police administrators, judges, and correctional officials, it is not too surprising that the Commission's recommendations emphasized reform of the criminal justice system.

The conservative approach to crime reduction was stressed by the Commission. The first sentence of the summary chapter of its final report stated that "America can *control* crime" (President's Commission on Law Enforcement and Administration of Justice, 1967: 279; emphasis added here). The Commission did give passing attention to the liberal approach:

> [C]rime flourishes where the conditions of life are the worst, and ... therefore the foundation of a national strategy against crime is an unremitting national effort for social justice. Reducing poverty, discrimination, ignorance, disease and urban blight, and the anger, cynicism or despair those conditions can inspire, is one great step toward reducing crime. *It is not the task, indeed it is not within the competence, of a Commission on Law Enforcement and Administration of Justice to make detailed proposals about housing or education or civil rights, unemployment or welfare or health.* However, it is the Commission's clear and urgent duty to stress that forceful action in these fields is essential to crime prevention, and to adjure the officials of every agency of criminal justice—policemen, prosecutors, judges, correctional authorities—to associate themselves with and labor for the success of programs that will improve the quality of American life. (President's Commission on Law Enforcement and Administration of Justice, 1967: 279; emphasis added here)

Why the Commission thought its broad mandate from the President to devise a national policy to reduce crime allowed it to avoid detailed proposals about the social causes of crime is a puzzle.

To reduce crime in America, the Commission recommended federal support to meet eight major goals:

1. State and local planning.
2. Education and training of criminal justice personnel.
3. Surveys and advisory services concerning organization and operation of criminal justice agencies.
4. Development of coordinated national information systems.
5. Development of a limited number of demonstration programs in agencies of justice.
6. Scientific and technological research and development.
7. Institutes for research and training personnel.
8. Grants-in-aid for operational innovations. (President's Commission on Law Enforcement and Administration of Justice, 1967: 285)

The implementation of these general proposals might have produced a more streamlined and better-funded system of criminal justice, but there is little evidence from criminological research that such changes would have reduced the crime rate.

The Law Enforcement Assistance Administration

The work of the Commission led to a 1968 law, the Omnibus Crime Control and Safe Streets Act, which established the Law Enforcement Assistance Administration (LEAA) in the United States Department of Justice. LEAA's goals were to stimulate comprehensive criminal justice planning at the state and municipal levels and to improve law enforcement through direct grants and support for research and development. At first, most of LEAA's funds were spent on the police, sometimes for such controversial purposes as establishing a computerized file of "suspected subversives" and purchasing an armored personnel carrier for use during riots. Over time, funds were increasingly used for correctional programs rather than for police crime-control measures. In 1971, President Richard Nixon announced a war on crime and increased LEAA's funding, raising expectations that the agency would reduce crime. When crime rates continued to rise in the 1970s, LEAA was attacked as ineffective and wasteful and for not having an overall guiding philosophy behind its disbursement of funds. LEAA was unable to demonstrate convincingly that it had reduced crime, and it was dismantled in 1981.

Experts disagree about what LEAA accomplished. A study based on interviews with federal officials concluded that LEAA's impact was primarily negative: it helped weaken the belief that capital punishment was a deterrent; it undermined faith in rehabilitation as a solution to the crime problem; and it showed that the crime rate would not be reduced by such changes in police methods as saturation patrolling, faster response time, and more education for officers (Cronin, Cronin, and Milakovich, 1981). Others have seen more benefits from LEAA's efforts, including the following:

- sting operations that recovered stolen goods and arrested thieves and fences;
- witness assistance programs that made it easier to prosecute cases;
- measures that helped businesses fight terrorism abroad;
- a program to prosecute white-collar crime that recovered ten times as much in fines and restitution as it cost;
- career criminal programs that gave priority to the prosecution and punishment of serious offenders; and
- correctional reforms that built new facilities and created prerelease programs. (Gordon and Morris, 1985)

LEAA was also able to get criminal justice agencies to work together, and more than 70 percent of the programs it sponsored were continued by the states in some form.

The 1968 and 1972 Presidential Elections

Crime was the major domestic issue in the 1968 presidential election, with the Vietnam War being the major foreign policy concern. Two of the candidates, Richard Nixon and George Wallace, were ardent and vocal advocates of a law-and-order approach to crime that was based on the conservative belief that crime could be reduced by strengthening the criminal justice system. Nixon and Wallace claimed that the Democrats, incumbents for eight years, had been "soft" on street crime, ghetto rioting, and campus violence. The Democratic candidate, Hubert Humphrey, did not support such violence, but Nixon and Wallace were able to parlay the issue of "crime in the streets" into millions of votes in November. Many voters switched their traditionally Democratic votes to the Republican party or the American Independent party because of the crime issue.

The burglary at the Watergate complex occurred in 1972, the year of another presidential election. The power of the office of the presidency was great enough to allow President Nixon to cover up this crime until he was reelected. Ironically, surveys show that a major reason for his victory in 1972, as well as in 1968, was the law-and-order vote (Gallup, 1972). People who would otherwise have voted for the Democratic candidate, Senator George McGovern, voted for President Nixon because of his opposition to crime in the streets. Nixon resigned in 1974 after a congressional committee voted bills of impeachment against him for obstruction of justice and other illegal acts.

The National Advisory Commission on Criminal Justice Standards and Goals

In 1971, the National Advisory Commission on Criminal Justice Standards and Goals (1973) was established to formulate policies to reduce crime. The Commission's recommendations were similar to those of the 1967 President's Commission on Law Enforcement and Administration of Justice, for they also emphasized criminal justice reforms as the way to reduce crime. Neither commission approached the problem of crime reduction by searching for the underlying causes of crime and then proposing ways to eradicate those causes. Both assumed that the existing criminal justice system was the appropriate apparatus for dealing with crime and that this system only needed improvement to solve the crime problem.

The Crime Issue during the Reagan Administration

Crime was not the major issue in the 1980 and 1984 presidential elections, but President Ronald Reagan made occasional use of the issue during his time in office. In a speech before the International Association of Chiefs of Police in 1981, he incorporated several recommendations made by the Attorney General's Task Force on Violent Crime (U.S. Department of Justice, 1981). He called for capital punishment, the use of mandatory prison terms for people convicted of using handguns during felonies, and the denial of bail for defendants who were likely to commit more crime if released. He called crime "ultimately a moral dilemma," rather than simply a question of more funds for the criminal justice system, and said that the war on crime would be won only when truths such as right and wrong, individual responsibility, and swift and certain punishment for wrongdoing take hold. He criticized social scientists, social workers, and psychiatrists who assert that poverty, disadvantaged childhoods, and a bad environment lead to crime, claiming instead that crime is a way of life that some people consciously choose, not because they are "seeking bread for their families," but because they "are driven crazy with desire for stuff they'll never be able to afford." Reagan believed that criminals commit crime because it is easy and not very risky, and because they believe they are entitled to what they steal.

In October 1984, Reagan signed into law the Comprehensive Crime Control Act, which he had recommended but which was also the product of bipartisan efforts in Congress. This law was wide-ranging in its reforms, but because it applied just to federal law, under which only 5 percent of all criminal defendants are tried, it has had little impact on the nation's crime problem. The law introduced preventive detention on the federal level in order to reduce bail crime. It led to the elimination of parole for federal prisoners and created a committee that in 1987 established sentencing guidelines designed to limit judicial discretion and reduce sentence disparity. The law restricted the insanity defense to people who were unable to appreciate the wrongfulness of their acts. It also created a victim-compensation program, expanded federal jurisdiction over credit-card fraud, made it easier for the government to seize the illegal profits of drug dealers and organized criminals, and lengthened penalties for drug dealers and repeat offenders.

The Reagan administration waged a "War on Drugs" that emphasized law enforcement rather than education, treatment, and research. For example, the 1986 Anti-Drug Abuse Act allocated $1.7 billion to fight drugs; 12 percent of that amount was for drug education, 22 percent was for treatment and research, and most of the remainder was for federal and state law-enforcement agencies. The burgeoning of the prison population during the 1980s was a direct result of the Reagan administration's policy of arresting and incarcerating more drug offenders (Tonry, 1995).

The 1988 Presidential Election and the Bush Administration

In his 1988 campaign for the presidency, Vice President George Bush effectively used the crime issue to help defeat Massachusetts Governor Michael Dukakis. Bush embarrassed Dukakis by accepting an endorsement from the Springfield, Massachusetts, police union. Dukakis's weak response to a question during a presidential debate about how he would react to the rape of his wife reinforced the perception that he was soft on crime. Most important were the Bush campaign's advertisements about a rape and assault committed by convicted first-degree murderer Willie Horton while he was on furlough from a Massachusetts prison. Dukakis was attacked by Bush for his willingness to furlough convicted murderers, even though the federal prison system and every state system also used furloughs, most systems even furloughing murderers. Because Horton was black and his rape victim white,

Democrats accused the Bush campaign of using the crime issue in a racially divisive way.

As did his predecessor in office, President Bush focused on the drug problem. One unsuccessful strategy was his April 1989 appointment of "drug czar" William Bennett to oversee a comprehensive attack on drug crime in Washington, D.C. This plan included construction of a new prison, use of National Guard troops to do clerical work so that police officers would be freed for street duty, and raids on crack houses. A year-and-a-half later, it was clear that these measures had been ineffective; drugs were still cheap and plentiful, and drug-related murders continued at a record pace. Bennett quit his job as Director of National Drug Control Policy in November 1990.

The 1992 and 1996 Elections and the Clinton Administration

The crime issue was frequently discussed by George Bush and Bill Clinton during the 1992 presidential campaign, but it was not a decisive issue. Because Democrats had been on the defensive on the crime issue since the 1960s, Clinton's ability to portray himself as being at least as tough on crime as George Bush was a kind of victory. Clinton supported capital punishment, a national police corps, a ban on some semiautomatic weapons, and a waiting period for the purchase of handguns. He attacked Bush for his inaction on handgun legislation and for his lack of support for increased funding of state and local law-enforcement agencies. Bush tried to portray Clinton as the governor of a state with a rising crime rate, but Clinton answered with evidence that the rate in Arkansas had fallen in the most recent period for which data were available. Clinton secured the endorsements of several police organizations to counteract Bush's endorsements from other police groups. Overall, neither candidate gained a strong advantage over the other on the crime issue.

In his first term, Clinton continued to stake his claim to being tough on crime. He supported and signed the Violent Crime Control and Law Enforcement Act of 1994, which provided money for additional police officers, expanded the number of federal crimes covered by the death penalty, banned the sale and possession of many assault weapons, and funded new research and evaluation efforts by the National Institute of Justice. Later, Clinton chided Republicans for being soft on crime when they sought to repeal the ban on assault weapons.

As in 1992, neither candidate in the 1996 presidential election had a clear advantage on the crime issue. Republican Bob Dole called for more prison construction, abolition of parole for violent offenders, harsher punishment for juvenile offenders, drug testing for inmates, and less violence in the movies (see the Crime and the Media box). Dole's charge that juvenile drug use had increased during President Clinton's first term was answered by Clinton's assertion that during that time crime rates had declined and tens of thousands of felons had been kept from buying firearms as a result of the Brady law. Clinton's victory was partly a result of his ability to neutralize Dole on the crime issue; Clinton did this by regularly supporting such measures as curfews for teenagers, school uniforms, a national registry of sex offenders, expansion of the death penalty, and a computerized system to track gun dealers who sell firearms to juveniles.

Crime and the Criminal Justice System

Many proposals for reducing crime seek to reform the criminal justice system by redefining the kinds of behavior over which the law should have jurisdiction or by changing the way that the police, courts, and prisons operate.

Overreach of the Criminal Law

Some critics claim that the criminal justice system would be more effective if it gave up jurisdiction over certain kinds of behavior. This assertion that efficiency is hindered by the "overreach" of the criminal law is often applied to victimless crimes, those offenses that are consensual and lack a complaining participant. Retributivists believe that acts that harm no one should not be punished. Others think that the limited resources of the criminal justice system could better be applied to conventional crimes than to victimless crimes such as gambling and prostitution.

Proposals to reduce the overreach of the law by decriminalizing drugs contend that

- citizens have the right to be protected from state interference in behavior that causes no societal harm,
- addicts should be offered treatment rather than prosecuted as criminals,
- the criminalization of drugs has not stopped drug use,
- the resources used to prosecute drug offenses could better be used to deal with more serious crimes, and
- the criminalization of drugs leads to such problems as the secondary crimes committed to support expensive habits (Farr, 1990).

By reducing the price of drugs, legalization might undercut the illegal drug trade as well as minimize the user's need to commit crime to support a habit. Critics of decriminalization claim that if drugs were legal, there would be more users because drugs would be less expensive and more readily available. Defenders of decriminalization reply that education and treatment could deal with any such increase in drug use, but critics of decriminalization say that we do not yet have reliable evidence that education and treatment can curb drug use. Critics of decriminalization also point out that there will always be a need for some controls on drugs, such as age limits on access to drugs similar to current laws that restrict the purchase of alcohol. If there were such age limits on access to drugs, those under the legal age would continue to provide a market for drug dealers. Opponents of decriminalization

CRIME AND THE MEDIA

Hollywood, American Values, and the 1996 Presidential Campaign

In May 1995, Bob Dole attracted public attention and conservative support for his strug-gling campaign for the Republican presidential nomination with a speech criticizing the "nightmare of depravity" in Hollywood films. Having assured himself of the nomination, in July 1996 he again made headlines with a more balanced speech. He criticized the film industry for using its considerable power to shape American values with "a con-stant stream of foul language offered as reality, rudeness palmed off as self-expres-sion, license hailed as liberation, and brutality disguised as strength" (Pertman, p. A17). He also complimented filmmakers for making some movies that had uplifting and posi-tive messages, claiming that the public rejects films that deride the nation and its val-ues and contain excessive sex and violence, even though violent films such as "Pulp Fiction" and the "Die Hard" series have been commercially successful. Dole praised "Forrest Gump," "Apollo 13," "Braveheart," "Babe," and "Independence Day," a film he had seen the day before and called a patriotic film of which Hollywood could be proud, despite the fact that it might have set a record for the number of people killed on screen. Dole said that he was not advocating government regulation of the film indus-try, nor did he think that all movies should be sentimental or even nonviolent; he simply wanted the industry voluntarily to reduce the amount of "gratuitous violence, casual sex, and generally cheap behavior" in movies (Nagourney, p. B7).

Jack Valenti, president of the Motion Picture Association of America, generally agreed with Dole, but suggested that politicians sometimes criticize the film industry as a high-reward, low-risk strategy to distract voters from problems with the federal bud-get and foreign affairs.

Dole probably gained little advantage in the presidential campaign with his second speech, because in his first term in office and during the campaign Bill Clinton consis-tently spoke against violence on television and, the day before Dole's second speech, announced an agreement with television networks to increase the educational content of children's shows.

Source: Based on Adam Pertman, "Dole Again Attacks Hollywood Values," *Boston Globe*, July 31, 1996, p. A17; Adam Nagourney, "Public Endorses Uplifting Movies, Dole Tells Hollywood," *New York Times*, July 31, 1996, p. B7.

also argue that many addicts committed crimes before they started using drugs, and they would probably continue to commit crimes even if the price of drugs dropped as a result of decriminalization. Opponents also suggest that drugs would have to be decriminalized selectively; the consequences of free access to crack would be quite different from the consequences of free access to marijuana.

The Police

Politicians and the public often claim that putting more police officers on the street will help solve the crime problem, even though evidence presented in Chapter 14 indicates that the number of officers per capita in a city makes little or no difference in its crime rate. Even if the presence of an officer does prevent an offender from committing a crime against a particular target, the offender can easily wait until the officer leaves or the offender can find another target. Street patrols might change the type of crime that an offender commits; for instance, a criminal might burglarize a house rather than rob a pedestrian. We cannot say that the police never prevent crime, but there is little evidence that they can have a major impact on crime.

A study by the Police Foundation concluded that rather than measure officers' productivity by the number of arrests they make, police administrators would contribute more to the reduction of crime by weighing the net impact of each arrest. Arrests of chronic criminals, who might commit five or more serious offenses per week, contribute more to curbing crime than arrests of occasional offenders. A weighted clearance rate that takes this into account would focus more attention on apprehending career criminals and would thus be a better way of measuring the performance of individual officers (Martin, 1986; Martin and Sherman, 1986).

Crime might also be reduced if the police established better relationships with the community and increased public trust so that more crimes were reported. Offenders might then realize that their crimes would be more likely to be reported and that they would therefore be more likely to be arrested. However, it is not clear that the reporting of crime can be increased enough for potential offenders to think that they face a significantly greater threat of punishment.

This police officer is lecturing a class of sixth graders who are participating in the Drug Abuse Resistance Education (D.A.R.E.) program.

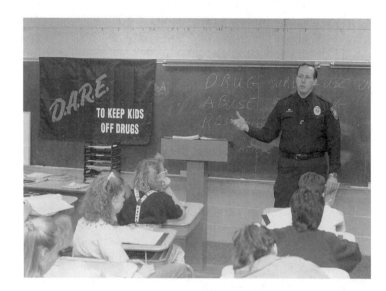

Federal Law Enforcement   The federal government's policy of dealing with drug use relies heavily on policing the nation's borders to prevent the importation of drugs. This approach has increased the amount of drugs confiscated at the borders, but even the increased amount that has been seized is a small proportion of the drugs that importers try to bring into the country. Importers typically increase their activity to compensate for what they lose to law-enforcement agents. Estimates of the proportion of all heroin, cocaine, and other illegal drugs seized at the borders range from 2 to 13 percent (Maitland, 1983). A 1994 Rand study recommended cutting the funds allocated to law enforcement for fighting the cocaine traffic, after concluding that treatment of abusers of the drug is a much more cost-effective strategy for curbing cocaine use (Rydell and Everingham, 1994).

The National Crime Information Center (NCIC) was established under the jurisdiction of the FBI in 1967. Despite concern about the accuracy of the NCIC's records and their threat to privacy, a national clearinghouse for information on crime is an important tool for law enforcement. Local police officers can get rapid responses to their inquiries about whether a car is stolen or a suspect they are questioning is wanted outside their state. The importance of a nationally coordinated system can be seen in the results of an FBI study that found that half of all offenders are arrested in more than one state during their criminal careers, and that 17.8 percent are arrested in three or more states (Kelley, 1976: 43). Many serial murderers wander from state to state killing their victims, and a centralized system of records can uncover patterns of similar crimes in different parts of the country. In response to this problem, the FBI in 1984 established the Violent Criminal Apprehension Program (VICAP) to collect and analyze standardized reports on violent crimes and missing persons.

The Courts

The primary way that the courts might reduce crime is by increasing the certainty of punishment, but it is not clear that certainty can be increased significantly without infringing on the constitutional rights of defendants or greatly expanding the resources of the criminal justice system.

Making Prosecution Easier   Because laws against sex offenses such as rape and child molestation have historically included impediments to prosecution and conviction, certainty of punishment might be increased by reforming those laws. For example, until recently rape victims were often asked in court about their past sexual conduct, making it seem that they, rather than the accused, were being tried. Most states now have "shield laws" that protect rape victims from this kind of cross-examination. Another reform that has made the prosecution of rape defendants easier is the division of this crime into several degrees of sexual assault, with different penalties for each of the three or four degrees of the offense. This makes it easier to get a conviction for sexual assault from a jury that believes that mitigating circumstances do not warrant the severe penalty that was previously attached to the single type of forcible rape.

Prosecuting Organized Crime   Legal reform and increased funding have made it possible for the federal government and local district attorneys to prosecute the leaders of organized crime more successfully. The FBI began to devote more of its resources to the prosecution of organized crime in the mid-1970s. The federal Racketeer Influenced and Corrupt Organizations law (RICO) has been an effective tool for prosecuting defendants who engage in a series of crimes. This law also permits the victims of financial fraud, either by organized crime or by white-collar offenders, to bring civil suits for treble damages. More use of undercover agents and informers, the pooling of resources by law-enforcement agencies, more concentration by the FBI on narcotics crimes, and the exchange of immunity and a new identity for a witness's testimony have all increased the prosecution and conviction of organized crime leaders.

Even though critics of these policies contend that imprisoned gangsters are simply replaced from within the organized crime "family," and that organized crime is not much affected by law-enforcement efforts, by the 1990s there was evidence that intensive efforts by prosecutors had weakened the Mafia.

Prosecuting White-Collar Crime   Federal, state, and local agencies lack the resources to prosecute many white-collar crime cases, and those that are prosecuted usually require years of investigation, so the certainty of punishment is low and penalties are not promptly administered. The penalties for corporate offenders also seem too lenient to deter white-collar crime. Fines are often minuscule compared with a corporation's total assets, and executives who are fined are often paid back by the company. Few executives are imprisoned, and when they are it is usually for a short term in a minimum-security prison. Punishment might be a more effective deterrent if fines were heavier, more offenders were incarcerated, and recidivists were prohibited from securing government contracts. Negative publicity about violations of the law could also affect corporate behavior, because firms are concerned with their public reputations (Fisse and Braithwaite, 1983). In extreme cases, an offending corporation might even be taken over by the federal government or prohibited from doing business.

Juvenile Courts   The search for solutions to the crime problem often focuses on young people, because many arrested suspects are juveniles, and juvenile delinquents are more likely than nondelinquents to go on to commit crime as adults.

Some have proposed that instead of incarcerating juveniles in reformatories, which should be reserved for those who repeatedly commit serious offenses, most young offenders should be placed in group homes in communities other than those in which their families live. These group homes can provide surrogate families for juveniles whose own families generate crime. Another proposal is to treat the entire family of the youthful offender, rather than isolate the juvenile for treatment, because the problems of delinquents often stem from poor relationships within their families.

Juvenile court records could be made more accessible than they now are, so that adults with histories of serious offenses as juveniles could be sentenced as persistent criminals rather than first-time offenders when they initially appear in adult criminal court. Others have suggested that the age at which adolescents can be prosecuted as adults should be lowered, although researchers have not found that this significantly reduces the crime rate.

The Prisons

A 1993 Canadian government report on crime prevention noted that "the United States affords a glaring example of the limited impact that criminal justice responses may have on crime," observing that "[i]f locking up those who violate the law contributed to safer societies, then the United States should be the safest country in the world" (cited in Proband, 1993: 2).

Because there is no compelling evidence that incarceration reduces crime through rehabilitation, some criminologists have argued that prison sentences should be based on the principle of just deserts. Treatment could be optional during a fixed period of confinement. Whenever possible, pretrial diversion and sanctions of warnings or probation might be substituted for imprisonment, which is both expensive and ineffective in curbing crime. Offenders who seem unlikely to commit more crimes might be left in the community where they can maintain ties to their families and jobs, but predicting which offenders are likely to commit more crimes is difficult, and leaving offenders in the community continues to expose them to the influences that led them to break the law in the first place.

Situational Crime Prevention

A second general strategy for solving the crime problem—in addition to relying on the criminal justice system to deter, incapacitate, and rehabilitate—is **situational crime prevention**. This involves opportunity-reducing measures "(1) directed at highly specific forms of crime (2) that involve the management, design, or manipulation of the immediate environment in as systematic and permanent a way as possible (3) so as to increase the effort and risks of crime and reduce the rewards as perceived by a wide range of offenders" (Clarke, 1992: 4). Influenced by the concepts of defensible space, crime prevention through environmental design, and problem-oriented policing, situational crime prevention includes the following:

1. *Techniques to increase the offender's effort* such as target-hardening (e.g., locks on steering columns and tougher glass), access-control (e.g., gates and identification badges), deflection of offenders (e.g., closing off streets), and control of facilitators (e.g., firearms).

One form of situational crime prevention is the scanning of students entering a school to prevent them from bringing weapons into the building.

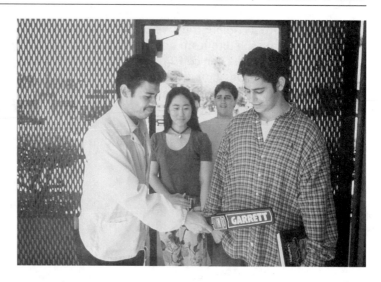

2. *Techniques that increase the offender's risks* such as entry/exit screening (e.g., border searches and merchandise tags), formal surveillance (e.g., security guards and burglar alarms), surveillance by employees (e.g., bus conductors and park attendants), and natural surveillance (e.g., defensible space design and Neighborhood Watches).

3. *Techniques that reduce the offender's rewards* such as target removal (e.g., removable car radios and reduced use of cash), property identification (e.g., property marking and stolen car location devices), removal of inducements (e.g., cleaning up graffiti and gender-neutral phone listings), and rule setting (e.g., drug-free school zones and library checkout procedures). (Clarke, 1992: 12–21)

Situational crime prevention has been criticized for displacing rather than preventing crime, but some research has identified measures that have "achieved reductions in crime with little apparent displacement" (Clarke, 1992: 23).

Target Hardening

One way to reduce opportunities for crime is to make it more difficult for an offender to carry out a crime against a particular target, a policy called **target hardening**. This includes the installation of bars and locks on doors and windows, the use of spotlights, the purchase of guard dogs, and the use of alarms. These measures might reduce the chance that the target-hardened building will be burglarized, but a burglar who is motivated to steal might simply move to another, less well-protected target.

An instance of target hardening that curbed bank robbery was the installation in New York City banks during the early 1980s of bulletproof Plexiglas shields to protect tellers, who could press an alarm button and ignore the robber's demands. According to police officials, these barriers were installed in about half of the city's banks by early 1983 and were partly responsible for a decline in bank robberies in the city from 848 in 1979 to 447 in 1982. The robbery rate at banks with protective shields was one-fourth that of the robbery rate at banks without the barriers (Buder, 1983).

A variation on target hardening is to remove from the home property that might be stolen by a burglar. In recent years, the high prices of gold and silver and gem and artwork investments have led many people to place their valuables in safe-deposit boxes. In some cities, private depositories that store property have developed to meet the demand for the safe-keeping of goods that banks are unable to fulfill. Private depositories reduce the risk of a major loss in a burglary, but they are inconvenient and expensive for property owners. Those who use depositories might simply be displacing burglars to their less well-protected neighbors' homes. If everyone used depositories, some marginally committed thieves might be deterred from crime altogether, but others might start burglarizing the depositories or robbing people who are on their way to deposit property.

Target-hardening measures have been proposed as a way to curb computer crime. Traditional safeguards against unauthorized access to computerized information include passwords and other electronic "locks," but these measures have been neutralized by "hackers" and by experienced computer operators who guess or steal passwords to gain access to information. Another way of making computers more impermeable is encryption, a method that translates information into code so that someone who gains access to the information cannot interpret its meaning. This method is not widely used, because executives are often nonchalant about the possibility of computer crime and because it is expensive to code and decode information for use within a company. Some companies protect computerized information with less burdensome methods, such as passwords that are difficult to guess and systems that require users to be called back before they are allowed access to the computer.

Self-Protective Measures

Some self-protective measures are much like target hardening, for they are aimed at making it harder for offenders to perpetrate a crime successfully against an individual. The sale of firearms after urban riots and during crime waves is based on a belief that gun owners will be less likely to be victimized, or more able to resist successfully if they are attacked or robbed. People also buy dogs, carry Mace, and take karate lessons to reduce their risk of victimization.

A study asked a sample of Seattle residents whether, at least two years prior to the interview, they had taken any of the following precautions to prevent crime: locking doors and leaving lights on when not home, asking neighbors to watch the house, installing extra locks or a burglar alarm, having a dog or a weapon in the home, and belonging to a Block Watch program. Those who had taken the most precautions were the least likely to have experienced a burglary; the risk of being the victim of vandalism or property theft was not affected by taking safety precautions. Safety measures taken by one person did not displace crime to nearby targets, nor did they reduce their neighbors' risk of being victimized (Miethe, 1991).

Informal Social Control

Opportunities for crime might be reduced by increasing informal social control over criminal behavior. This could be accomplished through defensible space architecture, although research indicates that this method is of limited value. Another proposed measure is improved street lighting, which makes public places more visible and draws more people to those places, which could then enhance informal control. There is, however, little research supporting the idea that crime can be reduced by better street lighting.

Another way to improve surveillance is to increase people's perception that the streets are safe and that uncivil behavior in their community is rare. Oakland, California, once adopted a program to erase signs of decay that might create the impression of a dangerous community, including graffiti, broken windows, open prostitution, panhandling, and loitering on street corners. The impact of this strategy is unclear, but such measures might reduce crime by enhancing informal social control if they manage to draw more people to the streets. For informal social control to be effective, people must act against criminals by intervening in a crime or by reporting it to the police.

Community Crime Prevention

Another strategy of situational crime prevention involves community organization. In 1976 a project was undertaken to reduce robbery and burglary in an area of Hartford, Connecticut, with the hope that changes in the community would reduce fear of crime and thereby enhance informal social control. This project altered the physical features of the community by changing roads to cul-de-sacs and one-way streets in order to reduce motorist traffic and define the neighborhood more clearly in a visual sense. A neighborhood police team was organized, and better communication was established between the community and the police. A formal neighborhood organization was also developed to deal with local problems.

In an evaluation of this project published six years later, the researchers concluded that environmental design can strengthen a neighborhood. Making the neighborhood more residential changed the degree to which people exercised informal control over the area and the way they felt about their neighbors. Strengthening informal control also helped reduce residents' fear and concern about crime. The evaluators of the Hartford project concluded that increased informal control does not, by itself, necessarily reduce robbery and burglary, but that it does help to curb crime if it is accompanied by aggressive and effective police practices (Fowler and Mangione, 1982).

Dealing with the Causes of Crime

Trying to reduce crime by relying on the criminal justice system is like relying on therapeutic rather than preventive medicine to deal with disease. Sick people do need help, but research into the causes of disease can lead to more effective treatment methods and even suggest ways to prevent the disease from occurring in the first place. A search for the causes of a disease might be more costly in the short run than using traditional methods to treat the disease, but the long-term benefits of a successful search for the causes of a disease are greater. Similarly, finding the causes of crime and attacking them is a more efficient way to reduce crime than waiting for crimes to occur and then using traditional methods to deal with offenders. The ineffectiveness of the criminal justice system in dealing with crime is suggested by James Q. Wilson, a political scientist who is an authority on crime and criminal justice, who says, "I doubt that a criminal justice system which I designed and I ran would have more than a small impact on the total crime rate" (cited in McCain, 1984: 2).

There is popular support for policies that focus on the causes of crime; prevention was the preferred method of crime reduction cited in a 1994 survey, although punishment and law enforcement together were favored by slightly more people (see Figure 15.2). Unfortunately, the causes of crime are not easily eradicated; as Gabriel Tarde said a century ago, "If the tree of crime, with all its roots and rootlets, could ever be torn out of our society, it would leave a vast abyss" (cited in Radzinowicz and King, 1977: 84). Even though social conditions are not easily changed, the solution to the crime problem lies in policies that deal with its underlying causes. Because social and economic factors distinguish societies with high crime rates from those with low rates, making countries with high crime rates more like those with low ones is a useful strategy for reducing crime.

Economic Factors

Usually countries undergoing economic development experience significant increases in their crime rates, but neither China nor Japan has had that experience. China has apparently avoided high crime rates through careful social planning that has been implemented by an authoritarian regime; this has provided a full-employment economy in which people are trained and given rewarding jobs. Workers in Japan have traditionally been employed by the same company for life, with employers taking a great interest in the welfare of their employees. Recently, job mobility has increased in Japan, but employee turnover is still less common there than in the United States.

The United States needs policies that create stable and meaningful jobs and provide retraining and job counseling when needed. At the national level there is no clear relationship between the unemployment rate and the crime rate, but many people who commit conventional crimes are without job skills and are unemployed. Perhaps even more importantly, they lack the social bond to the conventional order that work provides. Income subsidies that maintain an ex-convict's incentive to find full-time employment might reduce crime by making it more likely that such a bond will be formed (Rossi, Berk, and Lenihan, 1980). Job training is more likely to foster the development of such a bond if it includes socialization in job-related skills as well as in the techniques of the work; job-related skills include promptness, cooperativeness, and willingness to take orders (Cook, 1975). Measures that reduce job turnover and encourage loyalty to an employer also foster a worker's stake in conformity. Even more important than an ex-convict's getting a job is keeping one over time and becoming habituated to a work routine.

Nations with low crime rates commonly have less relative deprivation than nations with high rates. In China, control of the media limits citizens' access to information about the standard of living of the rest of the world, minimizing the "demonstration effect" that can increase expectations beyond the current level of well-being. The absolute level of economic well-being in a nation might be a less important influence on crime than relative deprivation, the gap between current economic well-being and economic expectations. The Chinese are absolutely deprived compared with Americans, but crime is relatively uncommon in China because expectations there have not been increased by constant exposure to higher standards of living.

In contrast to China, Americans at all economic levels are exposed to great wealth and are exhorted to work hard to achieve material success, which is seen as an indicator of individual worth. Thus, Americans who have higher absolute standards of living than most Chinese often see themselves as relatively disadvantaged compared with other Americans. These perceptions can generate both conventional property crime and white-collar crime. Policies that reduce American culture's emphasis on material well-being as a sign of personal worth might reduce crime, but those policies could also undercut the motivation to pursue material success through legitimate channels and thus harm the economy by lowering the demand for consumer goods.

Although reducing inequality between the poor and the rest of the population might reduce crime, measures that simply aim to alleviate poverty will not necessarily have that effect, because of the following problems with anti-poverty programs:

1. They will not normally succeed in lifting people out of poverty.
2. They foster cynicism and disappointment by raising expectations which they cannot fulfill.
3. They label people as disreputable and inferior.
4. Even if they do succeed in lifting people out of poverty, in a capitalist economy they typically do so at the expense of other people who are thrust into poverty.
5. Even if they do reduce the total number of poor people in a city, this is unlikely to reduce crime because cities with smaller numbers of poor people do not have lower crime rates. (Braithwaite, 1979: 232)

Relative deprivation and unmet expectations motivate people to break the law more than does absolute poverty, and policies to reduce poverty, although beneficial in other ways, might not curb crime in any dramatic way. Indeed, crime rates in the United States increased significantly during and just after the War on Poverty in the 1960s, even though this federal effort substantially reduced the proportion of Americans living in poverty.

The Process of Social Change

Crime might be curbed by policies that minimize the disruptive effects of social change. China and Japan have both experienced internal migration and urbanization, trends commonly associated with rising crime rates. In China, migration from rural areas to large cities is carefully planned so that those who move are provided with jobs in their new communities. Japan has urbanized without increased crime rates, apparently because group pressures to conform continue to exist, and are perhaps even enhanced, in large cities. Switzerland has also avoided a high crime rate through a slow process of urbanization that has minimized the disruption of individual lives (Clinard, 1978).

Countries such as China, Japan, and Switzerland that have experienced social change without increased crime rates have managed to maintain traditional attachments to relatives, friends, neighbors, and others who encourage conformity to the law. This is consistent with social control theory, which proposes that crime and delinquency are less common when people have a stake in conformity and are concerned with the good opinion of those close to them.

Political Factors

China's political ideology is conducive to a low crime rate. Before the Communist Revolution in 1949, China was composed of relatively autonomous regions; today it is a more integrated nation that commands its citizens' loyalty. People are attached to an institution with authority—the state—and this bond reduces their motivation to commit crime for selfish reasons.

Japan is similar in some ways, even though its political ideology is very different. As in China, the Japanese are subordinated to the nation, the family, and the community, as well as to the company for which they work. The Japanese are greatly concerned with the good opinion of other nations and censure behavior that brings shame on the country in the eyes of the rest of the world.

Because crimes are often committed to improve the situation of the offender, crime rates will be low where people learn supraindividual goals and high where people learn to pursue individual goals. It is difficult to suggest policies that would reduce the American culture's emphasis on individualism and increase its emphasis on national goals, but it is important to recognize that one cost of individualism is a high crime rate.

Community Ties

Crime rates are low in neighborhoods that are socially integrated, because this increases the attachment of individuals to one another and reduces crime by strengthening everyone's stake in conformity. In socially integrated neighborhoods, the surveillance of behavior is more likely, reducing crime by increasing the fear of being observed, reported, and arrested. Attachment to community is strong in Japan, China, and Switzerland, three nations with relatively low crime rates.

Programs that strengthen community ties might reduce crime rates, but it would be difficult to employ such measures in a nation such as the United States where individualism is a strongly held value and geographic mobility is common. Crime might be reduced by implementing a program tried in Puerto Rico that created a sense of community by allowing slum residents to take charge of their own lives and by requiring offenders to work to improve their community (Silberman, 1978: 429–466). Another approach is for the residents of well-to-do communities to develop "sister-neighborhood" or mentoring relationships with inner-city areas that have high crime rates. Those who control more resources could help the disadvantaged develop literacy, work, and social skills and find jobs for them. Broker organizations could recruit outside volunteers to help revitalize crime-ridden neighborhoods, but the volunteers would need to feel safe in those communities and would have to avoid patronizing attitudes that could alienate local residents. The ultimate goal of such a strategy would be to develop the human capital of those living in high-crime communities and integrate their neighborhoods into the larger society (Buerger, 1994).

The Family

The family is usually a strong institution in nations that have low crime rates. Chinese and Japanese families have traditionally had close attachments between children and their parents, whose "psychological presence" curbs the children's tendency toward delinquency. The Chinese family is organized on a hierarchical basis, emphasizing respect for elders while providing parental affection for children. As a result, the Chinese usually have low crime rates, whether they live in China or elsewhere (Count-van Manen, 1971). The Japanese family has similar characteristics. Japanese children are taught to be concerned about the good opinion of their family and to avoid bringing shame on it; this creates an investment in conformity and keeps children from delinquency. Swiss children also learn to be concerned about the good opinion of others and to avoid law-violating behavior that would bring public censure on themselves and their families.

In the United States, people who violate the law typically come from families that differ from the Chinese, Japanese, and Swiss families which have low crime rates. Policies might be implemented to strengthen the ability of American families to prevent delinquency and crime. The closeness of adolescents and their elders in Switzerland suggests the possibility of creating programs that integrate young people and adults in common activities (Clinard, 1978: 132–133). Family treatment programs should focus on child and spouse abuse, which are crimes themselves and which lead to later crimes by those who are abused as children. Teaching parents techniques of consistent but nonphysical discipline, training family members in communi-

Countries with low crime rates usually have strong families, suggesting that policies that strengthen the family can reduce crime.

cation and conflict-resolution skills, and treating entire families when one member gets into trouble with the law can reduce delinquency. These methods are most effective if they are directed at children when they first get into trouble and if they keep children in the community. One study estimated that a $1 million investment in parent-training programs would prevent 157 crimes per year, compared to only 60 that would be prevented by a similar investment in the construction and operation of prisons to house more career criminals for longer terms (Greenwood et al., 1996).

Welfare reform and income tax reform can also change the family. Crime could be reduced if the welfare system encouraged families to stay together, rather than taking a neutral stance toward family breakups or even encouraging family dissolution in order to become eligible for certain kinds of public assistance. A guaranteed minimum income might increase family stability and harmony. The income tax system could be redesigned to encourage family stability, which in turn would reduce crime. More flexible work hours and inexpensive day-care centers—and tax incentives to encourage those programs—could lead to better supervision of children and instill in them the "psychological presence" of adults that inhibits violation of the law.

Crime might also be curbed by providing instruction on child rearing to high school students and to prospective or new parents. Teachers and school administrators might teach child rearing by example, because they interact with schoolchildren on a daily basis, monitor their behavior, and punish misconduct (Hirschi, 1983). So far, it has proved difficult to teach methods of child rearing that are effective in curbing delinquent behavior, and it has been even harder to get parents to use those methods once they learn them (Wilson and Herrnstein, 1985). Nevertheless, there is some evidence that parent-training programs curb delinquent behavior, with greater impact on aggressive acts than on theft (Patterson, Chamberlain, and Reid, 1982).

The School

In China, the family's influence is reinforced by schools and government-run play centers, which tie children to adults who have authority. Schools and play centers also reduce the time that children have available to engage in delinquency and minimize the boredom that is sometimes mentioned as a cause of delinquency in the United States. In Japan, the tremendous academic pressure on students to succeed and not disappoint their families has been cited as a cause of recent increases in delinquency, although Japanese schools are quite effective in controlling students' behavior.

Delinquency can be curbed by improving academic performance through the preparation of disadvantaged children for school, the development of more structured classroom environments, and the adoption of student-centered teaching strategies. According to one study, money spent on a program that offers students incentives to graduate from high school will prevent four times as much crime as the same amount spent on more prison space for serious offenders (Greenwood et al., 1996). Reforms that tie students more closely to the school and its teachers can create a "psychological presence" that keeps young people from violating the law. If courses were made more relevant to the interests and needs of students, their attachment to the school might be strengthened. Curricula should provide students with the skills to achieve legitimate success but should also be designed to fit the needs and values of the community.

Nonacademic programs might also help reduce crime. Experiences such as wilderness survival training and discussion groups with elderly people in the community might develop students' self-confidence and broaden their perspectives. Programs that strengthen a sense of personal responsibility and create empathy with others might reduce crime by undermining the ability to use techniques of neutralization to justify violations of the law. Courses and tutoring can provide students with the social and emotional skills to control their anger and jealousy, negotiate with others, avoid confrontations, and develop relationships with peers and teachers.

Discrimination

Elimination of the discrimination that denies minority groups equal access to valued opportunities would help solve the crime problem, because minorities are disproportionately involved in crime. Discrimination weakens attachment to the conventional social order, increasing the chance that the group that is discriminated against will have a high crime rate. Obstacles to voting or organizing politically deny power to minority groups and thus weaken their ties to the political system. Schools that are segregated or poorly funded provide an inadequate education and leave minorities unprepared for good-paying jobs to which they can form strong ties. Job discrimination in which minority-group members are "the last hired and the first fired" can keep them from developing loyalty to an employer. Housing discrimination that relegates minorities to the most run-down areas of the city weakens their ties to the community.

Discrimination in education, work, and housing are sources of high poverty rates for minority groups. When poverty is combined with a cultural emphasis on material success, as it is in the United States, there is a strong motivation to commit property crime. Eliminating discrimination would open legitimate opportunities and create bonds to the conventional order among groups that traditionally have had high crime rates, and thus help reduce the overall crime rate.

Conclusion

Crime can be reduced by developing policies that enhance the social support available from families, schools, friends, employers, communities, and the government. Individuals use supportive relationships instrumentally to complete an education or get a job, and expressively to meet their needs for affection and sharing (Cullen, 1994). Policies that foster attachments to conventional people and institutions create a stake in conformity that makes the rewards of a law-abiding way of life and the risks of criminal behavior great enough to reduce violations of the law. Harsh or certain punishment is less likely to reduce crime than policies that make it more rewarding to abide by the law.

Summary

Three approaches to solving the crime problem differ in their ideas about crime causation and their recommendations for reducing the crime rate. The conservative approach focuses on conventional crime, which is attributed to the poor and to people who have been improperly socialized. Conservatives would solve the crime problem by using the criminal justice system to deter and incapacitate criminals, rather than by eliminating poverty or strengthening the family. The liberal approach also focuses on conventional crime, but it proposes that it can be reduced by alleviating poverty and providing legitimate opportunities for everyone. The radical approach looks at both conventional crime and white-collar crime, which are attributed to the structure of a capitalist system. According to this perspective, only the elimination of capitalism can solve the crime problem.

Since the 1960s, several national commissions have studied crime and recommended changes in the criminal justice system, rather than changes in social conditions, as the way to reduce crime. The Law Enforcement Assistance Administration was unable to reduce crime by changing the criminal justice system and was disbanded in 1981. Crime was a major issue in the 1968 and 1972 presidential campaigns, contributing in an important way to the victory of Richard Nixon in both elections. President Ronald Reagan occasionally raised the crime issue, and in 1984 he signed into law a sweeping set of reforms aimed at curbing crime. George Bush used the crime issue effectively in winning the presidency in 1988, and during his time in office he made numerous proposals to reduce crime in general and drug offenses in particular. In the 1992 and 1996 elections, neither Bill Clinton nor his opponents gained a strong advantage with their positions on the crime issue.

The first of three general recommendations for reducing crime is to change the criminal justice system. One way to do this is to reduce the overreach of the criminal law, so that the limited resources can be concentrated on the most serious crimes. The number of police officers in a city does not make much of a difference in its crime rate, but the kind of action the police take might make a difference. For years, the federal government has tried to stop the importation of drugs, but the amount of drugs entering the country does not seem to have decreased as a result. The courts might curb crime by increasing the certainty of punishment, but it is not clear that this can be done within the constraints of existing constitutional rights. Concentrated efforts to imprison organized crime leaders seem to have had an impact on the Mafia's criminal activities in recent years. Some have proposed that crime might be prevented if juvenile court records were more accessible to criminal court judges.

A second strategy is situational crime prevention. This involves target hardening to make buildings and property less vulnerable to theft. Self-protective measures might reduce the chance that an individual will be victimized; the carrying of tear gas sprays is an example. Strategies to increase informal social control can reduce crime, and community crime prevention has had some effect in curbing crime, especially when used in conjunction with aggressive police practices.

A third strategy is to deal with the causes of crime. Economic policies can provide offenders with work, and thus attach them more strongly to the conventional social order. Crime can also be curbed by minimizing the disruptive effects of social change. Attachment to the nation can keep a country's crime rate low, as it has in China and Japan; strong ties to the local community can have the same effect. Policies that strengthen the family and teach parents how to raise law-abiding children can reduce crime. Schools can reduce delinquency and crime by helping young people establish close ties to their teachers and by providing them with the skills to succeed in legitimate careers. Eliminating discrimination can reduce crime by strengthening the attachment to the conventional order of minority groups that have traditionally had high crime rates. In general, providing stronger ties to conventional people and institutions is an effective strategy for solving the crime problem.

Important Terms

conservative approach
liberal approach
radical approach

situational crime prevention
target hardening

Review Questions

1. What are the three ideological approaches to dealing with the crime problem? On which type of crime does each focus? How would each deal with crime?

2. What role has the crime issue played in presidential elections since the mid-1960s? How have presidential crime commissions addressed the problem of crime?

3. How can crime be reduced by reforming the criminal justice system?

4. How can situational crime prevention reduce crime?

5. How can crime be reduced by dealing with economic and political factors, the process of social change, community organization, the family, the school, and racial and ethnic discrimination?

GLOSSARY

Age-specific arrest rate   The number of arrests per 100,000 people in a given age category.

Aggravated assault   An unlawful attack by one person on another in which the purpose is to inflict severe bodily injury and in which a weapon typically is used.

Aggregate   People who happen to be in the same place at the same time but who do not interact much and have no sense of common identity.

Amenability issue   The possibility that certain kinds of offenders are amenable or suited to a particular type of treatment.

Anomie   Normlessness, or a disjunction between institutionalized means and culturally approved goals.

Appeal to higher loyalties   A technique of neutralization that justifies a violation of the law by the demands of a group that is smaller than the whole society but that requires of its members conformity to standards that may be incompatible with the law.

Argot   A specialized language that creates solidarity by differentiating a group from outsiders.

Arson   The willful burning of the building, motor vehicle, aircraft, or personal property of another person.

Assault   An unlawful attack by one person on another.

Atavism   A person "born out of time" and similar to primitive people or lower animals in his or her biological makeup; the basis of Lombroso's theory of the "born criminal."

Bail   A system of pretrial release designed to ensure that defendants will show up to face charges when the trial is scheduled, at the same time allowing them to remain free until the trial takes place.

Behavior modification   A treatment program that tries to change behavior, rather than personality, by rewarding desirable actions and punishing undesirable ones.

Biographical method   A research strategy in which the experiences of a single individual are examined in detail.

Boot camp   A military-style program designed to scare offenders away from crime by subjecting them to harsh discipline, rigorous exercise, and strenuous work.

Brawner rule   The legal rule that a person will be found not guilty by reason of insanity if at the time of such conduct as a result of mental disease or mental defect, he lacks substantial capacity either to appreciate the criminality of his conduct or to conform his conduct to the requirements of the law.

Bureaucracy   A formal organization that is rationally organized to pursue goals in an efficient manner.

Burglary   Unlawful entry of a building to commit a serious crime, usually the theft of property.

Business organization   A permanent structure that profits from extortion and the provision of illegal goods and services; more commonly called "organized crime."

Cartography   An approach to the study of crime that uses official data to map or chart patterns of crime.

Case attrition   A funnel or sieve effect that characterizes the criminal justice system, with cases being sorted out as they proceed through the system and with relatively few crimes ending with a perpetrator's conviction and imprisonment.

Casework   A treatment program designed to help offenders cope with specific problems they face.

Certification   The social verification by the criminal justice system or by conventional people that an offender is rehabilitated.

Classical school   An approach to crime that emphasizes free will and the deterrence of criminal behavior by the fear of punishment.

Clearance rate   The proportion of cases the police solve to their satisfaction.

Cohort   A carefully defined group of people who are in a common situation at one time.

Community policing   An approach that establishes two-way communication between citizens and the police through foot patrols, decentralized operations, storefront stations, community organizations, crime newsletters, and contacts with people at home and at work.

Comparative research   A research strategy that looks at crime in societies with different cultures and social structures.

Compensation   A system in which the state repays crime victims for their financial losses or physical injuries.

Computer crime   Any violation of the law in which a computer is the target or the means.

Concentric-zone model   A model of metropolitan areas that identifies concentric rings that have distinctive characteristics.

Concordance rate   A measure of the similarity of criminal behavior that is used in studies of twins.

Condemnation of the condemners   A technique of neutralization that asserts that it is the motives and behavior of the people who are condemning the offender, rather than the motives and behavior of the offender, that should be condemned.

Conflict perspective   An approach that sees the criminal law as closely intertwined with the distribution of political power and economic resources in a society.

Conformity   A mode of adaptation in which both cultural goals and the institutionalized means to reach those goals are accepted.

Consensus perspective   An approach that claims that the criminal law represents social consensus or agreement about what kinds of behavior should be punished by the state.

Conservative approach   An approach that seeks to preserve the status quo from criminals, who are seen as challengers to the existing social order.

Containment theory   The theory that people are insulated to various degrees against pressures to commit deviant acts by external and internal factors.

Contingency   A factor that determines movement from one criminal role to another, or from one crime to another.

Costs related to criminal violence   The financial losses that result from violent crimes in which victims are physically hurt.

Craft organization   A small and relatively permanent group of two or three thieves or confidence tricksters, each of whom plays a well-defined role in the specific type of crime that the group commits.

Crime   An act that violates the criminal law and is punishable by the state.

Crime index   The total number of eight serious crimes, which are defined by the FBI.

Crime rate   The number of reported crimes divided by the number of people in an area, often expressed as a rate of crimes per 100,000 people.

Criminal career   A sequence of criminal acts over time by one person.

Criminal intent   The willed or conscious desire to commit an act that violates a criminal law.

Criminology   A discipline that gathers and analyzes empirical data to explain violations of the criminal law and societal reactions to those violations.

Dark figure   The number of crimes that actually occur but are not recorded by the police.

Defensible space   The subdivision and design of housing to allow residents to distinguish stranger from neighbor and thus elicit a sense of territoriality, which can reduce crime by informal social control.

Delinquent gang   A gang that has a tight primary group structure and is organized to carry out specific profitable crimes.

Denial of injury   The technique of neutralization that claims that no one is hurt by an offender's crime, even if it technically violates the law.

Denial of responsibility   The technique of neutralization that involves the denial of personal responsibility for actions that violate the criminal law.

Denial of the victim   The technique of neutralization that claims that a crime is justified as a rightful retaliation against the victim.

Determinate sentence   A specified sentence meted out for an offense of a certain degree of harmfulness committed by someone with a particular prior record.

Deterrence   The inhibition of criminal activity by state-imposed penalties.

Differential association-reinforcement theory   A theory of crime and delinquency that states that learning occurs through operant conditioning in both nonsocial and social situations, even though most learning results from interaction with others.

Differential association theory   A theory that proposes that crime and delinquency are learned in face-to-face interaction and occur when there is an excess of definitions favorable to violation of the law over definitions unfavorable to violation of the law.

Differential identification theory   The theory that people engage in criminal or delinquent behavior because they identify with real or imaginary persons from whose perspective their crime or delinquency seems acceptable.

Differential opportunity theory   A theory of delinquency that focuses on the discrepancy between aspirations and access to both legitimate and illegitimate means to reach those goals.

Diffusion of responsibility   The situation that exists among groups of witnesses to an emergency or a crime, when people say that someone should act but that it need not be themselves because other potential helpers are present.

Direct loss   The result of a crime in which the stock of useful things is reduced, as in arson or vandalism.

Discretion   The use of judgment to decide what action to take.

Displacement effect   A change in the pattern of crime without a reduction in the total amount of crime that results from criminals' efforts to avoid punishment; displacement may be from one target to another, from one area to another, or from one kind of offense to another.

Doing gender   The idea that through their social behavior men develop and act out forms of masculinity, or masculinities, and women develop and act out forms of femininity, or femininities.

Drift   A condition of limbo between a conventional life style and a criminal life style with no strong attachment to either.

EFT crime   Any violation of the law involving an electronic fund transfer system.

Enforcement costs   The financial cost of crime that results from money spent on various criminal justice agencies.

Excuse   A defense to a criminal charge that denies criminal intent.

Exiting   A successful disengagement from a previous pattern of criminal behavior.

Experiment   A controlled study in which people are treated in different ways to determine the effects of that treatment on their attitudes and behavior.

Facilitating factor   A factor that increases the chance that a situation will lead to criminal violence or theft.

Family intervention   A program designed to improve communication and the expression of feelings within the family, change patterns of behavior within the family, or alter the way that parents manage their children.

Focal concern   A value or area of interest that elicits widespread, persistent attention and emotional involvement.

Forcible rape   Carnal knowledge of a female forcibly and against her will (FBI definition); some states define forcible rape in sex-neutral terms.

Formal organization   A large, complex secondary group that is deliberately created to achieve certain goals.

Formal social control   An effort to bring about conformity to the law by agents of the criminal justice system such as the police, the courts, and correctional institutions.

Fraud   The crime of obtaining money or property by false pretenses.

Gender ratio problem   The issue of why males commit more crime than females.

Gender structure   The institutional arrangements that treat men and women, and boys and girls, differently.

General deterrence   The inhibition of the desire to engage in crime among the general population through the punishment of certain offenders.

General strain theory   An expanded version of anomie theory that focuses on both positive and negative sources of strain, the various dimensions of strain, strategies for coping with strain, and factors that determine whether strain will be coped with in a delinquent or nondelinquent fashion.

Generalizability problem   The question of whether theories of crime, most of which were developed to explain offending by men and tested on male subjects, can be applied to crime by women.

Good Samaritan problem   The issue of how bystanders respond to emergencies such as crimes.

Group   A set of relationships among people who interact on a face-to-face basis over time.

Group counseling   A treatment program that allows several inmates to be treated at the same time and at a low cost; it involves the discussion of feelings and attitudes in an effort to create mutual acceptance and a supportive environment.

Hate crimes   Offenses in which victims are singled out because of their race, ethnicity, religion, sexual preference, or disability.

Historical research   A research strategy that examines the same society at different times and looks at the way crime has changed with economic and social development.

Illegal expenditures   The costs of crimes that divert money from the legitimate economy and represent a loss of potential revenue for people who produce and supply legal goods and services.

Incapacitation   The custodial control of convicted offenders so that they cannot commit crimes that affect the general public.

Incidence   The frequency with which offenders commit crime, or the average number of offenses per offender; it is measured by dividing the number of offenses by the number of offenders.

Indeterminate sentence   A penalty imposed under a system that establishes long maximum sentences for different crimes and allows judges to impose any penalty up to the maximum; sentences are often a range of years to be served in prison.

Individual therapy   A method of treatment commonly used in prison in which psychiatrists, psychologists, or psychiatric social workers help offenders solve psychological problems that are thought to be the cause of criminal behavior.

Informal social control   The reactions of individuals and groups that bring about conformity to norms and laws; it includes peer and community pressure, bystander intervention in a crime, and collective responses such as citizen patrol groups.

Innovation   The mode of adaptation in which cultural goals are accepted, but means are used that society regards as unacceptable.

Intensive offender   A person who engages in criminal activity that begins at an early age and is sustained over time, consciously planned, persistent, skilled, and frequent.

Intermittent offender   A person who engages in irregular and opportunistic crimes with low payoffs and great risks, and who does not think of himself or herself as a professional criminal.

Just deserts   The idea that offenders should be punished because they deserve to suffer for the harm they have caused.

Justification   A defense to a criminal charge that the law allows a person to act in a particular way.

Juvenile delinquent   A person below a legally specified age who has been adjudged by a juvenile court to have violated the law or committed a juvenile status offense.

Labeling perspective   The perspective on deviant behavior that emphasizes the effects that a socially imposed label has on a person who breaks a social rule.

Larceny   The unlawful taking, carrying, leading, or riding away of property from the possession of another.

Law   A kind of norm that is written down and formalized by the political system.

Learning disabilities   An impairment in sensory and motor functioning that leads to deviant classroom performance and is the result of an abnormal physical condition.

Left realism   A conflict theory that emphasizes the impact that crime by the lower and working class has on other members of the same class and that proposes a variety of pragmatic crime-reduction strategies.

Lex talionis   The principle of "an eye for an eye, a tooth for a tooth."

Liberal approach   The perspective that crime can be reduced by attacking its underlying causes through social reforms.

Machismo   The demonstration of masculinity through the manipulation and exploitation of women.

M'Naghten rule   The legal rule that a person will be found not guilty by reason of insanity if at the time of the crime the person was under a defect of reason so as to be unable to know the nature and the quality of the act, or if the person was aware of the nature of the act, he or she did not know that wrong was being done.

Marginal deterrent effect   The extent to which crime rates respond to incremental changes in the threat of sanctions.

Marxist or radical criminology   A conflict theory that focuses on social class, defined by the relationship of a group to the means of production, and that claims that capitalists, who own and control the means of production, use the law to protect their property from those who threaten it, the lower and working classes.

Master status   The situation in which other aspects of a person's behavior become submerged in a particular social identity, such as that of a deviant.

Mechanical solidarity   A unity based on shared values and norms and on the similarity of functions performed by all members of the society.

Milieu therapy   A treatment method that introduces the idea of rehabilitation into all aspects of an institution, including relations between inmates and staff members.

Mode of adaptation   A way that persons who occupy a particular social position adapt to cultural goals and the institutionalized means to reach those goals.

Motor vehicle theft   The theft of an automobile, truck, bus, or other type of vehicle.

Murder and nonnegligent manslaughter   The willful killing of a human being.

Networks   Ties among individual members of groups or among different groups.

Norm   A rule that makes explicit certain social expectations about what is appropriate behavior for a particular person in a specific situation.

Obscene material   Material, often pornographic in nature, that has been declared illegal because it poses a threat to the state or to organized religion, violates common morality, has no redeeming social value, or appeals to the prurient or lascivious interest.

Observation   A research strategy that involves the careful and systematic watching of behavior.

Organic solidarity   A unity based on an interdependence of functions, much as in a complex biological organism.

Organized crime   Criminal activity by an enduring structure or organization developed and devoted primarily to the pursuit of profits through illegal means (see *Business organization*).

Parole   A system under which inmates are released before they complete their full sentences and are then supervised in the community and sent back to prison if they violate the conditions of their release.

Patterns of crime   A research strategy that involves the use of data to determine where crime is committed, who commits crime, who is victimized, and what are the major dimensions of the criminal act.

Picaresque organization   A relatively permanent gang under the leadership of a single person who sometimes relies on the support and advice of a few officers.

Plea bargaining   An informal but structured process of negotiation in which the prosecutor and the defense attorney agree about a guilty plea and the sentence that the prosecutor will recommend to the judge.

Pluralistic ignorance   A situation in which witnesses in a group fail to help the victim of an emergency or a crime because they interpret the failure of other witnesses to help as a sign that no help is needed.

Pornography   Material that is intended to arouse people sexually by portraying sexual matters in visual or verbal terms.

Positivism   A perspective that relies on the scientific method to quantify and measure behavior and the social conditions associated with behavior.

Power-control theory   The theory that the class structure of the family explains the social distribution of delinquent behavior through the social reproduction of gender relations.

Premenstrual syndrome (PMS)   A set of symptoms associated with the onset of menstruation, including tension, nervousness, irritability, fatigue, headaches, cramps, and depressed moods.

Pretrial diversion   A program that allows a district attorney to recommend to a judge that a criminal proceeding be suspended while a suspect participates in a treatment program.

Prevalence   The proportion of a population that commits crime in a given period, measured by the number of offenders divided by the size of the population.

Prevention and protection costs   The financial costs of crimes that result from expenditures on alarm systems, spotlights, locks, bars, and other "target-hardening" devices, as well as the money that people spend on insurance premiums to cover their losses through theft.

Preventive detention   A system in which some defendants are held without bail while awaiting trial.

Primary deviation   An initial act of deviance that has not been socially labeled as deviant.

Primary group   A small and relatively permanent group characterized by intimate relationships.

Proactive police work   Efforts by the police to discover and deal with crime on their own initiative.

Probation   A form of supervised release imposed on convicted offenders by judges, without any time being served in jail or prison.

Professional thief   A skilled offender who is committed to crime as an occupation and thinks of himself or herself as a criminal.

Project organization   A group of several criminals who come together to commit one or a series of acts of robbery, burglary, fraud, or smuggling.

Protective neighboring   A combination of cooperative surveillance and willingness to intervene in a crime by the residents of a community.

Psychoanalytic perspective   A psychological approach to crime causation that sees crime as the behavior of people who are inadequately socialized.

Psychopath   A person who has a specific cluster of personality traits; is asocial, aggressive, highly impulsive, and unable to form lasting bonds of affection with others; and feels little or no guilt for antisocial activities.

Radical approach   A perspective that focuses on crime by both the underprivileged and the privileged, and attributes crime by both groups to the conditions of a capitalist society.

Radical nonintervention   A policy to minimize official reaction to delinquency in order to prevent the labeling of adolescents that could drive them into criminal careers.

Rape   See *Forcible rape*

Rational-choice perspective   A reward-risk model that emphasizes offenders' strategic thinking, the ways that they process information and evaluate opportunities and alternatives.

Reaction-formation   A repudiation of goals to which a person is emotionally attached but unable to attain, such as a reversal of middle-class goals by lower- or working-class delinquents.

Reactive police work   Efforts in which the police respond to a citizen's report of a crime.

Rebellion   A mode of adaptation in which people reject cultural goals and develop a new set of goals, and reject institutionalized means to reach cultural goals and develop a new set of means; behavior in which a person seeks to create a new social structure that will more effectively allow people to meet what the rebel considers appropriate goals.

Recidivism rate   The percentage of offenders who, during a specific period after their treatment has ended, are arrested and convicted of new offenses or have their punishment made more restrictive because they have failed to meet the conditions of a less restrictive sentence.

Rehabilitation   The restoration of criminals to a law-abiding way of life through treatment; the result of any planned intervention focused on the offender that reduces criminal activity.

Reintegrative shaming   A process that follows expressions of community disapproval of an offender's behavior with gestures of reacceptance by the larger law-abiding community.

Relative deprivation   The discrepancy between people's expectations about the goods and conditions of life to which they are rightfully entitled, and their capabilities, or the goods and conditions of life they believe they can attain and maintain under the current social system.

Restitution   A system that requires offenders to make monetary payments or provide services, either to the victim or to the community at large.

Retreatism   A mode of adaptation in which cultural goals are abandoned and institutionalized means are also rejected.

Retribution   The idea that offenders should be punished because they deserve to suffer for the harm they have caused.

Ritualism   A mode of adaptation in which cultural goals are scaled down or given up, while norms about the institutionalized means to reach cultural goals are accepted.

Robbery   The theft of property from another person by force or threat of force.

Routine activities approach   A perspective that sees crime as a function of people's everyday behavior, and stresses motivated offenders, target suitability, and guardianship.

Sanction   An effort to ensure future conformity to a norm and punish past nonconformity.

Schizophrenia   A psychosis that involves disordered thought patterns characterized by fantasy, delusion, and incoherence.

Secondary deviation   Deviant behavior that is the result of the labeling process.

Secondary group   A group that is usually larger, more complex, and less intimate than a primary group.

Selective incapacitation   A system of predictive restraint in which only those offenders who are the most likely to commit more crime if released are held.

Self-report study   Research that measures crime by having respondents report their own violations in confidential interviews or on anonymous self-administered questionnaires.

Sense of inequity   The belief that one's social position is not in as great a ratio to one's efforts as the social positions and efforts of other people.

Sentence disparity   The difference in the criminal sanctions that are handed out to people who are convicted of similar offenses and who have similar criminal records.

Simple assault   An unlawful attack by one person on another in which no weapon is used and no serious injury results.

Simultaneity   A reciprocal cause-and-effect relationship between two variables; for instance, sanctions by the criminal justice system may affect the crime rate, but the crime rate may also affect the sanctions that are handed out by the criminal justice system.

Situational crime prevention   Measures that involve the management, design, or manipulation of the environment in order to reduce opportunities for crime and increase the perceived risks of committing crime.

Social class   Social standing based on economic resources, occupational prestige, political power, or life style.

Social construction of crime   The way that crime is interpreted or given meaning by groups with different interests they seek to promote by using their resources to gain ownership of an issue.

Social control   A process that brings about conformity to society's norms and laws.

Social control theory   The theory that people who engage in crime or delinquency are relatively free of intimate attachments, aspirations, and moral beliefs that bind them to a conventional and law-abiding way of life.

Social gang   A gang that has a group identity, a relatively permanent structure, informal leadership based on popularity, and intimate interaction among members.

Social-skills training   A program that uses methods such as role-playing and modeling to help offenders take the perspective of other people, exercise greater self-control, negotiate solutions to interpersonal problems, and develop moral reasoning.

Social structure   Recurrent, stable patterns of interaction among people.

Somatotype   A body type that results from embryonic development and that is thought to be associated with a particular temperament and propensity to crime and delinquency.

Specific deterrence   The effect of a penalty that causes an individual who is punished for a crime not to commit that crime again because his or her reward-risk calculations have been altered by the punishment.

Status offense   An act defined as unacceptable for people below a given age and used as a basis for juvenile court proceedings; included are underage drinking, running away from home, and truancy.

Strain   The frustration and sense of injustice that result from experiencing socially structured incapacities as low capabilities.

Subculture   A patterned way of life similar in some ways but different in others from the dominant culture of a society.

Subculture-of-violence theory   The theory that the norms shared by a group of people may define violence as an appropriate response to certain circumstances and lead members of the group to engage in violent crime in order to conform to others' expectations.

Subterranean value   A value or ideal that is subordinate or below the surface in the dominant value system and is sought by most people only occasionally and in appropriate circumstances.

Survey   A research strategy in which a sample of people who are representative of a larger population are asked a series of prepared questions.

Target hardening   A policy of reducing opportunities for crime by making it more difficult for offenders to carry out crimes against particular targets.

Technique of neutralization   A justification used prior to a crime by an offender to render inoperative the social controls that would otherwise check law-violating behavior.

Transfer of property   The cost of crimes in which property is transferred from one person to another, such as from the victim of a theft to the thief.

Tutelage   Instruction or socialization in criminal motives and skills, including how to spot opportunities for theft, how to plan thefts, and how to carry out thefts.

Typology   A set of categories.

Vandalism   The willful or malicious destruction, injury, disfigurement, or defacement of property without consent of the owner.

Vengeance   A private and personal response to a wrong; it does not involve an established authority such as the state.

Victim compensation   See *Compensation*

Victim impact statement   A detailed written report based on an interview with a victim about the effects of a crime on him or her.

Victim precipitation   The situation that exists when a person who suffers eventual harm from a crime plays a direct role in causing the crime to be perpetrated.

Victim proneness   The tendency for certain people to be victimized repeatedly.

Victimization survey   A systematic effort to measure the experiences of the victims of crime by interviewing a cross section of a population.

Victimless crime   An offense that is consensual and lacks a complaining participant.

Violent gang   A fighting gang that emerges spontaneously to defend a territory against rival gangs, often resorting to violence over trivial provocations.

White-collar crime   An illegal act, punishable by a criminal sanction, that is committed in the course of a legitimate occupation or pursuit by a corporation or by an otherwise respectable individual of high social status.

Working personality   The police officer's distinctive approach to the situations and events that are encountered on the job.

XYY chromosome complement   A rare biological trait of some men that has been linked to a tendency to violate the law, or at least to be arrested for such violations.

BIBLIOGRAPHY

ABT ASSOCIATES, INC. *American Prisons and Jails*, Vol. 2: *Population Trends and Projections*. Washington, D.C.: U.S. Government Printing Office, 1980.

ADLER, FREDA. *Nations Not Obsessed with Crime*. Littleton, Colo.: Rothman, 1983.

——. *Sisters in Crime: The Rise of the New Female Criminal*. New York: McGraw-Hill, 1975.

——. "Socioeconomic Variables Influencing Jury Verdicts," *New York University Review of Law on Social Change* 3 (1973), 16–36.

ADLER, PATRICIA A. *Wheeling and Dealing: An Ethnography of an Upper-Level Drug Dealing and Smuggling Community*, 2nd ed. New York: Columbia University Press, 1993.

——, and PETER ADLER. "Shifts and Oscillations in Deviant Careers: The Case of Upper-Level Drug Dealers and Smugglers," *Social Problems* 31 (December 1983), 195–207.

AGETON, SUZANNE S., and DELBERT S. ELLIOTT. "The Effects of Legal Processing on Self-Concept." Boulder, Colo.: Institute of Behavioral Science, 1973.

AGNEW, ROBERT. "Adolescent Resources and Delinquency," *Criminology* 28 (November 1990), 535–566.

——. "Foundation for a General Strain Theory of Crime and Delinquency," *Criminology* 30 (February 1992), 47–87.

——. "The Interactive Effects of Peer Variables on Delinquency," *Criminology* 29 (February 1991a), 47–72.

——. "A Longitudinal Test of Social Control Theory and Delinquency," *Journal of Research in Crime and Delinquency* 28 (May 1991b), 126–156.

——. "Social Control Theory and Delinquency: A Longitudinal Test," *Criminology* 23 (February 1985), 47–61.

——. "The Techniques of Neutralization and Violence," *Criminology* 32 (November 1994), 555–580.

——. "Why Do They Do It? An Examination of the Intervening Mechanisms between 'Social Control' Variables and Delinquency," *Journal of Research in Crime and Delinquency* 30 (August 1993), 245–266.

——, and HELENE RASKIN WHITE. "An Empirical Test of General Strain Theory," *Criminology* 30 (November 1992), 475–499.

AICHHORN, AUGUST. *Wayward Youth*. New York: Viking, 1935, 1951.

AKERS, RONALD L. "Socioeconomic Status and Delinquent Behavior: A Re-Test," *Journal of Research in Crime and Delinquency* 1 (January 1964), 38–46.

——, et al. "Social Learning and Deviant Behavior: A Specific Test of a General Theory," *American Sociological Review* 44 (August 1979), 635–655.

AL-THAKEB, FAHAD. "Crime Trends in Kuwait," International Criminological Symposium, Stockholm, Sweden, 1978.

ALBINI, JOSEPH L. *The American Mafia: Genesis of a Legend*. New York: Appleton-Century-Crofts, 1971.

ALBRECHT, PETER-ALEXIS, CHRISTIAN PFEIFFER, and KLAUS ZAPKA. "Reactions of the Agencies of Social Control to Crimes of Young Foreigners in the Federal Republic of Germany," *International Summaries*. Washington, D.C.: U.S. Department of Justice, 1978.

ALDER, CHRISTINE. "An Exploration of Self-Reported Sexually Aggressive Behavior," *Crime and Delinquency* 31 (April 1985), 306–331.

ALLEN, FRANCIS A. "Criminal Justice, Legal Values and the Rehabilitative Ideal," in Stanley E. Grupp, ed., *Theories of Punishment*. Bloomington, Ind.: Indiana University Press, 1971, pp. 317–330.

ALLEN, VERNON L., and DAVID B. GREENBERGER. "An Aesthetic Theory of Vandalism," *Crime and Delinquency* 24 (July 1978), 309-321.

AMERICAN FRIENDS SERVICE COMMITTEE. *Struggle for Justice: A Report on Crime and Punishment in America*. New York: Hill and Wang, 1971.

AMIR, MENACHEM. *Patterns in Forcible Rape*. Chicago: University of Chicago Press, 1971.

ANDELMAN, DAVID A. "City Crime Wave Spreading to Suburbs," *New York Times*, January 30, 1972, p. 49.

ANDENAES, JOHANNES. *Punishment and Deterrence*. Ann Arbor: University of Michigan Press, 1974.

ANDREWS, D. A., et al. "Does Correctional Treatment Work? A Clinically Relevant and Psychologically Informed Meta-Analysis," *Criminology* 28 (August 1990a), 369–404.

——, et al. "A Human Science Approach or More Punishment and Pessimism: A Rejoinder to Lab and Whitehead," *Criminology* 28 (August 1990b), 419–429.

ANGEL, ARTHUR, et al. "Preventive Detention: An Empirical Analysis," *Harvard Civil Rights Civil Liberties Law Review* 6 (March 1971), 300–396.

ANGIER, NATALIE. "A Conference on Links of Violence to Heredity, a Calm after the Storm," *New York Times*, September 26, 1995, p. C8.

——. "Maybe It's Not a Gene Behind a Person's Thrill-Seeking Ways," *New York Times*, November 1, 1996a, p. A22.

——. "Variant Gene Tied to a Love of New Thrills," *New York Times*, January 2, 1996b, pp. A1, B11.

ANGLIN, M. DOUGLAS, and GEORGE SPECKART. "Narcotics Use and Crime: A Multisample, Multimethod Analysis," *Criminology* 26 (May 1988), 197–233.

APOSPORI, ELENI, and GEOFFREY ALPERT. "Research Note: The Role of Differential Experience with the Criminal Justice System in Changes in Perceptions of Severity of Legal Sanctions over Time," *Crime and Delinquency* 39 (April 1993), 184–194.

ARCHER, DANE, and ROSEMARY GARTNER. *Violence and Crime in Cross-National Perspective*. New Haven, Conn.: Yale University Press, 1984.

ARCHER, DANE, and ROSEMARY GARTNER. "Violent Acts and Violent Times: A Comparative Approach to Postwar Homicide Rates," *American Sociological Review* 41 (December 1976), 937–963.

ARCHER, DANE, ROSEMARY GARTNER, and MARC BEITTEL. "Homicide and the Death Penalty: A Cross-National Test of a Deterrence Hypothesis," *Journal of Criminal Law and Criminology* 74 (Fall 1983), 991–1013.

ARCHER, JOHN, ed. *Male Violence*. London: Routledge, 1994a.

——. "Violence between Men," in John Archer, ed., *Male Violence*. London: Routledge, 1994b.

ARMS, ROBERT L., GORDON W. RUSSELL, and MARK L. SANDILANDS. "Effects of Viewing Aggressive Sports on the Hostility of Spectators," *Social Psychology Quarterly* 42 (September 1979), 275–279.

ARMSTRONG, K. G. "The Retributivist Hits Back," in Stanley E. Grupp, ed., *Theories of Punishment*. Bloomington, Ind.: Indiana University Press, 1971, pp. 19–40.

ATTORNEY GENERAL'S COMMISSION ON PORNOGRAPHY. *Final Report*. Washington, D.C.: U.S. Department of Justice, 1986.

AULETTA, KEN. *The Underclass*. New York: Random House, 1982.

AUSTIN, JAMES, and JOHN IRWIN. *Who Goes to Prison?* San Francisco: National Council on Crime and Delinquency, 1990.

AUSTIN, ROY L. "Race, Father-Absence, and Female Delinquency," *Criminology* 15 (February 1978), 487–504.

——. "Women's Liberation and Increases in Minor, Major, and Occupational Offenses," *Criminology* 20 (November 1982), 407–430.

AUSTIN, WILLIAM. "Sex Differences in Bystander Intervention in a Theft," *Journal of Personality and Social Psychology* 37 (November 1979), 2110–2120.

AXENROTH, JOSEPH B. "Social Class and Delinquency in Cross-Cultural Perspective," *Journal of Research in Crime and Delinquency* 20 (July 1983), 164–182.

BACHMAN, RONET. *Crime Victimization in City, Suburban, and Rural Areas: A National Crime Victimization Survey Report*. Washington, D.C.: U.S. Department of Justice, June 1992.

——. *Elderly Victims*. Washington, D.C.: U.S. Department of Justice, October 1992.

BACON, MARGARET K., IRVIN L. CHILD, and HERBERT BARRY 3d. "A Cross-Cultural Study of Correlates of Crime," *Journal of Abnormal and Social Psychology* 66 (April 1963), 291–300.

BAILEY, WALTER C. "An Evaluation of 100 Studies of Correctional Outcome," *Journal of Criminal Law, Criminology and Police Science* 57 (June 1966), 153–160.

BAILEY, WILLIAM C. "Murder, Capital Punishment, and Television: Execution Publicity and Homicide Rates," *American Sociological Review* 55 (October 1990), 628–633.

——, and RUTH D. PETERSON. "Murder and Capital Punishment: A Monthly Time-Series Analysis of Execution Publicity," *American Sociological Review* 54 (October 1989), 722–743.

BAKER, WAYNE E., and ROBERT R. FAULKNER. "The Social Organization of Conspiracy: Illegal Networks in the Heavy Electrical Equipment Industry," *American Sociological Review* 58 (December 1993), 837–860.

BALDWIN, JOHN, and MICHAEL McCONVILLE. "Criminal Juries," in Norval Morris and Michael Tonry, eds., *Crime and Justice: An Annual Review of Research*, Vol. 2. Chicago: University of Chicago Press, 1980, pp. 269–319.

BALL-ROKEACH, SANDRA J. "Values and Violence: A Test of the Subculture of Violence Thesis," *American Sociological Review* 38 (December 1973), 736–749.

BARLOW, MELISSA HICKMAN, DAVID E. BARLOW, and THEODORE CHIRICOS. "Economic Conditions and Ideologies of Crime in the Media: A Content Analysis of Crime News," *Crime and Delinquency* 41 (January 1995), 3–19.

BARNETT, RANDY E. "Restitution: A New Paradigm of Criminal Justice," in Randy E. Barnett and John Hagel 3d, eds., *Assessing the Criminal: Restitution, Retribution, and the Legal Process*. Cambridge, Mass.: Ballinger, 1977, pp. 349–383.

BARR, ROBERT, and KEN PEASE. "Crime Placement, Displacement and Deflection," in Michael Tonry and Norval Morris, eds., *Crime and Justice: A Review of Research*, Vol. 12. Chicago: University of Chicago Press, 1990, pp. 277–318.

BASS, ALISON. "How Jocks View Women: Old Issue Gets New Scrutiny," *Boston Globe*, December 5, 1994, pp. 39, 52.

——. "Mental State No Sure Bet for Insanity Defense," *Boston Globe*, January 9, 1995, p. 4.

BASTIAN, LISA D. *Criminal Victimization 1993*. Washington, D.C.: U.S. Department of Justice, May 1995.

BAUMRIND, DIANA. "Parental Disciplinary Patterns and Social Competence in Children," *Youth and Society* 9 (1978), 239–276.

BAYLEY, DAVID H. "Police: History," in Sanford H. Kadish, ed., *Encyclopedia of Crime and Justice*, Vol. 3. New York: Free Press, 1983, pp. 1120–1125.

BECCARIA, CESARE. *On Crimes and Punishments*. Indianapolis, Ind.: Bobbs-Merrill, 1764, 1963.

BECK, ALLEN J., and BERNARD E. SHIPLEY. *Recidivism of Prisoners Released in 1983*. Washington, D.C.: U.S. Department of Justice, April 1989.

BECK, ALLEN, et al. *Survey of State Prison Inmates, 1991*. Washington, D.C.: U.S. Department of Justice, March 1993.

BECKER, HOWARD S. *Outsiders: Studies in the Sociology of Deviance*. New York: Free Press, 1973.

BEDAU, HUGO ADAM. "Concessions to Retribution in Punishment," in J. B. Cederblom and William L. Blizek, eds., *Justice and Punishment*. Cambridge, Mass.: Ballinger, 1977, pp. 51–73.

——. "Review of Walter Berns, *For Capital Punishment: Crime and the Morality of the Death Penalty*," *Ethics* 90 (April 1980), 457–466.

BEHN, NOEL. *Big Stick-Up at Brinks!* New York: G. P. Putnam's Sons, 1977.

BELL, DANIEL. "Crime as an American Way of Life: A Queer Ladder of Social Mobility," in *The End of Ideology: On the Exhaustion of Political Ideas in the Fifties*, rev. ed. New York: Free Press, 1962, pp. 127–150.

BELSON, WILLIAM A. *Juvenile Theft: The Causal Factors*. London: Harper & Row, 1975.

BENNET, JAMES. "New York Crime Statistics vs. Reality," *New York Times*, August 16, 1992, p. 39.

BENNETT, RICHARD R., and R. BRUCE WIEGAND. "Observations on Crime Reporting in a Developing Nation," *Criminology* 32 (February 1994), 135–148.

BENNETTS, LESLIE. "Do the Arts Inspire Violence in Real Life?" *New York Times*, April 26, 1981, pp. H1, H25.

BENSON, MICHAEL L. "Denying the Guilty Mind: Accounting for Involvement in a White-Collar Crime," *Criminology* 23 (November 1985), 583–607.

——, FRANCIS T. CULLEN, and WILLIAM J. MAAKESTAD. "Local Prosecutors and Corporate Crime," *Crime and Delinquency* 36 (July 1990), 356–372.

BERISTAIN, ANTONIO. "Capital Punishment and Catholicism," *International Journal of Criminology and Penology* 5 (November 1977), 321–335.

BERK, RICHARD A., and PHYLLIS J. NEWTON. "Does Arrest Really Deter Wife Battery? An Effort to Replicate the Findings of the Minneapolis Spouse Abuse Experiment," *American Sociological Review* 50 (April 1985), 253–262.

BERKOWITZ, LEONARD, and JACQUELINE MACAULAY. "The Contagion of Criminal Violence," *Sociometry* 34 (June 1971), 238–260.

BERNARD, THOMAS J. "Angry Aggression among the 'Truly Disadvantaged,'" *Criminology* 28 (February 1990), 73–96.

——, and R. RICHARD RITTI. "The Philadelphia Birth Cohort and Selective Incapacitation," *Journal of Research in Crime and Delinquency* 28 (February 1991), 33–54.

BERNS, WALTER C. *For Capital Punishment: Crime and the Morality of the Death Penalty*. New York: Basic Books, 1979.

BEST, JOEL. *Threatened Children: Rhetoric and Concern about Child-Victims*. Chicago: University of Chicago Press, 1990.

——, and DAVID F. LUCKENBILL. *Organizing Deviance*, 2nd ed. Englewood Cliffs, N.J.: Prentice-Hall, 1994.

BINDER, ARNOLD, and GILBERT GEIS. "*Ad Populum* Argumentation in Criminology: Juvenile Diversion as Rhetoric," *Crime and Delinquency* 30 (October 1984), 624–647.

BINDER, ARNOLD, and JAMES W. MEEKER. "Implications of the Failure to Replicate the Minneapolis Experimental Findings," *American Sociological Review* 58 (December 1993), 886–888.

BISHOP, DONNA M. "Legal and Extralegal Barriers to Delinquency: A Panel Analysis," *Criminology* 22 (August 1984), 403–419.

——, and CHARLES E. FRAZIER. "Gender Bias in Juvenile Justice Processing: Implications of the JJDP Act," *Journal of Criminal Law and Criminology* 82 (Winter 1992), 1162–1186.

——, and CHARLES E. FRAZIER. "The Influence of Race in Juvenile Justice Processing," *Journal of Research in Crime and Delinquency* 25 (August 1988), 242–263.

——, and CHARLES E. FRAZIER. "Race Effects in Juvenile Justice Decision-Making: Findings of a Statewide Analysis," *Journal of Criminal Law and Criminology* 86 (Winter 1996), 392–414.

BLACK, DONALD J. *The Behavior of Law*. New York: Academic Press, 1976.

——. "Crime as Social Control," *American Sociological Review* 48 (February 1983), 34–35.

——. *The Manners and Customs of the Police*. New York: Academic Press, 1980.

——. "Production of Crime Rates," *American Sociological Review* 35 (August 1970), 733–748.

——, and ALBERT J. REISS, JR. "Police Control of Juveniles," *American Sociological Review* 35 (February 1970), 63–78.

BLAU, JUDITH, and PETER BLAU. "The Cost of Inequality: Metropolitan Structure and Violent Crime," *American Sociological Review* 47 (February 1982), 114–129.

BLOCH, HERBERT A., and ARTHUR NIEDERHOFER. *The Gang: A Study in Adolescent Behavior*. New York: Philosophical Library, 1958.

BLOCK, ALAN A., and FRANK R. SCARPITTI. *Poisoning for Profit: The Mafia and Toxic Waste in America*. New York: Morrow, 1985.

BLOCK, CAROLYN REBECCA. *Homicide in Chicago*. Chicago: Center for Urban Policy, Loyola University of Chicago, 1987.

——. *Is Crime Seasonal?* Chicago: Illinois Criminal Justice Information Authority, 1984.

——, and ANTIGONE CHRISTAKOS. "Intimate Partner Homicide in Chicago over 29 Years," *Crime and Delinquency* 41 (October 1995), 496–526.

BLOCK, MICHAEL KENT, FREDERICK CARL NOLD, and JOSEPH GREGORY SIDAK. "The Deterrent Effect of Antitrust Enforcement," *Journal of Political Economy* 89 (June 1981), 429–445.

BLOCK, RICHARD. "Victim-Offender Dynamics in Violent Crime," *Journal of Criminal Law and Criminology* 72 (Summer 1981), 743–761.

——. *Violent Crime: Environment, Interaction, and Death*. Lexington, Mass.: D. C. Heath, 1977.

——, and CAROLYN R. BLOCK. "Decisions and Data: The Transformation of Robbery Incidents into Official Robbery Statistics," *Journal of Criminal Law and Criminology* 71 (Winter 1980), 622–636.

BLUM-WEST, STEPHEN ROBERT, and LARRY A. HEMBROFF. "The Effects of Intent, Motive, Fair Play, and Real Harm upon Judgments of Offense Seriousness." Paper presented at the Annual Meeting of the Southwestern Sociological Association, San Antonio, Tex., March 1982.

BLUMBERG, ABRAHAM S. "Crime and the Social Order," in Abraham S. Blumberg, ed., *Current Perspectives on Criminal Behavior: Original Essays on Criminology*. New York: Knopf, 1974, pp. 3–34.

——. *Criminal Justice: Issues & Ironies*, 2nd ed. New York: Viewpoints, 1979.

BLUMENTHAL, MONICA, et al. *Justifying Violence: Attitudes of American Men*. Ann Arbor, Mich.: Institute for Social Research, 1972.

BLUMSTEIN, ALFRED. "On the Racial Disproportionality of United States' Prison Populations," *Journal of Criminal Law and Criminology* 73 (Fall 1982), 1259–1281.

——. "Prisons: Population, Capacity, and Alternatives," in James Q. Wilson, ed., *Crime and Public Policy*. San Francisco: ICS Press, 1983, pp. 229–250.

——. "Violence by Young People: Why the Deadly Nexus?," *National Institute of Justice Journal*, August 1995, pp. 2–9.

——, and JACQUELINE COHEN. "Sentencing of Convicted Offenders: An Analysis of the Public's View," *Law and Society Review* 14 (Winter 1980), 223–261.

——, JACQUELINE COHEN, and DAVID P. FARRINGTON. "Criminal Career Research: Its Value for Criminology," *Criminology* 26 (February 1988), 1–35.

——, JACQUELINE COHEN, and WILLIAM GOODING. "The Influence of Capacity on Prison Population: A Critical Review of Some Recent Evidence," *Crime and Delinquency* 29 (January 1983), 1–51.

——, JACQUELINE COHEN, and DANIEL NAGIN. *Deterrence and Incapacitation: Estimating the Effects of Criminal Sanctions on Crime Rates*. Washington, D.C.: National Academy of Sciences, 1978.

——, DAVID P. FARRINGTON, and SOUMYO MOITRA. "Delinquency Careers: Innocents, Desisters, and Persisters," in Michael Tonry and Norval Morris, eds., *Crime and Justice: An Annual Review of Research*, Vol. 6. Chicago: University of Chicago Press, 1985, pp. 187–219.

——, and ELIZABETH GRADDY. "Prevalence and Recidivism in Index Arrests: A Feedback Model," *Law and Society Review* 16 (1981–82), 265–290.

——, et al. *Criminal Careers and "Career Criminals"*, Vols. 1 and 2. Washington, D.C.: National Academy Press, 1986.

BLUNDELL, WILLIAM E. "Equity Funding: 'I Did It for the Jollies,'" in Donald Moffitt, ed., *Swindled! Classic Business Frauds of the Seventies*. Princeton, N.J.: Dow Jones Books, 1976, pp. 42–89.

BOGGS, SARAH L. "Formal and Informal Crime Control: An Exploratory Study of Urban, Suburban, and Rural Orientations," *Sociological Quarterly* 12 (Summer 1971), 319–327.

BOHANNAN, PAUL, ed. *African Homicide and Suicide*. Princeton, N.J.: Princeton University Press, 1960.

BOISJOLY, RUSSELL, ELLEN FOSTER CURTIS, and EUGENE MELLICAN. "Roger Boisjoly and the *Challenger* Disaster: The Ethical Dimensions," *Journal of Business Ethics* 8 (1989), 217–230.

BOOTH, ALAN. "The Built Environment as a Crime Deterrent: A Reexamination of Defensible Space," *Criminology* 18 (February 1981), 557–570.

——, and D. WAYNE OSGOOD. "The Influence of Testosterone on Deviance in Adulthood: Assessing and Explaining the Relationship," *Criminology* 31 (February 1993), 93–117.

BORTNER, M. A. "Traditional Rhetoric, Organizational Realities: Remand of Juveniles to Adult Court," *Crime and Delinquency* 32 (January 1986), 53–73.

[*Boston Globe*]. "Ask the Globe," May 7, 1980, p. 86.

——. "Panel Says Criminals Launder Up to $150b," December 30, 1986, p. 10.

——. "Poll Finds Drop in Gun Owners' Support," May 21, 1995, p. 16.

——. "Race Held to Be Key in US Hate Crimes," November 5, 1996, p. A12.

BOWERS, WILLIAM J. "The Pervasiveness of Arbitrariness and Discrimination under Post-*Furman* Capital Statutes," *Journal of Criminal Law and Criminology* 74 (Winter 1983), 1067–1100.

——, and GLENN L. PIERCE. "Arbitrariness and Discrimination under Post-*Furman* Capital Statutes," *Crime and Delinquency* 26 (October 1980), 563–635.

——, with GLENN L. PIERCE and JOHN F. McDEVITT. *Legal Homicide: Death as Punishment in America, 1864–1982*. Boston: Northeastern University Press, 1984.

BOYDSTUN, JOHN E. *San Diego Field Interrogation: Final Report*. Washington, D.C.: Police Foundation, 1975.

BRADSHER, KEITH. "Gap in Wealth in U.S. Called Widest in West," *New York Times*, April 17, 1995, pp. A1, D4.

BRADY, JAMES P. "Arson, Fiscal Crisis, and Community Action: Dialectics of an Urban Crime and Popular Response," *Crime and Delinquency* 28 (April 1982), 247–270.

——. "Arson, Urban Economy, and Organized Crime: The Case of Boston," *Social Problems* 31 (October 1983), 1–27.

BRAITHWAITE, JOHN. *Crime, Shame, and Reintegration*. Cambridge, Eng.: Cambridge University Press, 1989.

——. *Inequality, Crime, and Public Policy*. London: Routledge and Kegan Paul, 1979.

——. "The Myth of Social Class and Criminality Reconsidered," *American Sociological Review* 46 (February 1981), 36–57.

——. "Reintegrative Shaming, Republicanism, and Policy," in Hugh D. Barlow, ed., *Crime and Public Policy: Putting Theory to Work*. Boulder, Colo.: Westview, 1995, pp. 191–205.

——. "White-Collar Crime, Competition, and Capitalism: Comment on Coleman," *American Journal of Sociology* 94 (November 1988), 627–632.

——, and GILBERT GEIS. "On Theory and Action for Corporate Crime Control," *Crime and Delinquency* 28 (April 1982), 292–314.

BRANTINGHAM, PAUL, and PATRICIA BRANTINGHAM. *Patterns in Crime*. New York: Macmillan, 1984.

BRATTON, WILLIAM J., and GEORGE L. KELLING. "Putting Police Officers Back on the Beat," *Boston Sunday Globe*, February 14, 1993, p. A2.

BREZINA, TIMOTHY. "Adapting to Strain: An Examination of Delinquent Coping Responses," *Criminology* 34 (February 1996), 39–60.

BRIDGES, JAMES H., JOHN T. GANDY, and JAMES D. JOR-GENSEN. "The Case for Creative Restitution in Corrections," *Federal Probation* 43 (September 1979), 28–35.

BRITT, CHESTER L. "Versatility," in Travis Hirschi and Michael R. Gottfredson, eds., *The Generality of Deviance*. New Brunswick, N.J.: Transaction Books, 1994, pp. 173–192.

BROWN, BAILEY. "Community Service as a Condition of Probation," *Federal Probation* 41 (December 1977), 7–9.

BROWN, JULIA S. "A Comparative Study of Deviations from Sexual Mores," *American Sociological Review* 17 (April 1952), 135–146.

BROWN, RICHARD MAXWELL. "The American Vigilante Tradition," in Hugh Davis Graham and Ted Robert Gurr, eds., *Violence in America: Historical and Comparative Perspectives*. Staff Report to the National Commission on the Causes and Prevention of Violence, Vol. 1. Washington, D.C.: U.S. Government Printing Office, 1969, pp. 121–169.

BUDER, LEONARD. "Sharp Drop in Bank Robberies Cited by New York City Police," *New York Times*, January 30, 1983, p. 22.

BUERGER, MICHAEL E. "A Tale of Two Targets: Limitations of Community Anticrime Actions," *Crime and Delinquency* 40 (July 1994), 411–436.

BUREAU OF JUSTICE STATISTICS. *Crime Prevention Measures*. Washington, D.C.: U.S. Department of Justice, March 1986.

——. *Criminal Victimization in the United States, 1990*. Washington, D.C.: U.S. Department of Justice, February 1992.

——. *The Economic Cost of Crime to Victims*. Washington, D.C.: U.S. Department of Justice, April 1984.

——. *Prisoners and Alcohol*. Washington, D.C.: U.S. Department of Justice, January 1983.

——. *Report to the Nation on Crime and Justice: The Data*. Washington, D.C.: U.S. Department of Justice, October 1983.

——. *Reporting Crimes to the Police*. Washington, D.C.: U.S. Department of Justice, December 1985.

——. *The Seasonality of Crime Victimization*. Washington, D.C.: U.S. Department of Justice, May 1988.

BURGESS, ANN WOLBERT, and LYNDA LYTLE HOLMSTROM. "Rape: Its Effect on Task Performance at Varying Stages in the Life Cycle," in Marcia J. Walker and Stanley L. Brodsky, eds., *Sexual Assault*. Lexington, Mass.: D. C. Heath, 1976, pp. 23–33.

BURGESS, ROBERT L., and RONALD L. AKERS. "A Differential Association-Reinforcement Theory of Criminal Behavior," *Social Problems* 14 (Fall 1966), 128–147.

BURNHAM, BONNIE. *The Art Crisis*. New York: St. Martin's Press, 1975.

BURNHAM, DAVID. "F.B.I. Says 12,000 Faulty Reports on Suspects Are Issued Each Day," *New York Times*, August 25, 1985, pp. 1, 30.

BURSIK, ROBERT J., JR., and HAROLD G. GRASMICK. "Economic Deprivation and Neighborhood Crime Rates, 1960–1980," *Law and Society Review* 27 (1993), 263–283.

BURSIK, ROBERT J., JR., and JIM WEBB. "Community Change and Patterns of Delinquency," *American Journal of Sociology* 88 (July 1982), 24–42.

BUTTERFIELD, FOX. "Are American Jails Becoming Shelters from the Storm?" *New York Times*, July 19, 1992, p. E4.

——. "How the Chinese Police Themselves," *New York Times Magazine*, April 18, 1982, pp. 32, 36–40, 50–56.

——. "States Revamping Laws on Juveniles as Felonies Soar," *New York Times*, May 12, 1996, pp. 1, 24.

BYNUM, TIM S., GARY W. CORDNER, and JACK R. GREENE. "Victim and Offense Characteristics: Impact on Police Investigative Decision-Making," *Criminology* 20 (November 1982), 301–318.

CALAVITA, KITTY, and HENRY N. PONTELL. "'Heads I Win, Tails You Lose': Deregulation, Crime, and Crisis in the Savings and Loan Industry," *Crime and Delinquency* 36 (July 1990), 309–341.

CALAVITA, KITTY, and HENRY N. PONTELL. "Savings and Loan Fraud as Organized Crime," *Criminology* 31 (November 1993), 519–548.

CAMERON, MARY OWEN. *The Booster and the Snitch: Department Store Shoplifting*. New York: Free Press, 1964.

CAMPBELL, ANNE. *Men, Women, and Aggression*. New York: Basic Books, 1993.

——, and STEVEN MUNCER. "Men and the Meaning of Violence," in John Archer, ed., *Male Violence*. London: Routledge, 1995, pp. 332–346.

CANTER, RACHELLE. "Family Correlates of Male and Female Delinquency," *Criminology* 20 (August 1982), 149–167.

CAPLAN, LINCOLN. "Annals of Law: The Insanity Defense," *New Yorker*, July 2, 1984, pp. 45–78.

CAPOTE, TRUMAN. *In Cold Blood: A True Account of a Multiple Murder and Its Consequences*. New York: Random House, 1965.

CARTER, BILL. "A New Report Becomes a Weapon in Debate on Censoring TV Violence," *New York Times*, February 7, 1996, pp. C1, C16.

CARTER, DANIEL L., ROBERT A. PRENTKY, and ANN W. BURGESS. "Victims: Lessons Learned for Responses to Sexual Violence," in Robert K. Ressler, Ann W. Burgess, and John E. Douglas, *Sexual Homicide: Patterns and Motives*. New York: Lexington Books, 1988, pp. 199–211.

CARTER, TIMOTHY, and DONALD CLELLAND. "A Neo-Marxian Critique, Formulation, and Test of Juvenile Dispositions as a Function of Social Class," *Social Problems* 27 (October 1979), 96–108.

CASPER, JONATHAN D. "Having Their Day in Court: Defendant Evaluations of the Fairness of Their Treatment," *Law and Society Review* 12 (Winter 1978), 237–249.

CASPI, AVSHALOM, et al. "Are Some People Crime-Prone? Replications of the Personality-Crime Relationship across Countries, Genders, Races, and Methods," *Criminology* 32 (May 1994), 163–195.

CERNKOVICH, STEPHEN A. "Conceptual and Empirical Ambiguity in Class-Oriented Theories of Crime and Delinquency," *International Journal of Criminology and Penology* 6 (May 1978a), 105–210.

——. "Evaluating Two Models of Delinquency Causation: Structural Theory and Control Theory," *Criminology* 16 (November 1978b), 335–352.

——. "Value Orientations and Delinquency Involvement," *Criminology* 15 (February 1978c), 443–458.

——, and PEGGY C. GIORDANO. "School Bonding, Race, and Delinquency," *Criminology* 30 (May 1992), 261–291.

——, PEGGY C. GIORDANO, and MEREDITH D. PUGH. "Chronic Offenders: The Missing Cases in Self-Report Delinquency Research," *Journal of Criminal Law and Criminology* 76 (Fall 1985), 705–732.

CHAIKEN, JAN M., and MARCIA R. CHAIKEN. "Drugs and Predatory Crime," in Michael Tonry and James Q. Wilson, eds., *Drugs and Crime*, Vol. 13 of *Crime and Justice: A Review of Research*. Chicago: University of Chicago Press, 1990, pp. 203–239.

CHAIKEN, MARCIA R., and JAN M. CHAIKEN. "Offender Types and Public Policy," *Crime and Delinquency* 30 (April 1984), 195–226.

CHAIKEN, MARCIA R., and JAN M. CHAIKEN. *Priority Prosecution of High-Rate Dangerous Offenders*. Washington, D.C.: U.S. Department of Justice, March 1991.

CHAMBLISS, WILLIAM J., ed. *Crime and the Legal Process*. New York: McGraw-Hill, 1969, pp. 360–378.

——. *On the Table: From Petty Crooks to Presidents*. Bloomington, Ind.: Indiana University Press, 1978.

CHAPMAN, WILLIAM. "Rising Delinquency in Japanese Junior High Schools," *Boston Globe*, April 5, 1983, p. 3.

CHEATWOOD, DERRAL. "Interactional Patterns in Multiple-Offender Homicides," *Justice Quarterly* 13 (March 1996), 107–128.

——. "Is There a Season for Homicide?" *Criminology* 26 (May 1988), 287–306.

CHEIN, ISIDOR, et al. *The Road to H: Narcotics, Delinquency, and Social Policy*. New York: Basic Books, 1964.

CHERMAK, STEVEN M. *Victims in the News: Crime and the American News Media*. Boulder, Colo.: Westview, 1995.

CHESNEY-LIND, MEDA. "Judicial Enforcement of the Female Sex Role: The Family Court and the Female Delinquent," *Issues in Criminology* 8 (Fall 1973), 51–69.

CHEVALIER, LOUIS. *Laboring Classes and Dangerous Classes in Paris during the First Half of the Nineteenth Century*. New York: Howard Fertig, 1973.

CHIBNALL, STEVE. *Law-and-Order News: An Analysis of Crime Reporting in the British Press*. London: Tavistock, 1977.

CHILTON, ROLAND J. "Delinquency Area Research in Baltimore, Detroit, and Indianapolis," *American Sociological Review* 29 (February 1964), 71–83.

——. "Persistent Problems of Crime Statistics," in Simon Dinitz and Walter C. Reckless, eds., *Critical Issues in the Study of Crime: A Book of Readings*. Boston: Little, Brown, 1968, pp. 89–95.

CHIRICOS, THEODORE G., and GORDON P. WALDO. "Socioeconomic Status and Criminal Sentencing: An Empirical Assessment of a Conflict Proposition," *American Sociological Review* 40 (December 1975), 753–772.

CHRISTIANSEN, KARL O. "A Preliminary Study of Criminality among Twins," in Sarnoff A. Mednick and Karl O. Christiansen, eds., *Biosocial Bases of Criminal Behavior*. New York: Gardner Press, 1977, pp. 80–108.

——. "Seriousness of Criminality and Concordance among Danish Twins," in Roger Hood, ed., *Crime, Criminology, and Public Policy: Essays in Honour of Sir Leon Radzinowicz*. New York: Free Press, 1974, pp. 63–77.

CHRISTIANSON, SCOTT. "Our Black Prisons," *Crime and Delinquency* 27 (July 1981), 364–375.

CLARK, JOHN P., and EDWARD H. HAUREK. "Age and Sex Roles of Adolescents and Their Involvement in Misconduct: A Reappraisal," *Sociology and Social Research* 50 (July 1966), 496–508.

CLARK, JOHN P., and LARRY L. TIFFT. "Polygraph and Interview Validation of Self-Reported Deviant Behavior," *American Sociological Review* 31 (August 1966), 516–523.

CLARKE, RONALD V., ed. *Situational Crime Prevention: Successful Case Studies*. Albany, N.Y.: Harrow and Heston, 1992.

——, and PATRICIA M. HARRIS. "Auto Theft and Its Prevention," in Michael Tonry, ed., *Crime and Justice: A Review of Research*, Vol. 16. Chicago: University of Chicago Press, 1992, pp. 1–54.

CLARKE, STEVENS H., and GARY G. KOCH. "The Influence of Income and Other Factors on Whether Criminal Defendants Go to Prison," *Law and Society Review* 11 (Fall 1976), 57–92.

——, and GARY G. KOCH. "Juvenile Court: Therapy or Crime Control, and Do Lawyers Make a Difference?" *Law and Society Review* 14 (Winter 1980), 263–308.

CLEAVER, ELDRIDGE. *Soul On Ice*. New York: Dell, 1968.

CLELLAND, DONALD, and TIMOTHY J. CARTER. "The New Myth of Class and Crime," *Criminology* 18 (November 1980), 319–336.

CLIFFORD, WILLIAM. *Crime Control in Japan*. Lexington, Mass.: D. C. Heath, 1976.

——. "Culture and Crime—In Global Perspective," *International Journal of Criminology and Penology* 6 (February 1978), 61–80.

CLINARD, MARSHALL B. *The Black Market: A Study of White-Collar Crime*. Montclair, N.J.: Patterson Smith, 1952, 1969.

——. *Cities with Little Crime: The Case of Switzerland*. Cambridge, Eng.: Cambridge University Press, 1978.

——. *Corporate Ethics and Crime: The Role of Middle Management*. Beverly Hills, Calif.: Sage Publications, 1983.

——. "The Process of Urbanization and Criminal Behavior," *American Journal of Sociology* 48 (September 1942), 202–213.

——. "Rural Criminal Offenders," *American Journal of Sociology* 50 (July 1944), 38–45.

——, and DANIEL J. ABBOTT. *Crime in Developing Countries: A Comparative Perspective*. New York: Wiley, 1973.

CLOWARD, RICHARD A., and LLOYD E. OHLIN. *Delinquency and Opportunity: A Theory of Delinquent Gangs*. New York: Free Press, 1960.

COCOZZA, JOSEPH J., and HENRY J. STEADMAN. "Prediction in Psychiatry: An Example of Misplaced Confidence in Experts," *Social Problems* 25 (February 1978), 265–276.

COHEN, ALBERT K. *Delinquent Boys: The Culture of the Gang.* New York: Free Press, 1955.

COHEN, JACQUELINE. *Incapacitating Criminals: Recent Research Findings.* Washington, D.C.: National Institute of Justice, U.S. Department of Justice, December 1983a.

———. "Incapacitation as a Strategy for Crime Control: Possibilities and Pitfalls," in Michael Tonry and Norval Morris, eds., *Crime and Justice: An Annual Review of Research,* Vol. 5. Chicago: University of Chicago Press, 1983b, pp. 1–84.

COHEN, LAWRENCE E. "Modeling Crime Trends: A Criminal Opportunity Perspective," *Journal of Research in Crime and Delinquency* 18 (January 1981), 138–162.

———, and DAVID CANTOR. "Residential Burglary in the United States: Life-Style and Demographic Factors Associated with the Probability of Victimization," *Journal of Research in Crime and Delinquency* 18 (January 1981), 113–127.

———, and MARCUS FELSON. "Social Change and Crime Rate Trends: A Routine Activity Approach," *American Sociological Review* 44 (August 1979), 588–608.

———, and JAMES R. KLUEGEL. "Determinants of Juvenile Court Disposition: Ascriptive and Achieved Factors in Two Metropolitan Courts," *American Sociological Review* 43 (April 1978), 162–176.

———, and KENNETH C. LAND. "Age Structure and Crime: Symmetry versus Asymmetry and the Projection of Crime Rates through the 1990s," *American Sociological Review* 52 (April 1987), 170–183.

COHEN, MARK A. "Some New Evidence on the Seriousness of Crime," *Criminology* 26 (May 1988), 343–353.

———, TED R. MILLER, and BRIAN WIERSEMA. *Victim Costs and Consequences: A New Look.* Washington, D.C.: U.S. Department of Justice, 1996.

COLEMAN, JAMES S., THOMAS HOFFER, and SALLY KILGORE. *High School Achievement: Public, Catholic, and Private Schools Compared.* New York: Basic Books, 1982.

COLEMAN, JAMES WILLIAM. *The Criminal Elite: The Sociology of White Collar Crime,* 3rd ed. New York: St. Martin's Press, 1994.

COLLINS, JAMES J., JR. *Alcohol Use and Criminal Behavior: An Executive Summary.* Washington, D.C.: U.S. Department of Justice, National Institute of Justice, 1981a.

———. "The Disposition of Adult Arrests: Legal and Extralegal Determinants of Outcomes," in Marvin E. Wolfgang, Terence P. Thornberry, and Robert M. Figlio, *From Boy to Man, from Delinquency to Crime.* Chicago: University of Chicago Press, 1987, pp. 68–75.

———, ed. *Drinking and Crime: Perspectives on the Relationships between Alcohol Consumption and Criminal Behavior.* New York: Guilford Press, 1981b.

———, ROBERT L. HUBBARD, and J. VALLEY RACHAL. "Expensive Drug Use and Illegal Income: A Test of Explanatory Hypotheses," *Criminology* 23 (November 1985), 743–764.

COLTON, KENT W., et al. *Computer Crime: Electronic Fund Transfer Systems and Crime.* Washington, D.C.: U.S. Government Printing Office, 1982.

CONKLIN, JOHN E. *Art Crime.* Westport, Conn.: Praeger, 1994.

———. *"Illegal but Not Criminal": Business Crime in America.* Englewood Cliffs, N.J.: Prentice-Hall, 1977.

———. *Robbery and the Criminal Justice System.* Philadelphia: Lippincott, 1972.

CONNELL, R. W. "Foreword," in James W. Messerschmidt, *Masculinities and Crime: Critique and Reconceptualization of Theory.* Lanham, Md.: Rowman and Littlefield, 1993, pp. vii–xv.

CONRAD, PETER, and JOSEPH W. SCHNEIDER. *Deviance and Medicalization: From Badness to Sickness.* St. Louis: C. V. Mosby, 1980.

COOK, PHILIP J. "The Correctional Carrot: Better Jobs for Parolees," *Policy Analysis* 1 (1975), 11–54.

———. "The Influence of Gun Availability on Violent Crime Patterns," in Michael Tonry and Norval Morris, eds., *Crime and Justice: An Annual Review of Research,* Vol. 4. Chicago: University of Chicago Press, 1983, pp. 49–89.

———. "Robbery Violence," *Journal of Criminal Law and Criminology* 78 (Summer 1987), 357–376.

———. "The Technology of Personal Violence," in Michael Tonry, ed., *Crime and Justice: A Review of Research,* Vol. 14. Chicago: University of Chicago Press, 1991, pp. 1–71.

CORDILIA, ANN. *The Making of an Inmate: Prison as a Way of Life.* Cambridge, Mass.: Schenkman, 1983.

COUNT-van MANEN, GLORIA. "A Deviant Case of Deviance: Singapore," *Law and Society Review* 5 (February 1971), 389–406.

CRESSEY, DONALD R. *Criminal Organization.* New York: Harper & Row, 1972.

———. *Other People's Money: A Study in the Social Psychology of Embezzlement.* Belmont, Calif.: Wadsworth, 1953, 1971.

———. *Theft of the Nation: The Structure and Operations of Organized Crime in America.* New York: Harper & Row, 1969.

CRIMINAL DIVISION, U.S. DEPARTMENT OF JUSTICE. Cited in *Congressional Record—Senate* 114 (July 18, 1968), 21986.

CROMWELL, PAUL F., JAMES N. OLSON, and D'AUNN WESTER AVARY. *Breaking and Entering: An Ethnographic Analysis of Burglary.* Newbury Park, Calif.: Sage, 1991.

CRONIN, ROBERTA C., et al. *Evaluation of the Habitual Serious and Violent Juvenile Offender Program.* Washington, D.C.: Office of Juvenile Justice and Delinquency Prevention, U.S. Department of Justice, January 1988.

CRONIN, THOMAS E., TANIA Z. CRONIN, and MICHAEL E. MILAKOVICH. *U.S. v. Crime in the Streets.* Bloomington, Ind.: Indiana University Press, 1981.

CRUTCHFIELD, ROBERT D., MICHAEL R. GEERKEN, and WALTER R. GOVE. "Crime Rate and Social Integration: The Impact of Metropolitan Mobility," *Criminology* 20 (November 1982), 467–478.

CSIKSZENTMIHALYI, MIHALY, and REED LARSON. "Intrinsic Rewards in School Crime," *Crime and Delinquency* 24 (July 1978), 322–335.

CULLEN, FRANCIS T. "Social Support as an Organizing Concept for Criminology: Presidential Address to the Academy of Criminal Justice Sciences," *Justice Quarterly* 11 (December 1994), 527–559.

——, and KAREN E. GILBERT. *Reaffirming Rehabilitation.* Cincinnati, Ohio: Anderson, 1982.

CULLEN, FRANCIS T., WILLIAM J. MAAKESTAD, and GRAY CAVENDER. *Corporate Crime under Attack: The Ford Pinto Case and Beyond.* Cincinnati, Ohio: Anderson, 1987.

CULLEN, FRANCIS T., WILLIAM J. MAAKESTAD, and GRAY CAVENDER. "The Ford Pinto Case and Beyond: Corporate Crime, Moral Boundaries, and the Criminal Sanction," in Ellen Hochstedler, ed., *Corporations as Criminals.* Beverly Hills, Calif.: Sage Publications, 1984, pp. 107–130.

CURRAN, DEBRA A. "Judicial Discretion and Defendant's Sex," *Criminology* 21 (February 1983), 41–58.

CURRIE, ELLIOTT. *Confronting Crime: An American Challenge.* New York: Pantheon, 1985.

CURTIS, LYNN A. *Criminal Violence: National Patterns and Behavior.* Lexington, Mass.: D. C. Heath, 1974.

——. *Violence, Race and Culture.* Lexington, Mass.: D. C. Heath, 1975.

CUSHMAN, PAUL, JR. "Relationship between Narcotic Addiction and Crime," *Federal Probation* 38 (September 1974), 38–43.

DALEY, SUZANNE. "As Crime Soars, South African Whites Leave," *New York Times*, December 12, 1995, pp. A1, A14.

DALGAARD, ODD STEFFEN, and EINAR KRINGLEN. "A Norwegian Twin Study of Criminality," *British Journal of Criminology* 16 (June 1976), 213–232.

DALY, KATHLEEN. "Gender and Varieties of White-Collar Crime," *Criminology* 27 (November 1989), 769–794.

——. *Gender, Crime, and Punishment.* New Haven, Conn.: Yale University Press, 1994.

——, and MEDA CHESNEY-LIND. "Feminism and Criminology," *Justice Quarterly* 5 (December 1988), 497–538.

DANNEFER, DALE, and RUSSELL K. SCHUTT. "Race and Juvenile Justice Processing in Court and Police Agencies," *American Journal of Sociology* 87 (March 1982), 1113–1132.

DANZIGER, SHELDON, and DAVID WHEELER. "The Economics of Crime: Punishment or Income Redistribution," *Review of Social Economy* 33 (October 1975), 113–131.

DARLEY, JOHN M., and C. DANIEL BATSON. "'From Jerusalem to Jericho': A Study of Situational and Dispositional Variables in Helping Behavior," *Journal of Personality and Social Psychology* 27 (July 1973), 100–108.

DATESMAN, SUSAN K., and MIKEL AICKIN. "Offense Specialization and Escalation among Status Offenders," *Journal of Criminal Law and Criminology* 75 (Winter 1984), 1246–1275.

DAVIES, CHRISTIE. "Crime, Bureaucracy, and Equality," *Policy Review* 23 (Winter 1983), 89–105.

DAVIS, JOHN A. "Justification for No Obligation: Views of Black Males toward Crime and the Criminal Law," *Issues in Criminology* 9 (Fall 1974), 69–87.

DAWSON, JOHN M., and PATRICK A. LANGAN. *Murder in Families.* Washington, D.C.: U.S. Department of Justice, July 1994.

DECKER, SCOTT H. "Collective and Normative Features of Gang Violence," *Justice Quarterly* 13 (June 1996), 243–264.

——, and BARBARA SALERT. "Predicting the Career Criminal: An Empirical Test of the Greenwood Scale," *Journal of Criminal Law and Criminology* 77 (Spring 1986), 215–236.

——, RICHARD WRIGHT, and ROBERT LOGIE. "Perceptual Deterrence among Active Residential Burglars: A Research Note," *Criminology* 31 (February 1993), 135–147.

DeFLEUR, LOIS B. "Biasing Influences on Drug Arrest Records: Implications for Deviance Research," *American Sociological Review* 40 (February 1975), 88–103.

DeFRANCO, EDWARD J. *Anatomy of a Scam: A Case Study of a Planned Bankruptcy by Organized Crime.* Washington, D.C.: U.S. Government Printing Office, 1973.

DEMING, ROMINE R. "Correctional Restitution: A Strategy for Correctional Conflict Management," *Federal Probation* 40 (September 1976), 27–32.

DENNO, DEBORAH W. *Biology and Violence: From Birth to Adulthood.* Cambridge, Eng.: Cambridge University Press, 1990.

——. "Gender, Crime, and the Criminal Law Defenses," *Journal of Criminal Law and Criminology* 85 (Summer 1994), 80–180.

DENTLER, ROBERT A., and LAWRENCE J. MONROE. "Social Correlates of Early Adolescent Theft," *American Sociological Review* 26 (October 1961), 733–743.

DERSHOWITZ, ALAN M. *The Abuse Excuse and Other Copouts, Sob Stories, and Evasions of Responsibility.* Boston: Little, Brown, 1994.

DESROCHES, FREDERICK J. *Force & Fear: Robbery in Canada.* Toronto: Nelson Canada, 1995.

DIETZ, MARY LORENZ. *Killing for Profit: The Social Organization of Felony Homicide.* Chicago: Nelson-Hall, 1983.

DINITZ, SIMON, FRANK R. SCARPITTI, and WALTER C. RECKLESS. "Delinquency Vulnerability: A Cross Group and Longitudinal Analysis," *American Sociological Review* 27 (August 1962), 515–517.

DIXON, JO, and ALAN J. LIZOTTE. "Gun Ownership and the 'Southern Subculture of Violence,'" *American Journal of Sociology* 93 (September 1987), 383–405.

DOBINSON, IAN. "Pinning a Tail on the Dragon: The Chinese and the International Heroin Trade," *Crime and Delinquency* 39 (July 1993), 373–384.

DOERNER, WILLIAM G. "The Index of Southernness Revisited: The Influence of Wherefrom upon Whodunnit," *Criminology* 16 (May 1978), 47–56.

DOMBRINK, JOHN. "Organized Crime: Gangsters and Godfathers," in Joseph E. Scott and Travis Hirschi, eds., *Controversial Issues in Crime and Justice.* Newbury Park, Calif.: Sage Publications, 1988, pp. 54–75.

DONNERSTEIN, EDWARD, DANIEL LINZ, and STEVEN PENROD. *The Question of Pornography: Research Findings and Policy Implications.* New York: Free Press, 1987.

DONNERSTEIN, EDWARD, RONALD G. SLABY, and LEONARD D. ERON. "The Mass Media and Youth Aggression," in Leonard D. Eron, Jacquelyn H. Gentry, and Peggy Schlegel, eds., *Reason to Hope: A Psychosocial Perspective on Violence & Youth.* Washington, D.C.: American Psychological Association, 1994, pp. 219–250.

DONZIGER, STEVEN R., ed. *The Real War on Crime: The Report of the National Criminal Justice Commission.* New York: Harper Perennial, 1996.

DUNFORD, FRANKLYN W., DAVID HUIZINGA, and DELBERT S. ELLIOTT. "The Role of Arrest in Domestic Assault: The Omaha Police Experiment," *Criminology* 28 (May 1990), 183–206.

DURKHEIM, EMILE. *The Division of Labor in Society,* trans. by George Simpson. Glencoe, Ill.: Free Press, 1895, 1933.

———. *The Rules of the Sociological Method,* trans. by Sarah A. Solovay and John H. Mueller; ed. by George E. G. Catlin. New York: Free Press, 1895, 1938.

DUSTER, TROY. "Crime, Youth Unemployment, and the Black Underclass," *Crime and Delinquency* 33 (April 1987), 300–316.

ECK, JOHN. "Solving Crimes," *NIJ Reports,* March 1984, pp. 4–8.

ECKHOLM, ERIK. "A Basic Issue: Whose Hands Should Guns Be Kept Out Of?" *New York Times,* April 3, 1992, pp. A1, A15.

EDELHERTZ, HERBERT. *The Nature, Impact and Prosecution of White-Collar Crime.* Washington, D.C.: U.S. Government Printing Office, 1970.

EDWARDS, ANNE. "Sex and Area Variations in Delinquency Rates in an English City," *British Journal of Criminology* 13 (April 1973), 121–137.

EGAN, JOHN W. "The Internal Revenue Service and Corporate Slush Funds: Some Fifth Amendment Problems," *Journal of Criminal Law and Criminology* 69 (Spring 1978), 59–74.

EHRLICH, ISAAC. "The Deterrent Effect of Capital Punishment: A Question of Life and Death," *American Economic Review* (June 1975), 397–417.

ELIAS, ROBERT. "Alienating the Victim: Compensation and Victim Attitudes," *Journal of Social Issues* 40 (1984), 103–116.

———. *Victims of the System: Crime Victims and Compensation in American Politics and Criminal Justice.* New Brunswick, N.J.: Transaction Books, 1983.

ELIFSON, KIRK W., DAVID M. PETERSEN, and C. KIRK HADAWAY. "Religiosity and Delinquency: A Contextual Analysis," *Criminology* 21 (November 1983), 505–527.

ELLIOTT, DELBERT S. "Serious Violent Offenders: Onset, Developmental Course, and Termination—The American Society of Criminology 1993 Presidential Address," *Criminology* 32 (February 1994), 1–21.

———, and SUZANNE S. AGETON. "Reconciling Race and Class Differences in Self-Reported and Official Estimates of Delinquency," *American Sociological Review* 45 (February 1980), 95–110.

ELLIOTT, DELBERT S., and DAVID HUIZINGA. "Social Class and Delinquent Behavior in a National Youth Panel: 1976–1980," *Criminology* 21 (May 1983), 149–177.

ELLIOTT, DELBERT S., DAVID HUIZINGA, and SUZANNE S. AGETON. *Explaining Delinquency and Drug Use.* Beverly Hills, Calif.: Sage Publications, 1985.

ELLIOTT, DELBERT S., and HARWIN L. VOSS. *Delinquency and Dropout.* Lexington, Mass.: D. C. Heath, 1974.

ELLIS, LEE. "Genetics and Criminal Behavior: Evidence through the End of the 1970s," *Criminology* 20 (May 1982), 43–66.

———. "Monoamine Oxidase and Criminality: Identifying an Apparent Biological Marker for Antisocial Behavior," *Journal of Research in Crime and Delinquency* 28 (May 1991), 227–251.

———. "Neurohormonal Bases of Varying Tendencies to Learn Delinquent and Criminal Behavior," in E. K. Morris and C. J. Braukman, eds., *Behavioral Approaches to Crime and Delinquency.* New York: Plenum, 1987, pp. 499–518.

———. "Religiosity and Criminality: Evidence and Explanations of Complex Relationships," *Sociological Perspectives* 28 (October 1985), 501–520.

ELLISON, CHRISTOPHER G., and PATRICIA L. McCALL. "Region and Violent Attitudes Reconsidered: Comment on Dixon and Lizotte," *American Journal of Sociology* 95 (July 1989), 174–178.

ELLSWORTH, PHOEBE C., and LEE ROSS. "Public Opinion and Capital Punishment: A Close Examination of the Views of Abolitionists and Retentionists," *Crime and Delinquency* 29 (January 1983), 116–169.

ELMHORN, KERSTIN. "Study in Self-Reported Delinquency among Schoolchildren in Stockholm," in Karl O. Christiansen, ed., *Scandinavian Studies in Criminology,* Vol. 1. London: Tavistock, 1965, pp. 117–146.

EMPEY, LAMAR T., and STEVEN G. LUBECK, with RONALD L. LaPORTE. *Explaining Delinquency: Construction, Test, and Reformulation of a Sociological Theory.* Lexington, Mass.: D. C. Heath, 1971.

ENNIS, PHILIP H. *Criminal Victimization in the United States: A Report of a National Survey.* Field Surveys II of the President's Commission on Law Enforcement and Administration of Justice. Washington, D.C.: U.S. Government Printing Office, 1967.

EREZ, EDNA, and PAMELA TONTODONATO. "The Effect of Victim Participation in Sentencing on Sentence Outcome," *Criminology* 28 (August 1990), 451–474.

ERICKSON, MAYNARD L., and JACK P. GIBBS. "On the Perceived Severity of Legal Penalties," *Journal of Criminal Law and Criminology* 70 (Spring 1979), 102–116.

ERICKSON, MAYNARD L., and GARY F. JENSEN. "'Delinquency Is Still Group Behavior!': Toward Revitalizing the Group Premise in the Sociology of Deviance," *Journal of Criminal Law and Criminology* 68 (June 1977), 262–273.

ERICKSON, PATRICIA G., and MICHAEL S. GOODSTADT. "Legal Stigma for Marijuana Possession," *Criminology* 17 (August 1979), 208–216.

ERIKSON, KAI T. *Wayward Puritans: A Study in the Sociology of Deviance.* New York: Wiley, 1966.

ERLANGER, HOWARD S. "The Empirical Status of the Subculture of Violence Thesis," *Social Problems* 22 (December 1974), 280–292.

——. "Is There a 'Subculture of Violence' in the South?" *Journal of Criminal Law and Criminology* 66 (December 1975), 483–490.

ERMANN, M. DAVID, and RICHARD J. LUNDMAN. *Corporate Deviance.* New York: Holt, Rinehart and Winston, 1982.

EVANS, SANDRA S., and JOSEPH E. SCOTT. "The Seriousness of Crime Cross-Culturally: The Impact of Religiosity," *Criminology* 22 (February 1984), 39–59.

EVANS, T. DAVID, et al. "Religion and Crime Reexamined: The Impact of Religion, Secular Controls, and Social Ecology on Adult Criminality," *Criminology* 33 (May 1995), 195–224.

EYSENCK, HANS. *Crime and Personality,* 3rd ed. London: Routledge and Kegan Paul, 1977.

——, and GISLI H. GUDJONSSON. *The Causes and Cures of Criminality.* New York: Plenum, 1989.

FAGAN, JEFFREY, and MARTIN GUGGENHEIM. "Preventive Detention and the Judicial Prediction of Dangerousness for Juveniles: A Natural Experiment," *Journal of Criminal Law and Criminology* 86 (Winter 1996), 415–448.

FAGAN, JEFFREY, and SANDRA WEXLER. "Family Origins of Violent Delinquents," *Criminology* 25 (August 1987), 643–669.

FAISON, SETH. "Copyright Pirates Prosper in China Despite Promises," *New York Times,* February 20, 1996, pp. A1, A6.

——. "Crackdown Fails to Stem Smuggling of Chinese to U.S.," *New York Times,* August 23, 1993a, pp. A1, B2.

——. "Hunt Goes on for Smugglers in Fatal Trip," *New York Times,* July 18, 1993b, pp. 27, 30.

FARBER, M. A. "Big Push on Crime Merely Pushes It Elsewhere, Many Officers Feel," *New York Times,* June 1, 1982, pp. Bl, B6.

FARHI, PAUL. "Researchers Link Psychological Harm to Violence on TV," *Boston Globe,* February 7, 1996, p. 3.

FARNSWORTH, CLYDE H. "Imitation Goods Costly to the U.S.," *New York Times,* February 5, 1984, p. 4.

FARR, KATHRYN ANN. "Revitalizing the Drug Decriminalization Debate," *Crime and Delinquency* 36 (April 1990), 223–237.

FARRELL, RONALD A., and JAMES F. NELSON. "A Sequential Analysis of Delinquency," *International Journal of Criminology and Penology* 6 (August 1978), 255–268.

FARRELL, RONALD A., and VICTORIA LYNN SWIGERT. "Prior Offense Record as a Self-Fulfilling Prophecy," *Law and Society Review* 12 (Spring 1978), 437–453.

FARRINGTON, DAVID P. "Self-Reports of Deviant Behavior: Predictive and Stable?" *Journal of Criminal Law and Criminology* 64 (March 1973), 99–110.

——, LLOYD E. OHLIN, and JAMES Q. WILSON. *Understanding and Controlling Crime: Toward a New Research Strategy.* New York: Springer-Verlag, 1986.

——, HOWARD N. SNYDER, and TERRENCE A. FINNEGAN. "Specialization in Juvenile Court Careers," *Criminology* 26 (August 1988), 461–485.

FEDERAL BUREAU OF INVESTIGATION. *Crime in the United States, 1995: Uniform Crime Reports.* Washington, D.C.: U.S. Government Printing Office, 1996.

FEENEY, FLOYD, and ADRIANNE WEIR, eds. *The Prevention and Control of Robbery.* Davis: Center on Administration of Criminal Justice, University of California at Davis, 1973.

FELD, BARRY C. "Criminalizing the American Juvenile Court," in Michael Tonry, ed., *Crime and Justice: A Review of Research,* Vol. 17. Chicago: University of Chicago Press, 1993, pp. 197–280.

——. "Delinquent Careers and Criminal Policy: Just Deserts and the Waiver Decision," *Criminology* 21 (May 1983), 195–212.

FELSON, MARCUS. "Routine Activities and Crime Prevention in the Developing Metropolis," *Criminology* 25 (November 1987), 911–931.

FELSON, RICHARD B., and HENRY J. STEADMAN. "Situational Factors in Disputes Leading to Criminal Violence," *Criminology* 21 (February 1983), 59–74.

FERRACUTI, FRANCO, SIMON DINITZ, and ESPERANZA ACOSTA De BRENES. *Delinquents and Nondelinquents in the Puerto Rican Slum Culture.* Columbus: Ohio State University Press, 1975.

FERRARO, KENNETH F. *Fear of Crime: Interpreting Victimization Risk.* Albany: State University of New York Press, 1995.

FIGUEIRA-McDONOUGH, JOSEFINA. "Discrimination or Sex Differences? Criteria for Evaluating the Juvenile Justice System's Handling of Minor Offenses," *Crime and Delinquency* 33 (July 1987), 403–424.

——, and ELAINE SELO. "A Reformulation of the 'Equal Opportunity' Explanation of Female Delinquency," *Crime and Delinquency* 26 (July 1980), 333–343.

FINCKENAUER, JAMES O. *Scared Straight! and the Panacea Phenomenon.* Englewood Cliffs, N.J.: Prentice-Hall, 1982.

FINKELHOR, DAVID, GERALD HOTALING, and ANDREA SEDLAK. *Missing, Abducted, Runaway, and Throwaway Children in America: First Report— Numbers and Characteristics, National Incidence Statistics.* Washington, D.C.: U.S. Department of Justice, May 1990.

FISHBEIN, DIANA H. "Biological Perspectives in Criminology," *Criminology* 28 (February 1990), 27–72.

——. "The Biology of Antisocial Behavior," in John E. Conklin, ed., *New Perspectives in Criminology.* Boston: Allyn and Bacon, 1996, pp. 26–38.

——, and ROBERT W. THATCHER. "New Diagnostic Methods in Criminology: Assessing Organic Sources of Behavioral Disorders," *Journal of Research in Crime and Delinquency* 23 (August 1986), 240–267.

FISHER, BONNIE, and JACK L. NASAR. "Fear of Crime in Relation to Three Exterior Site Features: Prospect, Refuge, and Escape," *Environment and Behavior* 24 (1992), 35–65.

FISHER, JOSEPH C. "Homicide in Detroit: The Role of Firearms," *Criminology* 14 (November 1976), 387–400.

FISHMAN, SIMA, KATHLEEN RODENRYS, and GEORGE SCHINK. "The Income of Organized Crime," in President's Commission on Organized Crime, *The Impact: Organized Crime Today.* Washington, D.C.: U.S. Government Printing Office, April 1986, pp. 413–494.

FISSE, BRENT, and JOHN BRAITHWAITE. *The Impact of Publicity on Corporate Offenders.* Albany: State University of New York Press, 1983.

FOREMAN, JUDY. "How to Tell If You Are 'Muggable,'" *Boston Globe,* January 20, 1981, pp. 20, 21.

——. "Violence Called Top Killer of Youth," *Boston Globe,* June 26, 1987, pp. 1, 84.

FORST, BRIAN E., and JOLENE C. HERNON. *The Criminal Justice Response To Victim Harm.* Washington, D.C.: U.S. Department of Justice, June 1985.

FOSTER, JACK D., SIMON DINITZ, and WALTER C. RECK-LESS. "Perceptions of Stigma Following Public Intervention for Delinquent Behavior," *Social Problems* 20 (Fall 1972), 202–209.

FOUCAULT, MICHEL. *Discipline and Punish,* trans. by Alan Sheridan. New York: Pantheon, 1978.

FOWLER, FLOYD J., JR., and THOMAS W. MANGIONE. *Neighborhood Crime, Fear and Social Control: A Second Look at the Hartford Program.* Washington, D.C.: National Institute of Justice, U.S. Department of Justice, 1982.

FOWLER, GLENN. "More 'Career Criminals' Convicted in State Effort," *New York Times,* January 8, 1981, p. B7.

FOWLES, RICHARD, and MARY MERVA. "Wage Inequality and Criminal Activity: An Extreme Bounds Analysis for the United States, 1975–1990," *Criminology* 34 (May 1996), 163–182.

FOX, JAMES ALAN. "A Disturbing Trend in Youth Crime," *Boston Globe,* June 1, 1995, p. 19.

——, ed. *Methods in Quantitative Criminology.* New York: Academic Press, 1981a.

——. *Models in Quantitative Criminology.* New York: Academic Press, 1981b.

——, and JACK LEVIN. "Termination Can Be Murder," *Boston Globe,* May 2, 1993, p. 71.

——, and MICHAEL L. RADELET. "Persistent Flaws in Econometric Studies of the Deterrent Effect of the Death Penalty," *Loyola of Los Angeles Law Review* 23 (November 1989), 29–44.

FRANKLIN, ALICE. "Criminality in the Work Place: A Comparison of Male and Female Offenders," in Freda Adler and Rita James Simon, eds., *The Criminology of Deviant Women.* Boston: Houghton Mifflin, 1979, pp. 167–170.

FRANKLIN, JAMES L. "The Churches and the Death Penalty," *Boston Globe,* March 14, 1982, p. 30.

FREEDMAN, LAWRENCE ZELIC. "No Response to the Cry for Help," in James M. Ratcliffe, ed., *The Good Samaritan and the Law.* Garden City, N.Y.: Doubleday, 1966, pp. 171–182.

FREEMAN, RICHARD B. "Crime and Unemployment," in James Q. Wilson, ed., *Crime and Public Policy.* San Francisco: ICS Press, 1983, pp. 89–106.

FREUD, SIGMUND. *Civilization and Its Discontents,* trans. by James Strachey. New York: Norton, 1930, 1962.

——. *New Introductory Lectures on Psycho-analysis,* ed. and trans. by James Strachey. New York: Norton, 1933.

FYFE, JAMES J. "Observations on Police Deadly Force," *Crime and Delinquency* 27 (July 1981), 376–389.

GAES, GERALD G. "The Effects of Overcrowding in Prison," in Michael Tonry and Norval Morris, eds., *Crime and Justice: An Annual Review of Research,* Vol. 6. Chicago: University of Chicago Press, 1985, pp. 95–146.

GAGNON, JOHN H. "Sexual Conduct and Crime," in Daniel Glaser, ed., *Handbook of Criminology.* Chicago: Rand McNally, 1974, pp. 233–272.

GALLUP, GEORGE. "Safety Fears Swelled Nixon Vote," *Boston Globe,* November 11, 1972, p. 7.

GARDINER, MURIEL. *The Deadly Innocents: Portraits of Children Who Kill.* New Haven, Conn.: Yale University Press, 1985.

GARFINKEL, HAROLD. "Conditions of Successful Degradation Ceremonies," *American Journal of Sociology* 61 (March 1956), 420–424.

GARNER, JOEL H., and CHRISTY A. VISHER. "Policy Experiments Come of Age," *NIJ Reports,* September/October 1988, pp. 2–8.

GAROFALO, JAMES. "Reassessing the Lifestyle Model of Criminal Victimization," in Michael Gottfredson and Travis Hirschi, eds., *Positive Criminology.* Newbury Park, Calif.: Sage Publications, 1987, pp. 23–42.

——, and MAUREEN McLEOD. "The Structure and Operations of Neighborhood Watch Programs in the United States," *Crime and Delinquency* 35 (July 1989), 326–344.

GASTIL, RAYMOND D. "Homicide and a Regional Culture of Violence," *American Sociological Review* 36 (June 1971), 412–427.

GEBHARD, PAUL H., et al. *Sex Offenders.* New York: Harper & Row, 1965.

GEIS, GILBERT. "Avocational Crime," in Daniel Glaser, ed., *Handbook of Criminology.* Chicago: Rand McNally, 1974, pp. 273–298.

——. "The Crime Intervenor: Samaritan or Superman?" Lecture presented at University of California, Irvine, February 5, 1981.

——. "White Collar Crime: The Heavy Electrical Equipment Antitrust Cases of 1961," in Marshall B. Clinard and Richard Quinney, eds., *Criminal Behavior Systems: A Typology.* New York: Holt, Rinehart and Winston, 1967, pp. 139–151.

GELFAND, DONNA M., et al. "Who Reports Shoplifters?" *Journal of Personality and Social Psychology* 25 (February 1973), 276–283.

GELLER, WILLIAM, and KEVIN J. KARALES. "Shootings of and by Chicago Police: Uncommon Crises. Part I: Shootings by Chicago Police," *Journal of Criminal Law and Criminology* 72 (Winter 1981), 1813–1866.

GELLES, RICHARD, and MURRAY A. STRAUS. *Intimate Violence.* New York: Simon and Schuster, 1988.

GENDREAU, PAUL, and BOB ROSS. "Effective Correctional Treatment: Bibliotherapy for Cynics," *Crime and Delinquency* 25 (October 1979), 463–489.

GEORGES-ABEYIE, DANIEL E., and KEITH D. HARRIES, eds. *Crime: A Spatial Perspective*. New York: Columbia University Press, 1980.

GERBNER, GEORGE, and LARRY GROSS. "Living with Television: The Violence Profile," *Journal of Communication* 26 (Spring 1976), 173–199.

GIBBONS, DON C. "Crime and Punishment: A Study of Social Attitudes," *Social Forces* 47 (June 1969), 391–397.

——. *Society, Crime, and Criminal Behavior*, 6th ed. Englewood Cliffs, N.J.: Prentice-Hall, 1992.

GIBBS, JACK P. *Crime, Punishment, and Deterrence*. New York: Elsevier, 1975.

GIBBS, JOHN J., and PEGGY L. SHELLY. "Life in the Fast Lane: A Retrospective View by Commercial Thieves," *Journal of Research in Crime and Delinquency* 19 (July 1982), 299–330.

GILLESPIE, ROBERT W. *Economic Factors in Crime and Delinquency: A Critical Review of the Empirical Evidence*. Washington, D.C.: National Institute of Law Enforcement and Criminal Justice, Department of Justice, 1975.

GILLIARD, DARRELL K., and ALLEN J. BECK. *Prison and Jail Inmates, 1995*. Washington, D.C.: U.S. Department of Justice, August 1996.

GILLIS, A. R., and JOHN HAGAN. "Density, Delinquency, and Design: Formal and Informal Control and the Built Environment," *Criminology* 19 (February 1982), 514–529.

GINSBURG, B. E., and B. F. CARTER. *Premenstrual Syndrome: Ethical and Legal Implications in a Biomedical Perspective*. New York: Bantam, 1987.

GIORDANO, PEGGY C. "Girls, Guys and Gangs: The Changing Social Context of Female Delinquency," *Journal of Criminal Law and Criminology* 69 (Spring 1978), 126–132.

——, STEPHEN A. CERNKOVICH, and M. D. PUGH. "Friendships and Delinquency," *American Journal of Sociology* 91 (March 1986), 1170–1202.

GLASER, DANIEL. "The Classification of Offenses and Offenders," in Daniel Glaser, ed., *Handbook of Criminology*. Chicago: Rand McNally, 1974, pp. 45–83.

——. *Crime in Our Changing Society*. New York: Holt, Rinehart and Winston, 1978.

——. "Criminal Theories and Behavioral Images," *American Journal of Sociology* 61 (March 1956), 433–444.

——. "A Review of Crime-Causation Theory and Its Application," in Norval Morris and Michael Tonry, eds., *Crime and Justice: An Annual Review of Research*, Vol. 1. Chicago: University of Chicago Press, 1979, pp. 203–237.

GLUECK, SHELDON, and ELEANOR GLUECK. *Physique and Delinquency*. New York: Harper & Brothers, 1956.

GLUECK, SHELDON, and ELEANOR GLUECK. *Unraveling Juvenile Delinquency*. Cambridge, Mass.: Harvard University Press, 1950.

GOLD, MARTIN. *Delinquent Behavior in an American City*. Belmont, Calif.: Brooks/Cole, 1970.

GOLDEN, DANIEL. "It's a Crime," *Boston Globe*, September 11, 1995, pp. 39, 52.

GOLDKAMP, JOHN S. "Questioning the Practice of Pretrial Detention: Some Empirical Evidence from Philadelphia," *Journal of Criminal Law and Criminology* 74 (Winter 1983), 1556–1588.

GOLDSTEIN, JEFFREY H. *Aggression and Crimes of Violence*, 2nd ed. New York: Oxford University Press, 1986.

——, ed. *Sports Violence*. New York: Springer-Verlag, 1983.

GOLDSTEIN, MICHAEL J., and HAROLD S. KANT. *Pornography and Sexual Deviance*. Berkeley: University of California Press, 1973.

GOLEMAN, DANIEL. "Brutal Sports and Brutal Fans," *New York Times*, August 13, 1985, pp. Cl, C3.

GONZALEZ, DAVID. "Sliwa Admits Faking Crimes for Publicity," *New York Times*, November 25, 1992, pp. B1, B2.

GORDON, ALAN R., and NORVAL MORRIS. "Presidential Commissions and the Law Enforcement Assistance Administration," in Lynn A. Curtis, ed., *American Violence and Public Policy: An Update of the National Commission on the Causes and Prevention of Violence*. New Haven, Conn.: Yale University Press, 1985, pp. 117–132.

GORDON, DAVID M. "Capitalism, Class, and Crime in America," *Crime and Delinquency* 19 (April 1973), 163–186.

GORDON, MARGARET T., and STEPHANIE RIGER. *The Female Fear*. New York: Free Press, 1989.

GORING, CHARLES. *The English Convict: A Statistical Study*. London: His Majesty's Stationery Office, 1913.

GOTTFREDSON, MICHAEL R. "Treatment Destruction Techniques," *Journal of Research in Crime and Delinquency* 16 (January 1979), 39–54.

——, and TRAVIS HIRSCHI. *A General Theory of Crime*. Stanford, Calif.: Stanford University Press, 1990.

——, and TRAVIS HIRSCHI. "Science, Public Policy, and the Career Paradigm," *Criminology* 26 (February 1988), 37–55.

GOVE, WALTER R., MICHAEL HUGHES, and MICHAEL GEERKEN. "Are Uniform Crime Reports a Valid Indicator of the Index Crimes? An Affirmative Answer with Minor Qualifications," *Criminology* 23 (August 1985), 451–501.

GRAHAM, MARY G. "Controlling Drug Abuse and Crime: A Research Update," *NIJ Reports*, March/April 1987, pp. 2–7.

GRASMICK, HAROLD G., and DONALD E. GREEN. "Legal Punishment, Social Disapproval and Internalization as Inhibitors of Illegal Behavior," *Journal of Criminal Law and Criminology* 71 (Fall 1980), 325–335.

GRASMICK, HAROLD G., et al. "Testing the Core Empirical Implications of Gottfredson and Hirschi's General Theory of Crime," *Journal of Research in Crime and Delinquency* 30 (February 1993), 5–29.

GREEN, DONALD E. "Measures of Illegal Behavior in Individual-Level Deterrence Research," *Journal of Research in Crime and Delinquency* 26 (August 1989a), 253–275.

——. "Past Behavior as a Measure of Actual Future Behavior: An Unresolved Issue in Perceptual Deterrence Research," *Journal of Criminal Law and Criminology* 80 (Fall 1989b), 781–804.

GREEN, EDWARD. "Race, Social Status, and Criminal Arrest," *American Sociological Review* 35 (June 1970), 476–490.

GREEN, GARY S. "Citizen Gun Ownership and Criminal Deterrence: Theory, Research, and Policy," *Criminology* 25 (February 1987), 63–81.

GREEN, PENNY A., and H. DAVID ALLEN. "Severity of Societal Response to Crime: A Synthesis of Models," *Law and Society Review* 16 (1981–82), 181–205.

GREENBERG, DAVID F. "Comparing Criminal Career Models," *Criminology* 30 (February 1992), 141–147.

——. "The Correctional Effects of Corrections: A Survey of Evaluations," in David F. Greenberg, ed., *Corrections and Punishment*. Beverly Hills, Calif.: Sage Publications, 1977a, pp. 111–148.

——. "Delinquency and the Age Structure of Society," *Contemporary Crises* 1 (April 1977b), 189–223.

——. "Methodological Issues in Survey Research on the Inhibition of Crime," *Journal of Criminal Law and Criminology* 72 (Fall 1981), 1094–1101.

——. "Modeling Criminal Careers," *Criminology* 29 (February 1991), 17–46.

——, and DREW HUMPHRIES. "Economic Crisis and the Justice Model: A Skeptical View," *Crime and Delinquency* 28 (October 1982), 601–609.

——, and RONALD C. KESSLER. "The Effects of Arrests on Crime: A Multivariate Panel Analysis," *Social Problems* 60 (March 1982), 771–790.

——, RONALD C. KESSLER, and COLIN LOFTIN. "The Effects of Police Employment on Crime," *Criminology* 21 (August 1983), 375–394.

——, RONALD C. KESSLER, and COLIN LOFTIN. "Social Inequality and Crime Control," *Journal of Criminal Law and Criminology* 76 (Fall 1985), 684–704.

GREENBERG, MARK S., and R. BARRY RUBACK. *After the Crime: Victim Decision Making*. New York: Plenum, 1992.

GREENBERG, STEPHANIE W. "Alcohol and Crime: A Methodological Critique of the Literature," in James J. Collins, Jr., ed., *Drinking and Crime: Perspectives on the Relationships between Alcohol Consumption and Criminal Behavior*. New York: Guilford Press, 1981, pp. 71–109.

——, and FREDA ADLER. "Crime and Addiction: An Empirical Analysis of the Literature, 1920–1973," *Contemporary Drug Problems* 3 (Summer 1974), 221–269.

GREENHOUSE, STEVEN. "Poles Find Crime Replacing Police State," *New York Times*, March 4, 1990, p. 20.

GREENWOOD, PETER W. "Differences in Criminal Behavior and Court Responses among Juvenile and Young Adult Defendants," in Michael Tonry and Norval Morris, eds., *Crime and Justice: An Annual Review of Research*, Vol. 7. Chicago: University of Chicago Press, 1986, pp. 151–187.

——. "Selective Incapacitation: A Method of Using Our Prisons More Effectively," *NIJ Reports*, January 1984, pp. 4–7.

——, et al. *Diverting Children from a Life of Crime: Measuring Costs and Benefits*. Santa Monica, Calif.: Rand, 1996.

——, et al. *Three Strikes and You're Out: Estimated Benefits and Costs of California's New Mandatory-Sentencing Law*. Santa Monica, Calif.: Rand, 1994.

——, with ALLAN ABRAHAMSE. *Selective Incapacitation*. Santa Monica, Calif.: Rand, 1982.

GREER, WILLIAM R. "Most Burglars Look for Easy Ways to Slip Unseen into Empty Homes and Head Straight for the Bedroom," *New York Times*, July 10, 1986, pp. C1, C6.

GRILLO, E. G. *Delincuencia en Caracas*. Caracas, Venezuela: Universidad del Zulia, 1970.

GRINNELL, RICHARD M., JR., and CHERYL A. CHAMBERS. "Broken Homes and Middle-Class Delinquency: A Comparison," *Criminology* 17 (November 1979), 395–400.

GROSS, SAMUEL R., and ROBERT MAURO. *Racial Disparities in Capital Sentencing*. Boston: Northeastern University Press, 1988.

GROTH, A. NICHOLAS, ROBERT E. LONGO, and J. BRADLEY McFADIN. "Undetected Recidivism among Rapists and Child Molesters," *Crime and Delinquency* 28 (July 1982), 450–458.

GURR, TED ROBERT. "Historical Trends in Violent Crime: A Critical Review of the Evidence," in Michael Tonry and Norval Morris, eds., *Crime and Justice: An Annual Review of Research*, Vol. 3. Chicago: University of Chicago Press, 1981, pp. 295–353.

——. *Why Men Rebel*. Princeton, N.J.: Princeton University Press, 1970.

HACKNEY, SHELDON. "Southern Violence," in Hugh Davis Graham and Ted Robert Gurr, eds., *Violence in America: Historical and Comparative Perspectives*. Staff Report to the National Commission on the Causes and Prevention of Violence, Vol. 2. Washington, D.C.: U.S. Government Printing Office, 1969, pp. 387–404.

HAFNER, KATIE, and JOHN MARKOFF. *Cyberpunk: Outlaws and Hackers on the Computer Frontier*. New York: Simon and Schuster, 1991.

HAGAN, JOHN. "The Social Embeddedness of Crime and Unemployment," *Criminology* 31 (November 1993), pp. 465–491.

——. *Structural Criminology*. New Brunswick, N.J.: Rutgers University Press, 1989.

——, and ALBERTO PALLONI. "The Social Reproduction of a Criminal Class in Working-Class London, circa 1950–1980," *American Journal of Sociology* 96 (September 1990), 265–299.

HAGEDORN, JOHN M. "Homeboys, Dope Fiends, Legits, and New Jacks," *Criminology* 32 (May 1994), 197–219.

HAKIM, SIMON, and GEORGE F. RENGERT, eds. *Crime Spillover*. Beverly Hills, Calif.: Sage Publications, 1981.

HAMILTON, V. LEE, and LAURENCE ROTKIN. "Interpreting the Eighth Amendment: Perceived Seriousness of Crime and Severity of Punishment," in Hugo Adam Bedau and Chester M. Pierce, eds., *Capital Punishment in the United States*. New York: AMS Press, 1976, pp. 502–524.

HAMILTON, V. LEE, and STEVE RYTINA. "Social Consensus on Norms of Justice: Should the Punishment Fit the Crime?" *American Journal of Sociology* 85 (March 1980), 1117–1144.

HAMILTON, V. LEE, and JOSEPH SANDERS. *Everyday Justice: Responsibility and the Individual in Japan and the United States.* New Haven, Conn.: Yale University Press, 1992.

HAMILTON, V. LEE, and JOSEPH SANDERS, et al. "Punishment and the Individual in the United States and Japan," *Law and Society Review* 22 (1988), 301–328.

HAMLIN, JOHN E. "The Misplaced Role of Rational Choice in Neutralization Theory," *Criminology* 26 (August 1988), 425–438.

HAMPARIAN, DONNA MARTIN, et al. *The Young Criminal Years of the Violent Few.* Washington, D.C.: U.S. Department of Justice, June 1985.

HANEY, CRAIG, CURTIS BANKS, and PHILIP ZIMBARDO. "Interpersonal Dynamics in a Simulated Prison," *International Journal of Criminology and Penology* 1 (February 1973), 69–97.

HANSON, BILL, et al. *Life with Heroin: Voices from the Inner City.* Lexington, Mass.: D. C. Heath, 1985.

HARE, ROBERT D., and JEFFREY W. JUTAI. "Psychopathy and Cerebral Asymmetry in Semantic Processing," *Personality and Individual Differences* 9 (1988), 329–337.

HARLOW, CAROLINE WOLF. *Injuries from Crime.* Washington, D.C.: U.S. Department of Justice, May 1989.

HARRING, SIDNEY L. "Policing a Class Society: The Expansion of the Urban Police in the Late Nineteenth and Early Twentieth Centuries," in David F. Greenberg, ed., *Crime & Capitalism.* Palo Alto, Calif.: Mayfield, 1981, pp. 292–313.

——. *Policing a Class Society: The Experience of American Cities, 1865–1915.* New Brunswick, N.J.: Rutgers University Press, 1983.

HARRISON, LANA, and JOSEPH GFROERER. "The Intersection of Drug Use and Criminal Behavior: Results from the National Household Survey on Drug Abuse," *Crime and Delinquency* 38 (October 1992), 422–443.

HARTJEN, CLAYTON A., and DON C. GIBBONS. "An Empirical Investigation of a Criminal Typology," *Sociology and Social Research* 54 (October 1969), 56–62.

HATHAWAY, STARKE R., and ELIO D. MONACHESI. *Analyzing and Predicting Juvenile Delinquency with the MMPI.* Minneapolis: University of Minnesota Press, 1953.

HAWKINS, GORDON. "God and the Mafia," *The Public Interest* No. 14 (Winter 1969), 24–51.

HEINZ, ANNE M., and WAYNE A. KERSTETTER. "Pretrial Settlement Conference: Evaluation of a Reform in Plea Bargaining," in Burt Galaway and Joe Hudson, eds., *Perspectives on Crime Victims.* St. Louis: C. V. Mosby, 1981, pp. 266–276.

HEMBROFF, LARRY A. "The Seriousness of Acts and Social Contexts: A Test of Black's Theory of the Behavior of Law," *American Journal of Sociology* 93 (September 1987), 322–347.

HENNESSY, MICHAEL, PAMELA J. RICHARDS, and RICHARD A. BERK. "Broken Homes and Middle Class Delinquency," *Criminology* 15 (February 1978), 505–528.

HENRY, ANDREW F., and JAMES F. SHORT, JR. *Suicide and Homicide: Some Economic, Sociological and Psychological Aspects of Aggression.* New York: Free Press, 1954.

HEPBURN, JOHN R. "The Impact of Police Intervention upon Juvenile Delinquents," *Criminology* 15 (August 1977), 225–262.

HERBERS, JOHN. "Fear of Crime Leads in Survey of Reasons to Leave Big Cities," *New York Times,* May 16, 1981, p. 8.

HERBERT, BOB. "In America: Deadly Data on Handguns," *New York Times,* March 2, 1994, p. A15.

HERSHEY, ROBERT D., JR. "I.R.S. Fraud Found to Net Big Refunds," *New York Times,* October 6, 1994, p. A21.

HICKEY, ERIC W. *Serial Murderers and Their Victims,* 2nd ed. Belmont, Calif.: Wadsworth, 1997.

HILLS, STUART L. *Demystifying Social Deviance.* New York: McGraw-Hill, 1980.

HILTS, PHILIP J. "Agency Rejects Study Linking Genes to Crime," *New York Times,* September 5, 1992, p. 8.

HINDELANG, MICHAEL J. "Causes of Delinquency: A Partial Replication and Extension," *Social Problems* 20 (Spring 1973), 471–487.

——. "Class and Crime," in Sanford H. Kadish, ed., *Encyclopedia of Crime and Justice,* Vol. 1. New York: Free Press, 1983, pp. 175–181.

——. *Criminal Victimization in Eight American Cities: A Descriptive Analysis of Common Theft and Assault.* Cambridge, Mass.: Ballinger, 1976.

——. "Race and Involvement in Common Law Personal Crimes," *American Sociological Review* 43 (February 1978), 93–109.

——, MICHAEL R. GOTTFREDSON, and JAMES GAROFALO. *Victims of Personal Crime: An Empirical Foundation for a Theory of Personal Victimization.* Cambridge, Mass.: Ballinger, 1978.

——, TRAVIS HIRSCHI, and JOSEPH G. WEIS. "Correlates of Delinquency: The Illusion of Discrepancy between Self-Report and Official Measures," *American Sociological Review* 44 (December 1979), 995–1014.

HIRSCHEL, J. DAVID, and IRA W. HUTCHISON 3d. "Female Spouse Abuse and the Police Response: The Charlotte, North Carolina Experiment," *Journal of Criminal Law and Criminology* 83 (Spring 1992), 73–119.

HIRSCHI, TRAVIS. *Causes of Delinquency.* Berkeley: University of California Press, 1969.

——. "Crime and the Family," in James Q. Wilson, ed., *Crime and Public Policy.* San Francisco: ICS Press, 1983, pp. 53–68.

——, and MICHAEL J. HINDELANG. "Intelligence and Delinquency: A Revisionist Review," *American Sociological Review* 42 (August 1977), 571–587.

HOFFMAN-BUSTAMANTE, DALE. "The Nature of Female Criminality," *Issues in Criminology* 8 (Fall 1973), 117–136.

HOHLER, BOB. "N.H. Neighbors React to a Rape and Witnesses Who Did Not Act," *Boston Globe,* August 16, 1987, p. 44.

HOLLINGER, RICHARD C., and JOHN P. CLARK. *Theft by Employees.* Lexington, Mass.: D. C. Heath, 1983.

HOLMES, STEVEN A. "Income Disparity between Poorest and Richest Rises," *New York Times,* June 20, 1996, pp. A1, A18.

HOLZMAN, HAROLD R. "Learning Disabilities and Juvenile Delinquency: Biological and Sociological Theories," in C. R. Jeffery, ed., *Biology and Crime.* Beverly Hills, Calif.: Sage Publications, 1979, pp. 77–86.

HOOTON, EARNEST A. *The American Criminal: An Anthropological Study.* Cambridge, Mass.: Harvard University Press, 1939.

HOPKINS, ANDREW. "Controlling Corporate Deviance," *Criminology* 18 (August 1980), 198–214.

HORNEY, JULIE D., WAYNE OSGOOD, and INEKE HAEN MARSHALL. "Criminal Careers in the Short-Term: Intra-Individual Variability in Crime and Its Relation to Local Life Circumstances," *American Sociological Review* 60 (October 1995), 655–673.

HORNING, DONALD N. M. "Blue-Collar Theft: Conceptions of Property, Attitudes toward Pilfering, and Work Group Norms in a Modern Industrial Plant," in Erwin O. Smigel and H. Laurence Ross, eds., *Crimes against Bureaucracy.* New York: Van Nostrand Reinhold, 1970, pp. 46–64.

HOROWITZ, RUTH. *Honor and the American Dream: Culture and Social Identity in a Chicano Community.* New Brunswick, N.J.: Rutgers University Press, 1983.

——, and GARY SCHWARTZ. "Honor, Normative Ambiguity and Gang Violence," *American Sociological Review* 39 (April 1974), 238–251.

HOWARD, JAN, and PHILLIP BORGES. "Needle-Sharing in the Haight: Some Social and Psychological Functions," in David E. Smith and George R. Gay, eds., *"It's So Good, Don't Even Try It Once" : Heroin in Perspective.* Englewood Cliffs, N.J.: Prentice-Hall, 1972, pp. 125–136.

HUNT, LEON GIBSON, and CARL D. CHAMBERS. *The Heroin Epidemics: A Study of Heroin Use in the U.S., 1965–75.* New York: Spectrum, 1976.

HYMAN, HERBERT A. "The Value Systems of Different Classes," in Reinhard Bendix and Seymour Martin Lipset, eds., *Class, Status and Power: Social Stratification in Comparative Perspective,* 2nd ed. New York: Free Press, 1966, pp. 488–499.

IANNI, FRANCIS A. J., with ELIZABETH REUSS-IANNI. *A Family Business: Kinship and Social Control in Organized Crime.* New York: Russell Sage Foundation, 1972.

IGNATIEFF, MICHAEL. *A Just Measure of Pain: The Penitentiary in the Industrial Revolution, 1750–1850.* New York: Pantheon, 1978.

INCIARDI, JAMES A. *Careers in Crime.* Chicago: Rand McNally, 1975.

——. "Heroin Use and Street Crime," *Crime and Delinquency* 25 (July 1979), 335–346.

——, RUTH HOROWITZ, and ANNE E. POTTIEGER. *Street Kids, Street Drugs, Street Crime: An Examination of Drug Use and Serious Delinquency in Miami.* Belmont, Calif.: Wadsworth, 1993.

INNES, CHRISTOPHER A. *Drug Use and Crime.* Washington, D.C.: U.S. Department of Justice, July 1988.

IRELAND, TIMOTHY, and CATHY SPATZ WIDOM. "Childhood Victimization and Risk for Alcohol and Drug Arrests," *International Journal of the Addictions* 29 (1994), 235–274.

IRWIN, JOHN. "Adaptation to Being Corrected: Corrections from the Convict's Perspective," in Daniel Glaser, ed., *Handbook of Criminology.* Chicago: Rand McNally, 1974, pp. 971–993.

——. *The Felon.* Englewood Cliffs, N.J.: Prentice-Hall, 1970.

JACKSON, BRUCE. *A Thief's Primer.* New York: Macmillan, 1969.

JACKSON, PAMELA IRVING, and LEO CARROLL. "Race and the War on Crime: The Sociopolitical Determinants of Municipal Police Expenditures in 90 Non-Southern U.S. Cities," *American Sociological Review* 46 (June 1981), 290–305.

JACOBS, JANE. *The Death and Life of Great American Cities.* N.Y.: Vintage, 1961.

JAMES, JENNIFER, and WILLIAM THORNTON. "Women's Liberation and the Female Delinquent," *Journal of Research in Crime and Delinquency* 17 (July 1980), 230–244.

JANKOWSKI, MARTIN SANCHEZ. *Islands in the Street: Gangs and American Urban Society.* Berkeley: University of California Press, 1991.

JARVIS, G. K., and H. B. MESSINGER. "Social and Economic Correlates of Juvenile Delinquency Rates: A Canadian Case," *Canadian Journal of Criminology and Corrections* 16 (1974), 361–372.

JASPAN, NORMAN. *Mind Your Own Business.* Englewood Cliffs, N.J.: Prentice-Hall, 1974.

JEFFERY, C. RAY. "Biology and Crime: The New Neo-Lombrosians," in C. R. Jeffery, ed., *Biology and Crime.* Beverly Hills, Calif.: Sage Publications, 1979, p. 7–18.

——. "The Genetics and Crime Conference Revisited," *The Criminologist,* March/April 1996, pp. 1, 3.

JENKINS, PHILIP. *Using Murder: The Social Construction of Serial Homicide.* New York: Aldine de Gruyter, 1994.

JENNINGS, JONATHAN S. "Trademark Counterfeiting: An Unpunished Crime," *Journal of Criminal Law and Criminology* 80 (Fall 1989), 805–841.

JENSEN, GARY F. "Inner Containment and Delinquency," *Journal of Criminal Law and Criminology* 64 (December 1973), 464–470.

——. "Power-Control vs. Social-Control Theories of Common Delinquency: A Comparative Analysis," in Freda Adler and William S. Laufer, eds., *New Directions in Criminological Theory: Advances in Criminological Theory,* Vol. 4. New Brunswick, N.J.: Transaction, 1993, pp. 363–380.

——, and DAVID BROWNFIELD. "Gender, Lifestyles and Victimization: Beyond Routine Activities," *Violence and Victims* 1 (1986), 85–99.

——, and KEVIN THOMPSON. "What's Class Got to Do with It? Further Examination of Power-Control Theory," *American Journal of Sociology* 95 (January 1990), 1009–1023.

JENSEN, MICHAEL C. "Business Students Disagree on Bribes," *New York Times,* March 27, 1976, p. 37.

JESILOW, PAUL, HENRY N. PONTELL, and GILBERT GEIS. *Prescription for Profit: How Doctors Defraud Medicaid.* Berkeley: University of California Press, 1993.

JOE, DELBERT, and NORMAN ROBINSON. "Chinatown's Immigrant Gangs: The New Young Warrior Class," *Criminology* 18 (November 1980), 337–345.

JOHNSON, DAVID R., and LAURIE K. SCHEUBLE. "Gender Bias in the Disposition of Juvenile Court Referrals: The Effects of Time and Location," *Criminology* 29 (November 1991), 677–699.

JOHNSON, ELMER H., and ISRAEL L. BARAK-GLANTZ. "Introduction," in Israel L. Barak-Glantz and Elmer H. Johnson, eds., *Comparative Criminology.* Beverly Hills, Calif.: Sage Publications, 1983, pp. 7–17.

JOHNSON, KIRK ALAN, and PATRICIA L. WASIELEWSKI. "A Commentary on Victimization Research and the Importance of Meaning Structures," *Criminology* 20 (August 1982), 205–222.

JOHNSON, RICHARD E. "Social Class and Delinquent Behavior: A New Test," *Criminology* 18 (May 1980), 86–93.

JOINT COMMITTEE ON NEW YORK DRUG LAW EVALUATiON. *The Nation's Toughest Drug Law: Evaluating the New York Experience.* Washington, D.C.: U.S. Government Printing Office, 1978.

JOYCE, FAY S. "Some Victims' Families Find Relief in Executions," *New York Times,* January 19, 1984, p. A18.

JUDSON, HORACE FREELAND. *Heroin Addiction in Britain: What Americans Can Learn from the English Experience.* New York: Harcourt Brace Jovanovich, 1974.

JUTAI, JEFREY W., ROBERT D. HARE, and JOHN F. CON-NOLLY. "Psychopathy and Event-Related Brain Potentials (ERPS) Associated with Attention to Speech Stimuli," *Personality and Individual Differences* 8 (1987), 175–184.

KALVEN, HARRY, JR., and HANS ZEISEL. *The American Jury.* Boston: Little, Brown, 1966.

KANDEL, DENISE B., and ISRAEL ADLER. "Socialization into Marijuana Use among French Adolescents: A Cross-Cultural Comparison with the United States," *Journal of Health and Social Behavior* 23 (December 1982), 295–309.

KAPLAN, FRED. "Patrols Say They Keep NYC Streets Safe," *Boston Globe,* June 10, 1996, p. 3.

KAPLAN, HOWARD B., STEVEN S. MARTIN, and ROBERT J. JOHNSON. "Self-Rejection and the Explanation of Deviance: Specification of the Structure among Latent Constructs," *American Journal of Sociology* (September 1986), 384–411.

KAPPELER, VICTOR E., MARK BLUMBERG, and GARY W. POTTER. *The Mythology of Crime and Criminal Justice,* 2nd ed. Prospect Heights, Ill.: Waveland Press, 1996.

KASSEBAUM, GENE, DAVID A. WARD, and DANIEL M. WILNER. *Prison Treatment and Parole Survival: An Empirical Assessment.* New York: Wiley, 1971.

KATZ, JACK. *Seductions of Crime: Moral and Sensual Attractions in Doing Evil.* New York: Basic Books, 1988.

KEIL, THOMAS J., and GENNARO F. VITO. "Race, Homicide Severity, and Application of the Death Penalty: A Consideration of the Barnett Scale," *Criminology* 27 (August 1989), 511–535.

KELLERMANN, ARTHUR L., et al. "Gun Ownership as a Risk Factor for Homicide in the Home," *New England Journal of Medicine* 329 (October 7, 1993), 1084–1091.

KELLEY, CLARENCE M. *Crime in the United States, 1975: Uniform Crime Reports.* Washington, D.C.: U.S. Government Printing Office, 1976.

KELLEY, THOMAS M. "Status Offenders Can Be Different: A Comparative Study of Delinquent Careers," *Crime and Delinquency* 29 (July 1983), 365–380.

KELLING, GEORGE L., et al. *The Kansas City Preventive Patrol Experiment.* Washington, D.C.: Police Foundation, 1974.

KEMPF, KIMBERLY L. "Crime Severity and Criminal Career Progression," *Journal of Criminal Law and Criminology* 79 (Summer 1988), 524–540.

——. "Offense Specialization: Does It Exist?" in Derek B. Cornish and Ronald V. Clarke, eds., *The Reasoning Criminal: Rational Choice Perspectives on Offending.* New York: Springer-Verlag, 1986, pp. 186–201.

——. "Specialization and the Criminal Career," *Criminology* 25 (May 1987), 399–420.

KENNEDY, LESLIE W., and DAVID R. FORDE. "Routine Activities and Crime: An Analysis of Victimization in Canada," *Criminology* 28 (February 1990), 137–152.

KENNEY, DENNIS JAY. *Crime, Fear, and the New York City Subways: The Role of Citizen Action.* New York: Praeger, 1987.

KERR, PETER. "'Ghost Riders' Are Target of an Insurance Sting," *New York Times,* August 18, 1993, pp. A1, D2.

KIFNER, JOHN. "New Immigrant Wave from Asia Gives the Underworld New Faces," *New York Times,* January 6, 1991, pp. 1, 20.

KING, HARRY, and WILLIAM J. CHAMBLISS. *Harry King: A Professional Thief's Journey.* New York: Wiley, 1984.

KIRKPATRICK, JOHN T., and JOHN A. HUMPHREY. "Stress in the Lives of Female Criminal Homicide Offenders in North Carolina," in James H. Humphrey, ed., *Human Stress: Current Selected Research,* Vol. 3. New York: AMS Press, 1989, pp. 109–120.

KIRKPATRICK, SIDNEY D. *Lords of Sipán: A True Story of Pre-Inca Tombs, Archaeology, and Crime.* New York: Morrow, 1992.

KITCHENER, HOWARD, ANNESLEY K. SCHMIDT, and DANIEL GLASER. "How Persistent Is Post-Prison Success?" *Federal Probation* 41 (March 1977), 9–15.

KITSUSE, JOHN I., and AARON V. CICOUREL. "A Note on the Use of Official Statistics," *Social Problems* 11 (Fall 1963), 131–138.

KITTRIE, NICHOLAS N. *The Right to Be Different: Deviance and Enforced Therapy.* Baltimore, Md.: Johns Hopkins University Press, 1971.

KLAUS, PATSY A. *The Costs of Crime to Victims.* Washington, D.C.: U.S. Department of Justice, February 1994.

KLECK, GARY. "Life Support for Ailing Hypotheses: Modes of Summarizing the Evidence for Racial Discrimination in Sentencing," *Law and Human Behavior* 9 (1985), 271–285.

——. *Point Blank: Guns and Violence in America.* New York: Aldine de Gruyter, 1991.

——. "Racial Discrimination in Criminal Sentencing: A Critical Evaluation of the Evidence with Additional Evidence on the Death Penalty," *American Sociological Review* 46 (December 1981), 783–805.

——, and MARK GERTZ. "Armed Resistance to Crime: The Prevalence and Nature of Self-Defense with a Gun," *Journal of Criminal Law and Criminology* 86 (Fall 1995), 150–187.

KLEIN, STEPHEN P., SUSAN TURNER, and JOAN PETERSILIA. *Racial Equity in Sentencing.* Santa Monica, Calif.: Rand, 1988.

KLEMKE, LLOYD W. "Does Apprehension for Shoplifting Amplify or Terminate Shoplifting Activity?" *Law and Society Review* 12 (Spring 1978), 391–403.

KLINGER, DAVID A. "Demeanor or Crime? Why 'Hostile' Citizens Are More Likely to Be Arrested," *Criminology* 32 (August 1994), 475–493.

——. "More on Demeanor and Arrest in Dade County," *Criminology* 34 (February 1996), 61–82.

KLOCKARS, CARL B. *The Professional Fence.* New York: Free Press, 1974.

KNORR, STEPHEN J. "Deterrence and the Death Penalty: A Temporal Cross-Sectional Approach," *Journal of Criminal Law and Criminology* 70 (Summer 1979), 235–254.

KOHLMEIER, LOUIS M. "The Bribe Busters," *New York Times Magazine*, September 26, 1976, pp. 47–60.

KOLATA, GINA. "Racial Bias Seen on Pregnant Addicts," *New York Times*, July 20, 1990, p. 13.

KOLBERT, ELIZABETH. "Television Gets Closer Look as a Factor in Real Violence," *New York Times*, December 14, 1994, pp. A1, D20.

KRAMER, JOHN H., and JEFFREY T. ULMER. "Sentencing Disparity and Departures from Guidelines," *Justice Quarterly* 13 (March 1996), 81–106.

KRAMER, RONALD C. "Corporate Crime: An Organizational Perspective," in Peter Wickman and Timothy Dailey, eds., *White-Collar and Economic Crime.* Lexington, Mass.: D. C. Heath, 1982, pp. 75–94.

KRAUSS, CLIFFORD. "Shootings Fall as More Guns Stay at Home," *New York Times*, July 30, 1995, pp. 29, 32.

KROHN, MARVIN D., JAMES P. CURRY, and SHIRLEY NELSON-KILGER. "Is Chivalry Dead? An Analysis of Changes in Police Dispositions of Males and Females," *Criminology* 21 (August 1983), 417–437.

KROHN, MARVIN D., et al. "Social Status and Deviance: Class Context of School, Social Status, and Delinquent Behavior," *Criminology* 18 (November 1980), 303–318.

KROST, JACK. "He Tries to Determine What Makes Criminals Tick," *Boston Globe*, October 24, 1982, p. 8.

KRUTTSCHNITT, CANDACE. "Women, Crime, and Dependency: An Application of the Theory of Law," *Criminology* 19 (February 1982), 495–513.

KUTCHINSKY, BERL. "Pornography and Sexual Violence: The Criminological Evidence from Aggregate Data in Several Countries." Paper presented at the Fourteenth International Congress on Law And Mental Health, Montreal, Canada, 1988.

KVÅLSETH, TARALD O. "Seriousness of Offenses: An Experimental Study Based on a Psychological Scaling Technique," *Criminology* 18 (August 1980), 237–244.

LAB, STEVEN P. "Patterns in Juvenile Misbehavior," *Crime and Delinquency* 30 (April 1984), 293–308.

——, and JOHN T. WHITEHEAD. "An Analysis of Juvenile Correctional Treatment," *Crime and Delinquency* 34 (January 1988), 60–83.

——, and JOHN T. WHITEHEAD. "From 'Nothing Works' to 'The Appropriate Works': The Latest Stop on the Search for the Secular Grail," *Criminology* 28 (August 1990), 405–417.

LABATON, STEPHEN. "The Cost of Drug Abuse: $60 Billion a Year," *New York Times*, December 5, 1989, pp. D1, D6.

——. "Milken's Sentence," *New York Times*, April 26, 1990, pp. D1, D11.

LaFREE, GARY D. "Adversarial and Nonadversarial Justice: Comparison of Guilty Pleas and Trials," *Criminology* 23 (May 1985), 289–312.

——. "The Effect of Sexual Stratification by Race on Official Reactions to Rape," *American Sociological Review* 45 (October 1980), 842–854.

——. *Rape and Criminal Justice: The Social Construction of Sexual Assault.* Belmont, Calif.: Wadsworth, 1989.

——, and KRISS A. DRASS. "The Effect of Changes in Intraracial Income Inequality and Educational Attainment on Changes in Arrest Rates for African Americans and Whites, 1957 to 1990," *American Sociological Review* 61 (August 1996), 614–634.

LaGRANGE, RANDY L., and HELENE RASKIN WHITE. "Age Differences in Delinquency: A Test of Theory," *Criminology* 23 (February 1985), 19–45.

LANDIS, DYLAN. "Insurance Fraud: Billions in Losses," *New York Times*, July 6, 1982, pp. D1, D2.

LANGAN, PATRICK A. "Racism on Trial: New Evidence to Explain the Racial Composition of Prisons in the United States," *Journal of Criminal Law and Criminology* 76 (Fall 1985), 666–683.

——, and JOHN M. DAWSON. *Spouse Murder Defendants in Large Urban Counties.* Washington, D.C.: U.S. Department of Justice, September 1995.

LANGER, SIDNEY. *The Rahway State Prison Lifers' Group: A Critical Analysis.* Union, N.J.: Kean College Department of Sociology, October, 1979.

LARZELERE, ROBERT E., and GERALD R. PATTERSON. "Parental Management: Mediator of the Effect of Socioeconomic Status on Early Delinquency," *Criminology* 28 (May 1990), 301–323.

LATANE, BIBB, and JOHN M. DARLEY. *The Unresponsive Bystander: Why Doesn't He Help?* New York: Appleton-Century-Crofts, 1970.

LAUDON, KENNETH C. *Dossier Society: Value Choices in the Design of National Information Systems.* New York: Columbia University Press, 1986.

——. "A Risky Index of Crime," *New York Times*, July 24, 1981, p. A27.

LAURITSEN, JANET L., ROBERT J. SAMPSON, and JOHN H. LAUB. "The Link between Offending and Victimization among Adolescents," *Criminology* 29 (May 1991), 265–291.

LAVRAKAS, PAUL J. "Fear of Crime and Behavioral Restrictions in Urban and Suburban Neighborhoods," *Population and Environment* 5 (1982), 242–264.

——, and ELICIA J. HERZ. "Citizen Participation in Neighborhood Crime Prevention," *Criminology* 20 (November 1982), 479–498.

LAYSON, STEPHEN K. "Homicide and Deterrence: A Reexamination of the United States Time-Series Evidence," *Southern Economic Journal* 52 (July 1985), 68–89.

LEA, JOHN, and JOCK YOUNG. "A Realistic Approach to Law and Order," in Brian MacLean, ed., *The Political Economy of Crime: Readings for a Critical Criminology.* Englewood Cliffs, N.J.: Prentice-Hall, 1986, pp. 158–164.

LEA, JOHN, and JOCK YOUNG. *What Is to Be Done about Law and Order?* New York: Penguin, 1984.

LeBLANC, MARC, and LOUISE BIRON. "Status Offenses: A Legal Term without Meaning: An Empirical Demonstration," *Journal of Research in Crime and Delinquency* 17 (January 1980), 114–125.

LEFKOWITZ, MONROE M., et al. *Growing Up to Be Violent: A Longitudinal Study of the Development of Aggression.* New York: Pergamon, 1977.

LEJEUNE, ROBERT. "The Management of a Mugging," *Urban Life* 6 (July 1977), 123–148.

LEMERT, EDWIN M. "Isolation and Closure Theory of Naive Check Forgery," *Journal of Criminal Law, Criminology and Police Science* 44 (September-October 1953), 293–307.

——. *Social Pathology.* New York: McGraw-Hill, 1951.

LEONARD, EILEEN B. *Women, Crime, and Society: A Critique of Criminology Theory.* New York: Longman, 1982.

LEONARD, WILLIAM N., and MARVIN GLENN WEBER. "Automakers and Dealers: A Study of Criminogenic Market Forces," *Law and Society Review* 4 (February 1970), 407–424.

LESIEUR, HENRY R. "Compulsive Gambling," *Society* 29 (May/June 1992), 43–50.

——. "Gambling, Pathological Gambling and Crime," in Thomas Galski, ed., *The Handbook of Pathological Gambling.* Springfield, Ill.: Charles C Thomas, 1987, pp. 89–110.

LETKEMANN, PETER. *Crime as Work.* Englewood Cliffs, N.J.: Prentice-Hall, 1973.

LEVINE, DENNIS B. *Inside Out: An Insider's Account of Wall Street.* New York: Putnam, 1991.

LEVINE, JAMES P. "Jury Toughness: The Impact of Conservatism on Criminal Court Verdicts," *Crime and Delinquency* 29 (January 1983), 71–87.

LEWIS, DAN A., JANE A. GRANT, and DENNIS P. ROSEN-BAUM. *Social Construction of Reform: Crime Prevention and Community Organizations.* New Brunswick, N.J.: Transaction Books, 1988.

LEWIS, DAN A., and GRETA SALEM. "Community Crime Prevention: An Analysis of a Developing Strategy," *Crime and Delinquency* 27 (July 1981), 405–421.

LEWIS, DAN A., and GRETA SALEM. *Fear of Crime: Incivility and the Production of a Social Problem.* New Brunswick, N.J.: Transaction Books, 1986.

LEWIS, DOROTHY OTNOW, et al. "Homicidally Aggressive Young Children: Neuropsychiatric and Experiential Correlates," *American Journal of Psychiatry* 140 (February 1983), 148–153.

LEWIS, DOROTHY OTNOW, et al. "Violent Juvenile Delinquents: Psychiatric, Neurological, Psychological and Abuse Factors," *Journal of the American Academy of Child Psychiatry* 18 (1979), 307–319.

LICHTER, LINDA S., and S. ROBERT LICHTER. *Prime Time Crime: Criminals and Law Enforcers in TV Entertainment.* Washington, D.C.: Media Institute, 1983.

LIND, ANDREW. "Some Ecological Patterns of Community Disorganization in Honolulu," *American Journal of Sociology* 36 (September 1930), 206–220.

LINDESMITH, ALFRED R. *Addiction and Opiates.* Chicago: Aldine, 1968.

——. "A Sociological Theory of Drug Addiction," *American Journal of Sociology* 43 (January 1938), 593–613.

LINK, BRUCE G., HOWARD ANDREWS, and FRANCIS T. CULLEN. "The Violent and Illegal Behavior of Mental Patients Reconsidered," *American Sociological Review* 57 (June 1992), 275–292.

LIPSEY, MARK W. *Juvenile Delinquency Treatment: A Meta-Analytic Inquiry into the Viability of Effects.* New York: Russell Sage, 1991.

LIPTON, DOUGLAS, ROBERT MARTINSON, and JUDITH WILKS. *The Effectiveness of Correctional Treatment: A Survey of Treatment Evaluation Studies.* New York: Praeger, 1975.

LISKA, ALLEN E., and MARK D. REED. "Ties to Conventional Institutions and Delinquency: Estimating Reciprocal Effects," *American Sociological Review* 50 (August 1985), 547–560.

LISKA, ALLEN E., and BARBARA D. WARNER. "Functions of Crime: A Paradoxical Process," *American Journal of Sociology* 96 (May 1991), 1441–1463.

LITTLE, CRAIG B., and CHRISTOPHER P. SHEFFIELD. "Frontiers and Criminal Justice: English Private Prosecution Societies and American Vigilantism in the Eighteenth and Nineteenth Centuries," *American Sociological Review* 48 (December 1983), 796–808.

LIZOTTE, ALAN J. "Extra-Legal Factors in Chicago's Criminal Courts: Testing the Conflict Model of Criminal Justice," *Social Problems* 25 (June 1978), 564–580.

LOEBER, ROLF, et al. "Initiation, Escalation, and Desistance in Juvenile Offending and Their Correlates," *Journal of Criminal Law and Criminology* 82 (Spring 1991), 36–82.

LOFTIN, COLIN, MILTON HEUMANN, and DAVID McDOWALL. "Mandatory Sentencing and Firearms Violence: Evaluating an Alternative to Gun Control," *Law and Society Review* 17 (1983), 287–318.

LOFTIN, COLIN, and ROBERT H. HILL. "Regional Subculture and Homicide: An Examination of the Gastil-Hackney Thesis," *American Sociological Review* 39 (October 1974), 714–724.

LOFTIN, COLIN, and DAVID McDOWALL. "'One with a Gun Gets You Two': Mandatory Sentencing and Firearms Violence in Detroit," *Annals of the American Academy of Political and Social Science* 455 (May 1981), 150–167.

LOFTIN, COLIN, and DAVID McDOWALL. "The Police, Crime and Economic Theory: An Assessment," *American Sociological Review* 47 (June 1982), 393–401.

LOFTIN, COLIN, et al. "Effects of Restrictive Licensing of Handguns on Homicide and Suicide in the District of Columbia," *New England Journal of Medicine* 325 (December 5, 1991), 1615–1620.

LOGAN, CHARLES H. "Arrest Rates and Deterrence," *Social Science Quarterly* 56 (December 1975), 376–389.

——, and GERALD G. GAES. "Meta-Analysis and the Rehabilitation of Punishment," *Justice Quarterly* 10 (June 1993), 245–263.

LOMBROSO, CESARE. "Introduction," to Gina Lombroso Ferrara, *Criminal Man According to the Classification of Cesare Lombroso.* New York: Putnam, 1911.

LOWMAN, JOHN, and BRIAN D. MacLEAN, eds. *Realist Criminology: Crime Control and Policing in the 1990s.* Toronto: University of Toronto Press, 1992.

LUCKENBILL, DAVID F. "Criminal Homicide as a Situated Transaction," *Social Problems* 25 (December 1977), 176–186.

——, and JOEL BEST. "Careers in Deviance and Respectability: The Analogy's Limitations," *Social Problems* 29 (December 1981), 197–206.

——, and DANIEL P. DOYLE. "Structural Position and Violence: Developing a Cultural Explanation," *Criminology* 27 (August 1989), 419–436.

LUNDMAN, RICHARD J. "Demeanor or Crime? The Midwestern Police-Citizen Encounters Study," *Criminology* 32 (November 1994), 631–656.

LUNDQUIST, JOHN H., and JANICE M. DUKE. "The Elderly Victim at Risk: Explaining the Fear-Victimization Paradox," *Criminology* 29 (May 1982), 115–126.

LUPSHA, PETER A. "Individual Choice, Material Culture, and Organized Crime," *Criminology* 19 (May 1981), 3–24.

LYNCH, JAMES P. "A Comparison of Prison Use in England, Canada, West Germany, and the United States: A Limited Test of the Punitive Hypothesis," *Journal of Criminal Law and Criminology* 79 (Spring 1988), 180–217.

MacANDREW, CRAIG, and ROBERT B. EDGERTON. *Drunken Comportment: A Social Explanation.* Chicago: Aldine, 1969.

McAULIFFE, WILLIAM E., and ROBERT A. GORDON. "A Test of Lindesmith's Theory of Addiction: The Frequency of Euphoria among Long-Term Addicts," *American Journal of Sociology* 79 (January 1974), 795–840.

McCAGHY, CHARLES H. "Child Molesters: A Study of Their Careers as Deviants," in Marshall B. Clinard and Richard Quinney, eds., *Criminal Behavior Systems: A Typology.* New York: Holt, Rinehart and Winston, 1967, pp. 75–88.

——. "Drinking and Deviance Disavowal: The Case of Child Molesters," *Social Problems* 16 (Summer 1968), 43–49.

McCAIN, NINA. "James Q. Wilson Talks about Crime and Punishment in the U.S.," *Boston Globe*, August 11, 1984, p. 2.

McCARTHY, BELINDA R., and BRENT L. SMITH. "The Conceptualization of Discrimination in the Juvenile Justice Process: The Impact of Administrative Factors and Screening Decisions on Juvenile Court Dispositions," *Criminology* 24 (February 1986), 41–64.

McCARTHY, BILL. "Not Just 'For the Thrill of It': An Instrumentalist Elaboration of Katz's Explanation of Sneaky Thrill Property Crimes," *Criminology* 33 (November 1995), 519–538.

——, and JOHN HAGAN. "Mean Streets: The Theoretical Significance of Situational Delinquency among Homeless Youth," *American Journal of Sociology* 98 (November 1992), 597–627.

McCARTHY, JOHN D., and DEAN R. HOGE. "The Dynamics of Self-Esteem and Delinquency," *American Journal of Sociology* 90 (September 1984), 396–410.

McCLEARY, RICHARD, BARBARA C. NIENSTEDT, and JAMES M. ERVEN. "Uniform Crime Reports as Organizational Outcomes: Three Time-Series Experiments," *Social Problems* 29 (April 1982), 361–372.

MACCOBY, ELEANOR E., and CAROL NAGY JACKLIN. "Sex Differences in Aggression: A Rejoinder and a Reprise," *Child Development* 51 (December 1980), 964–980.

MACCOBY, ELEANOR E., JOSEPH P. JOHNSON, and RUSSELL M. CHURCH. "Community Integration and the Social Control of Juvenile Delinquency," *Journal of Social Issues* 14 (June 1958), 38–51.

McCORD, JOAN. "Family Relationships, Juvenile Delinquency, and Adult Criminality," *Criminology* 29 (August 1991), 397–417.

——. "A Longitudinal Perspective on Patterns of Crime," *Criminology* 19 (August 1981), 211–218.

——. "Some Child-Rearing Antecedents of Criminal Behavior in Adult Men," *Journal of Personality and Social Psychology* 37 (1979), 1477–1486.

——. "A Thirty-Year Follow-up of Treatment Effects," *American Psychologist* 33 (March 1978), 284–289.

McCORD, WILLIAM. "Psychopathy," in Sanford H. Kadish, ed., *Encyclopedia of Crime and Justice*, Vol. 4. New York: Free Press, 1983, pp. 1315–1318.

——, and JOAN McCORD. *Origins of Crime: A New Evaluation of the Cambridge-Somerville Youth Study.* New York: Columbia University Press, 1959.

McCORKLE, RICHARD C. "Research Note: Punish and Rehabilitate? Public Attitudes toward Six Common Crimes," *Crime and Delinquency* 39 (April 1993), 240–252.

McDOWALL, DAVID, ALAN J. LIZOTTE, and BRIAN WIERSEMA. "General Deterrence through Civilian Gun Ownership: An Evaluation of the Quasi-Experimental Evidence," *Criminology* 29 (November 1991), 541–559.

McDOWALL, DAVID, COLIN LOFTIN, and BRIAN WIERSEMA. "A Comparative Study of the Preventive Effects of Mandatory Sentencing Laws for Gun Crimes," *Journal of Criminal Law and Criminology* 83 (Summer 1992), 378–394.

McFARLAND, SAM G. "Is Capital Punishment a Short-Term Deterrent to Homicide? A Study of the Effects of Four Recent American Executions," *Journal of Criminal Law and Criminology* 74 (Winter 1983), 1014–1032.

McGAHEY, RICHARD M. "Economic Conditions, Neighborhood Organization, and Urban Crime," in Albert J. Reiss, Jr., and Michael Tonry, eds., *Communities and Crime.* Chicago: University of Chicago Press, 1986, pp. 231–270.

McGLOTHIN, WILLIAM H., M. DOUGLAS ANGLIN, and BRUCE D. WILSON. "Narcotic Addiction and Crime," *Criminology* 16 (November 1978), 293–315.

McINTOSH, MARY. *The Organisation of Crime*. London: Macmillan Press, Ltd., 1975.

MacKELLAR, F. LANDIS, and MACHIKO YANAGISHITA. *Homicide in the United States: Who's at Risk?* Washington, D.C.: Population Reference Bureau, February 1995.

MacKENZIE, DORIS LAYTON. "Boot Camp Prisons in 1993," *National Institute of Justice Journal*, November 1993, pp. 21–28.

McLARIN, KIMBERLY J. "Welfare Fingerprinting Finds Most People Are Telling Truth," *New York Times*, September 29, 1995, pp. B1, B4.

MacLEAN, BRIAN. *The Political Economy of Crime: Readings for a Critical Criminology*. Scarborough, Ontario, Canada: Prentice-Hall, 1986.

McMILLAN, JON. "The All-American Fire Trap," *New York Times*, April 17, 1995, p. A17.

McNAMARA, JOHN H. "Uncertainty in Police Work: The Relevance of Police Recruits' Backgrounds and Training," in David J. Bordua, ed., *The Police: Six Sociological Essays*. New York: Wiley, 1967, pp. 163–252.

McNAMARA, JOSEPH D. "Preface," in George L. Kelling et al., *The Kansas City Preventive Patrol Experiment*. Washington, D.C.: Police Foundation, 1974, pp. iii–iv.

MAGUIN, EUGENE, and ROLF LOEBER. "Academic Performance and Delinquency," in Michael Tonry, ed., *Crime and Justice: A Review of Research*, Vol. 20. Chicago: University of Chicago Press, 1996, pp. 145–264.

MAGUIRE, KATHLEEN, and ANN L. PASTORE. *Sourcebook of Criminal Justice Statistics—1994*. Washington, D.C.: Bureau of Justice Statistics, U.S. Department of Justice, 1995.

MAGUIRE, MIKE. "The Needs and Rights of Victims of Crime," in Michael Tonry, ed., *Crime and Justice: A Review of Research*, Vol. 14. Chicago: University of Chicago Press, 1991, pp. 363–433.

MAHONEY, ANNE RANKIN. "The Effect of Labeling upon Youths in the Juvenile Justice System: A Review of the Evidence," *Law and Society Review* 8 (Summer 1974), 583–614.

MAITLAND, LESLIE. "U.S. Tries New Tack in Drug Fight as Global Supply and Use Mount," *New York Times*, January 30, 1983, pp. 1, 18.

MANN, CORAMAE RICHEY. *When Women Kill*. Albany: State University of New York Press, 1996.

MARGOLICK, DAVID. "Chorus of Judicial Critics Assail Sentencing Guides," *New York Times*, April 12, 1992, pp. 1–40.

MARS, GERALD. "Dock Pilferage: A Case Study in Occupational Theft," in Paul Rock and Mary McIntosh, eds., *Deviance and Social Control*. London: Tavistock, 1974, pp. 209–228.

MARTIN, DOUGLAS. "Kitty Genovese: Would New York Still Turn Away?" *New York Times*, March 11, 1989, p. 29.

MARTIN, JOHN BARTLOW. *My Life in Crime*. New York: Harper, 1952.

MARTIN, MICHAEL J., THOMAS K. HUNT, and STEPHEN B. HULLEY. "The Cost of Hospitalization for Firearm Injuries," *Journal of the American Medical Association* 260 (November 25, 1988), 3048–3050.

MARTIN, SUSAN E. "'A Cross-Burning Is Not Just an Arson': Police Social Construction of Hate Crimes in Baltimore County," *Criminology* 33 (August 1995), 303–326.

——. "Policing Career Criminals: An Examination of an Innovative Crime Control Program," *Journal of Criminal Law and Criminology* 77 (Winter 1986), 1159–1182.

——, and LAWRENCE W. SHERMAN. "Selective Apprehension: A Police Strategy for Repeat Offenders," *Criminology* 24 (February 1986), 155–173.

MARTINSON, ROBERT. "New Findings, New Views: A Note of Caution Regarding Sentencing Reform," *Hofstra Law Review* 7 (Winter 1979), 243–258.

——. "What Works?—Questions and Answers about Prison Reform," *The Public Interest* No. 35 (Spring 1974), 22–54.

MARVELL, THOMAS B. "Sentencing Guidelines and Prison Population Growth," *Journal of Criminal Law and Criminology* 85 (Winter 1995), 696–709.

——, and CARLISLE E. MOODY. "Determinate Sentencing and Abolishing Parole: The Long-Term Impacts on Prisons and Crime," *Criminology* 34 (February 1996), 107–128.

MARX, GARY T., and DANE ARCHER. "Citizen Involvement in the Law Enforcement Process: The Case of Community Police Patrols," *American Behavioral Scientist* 15 (September–October 1971), 52–72.

MARX, GARY T., and DANE ARCHER. "Picking Up the Gun: Some Organizational and Survey Data on Community Police Patrols." Paper presented at the Symposium on Studies of Public Experience, Knowledge and Opinion of Crime and Justice. Washington, D.C.: Bureau of Social Science Research, Inc., March 1972.

MASSEY, JAMES L., MARVIN D. KROHN, and LISA M. BONATI. "Property Crime and the Routine Activities of Individuals," *Journal of Research in Crime and Delinquency* 26 (November 1989), 378–400.

MASTROFSKI, STEPHEN D., ROBERT E. WORDEN, and JEFFREY B. SNIPES. "Law Enforcement in a Time of Community Policing," *Criminology* 33 (November 1995), 539–563.

MATSUEDA, ROSS L. "Reflected Appraisals, Parental Labeling, and Delinquency: Specifying a Symbolic Interactionist Theory," *American Journal of Sociology* 97 (May 1992), 1577–1611.

——, and KAREN HEIMER. "Race, Family Structure, and Delinquency: A Test of Differential Association and Social Control Theories," *American Sociological Review* 52 (December 1987), 826–840.

MATTHEWS, ROGER. "Taking Realist Criminology Seriously," *Contemporary Crises* 11 (1987), 371–401.

——, and JOCK YOUNG, eds. *Issues in Realist Criminology*. London: Sage, 1992.

MATZA, DAVID. *Delinquency and Drift*. New York: Wiley, 1964.

——, and GRESHAM M. SYKES. "Juvenile Delinquency and Subterranean Values," *American Sociological Review* 26 (October 1961), 712–719.

MAURER, DAVID W. *The American Confidence Man.* Springfield, Ill.: Charles C Thomas, 1974.

——. *Whiz Mob: A Correlation of the Technical Argot of Pickpockets with Their Behavior Pattern.* New Haven, Conn.: College & University Press, 1955, 1964.

MAYNARD, DOUGLAS W. "The Structure of Discourse in Misdemeanor Plea Bargaining," *Law and Society Review* 18 (1984), 75–104.

MEADOW, ARNOLD, et al. "Self-Concept, Negative Family Affect, and Delinquency: A Comparison across Mexican Social Classes," *Criminology* 19 (November 1981), 434–448.

MEDINNUS, GENE R. "Delinquents' Perceptions of Their Parents," *Journal of Consulting Psychology* 29 (December 1965), 592–593.

MEDNICK, SARNOFF A., WILLIAM F. GABRIELLI, JR., and BARRY HUTCHINGS. "Genetic Factors in the Etiology of Criminal Behavior," in Sarnoff A. Mednick, Terrie E. Moffitt, and Susan A. Stack, eds., *The Causes of Crime: New Biological Approaches.* Cambridge, Eng.: Cambridge University Press, 1987, pp. 74–91.

MEDNICK, SARNOFF A., and JAN VOLAVKA. "Biology and Crime," in Norval Morris and Michael Tonry, eds., *Crime and Justice: An Annual Review of Research,* Vol. 2. Chicago: University of Chicago Press, 1980, pp. 85–158.

MEDNICK, SARNOFF A., et al. "Biology and Violence," in Marvin E. Wolfgang and Neil Alan Weiner, eds., *Criminal Violence.* Beverly Hills, Calif: Sage Publications, 1982, pp. 21–80.

MEDNICK, SARNOFF A., et al. "EEG as a Predictor of Antisocial Behavior," *Criminology* 19 (August 1981), 219–229.

MEGARGEE, EDWIN I. "Psychological Determinants and Correlates of Criminal Violence," in Marvin E. Wolfgang and Neil Alan Weiner, eds., *Criminal Violence.* Beverly Hills, Calif.: Sage Publications, 1982, pp. 81–170.

——, and MARTIN J. BOHN. *Classifying Criminal Offenders: A New System Based on the MMPI.* Beverly Hills, Calif.: Sage Publications, 1979.

MEISENHELDER, THOMAS. "An Exploratory Study of Exiting from Criminal Careers," *Criminology* 15 (November 1977), 319–334.

MENARD, SCOTT, and BARBARA J. MORSE. "A Structuralist Critique of the IQ-Delinquency Hypothesis: Theory and Evidence," *American Journal of Sociology* 89 (May 1984), 1347–1378.

MERTON, ROBERT K. "Social Structure and Anomie," in *Social Theory and Social Structure,* 1968 enlarged ed. New York: Free Press, 1968, pp. 185–214.

MESSERSCHMIDT, JAMES W. *Masculinities and Crime: Critique and Reconceptualization of Theory.* Lanham, Md.: Rowman and Littlefield, 1993.

MESSNER, STEVEN F. "Economic Discrimination and Societal Homicide Rates: Further Evidence on the Cost of Inequality," *American Sociological Review* 54 (August 1989), 597–611.

——. "Poverty, Inequality, and the Urban Homicide Rate: Some Unexpected Findings," *Criminology* 20 (May 1982), 103–114.

——. "Regional and Racial Effects on the Urban Homicide Rate: The Subculture of Violence Revisited," *American Journal of Sociology* 88 (March 1983a), 997–1007.

——. "Regional Differences in the Economic Correlates of the Urban Homicide Rate: Some Evidence on the Importance of Cultural Context," *Criminology* 21 (November 1983b), 477–488.

——, and KENNETH TARDIFF. "The Social Ecology of Urban Homicide: An Application of the 'Routine Activities' Approach," *Criminology* 23 (May 1985), 241–267.

MIETHE, TERANCE D. "Citizen-Based Crime Control Activity and Victimization Risks: An Examination of Displacement and Free-Rider Effects," *Criminology* 29 (August 1991), 419–439.

——, and ROBERT F. MEIER. *Crime and Its Social Context: Toward an Integrated Theory of Offenders, Victims, and Situations.* Albany: State University of New York Press, 1994.

——, MARK C. STAFFORD, and J. SCOTT LONG. "Social Differentiation in Criminal Victimization: A Test of Routine Activities/Lifestyle Theories," *American Sociological Review* 52 (April 1987), 184–194.

MILGRAM, STANLEY. "The Experience of Living in Cities: A Psychological Analysis," *Science* 167 (March 13, 1970), 1461–1468.

——, and PAUL HOLLANDER. "The Murder They Heard," in Renatus Hartogs and Eric Artzt, eds., *Violence: Causes & Solutions.* New York: Dell, 1970, pp. 206–212.

MILLER, J. L., PETER H. ROSSI, and JON E. SIMPSON. "Perceptions of Justice: Race and Gender Differences in Judgments of Appropriate Prison Sentences," *Law and Society Review* 20 (1986), 313–334.

MILLER, STUART J., SIMON DINITZ, and JOHN P. CONRAD. *Careers of the Violent: The Dangerous Offender and Criminal Justice.* Lexington, Mass.: D. C. Heath, 1982.

MILLER, TED R., and MARK A. COHEN. "Costs of Penetrating Injury," in Rao Ivatury and C. Gene Cayten, eds., *Textbook of Penetrating Trauma.* Philadelphia: Lee and Civiga, 1995.

MILLER, WALTER B. "American Youth Gangs: Past and Present," in Abraham S. Blumberg, ed., *Current Perspectives on Criminal Behavior: Original Essays in Criminology.* New York: Knopf, 1974, pp. 210–239.

——. "Ideology and Criminal Justice Policy: Some Current Issues," *Journal of Criminal Law and Criminology* 64 (June 1973), 141–162.

——. "Lower Class Culture as a Generating Milieu of Gang Delinquency," *Journal of Social Issues* 14 (No. 3, 1958), 5–19.

MILLS, C. WRIGHT. *The Power Elite.* New York: Oxford University Press, 1956.

MINOR, W. WILLIAM. "Techniques of Neutralization: A Reconceptualization and Empirical Examination," *Journal of Research in Crime and Delinquency* 18 (July 1981), 295–318.

MINSKY, TERRY. "The Odds on Being Slain—Worse for Young Black Males," *Boston Globe,* February 23, 1984, pp. 1, 47.

MIRANNE, ALFRED C., and MICHAEL R. GEERKEN. "The New Orleans Inmate Survey: A Test of Greenwood's Predictive Scale," *Criminology* 29 (August 1991), 497–518.

MITFORD, JESSICA. *Kind & Usual Punishment: The Prison Business.* New York: Knopf, 1973.

MOFFITT, TERRIE E. "The Neuropsychology of Conduct Disorder," *Development and Psychopathology* 5 (1993), 133–151.

——, DONALD R. LYNAM, and PHIL A. SILVA. "Neuropsychological Tests Predicting Persistent Male Delinquency," *Criminology* 32 (May 1994), 277–300.

MONACHESI, ELIO D., and STARKE R. HATHAWAY. "The Personality of Delinquents," in J. N. Butcher, ed., *MMPI: Research Developments and Clinical Applications.* New York: McGraw-Hill, 1969, pp. 207–219.

MOORE, CHARLES A. "Taming the Giant Corporation? Some Cautionary Remarks on the Deterrability of Corporate Crime," *Crime and Delinquency* 33 (July 1987), 379–402.

MOORE, ELIZABETH, and MICHAEL MILLS. "The Neglected Victims and Unexamined Costs of White-Collar Crime," *Crime and Delinquency* 36 (July 1990), 408–418.

MOORE, JOAN W. *Homeboys.* Philadelphia: Temple University Press, 1978.

MORAN, RICHARD. "The Insanity Defense: Five Years after Hinckley," in Robert J. Kelly and Donal E. J. MacNamara, eds., *Perspectives on Deviance: Dominance, Degradation and Denigration.* Cincinnati, Ohio: Anderson, 1991, p. 77–87.

MORASH, MERRY, and MEDA CHESNEY-LIND. "A Re-Formulation and Partial Test of the Power-Control Theory of Delinquency," *Justice Quarterly* 8 (1991), 347–377.

——, ROBIN N. HAARR, and LILA RUCKER. "A Comparison of Programming for Women and Men in U.S. Prisons in the 1980s," *Crime and Delinquency* 40 (April 1994), 197–221.

——, and LILA RUCKER. "A Critical Look at the Idea of Boot Camp as a Correctional Reform," *Crime and Delinquency* 36 (April 1990), 204–222.

MORIARITY, THOMAS. "Crime, Commitment, and the Responsive Bystander: Two Field Experiments," *Journal of Personality and Social Psychology* 31 (February 1975), 370–376.

MORRIS, NORVAL. "Punishment, Desert, and Rehabilitation," in Hyman Gross and Andrew von Hirsch, eds., *Sentencing.* New York: Oxford University Press, 1981, pp. 257–271.

——, and GORDON HAWKINS. *The Honest Politician's Guide to Crime Control.* Chicago: University of Chicago Press, 1970.

MORSCH, JAMES. "The Problem of Motive in Hate Crimes: The Argument against Presumptions of Racial Motivation," *Journal of Criminal Law and Criminology* 82 (Fall 1991), 659–689.

MOSHER, DONALD L., and RONALD D. ANDERSON. "Macho Personality, Sexual Aggression, and Reactions to Guided Imagery of Realistic Rape," *Journal of Research in Personality* 20 (March 1986), 77–94.

MOSHER, DONALD L., and MARK SIRKIN. "Measuring a Macho Personality Constellation," *Journal of Research in Personality* 18 (June 1984), 150–163.

MURRAY, CHARLES A., and LOUIS A. COX, JR. *Beyond Probation: Juvenile Corrections and the Chronic Delinquent.* Beverly Hills, Calif.: Sage Publications, 1979.

MYDANS, SETH. "Videotape of Beating by Officers Puts Full Glare on Brutality Issue," *New York Times*, March 18, 1991, pp. A1, B7.

MYERS, MARTHA A. "Symbolic Policy and the Sentencing of Drug Offenders," *Law and Society Review* 23 (1989), 295–315.

MYERS, STEVEN LEE. "Captain and Crew Charged in Voyage of Chinese to U.S.," *New York Times*, June 8, 1993, pp. A1, B2.

NAGEL, ILENE H., and JOHN HAGAN. "Gender and Crime: Offense Patterns and Criminal Court Sanctions," in Michael Tonry and Norval Morris, eds., *Crime and Justice: An Annual Review of Research*, Vol. 4. Chicago: University of Chicago Press, 1983, pp. 91–144.

NAGIN, CARL. "The Peruvian Gold Rush," *Art & Antiquities*, May 1990, pp. 98–105, 134–135.

NAGIN, DANIEL. "Crime Rates, Sanction Levels, and Constraints on Prison Population," *Law and Society Review* 12 (Spring 1978), 341–366.

——, and DAVID P. FARRINGTON. "The Onset and Persistence of Offending," *Criminology* 30 (November 1992a), 501–523.

——, and DAVID P. FARRINGTON. "The Stability of Criminal Potential from Childhood to Adulthood," *Criminology* 30 (May 1992b), 235–260.

——, and RAYMOND PATERNOSTER. "Enduring Individual Differences and Rational Choice Theories of Crime," *Law and Society Review* 27 (1993), 467–496.

——, and RAYMOND PATERNOSTER. "On the Relationship of Past to Future Participation in Delinquency," *Criminology* 29 (May 1991), 163–189.

NATIONAL ADVISORY COMMISSION ON CRIMINAL JUSTICE STANDARDS AND GOALS. *A National Strategy to Reduce Crime.* Washington, D.C.: U.S. Government Printing Office, 1973.

NATIONAL INSTITUTE OF JUSTICE. *Drug Use Forecasting: 1994 Annual Report on Adult and Juvenile Arrestees.* Washington, D.C.: National Institute of Justice, November 1995.

NATIONAL RESEARCH COUNCIL. *Understanding and Preventing Violence.* Washington, D.C.: National Academy Press, 1993.

NAVARRO, MIREYA. "After Carjacking Surge, Puerto Rico Is Wary Behind the Wheel," *New York Times*, July 31, 1994, p. 28.

NELSEN, CANDICE, JAY CORZINE, and LIN HUFF-CORZINE. "The Violent West Reexamined: A Research Note on Regional Homicide Rates," *Criminology* 32 (February 1994), 149–161.

NELSON, JAMES F. "Multiple Victimization in American Cities: A Statistical Analysis of Rare Events," *American Journal of Sociology* 85 (January 1980), 870–891.

NEUBAUER, DAVID W. *Criminal Justice in Middle America.* Morristown, N.J.: General Learning Press, 1974.

[*New York Times*]. "F.B.I. Forms Unit To Battle "Carjacking," September 16, 1992, p. A21.

——. "Hostility Taints Postal Service, New Study Says," October 28, 1994, p. A24.

——. "How U.S. Plans to Fight Violence of Carjacking," November 15, 1992, p. 52.

——. "A Law Distinguishing Crack from Other Cocaine Is Upset," December 29, 1990, p. 13.

——. "Morgenthau Says Data Link a Third of Crimes to the Career Criminal," April 9, 1981, p. B3.

——. "Report Cites Heavy Toll of Rapes on Young," June 23, 1994, p. A12.

——. "Street Crime Hits Prague Daily Life," December 18, 1991, p. A21.

NEWBURN, TIM, and ELIZABETH A. STANKO, eds. *Just Boys Doing Business? Men, Masculinities and Crime.* London: Routledge, 1994.

NEWMAN, GRAEME. *Comparative Deviance: Perception and Law in Six Cultures.* New York: Elsevier, 1976.

NEWMAN, OSCAR. *Architectural Design for Crime Prevention.* Washington, D.C.: U.S. Government Printing Office, 1973.

——. *Creating Defensible Space.* Wanshington, D.C.: U.S. Department of Housing and Urban Development, Office of Policy Development and Research, April 1996.

——. *Defensible Space: Crime Prevention through Urban Design.* New York: Macmillan, 1972.

——, and K. A. FRANCK. "The Effects of Building Size on Personal Crime and Fear of Crime," *Probation and Environment* 5 (1982), 203–220.

NORMANDEAU, ANDRE. *Trends and Patterns in Crimes of Robbery.* Ph.D. dissertation. Philadelphia: University of Pennsylvania, 1968.

NYE, F. IVAN. *Family Relationships and Delinquent Behavior.* Westport, Conn.: Greenwood Press, 1958.

O'BRIEN, ROBERT M. "The Interracial Nature of Violent Crimes: A Reexamination," *American Journal of Sociology* 92 (January 1987), 817–835.

O'CARROLL, PATRICK W., and JAMES A. MERCY. "Regional Variation in Homicide Rates: Why is the *West* So Violent?" *Violence and Victims* 4 (1989), 17–25.

O'CONNOR, JAMES F., and ALAN LIZOTTE. "The 'Southern Subculture of Violence' Thesis and Patterns of Gun Ownership," *Social Problems* 25 (April 1978), 420–429.

OFFICE OF JUSTICE PROGRAMS, NATIONAL INSTITUTE OF JUSTICE. *The Extent and Costs of Crime Victimization: A New Look.* Washington, D.C.: U.S. Department of Justice, January 1996.

OFFICE OF JUVENILE JUSTICE AND DELINQUENCY PRE-VENTION. "Targeting Serious Juvenile Offenders for Prosecution Can Make a Difference," *NIJ Reports,* September/October 1988, pp. 9–12.

ONISHI, NORIMITSU. "Stolen Cars Find a World of Welcome," *New York Times,* July 10, 1995, pp. B1, B2.

ORCUTT, JAMES D. "Differential Association and Marijuana Use: A Closer Look at Sutherland (with a Little Help from Becker)," *Criminology* 25 (May 1987), 341–358.

ORSAGH, THOMAS, and ANN DRYDEN WITTE. "Economic Status and Crime: Implications for Offender Rehabilitation," *Journal of Criminal Law and Criminology* 72 (Fall 1981), 1055–1071.

OSBUN, LEE ANN, and PETER A. RODE. "Prosecuting Juveniles as Adults: The Quest for 'Objective' Decisions," *Criminology* 22 (May 1984), 187–202.

OSGOOD, D. WAYNE, et al. "Routine Activities and Individual Deviant Behavior," *American Sociological Review* 61 (August 1996), 635–655.

PACE, ERIC. "Crime's Lingering Allure," *New York Times,* June 6, 1982, p. F9.

PADILLA, FELIX M. *The Gang as an American Enterprise.* New Brunswick, N.J.: Rutgers University Press, 1992.

PAIK, HAEJUNG, and GEORGE COMSTOCK. "The Effects of Television Violence on Antisocial Behavior: A Meta-Analysis," *Communication Research* 21 (August 1994), 516–546.

PALMER, TED. "The Effectiveness of Intervention: Recent Trends and Current Issues," *Crime and Delinquency* 3 (July 1991), 330–346.

——. "Martinson Revisited," *Journal of Research in Crime and Delinquency* 12 (July 1975), 133–152.

——. *A Profile of Correctional Effectiveness and New Directions for Research.* Albany: State University of New York Press, 1994.

PARISI, NICOLETTE. "Are Females Treated Differently? A Review of the Theories and Evidence on Sentencing and Parole Decisions," in Nicole Hahn Rafter and Elizabeth Anne Stanko, eds., *Judge, Lawyer, Victim, Thief: Women, Gender Roles, and Criminal Justice.* Boston: Northeastern University Press, 1982, pp. 205–220.

——. "A Taste of the Bars?" *Journal of Criminal Law and Criminology* 72 (Fall 1981), 1109–1123.

PARKER, DONN B. *Crime by Computer.* New York: Scribner's, 1976.

PATERNOSTER, RAYMOND. "Examining Three-Wave Deterrence Models: A Question of Temporal Order and Specification," *Journal of Criminal Law and Criminology* 79 (Spring 1988), 135–179.

——. "Race of Victim and Location of Crime: The Decision to Seek the Death Penalty in South Carolina," *Journal of Criminal Law and Criminology* 74 (Winter 1983), 754–785.

PATTERSON, GERALD R. "Children Who Steal," in Travis Hirschi and Michael Gottfredson, eds., *Understanding Crime: Current Theory and Research.* Beverly Hills, Calif.: Sage Publications, 1980, pp. 73–90.

——, P. CHAMBERLAIN, and J. B. REID. "A Comparative Evaluation of a Parent-Training Program," *Behavior Therapy* 13 (1982), 638–650.

——, and THOMAS J. DISHION. "Contributions of Families and Peers to Delinquency," *Criminology* 23 (February 1985), 63–79.

PENNELL, SUSAN, et al. "Guardian Angels: A Unique Approach to Crime Prevention," *Crime and Delinquency* 35 (July 1989), 378–400.

PEREZ, JACOB. *Tracking Offenders.* Washington, D.C.: U.S. Department of Justice, October 1990.

PERKINS, CRAIG, and PATSY KLAUS. *Criminal Victimization 1994.* Washington, D.C.: U.S. Department of Justice, April 1996.

PETERSILIA, JOAN. "Criminal Career Research: A Review of Recent Evidence," in Norval Morris and Michael Tonry, eds., *Crime and Justice: An Annual Review of Research*, Vol. 2. Chicago: University of Chicago Press, 1980, pp. 321–379.

——. *Racial Disparities in the Criminal Justice System*. Santa Monica, Calif.: Rand, 1983.

——, PETER W. GREENWOOD, and MARVIN LAVIN. *Criminal Careers of Habitual Felons*. Santa Monica, Calif.: Rand, 1977.

PETERSON, MARK A., and HARRIET BRAIKER, with SUZANNE M. POLICH. *Who Commits Crimes: A Survey of Prison Inmates*. Boston: Oelgeschlager, Gunn & Hain, 1981.

PETERSON, RUTH D., and WILLIAM C. BAILEY. "Felony Murder and Capital Punishment: An Examination of the Deterrence Question," *Criminology* 29 (August 1991), 367–395.

PETERSON, RUTH D., and WILLIAM C. BAILEY. "Murder and Capital Punishment in the Evolving Context of the Post-Furman Era," *Social Forces* 66 (March 1988), 774–807.

PFUHL, ERDWIN H., JR. "Police Strikes and Conventional Crime: A Look at the Data," *Criminology* 21 (November 1983), 489–503.

PHILLIPS, DAVID P. "The Deterrent Effect of Capital Punishment: New Evidence on an Old Controversy," *American Journal of Sociology* 86 (July 1980), 139–148.

——. "The Impact of Mass Media Violence on U.S. Homicides," *American Sociological Review* 48 (August 1983), 560–568.

——, and JOHN E. HENSLEY. "When Violence Is Rewarded or Punished: The Impact of Mass Media Stories on Homicide," *Journal of Communication* 34 (Summer 1984), 101–116.

PHILLIPS, LLAD, and HAROLD L. VOTEY, JR. *The Economics of Crime Control*. Beverly Hills, Calif.: Sage Publications, 1981.

PHILLIPS, PHILLIP D. "Characteristics and Typology of the Journey to Crime," in Daniel E. Georges-Abeyie and Keith D. Harries, eds., *Crime: A Spatial Perspective*. New York: Columbia University Press, 1980, pp. 167–180.

PIERCE, GLENN, and WILLIAM J. BOWERS. "The Bartley-Fox Gun Law's Short-Term Impact on Crime in Boston," *Annals of the American Academy of Political and Social Science* 455 (May 1981), 120–137.

PILIAVIN, IRVING, and SCOTT BRIAR. "Police Encounters with Juveniles," *American Journal of Sociology* 70 (September 1964), 206–214.

PLATT, ANTHONY M. "Prospects for a Radical Criminology in the USA," in Ian Taylor, Paul Walton, and Jock Young, eds., *Critical Criminology*. London: Routledge and Kegan Paul, 1975, pp. 95–112.

PODOLEFSKY, AARON, and FREDRICK DuBOW. *Strategies for Community Crime Prevention: Collective Responses to Crime in Urban America*. Springfield, Ill.: Charles C Thomas Publisher, 1981.

POLK, KENNETH. "Delinquency and Adult Criminal Careers," in Delos H. Kelly, ed., *Criminal Behavior: Readings in Criminology*. New York: St. Martin's Press, 1980, pp. 143–150.

——. *When Men Kill: Scenarios of Masculine Violence*. Cambridge, Eng.: Cambridge University Press, 1994.

POLLARD, PAUL. "Sexual Violence against Women: Characteristics of Typical Perpetrators," in John Archer, ed., *Male Violence*. London: Routledge, 1994, pp. 170–194.

POLLOCK, VICKI, SARNOFF A. MEDNICK, and WILLIAM F. GABRIELLI, JR. "Crime Causation: Biological Theories," in Sanford H. Kadish, ed., *Encyclopedia of Crime and Justice*, Vol. 1. New York: Free Press, 1983, pp. 308–315.

POOLE, ERIC D., and ROBERT M. REGOLI. "Parental Support, Delinquent Friends, and Delinquency: A Test of Interaction Effects," *Journal of Criminal Law and Criminology* 70 (Summer 1979), 188–193.

PORTERFIELD, AUSTIN L. *Youth in Trouble: Studies in Delinquency and Despair, with Plans for Prevention*. Fort Worth, Tex.: Leo Potishman Foundation, 1946.

POWERS, EDWIN, and HELEN L. WITMER. *An Experiment in the Prevention of Delinquency: The Cambridge-Somerville Youth Study*. New York: Columbia University Press, 1951.

PRENTKY, ROBERT ALAN, MURRAY L. COHEN, and THEO-HARIS K. SEGHORN. "Development of a Rational Taxonomy for the Classification of Rapists: The Massachusetts Treatment Center System," *Bulletin of the American Academy of Psychiatry and the Law* 13 (1985), 39–70.

PRESIDENT'S COMMISSION ON LAW ENFORCEMENT AND ADMINISTRATION OF JUSTICE. *The Challenge of Crime in a Free Society*. Washington, D.C.: U.S. Government Printing Office, 1967.

PRESIDENT'S COMMISSION ON OBSCENITY AND PORNOGRAPHY. *Report*. Washington, D.C.: U.S. Government Printing Office, 1970.

PROBAND, STAN C. "Canadian Parliamentary Report Rejects U.S. Crime Control Approach," *Overcrowded Times: Solving the Prison Problem* 4 (April 1993), 2.

PRUGH, JEFF. "In Atlanta, a Pall of Fear," *Boston Globe*, February 14, 1981, p. 3.

PRUITT, CHARLES R., and JAMES Q. WILSON. "A Longitudinal Study of the Effect of Race on Sentencing," *Law and Society Review* 17 (1983), 613–635.

QUINNEY, RICHARD. *The Social Reality of Crime*. Boston: Little, Brown, 1970.

RADELET, MICHAEL L. "Racial Characteristics and the Imposition of the Death Penalty," *American Sociological Review* 46 (December 1981), 918–927.

——, HUGO ADAM BEDAU, and CONSTANCE E. PUTNAM. *In Spite of Innocence: Erroneous Convictions in Capital Cases*. Boston: Northeastern University Press, 1994.

——, and GLENN L. PIERCE. "Race and Prosecutorial Discretion in Homicide Cases," *Law and Society Review* 19 (1985), 587–621.

RADZINOWICZ, SIR LEON, and JOAN KING. *The Growth of Crime: The International Experience*. New York: Basic Books, 1977.

RAND, MICHAEL, et al. *The Use of Weapons in Committing Crimes*. Washington, D.C.: U.S. Department of Justice, January 1986.

RANKIN, JOSEPH H. "The Family Context of Delinquency," *Social Problems* 30 (April 1983), 466–479.

——, and ROGER KERN. "Parental Attachments and Delinquency," *Criminology* 32 (November 1994), 495–515.

RAPAPORT, ELIZABETH. "The Death Penalty and Gender Discrimination," *Law and Society Review* 25 (1991), 367–382.

RATCLIFFE, JAMES M., ed. *The Good Samaritan and the Law*. Garden City, N.Y.: Doubleday, 1966.

RAUSCH, SHARLA. "Court Processing versus Diversion of Status Offenders: A Test of Deterrence and Labeling Theories," *Journal of Research in Crime and Delinquency* 20 (January 1983), 39–54.

RAWLS, WENDELL, JR. "Fear Linked to Killings Rises among Atlanta Youths," *New York Times*, March 22, 1981, p. 24.

RECKLESS, WALTER C. "Containment Theory," in Barry Krisberg and James Austin, eds., *The Children of Ishmael: Critical Perspectives on Juvenile Justice*. Palo Alto, Calif.: Mayfield, 1978, pp. 187–193.

——. *The Crime Problem*, 5th ed. New York: Appleton-Century-Crofts, 1973.

REED, GARY E., and PETER CLEARY YEAGER. "Organizational Offending and Neoclassical Criminology: Challenging the Reach of a General Theory of Crime," *Criminology* 34 (August 1996), 357–382.

REED, JOHN SHELTON. "To Live—and Die—in Dixie: A Contribution to the Study of Southern Violence," *Political Science Quarterly* 86 (September 1971), 429–443.

REICHMAN, NANCY. "Insider Trading," in Michael Tonry and Albert J. Reiss, Jr., eds. *Beyond the Law: Crime in Complex Organizations*, Vol. 18 of *Crime and Justice: A Review of Research*. Chicago: University of Chicago Press, 1993, pp. 55–86.

REIMAN, JEFFREY H. "Marxist Explanations and Radical Misinterpretations: A Reply to Greenberg and Humphries," *Crime and Delinquency* 28 (October 1982), 610–617.

——. *The Rich Get Richer and the Poor Get Prison: Ideology, Class, and Criminal Justice*, 4th ed. Boston: Allyn and Bacon, 1995.

——, and SUE HEADLEE. "Marxism and Criminal Justice Policy," *Crime and Delinquency* 27 (January 1981), 24–47.

REISS, ALBERT J., JR. "Inappropriate Theories and Inadequate Methods as Policy Plagues: Self-Reported Delinquency and the Law," in N. J. Demerath 3d, Otto Larsen, and Karl F. Schuessler, eds., *Social Policy and Sociology*. New York: Academic Press, 1975, pp. 211–222.

——. *The Police and the Public*. New Haven, Conn.: Yale University Press, 1971.

——. "Police Brutality—Answers to Key Questions," *Trans-Action* 5 (July/August 1968), 10–19.

——, and DAVID J. BORDUA. "Environment and Organization: A Perspective on the Police," in David J. Bordua, ed., *The Police: Six Sociological Essays*. New York: Wiley, 1968, pp. 25–55.

——, and ALBERT LEWIS RHODES. "The Distribution of Juvenile Delinquency in the Social Class Structure," *American Sociological Review* 26 (October 1961), 720–732.

REPPETTO, THOMAS A. *Residential Crime*. Cambridge, Mass.: Ballinger, 1974.

RESSLER, ROBERT K., ANN W. BURGESS, and JOHN E. DOUGLAS. *Sexual Homicide: Patterns and Motives*. New York: Lexington Books, 1988.

RETTIG, RICHARD P., MANUAL J. TORRES, and GERALD R. GARRETT. *Manny: A Criminal-Addict's Story*. Boston: Houghton Mifflin, 1977.

REUSS-IANNI, ELIZABETH. *Two Cultures of Policing: Street Cops and Management Cops*. New Brunswick, N.J.: Transaction Books, 1983.

REUTER, PETER. "The Cartage Industry in New York," in Michael Tonry and Albert J. Reiss, Jr., eds., *Beyond the Law: Crime in Complex Organizations*, Vol. 18 of *Crime and Justice: A Review of Research*. Chicago: University of Chicago Press, 1993, pp. 149–201.

——. *Disorganized Crime: The Economics of the Visible Hand*. Cambridge, Mass.: MIT Press, 1983.

——, and JONATHAN B. RUBINSTEIN. "Fact, Fancy, and Organized Crime," *The Public Interest* No. 53 (Fall 1978), 45–67.

REZENDES, MICHAEL. "Jackson's New Target: Black-on-Black Crime," *Boston Globe*, November 6, 1993, pp. 1, 4.

——. "Reading Their Rights: Gun Lobby Challenging 2d Amendment's Interpretation," *Boston Globe*, September 10, 1995, pp. A1, A3.

RHODES, WILLIAM C. *Behavioral Threat and Community Response*. New York: Behavioral Publications, 1972.

RICHARDS, PAMELA, RICHARD A. BERK, and BRENDA FOSTER. *Crime as Play: Delinquency in a Middle Class Suburb*. Cambridge, Mass.: Ballinger, 1979.

ROBERTS, SAM. "Mafia Infiltration of Business Costing Consumers Millions," *New York Times*, December 19, 1985, p. B13.

——. "Why a Sure Way to a Prison Term Is Not Very Sure," *New York Times*, January 29, 1990, p. B1.

ROBIN, GERALD D. "Patterns of Department Store Shoplifting," *Crime and Delinquency* 9 (April 1963), 163–172.

ROBISON, JAMES, and GERALD SMITH. "The Effectiveness of Correctional Programs," *Crime and Delinquency* 17 (January 1971), 67–80.

ROGERS, JOSEPH W. *Why Are You Not a Criminal?* Englewood Cliffs, N.J.: Prentice-Hall, 1977.

ROIPHE, KATIE. *The Morning After: Sex, Fear, and Feminism on Campus*. Boston: Little, Brown, 1993.

ROJEK, DEAN G., and MAYNARD L. ERICKSON. "Delinquent Careers: A Test of the Career Escalation Model," *Criminology* 20 (May 1982), 5–28.

ROJEK, DEAN G., and MAYNARD L. ERICKSON. "Reforming the Juvenile Justice System: The Diversion of Status Offenders," *Law and Society Review* 16 (1981–82), 241–264.

RONCEK, DENNIS W., and PAMELA A. MAIER. "Bars, Blocks, and Crimes Revisited: Linking the Theory of Routine Activities to the Empiricism of 'Hot Spots,'" *Criminology* 29 (November 1991), 725–753.

ROSENBAUM, DENNIS P. "Community Crime Prevention: A Review and Synthesis of the Literature," *Justice Quarterly* 5 (September 1988), 323–395.

——. "The Theory and Research behind Neighborhood Watch: Is It a Sound Fear and Crime Reduction Strategy?" *Crime and Delinquency* 33 (January 1987), 103–134.

——, and LINDA HEATH. "The 'Psycho-Logic' of Fear-Reduction and Crime-Prevention Programs," in John Edwards et al., eds., *Social Influence Processes and Prevention*. New York: Plenum, 1990, pp. 221–247.

ROSENQUIST, CARL M., and EDWIN I. MEGARGEE. *Delinquency in Three Cultures*. Austin: University of Texas Press, 1969.

ROSENTHAL, ELIZABETH. "Health Insurers Say Rising Fraud Is Costing Them Tens of Billions," *New York Times*, July 5, 1990, pp. A1, B7.

ROSETT, ARTHUR, and DONALD R. CRESSEY. *Justice by Consent: Plea Bargains in the American Courthouse*. Philadelphia: Lippincott, 1976.

ROSS, R. R., and H. B. McKAY. "Behavioral Approaches to Treatment in Corrections: Requiem for a Panacea," *Canadian Journal of Criminology* 20 (1978), 279–298.

ROSSI, PETER H., RICHARD A. BERK, and KENNETH J. LENIHAN. *Money, Work, and Crime: Experimental Evidence*. New York: Academic Press, 1980.

ROTH, JEFFREY A. "Prosecutor Perceptions of Crime Seriousness," *Journal of Criminal Law and Criminology* 69 (Summer 1978), 232–242.

ROTHMAN, DAVID J. *The Discovery of the Asylum*. Boston: Little, Brown, 1971.

ROWE, DAVID C. "Biometrical Genetic Models of Self-Reported Delinquent Behavior: A Twin Study," *Behavior Genetics* 13 (1983), 473–489.

——, and D. WAYNE OSGOOD. "Heredity and Sociological Theories of Delinquency: A Reconsideration," *American Sociological Review* 49 (August 1984), 526–540.

RUBIN, ROBERT T. "The Neuroendocrinology and Neurochemistry of Antisocial Behavior," in Sarnoff A. Mednick, Terrie E. Moffitt, and Susan A. Stack, eds., *The Causes of Crime: New Biological Approaches*. Cambridge, Eng.: Cambridge University Press, 1987, pp. 239–262.

RUSSELL, DIANA E. H. *The Politics of Rape: The Victim's Perspective*. New York: Stein and Day, 1975.

——. *Rape in Marriage*. New York: Macmillan, 1982.

RUSSELL, GORDON W. "Psychological Issues in Sports Aggression," in Jeffrey H. Goldstein, ed., *Sports Violence*. New York: Springer-Verlag, 1983, pp. 157–181.

RUTTER, MICHAEL, et al. *Fifteen Thousand Hours: Secondary Schools and Their Effects on Children*. Cambridge, Mass.: Harvard University Press, 1979.

RYDELL, C. PETER, and SUSAN S. EVERINGHAM. *Controlling Cocaine: Supply Versus Demand Programs*. Santa Monica, Calif.: Rand, 1994.

SAMENOW, STANTON E. *Inside the Criminal Mind*. New York: Times Books, 1984.

SAMPSON, ROBERT J. "Crime in Cities: The Effects of Formal and Informal Social Control," in Albert J. Reiss, Jr., and Michael Tonry, eds., *Communities and Crime*. Chicago: University of Chicago Press, 1986, pp. 271–311.

——. "Structural Sources of Variation in Race-Age-Specific Rates of Offending across Major U.S. Cities," *Criminology* 23 (November 1985), 647–673.

——, and JACQUELINE COHEN. "Deterrent Effects of the Police on Crime: A Replication and Theoretical Extension," *Law and Society Review* 22 (1988), 163–189.

——, and W. BYRON GROVES. "Community Structure and Crime: Testing Social-Disorganization Theory," *American Journal of Sociology* (January 1989), 774–802.

——, and JOHN H. LAUB. *Crime in the Making: Pathways and Turning Points through Life*. Cambridge, Mass.: Harvard University Press, 1993.

——, and JANET L. LAURITSEN. "Deviant Lifestyles, Proximity to Crime, and the Offender-Victim Link in Personal Violence," *Journal of Research in Crime and Delinquency* 27 (May 1990), 110–139.

SAMUEL, WILLIAM, and ELIZABETH MOULDS. "The Effect of Crime Severity on Perceptions of Fair Punishment: A California Case Study," *Journal of Criminal Law and Criminology* 77 (Fall 1986), 931–948.

SANDAY, PEGGY REEVES. *Fraternity Gang Rape: Sex, Brotherhood, and Privilege on Campus*. New York: New York University Press, 1990.

SANDERS, WILLIAM B. *Gangbangs and Drive-Bys: Grounded Culture and Juvenile Gang Violence*. New York: Aldine de Gruyter, 1994.

SANGER, DAVID E. "Money Laundering, New and Improved," *New York Times*, December 24, 1995, p. E4.

SATTERFIELD, JAMES H. "Childhood Diagnostic and Neurophysiological Predictors of Teenage Arrest Rates: An Eight-Year Prospective Study," in Sarnoff A. Mednick, Terrie E. Moffitt, and Susan A. Stack, eds., *The Causes of Crime: New Biological Approaches*. Cambridge, Eng.: Cambridge University Press, 1987, pp. 146–167.

SAVITZ, LEONARD D. *Delinquency and Migration*. Ph.D. dissertation. Philadelphia: University of Pennsylvania, 1960.

SCHAFER, STEPHEN. *The Political Criminal: The Problem of Morality and Crime*. New York: Free Press, 1974.

——. *The Victim and His Criminal: A Study in Functional Responsibility*. Englewood Cliffs, N.J.: Prentice-Hall, 1968.

SCHLESINGER, PHILIP, and HOWARD TUMBER. *Reporting Crime: The Media Politics of Criminal Justice*. New York: Oxford University Press, 1994.

SCHLESINGER, STEVEN R. "Prison Crowding in the United States: The Data," *Criminal Justice Research Bulletin* 3 (1987), 1–3.

SCHNEIDER, ANNE L., and PETER R. SCHNEIDER. *Private and Public Minded Citizen Responses to a Neighborhood-Based Crime Prevention Strategy*. Eugene, Ore.: Institute of Policy Analysis, 1978.

SCHUESSLER, KARL F., and DONALD R. CRESSEY. "Personality Characteristics of Criminals," *American Journal of Sociology* 55 (July-August 1953), 166–176.

SCHULTZ, LEROY G. "Why the Negro Carries Weapons," *Journal of Criminal Law, Criminology and Police Science* 53 (December 1962), 476–483.

SCHUR, EDWIN M. *Crimes without Victims: Deviant Behavior and Public Policy.* Englewood Cliffs, N.J.: Prentice-Hall, 1965.

——. *Narcotic Addiction in Britain & America.* London: Tavistock, 1962.

——. *Our Criminal Society: The Social and Legal Sources of Crime in America.* Englewood Cliffs, N.J.: Prentice-Hall, 1969.

——. *Radical Nonintervention: Rethinking the Delinquency Problem.* Englewood Cliffs, N.J.: Prentice-Hall, 1973.

——, and HUGO ADAM BEDAU. *Victimless Ctimes: Two Sides of a Controversy.* Englewood Cliffs, N.J.: Prentice-Hall, 1974.

SCHWARTZ, RICHARD D. "Social Factors in the Development of Legal Controls: A Case Study of Two Israeli Settlements, " *Yale Law Journal* 63 (February 1954), 471–491.

——, and JEROME H. SKOLNICK. "Two Studies of Legal Stigma," *Social Problems* 10 (Fall 1962), 133–142.

SCHWENDINGER, HERMAN, and JULIA SCHWENDINGER. "Defenders of Order or Guardians of Human Rights?" in Ian Taylor, Paul Walton, and Jock Young, eds., *Critical Criminology.* London: Routledge and Kegan Paul, 1975, pp. 113–146.

SCHWENDINGER, JULIA R., and HERMAN SCHWENDINGER. *Rape and Inequality.* Beverly Hills, Calif: Sage Publications, 1983.

SCIMECCA, JOSEPH A. "Labeling Theory and Personal Construct Theory: Toward the Measurement of Individual Variation," *Journal of Criminal Law and Criminology* 68 (December 1977), 652–659.

SCOTT, JOSEPH E., and FAHAD AL-THAKEB. "The Public's Perceptions of Crime: Scandinavia, Western Europe, the Middle East, and the United States," in C. Ronald Huff, ed., *Contemporary Corrections: Social Control and Conflict.* Beverly Hills, Calif.: Sage Publications, 1977, pp. 77–88.

SCULLY, DIANA, and JOSEPH MAROLLA. "Convicted Rapists' Vocabulary of Motive: Excuses and Justifications," *Social Problems* 31 (1984), 530–544.

SECHREST, LEE, SUSAN O. WHITE, and ELIZABETH D. BROWN, eds. *The Rehabilitation of Criminal Offenders: Problems and Prospects.* Washington, D.C.: National Academy of Sciences, 1979.

SEIDMAN, DAVID, and MICHAEL COUZENS. "Getting the Crime Rate Down: Political Pressure and Crime Reporting," *Law and Society Review* 8 (Spring 1974), 457–493.

SEITZ, STEVEN THOMAS. "Firearms, Homicides, and Gun Control Effectiveness," *Law and Society Review* 6 (May 1972), 595–613.

SELLIN, THORSTEN. "The Basis of a Crime Index," *Journal of Criminal Law and Criminology* 22 (September 1931), 335–356.

——. *Culture Conflict and Crime.* New York: Social Science Research Council, 1938.

——, and MARVIN E. WOLFGANG. *The Measurement of Delinquency.* New York: Wiley, 1964.

SERRILL, MICHAEL S. "A Cold New Look at the Criminal Mind," *Psychology Today* 11 (February 1978), 86–92, 106.

SHAH, SALEEM A., and LOREN H. ROTH. "Biological and Psychophysiological Factors in Criminality," in Daniel Glaser, ed., *Handbook of Criminology.* Chicago: Rand McNally, 1974, pp. 101–173.

SHANNON, LYLE W. *Assessing the Relationship of Adult Criminal Careers to Juvenile Careers: A Summary.* Washington, D.C.: U.S. Government Printing Office, June 1982.

——, with JUDITH L. McKIM, et al. *Criminal Career Continuity: Its Social Context.* New York: Human Sciences Press, 1988.

SHAPIRO, SUSAN P. "Collaring the Crime, Not the Criminal: Reconsidering the Concept of White-Collar Crime," *American Sociological Review* 55 (June 1990), 346–365.

SHAW, CLIFFORD R., and HENRY D. McKAY. *Juvenile Delinquency and Urban Areas,* rev. ed. Chicago: University of Chicago Press, 1942, 1969.

SHELDEN, RANDALL G., JOHN A. HORVATH, and SHARON TRACY. "Do Status Offenders Get Worse? Some Clarifications on the Question of Escalation," *Crime and Delinquency* 35 (April 1989), 202–216.

SHELEY, JOSEPH F., and JOHN J. HANLON. "Unintended Consequences of Police Decisions to Actively Enforce Laws: Implications for Analysis of Crime Trends," *Contemporary Crises* 2 (July 1978), 265–275.

SHELEY, JOSEPH F., and JAMES D. WRIGHT. *In the Line of Fire: Youth, Guns, and Violence in Urban America.* New York: Aldine de Gruyter, 1995.

SHELLEY, LOUISE I. *Crime and Modernization: The Impact of Industrialization and Urbanization on Crime.* Carbondale: Southern Illinois University Press, 1981a.

——. "Urbanization and Crime: The Soviet Case in Cross-Cultural Perspective," in Louise I. Shelley, ed., *Readings in Comparative Criminology.* Carbondale: Southern Illinois University Press, 1981b, pp. 141–152.

SHENON, PHILIP. "The Mobsters Who Lurk behind the Corporate Veil," *New York Times,* December 8, 1985, p. E4.

SHERMAN, LAWRENCE W. "Attacking Crime: Police and Crime Control," in Michael Tonry and Norval Morris, eds., *Modern Policing,* Vol. 15 of *Crime and Justice: A Review of Research.* Chicago: University of Chicago Press, 1992a, 159–230.

——. "The Influence of Criminology on Criminal Law: Evaluating Arrests for Misdemeanor Domestic Violence," *Journal of Criminal Law and Criminology* 83 (Spring 1992b), 1–45.

——. *The Kansas City Gun Experiment.* Washington, D.C.; National Institute of Justice, January 1995.

——. "Police Crackdowns: Initial and Residual Deterrence," in Michael Tonry and Norval Morris, eds., *Crime and Justice: A Review of Research,* Vol. 12. Chicago: University of Chicago Press, 1990, pp. 1–48.

——. "Policing Communities: What Works?" in Albert J. Reiss, Jr., and Michael Tonry, eds., *Communities and Crime.* Chicago: University of Chicago Press, 1986, pp. 343–386.

——. *Policing Domestic Violence: Experiments and Dilemmas.* New York: Free Press, 1992c.

——, and RICHARD A. BERK. "The Specific Deterrent Effects of Arrest for Domestic Assault," *American Sociological Review* 49 (April 1984), 261–272.

——, PATRICK R. GARTIN, and MICHAEL E. BUERGER. "Hot Spots of Predatory Crime: Routine Activities and the Criminology of Place," *Criminology* 27 (February 1989), 27–55.

——, and BARRY D. GLICK. *The Quality of Police Arrest Statistics*, Police Foundation Reports 2. Washington, D.C.: Police Foundation, August 1984.

——, et al. "From Initial Deterrence to Long-Term Escalation: Short-Custody Arrest for Poverty Ghetto Domestic Violence," *Criminology* 29 (November 1991), 821–850.

SHORT, JAMES F., JR. "Introduction to the Revised Edition," in Clifford R. Shaw and Henry D. McKay, *Juvenile Delinquency and Urban Areas*, rev. ed. Chicago: University of Chicago Press, 1942, 1969, pp. xxv–liv.

——, and F. IVAN NYE. "Extent of Unrecorded Juvenile Delinquency: Tentative Conclusions," *Journal of Criminal Law, Criminology and Police Science* 49 (December 1958), 296–302.

——, and F. IVAN NYE. "Reported Behavior as a Criterion of Deviant Behavior," *Social Problems* 5 (Winter 1957), 207–213.

——, and FRED L. STRODTBECK. *Group Process and Gang Delinquency*. Chicago: University of Chicago Press, 1965.

SHOTLAND, R. LANCE, and MARGRET K. STRAW. "Bystander Response to an Assault: When a Man Attacks a Woman," *Journal of Personality and Social Psychology* 34 (November 1976), 990–999.

SHOVER, NEAL. *Aging Criminals*. Beverly Hills, Calif.: Sage Publications, 1985.

——. *Great Pretenders: Pursuits and Careers of Persistent Thieves*. Boulder, Colo.: Westview, 1996.

——. "The Later Stages of Ordinary Property Offender Careers," *Social Problems* 31 (December 1983), 208–218.

——. "The Social Organization of Burglary," *Social Problems* 20 (Spring 1973), 499–514.

——, GREER LITTON FOX, and MICHAEL MILLS. "Long-Term Consequences of Victimization by White-Collar Crime," *Justice Quarterly* 11 (March 1994), 301–324.

——, and DAVID HONAKER. "The Socially Bounded Decision Making of Persistent Property Offenders," *Howard Journal of Criminal Justice* 31 (November 1992), 276–293.

——. and CAROL Y. THOMPSON. "Age, Differential Expectations, and Crime Desistance," *Criminology* 30 (February 1992), 89–104.

SILBERMAN, CHARLES E. *Criminal Violence, Criminal Justice*. New York: Random House, 1978.

SIMON, RITA J., and DAVID E. AARONSON. *The Insanity Defense: A Critical Assessment of Law and Policy in the Post-Hinckley Era*. New York: Praeger, 1988.

SIMONS, RONALD L., et al. "A Test of Various Perspectives on the Intergenerational Transmission of Domestic Violence," *Criminology* 33 (1995), 141–172.

SIMPSON, SALLY S., and CHRISTOPHER S. KOPER. "Deterring Corporate Crime," *Criminology* 30 (August 1992), 347–375.

SINGER, SIMON I., and MURRAY LEVINE. "Power-Control Theory, Gender, and Delinquency: A Partial Replication with Additional Evidence on the Role of Peers," *Criminology* 26 (November 1988), 627–647.

SKOGAN, WESLEY G. "Citizen Reporting of Crime: Some National Panel Data," *Criminology* 13 (February 1976a), 535–549.

——. "Crime and Crime Rates," in Wesley G. Skogan, ed., *Sample Surveys of the Victims of Crime*. Cambridge, Mass.: Ballinger, 1976b, pp. 105–119.

——. *Disorder and Decline: Crime and the Spiral of Decay in American Neighborhoods*. Berkeley: University of California Press, 1990.

——. "Fear of Crime and Neighborhood Change," in Albert J. Reiss, Jr., and Michael Tonry, eds., *Communities and Crime*. Chicago: University of Chicago Press, 1986, pp. 203–229.

——. "On Attitudes and Behaviors," in Dan A. Lewis, ed., *Reactions to Crime*. Beverly Hills, Calif.: Sage Publications, 1981, pp. 19–45.

——. "Reporting Crimes to the Police: The Status of World Research," *Journal of Research in Crime and Delinquency* 21 (May 1984), 113–137.

——, and ARTHUR J. LURIGIO. "The Correlates of Community Antidrug Activism," *Crime and Delinquency* 38 (October 1992), 510–521.

SKOLNICK, JEROME H. *Justice without Trial: Law Enforcement in Democratic Society*, 2nd ed. New York: Wiley, 1975.

——, and JAMES J. FYFE. *Above the Law: Police and the Excessive Use of Force*. New York: Free Press, 1993.

SKORNECK, CAROLYN. "683,000 Women Raped in 1990, New Government Study Finds," *Boston Globe*, April 24, 1992, pp. 1, 32.

SLOAN, JOHN HENRY, et al. "Handgun Regulation, Crime, Assaults, and Homicide: A Tale of Two Cities," *New England Journal of Medicine* 319 (November 10, 1988), 1256–1262.

SMIGEL, ERWIN O. "Public Attitudes toward Stealing as Related to the Size of the Victim Organization," *American Sociological Review* 21 (June 1956), 320–327.

——, and H. LAURENCE ROSS. "Introduction," in *Crimes against Bureaucracy*. New York: Van Nostrand Reinhold, 1970, pp. 1–14.

SMITH, BRENT L., and KELLY R. DAMPHOUSSE. "Punishing Political Offenders: The Effect of Political Motive on Federal Sentencing Decisions," *Criminology* 34 (August 1996), 289–321.

SMITH, CAROLYN, and TERENCE P. THORNBERRY. "The Relationship Between Childhood Maltreatment and Adolescent Involvement in Delinquency," *Criminology* 33 (November 1995), 451–481.

SMITH, DAVID E., and GEORGE R. GAY, eds. *"It's So Good, Don't Even Try It Once": Heroin in Perspective*. Englewood Cliffs, N.J.: Prentice-Hall, 1972.

SMITH, DOUGLAS A. "The Plea Bargaining Controversy," *Journal of Criminal Law and Criminology* 77 (Fall 1986), 949–967.

——, and ROBERT BRAME. "On the Initiation and Continuation of Delinquency," *Criminology* 32 (November 1994), 607–629.

——, and PATRICK A. GARTIN. "Specifying Specific Deterrence: The Influence of Arrest on Future Criminal Activity," *American Sociological Review* 54 (February 1989), 94–106.

——, and CHRISTY A. VISHER. "Street-Level Justice: Situational Determinants of Police Arrest Decisions," *Social Problems* 29 (December 1981), 167–177.

SMITH, DWIGHT C., JR. "Organized Crime and Entrepreneurship," *International Journal of Criminology and Penology* 6 (May 1978), 161–177.

——. "Paragons, Pariahs, and Pirates: A Spectrum-Based Theory of Enterprise," *Crime and Delinquency* 26 (July 1980), 358–386.

SPARKS, RICHARD F. "A Critique of Marxist Criminology," in Norval Morris and Michael Tonry, eds., *Crime and Justice: An Annual Review of Research*, Vol. 2. Chicago: University of Chicago Press, 1980, pp. 159–210.

——. "Multiple Victimization: Evidence, Theory, and Future Research," *Journal of Criminal Law and Criminology* 72 (Summer 1981), 762–778.

——. *Research on Victims of Crime: Accomplishments, Issues, and New Directions*. Washington, D.C.: U.S. Government Printing Office, 1982.

SPECTER, MICHAEL. "Latest Films for $2: Video Piracy Booms in Russia," *New York Times*, April 11, 1995, p. A3.

SPITZER, STEVEN. "The Political Economy of Policing," in David F. Greenberg, ed., *Crime & Capitalism*. Palo Alto, Calif.: Mayfield, 1981, pp. 314–340.

SPOHN, CASSIA. "Crime and the Social Control of Blacks: Offender/Victim Race and the Sentencing of Violent Offenders," in George S. Bridges and Martha A. Myers, eds., *Inequality, Crime, & Social Control*. Boulder, Colo.: Westview, 1994, pp. 249–268.

STACK, STEVEN. "Publicized Executions and Homicide, 1950–1980," *American Sociological Review* 52 (August 1987), 532–540.

——. "Social Structure and Swedish Crime Rates: A Time-Series Analysis, 1950–1979," *Criminology* 20 (November 1982), 499–513.

STAFFORD, MARK C., and OMER R. GALLE. "Victimization Rates, Exposure to Risk, and Fear of Crime," *Criminology* 22 (May 1984), 173–185.

STANKO, ELIZABETH ANNE. "The Impact of Victim Assessment on Prosecutors' Screening Decisions: The Case of the New York County District Attorney's Office," *Law and Society Review* 16 (1981–82), 225–239.

STARK, RODNEY. "Deviant Places: A Theory of the Ecology of Crime," *Criminology* 25 (November 1987), 893–909.

——, et al. "Crime and Delinquency in the Roaring Twenties," *Journal of Research in Crime and Delinquency* 20 (January 1983), 4–23.

STATTIN, HÅKAN, and DAVID MAGNUSSON. "The Role of Early Aggressive Behavior in the Frequency, Seriousness, and Types of Later Crime," *Journal of Consulting and Clinical Psychology* 57 (December 1989), 710–718.

STEADMAN, HENRY J. "Empirical Research on the Insanity Defense," *Annals of the American Academy of Political and Social Sciences* 477 (January 1985), 58–71.

STEFFENSMEIER, DARRELL J. "Assessing the Impact of the Women's Movement on Sex-Based Differences in the Handling of Adult Criminal Defendants," *Crime and Delinquency* 26 (July 1980), 344–357.

——. *The Fence: In the Shadow of Two Worlds*. Totowa, N.J.: Rowman and Littlefield, 1986.

——. "Organization Properties and Sex-Segregation in the Underworld: Building a Sociological Theory of Sex Differences in Crime," *Social Forces* 61 (June 1983), 1010–1032.

——, and MICHAEL J. COBB. "Sex Differences in Urban Arrest Patterns," *Social Problems* 29 (October 1981), 37–50.

——, and MILES D. HARER. "Is the Crime Rate Really Falling? An Aging U.S. Population and Its Impact on the Nation's Crime Rate, 1980–1984," *Journal of Research in Crime and Delinquency* 24 (February 1987), 23–48.

——, JOHN KRAMER, and CATHY STREIFEL. "Gender and Imprisonment Decisions," *Criminology* 31 (August 1993), 411–446.

STEINHART, DAVID. "California Opinion Poll: Public Attitudes on Youth Crime," *NCCD Focus*, December 1988, pp. 1–7.

STENROSS, BARBARA. "Police Response to Residential Burglaries: Dusting for Prints as a Negative Rite," *Criminology* 22 (August 1984), 389–402.

STEPHAN, JAMES J., and TRACY L. SNELL. *Capital Punishment 1994*. Washington, D.C.: U.S. Department of Justice, 1996.

STEPHENS, RICHARD C., and ROSALIND D. ELLIS. "Narcotic Addicts and Crime: Analysis of Recent Trends," *Criminology* 12 (February 1975), 474–488.

STERNGOLD, JAMES. "Firms Act in Wake of 2 Scandals," *New York Times*, June 7, 1986, pp. 33, 36.

STODDART, KENNETH. "The Enforcement of Narcotics Violations in a Canadian City: Heroin Users' Perspectives on the Production of Official Statistics," *Canadian Journal of Criminology* 23 (October 1982), 425–438.

STOLZENBERG, LISA, and STEWART J. D'ALESSIO. "Sentencing and Unwarranted Disparity: An Empirical Assessment of the Long-Term Impact of Sentencing Guidelines in Minnesota," *Criminology* 32 (May 1994), 301–310.

STOOKEY, JOHN ALAN. "A Cost Theory of Victim Justice," in Burt Galaway and Joe Hudson, eds., *Perspectives on Crime Victims*. St. Louis: C. V. Mosby, 1981, pp. 80–89.

STRASBURG, PAUL A. *Violent Delinquents: A Report to the Ford Foundation from the Vera Institute of Justice*. New York: Monarch, 1978.

STUART, REGINALD. "Atlanta Deaths: Fear Felt by Young," *New York Times*, January 26, 1981, pp. A1, A12.

SUTHERLAND, EDWIN H. *The Professional Thief*. Chicago: University of Chicago Press, 1937.

——. *White Collar Crime: The Uncut Version*. New Haven, Conn.: Yale University Press, 1949, 1983.

—— and DONALD R. CRESSEY. *Criminology*, 10th ed. Philadelphia: Lippincott, 1978.

——, DONALD R. CRESSEY, and DAVID F. LUCKENBILL. *Principles of Criminology*, 11th edition. Dix Hills, N.Y.: General Hall, 1992.

SUTTLES, GERALD D. *The Social Order of the Slum: Ethnicity and Territory in the Inner City*. Chicago: University of Chicago Press, 1968.

SVIRIDOFF, MICHELLE, and JAMES W. THOMPSON. "Links between Employment and Crime: A Qualitative Study of Rikers Island Releasees," *Crime and Delinquency* 29 (April 1983), 195–212.

SWIGERT, VICTORIA LYNN, and RONALD A. FARRELL. *Murder, Inequality, and the Law*. Lexington, Mass.: D. C. Heath, 1976.

SWIGERT, VICTORIA LYNN, and RONALD A. FARRELL. "Normal Homicides and the Law," *American Sociological Review* 42 (February 1977), 16–32.

SYKES, CHARLES J. *A Nation of Victims: The Decay of the American Character*. New York: St. Martin's, 1992.

SYKES, GRESHAM M. *The Society of Captives: A Study of a Maximum Security Prison*. Princeton, N.J.: Princeton University Press, 1958.

——, and DAVID MATZA. "Techniques of Neutralization: A Theory of Delinquency," *American Sociological Review* 22 (December 1957), 664–670.

SZASZ, ANDREW. "Corporations, Organized Crime, and the Disposal of Hazardous Waste: An Examination of the Making of a Criminogenic Regulatory Structure," *Criminology* 24 (February 1986), 1–27.

TAYLOR, IAN, PAUL WALTON, and JOCK YOUNG, eds. *Critical Criminology*. London: Routledge and Kegan Paul, 1975a.

TAYLOR, IAN, PAUL WALTON, and JOCK YOUNG. "Critical Criminology in Britain: Review and Prospects," in Ian Taylor, Paul Walton, and Jock Young, eds., *Critical Criminology*. London: Routledge and Kegan Paul, 1975b, pp. 6–62.

TAYLOR, IAN, PAUL WALTON, and JOCK YOUNG. *The New Criminology: For a Social Theory of Deviance*. London: Routledge and Kegan Paul, 1973.

TAYLOR, RALPH B., and STEVEN GOTTFREDSON. "Environmental Design, Crime, and Prevention: An Examination of Community Dynamics," in Albert J. Reiss, Jr., and Michael Tonry, eds. *Communities and Crime*. Chicago: University of Chicago Press, 1986, pp. 387–416.

TAYLOR, RALPH B., STEPHEN D. GOTTFREDSON, and SIDNEY BROWER. "The Defensibility of Defensible Space: A Critical Review and a Synthetic Framework for Future Research," in Travis Hirschi and Michael Gottfredson, eds., *Understanding Crime: Current Theory and Research*. Beverly Hills, Calif: Sage Publications, 1980, pp. 53–71.

TAYLOR, RALPH B., and ADELE V. HARRELL. *Physical Environment and Crime*. Washington, D.C.: U.S. Department of Justice, May 1996.

TEILMAN, KATHERINE S., and PIERRE H. LANDRY, JR. "Gender Bias in Juvenile Justice," *Journal of Research in Crime and Delinquency* 18 (January 1981), 47–80.

TENNENBAUM, ABRAHAM N. "The Influence of the *Garner* Decision on Police Use of Deadly Force," *Journal of Criminal Law and Criminology* 85 (Summer 1994), 241–260.

TERRY, DON. "Carjacking: New Name for Old Crime," *New York Times*, December 9, 1992, p. A18.

THOMPSON, JAMES W., et al. *Employment and Crime: A Review of Theories and Research*. Washington, D.C.: National Institute of Justice, U.S. Department of Justice, 1981.

THOMSON, DOUGLAS R., and ANTHONY J. RAGONA. "Popular Moderation versus Governmental Authoritarianism: An Interactionist View of Public Sentiments toward Criminal Sanctions," *Crime and Delinquency* 33 (July 1987), 337–357.

THORNBERRY, TERENCE P. "Sentencing Disparities in the Juvenile Justice System," *Journal of Criminal Law and Criminology* 70 (Summer 1979), 164–171.

——, and R. L. CHRISTENSON. "Unemployment and Criminal Involvement: An Investigation of Reciprocal Causal Structures," *American Sociological Review* 49 (June 1984), 398–411.

——, et al. "Delinquent Peers, Beliefs, and Delinquent Behavior: A Longitudinal Test of Interactional Theory," *Criminology* 32 (February 1994), 47–81.

——, et al. "Testing Interactional Theory: An Examination of Reciprocal Causal Relationships among Family, School, and Delinquency," *Journal of Criminal Law and Criminology* 82 (Spring 1991), 3–35.

THORSELL, BERNARD A., and LLOYD W. KLEMKE. "The Labeling Process: Reinforcement and Deterrent?" *Law and Society Review* 6 (February 1972), 393–403.

THRASHER, FREDERIC M. *The Gang: A Study of l,313 Gangs in Chicago*, abridged ed. Chicago: University of Chicago Press, 1927, 1963.

TIEN, JAMES M., THOMAS F. RICH, and MICHAEL F. CAHN. *Electronic Fund Transfer Systems Fraud: Computer Crime*. Washington, D.C.: U.S. Department of Justice, April 1986.

TILLMAN, ROBERT. "The Size of the 'Criminal Population': The Prevalence and Incidence of Adult Arrest," *Criminology* 25 (August 1987), 561–579.

TIMNICK, LOIS. "Psychic Trauma Follows Chowchilla Kidnapping," *Boston Globe*, January 24, 1981, p. 3.

TIMROTS, ANITA D., and MICHAEL R. RAND. *Violent Crime by Strangers and Nonstrangers*. Washington, D.C.: U.S. Department of Justice, January 1987.

TITTLE, CHARLES R. "Social Class and Criminal Behavior: A Critique of the Theoretical Foundation," *Social Forces* 62 (December 1983), 334–358.

——, and ROBERT F. MEIER. "Specifying the SES/Delinquency Relationship," *Criminology* 28 (May 1990), 271–299.

——, and RAYMOND PATERNOSTER. "Geographic Mobility and Criminal Behavior," *Journal of Research in Crime and Delinquency* 25 (August 1988), 301–343.

——, and ALAN R. ROWE. "Certainty of Arrest and Crime Rates: A Further Test of the Deterrence Hypothesis," *Social Forces* 52 (June 1974), 455–462.

——, WAYNE J. VILLEMEZ, and DOUGLAS A. SMITH. "The Myth of Social Class and Criminality: An Empirical Assessment of the Empirical Evidence," *American Sociological Review* 43 (October 1978), 643–656.

TITUS, RICHARD M., FRED HEINZELMANN, and JOHN M. BOYLE. "Victimization of Persons by Fraud," *Crime and Delinquency* 41 (January 1995), 54–72.

TOBIAS, J. J. *Crime and Industrial Society in the 19th Century*. New York: Schocken, 1967.

TOBY, JACKSON. "The Differential Impact of Family Disorganization," *American Sociological Review* 22 (October 1957), 505–512.

——. "The Socialization and Control of Deviant Motivation," in Daniel Glaser, ed., *Handbook of Criminology*. Chicago: Rand McNally, 1974, pp. 85–100.

TONRY, MICHAEL. "The Failure of the U.S. Sentencing Commission's Guidelines," *Crime and Delinquency* 39 (April 1993), 131–149.

——. *Malign Neglect: Race, Crime, and Punishment in America*. New York: Oxford University Press, 1995.

TONTODONATO, PAMELA. "Explaining Rate Changes in Delinquent Arrest Transitions Using Event History Analysis," *Criminology* 26 (August 1988), 439–459.

TRACY, PAUL E., JR. "Race and Class Differences in Official and Self-Reported Delinquency," in Marvin E. Wolfgang, Terence P. Thornberry, and Robert M. Figlio, *From Boy to Man, from Delinquency to Crime*. Chicago: University of Chicago Press, 1987, pp. 87–121.

——, MARVIN E. WOLFGANG, and ROBERT M. FIGLIO. *Delinquency in Two Birth Cohorts: Executive Summary*. Washington, D.C.: U.S. Department of Justice, September 1985.

TRAUB, STUART H. "Battling Employee Crime: A Review of Corporate Strategies and Programs," *Crime and Delinquency* 42 (April 1996), 244–256.

TREASTER, JOSEPH B. "Behind Immigrants' Voyage, Long Reach of Chinese Gang," *New York Times*, June 9, 1993, pp. A1, B2.

TUNNELL, KENNETH D. *Choosing Crime: The Criminal Calculus of Property Offenders*. Chicago: Nelson-Hall, 1992.

TURK, AUSTIN. "Back on Track: Asking and Answering the Right Questions," *Law and Society Review* 27 (1993), 355–359.

——. *Criminality and Legal Order*. Chicago: Rand McNally, 1969.

——. "Law, Conflict, and Order: From Theorizing toward Theories," *Canadian Review of Sociology and Anthropology* 13 (1976), 282–294.

TURNER, STANLEY. "The Ecology of Delinquency," in Thorsten Sellin and Marvin E. Wolfgang, eds., *Delinquency: Selected Studies*. New York: Wiley, 1969, pp. 27–60.

UHLMAN, THOMAS M., and N. DARLENE WALKER. "'He Takes Some of My Time; I Take Some of His': An Analysis of Sentencing Patterns in Jury Cases," *Law and Society Review* 14 (Winter 1980), 323–341.

U.S. DEPARTMENT OF JUSTICE, ATTORNEY GENERAL'S TASK FORCE ON VIOLENT CRIME. *Final Report*. Washington, D.C.: U.S. Government Printing Office, 1981.

UNNEVER, JAMES D. "Direct and Organizational Discrimination in the Sentencing of Drug Offenders," *Social Problems* 30 (December 1982), 212–225.

——, and LARRY A. HEMBROFF. "The Prediction of Racial/Ethnic Sentencing Disparities: An Expectation States Approach," *Journal of Research in Crime and Delinquency* 25 (February 1988), 53–82.

van den HAAG, ERNEST. *Punishing Criminals: Concerning a Very Old and Painful Question*. New York: Basic Books, 1975.

van DINE, STEVE, JOHN P. CONRAD, and SIMON DINITZ. "The Incapacitation of the Chronic Thug," *Journal of Criminal Law and Criminology* 70 (Spring 1979), 125–135.

van VOORHIS, PATRICIA, et al. "The Impact of Family Structure and Quality on Delinquency: A Comparative Assessment of Structural and Functional Factors," *Criminology* 26 (May 1988), 235–261.

VISCUSI, W. KIP. "Market Incentives for Criminal Behavior," in Richard B. Freeman and Harry J. Holzer, eds., *The Black Youth Employment Crisis*. Chicago: University of Chicago Press, 1986, pp. 301–346.

VISHER, CHRISTY A. "The Rand Inmate Survey: A Reanalysis," in Alfred Blumstein et al., eds., *Criminal Careers and "Career Criminals"*, Vol. 2. Washington, D.C.: National Academy Press, 1986, pp. 161–211.

VITO, GENNARO F., and THOMAS J. KEIL. "Capital Sentencing in Kentucky: An Analysis of the Factors Influencing Decision Making in the Post-Gregg Period," *Journal of Criminal Law and Criminology* 79 (Summer 1988), 483–503.

VOLAVKA, JAN, et al. "EEGs of XYY and XXY Men Found in a Large Birth Cohort," in Sarnoff A. Mednick and Karl O. Christiansen, eds., *Biosocial Bases of Criminal Behavior*. New York: Gardner Press, 1977, pp. 189–198.

von HIRSCH, ANDREW. *Doing Justice: The Choice of Punishments*. New York: Hill and Wang, 1976.

——. *Past or Future Crimes: Deservedness and Dangerousness in the Sentencing of Criminals*. New Brunswick, N.J.: Rutgers University Press, 1985.

——. "Proportionality in the Philosophy of Punishment," in Michael Tonry, ed., *Crime and Justice: A Review of Research*, Vol. 16. Chicago: University of Chicago Press, 1992, pp. 55–98.

——. "Selective Incapacitation: A Critique," *NIJ Reports*, January 1984, pp. 5–8.

——. "Utilitarian Sentencing Resuscitated: The American Bar Association's Second Report on Criminal Sentencing," *Rutgers Law Review* 33 (Spring 1981), 772–789.

VOSS, HARWIN L. "Ethnic Differentials in Delinquency in Honolulu," *Journal of Criminal Law, Criminology and Police Science* 54 (September 1963), 322–327.

——, and JOHN R. HEPBURN. "Patterns in Criminal Homicide in Chicago," *Journal of Criminal Law, Criminology and Police Science* 59 (December 1968), 499–508.

VOTEY, HAROLD L., JR., and LLAD PHILLIPS. "The Control of Criminal Activity: An Economic Analysis," in Daniel Glaser, ed., *Handbook of Criminology*. Chicago: Rand McNally, 1974, pp. 1055–1093.

WAEGEL, WILLIAM B. "The Use of Lethal Force by Police: The Effect of Statutory Change," *Crime and Delinquency* 30 (January 1984), 121–140.

WALDO, GORDON P., and SIMON DINITZ. "Personality Attributes of the Criminal: An Analysis of Research Studies, 1950–1965," *Journal of Research in Crime and Delinquency* 4 (July 1967), 185–201.

WALKER, NIGEL. "Lost Causes in Criminology," in Roger Hood, ed., *Crime, Criminology and Public Policy: Essays in Honour of Sir Leon Radzinowicz.* New York: Free Press, 1974, pp. 47–62.

WALLERSTEIN, JAMES S., and CLEMENT J. WYLE. "Our Law-Abiding Law-Breakers," *Probation* 35 (April 1947), 107–112.

WALLIS, C. P., and R. MALIPHANT. "Delinquent Areas in the County of London: Ecological Factors," *British Journal of Criminology* 7 (July 1967), 250–284.

WALSH, ANTHONY. "Placebo Justice: Victim Recommendations and Offender Sentences in Sexual Assault Cases," *Journal of Criminal Law and Criminology* 77 (Winter 1986), 1126–1141.

WALSH, MARILYN E. *The Fence: A New Look at the World of Property Theft.* Westport, Conn.: Greenwood, 1977.

WALTERS, GLENN D. *The Criminal Lifestyle: Patterns of Serious Criminal Conduct.* Newbury Park, Calif.: Sage Publications, 1990.

——. "A Meta-Analysis of the Gene-Crime Relationship," *Criminology* 30 (November 1992), 595–613.

——, and THOMAS W. WHITE. "The Thinking Criminal: A Cognitive Model of Lifestyle Criminality," *Criminal Justice Research Bulletin* 4 (1989), 1–10.

WARR, MARK. "Age, Peers, and Delinquency," *Criminology* 31 (February 1993), 17–40.

——, and MARK STAFFORD. "The Influence of Delinquent Peers: What They Think or What They Do?" *Criminology* 29 (November 1991), 851–866.

WARREN, DONALD I. "Neighborhood Structure and Riot Behavior in Detroit: Some Exploratory Findings," *Social Problems* 16 (Spring 1969), 464–484.

WEBER, MAX. *Economy and Society: An Outline of Interpretive Sociology.* Berkeley, Calif.: University of California Press, 1979.

WEIS, JOSEPH G. "Crime Statistics: Reporting Systems and Methods," in Sanford H. Kadish, ed., *Encyclopedia of Crime and Justice,* Vol. 1. New York: Free Press, 1983, pp. 378–392.

WEISBURD, DAVID, ELIN WARING, and ELLEN CHAYET. "Specific Deterrence in a Sample of Offenders Convicted of White-Collar Crimes," *Criminology* 33 (November 1995), 587–607.

WEISBURD, DAVID, et al. *Crimes of the Middle Classes: White-Collar Offenders in the Federal Courts.* New Haven, Conn.: Yale University Press, 1991.

WELLS, L. EDWARD. "Self-Enhancement through Delinquency: A Conditional Test of Self-Derogation Theory," *Journal of Research in Crime and Delinquency* 26 (August 1989), 226–252.

——, and JOSEPH H. RANKIN. "The Broken Home Model of Delinquency: Analytic Issues," *Journal of Research in Crime and Delinquency* 23 (February 1986), 68–93.

——, and JOSEPH H. RANKIN. "Direct Parental Controls and Delinquency," *Criminology* 26 (May 1988), 263–285.

——, and JOSEPH H. RANKIN. "Families and Delinquency: A Meta-Analysis of the Impact of Broken Homes," *Social Problems* 38 (1991), 71–93.

WEST, D. J. *Delinquency: Its Roots, Careers and Prospects.* Cambridge, Mass.: Harvard University Press, 1982.

——. *Present Conduct and Future Delinquency.* London: Heinemann, 1969.

——, and D. P. FARRINGTON. *The Delinquent Way of Life.* London: Heinemann, 1977.

——, and D. P. FARRINGTON. *Who Becomes Delinquent?* London: Heinemann, 1973.

WHITAKER, CATHERINE J. *Black Victims.* Washington, D.C.: U.S. Department of Justice, April 1990.

WIATROWSKI, MICHAEL D., DAVID B. GRISWOLD, and MARY K. ROBERTS. "Social Control Theory and Delinquency," *American Sociological Review* 46 (October 1981), 525–541.

WIDOM, CATHY SPATZ. "The Cycle of Violence," *Science* 244 (April 14, 1989), 160–166.

——. *The Cycle of Violence Revisited.* Washington, D.C.: U.S. Department of Justice, February 1996.

——. *Victims of Childhood Sexual Abuse—Later Criminal Consequences.* Washington, D.C.: U.S. Department of Justice, March 1995.

WIEHOFEN, HENRY. "Punishment and Treatment: Rehabilitation," in Stanley E. Grupp, ed., *Theories of Punishment.* Bloomington, Ind.: Indiana University Press, 1971, pp. 255–263.

WILBANKS, WILLIAM. *Murder in Miami.* Lanham, Md.: University Press of America, 1984.

WILEY, NORBERT. "The Ethnic Mobility Trap and Stratification Theory," *Social Problems* 15 (Fall 1967), 147–159.

WILKERSON, ISABEL. "'Crack House' Fire: Justice or Vigilantism?" *New York Times,* October 22, 1988, pp. 1, 6.

WILKINSON, KAREN. "The Broken Home and Delinquent Behavior: An Alternative Interpretation of Contradictory Findings," in Travis Hirschi and Michael Gottfredson, eds., *Understanding Crime: Current Theory and Research.* Beverly Hills, Calif.: Sage Publications, 1980, pp. 21–42.

WILLIAMS, FRANKLIN P., 3d. "Conflict Theory and Differential Processing: An Analysis of the Research Literature," in James A. Inciardi, ed., *Radical Criminology: The Coming Crisis.* Beverly Hills, Calif.: Sage, 1980, pp. 213–232.

WILLIAMS, JAY R., and MARTIN GOLD. "From Delinquent Behavior to Official Delinquency," *Social Problems* 20 (Fall 1972), 209–229.

WILLIAMS, TERRY. *The Cocaine Kids: The Inside Story of a Teenage Drug Ring.* Reading, Mass.: Addison-Wesley, 1989.

——. *Crack House: Notes from the End of the Line.* Reading, Mass.: Addison-Wesley, 1992.

WILSON, JAMES Q. *Thinking about Crime,* rev. ed. New York: Basic Books, 1983.

——. *Varieties of Police Behavior: The Management of Law and Order in Eight Communities.* Cambridge, Mass.: Harvard University Press, 1968.

——, and BARBARA BOLAND. "Crime," in William Gorham and Nathan Glazer, eds., *The Urban Predicament.* Washington, D.C.: Urban Institute, 1976, pp. 179–230.

——, and RICHARD J. HERRNSTEIN. *Crime & Human Nature.* New York: Simon and Schuster, 1985.

WILSON, MARGO I., and MARTIN DALY. "Who Kills Whom in Spouse Killings? On the Exceptional Sex Ratio of Spousal Homicides in the United States," *Criminology* 30 (May 1992), 189–215.

WILSON, WILLIAM JULIUS. *The Truly Disadvantaged.* Chicago: University of Chicago Press, 1987.

WINICK, CHARLES. "Physician Narcotic Addicts," in Howard S. Becker, ed., *The Other Side: Perspectives on Deviance.* New York: Free Press, 1964, pp. 261–279.

WISE, NANCY BARTON. "Juvenile Delinquency among Middle-Class Girls," in Edmund W. Vaz, ed., *Middle-Class Juvenile Delinquency.* New York: Harper & Row, 1967, pp. 179–188.

WITKIN, HERMAN A., et al. "Criminality in XYY and XXY Men," *Science* 193 (August 13, 1976), 547–555.

WOLFGANG, MARVIN E. *Patterns in Criminal Homicide.* Philadelphia: University of Pennsylvania Press, 1958.

——. "Urban Crime," in James Q. Wilson, ed., *The Metropolitan Enigma.* Garden City, N.Y.: Doubleday, 1968, pp. 270–311.

——, and FRANCO FERRACUTI. *The Subculture of Violence: Towards an Integrated Theory in Criminology.* Beverly Hills, Calif.: Sage Publications, 1967, 1982.

——, ROBERT M. FIGLIO, and THORSTEN SELLIN. *Delinquency in a Birth Cohort.* Chicago: University of Chicago Press, 1972.

——, TERENCE P. THORNBERRY, and ROBERT M. FIGLIO. *From Boy to Man, from Delinquency to Crime.* Chicago: University of Chicago Press, 1987.

——, et al. *The National Survey of Crime Severity.* Washington, D.C.: U.S. Department of Justice, June 1985.

WOOTTON, BARBARA. *Social Science and Social Pathology.* London: George Allen and Unwin, 1959.

WORDEN, ROBERT E., and ROBIN L. SHEPARD. "Demeanor, Crime, and Police Behavior: A Reexamination of the Police Services Study Data," *Criminology* 34 (February 1996), 83–105.

WRIGHT, JAMES D., and PETER H. ROSSI. *Armed and Considered Dangerous: A Survey of Felons and Their Firearms.* New York: Aldine de Gruyter, 1986.

WRIGHT, JAMES D., PETER H. ROSSI, and KATHLEEN DALY. *Under the Gun: Weapons, Crime, and Violence in America.* New York: Aldine, 1983.

WRIGHT, JAMES D., and ELEANOR WEBER. *Homelessness and Health.* Washington, D.C.: McGraw-Hill's Healthcare Information Center, 1987.

WRIGHT, JOHN P., FRANCIS T. CULLEN, and MICHAEL B. BLANKENSHIP. "The Social Construction of Corporate Violence: Media Coverage of the Imperial Food Products Fire," *Crime and Delinquency* 41 (January 1995), 20–36.

WRIGHT, RICHARD T., and SCOTT H. DECKER. *Burglars on the Job: Streetlife and Residential Break-ins.* Boston: Northeastern University Press, 1994.

YABLONSKY, LEWIS. *The Violent Gang.* New York: Macmillan, 1966.

YOCHELSON, SAMUEL, and STANTON E. SAMENOW. *The Criminal Personality,* Vol. 1: *A Profile for Change.* New York: Jason Aronson, 1976.

YOCHELSON, SAMUEL, and STANTON E. SAMENOW. *The Criminal Personality,* Vol. 2: *The Change Process.* New York: Jason Aronson, 1977.

YODER, STEPHEN A. "Criminal Sanctions for Corporate Illegality," *Journal of Criminal Law and Criminology* 69 (Spring 1978), 40–58.

YOUNG, ROBERT L., DAVID McDOWALL, and COLIN LOFTIN. "Collective Security and the Ownership of Firearms for Protection," *Criminology* 25 (February 1987), 47–62.

YOUNG, WARREN, and MARK BROWN. "Cross-National Comparisons of Imprisonment," in Michael Tonry, ed. *Crime and Justice: A Review of Research,* Vol. 17. Chicago: University of Chicago Press, 1993, pp. 1–49.

YU, JIANG, and ALLEN E. LISKA. "The Certainty of Punishment: A Reference Group Effect and Its Functional Form," *Criminology* 31 (August 1993), 447–464.

ZARR, GERALD H. "Liberia," in Alan Milner, ed., *African Penal Systems.* London: Routledge and Kegan Paul, 1969.

ZATZ, MARJORIE S. "The Changing Forms of Racial/Ethnic Biases in Sentencing," *Journal of Research in Crime and Delinquency* 24 (February 1987), 69–92.

——. "Race, Ethnicity, and Determinate Sentencing: A New Dimension to an Old Controversy," *Criminology* 22 (May 1984), 147–171.

ZEISEL, HANS. "A Comment on 'The Deterrent Effect of Capital Punishment' by Phillips," *American Journal of Sociology* 88 (July 1982), 167–169.

ZEITLIN, LAWRENCE R. "A Little Larceny Can Do a Lot for Employee Morale," *Psychology Today* 5 (June 1971), 22–26, 64.

ZEITZ, DOROTHY. *Women Who Embezzle or Defraud: A Study of Convicted Felons.* New York: Praeger, 1981.

ZENOFF, ELYCE H., and ALAN B. ZIENTS. "Juvenile Murderers: Should the Punishment Fit the Crime?" *International Journal of Law and Psychiatry* 2 (1979), 533–553.

ZHANG, LENING, and STEVEN F. MESSNER. "Family Deviance and Delinquency in China," *Criminology* 33 (August 1995), 359–387.

ZHANG, LENING, et al. "Crime Prevention in a Communitarian Society: *Bang-Jiao* and *Tiao-jie* in the People's Republic of China," *Justice Quarterly* 13 (June 1996), 199–222.

ZILLMANN, DOLF, and JENNINGS BRYANT. "Effects of Massive Exposure to Pornography," in Neil M. Malamuth and Edward Donnerstein, eds., *Pornography and Sexual Aggression.* New York: Academic Press, 1984, pp. 115–138.

ZIMBARDO, PHILIP G. "Pathology of Imprisonment," *Society* 9 (April 1972), 4–8.

ZINGRAFF, MATTHEW T., et al. Child Maltreatment and Youthful Problem Behavior," *Criminology* 31 (May 1993), 173–202.

NAME INDEX

SUBJECT INDEX